Critical Praise for

Sowing the Gospel

"Tolbert has articulated well a method for interpretation which is quite interesting and illuminating. . . . By the rigors of her methods she has brought many mysteries to light and illumined much for us about the audience of the Gospel and the contours of its story. For anyone interested in probing the conundra of Mark's Gospel, this volume is well worth reading."
　　—David Rhoads, *Currents in Theology and Mission*

"This is a provocative, well-reasoned, and well-written analysis of Mark's Gospel. Whether or not she has gathered up all the mysterious strands that make up the earliest Gospel is certainly debatable. But no informed reader of Mark can overlook this book. It will richly reward careful study."
　　—Bernard Brandon Scott, *Theological Studies*

"I have found Tolbert's interpretation 'illuminating and interesting' —and that unfailingly. She hears and sees new things in this old story, and she reflects thoughtfully on how we see and hear."
　　—Elizabeth Struthers Malbon, *The Journal of Religion*

Tolbert's exegesis . . . is consistently ingenious. . . . Throughout, her attention to the rhetorical conventions of the work and her good eye for exegetical detail assist her in her effort to provide a *coherent* interpretation. . . . *Sowing the Gospel* contains a rich harvest for students, pastors, theologians, and biblical scholars."
　　—Susan R. Garrett, *Princeton Seminary Bulletin*

"The strength of this book lies not only in the solid and consistent interpretation of the Gospel which is offered, but also in the way in which this reading of Mark opens up all kinds of avenues for further theological reflection. . . . Tolbert's respect for her audience has helped to produce a book which is provocative in the best sense, inviting the reader on a journey which engages both mind and imagination, and whose benefits are to be found not simply in reaching the stated goal but also in having traveled the road to get there."
　　—Katherine P. Mey

Sowing
❧ the Gospel

MARK'S WORLD IN
LITERARY-HISTORICAL
PERSPECTIVE

Mary Ann Tolbert

FORTRESS PRESS　　　　　　　　MINNEAPOLIS

SOWING THE GOSPEL
Mark's World in Literary-Historical Perspective

First paperback edition 1996

Cover design: Helen Melnis Cherullo/David Meyer
Internal design: Polebridge Press

The Library of Congress has cataloged the hardcover edition as follows:

Tolbert, Mary Ann, 1947–
     Sowing the gospel : Mark's World in literary-historical
perspective / by Mary Ann Tolbert.
         p.   cm.
     ISBN 0-8006-2412-2
     1. Bible. N.T. Mark—Criticism, interpretation, etc.
     2. Narration in the Bible. I. Title.
     BS2585.2.T62   1989
     226.3´066—dc20   89–37503
                                                                            CIP

     ISBN 0-8006-2974-4 (paperback; alk. paper)

The paper used in this publication meets the minimum requirements of American National Standard for Information Sciences—Permanence of Paper for Printed Library Materials, ANSI Z329.48–1984.

Manufactured in the U.S.A.   AF 1-2974

00   99   98   97   2   3   4   5   6   7   8   9   10

To Mary Cloe Tolbert
and G. Ray Tolbert

Contents

Preface

This book intends to be a work of *literary history;* that is, it attempts to situate the Gospel of Mark within the literary currents of its own historical milieu. The special combination of a literary and a historical approach to the Gospel is needed, I wish to argue, in order to answer the two most persistent complaints about Mark in modern scholarship: (1) that no consistent interpretation of the Gospel in all its parts has yet been elicited from studies of it and (2) that the narrative as it now stands appears obscure or muddled. Literary perspectives are especially appropriate for exploring the overall design of a narrative and/or its effect on its audience. Hence the first complaint seems to call clearly for literary studies of the Gospel, and much recent scholarship on Mark has moved in that direction with excellent results.

Interestingly, some of these literary analyses have served to underscore the second complaint, for read as narrative the Gospel often sounds enigmatic, more of a secretive riddle than a story. If interpreting Mark as story tends to dramatize its narrative obscurity, how is the second complaint to be addressed? It is certainly possible simply to grant that the Gospel is and was intended to be an esoteric, hidden text. Yet contemporary literary theory also emphasizes the vital roles of both the reader and the conventions of reading used by the reader in the construction of the meaning of any text. Such theories made me begin to wonder whether or not current critical readers of Mark trained mainly on the narrative subtleties of the modern novel and molded by the fashions of post-Enlightenment biblical criticism might be reading the text in conventional ways very foreign to the narrative patterns of its ancient author and original audiences. Might it not then be equally possible that some of the muddle seen in Mark is actually the result of this mismatch in reading conventions? Such speculations generated this study.

Since the Gospel of Mark is a literary text, no matter how unsophisticated its "literary" nature might be, it must be located first within the literary conventions of its own day in order to be understood as its author hoped the original audience would be able to do. Neither historical reconstructions of early Christianity nor attempts to chart the social world of the ancient Mediterranean can provide this essential *literary* perspective. Although social conventions and literary conventions are often related, they are rarely the same (think, for example, of the vast differences between the popular literary and cinematic type of the cowboy with his ready gun and faithful horse and the actual historical and social experience of the early settlers of the North American West). Consequently, reading Mark within the literary world of its own milieu necessitates an imposing task of literary-historical reconstruction, only in its infancy in biblical studies. Especially given the fact that *conventional* literary practices are often just that—agreements about writing and reading/hearing *assumed* by cultures without much argument or even discussion—the data for such reconstructions are often indirect and widely scattered. Thus, throughout this book and particularly in Part I, I try to reconstruct, often quite laboriously, from whatever appropriate material has survived from the ancient world, typical patterns of popular Greek writing that would have been second nature to people of the Greco-Roman period. While the basic interpretation of the Gospel of Mark developed in Part II of the book can be read on its own, the hypotheses about genre, stylistic conventions, and narrative strategies upon which the interpretation stands—and is made, I hope, most persuasive—require study of Part I first.

Like a formal commentary, this work covers every episode in the Gospel of Mark, often at length and often in several different contexts; but as a literary study, consciously trying to move in harmony with Mark's own narrative rhythms, the typical verse-by-verse commentary format is completely alien to its approach. However, for those wishing to explore one particular passage in depth, a comprehensive biblical citation index for the Gospel of Mark has been provided to guide such research. I am firmly convinced that the study of any individual pericope is best carried out with some sense of the total narrative context in which it appears, but I also recognize that at this point I may be accused of having sharply vested interests.

Although this book cannot be forthrightly designated a work of feminist literary criticism, my own deeply held political commitments are by no means absent from its conception or goals. Literary history in the broader world of contemporary literary criticism is undergoing a revival of sorts under the banner of the "new historicism," a movement, especially evident in recent Renaissance studies, that proposes to relocate texts in the contexts out of which they were generated. While many—but not all—new historicist analyses evince obvious Marxist tendencies by their focus on the power relations in and around the text, a focus this particular book does not have, I share with the new historicists what Edward Pechter in a review ("The New Historicism and Its Discontents: Politicizing Renaissance Drama," *PMLA* 102 [May 1987]: 292–303) decried as their "most important characteristic," their "detachment from the text" (p. 298). This detachment, which Pechter fears will detract from a modern audience's appreciation of Renaissance drama, serves to reduce the power of the text and increase "the observer's power over the text—the power to see through the surface, penetrate its disguises" (p. 299). If it is the Bible and not Shakespearean drama that is at issue, gaining some detachment from the control of the text and its generations of institutional interpreters by rehistoricizing it is no mean political act, because the authority of this text has so often been employed to deny the full humanity of women and other oppressed groups. It is my hope that hearing the Gospel of Mark and other biblical writings with new ears may permit us to see ourselves and one another with new eyes.

The work recounted in the following pages evolved over several years and owes much to the support of many people and institutions. Encouraged by colleagues from the SBL Markan Seminar of the late 1970s, I applied for and received the American Council of Learned Societies Research Fellowship for Recent Ph.D. Recipients in the Spring of 1981, permitting me to spend that time at Union Theological Seminary in New York City beginning an intensive study of Mark. That early research was aided by the help of Professor Phyllis Trible and conversations with Professor Ray Brown. Later, in 1985–86 I was able to realize the bulk of both the research and writing of the book during my sabbatical leave in Cambridge, England. I am deeply grateful to the Research Council of Vanderbilt University for awarding me the Research Associate Professorship to fund that year and to Professor Morna Hooker, the Lady Margaret's Professor of Divinity at Cambridge University, for both her friendship and her sponsorship of my position as a Bye Fellow at Robinson College, Cambridge.

The greatest debt I owe, however, is undoubtedly to colleagues and students at Vanderbilt University Divinity School who have suffered with remarkably good grace through years of comments about Mark, lectures on Mark, or illustrations from Mark. My two colleagues in New Testament, Professors Daniel Patte and Fernando Segovia, have especially been sources of comradeship and challenge in the formulation of my own ideas. Vanderbilt has also provided me as a female scholar with the all too rare gift of having senior women faculty as colleagues and mentors. Professor Sallie McFague has read and critiqued this entire manuscript, while Professor

Peggy Way helped me adjust to the peculiarities of life in a divinity school. Although many students have contributed to my growing understanding of Mark, as the several footnotes in the following pages witness, I had the careful and skilled assistance of Jeff Tucker, a fine scholar in his own right, in the final preparation and editing of the manuscript. In addition, Judy Matthews-Taylor deserves real credit for transcribing my handwritten pages onto the computer and thus allowing me to pretend to be part of the modern world. That pretense has, moreover, been further aided and abetted by the careful production management of John Hollar and Timothy Staveteig of Fortress Press.

Finally, this book is dedicated to my parents, both of whom started their adult careers as schoolteachers, though later turning to other pursuits. They made sure that the family in which I began my life was one thoroughly permeated by the love of learning. Along with a good beginning, a major project like this one requires daily support and encouragement. That present strength I have received in large measure from Sallie McFague, with whom I shared the sabbatical year in which much of this work was done. Indeed, I owe her more than I can say, for she has in addition joyfully shared with me her friendship, her wisdom, her intellectual stamina, and last—but not at all least—her dog. Without such nurture, the seeds of this book would still lie dormant.

Mary Ann Tolbert

List of Abbreviations

AAA	American Anthropological Association
AB	Anchor Bible
AnBib	Analecta biblica
BETL	Bibliotheca ephemeridum theologicarum lovaniensium
BZNW	Beihefte zur Zeitschrift für die neutestamentliche Wissenschaft
CBQ	*Catholic Biblical Quarterly*
CBQMS	Catholic Biblical Quarterly—Monograph Series
EKKNT	Evangelisch-katholischer Kommentar zum Neuen Testament
ETL	*Ephemerides theologicae lovanienses*
FRLANT	Forschungen zur Religion und Literatur des Alten and Neuen Testaments
GBS	Guides to Biblical Scholarship, Fortress Press
HTKNT	Herders theologischer Kommentar zum Neuen Testament
IRT	Issues in Religion and Theology
JBL	*Journal of Biblical Literature*
JSNTSup	Journal for the Study of the New Testament—Supplement Series
LEC	Library of Early Christianity, Westminster Press
NTS	*New Testament Studies*
NTS	New Testament Studies, London
NVBS	New Voices in Biblical Studies, Harper & Row
PMLA	*Publications of the Modern Language Association of America*
SBLDS	SBL Dissertation Series
SBLMS	SBL Monograph Series
SBLSBS	SBL Sources for Biblical Study
SBLSP	SBL Seminar Papers

SBLSS   SBL Semeia Studies
SBT   Studies in Biblical Theology
SJLA   Studies in Judaism in Late Antiquity
SNT   Studien zum Neuen Testament
TS   *Theological Studies*
TWAS   Twayne's World Authors Series
USQR   *Union Seminary Quarterly Review*
WUNT   Wissenschaftliche Untersuchungen zum Neuen Testament
ZNW   *Zeitschrift für die neutestamentliche Wissenschaft*
ZTK   *Zeitschrift für Theologie und Kirche*

Introduction

In the process of analyzing Homer's *Odyssey,* Tzvetan Todorov confirms a fundamental law of all literature, no matter how ancient or how apparently primitive:

> No narrative is natural; a choice and a construction will always preside over its appearance; narrative is a discourse, not a series of events.[1]

The Gospel of Mark is a narrative. That simple observation and the fundamental law behind it have often been lost, ignored, or denied in the understandable desire of Christianity for theological clarity and dogmatic authority and in the primary concern of modern biblical scholarship for data upon which to build historical reconstructions of the life of Jesus or the earliest Christian communities. Choice and construction, however, do stand behind the story told by the Gospel of Mark. Moreover, it seems to be a mysterious, opaque, and peculiar story: Jesus is portrayed as a miracle-working but secretive Messiah, who selects as special disciples a remarkably obtuse group, who in the end flee, betray, or deny him. On the one hand his apparently preordained and inevitable death is at the hands of weak Romans influenced by a monolithically evil Jewish establishment, but on the other hand a centurion affirms that he is Son of God as he dies, while his women followers, when informed of his resurrection, rush away in fear from the tomb and tell no one what has happened. That such a paradoxical

1. "Primitive Narrative," in *The Poetics of Prose,* trans. R. Howard (Oxford: Basil Blackwell, 1977), 55.

and negative story should be proclaimed as the good news of Jesus Christ (Mark 1:1) has challenged the ingenuity of generations of biblical interpreters. One common response to the oddness of the Markan narrative has been to study it only in small segments, thus avoiding the difficulty of the overall sense. Yet the same choice and construction that put together the parables and the miracle stories also developed the theme of discipleship failure and the suffering Messiah. Sometimes the author of the Gospel is castigated as a muddler of tradition or a clumsy, incompetent writer. Or, the evangelist is excused for these faults by pointing to the presence of traditional oral or written materials in the early Christian communities that had to be preserved regardless of the detriment to the narrative. Unfortunately such excuses are often a case of damning by faint praise and another, albeit more sophisticated, way of evading the issue. If choice and construction, no matter how unpretentious, stand behind *any* parts of the story (e.g., the so-called "redactional units"), then that same choice and construction must have presided over the selection, placement, and development of all parts of the narrative.[2] However, it is precisely some overall sense of the continuity and unity of the Gospel of Mark that remains elusive in studies of it. As W. G. Kümmel noted in his review of research on Mark in the mid-1970s, "A clear explanation of the aim of the evangelist has not yet been elicited from the text."[3]

The Goal of the Study

Although the situation that Kümmel perceived has altered in the years since his assessment, primarily because of the introduction into the field of biblical studies of literary-critical[4] perspectives more amenable to discern-

---

2. For an introduction to the issues of tradition and redaction as they affect Mark, see, e.g., N. Perrin, *What Is Redaction Criticism?* (GBS; Philadelphia: Fortress Press, 1969).

For an example of excusing Mark's style because of the need to preserve traditional material, see E. Best, "Mark's Preservation of the Tradition," in *L'Evangile selon Marc: Tradition et rédaction,* ed. M. Sabbe (Gembloux: J. Duculot, 1974), 25–30.

For an example of castigating the author's competence, see J. Meagher, *Clumsy Construction in Mark's Gospel* (New York and Toronto: Edwin Mellen Press, 1979).

3. *Introduction to the New Testament,* trans. H. C. Kee (Nashville: Abingdon Press, 1975), 92.

4. Terminological confusion for this new area abounds in biblical studies at present primarily because nineteenth-century biblical scholars decided to call their study of the sources, locations, and possible authors of biblical books "literary criticism." In order to avoid confusing that earlier, basically historical exploration with current use of theories and methods drawn from the disciplines of literature and linguistics, many scholars today have suggested new labels for what they are doing. Narrative criticism, aesthetic criticism, rhetorical criticism, and composition criticism are just four of the most common proposals. All of these terms have elements to recommend them. However, I prefer not to employ another specialized label, recognizable only to the

ing narrative coherence, most of these recent discussions have still tended to analyze only limited portions of the text or the development of only one motif, literary structure, or set of characters. Since it continues to pose difficulties for many of the more traditional biblical methods such as source, form, and redaction criticism, Mark has been at the forefront of much of this new literary exploration.[5] Yet, for all of their excellent contributions to understanding the Gospel, few of these recent studies have attempted to develop a "perspective in which the Gospel in all its parts could be given a consistent interpretation."[6] Nevertheless, interpreting the whole is not only the special aptitude of literary criticism and the practical goal envisaged by most literary investigations, it is also the necessary context for adequately evaluating any of the individual parts. Consequently, in an attempt to address the current situation in Markan studies, this study intends primarily to articulate at least one possible "consistent interpretation" of "the Gospel in all its parts," using the perspectives and tools provided by literary criticism as the practical basis of analysis.

Since no one discussion of a text as ancient and as deeply involved in centuries of religious and historical debates as Mark is can hope to cover all issues or answer all questions, the selection of which concerns this particular work will address and which it will not, will be guided by a criterion

limited guild of biblical scholars, for I believe biblical studies needs to become fully and openly interdisciplinary. To assure the integrity of work on biblical texts, scholars across the disciplines of the humanities and social sciences should be able to read and evaluate these analyses. Consequently, in this book, "literary criticism" will always refer to the general literary approaches used to study ancient and modern writings. "Source criticism" will be adopted to refer to the special historical interests that nineteenth-century biblical scholars called "literary criticism."

5. Some recent works incorporate literary concerns in exploring aspects of the Gospel of Mark: E. Best, *Mark: The Gospel as Story* (Edinburgh: T. & T. Clark, 1983); J. Dewey, *Markan Public Debate: Literary Technique, Concentric Structure and Theology in Mark 2:1—3:6* (SBLDS 48; Chico, Calif.: Scholars Press, 1980); R. M. Fowler, *Loaves and Fishes: The Function of the Feeding Stories in the Gospel of Mark* (SBLDS 54; Chico, Calif.: Scholars Press, 1981); W. Kelber, *Mark's Story of Jesus* (Philadelphia: Fortress Press, 1979); idem, *The Oral and the Written Gospel: The Hermeneutics of Speaking and Writing in the Synoptic Tradition, Mark, Paul, and Q* (Philadelphia: Fortress Press, 1983); F. Kermode, *The Genesis of Secrecy: On the Interpretation of Narrative* (Cambridge, Mass., and London: Harvard University Press, 1979); J. D. Kingsbury, *The Christology of Mark's Gospel* (Philadelphia: Fortress Press, 1983); J. L. Magness, *Sense and Absence: Structure and Suspension in the Ending of Mark's Gospel* (Atlanta: Scholars Press, 1986); N. Petersen, *Literary Criticism for New Testament Critics* (Philadelphia: Fortress Press, 1978); D. Rhoads and D. Michie, *Mark as Story: An Introduction to the Narrative of a Gospel* (Philadelphia: Fortress Press, 1982); V. Robbins, *Jesus the Teacher: A Socio-Rhetorical Interpretation of Mark* (Philadelphia: Fortress Press, 1984); D. O. Via, Jr., *The Ethics of Mark's Gospel—In the Middle of Time* (Philadelphia: Fortress Press, 1985); and J. G. Williams, *Gospel Against Parable: Mark's Language of Mystery* (Bible and Literature Series 12; Sheffield: JSOT Press, 1985).

6. H. C. Kee, "Mark's Gospel in Recent Research," in *Interpreting the Gospels*, ed. J. L. Mays (Philadelphia: Fortress Press, 1981), 131–32.

of relevancy to the overarching goal of the study. Thus, while it will be necessary to explore the whole of the Gospel, literary analysis with its attendant assumptions of unity and intentionality is not consonant with either the verse-by-verse format or the encyclopedic aims of the traditional biblical commentary genre. Moreover, text, source, and form-critical problems, as vital as they are to reconstructing the life of the historical Jesus or the early Christians, will be raised only insofar as they clearly influence an assessment of the overall story Mark is telling. Certainly the results of literary analysis may well supply useful information for historical reconstructions of the milieu of the Gospel, but the determination of that information must logically follow, not precede, the completion of thorough literary evaluation.[7]

Because the goal of this study is the practical application of literary perspectives to a text in order to interpret it, concrete demonstration of literary techniques rather than theoretical speculations about narrative will be emphasized. Although some presentation of literary and historica! theory is mandatory, it will be limited to the required and the useful. The point is to use theory to illuminate the text, not to use the text to illustrate theories. Hence, whenever possible, the demands of the story, not the categories of literary criticism, will organize and focus the discussion. Furthermore, while the conflicting claims of different literary theories, and the debates engendered by their various loyal supporters, are vitally important for continuing insight into the creative process, most practical criticism remains basically eclectic in nature. Such eclecticism, however, need not be arbitrary. Literary approaches—or any other methods, for that matter—applied to a text should be guided by goal-specific and text-specific criteria; that is, one should select the method of study (in the case of biblical texts, the particular exegetical method, either historical or literary), first, on the basis of what one is seeking generally to learn from the text and, second, on the basis of the special aspects, circumstances, and characteristics making up the particular text under study.

For example, if the quest of the historical Jesus is the motivation for a study of Mark, some analysis combining source and form criticisms with criteria for determining the degree of historical probability of isolated units of material must be followed, but if, instead, one wishes to compare the

---

7. This is not at all an original observation. Indeed, William Wrede made the same point almost one hundred years ago, but it was not heeded by historical critics then: "The first task must always be the thorough illumination of the accounts in the spirit of those accounts themselves, to ask what the narrator in his own time wanted to say to his readers, and this task must be carried to its conclusion and made the foundation of critical historiography" (Wrede, *Das Messiasgeheimnis in den Evangelien* [Göttingen: Vandenhoeck & Ruprecht, 1901; ET: *The Messianic Secret,* trans. J. C. Greig (Greenwood, S.C.: Attic Press, 1971)], 2–3).

portrayal of Jesus' ministry in Mark with that of Matthew or Luke, then very different redactional, literary, and comparative procedures are called for. Moreover, the special characteristics of a particular text, including such crucial issues as genre, language, style, historical milieu, conventions, and so forth, often far from self-evident, are critical to forming a reasonable interpretation. Especially with ancient and culturally alien texts like Mark, careful attention must be given to the particularities of the work and the literary and historical milieu in which it was produced, establishing plausible hypotheses where reliable knowledge is lacking. Finally, the methodological approach selected should be adapted as far as possible to conform to the requirements determined for that specific text. A historical analysis of ancient speeches, for instance, that assumes a model of verbal transcription based on twentieth-century concerns for accuracy is obviously not compatible with the cultural milieu of ancient historiography. Similarly, the increasing complexity of the modern novel has generated narrative theories capable of awesomely detailed analyses of all the vagaries of point of view and composition, but much of this arsenal is unnecessary, and indeed occasionally distracting, when the text under study lacks the subtleties of narrative development typical of contemporary literature.[8]

How goal-specific and text-specific criteria shape the literary approach to the Gospel of Mark followed in this book will be explored at length in Part I: Delineating the Approach. The five chapters of Part I will outline the major methodological orientation, theoretical assumptions, and historical hypotheses, including issues of milieu and genre, that will be used to guide the practical interpretation of the Gospel. Part II: Interpreting the Gospel will concentrate on the text of Mark itself, starting in chapter 7 with an overview of rhetorical structure that suggests the basic interrelationships of the different strands of the Gospel. Chapters 8 through 11 will then develop those interrelationships fully and in the process attempt to articulate one possible interpretation of "the Gospel in all its parts." Although Part II is comprehensible without reading Part I first, much of the argument upon which Part II is based and, consequently, much of the persuasiveness of its interpretation depends on the discussions in Part I.

The organization of the book attempts to explain in an orderly, reason-

8. Some current theorists like Gerard Genette (*Narrative Discourse: An Essay in Method,* trans. J. Lewin [Ithaca, N.Y.: Cornell University Press, 1980]), Boris Uspensky (*A Poetics of Composition,* trans. V. Zavarin and S. Wittig [Berkeley and Los Angeles: University of California Press, 1973]), and Umberto Eco (*The Role of the Reader* [Bloomington, Ind.: Indiana University Press, 1979]) have been used with benefit by biblical scholars when they are substantially reduced in complexity. On this issue, see the discussion in R. A. Culpepper, *Anatomy of the Fourth Gospel: A Study in Literary Design* (Philadelphia: Fortress Press, 1983), 6–10, and his use of some of these theorists (pp. 20–49).

able, and clear fashion what the author, admittedly, has discovered about the Gospel of Mark in a disorganized, tangential, and occasionally even illogical manner. Thus, what one hopes will be the persuasive progression of the argument should in no way be taken as a pattern for "doing" literary criticism or even as a reliable guide to how this particular literary analysis was "done." It represents, instead, only a way of providing clarity in explanation.[9]

Scholarship is, or ideally ought to be, a continuing dialogue among interested parties, and that disciplined fellowship has helpful implications for a study such as this one. Unlike the classic parental lament that each new generation insists on learning all over again for itself the basic "facts of life" rather than heeding experienced counsel, partners in scholarly pursuits can build upon the work of their colleagues instead of having to start from "first principles" each time. Since a number of excellent books already exist to introduce biblical scholars and students of the Bible to the aims, terms, and concerns of literary criticism,[10] those issues will not be rehearsed here; interested readers are encouraged to consult the work of others. Similarly, trends in recent research on all the various aspects of the Gospel of Mark are being assessed continually[11] and need not be repeated. In addition, because this study intends to interpret the whole of Mark, many aspects of it might be compared and contrasted with past and present scholarship on all parts of the Gospel. However, extensive cataloguing is beyond the scope of this book, and, consequently, except for striking examples of similarity or difference, the footnotes throughout the coming chapters will indicate only instances of dependence on the thought of others.

9. For a superb presentation of the difference between discovery and explanation in literary criticism, see Kermode, *The Genesis of Secrecy,* 137.

10. For helpful discussions related specifically to the New Testament Gospels, see Culpepper, *Anatomy of the Fourth Gospel;* Dewey, *Markan Public Debate,* esp. 5–39; Petersen, *Literary Criticism for New Testament Critics;* and Rhoads and Michie, *Mark as Story.*

For general discussions of literary approaches to biblical material, see R. Alter, *The Art of Biblical Narrative* (New York: Basic Books, 1981); G. A. Kennedy, *New Testament Interpretation Through Rhetorical Criticism* (Chapel Hill, N.C.: University of North Carolina Press, 1984); and E. V. McKnight, *The Bible and the Reader: An Introduction to Literary Criticism* (Philadelphia: Fortress Press, 1985). Note that Kennedy, a classicist, proposes a different designation for his approach because he thinks literary criticism does not deal with the historical milieu of a text. His error lies in taking only the New Critics and Northrop Frye as examples of literary criticism (see Kennedy, pp. 4–5). Hence, biblical scholars are not the only ones to suggest new titles for what the humanities in general understand literary criticism to do.

11. Two book-length studies of research on Mark are H. Humphrey, *A Bibliography for the Gospel of Mark: 1954–1980* (New York: Edwin Mellen Press, 1982), and S. Kealy, *Mark's Gospel: A History of Its Interpretation* (New York: Paulist Press, 1982). In addition, three recent article-length reviews of research are very useful: Kee, "Mark's Gospel in Recent Research"; J. D. Kingsbury, "The Gospel of Mark in Current Research," *Religious Studies Review* 5 (1979): 101–7; and D. Harrington, "A Map of Books on Mark (1975–1984)," *Biblical Theology Bulletin* 15 (1985): 12–16.

Viewing scholarship as a continuing dialogue also supplies the courage one needs to put forth yet another interpretation of an often interpreted text like Mark. Just as this discussion builds on the strengths and tries to avoid some of the limitations of earlier work, just so it, in turn, will encourage others to confirm, expand, and refute its own claims and in so doing explore yet again the odd story of the Gospel of Mark. Perhaps all efforts at critical interpretation find their most basic justification in assuming the role of gadfly to future and deeper textual studies. Thus, this book in no way intends to present a final or ultimate word on the interpretation of Mark; rather, it is only one further point in a continuing conversation.

Multiple Interpretations

Indeed, attempting to articulate "a consistent interpretation" of "the Gospel in all its parts," while requiring a certain amount of passionate defense, does not need to claim utter completeness, absolute truth, or finality. From both a theoretical and a practical standpoint, it is clear that more than one "consistent interpretation" of "the Gospel in all its parts" is possible. Multiple interpretations arise not only from the necessary historical conditionedness of both texts and readers but also from the very nature of narrative itself.[12] The intrinsic ambiguity of narrative, indeed of language, requires readers to judge continually the relationship of each sentence, each new incident, each character's next speech to what has gone before and what is likely to come after, demanding, quite often, reevaluations of the past and revisions of future expectations.[13] Inevitably, different readers will emphasize different aspects of the sequence in attempting to make sense of the whole, or they will fill in the narrative "gaps" in the story in different ways.[14] While narrative conventions, such as genre, stylistic features, type scenes, and reliable commentary, guide readers in making

12. On this issue, see the whole argument in Kermode, *The Genesis of Secrecy,* and for one evaluation of that argument, see M. A. Tolbert, "Frank Kermode, *The Genesis of Secrecy,*" *Religious Studies Review* 8 (1982): 1–6.

13. An excellent example of the popular manipulation of the dynamics of linear narrative occurred on one episode of the long-running American television series "M*A*S*H": An unexploded bomb had landed in the hospital compound and surgeons Hawkeye and Trapper John were attempting to disarm it while Colonel Blake read out the instructions sent by the Army. Blake read, "Now cut the two wires leading to the timing fuse," and then looked up. The two doctors carefully cut the wires. Blake looked back at the instructions and read, "But first remove the fuse." At that point, panic ensued, everyone ran for cover, and the bomb—a dummy, as it happened—exploded.

The entire humor of the episode was built on the ambiguities inherent in the linearity of narrative.

14. See W. Iser, *The Act of Reading: A Theory of Aesthetic Response* (Baltimore: Johns Hopkins University Press, 1978), 180–231, for an insightful discussion of the presence of "blanks" or "gaps" in narrative and the ways readers may potentially fill them.

these judgments, considerable room for debate still exists in even the most mundane of narratives. Self-consciously aesthetic works like James Joyce's *Ulysses* or Virginia Woolf's *To the Lighthouse* delight in multiplying ambiguities, but even humbler narratives like folktales, popular fiction, government reports, newspaper articles, and bicycle assembly instructions manage to immerse their readers in the work of interpretation. One does not have to accept the extreme position of some poststructuralists, that the text is an empty space made meaningful only by the act of reading, to grant that the process of reading is indeed a creative endeavor.[15]

Not only the intrinsic ambiguity of narrative but also the historical, cultural, and intellectual distance between current readers and the production of an ancient text like Mark encourages the growth of multiple interpretations. Neither the author of a text nor its readers stand outside the movement of history. The conventions guiding reading and writing, cultural, social, and intellectual values, and the very definition of truth itself along with the institutions that erect that definition shift from age to age, from culture to culture, from generation to generation. In reading a text like Mark, one may acknowledge the relatively simple changes in monetary system, government administration, agricultural practice, and the like, while failing to recognize the far more profound shifts in narrative conventions, values, patterns of thought, and social organization. These latter constitute an alien world, much of it an irrevocably lost world, that deeply divides the experience of a modern reader from that of the earliest readers and hearers of the Gospel.

From both a theoretical and a practical standpoint, then, multiple interpretations of a text are not only legitimate but inevitable. The ramifications of that assertion for the authority, validity, or evaluation of any single interpretation are considerable.[16] On one extreme lies the absolutely untenable view that all interpretations should cease. Only if we stop reading a text will we stop interpreting it, for every act of reading is an act of interpretation. The opposite extreme position, even if theoretically more supportable, is equally impracticable: every new reading is a new interpretation standing on an equal footing with every other interpretation. Reading in this view *creates* the text; without it no text exists. Between the theoretical purity of these two extremes lies the realm of messy, practical judgments

15. An excellent assessment of the various arguments on the nature of texts and their relation to readers among structural, poststructural, and audience-oriented critics can be found in F. Lentricchia, *After the New Criticism* (Chicago: University of Chicago Press, 1980).

16. For an insightful discussion of the various poles in the debate over "validity in interpretation" from E. D. Hirsch to the Yale School, see Lentricchia, *After the New Criticism*, 257–80. For a strong reader-response argument for multiple interpretations, see Iser, *Act of Reading*, 163–231.

and slippery criteria which can claim only transitory authority—in other words, the kind of world that human beings generally inhabit. In regard to biblical texts especially, some readers attempt to avoid this universal human condition by accepting a church decision as to which interpretation of a text is the correct one. Unfortunately for them, churches tended to make those determinations more readily in past centuries than they do in the present, and believers are often faced with antiquated authorized interpretations that themselves require as much interpretation as the original text.

Short of such institutional decrees, it is still possible to acknowledge the existence of conventional and publicly shared standards for interpretations.[17] While accepting the philosophical caveat that such standards may well be only fantasies of order covering the essential randomness that is reality, they are at least mutual fantasies, providing the shared conventions any era needs in order to support public discourse with some modicum of real communication. Clearly, such conventional standards are also highly susceptible to cultural change. For example, throughout the early centuries of Christian development, generations of teachers, preachers, and scholars understood allegory to be an entirely appropriate method for interpreting Scripture. The literal text was often seen as a veil which the true believer must penetrate in order to find the real meaning of the story. Origen, Augustine, the Venerable Bede, Hugh of St. Victor, even Dante, along with their contemporaries, predecessors, and followers, used and developed allegorical interpretation in ever more ingenious forms to explain Scripture. The fourfold allegorical method was summarized in Latin couplet by the thirteenth-century scholar Augustine of Dacia:

Littera gesta docet, quid credas allegoria
Moralis quid agas, quo tendas anagogia.[18]

Yet, with the rise of the scientific method and historical consciousness that marked the Enlightenment of the seventeenth and eighteenth centuries, the respectability of allegorical interpretation was severely undermined. In the

17. The fact that different readers can sometimes reach a consensus on the meaning of a work indicates that some publicly accepted standards are in operation. For an interesting discussion of conventions and readings, see J. Culler, *On Deconstruction: Theory and Criticism After Structuralism* (Ithaca, N.Y.: Cornell University Press, 1982), 31–83.

18. Kealy, *Mark's Gospel* (p. 33), gives a traditional loose English translation of the couplet as follows:

The letter shows what God and our fathers did;
The allegory shows where our faith is hid;
The moral meaning gives us rules of daily life;
The anagogy shows us where we end our strife.

See Kealy's full discussion of the medieval interpretation of Mark (pp. 31–57).

twentieth century it is no longer intellectually acceptable or valid as a method of interpreting Scripture.[19] The rise and fall of allegory stands as a striking example of the cultural relativity of conventional standards and should act as a warning against scholarly hubris in contemporary research. One must do as well as one can, recognizing that later generations may find little of value in those efforts.

Criteria for Adjudicating Interpretations

Armed with these qualifications, concerning the philosophical possibility that order itself is an illusion and concerning the inevitable cultural relativity of conventional judgments, we nevertheless submit that publicly accepted standards are available for evaluating the plethora of interpretations of a text. Such criteria function as parameters for judging readings and thus result, *not* in a definitive ruling of right or wrong, but rather in a general perception that some interpretations of a text are more *persuasive* to modern readers than others according to current cultural standards.

A tentative list of such criteria would probably include the following five points:

1. An interpretation of a text should be in accord with the standards of intellectual discourse of its age. It should reflect the contemporary status of scientific and philosophical knowledge.

The fourfold allegorical method would be ruled out for modern interpretations under this rubric. In addition, persuasive interpretations are ones that take seriously the changes in fundamental paradigms of understanding or major shifts in hermeneutical positions that occur in society. Liberation theology, feminist criticism, and the hermeneutics of suspicion are just a few present issues that ought to concern the interpreter of Scripture.[20] However, this criterion affects the interpreter and the interpretation, not the text. Ancient texts cannot always be expected to reflect current concerns, but interpreters *can* be expected to reflect upon the text self-consciously out of their own moment in history. Indeed, interpreters always actually do that; the point is how self-consciously and how honestly they go about their task.

2. The more fully an interpretation can demonstrate its points from the text itself, the more convincing it becomes.

---

19. See an earlier discussion of this whole issue in M. A. Tolbert, *Perspectives on the Parables: An Approach to Multiple Interpretations* (Philadelphia: Fortress Press, 1979), 62–91.

20. See the excellent discussion of the effect of some of these issues on biblical interpretation in E. Schüssler Fiorenza, *In Memory of Her: A Feminist Theological Reconstruction of Christian Origins* (New York: Crossroad, 1983), 3–36.

The literary structure of a text, its stylistic features, plot development, rhetorical figures, diction, conventional scenes, characters, narrative voice, point of view, and reliable commentary form the empirical base of all interpretations. While modern interpretations do, and indeed should, employ contemporary models of analysis and explanation—be they literary, linguistic, psychological, or sociological—in interpreting a text, the proof of the model's applicability and usefulness depends on the extent to which it can organize and illuminate these empirical textual elements. Although different readers can and do often disagree on the presence, function, and importance of these elements in any given story—either because of varying degrees of reading competence or because of varying perspectives—the basic "material" of the text still provides a fairly public ground for argument and evaluation.

3. The more coherence an interpretation can disclose in a text, the more persuasive it becomes. For example, in Mark an interpretation that explains discipleship failure by one hypothesis but must evolve a quite different rationale for the strange ending is less persuasive than an interpretation that can encompass and unify both elements.

This criterion assumes a logical unity within a text itself; it assumes that a text is not random but intentional, not scattered but coherent. Whether ontologically grounded in the text or in the reader, the presumption of intentionality, organization, coherence, and unity in a text underlies the whole process of reading and interpretation. As Frank Kermode points out, "Our whole practice of reading is founded on such expectations."[21] Indeed, so dominant is this convention that it requires "a more strenuous effort to believe that a narrative lacks coherence than to believe that somehow, if we could only find out, it doesn't."[22] At the same time, one must also admit that all interpretations are reductions of the text; they must be so, if they are not simply to repeat the text itself word for word. Interpretations stress some aspects of the story and necessarily ignore or neglect others. Thus, this criterion always functions in a relative sense, favoring those readings that integrate relatively more aspects of the narrative than others.

The negative version of this rubric also questions those interpretations that insist on omitting segments of the story in order to make sense of it. The practice of labeling material as "secondary," "traditional," or "an interpolation" in order to drop it from consideration is all too common in biblical exegesis. While some material may indeed be later additions to a text, the burden of proof falls on the interpreter, and interpretations that lean too heavily or too often on such labels are generally unconvincing.

21. Kermode, *The Genesis of Secrecy,* 53.
22. Ibid.

4. An interpretation should be cognizant of the general historical, literary, and sociological matrix out of which the text comes.

Earlier in this century, literary criticism especially in America was dominated by a critical theory that would have denied the relevance of this criterion. The New Critics insisted that each literary work was an autonomous aesthetic object and must therefore be studied in isolation from issues of author, audience, historical situation, and so forth.[23] New Criticism had developed as a reaction against the typical critical practices of previous centuries in which the explication of a literary work had become essentially the biography of the author or the response of an audience or the political situation it reflected. The work itself hardly needed to be mentioned. Such concepts as the intentional fallacy, the affective fallacy, the genetic fallacy, and, more recently, the representational fallacy were useful correctives for a critical practice that naively identified literature totally with the author's stated intentions or the audience's reaction or the sources it used or the "real world" it was supposed to represent.[24] Yet, by its own insistence on the absolute autonomy of a literary work, New Criticism itself eventually provoked reaction, for literature clearly is related in important ways to the historical and cultural milieu out of which it comes.[25]

Somewhere between total autonomy and total identification lies the more reasonable critical option. Interpretations need to be cognizant of the milieu of the text, but they do not need to be slavishly limited to it, even if that were actually possible. If an interpretation can demonstrate its grounding in the text, it has established its right to be taken seriously, but "grounding in the text" generally requires, especially for an ancient and culturally alien text like Mark, careful analysis of the literary conventions governing the text's historical milieu.[26]

23. R. Wellek and A. Warren, *Theory of Literature* (3d ed.; New York: Harcourt, Brace & World, 1956), is the theoretical Bible of New Criticism and presents its case in convincing detail. A good, brief discussion of the history of various critical theories from Plato to the New Critics can be found in M. H. Abrams, *The Mirror and the Lamp: Romantic Theory and the Critical Tradition* (New York: W. W. Norton, 1958), 3–29.

24. Much traditional biblical scholarship still bears unfortunate analogies with this type of naive critical practice, and insistence on many of the principles of New Criticism remains an important corrective for biblical scholars to hear. Given this situation, it is not at all surprising that literary studies of the Bible continue to exhibit strong ties with New Criticism, while at the same time attempting to adopt more recent critical theories.

25. For a discussion of the demise of New Criticism and the explosion of critical options since, see Lentricchia, *After the New Criticism,* esp. 3–26.

26. The common censure heard in biblical circles that an ancient author surely could not have intended this or that meaning suggested by an interpretation is wrongly applied to any interpretation that can demonstrate its points in the text itself. This critique ignores what the New Critics quite rightly pointed out: writers often say more than they intend or less than they intend or other than they intend. Moreover, modern

5. An interpretation should be illuminating and interesting.

The force of this criterion is twofold. First, presenting an interpretation for others to consider implies that something new or different has been seen in the text from what others have already perceived. Some illumination of the text is expected. While that illumination need not always be blinding, it should at least be interesting and engaging. Second, that an interpretation is interesting to others ensures its public character. Idiosyncratic, highly personal, or solipsistic readings rarely generate more than cursory notice. An interesting reading exhibits some communal (or institutional) acceptability.

Although other criteria might arguably be added to the list, these five already provide some fairly clear standards by which different interpretations of a text may be compared and adjudicated. To acknowledge the inevitability of multiple interpretations is neither to affirm the suggestion that "anything goes" in interpretation nor to strengthen the case for authoritative institutional decrees. One can enjoy, rather than fear, the creativity of reading because reasonable limits exist in the public sphere and can be used to evaluate the persuasiveness of any given interpretation. While obviously more than one may be judged highly persuasive, the result is not anarchy but disciplined plurality.

Justification for the Study

One final issue needs to be addressed before the main task of this book can begin. What justification exists for spending so much time and effort on a relatively brief, undistinguished text from so far away and so long ago as the Gospel of Mark? For some within the Christian community the justification is self-evident: it is a part of the canon of Holy Scripture. However, even in Christian circles the "house of authority" now appears to many to be founded on shifting sand and not rock.[27] Christian life in the twentieth or the twenty-first century cannot and should not look to first-century Greek writings for normative principles or authoritative moral judgments.

Why, then, continue to rehearse the past? Several reasons might be suggested. First, though Christians through the centuries have continued to articulate their faith in the light of the problems and concerns of their own times, the Gospel of Mark was one of the first of those articulations. While

interpretations of ancient texts must sometimes painstakingly reconstruct writing conventions that ancient authors simply assumed and absorbed from their cultures, making the modern interpretation look far more complicated than the situation actually was for the ancient writer.

27. See, e.g., E. Farley, *Ecclesial Reflection: An Anatomy of Theological Method* (Philadelphia: Fortress Press, 1982), 3–168.

being among the first does not confer perpetual relevance or value, it does establish a pattern of expression that others often follow. If the Bible is not an archetype, it still retains interest as a prototype.[28] In addition, because Christianity has, for better or worse, dominated so much of Western history and culture, the biblical writings not only have established patterns for theological reflection but also have shaped the development of the arts in the Western world. Painting, sculpture, drama, and literature all bear the images, themes, cadences, and figures of the Gospel stories.

Second, while many texts from the past may remain important as sources for later cultural developments, very few texts extend a living tradition through the centuries. In liturgy, homily, and Bible study, the Gospels, and much other biblical material, *live in the present.* They are not relics of a dead past but rather the continuing focus of debate and controversy. People still care passionately about their interpretation.[29] Moreover, such contemporary use of ancient texts raises forcefully all manner of hermeneutical questions: How can ancient narrative speak to contemporary issues? How does a text *mean* through history? Is there a transhistorical myth or core to a story that remains helpful to the general human situation in all times and places? What degree of translation of a text into contemporary language and thought is permissible? Although all literature raises these and similar questions to some extent, the degree of urgency with which biblical literature poses these issues is exceptional. Thus, working with the Gospels can become a vital, demanding, and exciting enterprise.

Third, *as religious texts,* the Gospels deal with basic human fears and concerns: death, suffering, illness, alienation, betrayal, failure, oppression. The power of any religion lies in its ability to counter these human experiences, either in the present or the future; either through altered consciousness, endurance, escape, or revolution; either by meditation, good works, faith, or obedience. The Gospel of Mark, like some of the other New Testament writings, is deeply involved in the dramatic portrayal of this fateful struggle between the forces of evil and the forces of good, between the persistence of fear and the possibility of faith. Whatever the cultural idiom, whatever the literary polish, such elements make for a good story.

---

28. See the discussion of archetype versus prototype in Schüssler Fiorenza, *In Memory of Her,* 33–36.

29. Other literature that often has a similar living tradition is drama—and especially Shakespeare's plays. Since the plays of Shakespeare are still performed yearly, their interpretation, their contemporary relevance, if any, is the subject of passionate argument. The point here is not that Shakespeare's plays are great literature and thus continue to attract interest, for there is much great literature that does not engender passionate contemporary debates. Rather, Shakespeare's plays live in the present through continual reinterpretation, performance, and even institutional support and development (e.g., The Royal Shakespeare Company).

Finally, the most persuasive justification for spending time and effort on this ancient text is well expressed in the words of Samuel Sandmel: "Mark fascinates me."[30]

30. "Prolegomena to a Commentary on Mark," in *Two Living Traditions: Essays on Religion* (Detroit: Wayne State University Press, 1972), 149.

PART I

Delineating the Approach

1

Introducing
the Approach

Whether because of the pervasive influence of Augustine's view that Mark was an abbreviation of Matthew or whether because of the baffling portrait it presented of Jesus, the Gospel of Mark received minimal attention throughout most of the centuries of church history. Only in the last two hundred years has Mark begun to attract extensive notice, and the reason for its recent rise to consciousness has more to do with forces within the world of biblical scholarship than the pressure of ecclesial need. Indeed, the development of modern biblical research and the increasing importance of Mark go hand in hand. Spurred on by challenges to the historical reliability of the Christian message hurled down first by H. S. Reimarus and second by the massive Gospel studies of D. F. Strauss, biblical scholars of the last century embarked on the careful critical explorations of the literary relationships among the canonical Gospels that finally resulted in the hypothesis of Markan priority.[1] Mark, they proposed, was not an abbreviation of Matthew or a muddled contraction of Matthew and Luke but the earliest extant Gospel and one of the sources used by the authors of Matthew and Luke.[2] From that moment on, Mark became the crucible of almost all new

1. For further discussion of this fascinating history up until the early years of this century, see A. Schweitzer, *Von Reimarus zu Wrede* (Tübingen: J. C. B. Mohr [Paul Siebeck], 1906; ET: *The Quest of the Historical Jesus,* trans. W. Montgomery [New York: Macmillan Co., 1961]).

2. While debate on Markan priority continues, and should continue, I still accept the Markan hypothesis as the best explanation of the relationships among the Synoptic Gospels. Although the results of this study, as will become clear later, really do not depend in any way on that hypothesis, my work with the text itself has confirmed in

experiments in New Testament study. Both scholars in quest of the historical Jesus and those who opposed the quest began with Mark. Early in this century Mark and the hypothetical Q document (material shared by Matthew and Luke not found in Mark) became the basic texts of New Testament form criticism, and in recent decades major studies in redaction criticism, and particularly the methodological development of redaction criticism,[3] have focused on Mark. It is thoroughly appropriate, then, that two of the most recent avenues of biblical research, sociological analysis and literary criticism, should find in the Gospel of Mark a primary text.[4]

As a contribution to these ongoing investigations of the Gospel of Mark, this study intends to develop an interpretation of the whole Gospel by using the perspectives and tools provided by literary criticism as the practical basis of analysis. As suggested in the Introduction, a practical literary approach to any text should be shaped by goal-specific and text-specific criteria. The purpose of Part I is to explore the theoretical and methodological ramifications of those criteria for fashioning a practical literary analysis of the Gospel of Mark. Given my stated goal, the first step will be to determine what directions and limitations such a goal assumes for the analysis, both in terms of the text of Mark itself and in terms of the use of literary-critical perspectives. The second step will be to investigate the special characteristics of the Gospel that need to be considered in this type of study. That investigation will be conducted in two chapters: the general features of the context and milieu of the Gospel that shaped its production will be considered, and then the specific indications of its generic affiliations will be detailed in order to suggest a new hypothesis for its genre to guide our interpretation. In the course of these text-specific considerations, a further refinement of the goal of the analysis will be made. Finally, with goal-specific and text-specific issues clarified, the contours of a responsible, practical literary approach to the Gospel of Mark can be sketched.

my own mind the general correctness of this position. For the best defense of the opposing view, see W. Farmer, *The Synoptic Problem: A Critical Analysis* (New York: Macmillan Co., 1964).

3. Because of the special problems Mark gave redaction critics (i.e., its *sources* were not known), careful criteria had to be developed in a self-conscious way to study Mark redactionally. Redaction criticism in Mark began to develop into a fuller composition criticism. See, e.g., J. R. Donahue, *Are You the Christ? The Trial Narrative in the Gospel of Mark* (SBLDS 10; Missoula, Mont.: Scholars Press, 1973); T. J. Weeden, *Mark—Traditions in Conflict* (Philadelphia: Fortress Press, 1971); and R. H. Stein, "The Proper Methodology for Ascertaining a Markan Redaction History," *Novum Testamentum* 13 (1971): 193–98.

4. For the use of sociological analysis in reconstructing the evangelist's community, see, e.g., H. C. Kee, *Community of the New Age: Studies in Mark's Gospel* (Philadelphia: Westminster Press, 1977); and R. Scroggs, "The Earliest Christian Communities as Sectarian Movements," in *Christianity, Judaism and Other Greco-Roman Cults, Part Two*, ed. J. Neusner (SJLA 12; Leiden: E. J. Brill, 1975), 1–23.

See the Introduction, p. 3 n. 5, for literary studies of Mark.

Goal-Specific Requirements

The goal chosen for this study, to articulate an interpretation of the whole Gospel of Mark using the perspectives of literary criticism, suggests two broad areas for consideration: what is involved in focusing on the whole of the Gospel of Mark and what is involved in applying literary-critical perspectives to it. In the first instance, what it means to interpret the whole Gospel of Mark might best be determined by describing what it does *not* mean; that is, in order to see what the goal requires, it might be easier to follow the *via negativa* and discover what the goal brackets out of consideration.

Circumventing the *Vorleben*

This exploration of the Gospel will not be concerned with the period before the Gospel was written. Study of the pre-Markan tradition, what might be called the *Vorleben* of the Gospel, has dominated much of the research on Mark in this century. Often the stimulus for this search for material prior to Mark's existence is a desire to capture some glimpse of the elusive historical Jesus behind the layers of church tradition. Occasionally the aim is a more general concern with the process of "traditioning"—how tradition evolves, changes, and gets passed on. Recently the important issue of the effect of transition from an oral to a written format on the meaning of traditions has been raised.[1] However, in all of these cases the focus is on

1. E.g., J. Jeremias, *The Parables of Jesus,* trans. S. Hooke (2d rev. ed.; New York: Charles Scribner's Sons, 1972), is not only concerned with finding the historical Jesus

the period *before* the Gospel comes into existence as a unified whole, and in order to probe the *Vorleben* of Mark it is necessary to dissect and fragment the text. By complicated and often debated criteria, traditional units are separated from redactional units, pre-Markan combinations of traditions are speculated upon and argued for, and, finally, various *Sitze im Leben* are postulated for the earlier material thus isolated. While the value of such procedures is that they provide our only disciplined access to periods, people, and issues existing prior to the written documents, their pervasiveness in biblical circles has not proven conducive to understanding what the Gospel of Mark as a whole is trying to communicate. Not surprisingly, concentrating on fragments of material in hypothetical contexts *other than* those formulated by the Gospel itself often leads scholars to question the unity of Mark or the literary, if not mental, competence of its author. If, so the argument goes, Jesus may have used this saying for such and such a purpose, Mark has muddled it royally to have it say something else.[2] Since our goal is to try to interpret what the Gospel of Mark is saying, speculation about the *Vorleben* of some of the material is certainly irrelevant and may indeed even be damaging to that end.

Not only are fragments of narrative used to reconstruct the historical Jesus or the early church tradition but early scholarly reconstructions of the Gospel community often relied primarily on fragments of the text as well. When traditional material was separated from the redactional summaries, connecting sentences, and elaborations, that redactional residue became the focus for reconstructions of the Gospel community. On the rather dubious assumption that the intention of a writer appears most clearly in these pieces of connecting material, the redactional units were analyzed to see what patterns of theological concern they evinced, if any.[3] This information could then be used to describe the major issues within the Markan

but also with the tendencies of the early church in modifying traditions. The works of major New Testament form critics such as R. Bultmann (*The History of the Synoptic Tradition,* trans. J. Marsh [New York: Harper & Row, 1963]) and M. Dibelius (*From Tradition to Gospel,* trans. B. L. Woolf [New York: Charles Scribner's Sons, 1935]) are the most encompassing examples of this work. The recent fascinating study by Werner Kelber (*The Oral and the Written Gospel: The Hermeneutics of Speaking and Writing in the Synoptic Tradition, Mark, Paul, and Q* [Philadelphia: Fortress Press, 1983]) explores the dynamics of the shift from oral tradition to written tradition.

2. The history of the interpretation of Mark 4:11–12 is a superb example of this type of reasoning. Mark seems to be saying rather clearly that the parables are intended to conceal their meaning from outsiders. Scholars beginning as far back as A. Jülicher in the last century have found such a meaning on the lips of Jesus to be unpalatable and impossible. Mark, they argue, must have utterly misunderstood and muddled the material. See, e.g., Jeremias, *The Parables of Jesus,* 13–18; see J. Drury, "The Sower, the Vineyard, and the Place of Allegory in the Interpretation of Mark's Parables," *Journal of Theological Studies* 24 (1973): 367–79, for a critique of this argument about Mark.

3. For the method of redaction criticism, see N. Perrin, *What Is Redaction*

community. Fortunately, as redaction-critical studies of all of the Gospels progressed during the past twenty-five years, it became evident that the intention of the writer can be perceived not only in the redactional residue but also in the selection, placement, and editing of the traditional units of material. Redaction criticism, perhaps best understood as a transitional discipline, has led directly to the beginnings of more broadly conceived literary examinations of the Gospels on one hand and to more sophisticated sociological analyses of the Gospels' communities on the other.

Circumventing Fragmentation

That reducing the Gospels to fragments rather than attempting to study them as wholes should form the dominant perspective of decades of modern biblical scholarship appears strange to many outside the biblical guild.[4] The most obvious reason for this obsession with dissolving the narrative lies in the strong desire of scholarship to reach the historical core of early Christianity in the life and teachings of Jesus. By the beginning of the twentieth century all of the canonical Gospels, even Mark, had been recognized as primarily documents of Christian dogmatic reflection rather than simple eyewitness accounts of the life of Jesus and the disciples. As one scholar ruefully remarked about the Gospels: "If the historical statements they make chance to be reliable, this is only coincidental."[5] Although the degree of skepticism about the historical trustworthiness of the Gospels varies greatly across the spectrum of biblical scholars, there are very few indeed who would not admit the need to press Gospel statements through fairly rigorous historical criteria before accepting them as reliable historical information. However, asserting that the tendency to read the Gospels only in fragments is a result of the quest for historical information raises a considerably more obscure—and, perhaps, political—question: Why is historical information so overwhelmingly important? Without embarking on a dissertation far beyond the limits of our present interests, we might suggest three possible reasons for this historical desideratum:

Criticism? (GBS; Philadelphia: Fortress Press, 1969). For studies of Mark, see, e.g., W. Marxsen, *Mark the Evangelist* (Nashville: Abingdon Press, 1969). To see the use of the separation of tradition from redaction in a commentary format, see, e.g., D. E. Nineham, *The Gospel of St. Mark* (Harmondsworth: Penguin Books, 1964).

4. Thus, when discussing the tendencies of biblical scholarship, Frank Kermode, a self-proclaimed outsider to the biblical guild, asserts, "But it is astonishing how much less there is of genuine literary criticism on the secular model than there ought to be" (*The Genesis of Secrecy: On the Interpretation of Narrative* [Cambridge, Mass., and London: Harvard University Press, 1979], 136).

5. Sandmel, "Prolegomena to a Commentary on Mark," in *Two Living Traditions: Essays on Religion* (Detroit: Wayne State University Press, 1972), 149.

1. From a theological perspective, the Christian claim that God's definitive revelation came in human form at a particular moment of world history clearly confers a special status to history itself and especially to the history of that particular moment. "The mighty acts of God in history," then, functions at least in modern times as an impetus to historical studies.

2. From a more openly political-theological perspective, the development of historical criticism in biblical studies has been one of the most effective and vital weapons against the spread of fundamentalism. Historical studies insist upon the *distance* between that past particular moment and the present. If God acted in history, then God acted in the limited, the changing, and the concrete, not in the infinite, the absolute, and the abstract. Thus, to generalize and absolutize that concrete action is to violate its very nature as *historical* revelation. Instead, ways need to be found to communicate that particular, concrete past event to present concrete situations and occasions. Such communication is the complex task of hermeneutics or interpretation. The normative, absolute, infinite authority of that past event is denied to fundamentalism by the results of historical research. And that is a desideratum.

3. From a revolutionary-theological perspective, the reliance of historical investigation on the disciplined speculations of "historical imagination" and thus its freedom from the empirical chains of extant textual formulations make it an excellent medium for change. For example, in reconstructing the historical Jesus, one is not limited to the view of Jesus found in Mark, Matthew, Luke, John, or the Coptic *Gospel of Thomas;* rather, one may extract material from one or all of these texts, combine it with various models of Jewish or Hellenistic teacher-reformers, and fashion a quite different picture of the historical Jesus, a picture that has, in fact, an equal, if not better, claim to historical reliability than those found in any of the Gospels. Such a reconstruction can then be used to challenge the present patterns of religious institutions. From traditional scholars like Joachim Jeremias, who in the 1940s struggled to reconstruct the Jesus of the parables to give power back to Protestant preaching,[6] to revolutionary scholars like Elisabeth Schüssler Fiorenza, who in the 1980s reconstructed the egalitarian community called into existence by Jesus "to undermine the legitimization of patriarchal religious structures" and "to empower women in their struggle against such oppressive structures,"[7] historical studies have functioned as advocacy stances, overtly or more often covertly, toward the current religious establishment. And that too is a desideratum.

6. *The Parables of Jesus,* 9, 22,
7. *In Memory of Her: A Feminist Theological Reconstruction of Christian Origins* (New York: Crossroad, 1983), xx.

In addition to these three underlying supports for historical-critical research, methods that chop biblical texts up into small pieces are encouraged in a less obvious way by the traditional patterns of Bible use within actual worshiping communities. From very early centuries to the present the Bible has been read and studied during Christian worship in lectionary format. One or two brief, separate episodes of the longer Gospel narrative generally form the basis of Scripture reading and sermon in most worship services. Consequently, scholarship that focuses its major interest on smaller units of material conforms well to the social datum of institutional use. The popularity of the biblical commentary genre is a further expression of this pattern. Ministers who must plan homilies and liturgies around a brief lectionary reading want resources that present the widest possible discussion of small sections of material. While the overall story of a Gospel might be of interest to them, it is often of less practical value in their day-to-day activities than the fragments.

Since our goal is a study of the whole of Mark, approaches that tend to dissolve the narrative into separate pieces do not support that task as well as approaches that emphasize the unity and overall integrity of the story. Thus, for our goal literary-critical rather than historical-critical methods are preferable. However, the desiderata of historical criticism ought not to be lost through choosing a different perspective. Literary criticism, done honestly, also insists on the *distance* between the text and the reader as well as their interaction. Moreover, it thoroughly underlines the considerable distance between the *story* presented by the text and any possible "real" events that the story might resemble. Literary criticism understands the biblical text as *fiction,* the result of literary imagination, not of photographic recall. Failure to declare openly the fictional nature of biblical writings has allowed some scholars to use literary terminology to promote neo-conservatism.[8] Such an abuse of literary criticism must not be allowed to destroy its potential value for biblical scholarship. Instead, biblical literary critics must be clear about the assumptions upon which their work is based. For concepts such as style, plot movement, character development, or rhetorical

8. The work of Hans Frei and George Lindbeck is one example of an attempt to preserve the traditional authority of Scripture through the use of what is called "realistic narrative." Lindbeck's position depends on Frei's work on narrative, especially in Frei's *The Eclipse of Biblical Narrative: A Study in Eighteenth- and Nineteenth-Century Hermeneutics* (New Haven: Yale University Press, 1974) and a number of essays. See, e.g., "The 'Literal Reading' of Biblical Narrative in the Christian Tradition," in *The Bible and the Narrative Tradition,* ed. F. McConnell (Oxford: Oxford University Press, 1986). Lindbeck's book, *The Nature of Doctrine: Religion and Theology in a Postliberal Age* (Philadelphia: Westminster Press, 1984), describes the importance of this view of narrative for what he calls the "cultural-linguistic alternative" to liberal theology. See esp. chap. 6, "Toward a Postliberal Theology."

patterning to have any meaning, it is necessary to assume that the story *can be told differently,* that there is "choice and construction" behind the narrative—in other words, that the Gospels are fictions. Thus, literary criticism also undercuts the attribution of normative, absolute authority to the text by its insistence that "simple narrative" is not a series of events but a biased discourse; it is not a transparent mediation of some divine historical act but a consciously manipulated and conventionally formulated story that can be, and indeed has been, told differently.

Furthermore, by delineating the considerable role of readers in formulating all interpretations of a story, by emphasizing the inherent ambiguity of narrative, and by acknowledging the inevitability of multiple interpretations, literary criticism not only destroys the claim of any one reading to be final, transcendent, or authoritative, but it also offers the possibility for the development of persuasive, new interpretations that can challenge contemporary institutional practice. Just as the "historical imagination" allows for potentially revolutionary reassessments of the past, the "literary imagination" of readers from vastly different cultures, social classes, races, and experiences in interaction with the story can generate revolutionary interpretations of the text. Moreover, these new interpretations are to be evaluated on an equal footing with institutionally sanctioned readings to determine which ones are more persuasive under current cultural standards.[9]

All too often traditional understandings of biblical material rest mainly on the authority of institutional fiat rather than on any publicly debated standards of judgment or evaluation, and, not surprisingly, the institutional powers-that-be favor interpretations that promote their vested interests. By insisting on the incomplete and relative nature of *any* reading of a text, literary critics are free to develop new interpretations and subject *all* of them—including those cherished by the power structure—to evaluation, testing, and debate. In addition, since all literate people possess some rudimentary knowledge of literary concepts such as plot, character, and narrator, these debates become far more accessible to those outside the biblical guild or the religious hierarchy than the rarefied philological and historical controversies of the past. The authority granted to priest and scholar by the possession of specialized, obscure knowledge is democratized when they must use the language of all readers. Literary criticism permits, indeed implies, an impressive political agenda. It does not sacrifice the desiderata of historical research. Even the practical needs of homiletics

9. An excellent example of rereading a text to develop a revolutionary interpretation that thoroughly challenges and indeed routs the traditional, institutionally sanctioned reading can be found in Phyllis Trible's careful literary analysis of the creation story in Genesis 2—3, in her *God and the Rhetoric of Sexuality* (Philadelphia: Fortress Press, 1978), 72–143.

and liturgy can benefit from literary approaches that stress the integrity rather than the disparity of the narrative, for an individual part is really best understood in the light of the whole story, and not in isolation from it.

Circumventing the *Nachleben*

Because our predetermined goal is the interpretation of the whole of the Gospel of Mark, we must obviously bracket out of consideration issues concerning the *Vorleben* of some Markan material, and we must avoid methods that fragment the text. To put it positively, our goal specifies study of the narrative in its final form, and it specifies the use of literary approaches that preserve the integrity of the story. Furthermore, because our subject is the Gospel of Mark, and not Gospel traditions in general or other formulations of the story, we must also avoid another highly prevalent, if less obvious, tendency in Markan studies: the use of the Gospels of Matthew and Luke to interpret Mark. Just as the author of Mark[10] used previously existing sources, probably oral, in formulating his story, just so Matthew and Luke probably used Mark as a source for their stories. These two later Gospels are the earliest extant examples of the *Nachleben* of Mark, the tradition of use, adaptation, and influence that followed the production of the Gospel itself.

Many literary works generate a *Nachleben;* later authors borrow, revise, adapt, or are heavily influenced by the plots, characters, episodes, and speeches of their predecessors. When the *Nachleben* of a work becomes totally conventionalized or stereotypical, it begins to function as a commonplace or topos.[11] That later writers depend on earlier material presents no difficulty; the problem arises in using later adaptations to interpret the earlier work. It is certainly possible that a later use of material will be in basic harmony and continuity with its earlier formulation. It is also possible, and perhaps more probable, that it will not be. Later generations of writers, living in different historical and cultural contexts, addressing differ-

10. Even though the tradition stating that Mark, a disciple of Peter's, wrote this Gospel is the oldest authorship tradition for any of the canonical Gospels, I find it equally unsatisfactory as the slightly later traditions for Luke and Matthew. The most probable case concerning authorship is that all of the Gospels were originally anonymous documents to which names were attached by later generations of Christians. However, as a matter of convenience, I will throughout this book use the conventional designation "Mark" for this anonymous first-century writer. Since there had been a slight upsurge in literacy among women beginning in the third to second centuries B.C.E., there is a slight possibility that the author of Mark might have been a woman. I continue to use the pronoun "he" for the author, then, with some ambivalence, although I judge the probability of female authorship to be quite low.

11. For the importance of classical topoi for later literature, see E. Curtius, *European Literature and the Latin Middle Ages,* trans. W. R. Trask (London: Routledge & Kegan Paul, 1953).

ent audiences from different social settings may employ the plot, characters, or design of an earlier story for the same purpose and goal as the earlier author, but it is more likely that the purpose, goal, and intention will be different to fit changed circumstances, genre, or viewpoint. For example, Shakespeare may have been influenced by the classical Roman historians and the formulations of other earlier playwrights in producing *Julius Caesar,* but using his *Julius Caesar* to clarify the meaning or design of Tacitus or Suetonius would be foolhardy.

Canonizing four separate Gospels and placing them side by side in New Testament manuscripts encouraged from a quite early time the relatively unselfconscious tendency to read passages in one in the light of similar material in the others. This harmonizing principle, while completely understandable, was particularly disastrous for Mark because about 93 percent of its material is paralleled, although not exactly, in the Gospel of Matthew.[12] Furthermore, Matthew's version is often in more acceptable Greek syntax and provides a richer context than Mark's. Thus Augustine's inclination to dismiss Mark in favor of Matthew is not at all surprising. The reversal of Augustine's position and the recent rise to prominence of Mark in modern biblical studies has, oddly enough, not challenged the general practice of interpreting Mark in the light of Matthew and Luke. Indeed, the development of redaction criticism has somewhat unintentionally encouraged this long-standing practice. Early redaction-critical research, founded on the hypothesis of Markan priority, examined the omissions, additions, and alterations made by Matthew and Luke in incorporating Markan material in order to establish the theological concerns of these later evangelists. However, such concentration on Matthew's and Luke's interpretations and use of Mark inevitably, if unjustifiably, increased the tendency to see Mark mainly through their eyes.

Redaction criticism has focused careful, detailed attention on the differences between the three Synoptic Gospels. The broader, and perhaps more interesting, issue of why three writings relatively close in time should contain so much *similar* material has generally been ignored. Many current New Testament scholars appear to assume without much argument or analysis that Matthew and Luke simply intended to extend and clarify Mark's vision for their own communities. Hence, these later writers can be used to interpret Mark's occasionally muddled presentation. But suppose Matthew and Luke, for different reasons and in different ways, were attempting not to clarify and extend Mark's vision but to refute and undermine it. In the rhetorical fashion of the first century one very effective way of refut-

12. R. H. Lightfoot noted that "Mark, in the English Revised Version, from 1:1 to 16:8, contains 666 verses; of these only some 50 verses find no parallel in Matthew" (*The Gospel Message of St. Mark* [London: Oxford University Press, 1950], 2).

ing one's opponents was to incorporate their arguments in one's own presentation and then demonstrate how faulty their conclusions were.[13] It is just possible that some of the muddle that scholars have detected in Mark, and used Matthew and Luke to clarify, is actually the *result* of reading Mark in the light of Matthew and Luke in the first place. That Matthew and Luke intended to refute and supplant Mark rather than clarify and extend it is a less often voiced but equally likely possibility.[14] Until clearer evidence and fuller discussions permit a reasoned judgment on whether the relationship of Matthew and Luke to Mark is benign or malign, to be sure we are interpreting Mark in the light of its own intentions, those other two writings should not be used as controls on its interpretation.

The ramifications of choosing as one's goal an interpretation of the whole of the Gospel of Mark are finally beginning to become clear. First, the Gospel must be studied in its final form rather than through the hypothetical development of its *Vorleben*. Second, it must be explored by approaches that preserve and conserve its integrity rather than shatter the narrative into fragments. And third, it must be read as much as possible on its own terms rather than on terms set out by manifestations of its *Nachleben*, especially the Gospels of Matthew and Luke. Since all three of these goal-specific requirements run counter to the predominant ways in which Mark has been approached in modern biblical research, the paucity of interpretations of the Gospel "in all its parts"[15] is not difficult to fathom. Furthermore, because scholars have not in the past tended to think about Mark in these ways, fulfilling the three requirements will demand an imaginative leap into new perspectives or, at the very least, an initial willingness to suspend old habits of thinking.

Assumptions of a Literary Perspective

The second part of our goal is to use the perspectives of literary criticism in articulating an interpretation of Mark. Although seeking to study the whole of the Gospel of Mark itself encourages the adoption of approaches

13. Paul, in fact, employs this strategy frequently in his letters. The opening chapters of 1 Corinthians provide several examples of Paul quoting the views of the Corinthians and then refuting their conclusions. See, e.g., 1 Cor. 1:10–17; 3:1–9, 18–23; 4:6–13; 5:9–13; 6:12–20.

14. A very strong argument for the view that Matthew and Luke wanted to refute Mark can be found in Sandmel, "Prolegomena," 152–53. That at least some within the Christian movement of the early second century C.E. were critical of the way Mark presents the story of Jesus can be gathered from the defensive tone of Papias's remarks on the authorship of Mark in Eusebius, *Historia ecclesiastica* 3.39.15. For a discussion of Papias's remarks, see M. Hengel, *Studies in the Gospel of Mark* (Philadelphia: Fortress Press, 1985), 47–50.

15. See Introduction, pp. 2–3.

that are especially designed to preserve the integrity of the story, as we have discovered above, our goal has additionally emphasized the use of literary-critical perspectives in order to demonstrate their effectiveness for this type of investigation. However, adopting literary perspectives, just like adopting historical perspectives, carries with it certain assumptions about the text and the task.

The first and most important of these assumptions, as we have already noted, is that Mark is a self-consciously crafted narrative, a fiction, resulting from literary imagination, not photographic recall. To say it is a fiction does not necessarily mean that it has no connection with events in history; rather, describing Mark as fiction serves to underscore the selection, construction, and choice behind the story it tells.[16] What is there, what is not there, and how it is all depicted become extremely significant issues. For example, that Mark 16:7 suggests some future for the disciples and Peter with Jesus in Galilee is significant; that 16:8 suggests that the disciples never heard the message and that the Gospel ends without narrating the Galilee meeting are also significant. *Both* implying reconciliation *and* not presenting it must be accounted for in any discussion of the ending of Mark. However, unlike some earlier form critics who argued that Mark presented no version of a post-resurrection appearance of Jesus to the disciples simply because he did not have one in his bag of traditions,[17] a literary critic assumes that a writer could have added more or stopped earlier[18] or said it differently. Consequently, the *way it is said* is crucially important. Organization, emphasis, and style become the primary concerns of the literary interpreter of Mark, for the form of the Gospel develops its meaning.

The use of a literary approach also assumes that a narrative is unified and coherent. Unity and coherence do *not* entail utter harmony. Breaks, gaps, contradictions, and duplications are all literary devices that give narrative some quality of verisimilitude;[19] an utterly harmonious narrative, besides

16. Much the same point is made about material in the Hebrew Bible by Robert Alter, who thinks the best label for biblical literature is "historicized fiction" (see his discussion in *The Art of Biblical Narrative* [New York: Basic Books, 1981], 24–27, 32, 36, 41).

17. See, e.g., R. H. Fuller, *The Formation of the Resurrection Narratives* (New York: Macmillan Co., 1971; Philadelphia: Fortress Press, 1980), 65–66; and A. Lindemann, "Die Osterbotschaft des Markus: Zur theologischen Interpretation von Mark 16:1–8," *NTS* 26 (1980): 300–302.

18. Actually, one does not, as the early church did, have to add new endings to Mark to force it to conclude triumphantly; all one need do is remove Mark 16:8. Had the author of Mark wanted to imply *unambiguously* that reconciliation with Peter and the disciples would undoubtedly occur, the story could have ended at 16:7. But it does not. For further discussion of the ending, see pp. 288–99 below.

19. As Todorov points out in his "Introduction to Verisimilitude," it is a very old literary device, for discussions of it can be found in Corax, Plato, and Aristotle. For these early writers, however, verisimilitude was not a naive copying of reality as it often

being unbelievable, would be utterly boring. However, the presumption of unity and coherence does indicate an internal rationale for most elements of the story. In other words, the reason why a certain part of the narrative exists is to be discovered within the narrative itself and not generally in some realm external to the narrative.[20] For Mark, such an assumption would again challenge the predominant tradition of Gospel research: form and redaction critics tend to move very quickly out from the text to the life of Jesus, the history of the early church, or theological issues in the Markan community. Indeed, the primary explanatory grid for any element in the Gospel is often an extratextual one. The assumption of unity and coherence shifts the primary explanatory grid to an internal literary or narrative one. The meaning or reason for any aspect of the story should be sought *first inside the story itself* before external references are considered.

For example, a fairly common explanation of the brief, apparently irrelevant reference in Mark 15:27 to robbers crucified with Jesus, "one on his right and one on his left" (ἕνα ἐκ δεξιῶν καὶ ἕνα ἐξ εὐωνύμων αὐτοῦ),[21] is quite simply that it really happened that way.[22] Whether such is the case or not, the presence of an element that appears not to be necessary for the current scene, beyond giving it a further touch of verisimilitude, should raise for a literary critic the question of connection with earlier or later material. Here the phrase "on his right and on his left" occurs strikingly one other time in the Gospel of Mark. Earlier at Mark 10:35–40, immediately after Jesus' third and most detailed prediction of his passion in Jerusalem, James and John come to him privately to ask a favor: "Grant us to sit, one at your right hand and one at your left, in your glory." While Jesus can promise them

---

is in modern realism, but "verisimilitude was a relation . . . with what most people believe to be reality—in other words, with public opinion" (Todorov, *The Poetics of Prose,* trans. R. Howard (Oxford: Basil Blackwell, 1977), 81–82.

20. A narrative, of course, may allude to other texts specifically (intertextuality), or it may assume common conventions that members of the same society could be expected to recognize (extratextual repertoire), but indications of these "external" elements appear *in the narrative itself.* Such narrative allusions or conventions are not the issue here. For a careful working out of these external narrative elements for a study of Jesus and Herod in Luke, see J. Darr, "'Glorified in the Presence of Kings': A Literary-Critical Study of Herod the Tetrarch in Luke-Acts" (Ph.D. diss., Vanderbilt University, 1987).

21. Because of the importance for my interpretation of the rhetorical patterns of repetition, wordplay, and sound in the Greek of the Gospel of Mark, many translations of the text throughout this book are my own. If the English translation is not my own, it is from the Revised Standard Version. To distinguish between the two, all quotations from the RSV are set off by quotation marks as well as chapter and verse numbers, while my own translations indicate only chapter and verse numbers. Unless otherwise noted, all Greek quotations are from the Nestle-Aland 26th revised edition main text. The use of variant readings is always indicated.

22. See, e.g., H. Anderson, *The Gospel of Mark* (New Century Bible Commentary; Grand Rapids: Wm. B. Eerdmans, 1976), 342–43.

strife and persecution, he cannot grant them "to sit at my right hand or at my left" (ἐκ δεξιῶν μου ἢ ἐξ εὐωνύμων), for that honor is "for those for whom it has been prepared." Later in the midst of the crucifixion, all the disciples having fled, the reader meets "those for whom it has been prepared," the robbers, not James and John, and the reader also realizes clearly that in the Gospel of Mark, despite what the disciples might wish, Jesus' coming "in his glory" is Jesus crucified on a cross. The narrative develops its own sense and coherence, if one will but look for it before rushing too quickly out of the text into history.

Although understanding Mark to be fiction and to develop its own coherence and unity does not mean that what is related in the story bears no relationship whatsoever to the events of the external world, it does mean that the nature of that relationship is complex and difficult to ascertain. Even in modern views of history writing as a factual record of "what really happened," the constraints of narrative form on historiography blur the distinction between history and fiction. The simultaneous convergence of events, actions, characters, and the constant bombardment of visual, aural, and vocal stimuli that all together constitute every moment of real life simply cannot be represented by linear narrative with its ordered sequence and grammatical requirements. Thus, even modern, scientific history is but a highly selective distillation of "what really happened."²³ It is an interpretation of an event. Ancient historiography, particularly Hellenistic historiography, never pretended to be anything other than an interpretation. Speeches, characters, and even whole incidents could be created by the Hellenistic historian, and events for which records or sources existed were often thoroughly embellished. The aim of ancient history writing was rarely to produce an accurate chronicle or record; rather, its purposes were moral edification, apologetics, glorification of certain families, and mainly entertainment.²⁴ Indeed, if one were to assume that the Gospel of Mark

23. Needless to say, philosophers of history debate this issue constantly. It has also been analyzed from the side of literary critics. A useful summary of the various positions and issues can be found in R. Seamon, "Narrative Practice and the Theoretical Distinction Between History and Fiction," *Genre* 16 (1983): 197–218. Also see the delightful discussion in Kermode, *The Genesis of Secrecy*, 101–23; and W. Iser, *The Act of Reading: A Theory of Aesthetic Response* (Baltimore: Johns Hopkins University Press, 1978), 53–85. Paul Ricoeur in an essay, "The Narrative Fiction" (in *Hermeneutics and the Human Sciences*, ed. and trans. J. B. Thompson [Cambridge: Cambridge University Press, 1981], 274–96), argues that history and fiction share narrative functions and natures and both depend upon plot, but they differ in the claims they make to refer to reality.

24. See, e.g., H. Cadbury, "The Greek and Jewish Traditions of Writing History," in *The Beginnings of Christianity. Part I: The Acts of the Apostles,* ed. F. Foakes Jackson and K. Lake, vol. 2, Prolegomena II (London: Macmillan & Co., 1922), 7–29. More recently, see K. Sacks, "Rhetorical Approaches to Greek History Writing in the Hellenistic Period," in *SBL Seminar Papers 1984,* ed. K. Richards (SBLSP 23; Chico,

belonged to the genre of Hellenistic historiography, one would still be involved in the dynamics of fiction.

Furthermore, as unified and coherent fiction, Mark can be read within the context of other related fictions of the period. While reconstructions of the historical Jesus or of the theological disputes of early Christianity ought not to be employed too quickly as a means for explaining puzzling aspects of the narrative, the universe of Hellenistic literature may be able to provide assistance in clarifying conventional modes of writing, reading, and hearing. Texts from similar genres, especially, may illuminate narrative patterns in Mark, and for that reason some hypothesis concerning the genre of the Gospel of Mark is necessary for any literary interpretation of it. Thus the assumptions behind adopting a literary approach to Mark define the main area of analysis to be the internal emphases, patterns, and constructs of the narrative and define the main context of study to be other related literature of the Hellenistic period. However, affirming these limits does not fence the Gospel off into a tiny, rarefied aesthetic domain, for literature is produced by people for people; it is influenced by economic and political factors at work both on the writers and their audiences and on their access to means of production and transmission. Writing, like any form of communication, is a deeply social activity, and exploring the matrix of ideas, conventions, social, educational, and political dynamics in which every text is rooted is also part of employing a literary perspective.

Summary

To have chosen as the goal of this contribution to Markan scholarship an interpretation of the whole of the Gospel using perspectives provided by literary criticism as the practical basis of analysis determines a wide array of interpretive issues. Although the Gospel surely relies on a variety of sources and became itself a source for later writers, neither its *Vorleben* nor its *Nachleben* will be the subject of our analysis. Furthermore, methods of research that dissolve the narrative into isolated fragments will be avoided, while approaches that encourage integration and synthesis will be adopted. The very use of literary-critical perspectives also posits some clear assumptions about the text under study. As fiction, its internal organization, style, plot development, character types, and overall configuration must be explored carefully as guides to emphasis and meaning, and its connections

---

Calif.: Scholars Press, 1984), 123–33; P. Segal, "Manifestations of Hellenistic Historiography in Select Judaic Literature," in ibid., 161–85; and B. E. Perry, *The Ancient Romances: A Literary-Historical Account of Their Origins* (Berkeley and Los Angeles: University of California Press, 1967), 66–70, 77–79.

to its own literary milieu must be charted as the context for understanding patterns of expression and conventional usage.

All of these issues now become part of the preunderstanding *(Vorverständnis)* with which we approach the Gospel of Mark. No reader comes to a text with a completely blank mind; instead, readers of whatever competence begin reading with certain expectations and often certain questions which affect what they then see in the text. No reading of a text is ever innocent or unbiased or without such preconceptions. By consciously fashioning a preunderstanding of Mark different from those generally held by biblical scholars, we should expect a somewhat different view of the Gospel to emerge. While it is not theoretically required for the preunderstanding that is brought to a text to bear a close relationship to the text itself[25] and in fact the historical distance between text and interpreter makes difference inevitable, establishing some congruence between the interpreter's presuppositions and the text probably results in an interpretation that is more persuasive to other readers. In order to develop that congruence, we must examine the specific characteristics of the text under analysis.

25. Some literary critics would argue that the most interesting interpretations derive from beginning at a wide angle or an odd perspective on the text. Psychoanalytic and Marxist interpretations often achieve fascinating results from their very different assumptions about literature. (See, e.g., the discussion in Kermode, *The Genesis of Secrecy,* 4–12.) It should be noted, however, that both psychological readings and Marxist readings justify their appropriateness to texts of all eras, not on the basis of congruence with the text or the text's literary milieu, but rather on the basis of their own claims to universal applicability. The psychological dynamics of humanity and human society or the economic forces molding history, while only articulated in the last two centuries, are posited as *universal* aspects of human development. Thus their categories are as applicable to ancient as to modern texts.

Text-Specific
Requirements:
General

Author, Date, and Place

In a broad discussion of current views of genre to be found among literary theorists, Thomas Kent comments: "Certain of our generic expectations, or what we expect to encounter when we begin to read a text, is determined in part by what we know about a text's . . . history, its author, its genre."[1] Such a claim leaves the interpreter of the Gospel of Mark in some despair, for the history of the production of the text, its intended audience, its location, its date, and its author have all been lost in the dust of centuries. During the second through the fourth century C.E., Christian writers speculated on many of these issues and developed suggestions, often conflicting, that became part of the tradition about Mark.[2] Most guesses about these matters, however, have to be argued from the text itself, and it, unhelpfully, never names its author or indicates where it was written. From the implication of Mark 13 that persecutions and conflicts were besetting the probable audience, scholars, both ancient and modern, tend to date the Gospel in the 60s–70s of the first century C.E. when Nero's persecutions of Christians in Rome were quickly followed by the Roman war against the Jews in Palestine; so, whether the audience was closer to Palestine or to

---

1. "The Classification of Genres," *Genre* 16 (1983): 8.
2. Evidence from the church fathers on the authorship, location, and date of Mark is summarized in many commentaries. See, e.g., V. Taylor, *The Gospel According to St. Mark* (2d ed. reprint 1966; Grand Rapids: Baker Book House, 1981), 1–8.

Rome, persecution and war would be the state of the day. Since the Gospel was written in Greek and since the few Aramaic words added (e.g., Mark 5:41; 7:34; 15:34) are always translated into Greek, the presumed audience was probably mostly Greek-speaking and not familiar with Semitic languages. Since the type of Greek in the Gospel is common or *koine* Greek, the main language of commerce and travel across the entire Roman Empire, the fact that the Gospel was written in Greek does not help locate its point of origin. The occasional attempt by the Gospel to explain, with notable lack of clarity, Jewish customs and practices (e.g., Mark 7:3–4) suggests that the intended audience, and perhaps the author as well, were at some distance from the more established practices of Judaism.

An anonymous author writing in *koine* Greek to a Greek-speaking, predominantly Gentile audience during the second half of the first century C.E. is about as specific as our knowledge can be concerning the history of the Gospel's production. Nevertheless, that the author had been taught to write in Greek does give us an opportunity to sketch the Gospel's context a little more fully, for the educational system for teaching Greek grammar remained amazingly stable over many centuries throughout the Roman Empire.[3] The first two stages of education, grammar and rhetoric, were taught by a system founded upon imitation of past writers, especially Homer. Students were given increasingly difficult tasks of first copying and then imitating in their own words the forms, practices, and figures of the past. Even at the earliest stages of grammatical training, study of correct word choice and arrangement and the use of figures was accomplished by detailed interpretation of classical writers.[4] The pervasiveness of this educational practice means that writers and readers of Greek across the empire at the earliest levels of competence were accustomed to conventional figures

---

3. The classic study of education in antiquity is H. I. Marrou, *A History of Education in Antiquity* (New York: Sheed & Ward, 1956). See also for the discussion that follows, D. L. Clark, *Rhetoric in Greco-Roman Education* (New York: Columbia University Press, 1957); G. A. Kennedy, *New Testament Interpretation Through Rhetorical Criticism* (Chapel Hill, N.C.: University of North Carolina Press, 1984), 8–10; G. M. A. Grube, *The Greek and Roman Critics* (Toronto: University of Toronto Press, 1965), v–x; and S. F. Bonner, *Education in Ancient Rome: From the Elder Cato to the Younger Pliny* (Berkeley and Los Angeles: University of California Press, 1977), 250–76.

4. D. A. Russell, *Criticism in Antiquity* (London: Gerald Duckworth & Co., 1981), 115. Russell quotes an author known as Heraclitus who wrote probably sometime during the first century C.E. on the continuing importance of Homer: "From the earliest stage of life, our infant children in their first moments of learning are suckled on him; we are wrapped in his poems, one might also say, as babies, and nourish our minds on their milk. As the child grows and comes to manhood Homer is at his side. Homer shares his mature years, and the man is never weary of him even in old age. When we leave him, we feel the thirst again. The end of Homer is the end of life for us" (p. 191).

and rhetorical patterns and could use them in their own writing and speaking and recognize them in the presentations of others. In order to perceive more clearly the literary milieu of the Gospel of Mark, we need to survey in fairly general terms some of these conventions of Hellenistic literature that might have affected the production of the Gospel, and then, in a more specific way, the next chapter can develop a hypothesis about the genre of Mark to guide our reading of it.

Hellenism

A number of very fine studies of Hellenistic culture exist, and while we need not repeat that material fully, a few of the major aspects of the period clarify why and how people wrote, read, and heard.[5] Beginning with the conquests of Alexander in the fourth century B.C.E., Greek language, philosophy, political organization, and values swept over the Mediterranean world. From India to Egypt to Asia Minor, Greek education and culture reigned, mixing in various combinations with native civilizations already present. Even the establishment of the Roman Empire in the first century B.C.E. did not shake the dominance of Greek culture. The Romans too adopted, in a suitably altered version, Greek educational practices, artistic and literary values, and general philosophical perspectives. Not until the "triumph of Christianity" in the fourth century C.E. did the eminence of Greek culture begin to wane. It is a tribute to the importance of this culture that, next to copies and fragments of the New Testament, the greatest number of manuscripts of any work that have survived from the ancient world are copies of Homer's *Iliad*.[6]

Judaism too, by the time of the first century C.E., was thoroughly Hellenized, both in Palestine and especially in the Diaspora.[7] Attempts to divide

5. Major studies of Hellenistic culture can be found in W. W. Tarn and G. T. Griffith, *Hellenistic Civilization* (3d ed. rev.; London: University Paperbacks, 1966); V. A. Tcherikover, *Hellenistic Civilization and the Jews,* trans. S. Applebaum (Philadelphia: Jewish Publication Society of America, 1959); W. Jaeger, *Early Christianity and Greek Paideia* (Cambridge: Harvard University Press, 1962); M. Hadas, *Hellenistic Culture: Fusion and Diffusion* (New York: Columbia University Press, 1959); and especially for biblical studies, see H. Koester, *Introduction to the New Testament* (Philadelphia: Fortress Press; Berlin and New York: Walter de Gruyter, 1982), vol. 1.

Some scholars, often focusing primarily on political influence, prefer to end the Hellenistic period with the rise of the Roman Empire in the first century B.C.E. Since our interest is in the dominance of Greek culture that extended into the early centuries of the Roman period, we will date the end of Hellenism to the "triumph of Christianity" in the fourth century C.E.

6. B. Metzger, *The Text of the New Testament: Its Transmission, Corruption, and Restoration* (New York and London: Oxford University Press, 1964), 34.

7. Many studies have made this point recently. See, e.g., M. Hengel, *Judaism and Hellenism: Studies in Their Encounter in Palestine During the Early Hellenistic Period,*

sharply the Jewish heritage of Christianity from the Greek heritage fail to recognize the degree of Hellenization already a part of Jewish culture. Instead of Jew versus Greek or Egyptian versus Greek, Hellenistic culture displayed·a spectrum of cultural assimilation from more consciously native to more consciously Hellenized, but the positions along this spectrum were matters of differences in degree, not in kind—all were Hellenized. Vernon Robbins's recent careful and detailed comparison of the teacher/disciple cycles in both Greco-Roman and Jewish literature demonstrates over-whelmingly the blending of those past traditions in Mark to produce a work intimately connected to its own Hellenistic milieu.[8]

Mobility

The ability of that milieu to establish a common language, *koine* Greek, and a common sensibility, Greek *paideia*,[9] throughout many disparate regions of the known world had revolutionary consequences, three of which may affect our understanding of the Gospel of Mark. In the first place, the Greek ideal of adventurous journey, so central to Homer's *Odyssey*, became a general reality in the Hellenistic period. Trade and cultural exchange flourished. Physical, ethnic, and social mobility were the order of the day. People traveled by sea and by land in pursuit of trade, better working conditions, and of course adventure. Large cities like Rome, Antioch, or Alexandria attracted communities of people from other lands and other religions. Trade associations often ran hotels for traveling mem-bers and assisted foreign members moving into a region to find homes and new jobs.[10] Such mobility fired cultural exchange and assimilation (and reaction *against* assimilation) to hitherto unheard of levels. Religions from the east spread west, carried by traveling native believers and new "foreign" converts. Judaism, the cult of Isis, and Christianity are but three major

vol. 1–2, trans. J. Bowden (Philadelphia: Fortress Press, 1974); idem, *Jews, Greeks, and Barbarians: Aspects of the Hellenization of Judaism in the Pre-Christian Period,* trans. J. Bowden (Philadelphia: Fortress Press, 1980); H. Fischel, *Rabbinic Literature and Greco-Roman Philosophy: A Study of Epicurea and Rhetoric in Early Midrashic Writings* (SPB 21; Leiden: E. J. Brill, 1973); and E. Bickerman, *From Ezra to the Last of the Maccabees* (New York: Schocken Books, 1970).

8. *Jesus the Teacher* (Philadelphia: Fortress Press, 1984), 113–19, 166–68, 185–93. See also B. Standaert, *L'Evangile selon Marc: Composition et genre littéraire* (Nijmegen: Stichting Studentenpers Nijmegen, 1978), for a careful literary study of the Gospel that emphasizes its connections to Greek rhetorical tradition and especially Greek dramatic style.

9. *Paideia* (παιδεία) is more than the idea of narrow learning or education; it is a whole system of formation, based on similar ideals, values, and texts. It is the development of a full sensibility. See Jaeger, *Early Christianity and Greek Paideia.*

10. See Koester, *Introduction to the New Testament,* 1:65–67, for the great impor-tance of these associations.

examples among many of this pervasive mobility. The missionary teachers of these religions could no longer count on traditional, tribal knowledge in their new and very mixed audiences. Yet some minimal acquaintance with Greek *paideia* could often be assumed; thus, while Paul needed to say very different things to the very different Christian communities at Corinth or Galatia or Rome, depending on their special problems, cultural backgrounds, and relationships to him, he could use Greek epistolary style and rhetorical strategies for all.[11] To find Hellenistic patterns and rhetorical devices at work in the Gospel of Mark along with explanations of Aramaic words and Jewish practices indicates its mixed Hellenistic home. Moreover, Mark's portrayal of Jesus as a traveler, constantly journeying from town to town and finally to Jerusalem, whatever its historical or sociological[12] significance, also connects the Gospel to the mobility of Hellenistic times.

Insecurity

This increase in mobility was, in the second place, accompanied by an increase in insecurity.[13] As native cultures and tribal allegiances began to break down under the influx of new ideas and the emigration of established families either by choice or by force[14] to other regions, the sense of living in a stable universe with familial or tribal solidarity also diminished. Alienation, isolation, and anxiety became the common experiences of the Hellene. The cosmos bristled with hostile supernatural powers bent on making

11. For studies of Paul's use of rhetorical principles, see, e.g., H. D. Betz, *Galatians: A Commentary on Paul's Letter to the Churches in Galatia* (Philadelphia: Fortress Press, 1979), 14–25; K. A. Plank, *Paul and the Irony of Affliction* (SBLSS; Atlanta: Scholars Press, 1987); W. Wuellner, "Paul's Rhetoric of Argumentation in Romans: An Alternative to the Donfried-Karris Debate over Romans," *CBQ* 38 (1976): 330–51; and H. D. Betz, "The Literary Composition and Function of Paul's Letter to the Galatians," *NTS* 21 (1975): 353–79.

12. The Gospel of Luke and the Acts of the Apostles extend and emphasize the "journeying motif" for Jesus and for Paul, respectively. While this motif may be related to the sociological development of the Jesus movement as Gerd Theissen has argued (*Sociology of Early Palestinian Christianity,* trans. J. Bowden [Philadelphia: Fortress Press, 1978]), it most certainly ties Mark and Luke-Acts to Greek literature with Homer's *Iliad* and *Odyssey* at its apex. The hero who journeys from place to place encountering trials and miraculous occurrences is a constant element in Greco-Roman literature.

13. See, e.g., E. R. Dodds, *Pagan and Christian in an Age of Anxiety* (Cambridge: Cambridge University Press, 1965); idem, *The Greeks and the Irrational* (Berkeley and Los Angeles: University of California Press, 1951); and A. D. Nock, *Conversion: The Old and New in Religion from Alexander the Great to Augustine of Hippo* (London: Oxford University Press, 1961).

14. War and abduction were constant realities that fed the ranks of slavery in the Roman Empire. Often the best educated, most attractive, and most cultured were at the greatest risk for becoming slaves. See, e.g., R. MacMullen, *Roman Social Relations 50 B.C. to A.D. 284* (New Haven: Yale University Press, 1974).

human life as unbearable and dangerous as possible, and an inexorable Fate controlled the destiny of everyone. Whether by consulting oracles or astrological charts or by participating in mystery cult initiations or the new salvationist religions, the Hellene struggled against a debilitating cosmic paranoia.[15] Among the aristocratic literati where public displays of such superstitions were sometimes condemned as vulgar and common, solace might be found in various philosophical schools like the Stoics, the Cynics, and the Epicureans or in the nostalgic yearning for the ordered and secure past that characterized the Second Sophistic, the Greek cultural revival of the first centuries C.E. Whichever path was chosen, the underlying desire was for escape from isolation, danger, and death. Paul's stirring affirmation in Rom. 8:38–39 is the Christian response to precisely this deep-seated longing in the Hellenistic soul: "For I am sure that neither death, nor life, nor angels, nor principalities, nor things present, nor things to come, nor powers, nor height, nor depth, nor anything else in all creation, will be able to separate us from the love of God in Christ Jesus our Lord."

The individual's experience of an increasingly immense, alienating, and hostile universe fueled feelings of isolation, loneliness, and helplessness. Consequently most people in the Greco-Roman world were on a quest for security, "in God or in some other human being. The escape from isolation, the way to salvation, is to find the God or human being who cares about you as an individual. In this way only can you find your social identity; the time has passed when the individual felt he had a meaningful position in society as a 'citizen.'"[16] The breakdown of many traditional regional, tribal, and familial connections focused attention on the individual, alone, searching for salvation without the social props that had undergirded his or her ancestors. The image of the lonely Jesus of the Gospel of Mark, accompanied on his way by confused disciples who misunderstand his teachings and then flee when active persecution finally arrives, reverberates with this sense of alienation, isolation, and individual questing that so marks the Hellenistic period. The Jesus of Mark clearly speaks to the dynamics of his own time.

---

15. Studies of the development of religion in the Hellenistic and early Imperial periods can be found in, e.g., F. C. Grant, *Hellenistic Religions: The Age of Syncretism* (New York: Bobbs-Merrill, 1953); Nock, *Conversion;* D. G. Rice and J. E. Stambaugh, *Sources for the Study of Greek Religion* (SBLSBS 14; Missoula, Mont.: Scholars Press, 1979); F. Solmsen, *Isis Among the Greeks and Romans* (Cambridge: Harvard University Press, 1979); S. K. Heyob, *The Cult of Isis Among Women in the Greco-Roman World* (Leiden: E. J. Brill, 1975); and L. Martin, *Hellenistic Religions: An Introduction* (Oxford: Oxford University Press, 1987).

16. T. Hägg, *The Novel in Antiquity* (Oxford: Basil Blackwell, 1983), 89–90.

Rhetoric

In the third place, the increased mobility of the era stressed the value of communication. Skill in speaking persuasively became the most sought after and admired ability in society. Indeed, the Hellenistic period was, above all, the age of rhetoric. Whether rhetoric is defined broadly as the art of speaking well or more narrowly as the art of persuasion,[17] it affected almost every aspect of public and private life. Anyone who learned to read and write Greek (or later Latin) studied rhetorical theory from the earliest grammatical lessons. Yet, even for the majority of people, who remained illiterate, rhetorical conventions permeated their universe and their culture, the way they heard and the way they spoke,

> for the rhetorical theory of the schools found its immediate application in almost every form of oral and written communication: in official documents and public letters, in private correspondence, in the law courts and assemblies, in speeches at festivals and commemorations, and in literary composition in both prose and verse.[18]

The goal of rhetorical training was eloquence, but in part eloquence is achieved by balancing one's style of speaking with one's aims. In the classic formulation popularized by Cicero and later appropriated by Augustine for Christian speaking, the ends of rhetoric were to teach, to delight, and to persuade, and the concomitant styles were, respectively, the plain (clear, ordinary, unpretentious), the middle or moderate (decorative, polished, beautiful), and the grand style (ornate, weighty, fierce).[19] Rhetorical handbooks explaining and illustrating these theories of decorum were quite common, the oldest text that has survived in full, *Rhetorica ad Herennium,* being dated early in the first century B.C.E. Around the same time, Demetrius's *On Style* was written in Greek.[20] Like the rhetorical handbooks,

17. Kennedy, *Rhetorical Criticism,* 13. See also idem, *Classical Rhetoric and Its Christian and Secular Tradition from Ancient to Modern Times* (Chapel Hill, N.C.: University of North Carolina Press, 1980).

18. Kennedy, *Rhetorical Criticism,* 10.

19. Cicero, *Orator* 75–99. See also Augustine, *De doctrina christiana* 4.12.27–4.25.55. The late Roman and early medieval periods developed this theory of styles further to include subject matter and characterization. In the thirteenth century, John of Garland designated such decorum as "the Wheel of Virgil," in which peasant stories with rustic characters were to be written in the plain style (e.g., Virgil's *Bucolics*); middle-class stories with good, somewhat educated characters were to be written in the moderate style (e.g., Virgil's *Georgics*); and epic stories with heroic characters were to be written in the grand style (e.g., Virgil's *Aeneid*).

20. For issues of dating, authorship, and importance, see "Demetrius, *On Style,*" trans. D. C. Innes, in *Ancient Literary Criticism: The Principal Texts in New Transla-*

Demetrius's essay begins with basic grammatical issues of word choice, the structure of sentences, the use of clauses, and the development of periods ("a combination of clauses and phrases which has brought the underlying thought to a conclusion with a neatly turned ending")[21] before turning to the practical uses and abuses of styles.[22] Writers of whatever competence in Greek would almost surely have been aware of some of these discussions in even the beginning stages of their grammatical training. Thus the rhetorical directives, practices, and admonitions found especially in Demetrius and *Rhetorica ad Herennium* but also in Cicero and Quintilian may provide an insightful context for studying the Greek of Mark. That Mark lacks graceful periods, extended figures, or light pleasantries does not indicate that the narrative is without rhetorical development, if one understands the variety of styles available to a Hellenistic author.[23]

For example, although Demetrius applauds the artistic polish of the periodic sentence, he also finds that its use can lead to artificiality, and so it should be balanced by the "disjointed style" of sentences, which he defines as "loosely related clauses with little interlocking" or as clauses "piled one on top of the other and thrown together without any integration and interdependence."[24] Such disjointed sentence construction achieves the simplicity of speech but often lacks clarity, as Demetrius later points out in his discussion of the plain style. The use of basic connectives can, then, help clarify the material, while at the same time preserving the effect of ordinary speech. However, for truly dramatic delivery and great emotion all connectives ought to be omitted.[25] Two of the most striking and common features of Mark's Greek style are the presence of parataxis, "the simple co-ordination of clauses with καὶ instead of the use of participles or subordinate clauses," and asyndeta, the absence "of the connecting links supplied by particles and conjunctions."[26] In Demetrius's terms the Gospel's style attempts to blend the clarity and simplicity of ordinary speech with the emotion of dramatic delivery. And why choose ordinary speech for so

tions, ed. D. A. Russell and M. Winterbottom (Oxford: Clarendon Press, 1972), 171–73.

21. *On Style* 10–11.

22. Demetrius lists four, rather than three, styles and also illustrates their faults: (1) the grand (or elevated) style—fault: the frigid style; (2) the elegant style—fault: the affected style; (3) the plain style—fault: the arid style; and (4) the forceful style—fault: the unpleasant style.

23. Indeed, Demetrius not only provides four styles rather than three but he also suggests that most of the four can be mixed with one another to form even more alternatives (*On Style* 36–37).

24. *On Style* 12–15.

25. Ibid., 190–95.

26. Taylor (*The Gospel According to St. Mark,* 48–49) gives many specific examples of these two characteristic traits.

momentous a message as the good news of Jesus Christ? Demetrius, again, suggests a possible reason: persuasiveness.

> Persuasiveness has two characteristics, clarity and ordinary language. Anything obscure and out of the ordinary is unconvincing. For persuasive effect then, we must aim to avoid diction which is ornate and pretentious. . . . In addition to these factors . . . not everything should be given lengthy treatment with full details but some points should be left for our hearer to grasp and infer for himself. If he infers what you have omitted, he no longer just listens to you but acts as your witness, one too who is predisposed in your favor since he feels he has been intelligent and you are the person who has given him this opportunity to exercise his intelligence. In fact, to tell your hearer everything as if he were a fool is to reveal that you think him one.[27]

Hence Mark's use of parataxis, asyndeta, ordinary diction, and brevity of narration, allowing the hearer/reader to fill in the "gaps," all find a home in Greek rhetorical theory. With the additional catalogues of Markan rhetorical figures, strategies, and styles supplied by a number of recent studies of the Gospel, there can be no doubt of Mark's thorough immersion in the realm of rhetoric.[28]

The fundamental basis of rhetoric is *amplification* of a speaker's positions, arguments, or theses.[29] Such amplification is necessary because of the oral nature of ancient discourse. Speaking and writing in the Greco-Roman world were done *for the ear, not the eye.* Many of the figures listed by rhetorical handbooks concern the *sound* of language, not the visual image presented, and since one is composing for the ear, many rhetorical strategies concern the use of repetition,[30] in small and large ways, without eliciting boredom.[31] The line between speaking and writing, hearing and

---

27. *On Style* 221–22. Modern reader-response critics like Wolfgang Iser would certainly find Demetrius's advice on involving the hearer in the presentation to be in total harmony with their own views.

28. See, e.g., D. Rhoads and D. Michie, *Mark as Story: An Introduction to the Narrative of a Gospel* (Philadelphia: Fortress Press, 1982), 35–62; T. Boomershine, "Mark, the Storyteller: A Rhetorical-Critical Investigation of Mark's Passion and Resurrection Narrative" (Ph.D. diss., Union Theological Seminary, New York, 1974); F. Neirynck, *Duality in Mark: Contributions to the Study of the Markan Redaction* (BETL 31; Louvain: Louvain University Press, 1972); and Robbins, *Jesus the Teacher.*

29. Kennedy, *Rhetorical Criticism,* 21–22.

30. Homoioteleuton (similar end sounds), onomatopoeia (words that also express sounds), and parechesis (repetition of same sound in successive words) are examples of sound figures, while chiasmus (crosswise repetition), antistrophe (repetition of the same word at the end of clauses), anaphora (repetition of the same word at the beginning of clauses), and pleonasm (redundancy) all feature repetition.

31. The rule as presented in *Rhetorica ad Herennium* (4.42.54) is quite specific: "We shall not repeat the same thing precisely—for that, to be sure, would weary the hearer and not elaborate the idea—but with changes."

reading was a very narrow one. All reading in the Greco-Roman world was done aloud, and often the author would be the reader of the piece to the audience. Demosthenes and Cicero, for example, wrote their speeches and also performed them orally. Indeed, of the five stages of rhetoric, the first three—invention, arrangement, and style—had to do with the composition of the work, while the last two—memory and delivery—controlled its oral performance.[32] Composing and performing were part of one complex task and were intimately related to each other. The difficulty of distinguishing between speaking and writing is well illustrated by the case of Isocrates. Isocrates was revered as one of the finest rhetoricians in Greek history; his theories of rhetoric probably had greater influence over Hellenistic schools of rhetoric than the work of either Plato or Aristotle, and yet Isocrates *never* delivered a speech orally. His entire reputation rested on speeches he composed for others to deliver, but *he* was hailed as a great orator.[33]

Not speeches alone but histories, poems, biographies, and of course drama were all performed orally and were composed and judged by rhetorical principles.[34] The reading aloud of all types of texts was a fairly common practice during meals in wealthy homes, and even when one was alone, one would read aloud.[35] Thus all ancient discourse had a *speaking voice* behind it, even if the speaking voice was the reader's own. The Gospel of Mark, then, like its counterparts up and down the aesthetic scale of Hellenistic literature, was an *aural text,* a spoken writing, a performed story.[36] This

32. Kennedy, *Rhetorical Criticism,* 13–14.

33. Either a speech defect or shyness was behind Isocrates's refusal to speak orally. See Clark, *Rhetoric in Greco-Roman Education,* 7–10; see also Quintilian's discussion, *Institutio Oratoria* 12.10.49–50.

34. Kennedy, *Rhetorical Criticism,* 13.

35. H. I. Marrou, "Education and Rhetoric," in *The Legacy of Greece: A New Appraisal,* ed. M. I. Finley (Oxford: Clarendon Press, 1981), 196. An excellent New Testament example of this practice can be found in Acts 8:28–31. Philip *hears* the Ethiopian reading alone in his chariot because he was, obviously, reading aloud. Other reading aloud scenes are, e.g., Luke 4:16 and Acts 15:21. The first person from antiquity who is actually reported to have read without sound is St. Ambrose (see Augustine, *Confessions* 6.3).

36. See also Aristotle, *Rhetoric* 3.1407b: "Generally speaking, a written work should be easy to read aloud and to deliver, which is really the same thing."
My position throughout this section contrasts with the interesting thesis recently argued by Werner Kelber concerning the dramatic hermeneutical shift which occurred in the Christian tradition when early *oral* material was transformed into a *written* text (Kelber, *The Oral and the Written Gospel*). Kelber is most certainly right to emphasize the distinctive act of creation that produced the Gospel of Mark in opposition to the form-critical opinion that Mark was merely the natural end product of a traditioning process growing from the oral use of earlier material by Christian communities. However, to posit such a radical gap between oral and written dynamics as he does seems to ignore the rhetorical nature of the Hellenistic milieu.
While even in the Hellenistic period some distinction must be drawn between

aural nature of the Gospel is one source of hermeneutical difficulty to modern readers, for the contemporary sensibility is dominantly visual, not aural.[37] For us, "to see" metaphorically means "to understand" or "to comprehend," but for the author of Mark, "to hear" meant "to understand" (see Mark 4:12); those who have ears to hear must hear (4:9, 23), and it is the word that they hear. Not only the style of the Gospel but also its content, its vision of existence, to use a singularly inappropriate modern

completely oral situations and aural texts (see, e.g., Aristotle, *Rhetoric* 3.1413b but contrast 3.1407b), the dominance of rhetorical concerns in both makes the line between them narrow and blurred. Quintilian, who had a word to say on practically everything involving rhetoric, actually discusses whether there is or should be a difference between written speeches and spoken speeches (*Institutio oratoria* 12.10.49–57) and, at another place, the differences between hearing and reading (10.1.16–19). In the first instance, Quintilian states categorically: "It is one and the same thing to speak well and to write well: and a written speech is merely the record of a delivered speech" (12.10.51). In the second instance, he does think hearing and reading have somewhat different virtues, related primarily to *time:* readers have more time to go over the book and thus their judgment can be more reliable, while the hearer is taken up by the emotions of the moment and may not judge as wisely. The point of reading, for Quintilian, is to commit material to memory for later use in one's own oral performances. Again, the line between hearing and reading begins to blur.

Only very briefly at the end of the last chapter in his study does Kelber raise the issue of the oral performance of written texts in antiquity (pp. 217–18), and his suggestion of a "secondary orality," while intriguing, is not at all developed. Yet, even to admit that ancient texts may partake of "secondary orality" is to undercut somewhat his thesis concerning the radical difference between oral and written.

The basic problematic in applying Kelber's thesis to the Gospel of Mark is not, I think, his model of orality (pp. 44–89), for what he calls Mark's "oral legacy," I would call Mark's rhetorical intention; indeed, a number of the rules of oral communication (e.g., constant variation in repetition, pp. 45–46, 67–68) that Kelber cites are precisely the recommendations of rhetorical handbooks (see p. 43 n. 31 for *Rhetorica ad Herennium* 4.42.54, on repetition with variation). The problem occurs in his model of textuality (pp. 90–139) which is an adequate presentation of modern, Western textuality but is totally inappropriate for Mark. His first point, that Mark disrupts "the oral lifeworld" by "the textually induced eclipse of voices and sound" (p. 91) ignores the oral performance of ancient texts: sound and voice were *always* present. If the medium really is the message, as Kelber insists (p. 91 and passim), then a careful description and analysis of the medium in its historical matrix is necessary. While there may well be some transhistorical, transcultural elements to oral and written discourse, forms of speaking and forms of writing are deeply embedded in the change and movement of history, and models that ignore historical constraints risk ignoring the real dynamics of the medium. Kelber's thesis may well reflect the way modern, Western readers read Mark, but establishing that modern model of textuality as the experience of early Christians as well will require considerably more evidence and argument.

37. Whenever and however the shift from aural to visual hermeneutics came about, contemporary existence is overwhelmingly visual. That last bastion of aural aesthetics, music, has now moved into the visual universe with music videos. Moreover, ancient manuscripts evince their aural orientation by allowing no spacing between words or sections and little punctuation, relying on the ear to hear the proper stops and starts. Modern books, on the other hand, replete with illustrations, labels between sections, and that most visual of all grammatical requirements, paragraphing, clearly show their eye dependence.

phrase, is primarily aural. Becoming sensitive to the ear orientation of the Gospel is one important way to begin to hear it differently.[38]

One final word on ancient rhetoric: as oral performance, rhetorical works of all genres aimed to persuade by *entertaining*. To please the hearers, to entertain them, was the sine qua non of persuasive speaking and writing. Plato called rhetoric "amusement" (ψυχαγωγία),[39] and the desire to entertain was at one with the desire to influence the audience. Although this amusing quality of rhetoric occasionally had to be defended against attacks on its moral or didactic adequacy,[40] the view that writing or speaking needed to please in order to persuade was widespread in Hellenistic times. The first-century C.E. Jewish scholar Philo suggested that the goal of historiography in his day was "to please" (ψυχαγωγῆσαι),[41] and the author of 2 Maccabees quite forthrightly in the preface (2 Macc. 2:24–32) describes the purpose of the writing: "We have aimed to please those who wish to read, to make it easy for those who are inclined to memorize, and to profit all readers" (v. 25). To please, to entertain, was necessary to persuasion and thus "to profit all readers." While we do not often consider the entertainment value of biblical texts like Mark, perhaps because we have accepted the position of classical writers like Plato and Eratosthenes, who argued that serious moral issues are not commensurate with pleasure, we may need to revise our position in the light of the intimate connection between pleasing and persuading. The macabre details of the beheading of John the Baptist (Mark 6:17–29), the narrative relish of the herd of swine hurling themselves over the cliff in the healing of the demoniac (5:1–20), or the increasingly nitwit responses of the disciples throughout the Gospel may serve the purpose of entertainment as well as moral instruction, for that combination is a special grace of Hellenistic rhetoric.

Summary

The complex cultural phenomenon that was Hellenism shifted the entire Mediterranean world into a different key. Encouraged by a common lan-

38. One pervasive tendency in modern homiletics is to develop sermons on Gospel stories by "painting a picture" of the episode; so, the warmth of the day is described, the weariness of the crowd, the little boy with his fish or the little girl with her bread, and so on until the congregation can *see* the story of the feeding of the multitudes. However, that is not the way the story is presented in the Gospels. What is happening between the Gospel story and the sermon is the shift from aural hermeneutics to visual hermeneutics, for it is *visually* that a modern congregation understands stories. The minister is functioning, often unconsciously, as a mediator between hearing the word and seeing it. Such a necessary task might be more effectively done if the minister were actually clearly aware of what she or he was doing.

39. *Phaedrus* 261a.

40. See, e.g., the Stoic Strabo's defense of entertainment as an absolute support for moral instruction in *Geography* 1.2.3 (written about 17 C.E.).

41. *De vita Moses* 11.8.

guage and a common *paideia,* mobility increased. People moved from one region to another, one city to another, either by force or by choice; they also moved up and down the social ladder. Such movement brought with it the inevitable breakdown of older, more stable native traditions, families, and tribes and thus engendered increased anxiety, insecurity, and alienation. Without familial or tribal solidarity, the isolated individual sought security either in new sects and religious cults, which promised fellowship, salvation, or escape from death, or in philosophies of endurance or freedom, or in the magical manipulation of oracles and astrology. Above all, this new-found mobility meant an increased emphasis on communication; the gifted rhetor significantly increased his or her social ranking, and the art of speaking well and persuasively flourished in schools, law courts, assemblies, and marketplaces. This cultural environment is the historical home of the Gospel of Mark. Like others of his age, Mark's constantly journeying Jesus is divided from his own family and hometown (Mark 3:31–35; 6:1–6), rejected by the traditional leaders of his religion, and thus leads the way to a new family and a new faith, based on a new word for all to hear. In so many ways, Jesus, as Mark characterizes him, epitomizes the situation of the Hellene, caught between suffering and hope, the breakdown of the old and the promise of the new.

Text-Specific
Requirements:
Genre

By comparing generalized features of Hellenistic culture with generalized comments about Mark's story of Jesus, it is possible to perceive their complementarity and perhaps to gain a fuller sense of the setting within which the Gospel was written and first heard. In order to study the Gospel with greater specificity and depth, however, we need to have some idea of its genre. Generic expectations of works are often the single most important guide to their interpretations.[1] What readers conceive the genre of a text to be—newspaper article, poem, detective story, telephone book—determines how they read it, what they expect to find, and what they learn from it. Unfortunately one of the thorniest and most contested issues in Gospel research is precisely this one: What genre or genres are the canonical Gospels? Suggestions run the gamut from unique, totally new forms of proclamation (required by the totally new revelation of Jesus Christ) to types of ancient aretalogies (accounts of the miraculous deeds of divine men) to midrashic lectionary texts to types of ancient biography. In order to sort through the welter of proposals and counterproposals to a productive result, we must first establish some basic working definitions for genre, author, and audience. After this exercise in definition, we can then look

---

1. See Kent, "Classification of Genres," 1–2; S. Mailloux, *Interpretive Conventions: The Reader in the Study of American Fiction* (Ithaca, N.Y.: Cornell University Press, 1982), 126–39; and E. D. Hirsch, *Validity in Interpretation* (New Haven: Yale University Press, 1967).

briefly at suggestions concerning the genre of the Gospel of Mark and begin to construct a hypothesis for it which can be used to guide the literary analysis.

Definitions—Genre

Confusion in discussions of Gospel genre arises from two different areas: the compass of the term "genre" and its force. Genre can be used to encompass at least three distinct levels of literary endeavor. In its broadest sense, genre can refer to overarching, almost archetypal, plot patterns such as tragedy, comedy, and romance. If the focus is somewhat narrower, genre delineates sets of related texts that display similar conventions of plotting, characterization, and motifs such as novels, drama, biographies, detective stories, and lyric poetry; moreover, subsets can be designated by combining these first two levels to reveal tragic novels, comic poetry, romantic biographies, and on and on. At its narrowest focus, genre can describe the individuality of each separate text, for each literary work establishes its own special intrinsic genre by its unique combination of motifs, characters, and plot. At this minimal level, however, the idea of genre becomes so particularized that it ceases to have any useful function. Hence, for example, when people argue that the Gospel is a unique genre because it is the only writing that presents Jesus as its main character, they are developing an intrinsic understanding of genre, and since the same claim can be made for any other literary work (Dickens's *Oliver Twist* is a unique genre because it is the only story that has Oliver Twist as its main character), the argument, while sounding impressive, is fairly useless.

Nevertheless, the two broader levels of genre do function practically, for they point to shared conventions in groups of texts that readers can recognize and identify. Because readers have read texts with similar patterns, themes, and motifs before this one, they will read with definite generic expectations that the author can count on in creating the work. Through the experience of previous texts readers build up a repertoire of conventional expectations that they bring to each new text of similar design. Thus, along with many contemporary critics, we may define "genre" as a prior agreement between authors and readers or as a set of shared expectations or as a consensus "of fore-understandings exterior to a text which enable us to follow that text."[2] With this general definition in mind, let us turn to the

---

2. Kermode, *The Genesis of Secrecy,* 163; see also J. Culler, *Structuralist Poetics: Structuralism, Linguistics, and the Study of Literature* (Ithaca, N.Y.: Cornell University Press, 1975), 30; Mailloux, *Interpretive Conventions,* 126–37; and Kent, "Classification of Genres," 8–19.

second major source of confusion in discussions of Gospel genre: force. Are genres descriptions of shared expectations, or are they prescriptions of sharply defined rules? Do they guide reading, or do they constrict options? A number of studies of the Gospel of Mark have argued that it could not be a biography or the memorabilia of a sage because it does not fit all the rules prescribed for these genres in ancient literature.[3] Conventional expectations, however, become prescribed requirements only through the imposition of institutional power.[4] The established literati or the ecclesial hierarchy may have the ability to transform the normal into the normative for those under their control, but at the early stages of such institutions or for groups only loosely associated with them, their regulative force is minimal. The rigid rules of late antiquity or the medieval period do not cover the production of early Christian literature! Both the tendency to reject generic proposals because of their lack of exact "fit" to some supposed prescribed format and the tendency to construct generic proposals by sharp delineation of precise types or "kinds" misconstrue the nature of genre.[5]

If we understand genre as a repertoire of shared conventions that guides readers and writers, we immediately resolve two issues prevalent in earlier discussion of the Gospels' genres. First, no unique genre can exist almost by definition, for as a set of agreed expectations, a genre that is unique would also be unfollowable. Second, genres, as opposed to institutionally prescribed "kinds," are fluid patterns, capable of adopting and adapting aspects of earlier works:

> New genres are formed from realignments of existing genres. To prove that a gospel is evidently not a *chria* or an aretalogy or a *baracah* or an apocalypse is by no means to demonstrate that these genres did not contribute to the set of expectations within which Mark wrote and his audience read or listened.[6]

Thus, biography, memorabilia, and other related forms need to be studied for what they suggest about the conventions shared by the author and hearers of the Gospel of Mark.

---

3. See the use of this kind of argument in Kee, *Community of the New Age,* 17–30; see also A. N. Wilder, *Early Christian Rhetoric: The Language of the Gospel* (1964; reprint, Cambridge: Harvard University Press, 1971), 28.

4. See Mailloux, *Interpretive Conventions,* 126–29; Kermode, *The Genesis of Secrecy,* 162; and K. Jamieson, "The Standardization and Modification of Rhetorical Genres: A Perspective," *Genre* 8 (1975): 183–93.

5. C. H. Talbert's proposals to fit each Gospel to carefully delineated types of Greco-Roman biography would be considerably more persuasive were it not quite as precise and rigid (*What Is a Gospel? The Genre of the Canonical Gospels* [Philadelphia: Fortress Press, 1977]).

6. Kermode, *The Genesis of Secrecy,* 162–63.

Definitions—Author, Audience

Defining genre in terms of conventional expectations shared by authors and readers raises another definitional problem. What is meant by the terms "author" and "readers" for the Gospel of Mark? We cannot know the real flesh-and-blood author or first hearers of the Gospel, and even if we could, that information might be of little practical assistance in interpreting Mark. The terms "author" and "readers" (or "audience") function in a literary study as heuristic constructs, built up from observable configurations in the text itself combined with theories elaborating the dynamics of the reading (or hearing) process as a whole. "Author" refers to that ideal version of the writer created by the sum of choices making up the text.[7] In the case of Mark, this implied, ideal author is based not only on the identical ideological points of view articulated by the third-person omniscient narrator and the main character, Jesus,[8] but also on the overall selection and placement of material, the crafting of the story as a whole. Thus the evaluative perspective that dominates the Gospel and is found in the narrator, Jesus, and all other reliable commentary (e.g., the voice from heaven in Mark 1:11 and 9:7) is the point of view of the implied author, but, moreover, the implied author stands outside the story as well in the capacity of creator. Whenever we use the term "author" of Mark, we will be referring to this sum of choices perceived in and around the text.

Similarly, the "reader" of Mark is also a theoretical construct. In this case, however, the current prominence of reader-response or audience-oriented criticism has produced a mass of theoretical "readers."[9] Differences among the various "reader" theories arise primarily over the degrees of influence each position allows to text and reader vis-à-vis each other. Does the text control the reading process, with each reader as a passive receptacle? Or

7. W. Booth, *The Rhetoric of Fiction* (Chicago: University of Chicago Press, 1961), 71–77.

8. For a careful working out of the identical viewpoints of Jesus and the narrator of Mark, see N. Petersen, "'Point of View' in Mark's Narrative," *Semeia* 12 (1978): 97–121.

9. The "mock reader," the "ideal reader," the "informed reader," the "subjective reader," and the "implied reader" are just a few of the current options. Useful overviews of these possibilities in reader-response criticism can be found in J. P. Tompkins, "An Introduction to Reader-Response Criticism," in *Reader-Response Criticism: From Formalism to Post-Structuralism,* ed. J. P. Tompkins (Baltimore: Johns Hopkins University Press, 1980), ix–xxvi; and S. Suleiman, "Introduction: Varieties of Audience-Oriented Criticism," in *The Reader in the Text: Essays on Audience and Interpretation,* ed. S. Suleiman and I. Crosman (Princeton: Princeton University Press, 1980), 3–45; see also E. V. McKnight, *The Bible and the Reader: An Introduction to Literary Criticism* (Philadelphia: Fortress Press, 1985); and R. M. Fowler, "Who Is 'the reader' of Mark's Gospel," in *SBL Seminar Papers 1983,* ed. K. Richards (SBLSP 22; Chico, Calif.: Scholars Press, 1983), 31–53.

does the reader create the text, which on its own is simply a set of arbitrary signs? For the purposes of practical criticism, some moderating view between these extremes is the most useful: meaning occurs in the interaction of text and reader.[10] The text is both determinate and indeterminate in that it provides structures and clues to guide the reader while at the same time presenting blanks or gaps that each reader must fill in for himself or herself. Correspondingly, each reader is both controlled by the text and free of it, for the text creates a role for the reader, but each real reader fulfills that role differently, depending on historical or individual circumstances.[11] The role of the reader implied by the text, and the ideal version of the author, can both be the subject of critical analysis because they are *textual functions* (i.e., they are *in* the text). However, since the role of the reader can be concretized or actualized by different real readers in different ways, textual analyses only *clarify the potential of the text* rather than determining its absolute meaning.[12]

Definitions—Authorial Audience

One further distinction is necessary to uncover the particular interests of this study of Mark. While the implied reader is a textual role fulfilled by real readers in quite different ways throughout the long history of the Gospel, the real author of Mark had a fairly specific audience in mind in composing it. A writer "cannot write without making certain assumptions about his readers' beliefs, knowledge, and familiarity with conventions."[13] Although we cannot detail the exact historical community the Gospel was written to address,[14] we can reasonably assume that it, indeed, was designed "rhetor-

10. My position is closest to that of Iser *(Act of Reading)*, although I modify his theory of reading toward a more sociological perspective by emphasizing as well the interpretive conventions that guide the process. For a reading theory based on conventions, see Culler, *Structuralist Poetics;* and Mailloux, *Interpretive Conventions.*

11. Iser, *Act of Reading,* 36–37. One of the possible circumstances that affects the actual reader's fulfillment of the reader's role created by the text is reading competency. At the far end of the spectrum is the critic, or highly informed reader, whose experience of reading a text is different from that of the general reader. Lack of awareness of this difference sometimes leads critics to argue for reading clues in the text that most readers would never notice. Especially in biblical texts where each verse is minutely examined, critics tend to see highly subtle hints and clues as quite major signposts for meaning.

12. Ibid., 18–19. Understanding the process of reading to be both a textual function and an individual act by real readers fulfilling that function in different ways provides both a theoretical and a practical foundation for multiple interpretations.

13. P. J. Rabinowitz, "Truth in Fiction: A Reexamination of Audience," *Critical Inquiry* 4 (1977): 126.

14. For an attempt to use reader-response categories to begin to build a picture of the historical community, see N. Petersen, "The Reader in the Gospel," *Neotestamentica* 18 (1984): 38–51.

ically for a specific hypothetical audience"[15] which could be expected to recognize the conventions, to follow the plot structure, and generally to possess the necessary competencies to understand the text. We will call this audience imagined by the author the "authorial audience" or "authorial reader." It too is a heuristic literary construct, which we might conceive as the writer's vision of an ideal reader, the reader who would fulfill the reader's role implied in the text in the way it was designed to be done. Even the real flesh-and-blood first hearers of the Gospel may well not have been able to actualize successfully what the author envisioned, but they were considerably better prepared to accomplish that act than modern readers are. As Peter Rabinowitz points out: "If historically or culturally distant texts are hard to understand, it is often precisely because we do not possess the knowledge required to join the authorial audience."[16] In our concern with the culture out of which the Gospel came and with the possible shared expectations, or generic conventions, presupposed by the Gospel, we are attempting to enter the authorial audience, to actualize the implied reader in terms of the possible authorial reader, and to clarify the potential of the Gospel for its authorial audience. Thus we may restate the goal of this literary-critical analysis of the Gospel of Mark as an attempt to articulate one possible interpretation of the Gospel in all its parts *in the light of its authorial audience.*

Asserted in that way, of course, the goal is not only a formidable literary-historical task but also quite impossible. It is impossible because much of the knowledge necessary to join the authorial audience is simply lost to us. Whether out of ideological disagreement or simple unconcern or ignorance, many of the writings of the Greco-Roman world were destroyed during the long process of scribal copying and transmitting from the ancient world through the Middle Ages. The Gospel of Mark and other Greek and Latin texts are, then, the remnants of a lost world. And the dimensions of the loss are overwhelming. For example, many ancient writers mention the great importance of the development of New Comedy in the plays of Menander. He revealed the dramatic and comic possibilities of ordinary people using ordinary speech with revolutionary consequences for the literature and drama of the Hellenistic age. Yet not one full play of Menander's has survived. Our knowledge of him comes only through the praise of others, the occasional lines they quote from his many works, and

15. Rabinowitz, "Truth in Fiction," 126.
16. Ibid., 127. See also R. Scholes and R. Kellogg, *The Nature of Narrative* (London: Oxford University Press, 1966), 83: "To understand a literary work, then, we must first attempt to bring our own view of reality into as close an alignment as possible with the prevailing view in the time of the work's composition. . . . Thus, the approach of a modern reader to a work from an alien milieu, ancient or modern, must depend to some extent upon historical scholarship or what used to be called 'learning.'"

tattered papyrus fragments. The loss of Menander is only one instance of many, although it may be one of special importance for the Gospel of Mark, because Quintilian says that grammatical training in Greek often employed Menander as a model to be imitated by students.[17] If we could compare the rhetorical style of Mark to some of Menander's plays, we might understand Mark far more clearly than we do. Because so much that might elucidate the authorial audience of the Gospel is irrevocably lost, the possibility of modern readers joining that group to any great extent has also been lost.

While honesty compels the admission that any attempt to participate fully in the authorial audience of the Gospel of Mark is doomed to failure, given the lack of resources, that admission need not be taken as license to forget the whole matter. Enough information might be available from a careful study of the Gospel itself in the context of both Hellenistic rhetorical practice and other related works that have survived from the ancient world to obtain some glimpse of the possible competencies and shared expectations the authorial audience might have possessed. Furthermore, the thoughtful application of contemporary literary theory to this ancient text may be able to provide additional assistance in clarifying its conventions and dynamics. Insofar as modern theories of narrative illuminate the basic forces operative in all narratives of all historical epochs, their use in studying ancient literature needs no other justification; however, since most theorists, ancient and modern, naturally concentrate on the particular manifestations of narrative popular in their own times, contemporary literary theories may require some adjustment in dealing with ancient or culturally alien texts. Nevertheless, any insights that current literary, historical, or sociological theories can suggest for clarifying the potential of the Gospel of Mark in the light of its own literary and historical milieu should be warmly welcomed. Consequently, although full participation in the authorial audience is an impossibility, a modern literary-critical study of Mark may be able to draw together *enough* material from related ancient texts and appropriate current research to glimpse some aspects of the potential of the Gospel for its authorial audience, and as John Austin said, "Enough is enough, enough isn't everything."[18]

Before we consider various specific suggestions for the genre of the Gos-

17. *Institutio oratoria* 1.8.7–8. The later Latin playwrights Plautus and Terence made use of many of Menander's plots in their comedies; thus we do have some evidence of the structures of Menander's works, but that information does not provide insight into Menander's Greek style.

18. As quoted in H. Putnam, "The Craving for Objectivity," *New Literary History* 15 (1984): 230. In reflecting on the tendency to prefer to say nothing rather than advancing modest claims, Putnam notes, "That everything we say is false because everything falls short of being everything that could be said is an adolescent sort of error . . . [that] haunts the entire subject of interpretation" (p. 229).

pel of Mark, one final clarification of the restated goal of this study may be valuable. What is being proposed here about glimpsing the potential of the text for its authorial audience is *not* a return to the old, sharp division between "what it means" and "what it meant,"[19] for that position was based on the idea that "what it means" is contemporary subjective appropriation, while "what it meant" is scientific objective analysis. The model of interpretation and reading fundamental to this study insists that every reader participates in *creating* the meaning of the text in the process of interpreting it. Attempting to elucidate some of the competencies possibly possessed by the authorial audience is basically an acknowledgment that cultural change and historical distance do, in fact, exist in human society and ought not to be ignored. However, the resulting interpretation will still be that of a modern person reflecting from a late-twentieth-century perspective on what an ancient text might have communicated to an ancient audience. Indeed, I am the one who is the cocreator of the meaning of the text, but I choose to develop that meaning in the context of ancient conventions insofar as possible, because I suspect that some of the muddle and confusion that modern readers find in the Gospel of Mark may be the result of a failure to recognize those conventions for what they are. Thus, "what it means" and "what it meant" inevitably merge in interpretation even when historical distance is consciously acknowledged and allowed to modify the interpretive process.

The Genre of Mark

The agreements between authors and readers, their shared expectations that compose genres, arise from familiarity with previous similar texts. Thus many studies of the genre of the Gospels have quite rightly explored Greco-Roman literature for texts that parallel the Gospels. The difficulty that these studies encounter is that no extant ancient texts, written *prior* to the composition of the Gospels,[20] display any obvious overall resemblance

19. This division, a very important one for biblical scholarship over a number of decades, was given its classic formulation in K. Stendahl, "Biblical Theology, Contemporary," in *The Interpreter's Dictionary of the Bible,* ed. G. A. Buttrick (Nashville: Abingdon Press, 1962), 1:418–32.

20. The non-Christian text that is remarkably close to the pattern found in the canonical Gospels is Philostratus's *Life of Apollonius of Tyana,* the story of the sage, magician, and philosopher Apollonius, who travels the world with a small band of disciples healing the sick, raising the dead, and teaching. Apollonius contends with tyrant rulers, and after his death he reappears to his disciples to assure them of his immortality. Finally, he apparently ascends into heaven accompanied by angels. Although Apollonius is supposed to have lived in the first century C.E., Philostratus's story must be dated to the early third century C.E., 100 to 150 years *after* the canonical Gospels were written. Philostratus claims, however, to have based his work on the

to them. Three possible deductions can be drawn from this datum: (1) No prior texts exist that are similar to the Gospels because the canonical Gospels, especially Mark, if it was first, were a new genre; (2) prior texts similar to the Gospels did exist but have not survived; (3) the Gospels really do resemble extant ancient texts but in a debased or altered manner caused by their writers' lack of technical skill. One of these three deductions can be found at the basis of all current discussions of the genre of the Gospels. Since deductions 2 and 3 can be, and often are, merged together, the real divide in studies of the Gospels' genres falls between deduction 1 and the other two.

The claim that gospel was a new, or in its most extreme formulation unique, genre certainly owes some of its persistence in biblical studies to the theological temper of the post-World War I Christian world. The unique, utterly unparalleled divine revelation in Jesus Christ, so fiercely and persuasively proclaimed by Karl Barth, could hardly be expressed by any previously existing, pagan literary forms, mutated or not. Rudolf Bultmann's conclusion that the Gospels, as Christian kerygma expanded into narrative form, were distinctive *Christian* writings was a pervasive position in such a theological climate.[21] Moreover, the development of the "New Hermeneutic" in the 1950s and 60s, following the philosophy of the later Heidegger that language was "the house of Being," placed increased stress on the unique nature of Christian writings required to fit the unique nature of the Christian revelation in Jesus.[22] However, without that theological impetus and with a clearer understanding of the sociological function of genre in providing the common ground necessary to make texts intelligible to readers, the assertion of a totally new, or unique, genre for the Christian Gospels has little to recommend it. Indeed, the position has been under attack by a number of works investigating the Jewish and Greco-Roman milieu of the Gospels,[23] and however one may rate the separate alternatives suggested in these historical studies, their combined weight thoroughly undercuts any suggestion of a totally new Christian form.

Nevertheless, despite these careful comparative studies that demonstrate the rooting of the Gospel of Mark in Hellenistic literature, claims for a

writings of one of Apollonius's disciples, Damis, and thus to have eyewitness support for his account.

21. See *The History of the Synoptic Tradition,* 373–74.

22. For a discussion of Gospel literary forms deeply influenced by this position, see Wilder, *Early Christian Rhetoric.*

23. See Talbert, *What Is a Gospel?;* Robbins, *Jesus the Teacher;* P. L. Shuler, *A Genre for the Gospels: The Biographical Character of Matthew* (Philadelphia: Fortress Press, 1982); and M. D. Goulder, *The Evangelists' Calendar: A Lectionary Explanation of the Development of Scripture* (London: SPCK, 1978).

novel or unique genre persist. The recent proposal that the genre of Mark is "parable" is another, somewhat covert, example of the view.[24] While parables did exist in both Greek and Jewish writings of the time, neither culture supports any literary form longer than a brief illustrative story, riddle, oracle, allegory, or fable, and if characters are present at all, they are rarely named, historical, or specific.[25] So, although parables are present in the historical milieu, to describe the genre of Mark as parable is *not* a recognizable historical use of the term. However, "parable" has come to have a metaphorical meaning in current theology for the paradoxical, open-ended, and participatory nature of the Christian message. It is this metaphorical use that is being drawn upon in calling the Gospel a parable, and it is an understandable designation in a theological situation where the distinctive revelation of Jesus Christ is seen as "parabolic."[26]

Indeed, calling the Gospel of Mark a "parable" is thoroughly comprehensible, and perhaps even insightful, to contemporary theologians and students of the Bible who have already come to understand parable as a metaphor for Jesus' message and life. In other words, *Gospel as parable does fit the shared expectations of twentieth-century readers,* and herein may rest the real crux of the matter. As we have already argued, readers will actualize the role of the reader implied by a text according to their own historical situation and context. If the Gospels are to continue as *living* texts, then modern readers must always be able to interpret them in the light of current theological reflection and discourse. The terms used to describe the new or unique character of the Gospels by scholars (e.g., kerygma, parable) are not "new" or "unique" to their own peers and thus are suitable designations for the shared generic expectations of current readers. Those scholars who have explored the Greco-Roman and Jewish milieu of the Gospels, on the other hand, while still contemporary interpreters themselves, are attempting to read the Gospels in the light of their *authorial audience.* Thus the division between the two major streams of research on the gospel genre may be understood as attempts to clarify the reading process in terms of quite different, but equally legitimate, audiences, the contemporary and the authorial.

Since the interest of this particular literary-critical study of the Gospel of Mark is with the authorial audience insofar as possible, we need be concerned only with genre proposals that have arisen from analyses of Greco-

24. See, e.g., Kelber, *The Oral and the Written Gospel,* 211–20.

25. See M. A. Tolbert, *Perspectives on the Parables: An Approach to Multiple Interpretations* (Philadelphia: Fortress Press, 1979), 16–18.

26. See, e.g., J. R. Donahue, "Jesus as Parable of God in the Gospel of Mark," *Interpretation* 32 (1978): 369–86.

Roman and Jewish literary forms of the period. While "midrash" and "apocalypse" (or "midrashic lectionary"[27] and "apocalyptic drama"[28]) may describe types of material or, in the case of "apocalypse," points of view present in the Gospel of Mark, neither term as a description of an ancient literary genre fits the text of Mark. The heavily symbolic, esoteric styles of Daniel and Revelation and the Scripture interpretation characteristic of Jewish midrash occur only occasionally and in fairly limited contexts in Mark. Of the other three major hypotheses for genre—aretalogy,[29] biography,[30] and memorabilia[31]—all exhibit biographical tendencies of one sort or another, and all have objections lodged against them. Catalogues of the miracle-working activities of divine men in various literary forms may well have preexisted the Gospel of Mark, but no such complete text is known, nor does the label "aretalogy" appear to be a recognizable or consistent designation for this multiform group.[32] While biography (technically *bios*) is one of the earliest and most persistent scholarly hypotheses for the gospel genre,[33] it generally charts the entire course of life from birth to death, which Mark, at any rate, does not,[34] and its dominant and essential focus on the special character of the central figure seems to miss Mark's interest in the various responses to Jesus of the disciples, Jews, and crowds.[35] The

27. See M. D. Goulder, *Midrash and Lection in Matthew* (London: SPCK, 1974), 199–201.
28. See, e.g., N. Perrin, *The New Testament: An Introduction* (New York: Harcourt Brace Jovanovich, 1974), 143–45.
29. See, e.g., M. Smith, "Prolegomena to a Discussion of Aretalogies, Divine Men, the Gospels and Jesus," *JBL* 90 (1971): 174–99; and J. Z. Smith, "Good News Is No News! Aretalogy and Gospel," in Neusner, *Christianity, Judaism, and Other Greco-Roman Cults,* 21–38.
30. See, e.g., Talbert, *What Is a Gospel?*; and Shuler, *A Genre for the Gospels.*
31. Robbins, *Jesus the Teacher,* 60–69.
32. The most extensive criticisms of "aretalogy" as the designation of the gospel genre can be found in H. C. Kee, "Aretalogy and Gospel," *JBL* 92 (1973): 402–22; and D. L. Tiede, *The Charismatic Figure as Miracle Worker* (SBLDS 1; Missoula, Mont.: Scholars Press, 1972).
33. In modern times it was first proposed by C. W. Votaw, "The Gospels and Contemporary Biographies in the Greco-Roman World," *American Journal of Theology* 19 (1915): 45–73, 217–49. See also Talbert, *What Is a Gospel?*; and J. Drury, "What Are the Gospels?" *Expository Times* 87 (1976): 324–28; for an argument for encomium biography, a special laudatory subgenre of biography, see Shuler, *A Genre for the Gospels.*
34. Robbins, *Jesus the Teacher,* 62.
35. H. C. Kee, "Mark's Gospel in Recent Research," in *Interpreting the Gospels,* ed. J. L. Mays (Philadelphia: Fortress Press, 1981), 140. C. H. Talbert is most surely correct that the objections raised by Bultmann to categorizing the Gospels as ancient biography, namely, that the Gospels do not show development in the character of Jesus and that ancient biographies lack the mythical pattern and cultic use of the Gospels, are based on a confusion of modern with ancient biography and an ignorance of the uses of biography in the ancient world, respectively; see Talbert, *What Is a Gospel?* 1–8, 25–109.

recent generic suggestion by Vernon Robbins of the memorabilia of a sage (technically *apomnemoneumata*) has the advantages of focusing mainly on adult life and death, emphasizing the relationship of the sage to disciples, existing as a recognized genre well before the first century C.E., and being a term actually used of the Gospels by some later patristic authors.[36] From a literary standpoint it also has the considerable advantage of being the first generic hypothesis to be argued on structural or rhetorical grounds rather than simply on generalized content. Robbins concentrates on the formal patterning of the teaching process between sage and disciples as the feature that links the Gospel of Mark to this ancient genre.[37] The presence of the pattern raises certain conventional expectations in the hearer that the author can then either fulfill or frustrate. Thus Robbins's proposal takes seriously the sociological function of genre for the reading process.

Two basic objections to all of these generic hypotheses are obvious. First, each of the main three—aretalogy, biography, and memorabilia—by emphasizing so strongly one aspect of Mark's story, of necessity must omit or undervalue other parts of the story. In fact, if one could *combine* an aretalogy's focus on miracle-working, a biography's focus on the character of Jesus, and a memorabilia's focus on the teaching cycle between Jesus and the disciples, one would have almost created an adequate generic formulation for the Gospel of Mark. Second, the extant examples from the ancient world of all three of these genres exhibit far superior linguistic and technical skill, far more sophisticated literary and philosophical acumen, and far greater subtlety and sensitivity than anything found in the Gospel of Mark. This second, overarching objection is especially damaging to Robbins's thesis, for, regardless of possible similarity in the patterns of teaching cycles, the rhetorical, philosophical, and stylistic polish of Xenophon's *Memorabilia* is as different from the Gospel of Mark as day is from night.

A New Hypothesis for Genre

The simplicity of Greek style, the unpolished rhetorical development, the lack of philosophical or literary pretension, and the typological, conventional narration which characterize the Gospel of Mark—and, for that matter, the Gospels of Matthew, Luke, and John[38]—seem to place these texts on an entirely different plane from the majority of extant works from

36. Robbins, *Jesus the Teacher,* 60–67.
37. Ibid.
38. Luke-Acts is, of course, easily above the others in rhetorical development and literary self-consciousness, and John has some philosophical pretensions, but even these writings, compared to most of the texts from the Greco-Roman world, are far below standard.

the Greco-Roman world. Attempting to account for that difference may provide a new starting point for developing a plausible hypothesis concerning the genre of the Gospels: perhaps they belong to the realm of *popular culture and popular literature.*[39] If so, then Xenophon's *Memorabilia* stands in the same relationship to the Gospel of Mark that Dostoevsky's *Crime and Punishment* stands to Agatha Christie's *The Murder of Roger Ackroyd:* one is written for the literate elite of culture, the other is accessible to middle- and lower-class masses; one is individualized, subtle, ambiguous, and profound, the other is conventionalized, pellucid, stereotypical, and repetitious; one is an example of self-conscious literate culture, the other of popular culture. The study of popular culture has been a major component of literary scholarship for many years, but only relatively recently have scholars begun to realize that popular cultures existed alongside "elite" cultures well back in history, back behind the pulp novels of the nineteenth century, back behind the Middle English verse romances of the medieval period, back, in fact, at least to the classical world.[40] Both the Hellenistic and the Roman eras encouraged the growth of popular culture, especially in the large city centers, for popular culture can be linked to the development of certain political, economic, and social institutions that indicate the presence of a working class with money and some education but without the privileged leisure of the aristocracy: "Popular culture emerges along with

39. The distinction I am drawing between popular literature and elite literature in the Hellenistic period is not the same as that proposed by K. L. Schmidt in his influential essay "Die Stellung der Evangelien in der allgemeinen Literaturgeschichte" (in *Eucharisterion: Hermann Gunkel zum 60. Geburtstag,* ed. H. Schmidt [Göttingen: Vandenhoeck & Ruprecht, 1923], 50–134) between *Kleinliteratur* and *Hochliteratur.* Schmidt defined *Kleinliteratur,* a category that included the Gospels, as collectively created writings arising out of the cultic activities of a community, while *Hochliteratur* was literature produced for the public by individual authors (pp. 76, 124). All the extant texts and genres of Greco-Roman antiquity for Schmidt were examples of *Hochliteratur* and had no affinities with *Kleinliteratur* such as the Gospels.

Schmidt's category of *Kleinliteratur* would be similar to what literary scholars today might classify as folktales. Since most biblical critics now recognize the distinctive hands of individual authors behind each of the Gospels, they automatically become part of Schmidt's *Hochliteratur,* and the categorization that Schmidt proposed, as important as it was for form criticism, no longer serves any useful purpose in Gospel studies.

The distinction between elite and popular literatures I am suggesting does have affinities with the two types of ancient biography, historical and popular, discussed by Votaw in his insightful essay "The Gospels and Contemporary Biographies in the Greco-Roman World," which Schmidt's article was attempting to refute.

40. See the discussion in F. Schroeder, "The Discovery of Popular Culture Before Printing," in *5000 Years of Popular Culture: Popular Culture Before Printing* (Bowling Green, Ohio: Bowling Green University Popular Press, 1980), 4–15. See also N. Cantor and M. Wertham, eds., *The History of Popular Culture to 1815* (New York: Macmillan Co., 1968); and S. Chodorow and P. Stearns, *The Other Side of Western Civilization* (New York: Harcourt Brace Jovanovich, 1975); particularly for Greek literature, see B. P. Reardon, "Aspects of the Greek Novel," *Greece and Rome* 23 (1976): 130.

taxes, most of all. Taxation implies a political structure, an economic system and an ideology that transcends the natural units of family, tribe, and clan. It also implies extended lines of communication. . . . And it implies the metropolis."[41]

Taxation across the Roman Empire supported the enforcement of laws, the spread of education, the establishment of uniform administrative structures, and the possibility of patronage and aristocratic leisure. Privileged leisure and status mark the cultural division between "the elite, cultivated tradition of arts, thought, discourse and life styles,"[42] from which the vast majority of extant ancient texts come, and the popular, conventionalized, mass culture of the semieducated or uneducated lower-status working classes, whose contact with the cultivated tradition is always mediated, generalized, and secondhand. Whether popular culture should be seen as a pallid reflection of elite culture or as an independent entity brought about by standardized linguistic, political, and economic factors is a theoretical argument we need not enter,[43] for the practical result in either case is a conventionalized conformity suitable for mass communication. Popular literature, as one aspect of popular culture, is related in theme and overall patterning to elite literature, but it is written in an entirely different key. Its vocabulary, plot development, rhetorical strategies, and characterization are simpler, more conventionalized, more homogenized, and often more formulaic than the cultivated and self-conscious writings of the privileged classes. Rather than encouraging individuality and aesthetic excellence, popular literature stresses mass communication and the "artistic principle of variations on a theme."[44]

One of the reasons scholars were slow to recognize the existence of popular cultures in historical periods prior to the Middle Ages was that so little actual evidence of them survived. The groups that control the processes of preservation and transmission of manuscripts, paintings, sculptures, and all the other artistic artifacts of an age are the privileged upper classes with the leisure and financial resources necessary for such activities. In the Greco-Roman world, wealthy patrons subsidized the best and brightest artists, poets, and philosophers; they paid to have the classic writings of literary taste and judgment copied and preserved. This quite limited, well-educated minority, then, are the creators and conservers of the vast majority

41. Schroeder, "The Discovery of Popular Culture Before Printing," 8–9.
42. Ibid., 7.
43. See, e.g., R. Williams, *Culture and Society: 1780–1950* (New York: Columbia University Press, 1958); B. Rosenberg and D. White, eds., *Mass Culture* (Glencoe, Ill.: Free Press, 1957); idem, *Mass Culture Revisited* (New York: Van Nostrand Reinhold Co., 1971); and B. Ulanov, *The Two Worlds of American Art: The Private and the Popular* (New York: Macmillan Co., 1965).
44. J. G. Cawelti, *Adventure, Mystery and Romance: Formula Stories as Art and Popular Culture* (Chicago: University of Chicago Press, 1976), 10.

of surviving ancient texts. It was not from this group, however, that most of the earliest Christians and Christian missionaries came. They came instead from the growing middle stratum of society—the artisans, traders, and freed slaves crowding into the large cities of the age,[45] whose language was *koine* Greek and whose cultural tradition was the mediated, conventionalized, and homogenized result of popular experience. If the authors and original audiences of all the canonical Gospels—indeed, of almost all early Christian writings of any type—belonged in the main to the middle and lower levels of society, it would be extremely odd not to find the evidence of popular literary techniques stamped on their works.

Providentially, examples of one other Hellenistic popular prose literary genre have endured the ravages of manuscript transmission: the ancient novel.[46] By describing and exploring the patterns, techniques, and strategies of the Greek ancient novel, we may be able to discover what possible connections the Gospel of Mark might have had to Hellenistic popular literature. Five complete examples of the ancient novel exist, along with numerous papyrus fragments of other novels. The five are Chariton's *Chaereas and Callirhoe,* Xenophon's *An Ephesian Tale,* Longus's *Daphnis and Chloe,* Achilles Tatius's *Leucippe and Clitophon,* and Heliodorus's *An Ethiopian Tale.* Of the five, only the first two display little "Attic" influence from the Greek cultural revival of the first centuries C.E. known as the Second Sophistic, and it is these earlier, non-Sophistic novels that show the clearest parallels to the Gospels. Although dating is as difficult for these ancient novels as it is for Christian writings, papyrus fragments clearly date the genre to the first two centuries B.C.E. Chariton is usually dated between 100 B.C.E. and 50 C.E., while the dating of Xenophon varies from 50 C.E. to 263 C.E., with the earlier rather than the later end of the spectrum being most probable.[47] About the authors themselves we know little. Chariton states in

45. See, e.g., W. Meeks, *The First Urban Christians: The Social World of the Apostle Paul* (New Haven: Yale University Press, 1983), 51–73; and R. MacMullen, *Christianizing the Roman Empire (A.D. 100–400)* (New Haven: Yale University Press, 1984), 37–42.

46. This genre has also been called the "romance." No designation was created for it in antiquity, although it was evidently a prolific class of literature; as *popular* literature, however, it was not deemed important enough for the cultivated theorists and critics of the ancient world to describe and name. The term "romance" comes from the medieval world and was used initially to characterize writings done in vernacular languages ("Romance" languages) rather than Latin. Since the term "romance" has come to have such narrow connotations in the present, several classicists have argued that the designation should be dropped in favor of the broader term "ancient novel." For this argument, see Hägg, *The Novel in Antiquity,* 1–4.

I have some real misgivings about the use of the term "novel," because it carries with it assumptions about the modern novel that simply do not fit this ancient popular genre, as I will point out later. In order to avoid confusion as much as possible, I will always refer to this genre as either "the ancient novel" or "the erotic popular novel."

47. Hägg, *The Novel in Antiquity,* 3, 5–6, 20–21; G. L. Schmeling, *Xenophon of Ephesus* (TWAS 613; Boston: Twayne Publishers, 1980), 18–19; and Perry, *The*

his opening line that he is Chariton of Aphrodisias (a city in Caria in southwest Asia Minor) and works as a clerk to the rhetor Athenagoras, and this information may well be true.[48] Xenophon of Ephesus provides no personal reference, and the name Xenophon may be a pseudonym alluding to the famous Xenophon of Athens (author of the *Memorabilia*), who lived centuries earlier.[49] The location of the authors and actions in all of the earliest ancient novels is the eastern Mediterranean world from Asia Minor to Egypt.[50] Thus we have a popular Greek prose genre existing well before the Gospel of Mark and produced and distributed throughout the eastern Mediterranean, the home of early Christianity. From the standpoint of simple historical evidence, there is no obvious objection to suggesting that Mark's authorial audience might have been familiar with the patterns of this ancient popular genre.

The five extant texts are all of the erotic variety of the ancient novel; that is, their basic plot elements detail the familiar work of the god Eros: a young couple fall in love, are separated through evil or misadventure, endure great trials and testing, and are finally reunited. It would be a mistake, however, to think that the love theme is the primary focus of the story, for many ancient novelists, especially Xenophon, use the love-separation-reunion framework to concentrate on the exotic, painful, and thrilling adventures experienced by each of the lovers during their long separation. Travel, adventure, and violence are as much the point of these stories as love.[51] Furthermore, a number of scholars argue that even that combination of themes is too restrictive in describing the ancient novel, for also included in this genre are the later writings *Apollonius of Tyre* and the pre-Christian revision of the Pseudo-Clementine *Recognitions* as well as the Christian apocryphal *Acts of the Apostles,* especially the *Acts of Paul and Thecla* and the *Acts of Thomas.*[52] Neither *Apollonius of Tyre* nor the *Recognitions* contains the conventional pair of lovers, although both have travel and adventure in large measure, and some of the earliest papyrus fragments seem to exhibit similar adventure plots without the love theme. On the other hand, perhaps the most polished of the ancient novels, Longus's *Daphnis and Chloe,* lacks both adventure and travel, focusing solely on the seasonal, natural development of love between a shepherdess and a goatherd on Lesbos.

What unites these works are a common myth, a common heritage, and a

---

Ancient Romances, 343–46. See also the review of various dating theories in R. Hock, "The Greek Novel," in *Greco-Roman Literature and the New Testament,* ed. D. E. Aune (SBLSBS 21; Atlanta: Scholars Press, 1988), 127–29.

48. See Hägg, *The Novel in Antiquity,* 4.

49. Ibid., 18–19; and Schmeling, *Xenophon of Ephesus,* 15–17.

50. B. P. Reardon, "The Greek Novel," *Phoenix* 23 (1969): 292–93; and Hock, "The Greek Novel," 139.

51. Hägg, *The Novel in Antiquity,* 3.

52. Perry, *The Ancient Romances,* 27–36; and Hägg, *The Novel in Antiquity,* 147–65.

common conventionalized style, employed by the authors with varying degrees of sophistication. The myth is the Hellenistic myth of the isolated individual in a dangerous world:

> Unaccommodated man, man alone and thus without security, seeks security, in God or his fellow man, or woman. Lacking a social identity, he seeks to create for himself a personal one by becoming the object of the affections of his own kind or of the providence of the Almighty. He identifies himself by loving God or man or both.[53]

The novels are full of religious concerns and themes. It is the gods who often step in to save or damn the hero and heroine. Indeed, one major thesis concerning the origin of the novel, not widely accepted as yet, is that, with the exception of Chariton's, they are all *Mysterientexte,* cultic texts of Hellenistic mystery religions, fully understandable only to the initiated.[54] Whether one agrees with that hypothesis or not, the pattern of "the separation, wanderings, trials, apparent deaths, and final reunion of the two lovers" is strikingly close to the myth of Isis and Osiris so important to the cult of Isis.[55] Indeed, the gods or fate stand behind most of the action in these stories, and regardless of their clear relish for violence, exciting adventure, and entertainment, all of these ancient novels betray a very serious, very religious underlying concern: salvation from isolation, chaos, and death.

The literary heritage of the Greek novel combines Greek drama and historiography. As prose writing, it takes its basic narrative structure from historiography but blends the manners, styles, and concerns of drama and epic into its stories. The ancient novel is "fundamentally drama in substance and historiography in its outward form."[56] The major characters in the novels are often historical persons of earlier periods or the fictional sons

---

53. Reardon, "The Greek Novel," 294; see also Hägg, *The Novel in Antiquity,* 89–90.

54. The position is most strongly argued by R. Merkelbach, *Roman und Mysterium in der Antike* (Munich: C. H. Beck, 1962); see also R. E. Witt, "Xenophon's Isiac Romance," in *Isis in the Greco-Roman World* (Ithaca, N.Y.: Cornell University Press, 1971), 243–54. Compare A. D. Nock's assessment of the thesis in its earlier form in the work of K. Kerényi ("Die griechisch-orientalische Romanliteratur in religionsgeschichtlicher Beleuchtung," *Gnomon* 4 [1928]: 485–92) in "Greek Novels and Egyptian Religion," in *Essays on Religion and the Ancient World* (Cambridge: Harvard University Press, 1972), 1:169–75.

55. Hägg, *The Novel in Antiquity,* 101, and see Hägg's sympathetic rejection of Merkelbach's thesis in pp. 101–4; for another sympathetic discussion of Merkelbach, see Reardon, "Aspects of the Greek Novel," 127–31.

56. Perry, *The Ancient Romances,* 140. Much of Perry's study is given over to tracing the heritage of the ancient novel; see especially pp. 3–95. For an argument that moves the origin of the form more toward the practices of the rhetorical schools in rewriting poetry into prose, see G. Giangrande, "On the Origins of the Greek Romance: The Birth of a Literary Form," *Eranos* 60 (1962): 132–59; see also Hägg, *The Novel in Antiquity,* 109–24.

and daughters of actual historical figures. The action takes place in real cities and involves practices and groups that truly existed (e.g., shipwrecks, pirates, slavery, crucifixion). This essential historiographic form gives verisimilitude to the conventionalized and formulaic plots themselves.[57] The internal dynamics of the plots owe much to drama and epic: brief, dramatic scenes, dialogue with narrative summaries interspersed, episodic development, beginnings with minimal introductions or *in medias res,* central turning points, and final recognition scenes. The ancient novel, then, like the modern novel, is a remarkably synthesizing genre, pulling together a great variety of earlier forms and adapting and diluting them for a larger audience.[58]

The Gospel of Mark is obviously not an ancient novel of the erotic type. However, its mixing together of historiographic form and dramatic force, its synthesizing of earlier genres such as biography, memorabilia of a sage, aretalogy, and apocalypse, its stylistic techniques of episodic plot, beginning with minimal introduction, central turning point, and final recognition scene, and most of all, its fairly crude, repetitive, and conventionalized narrative display striking *stylistic* similarities to the popular Greek ancient novel. There is indeed some fragmentary evidence for a more biographical, as opposed to erotic, type of the ancient novel, with the *Cyropaedia* of Xenophon of Athens (rather than his *Memorabilia*) as its antecedent and the Alexander Romance and Philostratus's *Life of Apollonius of Tyana* as its heirs.[59] If such a historical/biographical type of ancient novel existed, it would clearly be the generic home of the Gospels and would explain why Mark and John, if they were indeed completely independent of

57. In his discussion of possible generic categories for the Gospels from the Greco-Roman world, Talbert dismisses the possibility of exploring the ancient novel (romance) because "the contents of a romance are fictitious, focusing on the experience and emotions of private individuals devoid of historical reality. Both history and biography, however legendary, claim to speak of actual people and events" (*What Is a Gospel?*, 17). Yet it is precisely the historiographic form that most distinguishes the ancient novel. Furthermore, it fulfills two of his requirements for the gospel genre: it is mythic and may well have had a cultic function (viz., R. Merkelbach). For the historical character of the ancient novel, see also Perry, *The Ancient Romances,* 74–79 and Schmeling, *Xenophon of Ephesus,* 106–8. It is, of course, a special kind of history, and here Talbert's point is well taken, for the ancient novel dramatizes *personal* history. The heroes and heroines may meet kings and generals, but the events they are involved in generally affect themselves alone and not the fate of nations, battles, or whole cities, although there are some notable exceptions to this rule.

58. Hägg (*The Novel in Antiquity,* 89) puts it this way: "The novel . . . is the least defined, the least concentrated, the least organic, and the most formless of all the so-called literary forms. It is the open form for the open society. This 'latter-day epic for Everyman' has everything for everybody, exactly as did the old heroic epic; only the difference now is that 'everybody' and 'everything' have become infinitely more varied entities." See also T. Hägg, *Narrative Technique in Ancient Greek Romances: Studies of Chariton, Xenophon Ephesius and Achilles Tatius* (Stockholm: Acta Instituti Atheniensis Regni Sueciae, 1971).

59. See Hägg, *The Novel in Antiquity,* 115, 125–40.

each other, should happen upon the same general format for the story of Jesus. Reference to ancient biographies of Pythagoras, a biography of Alexander (one of the possible sources of the later Alexander Romance), and perhaps the highly fragmentary *Ninus Romance,* dated to 100 B.C.E., would serve as possible candidates for this historical/biographical type of ancient novel.[60] However, since none of these texts survived, or survived in sufficient quantity to be studied, the supposition of a historical/biographical type of ancient novel must remain highly speculative; in fact, if the type existed, the only extant examples would be the Gospels themselves, and, of course, Christian monks made sure that they survived the medieval transcription process.[61]

It is not necessary to posit the existence of a historical/biographical type in order to compare the Gospel of Mark usefully and appropriately to extant examples of the ancient novel. Because genre refers to shared expectations between author and audience, all we need do is confirm the plausibility of the authorial audience of the Gospel having some previous experience of the ancient novel in any of its types. Then the kind of synthesizing style, rhetorical strategies, plot development, and so on, of the popular ancient novel could have been drawn upon by the author of Mark and recognized by authorial readers or hearers. Manifestly, the historical data available on the ancient novel establishes the *possibility* of its membership in the generic repertoire of the authorial audience. Determining the *plausibility* of its presence might best be accomplished simply by indicating some of the literary, stylistic, and rhetorical similarities between the Gospel and examples of the ancient novel.

Chariton and Xenophon of Ephesus, the authors of the non-Sophistic novels, provide the clearest comparisons in overall style, and while Chariton's work has strong similarities to Luke-Acts,[62] it is Xenophon of Ephesus, the crudest and least skillful of the ancient novelists, whose Greek style most resembles the Gospel of Mark.[63] Besides the factors already

60. Ibid.

61. There is firmer evidence for an epistolary type of the ancient novel built on a collection of letters. One of the other sources of the Alexander Romance may have been such an epistolary type and the so-called *Chion Novel* of the first century C.E. is also an example. Studies of the *collection* of Pauline letters might find some comparisons with this material helpful. See R. Merkelbach, *Die Quellen des griechischen Alexanderromans* (2d ed.; Munich: C. H. Beck, 1977); and Hägg, *The Novel in Antiquity,* 126–27.

62. See, e.g., S. M. Praeder, "Luke-Acts and the Ancient Novel," in *SBL Seminar Papers 1981,* ed. K. Richards (SBLSP 20; Chico, Calif.: Scholars Press, 1981), 269–92; R. I. Pervo, *Profit with Delight: The Literary Genre of the Acts of the Apostles* (Philadelphia: Fortress Press, 1987); and D. R. Edwards, "Acts of the Apostles and Chariton's Chaereas and Callirhoe" (Ph.D. diss., Boston University, 1987).

63. Only one manuscript of Xenophon's *Ephesiaca* survived the Middle Ages. It is

mentioned—beginning with minimal introduction, journey motif, episodic plot, central turning point *(peripeteia)*, and final recognition scene, all of which find their ultimate ancestor in Homer—Xenophon, like Mark, supplies little descriptive detail to characters, places, or events. Towns are only named; one stereotypical adjective, if that, is all most characters receive; and brief scenes of dialogue are surrounded by narrative summation.[64] There is a considerable amount of repetition, a characteristic of all the ancient novels, both in words and in similar episodes, whose major alterations are often simply that the actions take place in different towns. In Xenophon, as in Mark, these repetitions often take the form of doublets or pairs which help to structure the story.[65] Such repetitions with variation in both the ancient novel and the Gospel of Mark are indications of their rhetorical heritage and their status as aural texts. As with Mark, behind the human action in Xenophon stand divine decree and initiation which only occasionally concretely enter the story. This development of the action through both divine and human motivations simultaneously is another Homeric trait.[66] Suspense is not an element in the ancient novel or in Mark; early in the story, oracles or narrative reassurances of a successful conclusion are provided. The concern of the audience in both cases is not *what* is going to happen but *how* it will happen.[67] In general, all the ancient novels, like Mark, use day and night sequences either to bind a series of actions together or to separate actions from one another. In Xenophon, the day and night sequences appear and disappear rather arbitrarily until the final action of the recognition scene which is, like Mark's passion narrative, organized strictly and carefully over a definite period of days.[68]

On the negative side, the plot of *An Ephesian Tale,* and the plots of the

now in the Laurentian Library in Florence (a copy of it is held by the British Museum in London). For a critical edition of the text and French translation, see G. Dalmeyda, *Xenophon d'Ephèse Les Ephésiaques* (Paris: Société d'Edition "Les Belles Lettres," 1926). A select English translation appears in M. Hadas, ed., *Three Greek Romances* (Indianapolis: Bobbs-Merrill, 1953).

64. Hägg, *Narrative Technique in Ancient Greek Romances,* 97–100; and Schmeling, *Xenophon of Ephesus,* 75–76.

65. Schmeling, *Xenophon of Ephesus,* 78–79, 38, 104.

66. Hägg, *The Novel in Antiquity,* 6.

67. Schmeling, *Xenophon of Ephesus,* 27; Hägg, *The Novel in Antiquity,* 111; and G. Duckworth, *Foreshadowing and Suspense in the Epics of Homer, Apollonius, and Virgil* (Princeton: Princeton University Press, 1933), 116–22.

68. Hägg, *Narrative Technique in Ancient Greek Romances,* 50–63. Kelber argues that the careful plotting of the passion narrative in Mark in contrast to the redundancy of the earlier episodic sections during Jesus' life indicates the difference between basically oral (episodic) and basically textual (plotted) patterns (*The Oral and the Written Gospel,* 186–99). However, an episodic journeying section followed by a far more strictly plotted final recognition scene is a common feature of the popular erotic novel; that is, the *combination* of episodic and plotted sections is a conventional feature of ancient popular literature.

other erotic ancient novels, are considerably more complex than Mark's story line. The major reason for this greater complexity is the necessity of a *dual* plot in the erotic novels: one plot follows the heroine, the other the hero in their various separate adventures. Consequently, methods of alternation and transition play a larger part in the erotic novels than in the Gospels.[69] In Mark, only one plot line is followed, that of Jesus, and only rarely are transitions necessary (e.g., at Mark 6:14ff. in the episode of the death of John the Baptist and at 14:66ff. for Peter's denial), but in those few instances it might be helpful to compare the techniques of transition used by the novelists. While the novelists revel in exotic adventures like shipwrecks (present in Luke-Acts but not in Mark), pirates, slavery, and prostitution, all of which play little role in Mark,[70] they also abound in apparent deaths, with awakenings in the tomb after burial, and unjust trials resulting in crucifixion, a form of death rarely present in the elite literature of the Greco-Roman period.[71] These macabre devices and violent experiences serve the interests of entertainment, to be sure, but they also provide occasions for serious moral instruction on the power of the divine to save or punish.

Finally, for anyone familiar mostly with the elite literature of the Greco-Roman world, one of the most striking similarities between Xenophon and the Gospel of Mark is the Greek they both use.[72] While Xenophon writes in Attic Greek rather than Mark's *koine,* the style of Attic employed by Xenophon is far from pure and shows much influence from *koine.* Indeed, although people trained only in New Testament Greek are rarely able to read most classical Greek texts, they could read Xenophon with ease. The vocabulary is simple and the language generally clear. Like Mark, Xenophon uses a style that is basically paratactic rather than syntactic, and often it is even *kai*-paratactic.[73] In terms of language competency, Xenophon's

---

69. See, e.g., Hägg, *Narrative Technique in Ancient Greek Romances,* 138–88.

70. There are some exceptions to this judgment, for the dance of Herodias's daughter before Herod's banquet to win the head of John the Baptist could have come directly out of Xenophon's *An Ephesian Tale* in terms of exotic, violent adventure. Also, Mark's description of the healing of the demoniac in Mark 5:1–20 has a similar exotic, fantastic character to it.

71. While not often present in elite literature, it is common and thoroughly described in the ancient novel, contra the position of Kelber, *The Oral and the Written Gospel,* 193.

72. For documentation of this claim through a careful comparison of Mark's Greek and that found in Chariton, Xenophon of Ephesus, and Achilles Tatius, and in the Alexander Romance and other popular novels, see the insightful study of M. Reiser, *Syntax und Stil des Markusevangeliums im Licht der hellenistischen Volksliteratur* (WUNT 2, 11; Tübingen: J. C. B. Mohr [Paul Siebeck], 1984).

73. Schmeling, *Xenophon of Ephesus,* 78–79. Schmeling quotes P. Turner's judgment

authorial audience and Mark's authorial audience were on almost exactly the same level.

Whether these linguistic, stylistic, and rhetorical similarities between the Gospel and extant examples of the ancient novel arise from actual familiarity with the erotic novel or from generic participation in a now extinct historical/biographical subtype of the ancient novel or from general mutual involvement in Hellenistic popular literature, with its synthesizing and diluting stance toward elite culture, matters little for our analysis. What does matter is the plausibility of locating the Gospel of Mark (and the other gospels as well) within the realm of popular literature, for that hypothesis provides concrete benefits for further delineating the authorial audience of the Gospel, for uncovering some of the conventional features of narrative shared by other popular texts, for understanding more clearly the relationship of the Gospel to elite literary genres like memorabilia, biography, drama, and apocalypse, and for opening up a whole new world of theoretical and textual analysis through the study of popular culture. While we have argued that simple historical data establish the possibility of the Gospel's author and authorial audience having previous experience with the ancient novel and that stylistic similarities between extant ancient novels and Mark further indicate the plausibility of that hypothesis,[74] a fairly commonsense test for any generic suggestion is the degree of illumination it brings to interpreting a text. If the Gospel is an example of Hellenistic popular literature and Mark's authorial audience recognized in it many of the stylistic features of the ancient popular novel and thus related it to popular literary forms, the authorial audience would then have rightly interpreted the patterns and conventions used by the author; if our hypothesis of Mark's popular heritage is correct, then we too should be better able to identify and interpret the popular patterns and conventions contained in the Gospel than we have been in the past. The obscurity and muddle of

on Xenophon's Greek usage (p. 75): "The language of Xenophon is so inornate that he 'gives the impression of being almost illiterate.'"

74. We can be quite sure that by the second and third centuries C.E. many Christians were familiar with the erotic ancient novel, for so many of the stories collected in the apocryphal *Acts of the Apostles* use the basic plot patterns and motifs found in the novels. The tale of Thecla and Paul in the *Acts of Paul and Thecla* is especially interesting because it is almost an antitype of the erotic novel. Thecla suffers all sorts of horrible trials, not, as in the erotic novels, so that she can fulfill her marriage vows, but because she refuses marriage. It is her great desire to remain a virgin and serve God that propels her travels and adventures. Only when a genre is extremely conventionalized and well known can an antitype function effectively. Indeed, Hägg suggests that the real heirs of Chariton and Xenophon are not the later Sophistic erotic novels but rather the many Christian apocryphal stories about martyrs, saints, and apostles (*The Novel in Antiquity*, 159–61).

Mark for modern readers should begin to fade just a little. As a first step in the practical testing of this hypothesis, let us detail concretely some of its ramifications for understanding the Gospel and its authorial audience.

The Gospel of Mark as Popular Literature

If we classify the Gospel of Mark as an example of Hellenistic popular literature, then we have grounds for assuming that it shares some of the stylistic features and synthesizing, diluting dynamics of the ancient erotic popular novel. In order to begin to see what concrete advantages such a hypothesis provides, we need first to clarify the category "popular literature." Once that task is accomplished, we can discuss what information the hypothesis supplies concerning the authorial audience and the basic characteristics of the text itself.

In contemporary society, popular culture and popular literature are usually associated with mass communication and mass production. Although Hellenistic society achieved greater and wider levels of literacy, travel, and communication than any previous culture had, it would still certainly not qualify as a "mass culture" in any modern sense. Hence, for the Greco-Roman world the clearest definition of popular literature might be *literature composed in such a way as to be accessible to a wide spectrum of society,* both literate and illiterate. It is distinguishable, on the one hand, from elite literature which is composed by the canons of and for the approval of the artistic establishment and, on the other hand, from folktales which are mostly local and tribal in compass.[75] Popular literature, then, is educated, and it is quite possible for its authors and some of its readers to be highly educated, but it is not written solely for the highly educated, as elite literature often is; instead, it is also possible for its readers to be semieducated or uneducated. It is the necessity of covering this broad spectrum that makes popular literature conventionalized, formulaic, and repetitive, for it aims at putting fewer demands on its readers than elite literature does.[76]

The moderating, undemanding, conventionalized nature of popular literature has earned it the scorn of artistic establishments from the Greco-Roman world to the present. Since it is not considered "serious" literature, it is either passed over in silence or actively reviled. If the Gospels belong to

75. See Schroeder, "The Discovery of Popular Culture Before Printing," 7–8.

76. This low level of demand on the reader is one aspect of popular literature that makes it a suitable medium for "escape" and relaxation. Ironically, the same conventionalized, formulaic style that makes popular literature easily accessible to audiences in its own historical milieu makes it considerably less understandable and much more demanding for readers from an alien culture or a historical period whose reading conventions are different. Thus, some of the very elements that made Mark or the ancient novels easy for Hellenistic readers make them difficult for modern readers.

the tradition of Hellenistic popular literature, that fact alone would explain why no other closely similar texts have survived (popular literature is generally not preserved by the academy) and why none of the ancient critics specifically discuss texts like the Gospels (popular literature is not worth discussion). As B. P. Reardon commented about the ancient novel, "The Greek Academié appears to have regarded prose fiction as a thoroughbred racehorse might regard a camel, with puzzlement and disdain."[77] While it may not be acceptable to the academy, popular literature nevertheless is the perfect medium for religious edification because of its broad accessibility and appeal.[78]

If the Gospel of Mark is popular literature, composed in such a way as to be available to a wide spectrum of society, then its authorial audience and that of the ancient erotic popular novel, also written so as to be available to a wide spectrum of readers, would share many of the same general characteristics. A number of studies of the ancient novel have attempted to evaluate its Hellenistic audience.[79]

> Rootless, at a loss, restlessly searching—the people who needed and welcomed the novel are the same as those who were attracted by the mystery religions and Christianity: the people of Alexandria and other big cities round the Eastern Mediterranean.[80]

The Hellenistic period had seen an expanding level of literacy, especially in the fairly well-to-do sections of the working classes and among women. While their positions as artisans, traders, professional people, and administrators were not always associated with high status, many from this expanding mainly urban class could amass sufficient income for the purchase of books and had developed a taste for episodic adventure stories through the

77. "Aspects of the Greek Novel," 120.

78. Schroeder views religion as the main concern of popular culture prior to the invention of printing: "Religion is the common ground, or the pivot between popular culture before and after printing. Religious cultural materials and practices were mass-produced or mass-disseminated at an early time in history, because of the desirability of consistent value and conforming behavior among constituent, colonial or subservient peoples" ("The Discovery of Popular Culture Before Printing," 10).

79. See, e.g., Hägg, *The Novel in Antiquity,* 81–108; and Schmeling, *Xenophon of Ephesus,* 131–38. Contemporary literary criticism also provides a range of both theoretical and practical studies of the sociology of the reader; see, e.g., L. Goldmann, *The Hidden God: A Study of Tragic Vision in the "Pensées" of Pascal and the Tragedies of Racine,* trans. P. Thody (New York: Humanities Press, 1964); G. Mills, *Hamlet's Castle: The Study of Literature as a Social Experience* (Austin, Tex.: University of Texas Press, 1976); H. R. Jauss, "Theses on the Transition from the Aesthetics of Literary Works to a Theory of Aesthetic Experience," in *Interpretation of Narrative,* ed. M. Valdis and O. Miller (Toronto: University of Toronto Press, 1978), 137–47; and F.-J. Leenhardt, "Toward a Sociology of Reading," trans. B. Navelet and S. Suleiman, in *The Reader in the Text,* ed. Suleiman and Crosman, 205–24.

80. Hägg, *The Novel in Antiquity,* 90.

use of Homer in the schools of grammar and rhetoric.[81] Furthermore, since their fields of endeavor were primarily commercial, political, or administrative rather than aesthetic and academic, they were not bound by the critical sensibilities of the cultivated artistic tradition, nor were they likely to possess highly polished reading or writing skills. In addition to this newly literate group, the audience of the ancient novel probably also came from two other sections of Hellenistic society: the traditional upper-class, educated aristocracy and the illiterate. While they might not brag about it to their friends, members of the educated aristocracy who were willing to suspend their artistic judgments and intellectual requirements in the interests of exciting stories surely formed a part of the readership of ancient popular literature, as, in fact, they continue to do in contemporary society.[82]

The possibility of an illiterate component in the audience of the ancient novel has been proposed by Tomas Hägg in an interesting hypothesis about the use of the ancient novel as entertainment.[83] Hägg notes that the increased mobility of the Greco-Roman period forced an increasing dependence on written communication in letters, edicts, laws, and other sorts of documents. Since the majority of people were illiterate, a class of scribes or secretaries developed who earned their living by reading or writing for others. Chariton, who described himself as a secretary to a lawyer, would be an example of such a group. Hägg, then, hypothesizes a reasonable consequence of this situation:

> The ability to read, and read easily and for pleasure, in a milieu where true literacy was not common, no doubt carried with it the obligation to read aloud to members of the household, to a circle of friends, perhaps even to a wider audience.[84]

As literacy grew, the opportunities for illiterate people to attend such recitations would also have grown. As Hägg points out, the many instances of repetition, regular plot summaries, and foreshadowings present in the ancient novels support the suggestion of their oral performance. Since the Gospel of Mark shares these stylistic features with the ancient novel, Hägg's hypothesis may describe Mark's authorial audience as well. Indeed, the almost certain mixture of literate and illiterate people in the early Christian communities must have obliged the literate to read aloud for the benefit of all.[85]

81. Ibid., 91; and Schmeling, *Xenophon of Ephesus*, 132–33.
82. Schmeling, *Xenophon of Ephesus*, 133–34.
83. Hägg, *The Novel in Antiquity*, 91–93.
84. Ibid., 93. See also Marrou's comments on the custom of securing a "reader" (*anagnostes*) to read material aloud ("Education and Rhetoric," 196).
85. Several texts in the New Testament actually contain specific instructions that

The emerging consensus on the social description of early Christian communities seems to view them as a cross section of Greco-Roman society with the very top level and very bottom level omitted.[86] The majority of first- and second-century Christians, moreover, came from the expanding urban class of artisans, traders, and freed slaves, some of whom had considerable money and education. Speculations about the audience of the ancient novel point to precisely the same group. In addition, because of the general tendency of all the ancient erotic novels to portray the heroine as more admirable, more faithful, and more chaste than the hero,[87] some scholars have suggested that the rise of the popular novel should be linked to the increasing level of literacy among women and that women might have been the authors or formed a major part of the audience for the ancient novel.[88] Women, especially wealthy women, were clearly among the early leaders and patrons of the Christian movement as well and tended to be quite active in the propagation of eastern cults such as the cult of Isis.[89] Finally, one small but perhaps significant historical datum links the audiences of the ancient novel and the early Christian writings: the use of the codex form. Although the prestigious format for literature remained the scroll, in the first and second centuries C.E. the handier codex style began to be used for nonliterary material. Two other kinds of texts were soon frequently distributed in codex form: Christian writings and the ancient popular novel.[90]

Because social descriptions of readers of the ancient novel and of members of the early Christian communities must rest on internal analyses of both groups of writings, supported by whatever partial and incomplete historical data might be available, they must always remain speculative and tentative. Nevertheless, similarities between the two groups are apparent,

---

they be read aloud to the entire group; see, e.g., Col. 4:16; 1 Thess. 5:27; and Rev. 1:3. Indeed, the *anaginoskon* of Mark 13:14 may refer to the one who is reading the text aloud.

86. See, e.g., Meeks, *The First Urban Christians*, 72–73; and A. Malherbe, *Social Aspects of Early Christianity* (Baton Rouge: Louisiana State University Press, 1977), 29–59.

87. In the case of both of the earliest novels by Chariton and Xenophon, the male member of the couple is the one responsible for starting all the troubles in the first place. After marrying Callirhoe, Chaereas becomes falsely jealous of her, strikes her, and apparently kills her. She awakes in the tomb only to be carried off by grave robbers, and thus the long, painful separation begins. In Xenophon's *An Ephesian Tale*, Habrocomes is so smitten with his own beauty as a thing in itself, he offends the god Eros, who determines to punish him by having him fall madly in love and then be separated from his beloved, and that is just what happens.

88. Hägg, *The Novel in Antiquity*, 95–96.

89. See Meeks, *The First Urban Christians*, 23–25, 58–63. See also Schüssler Fiorenza, *In Memory of Her*.

90. Hägg, *The Novel in Antiquity*, 94–95.

and if one accepted the hypothesis that the Gospels are examples of Hellenistic popular literature and thus were directed to the same general populations as other Hellenistic popular literature, then studies of the readers of the ancient novel could be used to supplement social descriptions of early Christians. Since our purpose is not social description but literary analysis of the Gospel of Mark, the similarities between studies of the readers of the ancient novel and studies of early Christian communities only serve to strengthen our hypothesis that Mark's authorial audience would have been familiar with the techniques of popular literature and would have understood their appearance in the Gospel.

Having clarified the definition of popular literature for the ancient period and surveyed views of the authorial audience of the ancient novel, noting similarities to descriptions of adherents of early Christianity, we now need to outline the literary characteristics of ancient popular literature that might affect our interpretation of the Gospel of Mark. As Greek popular prose writings, both the Gospels and the ancient novels combine historiographic form with epic and dramatic substance. Thus the use of historical characters, locations, activities, and groups may be as much a *formal* element in the Gospel of Mark as a reflection of the actual historical situation. Mark's descriptions of the Jewish hierarchy and its practices, the Roman rulers, the crowds, the villages of Galilee, and even Jerusalem and the temple may well be set pieces, more stereotypical than typical. Such features give the plot verisimilitude, but verisimilitude for the ancient world was mainly a representation of generalized opinion, not a representation of reality, as modern realism insists.[91]

If the frame of popular prose was historiographic, the content was dramatic and epic. The episodic epic plot pattern uses the motif of journey to tie together separate encounters and adventures. Episodes are not necessarily connected to one another by cause and effect, as they are in developmental plot patterns; rather, they often cluster in sets defined by the needs of repetition or thematic expression. In the ancient novel, there are at least three possible points where this episodic clustering gives way to necessary placement: at the beginning of the action, the central turning point, and the final recognition scene. The beginning obviously needs to establish briefly both the divine and the human levels of the story. While the central turning point *(peripeteia)* is not necessarily the surprise shift that Aristotle posited for tragedy,[92] it does suggest some distinctive change and usually points toward the final recognition scene. In Chariton's novel, for example, the trial scene before the Persian king in which Chaereas first glimpses Callirhoe

---

91. See Todorov, "Introduction to Verisimilitude," in *The Poetics of Prose,* 81–82.
92. *Poetics* 1450a.

after their long and harrowing separation marks the central turning point in the story and foreshadows their final recognition scene when Chaereas, after defeating the Persian forces with his Egyptian fleet, recognizes an unknown female prisoner as his beloved Callirhoe.[93] Similarly, the Caesarea Philippi scene in Mark 8:27–30 marks the first time a human being, as opposed to a demon or spirit, has acknowledged Jesus' identity. Immediately after this central scene comes Jesus' first prediction of his passion in Jerusalem. Hence, the scene both marks a shift in emphasis toward Jerusalem and foreshadows the final recognition scene which begins with Jesus' trial before the Jewish leaders, when he openly proclaims his true identity (14:60–63).

Speaking of a final recognition *scene* may be somewhat misleading, for the final events in the ancient novel usually include a whole sequence of recognitions, culminating in the reunion of the lovers. In Xenophon's *An Ephesian Tale,* for example, Habrocomes, the hero, is recognized for who he is after answering a series of questions by his old and faithful servants. The question-and-answer motif in recognition scenes probably derives from Homer's *Odyssey* and is a common feature.[94] Later the servants recognize a lock of hair placed as a votive offering in the temple to belong to the heroine, Anthia. Still later the servants observe a strange woman in the temple and recognize her as Anthia, although Anthia does not recognize them until they remind her who they are. Finally, through the servants, Habrocomes and Anthia are reunited and tell each other of their adventures. The whole sequence is carefully plotted over a three-day period and tied together by references to time: "the following day," "when night came," and so forth.

At the heart of a recognition scene is the question of identity, and the recognition sequence in the Gospel of Mark focuses on the issue of Jesus' true identity. During the question-and-answer scene with the high priest, Jesus announces his identity (Mark 14:60–63): he is "the Christ, the Son of the Blessed." Later his rightful position as "King of the Jews" is given a backhanded acknowledgment by Pilate, and finally, after his death, the centurion recognizes him as "Son of God" (15:39). In this light, it is interesting to note that Peter's denial (14:66–72), following immediately after the trial of Jesus, is almost an exact antitype of the recognition scene. In a series of questions, a maid of the high priest recognizes Peter as one of Jesus' followers, but Peter three times denies this correct identification. To anyone familiar with the conventions of recognition scenes in the ancient world, such a denial of correct identification would rule out any final happy

93. Hägg, *The Novel in Antiquity,* 13.
94. Schmeling, *Xenophon of Ephesus,* 72–73. The recognition sequence in *An Ephesian Tale* begins at 5.11.2 and goes to 5.15.1.

reunion. The recognition sequence in Mark, like those of the ancient novels, is carefully plotted over a series of days and uses time references to tie the events together.

The episodic plot pattern in popular literature adopts techniques drawn from ancient drama to shape each episode. Brief dialogues surrounded by narrative explication are common, although they are less prominent in Xenophon's story than in the other ancient novels. Like New Comedy, the ancient novel additionally uses monologues at crucial moments to review past adventures and to reveal some of the internal agony of the characters.[95] While also employing brief dialogue surrounded by narrative, the Gospel of Mark contains only one brief monologue, Jesus' prayer in Gethsemane in Mark 14:32–42, but like the monologues in Xenophon's *An Ephesian Tale,* which can also be quite brief, Jesus' prayer comes at a crucial moment, expresses an internal state of dispute between desire and will, and resolves the situation in appropriate action.[96] Crowds are used in the ancient novel and in Mark, much as the chorus in a drama, to express general views or opinions on the action. With the exception of the hero and heroine and perhaps a couple of faithful servants (Xenophon) or a faithful friend (Chariton), all of the other characters in the ancient novels are minor and appear for an episode or two and then disappear. The central pair are the basic uniting force in the episodic plot from its beginning to its end. Yet even they are often portrayed in a flat, stereotypical, passive, and static manner.[97]

Such stereotypical depiction is the hallmark of ancient literature in general and probably one of its most significant differences from modern literature. Aristotle's comment that tragedy could not exist without plot but could exist without characters[98] baffles contemporary readers raised on the conventions of the modern novel, which is preeminently character study. "Character" for Aristotle and most ancient literature consisted of stereotypical mimetic attributes employed to "color" the figure or agents of the required action. In ancient literature, characters were more illustrative than representational:

> Illustration differs from representation in narrative art in that it does not seek to reproduce actuality but to present selected aspects of the actual, essences referable for their meaning not to historical, psychological, or sociological truth but to ethical and metaphysical truth. Illustrative characters are concepts in anthropoid shape. . . . Thus we are not called upon to

95. Schmeling, *Xenophon of Ephesus,* 103–4.
96. Scholes and Kellogg, *The Nature of Narrative,* 178–81.
97. See Schmeling, *Xenophon of Ephesus,* 118–24, for a blistering description of the incredible passivity of Xenophon's hero and heroine.
98. *Poetics* 1450a.

understand their motivation . . . but to understand the principles they illustrate through their actions in a narrative framework.[99]

The illustrative characters of ancient literature are static, monolithic figures who do not grow or develop psychologically. They have fundamentally the same characteristics at the end as at the beginning. They may, of course, change state, from good fortune to bad, from unknown to known, or from insider to outsider, for example, but such shifts are always implicit in the actions or principles the characters are illustrating. The Christian tradition, especially as focused through Augustine, with its concern for interior, psychological motivations and individuality, became one of the primary sources for the growth of representational characterization[100] and one can see it beginning to develop by the fourteenth century in the writings of Chaucer.[101] Nevertheless, the Gospel of Mark and the ancient erotic novels are children of an earlier age, and to read them in the light of their authorial audiences means to take very seriously their illustrative, symbolic, and monolithic manner of characterization. Illustrative characterization is not better or worse than representational; it is just different. However, it is a difference modern readers have special difficulty recognizing and acknowledging because of the importance of internal, psychological character development in the modern novel. Indeed, deciding to call ancient erotic popular narrative "novels" has the negative side effect of masking one of the striking differences between those ancient writings and what we today know as the "novel."[102] To avoid confusion, modern readers must be very clear

99. Scholes and Kellogg, *The Nature of Narrative,* 88; see also the discussion of character in ancient narrative as opposed to modern narrative in T. Todorov, "Narrative-Men," in *The Poetics of Prose,* 66–67.

100. Scholes and Kellogg, *The Nature of Narrative,* 164–70.

101. Ibid., 91–99.

102. As Scholes and Kellogg lament, "In the middle of the twentieth century, our view of narrative literature is almost hopelessly novel-centered. . . . The novel-centered view of narrative literature is an unfortunate one for two important reasons. First, it cuts us off from the narrative literature of the past and the culture of the past. Second, it cuts us off from the literature of the future and even from the advance guard of our own day" (*The Nature of Narrative,* 8). Their recommendation that in order to appreciate past (and future) literature we must "put the novel in its place" is especially important for interpreters of New Testament narratives. We must try to recognize the differences in narratives of the past from our present reading conventions (see also Kermode, *The Genesis of Secrecy,* 138).

That ancient narratives emphasized plot (actions with agents) as the primary concern, while the modern novel emphasizes the psychological development and expression of character as primary, is just one of many conventional differences that need to be consciously acknowledged in the reading of ancient works. Other important differences include the virtual dominance of reliable narrators in ancient literature versus the prevalence of unreliable narrators in modern narrative (see Booth, *The Rhetoric of Fiction,* 6–7; and Scholes and Kellogg, *The Nature of Narrative,* 51–56,

about the illustrative, static characterization of ancient literature. The specific implications of this feature for understanding the Gospel of Mark will become very clear in our literary analysis.

Summary

By recognizing the sociological function of genre as the common ground or shared expectations of authors and audiences, we can move the discussion of the genre of the Gospels to a more productive level. While we cannot know the real author or authorial audience of the Gospel of Mark, by examining the text itself we can develop some sense of the implied author and the implied audience. Furthermore, by exploring similar literature contemporary with Mark, we may begin to discover some of the conventions and patterns that might have been present in the generic repertoire of the authorial audience. Although the generic suggestions of aretalogy, biography, and memorabilia all clearly find resonances in the Gospel, none of them account for the simple, fairly crude, synthetic narrative Mark exhibits. However, locating Mark in the ranks of Hellenistic popular culture does appear to account for those qualities and at the same time helps clarify the Gospel's links to elite forms of aretalogy, biography, and memorabilia. Fortunately, one other example of Hellenistic popular literature survived the manuscript transmission process: the ancient erotic novel.

While the Gospel of Mark and the early examples of the ancient novel obviously do not share the same story line, their rhetorical, stylistic, and linguistic similarities are conspicuous. Both are synthetic, conventional narratives that combine historiographic form with epic and dramatic substance. Episodic plots, central turning points, final recognition sequences, dialogic scenes with narrative frames, sparing but crucial use of monologue, repetition, narrative summaries, foreshadowing, and monolithic, illustrative characters are some of the elements the Gospel and ancient novels have in common—and all of these features are presented in a simple, crude, conventionalized style suitable to popular dissemination across a broad spectrum of society. Indeed, if the Gospel of Mark is an example of Hellenistic popular literature, we have uncovered a major reason for its opacity and apparent muddle for modern readers. Popular literature is far more dependent than elite literature on conventions and formulas; it is therefore far less understandable outside its own cultural conventions than the more highly individualized literature of the cultivated tradition. If Mark is a

263–79); the presence of helps for the reader in ancient writing (e.g., repetitions, summaries, foreshadowings by oracles or dreams) versus the tendency of modern literature to let the reader draw his or her own conclusions; etc.

popular literary text, modern readers absolutely must discern some of the competencies of the authorial audience in order to have any hope of following the story. Thus our redefined goal of articulating a consistent interpretation of the Gospel in all its parts *in the light of its authorial audience* becomes critically important for modern appropriation of Mark as well as for the task of interpreting early Christian thought.

The Approach Delineated

Two basic issues motivated the choice of a goal for this study of the Gospel of Mark: the paucity in current research of successful attempts to interpret the Gospel in all its parts integrally and consistently and the prevailing judgment of modern readers of Mark concerning its opacity, confusion, and muddle. In the hope of addressing these issues in some way, we proposed to formulate a practical literary analysis of the whole Gospel as a foundation for articulating a consistent interpretation of it. While practical criticism is generally eclectic in nature, that eclecticism should not be arbitrary but should be guided by goal-specific and text-specific criteria. The purpose of this first part of our study has been to explore the ramifications of those criteria for developing a practical literary approach to the Gospel of Mark.

In the process of these theoretical and methodological explorations, several possible reasons for the current state of affairs in Markan studies have surfaced. The pervasive concern of much biblical research for historical reconstructions of the life and message of Jesus or of the beliefs and conflicts of early Christian communities has focused attention on the pre-Markan tradition. Since such a tradition can be discerned only in fragments of the text, the tendency of modern scholarship has been to dissolve the full narrative into smaller, separate, and isolated units. Clearly, this procedure mitigates against reading the text as a unified whole. Furthermore, speculating on possible settings and meanings for isolated units of material *outside* their Gospel context and supposedly prior to it has increased the inclination to condemn the author of Mark as an obscurantist and muddler of source material. In addition, when attempts have been made to interpret Mark's narrative, they have often been heavily influenced by Matthew's and Luke's use of Mark, on the assumption that these later evangelists only intended to clarify and extend Mark's Gospel for their own communities. It is possible, however, that the later writers had more malign than benign intentions in relationship to Mark and actually wished to supplant Mark's interpretation of Jesus with their own. If this latter possibility is the case, reading Mark through the eyes of Matthew and Luke will provide more distortion than clarification, and again Mark will appear to be confused and obscure.

Specific problems related to the historical milieu and genre of the Gospel of Mark may also be partly responsible for its peculiarity and difficulty for modern interpreters. The Hellenistic milieu out of which the Gospel comes was a time of great social and cultural change. Increased travel, trade, communication, literacy, and cultural amalgamation encouraged the growth of social alienation and personal insecurity as people left their native lands, tribes, and families and settled in the large urban centers around the Mediterranean. Mystery cults and salvationist religions offered relief from isolation through community and escape from death and the hostile universe through divine assistance. Moreover, the ability to speak persuasively and eloquently became one of the most prized and rewarded talents of all in law courts, political assemblies, and marketplaces, and thus the theory and practice of rhetoric dominated the culture. This insecure, mobile, and rhetorical universe was the birthplace of the Gospel of Mark, and it is a child of its own cultural milieu. Indeed, it may be even more rooted in its own age than many other extant literary works from the Greco-Roman world, if it is, as appears likely, an example of ancient popular literature. The stylistic, rhetorical, and linguistic similarities between Mark and examples of the only other surviving popular genre, the ancient novel, combined with its marked differences in sophistication, literary polish, and linguistic refinement from elite or cultivated Greco-Roman literature, make the hypothesis of its popular literary origins quite plausible. Since popular culture in all periods tends to be more conventional and more formulaic than its elite counterpart, failure to perceive the conventions readily understood by the Gospel's authorial audience will necessarily mar modern attempts to interpret Mark.

What, positively, do all of these goal-specific and text-specific speculations entail for delineating a practical, eclectic literary approach to the Gospel of Mark? First, as far as possible we must bracket out of consideration both issues relating to the pre-Markan tradition and interpretations resting primarily on the authority of Matthew or Luke. Second, we must choose literary procedures that preserve the integrity of the text and use its overall structure as a guide to emphasis and meaning. Third, we must clarify the potential of the text insofar as possible in the light of its authorial audience, and that task will require us to take very seriously the two major formative influences on its stylistic development that we have discerned: Greco-Roman rhetoric and popular culture. Finally, whatever modern literary theories we employ to supplement ancient works on rhetoric and popular literature must both blend well with these perspectives and also be altered to suit the differences between modern and ancient narratives in plot development, characterization, and the like. Let us survey briefly the types of material suggested by this methodological analysis as guides for a literary interpretation of the Gospel of Mark.

Textbooks and studies of ancient rhetoric are clearly important. Especially earlier works such as Demetrius's *On Style* and *Rhetorica ad Herennium* are essential, but even the summations of rhetorical theory in Cicero and Quintilian may prove useful for gaining some sense of the Hellenistic rhetorical milieu. Modern theories of rhetoric and studies of the rhetorical dynamics of narrative are possible appropriate supplements to ancient theory.[1] In addition, since the focus of rhetoric is on the persuasion of hearers and readers, modern audience-oriented criticism may supply helpful perspectives. However, in order to adapt these modern theories to the special aural and conventional characteristics of Mark, we need to select those viewpoints among the diversity of current critical options that fashion their theories on rhetorical or sociological models. Audience-oriented criticism built on speech-act theory or devoted to the study of reading conventions shared by groups are, then, especially good resources.[2]

Studies of the ancient novel and examples drawn from the novels themselves, as the only other extant popular genre from the Hellenistic period, obviously need to be explored as guides to stylistic conventions present in the Gospel. Modern discussions of popular literature also may be valuable, especially those works that attempt to develop typologies of popular genres

---

1. An excellent modern development of rhetorical theory is C. Perelman and L. Olbrechts-Tyteca, *The New Rhetoric: A Treatise on Argumentation*, trans. J. Wilkinson and P. Weaver (Notre Dame, Ind.: University of Notre Dame Press, 1969). Useful studies of the rhetorical dynamics of narrative can be found in the works of Booth (e.g., *The Rhetoric of Fiction* and *A Rhetoric of Irony* [Chicago: University of Chicago Press, 1975]).

2. W. Iser develops his perceptions of a reader's participation in the reading process on a modification of speech-act theory *(Act of Reading)* and S. Lanser details the formulation of narrative point-of-view through an analysis of speech-act theory *(The Narrative Act: Point of View in Prose Fiction* [Princeton: Princeton University Press, 1981]). Studies of the shared conventions assumed by reading can be found in Culler, *Structuralist Poetics,* and in Mailloux, *Interpretive Conventions.*

that can be applied across cultural boundaries.[3] Hence, studies of rhetoric, ancient and modern, and studies of popular literature, ancient and modern, form the background for the literary interpretation of Mark proposed in Part II: Interpreting the Gospel. Whether all of these theories, speculations, and hypotheses will be enlightening or not, the success or failure of the following pages will ultimately demonstrate. As Grandmother used to say, "The proof of the pudding is in the tasting."

3. See, e.g., Cawelti, *Adventure, Mystery, and Romance.*

Interpreting the Gospel

Beginning
the Interpretation

Is a lamp brought in to be put under a bushel, or under a bed, and not on a stand? For there is nothing hid, except to be made manifest; nor is anything secret, except to come to light. (Mark 4:21–22)

For the Gospel of Mark, secrecy or hiddenness is apparently intended to serve the purpose, not of obscurity, but of clarity and openness: nothing is secret except *for the purpose of* (ἵνα) coming into the open. While scholars certainly, and perhaps many religious persons as well, have a deep affection for mystery and enigma, and while the heart of the affirmation of divine presence in human experience is indeed a mystery beyond imagining, for one attempting to proclaim the good news of Jesus Christ, surely intentional obscurity or unintentional muddle would qualify as counterproductive effects. Perhaps, for the author of Mark, Jesus' early commands to secrecy and his explanations to insiders with only parables to outsiders (cf. Mark 4:11–12) were meant as necessary preconditions for his later revelation of identity (14:62) and his passion, much as secrecy concerning the identity of the guilty party in some murder mysteries provides the necessary motivation for the detective's quest and ultimate revelation of truth. Perhaps, moreover, the authorial audience of the Gospel was familiar with such conventions and followed them with understanding and ease.

For modern readers of the Gospel, unfortunately, the situation is quite different. Approaching Mark with contemporary preunderstandings about plot development, characterization, historical reliability, and theological dogma, one encounters an opaque and even intractable text. With praise-worthy human inventiveness, some have used this opportunity to detail the virtues of secrecy and obscurity[1] rather than simply complaining about the ineptness of the Gospel writer. However, attempting to clarify the potential of the Gospel of Mark for its authorial audience is a different kind of response to current problems in its interpretation. As a literary approach, it assumes that the Gospel writer intended to communicate something to an audience who had the necessary competencies to understand it, and thus the difficulty that modern audiences experience in reading the Gospel derives, at least in part, from their lack of knowledge concerning the ancient rhetorical and popular conventions shared by Mark's author and authorial audience. The purpose of Part I: Delineating the Approach was both to explore contemporary practices that may have obscured more than they clarified in the Gospel's story and to investigate ancient conventions of reading (hearing) and writing which may throw some light on the organization and stylistic features of Mark. The purpose of Part II: Interpreting the Gospel is to put those theoretical discussions and hypotheses into practical use for analyzing the Gospel of Mark and articulating one possible interpretation of the Gospel in all its parts.

The hypothesis developed in Part I concerning the generic home of Mark in Hellenistic rhetoric and Hellenistic popular literature suggests certain elements we should expect to discover in the text. If the text has been influenced by rhetorical practice, not only will common rhetorical devices and figures appear but the structure of the text as a whole, with its repetitions, summaries, and anticipations, should guide our interpretation of it. The narrative should provide markers to direct our understanding, and those markers will, generally speaking, be intended for the ear, not the eye. In commenting on the value of breaks and helps for an audience's ability to follow even something as brief as a sentence, Demetrius uses "the analogy of roads with many signposts and resting-places: the signposts act as guides, whereas a straight road without signposts, however short it is, seems aimless."[2] If the Gospel belongs to the realm of popular literature, then many of the stylistic features present in the ancient erotic novels will probably appear in the Gospel. In addition to elements like episodic plot, journey motif, central turning point, and final recognition scene, the story as a whole ought to be fairly obvious, straightforward, and repetitious rather than subtle and esoteric. Finally, since it is an ancient text, we should expect to find an illustrative narrative and not a representational one. Most of these expectations derive from the generic hypothesis, and the degree to

---

1. See, e.g., F. Kermode, *The Genesis of Secrecy: On the Interpretation of Narrative* (Cambridge, Mass., and London: Harvard University Press, 1979).
2. *On Style* 202.

which the Gospel fulfills them will demonstrate the advantages or disadvantages of that reasoning.

Because the overall structure of the Gospel is one of the most important guides to its interpretation, our literary analysis of Mark in chapters 7—11 will begin with an overview of the formal patterning of the whole Gospel. Chapter 7 will present that overview and begin to develop its implications. Using the analysis of structure as the basis of interpretation, chapters 8 and 9 will explore the first half of the Gospel and chapters 10 and 11 the final half. The main outlines of one possible interpretation of the Gospel in all its parts should begin to become clear by the end of chapter 7, but chapters 8—11 will provide the needed thoroughness and detail. It may be wise to recall at this point that the views to be presented constitute only *one possible* interpretation of Mark; many other analyses, using somewhat different developments of the overall structure or reading with different generic assumptions and different goals, can and should be expounded and evaluated. No final or authoritative word is intended here.

Overview of
the Gospel of Mark

As both a rhetorical and a popular Hellenistic text, the Gospel of Mark attempted to be a persuasive communication accessible to a broad spectrum of ancient Greek-speaking people. This concentration on affecting a variety of readers means that both the narrative point of view developed by the Gospel and its structuring of the story, revealing emphasis and intention, are constructed with the position of the reader in mind. Thus a general literary analysis of the dynamics of Mark needs, first, to reflect on the position of the audience in narrative discourse like Mark and how the narrative strategy of the Gospel affects audiences. Second, the rhetorical structure of the story must be determined and the implications of that structure for the reading process assessed. The rhetorical structure uncovered by the analysis can, then, become the foundation for an interpretation of the Gospel.

A Model of Narrative Discourse

Since the Gospel of Mark is an aural text, located in the intersection of speaking and writing, any model employed to help reveal its narrative dynamics needs to reflect its rhetorical character. Consequently, theories of narrative developed on a speech-act paradigm appear especially appropriate for Mark, for the use of speech-act theory for narrative "bridges the gap between poetics and rhetoric as well."[1] Building on the work of many

1. S. Lanser, *The Narrative Act: Point of View in Prose Fiction* (Princeton: Princeton University Press, 1981), 68.

90

literary theorists, Susan Lanser has constructed a very thorough and clear study of narrative dynamics using a speech-act model in *The Narrative Act: Point of View in Prose Fiction*. Her model will form the basis of our investigations of narrative dynamics in Mark.

One cannot move directly from speech-act theory to narrative, because the context of production, literary conventions, and medium of expression are somewhat different between speech and narrative. Speech-act theory, then, has to be adapted to narrative demands. Roman Jacobson's well-known model for communication is the foundation from which Lanser begins her discussion of "narrative-act":[2]

$$\text{context}$$

$$\text{ADDRESSER} \rightarrow \text{MESSAGE} \rightarrow \text{ADDRESSEE}$$

$$\text{contact}$$

$$\text{code}$$

A sender sends a message to a receiver, but whether the message is understood or not depends on the social context of communication, the shared knowledge of specific linguistic conventions (code), and the connection (contact) between addresser and addressee, which comprises not only the physical medium of the message (text or speech) but also the "psychological" relationship between participants, including images of ideal sender and receiver, authority of the message, sense of competence, reliability, and so on. As every good model should be, Jacobson's model of communication is a simple outline of a very complex activity. In addition, it has the benefit of stressing the fact that every communication takes place within a social context according to definite shared rules, expectations, and conventions. The Gospel of Mark was not written in a nebulous, transcendent ether but in a very specific social and cultural milieu that provided shared literary conventions capable of generally predictable effects on an audience. It is only by learning to perceive some of those conventions that the message itself can be clarified, although the vital role of context also means that all new contexts must inevitably influence interpretations. So, with speech-act theory as a model for narrative, discourse becomes, not a set of signs with an indelible and fixed meaning, but "a dynamic system of communicational 'instructors' with a variable meaning-potential which is defined by specifying co-texts and contexts."[3]

2. Ibid., 66–67. See also R. Jacobson, "Closing Statement: Linguistics and Poetics," in *Style and Language*, ed. T. Sebeok (Cambridge, Mass.: MIT Press, 1960), 350–57.
3. S. J. Schmidt, "Reception and Interpretation of Written Texts," in *Style and Text: Studies Presented to Nils Erik Enkvist* (Stockholm: Skriptor, 1975), 401, as cited in Lanser, *The Narrative Act*, 75.

Using speech-act theory as her model, Lanser proposes that prose narratives display a complex system of tellers or voices located on various levels of the discourse, and the dynamics among levels and among voices provide much of the complexity and effectiveness of prose writing. Moreover, these narrative levels are organized "after the fashion of 'Chinese boxes,'"[4] with each level being completely incorporated in the one before it. The levels are determined by who is telling the story and to whom it is being told. At the broadest level, the extrafictional level (i.e., what is going on *outside* the story world), the real author is telling the story to the real authorial audience, but this broadest level, as the one most deeply influenced by social, historical, and cultural constraints, is, in the case of Mark, the level most difficult to reconstruct. Our hypotheses concerning genre and literary-rhetorical conventions are part of the attempt to enter this level of the Gospel narrative. The next level, or "box," stands on the borderline of the fictional world, both in it and above it, and it is that of the implied author and the implied reader. In the fictional world proper, the first level belongs to the narrator and the narratee, who may even be characters in the story, as in Joseph Conrad's *Lord Jim;* inside the narrator's box comes the level containing what the characters say to one another. If any character, furthermore, were to tell a story that had independent agents and actions, that story would form the next inside level or box and so on. For the purposes of clarifying Mark, we might diagram this process as follows:

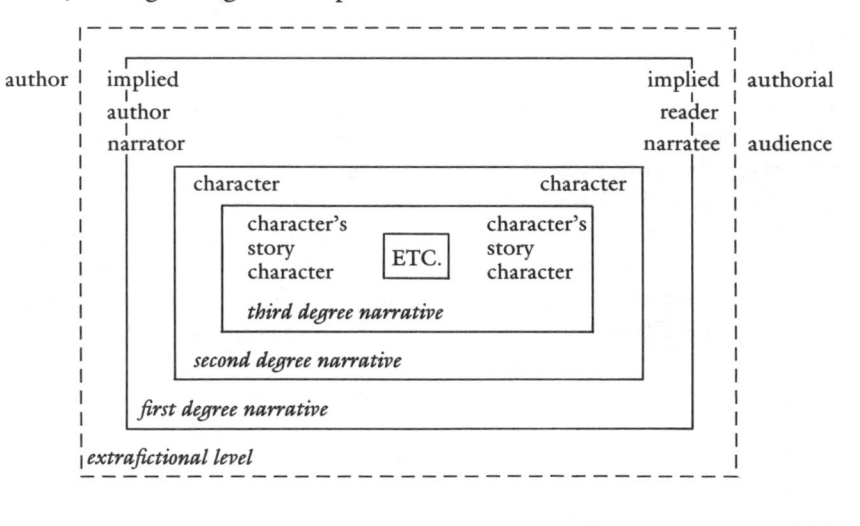

For Mark, neither the narrator nor the narratee exists as a persona within the fictional world. In Lanser's terms, the omniscient third person narrator

---

4. Lanser, *The Narrative Act,* 133–34. Much of the following discussion depends on this material.

in Mark is a "public narrator" who brings the fictional world into existence and addresses a narratee/implied reader who "represents the public, rather than another persona within the fictional world."[5] Thus, in the case of the Gospel, the levels of implied author–implied reader and narrator–narratee coalesce into one, the first degree narrative.[6] Whenever characters speak to one another in their own voice, second degree narrative occurs. Occasionally a character will actually begin to tell part of the story himself or herself. When a character in the second degree narrative functions in this manner, that character becomes what Lanser calls a "private narrator," one who is dependent on the fictional world for authority to speak and one who addresses the limited audience of other fictional characters rather than "the textual equivalent of the reading public."[7] While Jesus in Mark is a character speaking to the other characters and being addressed by them in second degree narrative, he also occasionally tells about the past or predicts the future, narrating himself elements of the overall story; thus the character Jesus also performs the role of private narrator in the Gospel. Furthermore, were any character himself or herself to tell another story with characters and actions, that character's story would be third degree narrative, and in principle the process could continue indefinitely. The Gospel of Mark is composed primarily of first and second degree narration and has a single, dominant third person, omniscient public narrative voice and one major private narrator, Jesus. Thus we might diagram it this way:

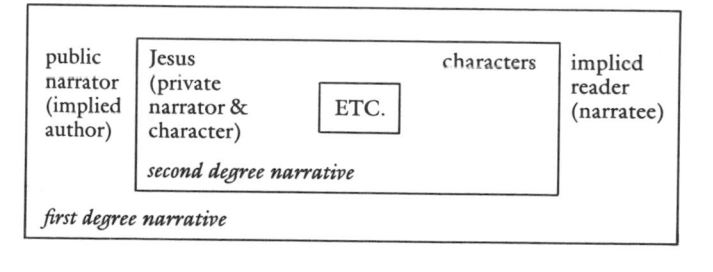

Narrative Levels

The usefulness of Lanser's model of narrative is the clarity it provides for understanding the differing amounts of knowledge and perception available to various levels and the ways in which the dynamics between levels can be manipulated. The Markan narrator knows everything: the past and the

5. Ibid., 138.
6. As a matter of convenience, I will generally hereafter refer to the participants in the first degree narrative as the narrator and the reader, meaning the implied author/narrator and implied reader/narratee, respectively.
7. Lanser, *The Narrative Act,* 138. See also G. Savran, "The Character as Narrator in Biblical Narrative," *Prooftexts* 5 (1985): 1–17.

future, the internal thoughts of characters (e.g., 2:6–7), decisions made away from the main action (e.g., 3:6), the words of the heavenly voice to Jesus (e.g., 1:11), the private words of Jesus (e.g., 14:35–36), the motivations for actions (e.g., 9:6; 11:18; 15:10), and the true identity of Jesus (1:1); and all of these things the public narrator communicates to the implied reader. On the other hand, characters in the story hear only what is given in the second degree narration; their knowledge when compared to that of the narrator or implied reader is strikingly limited. This difference in knowledge functions in several ways in the Gospel. In the first place, since the narrator tells the reader the identity of Jesus in the opening line, and in the first thirteen verses reinforces that identification by the authority of scriptural quotation, scriptural allusion, prophetic announcement, and a voice from heaven, the reader from the beginning has no doubt about who Jesus is or the basis of his authority. Hence the reader can quickly evaluate the reliability, perception, and goodness of other characters based upon their responses to Jesus. Those who respond in faith are good, and those who do not are not. Those who accept Jesus' authority are perceptive; those who do not are not. By establishing in the opening verses the divine authority of Jesus, the narrator has established the basic evaluative perspective of the Gospel.

Second, although Jesus, as a character in the story whose competence and authority must be constituted by the narrator, exists in the second degree narration, by allowing Jesus to share partially in the omniscience of the narrator Jesus' divine connection is heightened for the reader. As a character, Jesus evinces limitations in knowledge and power, especially power over other characters. His commands to people not to make him known are frequently blatantly disobeyed (e.g., 1:44–45; 7:36); his intentions to keep to himself are generally foiled (e.g., 6:32–34, 48–49; 7:24); even his ability to perform mighty works and his own understanding of his mission can be challenged (e.g., 6:5–6; 7:27–29). Yet the narrator also describes Jesus as one possessing superhuman abilities: he can heal and he can control nature. While healing is a gift evidently available to others as well, even to the disciples (e.g., 6:12–13; 9:38–39), Jesus' power over the forces of nature such as wind and sea amazes and startles them (e.g., 4:39–41; 6:50–51). Less obvious than these repeated depictions of Jesus' miracles is the narrator's effective portrayal of Jesus' participation in qualities that normally are solely the prerogative of an omniscient public narrator. Like the public narrator, Jesus can read the unspoken thoughts of others (e.g., 2:8) and predict future events that are later fulfilled in the narrative (e.g., 8:31; 9:31; 10:33–34; 11:1–6; 14:13–16). Hence, not only by describing Jesus as more powerful than other characters but also by showing Jesus functioning with abilities generally reserved to omniscient narrators, the implied author/

narrator creates a hero for the story who bridges the divine-human divide by appearing to rise above the limitations of second degree narrative in appropriating some of the all-seeing power of the public narrator.

Third, though differences in authority and knowledge do still exist between the implied author, the public narrator, and the private narrator of Mark, the boundary-crossing narrative techniques of the Gospel forge a unity among them that assures the presentation of a story with no moral or ideological ambiguity. The moral or ideological stance of a narrative—that is, what values or perspectives are deemed right, true, and important—can be made ambiguous by using the views of one narrative level to cast doubt on the reliability of another. For example, an implied author may develop a public narrator who comments on the morality of the characters; if in the course of the story those characters should act in ways that contradict the public narrator's assessment, the reader begins to doubt the narrator's reliability and must reevaluate the story, comparing what characters do with what the narrator says. Such tension or contradiction between narrative levels can produce considerable moral or ideological ambiguity. Modern novels adopt this type of technique in many complex configurations that place great demands on their readers. Not so Mark. The implied author of the Gospel is distinguished from the narrator only to the extent that the concept of implied author suggests some final overall molding of the story, including the narrator's role. Because the narrator is not a character within the fictional world and because everything the narrator describes and predicts is confirmed by the story itself, the stance of implied author and the stance of narrator are identical. That identity is further strengthened by the impersonal tone of the narration. While the Markan narrator interrupts the story line a number of times in the Gospel, those asides for the benefit of the reader almost always contain explanatory information concerning the meaning of a foreign word or unusual practice, often preceded by ὅ ἐστιν, "that is" (e.g., 3:17; 5:41; 7:2–4; 12:42; 15:16). Only at Mark 13:14, in the famous "wink" to the reader, does the narrator drop the formal tone and directly address the reader, ὁ ἀναγινώσκων νοείτω, "let the reader understand."[8] The dominance of this detached style of narration even in asides reinforces the identification of narrator with implied author.

Although both Chariton and Xenophon fashion third person omniscient narrators for their ancient novels, Chariton's narrator indulges in brief

---

8. If Hägg's hypothesis about public readings of the ancient novel, discussed in Part I (pp. 72–73), can be extended to the Gospel of Mark, this unusual slip to direct address might have been some type of "stage direction" to the one orally performing the Gospel for a group. Needless to say, whatever the reader is supposed to understand here has been lost in time. Some scholars have suggested that the anacoluthon in Mark 2:10 indicates the presence of another direct address from author to reader; for my reasons for disagreeing with this suggestion, see below p. 136 n. 18.

comments in the first person, evaluating characters and actions and providing universalizing information about human behavior or culture to
indicate the applicability of the story to the general human situation.[9]
Xenophon's narrator, on the other hand, displays the same aloof, distanced
perspective found in Mark. Rarely does Xenophon's narrator digress from
the story line, and when interruptions do occur, they are primarily to
present geographical or cultural information.[10] The result of such distance
is to fuse narrator with author and to increase the distance between the first
degree narrative and the second degree narrative. Since the reader is privy to
all the knowledge of the narrator, while the characters in the second degree
narrative are not, the reader shares the omniscience of the narrator and
judges all of the characters from that lofty perspective. As with Mark, the
dominance of such an aloof, impersonal, and distanced omniscient narrative voice allows no moral ambiguity to enter the story. The way the
author/narrator creates the (story) world is the way the (story) world is,
and no questioning of that perspective is permitted.[11]

Unlike Xenophon, whose characters uniformly display the limitations of
second degree narrative and hence remain at a great distance from the
reader, Mark, as we have already noted, portrays Jesus as possessing qualities usually reserved to omniscient public narrators. In Xenophon's *An
Ephesian Tale,* the disparity between the level of narrator and reader and the
level of the characters is so great that it becomes difficult for the reader to
sympathize or identify with any of the characters.[12] However, because of the
connection established between Jesus and the Markan narrator, the reader
of Mark, already allied with the perspective of the omniscient narrator, also
identifies with Jesus. Although clearly a part of the second degree narrative,
Jesus also apparently stands above it, addressing directly not only other
characters in the story but the reader as well (e.g., 13:37: "What I say to you
I say to all"). Not only can Jesus function in ways similar to the public
narrator, but the content of his understandings of other characters, his

9. T. Hägg, *Narrative Technique in Ancient Greek Romances: Studies of Chariton,
Xenophon Ephesius and Achilles Tatius* (Stockholm: Acta Instituti Atheniensis Regni
Sueciae, 1971), 293–94.

10. Ibid., 100–101. E.g., *An Ephesian Tale* 1.2.2–3; 1.6.4.

11. The aloof, distanced, almost hidden, character of the public narrative voice in
the Gospel of Mark is probably one of the elements of the story that has encouraged
modern readers to understand it as an "eye-witness" account (providing, of course,
that an omniscient eyewitness existed) or a compilation of material edited together by
community effort rather than as a consciously crafted narrative. For a rather different
approach to narrative point of view in Mark that arrives at similar conclusions, see N.
Petersen, "'Point of View' in Mark's Narrative," *Semeia* 12 (1978): 97–121; for a
general discussion of the characteristics of the Markan narrator, see D. Rhoads and D.
Michie, *Mark as Story: An Introduction to the Narrative of a Gospel* (Philadelphia:
Fortress Press, 1982), 35–44.

12. Cf. G. L. Schmeling, *Xenophon of Ephesus* (TWAS 613; Boston: Twayne
Publishers, 1980), 88, 118–20.

predictions of the future, and his teachings correspond exactly to the expressions of the public narrator. Thus, in form and in content the implied author, the public narrator, and the private narrator of the Gospel merge to present a clear, unambiguous, integrated ideological perspective, which the audience shares. The first degree narrative "box" which contains the author/narrator and reader/narratee provides a uniform point of view that is then further reinforced by the depiction of Jesus' abilities and message. The implied author/narrator/Jesus position forms the positive pole of the story with which the implied reader identifies and by which the reader evaluates all other characters and viewpoints found in the Gospel.[13]

Hence, analyzing the dynamics of narrative levels in Mark indicates, first, how the omniscient narrator establishes at the outset for the reader the identity and authority of Jesus, allowing that knowledge to then be used by the reader to evaluate other characters; second, how the narrator depicts Jesus as possessing levels of knowledge generally available only to the participants in first degree narrative, raising his status greatly above all the other members of second degree narrative; and third, how the blending of implied author/narrator/Jesus provides a single, dominant point of view shared by the audience that makes ideological or moral ambiguity in the story impossible. We might represent the Markan narrative in the following way, where the shaded area indicates those holding a uniform point of view.

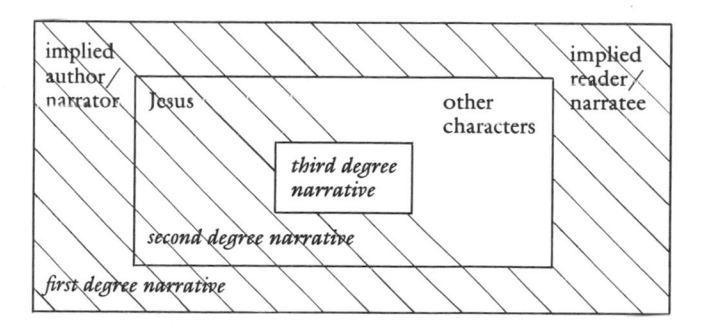

13. Analyzing the narrative levels of the Gospel in this way clarifies one of the points of debate in recent literary studies of Mark: whether or not the implied reader identifies with the disciples. According to this model, the reader identifies with the point of view of the implied author/narrator, which is clearly shown to be the point of view of Jesus as well. Thus the reader identifies with the perspective of Jesus. Only to the extent that the disciples *also* respond positively to Jesus and agree with his perspective will the reader identify with the disciples. The reader's view of the disciples, and all other characters in the Gospel, depends entirely on their affiliation with Jesus. See R. Tannehill, "The Disciples in Mark: The Function of a Narrative Role," *Journal of Religion* 57 (1977): 386–405; E. S. Malbon, "Fallible Followers: Women and Men in the Gospel of Mark," *Semeia* 28 (1983): 29–48; and Petersen, "'Point of View' in Mark's Narrative."

In any individual scene in the story, the positive or negative response of a given character to Jesus determines whether that particular character shares this dominant point of view, thus eliciting the approval or condemnation of the audience. Such a thoroughly unified point of view produces a very straightforward and clear narrative. The audience of Mark is never unsure who the hero is or how responses to him or events surrounding him should be evaluated. Indeed, the status of Jesus in the Gospel is such that without overstatement one could say that Jesus is the single major figure in the story; in comparison with him, all the other characters are minor, participating only in limited parts of the narrative.[14]

Irony

Two final issues concerning narrative levels, which will be developed more fully in later chapters, need to be introduced before we can begin to analyze the rhetorical structure of the Gospel: irony and the presence of third degree narrative. Because narrative levels are organized "after the fashion of 'Chinese boxes,'"[15] second degree narrative is completely encompassed by first degree narrative, and consequently the audience of the Gospel not only hears the omniscient insights of the public narrator but also sees and hears all the actions and words of the characters. Since the audience has far greater knowledge about what is going on than any of the characters, except possibly Jesus, the disparity in insight between first and second degree narrative participants opens the way for irony. Irony, a figure of speech with deep roots in the classical tradition, is notoriously difficult to define,[16] but it is generally related to differences in knowledge, so that what appears to be the case to some, others realize from their better vantage point is not the case at all. For narrative irony to work in a fairly stable and clear

14. The same point can be made about the ancient erotic novels as well. Chariton's Chaereas and Callirhoe and Xenophon's Habrocomes and Anthia are the dominant characters in each novel. Other characters appear for an episode or two and then disappear. Interestingly, both ancient novels also present a kind of middle-range character, who is not as dominant as the hero and heroine but who appears in a number of episodes and plays a larger part than most others. In Chariton's text it is Polycharmus, Chaereas's friend, and in Xenophon's story it is Hippothous, the friendly outlaw (see Schmeling, *Xenophon of Ephesus,* 118–24). One might argue that Peter, and perhaps James and John, occupy such a middle-range position in Mark.

15. Lanser, *The Narrative Act,* 133.

16. One of the best and most exhaustive attempts to define irony can be found in D. C. Muecke, *The Compass of Irony* (London: Methuen & Co., 1969). See also N. Knox, *The Word Irony and Its Context, 1500–1755* (Durham, N.C.: Duke University Press, 1961). A beginning study of irony in Mark can be found in R. M. Fowler, *Loaves and Fishes: The Function of the Feeding Stories in the Gospel of Mark* (SBLDS 54; Chico, Calif.: Scholars Press, 1981).

fashion, which it often does *not* do, narrators and readers must share sufficient knowledge for the reader to be able to recognize that what the story
appears to say is not what is intended.

The classic example of irony in Mark occurs in the mocking of the
soldiers and the chief priests at the crucifixion (15:18–32).[17] They call Jesus
"King of the Jews" and "Christ" to deride and ridicule him; they view what
they are saying as obviously false ascriptions, thrown at Jesus in mocking
irony. The reader, however, *knows* that Jesus *is* the "Christ," the "King of the
Jews." Thus, the reader perceives the true irony of the scene: what the
enemies of Jesus are calling at him mockingly is really who he is, and their
ridicule redounds on their own heads. The irony works in the episode
because the reader has been so thoroughly assured of the identity of Jesus
from the beginning of the Gospel up to this point by the narrator and,
indeed, by Jesus himself. While irony often has a victim, the person or
character in the second degree narrative with limited knowledge, the more
significant function of irony in narrative, according to Wayne Booth, is to
build community and connection between the author/narrator and
readers: "The building of amiable communities is often far more important
than the exclusion of naive victims. Often the predominant emotion when
reading stable ironies is that of joining, of finding and communing with
kindred spirits."[18] The irony of the Markan crucifixion scene is but one
further demonstration of the unified point of view shared by narrator and
reader.

Many other scenes in the Gospel exploit the disparity in knowledge and
perspective between the first and second degree narratives. Without actually
having to reject the apparent meaning of an exchange in the second degree
narrative, the reader of Mark is often called upon to recognize another,
broader implication to it that accords with the reader's greater knowledge.
For example, Mark 3:13–27 presents back-to-back accounts of Jesus'
appointment of the Twelve (vv. 13–19) and his controversy with "those
near him"[19] and scribes from Jerusalem (vv. 20–30). The first episode is
given completely by the narrator and is thus part of first degree narrative,

17. See the fine discussion of this scene in W. Booth, *A Rhetoric of Irony* (Chicago:
University of Chicago Press, 1975), 28–29; see also Rhoads and Michie, *Mark as Story*,
59–62.

18. Booth, *A Rhetoric of Irony*, 28.

19. It is not at all clear to me that οἱ παρ' αὐτοῦ in Mark 3:21 ought to be translated as "his family" as the RSV does. The phrase has considerably broader connotations of "adherent," "agents," "neighbors," as well as "relatives" in the LXX and papyri
(see the discussion of Greek usage in V. Taylor, *The Gospel According to St. Mark* [2d
ed. reprint 1966; Grand Rapids: Baker Book House, 1981], 236–37). Especially given
the argument that follows, the phrase could well include friends, followers, and
disciples, the οἱ περὶ αὐτὸν of Mark 4:10, as well as relatives.

while the second consists almost entirely of the direct speech of characters (second degree narrative). Jesus responds to the charge that he is possessed by "the prince of demons" (v. 22) by relating a number of sayings about the inevitable failure of divided kingdoms and houses (vv. 23–26). This retort works perfectly well on the level of second degree narrative; he is effectively answering his immediate opponents. However, the very last element the narrator reported to the reader about the appointment of the Twelve was "and Judas Iscariot, who betrayed him" (v. 19). Providing the reader with information about Jesus' own future "divided house" at just this point casts the whole of the following episode in a new light. The reader, privy to both first and second degree narration, understands Jesus' retort both to respond to his immediate opponents and also to point toward his end and the failure of his disciples, for his own most recently established "house" is divided as well.

Mark 3:27 is quite interesting in this regard, for while the verse fits with some difficulty into the immediate context of the controversy, if one identifies the "strong man" as Satan and Jesus as the one who has bound him and is now plundering his house, it also suggests a rather different allegory on the level of first degree narrative. If the house belongs to Jesus, then Jesus is the strong man, and the plunder of his house can occur only after he has been bound, for "no one can enter a strong man's house and plunder his goods, unless he first binds the strong man; then indeed he may plunder his house" (v. 27). That the disciples do flee right after Jesus is arrested (14:43–50) and that Peter's complete denial of Jesus (14:66–72) is followed immediately by the report of the scribes' sending Jesus off—*bound*—to Pilate (15:1) confirm the double entendre of these earlier words. Moreover, the conclusion of Jesus' speech in 3:28–30 is very awkward on the level of second degree narrative. Having apparently been speaking for four verses about the defeat of Satan at his hands, Jesus concludes by saying: "Truly, I say to you, all sins will be forgiven the sons of men, and whatever blasphemies they utter; but whoever blasphemes against the Holy Spirit never has forgiveness, but is guilty of an eternal sin" (vv. 28–29). The narrator attempts to smooth the abrupt change of topic by adding in verse 30, "for they had said, 'He has an unclean spirit.'" While the ending may be confusing on the level of second degree narrative, it fits quite well into the logic being developed in first degree narrative: the failure of Jesus' house, initiated by Judas's betrayal and accomplished by binding the strong man, provides the context for the denunciation of Jesus as a blasphemer by the chief priest at the trial (14:61–64). Indeed, this whole section of Mark 3:20–30 for the reader is filled with chilling forebodings concerning what is coming, and the twofold function of the passage rests on the greater knowledge about the future of Jesus' appointed disciples supplied to the reader by the narrator immediately prior to the controversy. Because the reader knows more than the characters, the reader can perceive the wider implications of Jesus' words.

If such double-dealing with episodes in the story is often fairly subtle and occasionally even downright confusing, then the pervasive use of irony to accentuate the opacity of the disciples is anything but subtle. In Mark 4, Jesus teaches the people and the disciples "in parables," but privately he explains the parables to his disciples (4:10–12), telling them that they have been given the "mystery" of the kingdom of God, while others receive only parables. The narrator concludes the scene by summarizing, "He did not speak to them without a parable, but privately to his own disciples he explained everything (πάντα)" (4:34). Immediately following the teaching session and connected closely to it by a time indicator, "on that day" (4:35), Jesus and the disciples enter a boat, and Jesus falls asleep. A storm comes up, and the disciples in a panic wake Jesus, who promptly calms the storm and rebukes the disciples for lack of faith (4:39–40). The audience, having just heard the narrator relate that Jesus had explained *everything* to his disciples, might expect the disciples at this point to show a modicum of insight; instead, the narrator reports that they were filled with great fear (φόβον μέγαν), and the disciples themselves ask one another, "Who then is this, that even wind and sea obey him?" (4:41). The audience would be quite justified in beginning to doubt the perspicacity of the disciples.

This type of irony in which a character naively believes or says something the reader knows to be untrue, or, in the case of the disciples, blindly refuses to believe or understand something the reader knows to be true, is often called "situational irony," for the irony arises not so much from verbal play (as in the mocking scene) as from the nature of the situation itself.[20] Xenophon's *An Ephesian Tale* is full of situational irony, especially in those sections where each of the two lovers believes the other to be dead, while the audience knows that neither is.[21] In Xenophon's novel, the knowledge of the audience is so superior to that of the characters that situational irony can easily broaden almost into satire, and the audience's affiliation with the hero and heroine can suffer: "Our superiority over Habrocomes and Anthia, however, is too great. It is almost the superiority of man over ventriloquist's dummy."[22]

The situational irony that stalks the disciples in Mark displays much the same tendency. For example, in Mark 6:35–44 Jesus is faced with a large

20. Rhoads and Michie, *Mark as Story,* 60–61.
21. See the discussion in Schmeling, *Xenophon of Ephesus,* 88, 120–21.
22. Ibid., 120.

crowd ("five thousand men") who are hungry and far away from areas in which they could purchase food. He tells the disciples to feed them, and the disciples can probably be forgiven for being taken aback by the command, for it does seem a lot to ask. They find five loaves and two fish; Jesus takes the food, blesses it, breaks it, and gives it to the disciples to distribute. All eat and are satisfied; moreover, the disciples take up twelve baskets of leftovers. The story provides the disciples and the audience with another example of Jesus' amazing power. A little later, in Mark 8:1–9, Jesus is "again" (πάλιν) faced with a large, hungry crowd ("four thousand people") in a deserted place. The narrator uses the πάλιν in 8:1 to remind the audience that this type of situation has occurred before. When Jesus broaches the issue of feeding the multitude, the disciples, rather than remembering what Jesus has done before and responding willingly, ask, "How can one feed these [people] with bread here in the desert?" For the audience the answer is shockingly plain: the same way he did in the past. Indeed, Jesus then proceeds to repeat his earlier feat. After the disciples discover seven loaves and "a few small fish," Jesus blesses them, breaks them, and gives them to the disciples to distribute. Everyone eats, and the disciples collect seven baskets of leftovers. The irony is manifest: Jesus had more food and a smaller crowd, but still the disciples, who *distributed* the food in the earlier episode, professed ignorance about how the crowd could be fed.[23]

As if the irony of these two feedings stories were not enough, the narrator adds a third episode, which moves irony close to the point of satire. Soon after the second feeding story in Mark 8:14–21, Jesus and the disciples are in a boat with only one loaf of bread. Jesus is trying to teach the disciples metaphorically to avoid "the leaven" of the Pharisees. Missing the metaphor altogether, the disciples get worried about not having bread. Sitting in the boat with one who has just fed four thousand people with seven loaves of bread and earlier fed five thousand people with five loaves, the disciples' worry over thirteen people with one loaf strikes the audience as absurd and also finally draws Jesus' exasperated rebuke: "Why do you discuss the fact that you have no bread? Do you not yet perceive or understand? Are your hearts hardened? Having eyes do you not see, and having ears do you not hear? And do you not remember?" (8:17–18). The comments of Jesus, Mark's specially privileged hero, define the nature of the audience's response to the disciples at this point. The irony of the situation is so broad that the reader could find it funny or view the disciples as hopeless dimwits, more suitable to stereotypical roles in New Comedy than disciples of the

---

23. A fine study of the irony of these feeding stories can be found in Fowler, *Loaves and Fishes*.

Messiah. However, Jesus' anger and stern words to the disciples indicate to the reader the seriousness and disappointment inherent in their present lack of comprehension.

The disciples in Mark, as victims of constant and increasingly broad doses of situational irony, become at the same time increasingly removed from the audience's sympathy. If irony serves to bind more closely together the audience and the narrator (and, of course, also Jesus, since he shares much of the narrator's status) by underscoring their joint knowledge and point of view, it also serves to distance the audience from the witless victims of irony, whether they be high priests or disciples. The rhetorical effect of irony, then, is twofold: it builds and strengthens community among those with superior knowledge, and it excludes and denigrates those with inferior knowledge. It thus appears to be a very appropriate literary strategy for a Gospel so seemingly concerned with "insiders" and "outsiders."

Third Degree Narrative

If one of the characters in the second degree narrative were to tell a story with independent agents and actions, that story would constitute third degree narrative, and it would be completely encompassed by second and first degree narrative. While the Gospel consists primarily of first and second degree narrative, Jesus as private narrator not only explains past actions (e.g., 9:11–13) and predicts future ones (e.g., 10:33–34; 11:2–3; 13:5–37) that carry forward the basic story line, he also on several occasions narrates independent stories with their own agents, actions, and even dialogue. These third degree narratives are the parables, the two longest of which occur near the beginning and near the ending of the Gospel. The parable of the Sower and its interpretation in Mark 4:3–8, 14–20 and the parable of the Tenants in Mark 12:1–11 are the major examples of third degree narrative in the Gospel and as such demand some special attention.

Compared to the Gospels of Matthew and Luke, Mark has relatively few parables. Moreover, it seems quite clear that, whatever the parables may or may not have been on the lips of the historical Jesus, for Mark they are primarily allegories.[24] To say that Mark's parables are allegories does not

---

24. Attempts to establish the message of the historical Jesus have been particularly destructive of any understanding of *Mark's use* of parables, because the argument about the historical Jesus' use of parables for so long castigated allegory and refused to admit even the possibility that Jesus may have employed it. See, e.g., J. Jeremias, *The Parables of Jesus*, trans. S. Hooke (2d rev. ed. New York: Charles Scribner's Sons, 1963), 18–19, 66–89; N. Perrin, *Jesus and the Language of the Kingdom* (Philadelphia: Fortress Press, 1976), 92–98; and M. A. Tolbert, *Perspectives on the Parables: An Approach to Multiple Interpretations* (Philadelphia: Fortress, 1979), 27–28. The allegorical nature of Mark's understanding of parables is definitively argued by

mean that a slavish one-to-one correspondence to every individual element
in these stories is intended but rather that in general the major figures or
elements in Mark's parables are meant to represent other characters or
actions that audiences, both in the second and first degree narratives, ought
to be able to identify. The first use of the word παραβολή occurs in Mark
3:23, beginning Jesus' retort about divided houses and kingdoms, which we
have already discussed. Mark 3:27 concerning the binding of the strong
man and the plunder of his house can be interpreted quite differently
depending on whether one identifies the strong man as Satan (implication
of the second degree narrative) or as Jesus (implication of the first degree
narrative). Either way, the verse is being read allegorically. In the case of the
parable of the Sower (4:3–8), a point-by-point allegorical explanation is
given to clarify its meaning, an issue we will be discussing at considerable
length later. It would be difficult for anyone to escape the allegorical reference of the parable of the Tenants (12:1–11), in which the owner of the
vineyard finally sends his own beloved son to the tenants and they decide to
kill him. Even the Jerusalem leaders recognize that the parable was told
"against them," and the narrator's report of their understanding also provides a clue to the allegory for any reader who might have missed it. Indeed,
that the author provides a clue to the allegorical correspondence for the
Tenants (i.e., tenants = Jewish leaders) and an interpretation for the Sower,
beginning with a clear correspondence (i.e., seed = the word; 4:14), suggests that these parables were *not* intended to be confusing, misleading, or
obscure to the reader—at least to the authorial reader, if not to the modern
reader.

The novels of both Xenophon and Chariton contain small amounts of
third degree narrative. These usually take the form of dreams or visions with
their own agents and actions, narrated by one of the characters, or, in
Xenophon's case, the narrator and character together.[25] Rarely do these
dreams or visions carry the story line forward; instead, they may contain
warnings or assurances about future events, or they may express the emotional state of mind of the character. In addition, Xenophon employs
oracles near the beginning and near the ending of his tale.[26] While not
technically third degree narratives,[27] the earlier oracle especially is dra-

M. Boucher, *The Mysterious Parable: A Literary Study* (CBQMS 6; Washington, D.C.:
Catholic Biblical Association of America, 1977); see also J. Drury, "The Sower, the
Vineyard, and the Place of Allegory in the Interpretation of Mark's Parables," *Journal
of Theological Studies* 24 (1973): 367–79; Rhoads and Michie, *Mark as Story*, 55–57.

25. See, e.g., Xenophon, *An Ephesian Tale* 1.12.4; 2.8.2; 5.8.5–8.

26. Ibid., 1.6.2 and 5.4.11.

27. Lanser herself recognizes "the impossibility of forcing all narration into clear-
cut categories" (*The Narrative Act*, 140) and thus often indicates that her model
should not be used in a rigid manner. The point of using such a narrative model at all
is the insight it provides into narrative dynamics, not its ability to label everything
definitively.

matically set apart from the rest of the prose narrative by appearing in nine lines of dactylic hexameter, the normal meter for Apollo's messages. These nine lines set out in concise form the outline of the entire plot of the novel, including its eventual happy ending.[28] The brief, one-line oracle in Book 5 of *An Ephesian Tale* simply signals the fast-approaching end of the story by assuring Anthia, the heroine, that she will soon be reunited with Habrocomes, the hero. The use of such devices to provide plot synopses close to the opening of stories is fairly common in ancient novels and is probably patterned on the prooemium of the epic, in which the entire plot is formally summarized *before* the actual telling of the tale begins.[29] These plot abstracts, along with other foreshadowing and summarizing techniques, including dreams and visions, serve the important practical function of assisting audiences in following aural texts, and their appearance in the narrative is usually set apart in some way like third degree narration to draw the audience's special attention.

In Lanser's model, shifts in narrative level bring corresponding changes in the type of authority the material exerts on the reader. The public narrative voice carries the greatest *"diegetic authority*—authority attached to an authorial voice."* A private narrator, insofar as he or she is also a character in the fictional world, carries greater *"mimetic authority*—authority that attaches to the acting persona."*[30] The distinction between *diēgesis* and *mimēsis* ultimately goes back to Plato's comparison of epic, which combines narrative (*diēgesis,* or narrated discourse in the author's own voice) with imitation (*mimēsis,* or direct discourse in the character's own voice), to lyric poetry (all *diēgesis*) and drama (all *mimēsis*).[31] In a somewhat oversimplified way, the distinction can be termed the difference between "telling" (*diēgesis*) and "showing" (*mimēsis*). The intellectual authority of "telling" belongs mostly to the omniscient public narrator; the private narrator, as a character in the story, bears the lived, experiential authority of "showing." The longer parables in Mark, as third degree narratives presented by the

---

28. Why do you want to know the cause and final outcome of the illness?
    One disease afflicts both youngsters, and one remedy will cure them both.
    Before the suffering is over I predict terrible experiences for them.
    Pirates will pursue and chase them over the sea;
    And they will wear the chains put on them by seamen;
    A grave will be a bridal chamber for both, and there will also be a terrible fire.
    Then later by the banks of the Nile you will deliver up
    Rich gifts to holy Isis, the savior.
    After all their suffering, both will enjoy a happier fate.
ET by Schmeling, in *Xenophon of Ephesus,* 26–27; see also his discussion of the oracle, 27, 89–90.

29. Hägg, *The Novel in Antiquity,* 111. See also Aristotle, *Rhetoric* 3.1415a.

30. Lanser, *The Narrative Act,* 142.

31. *Republic* 3.392a–394. In Aristotle's *Poetics* 1448a, this same distinction is codified as the three modes of discourse.

private narrator Jesus, are basically mimetic; that is, they function less to proclaim propositions than to *show* what the situation is. As mimetic narratives, they act out the experience of the fictional world, and the more felicity and skill they exhibit in doing so, the more effective their mimetic authority becomes.[32] Thus, from the standpoint of both their possible mimetic authority, derived from theoretical speculations concerning narrative levels, and their possible function in the Gospel, derived from comparisons with similar material in ancient novels, the parables obviously require further, careful attention and explication. The next step in that process is the delineation of the rhetorical structure of the Gospel as a whole to determine how the parables—and indeed all the other elements of the narrative—are integrated together into one story.

Introduction to Rhetorical Structure

Since understanding the structure of gospels or of any text is a very helpful interpretive tool, many attempts at outlining the overall organization of Mark have been made in the past and will assuredly continue to be made in the future.[33] Quite a few of these studies agree in their basic principles and findings, and such agreements are not at all unexpected, if, as we have argued, the Gospel is a popular text, designed to be clearly and widely accessible. The rhetorical structure to be presented in the following pages bears many resemblances to and some differences from past studies. What it will try to evaluate in more depth than some other studies have done is how structure affects the story. The analysis of structure for its own sake can be a useful exercise in technique, but it contributes little to under-

32. Lanser, *The Narrative Act,* 169–71.
33. See, e.g., V. Robbins, *Jesus the Teacher* (Philadelphia: Fortress Press, 1984), 19–51; E. Trocmé, *The Formation of the Gospel According to Mark,* trans. P. Gaughan (Philadelphia: Westminster Press, 1975), 215–59; N. Perrin, *The New Testament: An Introduction* (New York: Harcourt Brace Jovanovich, 1974), 151–61; R. Pesch, *Naherwartungen: Tradition und Redaktion in MK 13* (Düsseldorf: Patmos-Verlag, 1968), 48–73; C. E. Faw, "The Outline of Mark," *Journal of Bible and Religion* 25 (1957): 19–23; F. Neirynck, *Duality in Mark: Contributions to the Study of Markan Redaction* (BETL 31; Louvain: Louvain University Press, 1972); F. G. Lang, "Kompositionsanalyse des Markusevangeliums," *ZTK* 74 (1977): 1–24; M. P. Scott, "Chiastic Structure: A Key to the Interpretation of Mark's Gospel," *Biblical Theology Bulletin* 15 (1985): 17–26; N. Petersen, "The Composition of Mark 4:1—8:26," *Harvard Theological Review* 73 (1980): 185–217; A. Stock, "Hinge Transitions in Mark's Gospel," *Biblical Theology Bulletin* 15 (1985): 27–31; J. Dewey, *Markan Public Debate: Literary Technique, Concentric Structure, and Theology in Mark 2:1—3:6* (SBLDS 48; Chico, Calif.: Scholars Press, 1980); B. van Iersel, "De betekenis van Marcus vanuit zijn topografische structuur," *Tijdschrift voor Theologie* 22 (1982): 117–38; E. Schweizer, "The Portrayal of the Life of Faith in the Gospel of Mark," *Interpretation* 32 (1978): 387–89; and R. A. Culpepper, "An Outline of the Gospel According to Mark," *Review and Expositor* 75 (1978): 619–22.

standing the story, and interpreting the story is the primary goal of this analysis. That the Gospel of Mark is, in fact, consciously structured is an assumption grounded in the rhetorical nature of the text. If, as Demetrius argued in his discussion of the plain style, it is important for long sentences to be broken up into clearly defined groups "on the analogy of roads with many signposts and resting-places" so that the reader may be guided through the thought, how much more necessary are "signposts and resting-places" in full narratives, for "the signposts act as guides, whereas a straight road without signposts, however short it is, seems aimless."[34]

Because the fundamental dynamic of rhetoric is the amplification of positions, theses, or ideas, required by the aural orientation of communication in the ancient world,[35] repetitions of words, sentences, and episodes become very common signposts to guide audiences through material. However, these repetitions are rarely exact, for exact repetition was deemed boring by ancient rhetoricians.[36] Furthermore, elements of the story bound together in this manner often evince "variations on a theme," for the same general point needs to be presented several times for the ear to comprehend it. Other aural signposts available to writers were lexical indicators to remind audiences of similar events or indicate the presence of something special (e.g., Mark's use of πάλιν, "again"), notations of time (e.g., the day and night sequences of the ancient novels), shifts in geography or location, radical changes in style (e.g., from prose to poetry in Xenophon's first oracle), abrupt breaks in normal grammatical practice, and variations in narrative pace (e.g., from summary to detailed exposition).

With these and other aural signposts in mind, analysis of the narrative patterns of the Gospel of Mark reveals a general rhetorical structure which divides the Gospel into two major sections, the preaching tour in Galilee (1:14—10:52) and the events in Jerusalem (11:1—16:8), each of which is further organized into several shorter units of roughly similar length. However, before we proceed to delineate and explain this structure, two further introductory comments are in order. First, that a narrative displays apparent divisions or segments only witnesses to its intent to assist audiences in following the unfolding story. Just as the visual aids of chapter titles, subheadings, and paragraphing better enable the eye to understand and comprehend material in modern books, just so repetitions, summaries, and other aural signposts aid the ear in perceiving emphasis and organization in ancient rhetorical texts. Consequently, uncovering segmentation

34. *On Style* 202.
35. See G. A. Kennedy, *New Testament Interpretation Through Rhetorical Criticism* (Chapel Hill, N.C.: University of North Carolina Press, 1984), 21–23, and the discussion of rhetoric in Part I, pp. 41–46.
36. See, e.g., *Rhetorica ad Herennium* 4.42.54.

in an ancient narrative in no way implies complete separation or independence for any of the segments, for they are all part of the same developing plot; nor does segmentation necessarily imply the existence of separate sources any more than dividing a book into chapters implies separate authors. Source theories must be built on other bases. Second, the determination of rhetorical structure very much depends upon where one begins and where one ends. Analyses that focus on limited sections of a longer narrative may observe structural patterns that appear prominent when that section alone is in view but appear quite different when the whole narrative is considered. If one attempts, as we are, to investigate the overall rhetorical structure from the beginning to the ending of the story in order to perceive the emphases and relations of episodes and characters across the whole, then discerning separate divisions or units must always be justified against the backdrop of that whole, and we should not be surprised if the results differ from research that has concentrated on smaller units.

Major Rhetorical Divisions—The Prologue

Since almost every aspect of the rhetorical structure of Mark will be discussed in much more detail in later chapters of our study, our goal at this point is simply to introduce the major divisions, indicate the reasons for positing them, and relate some of the implications arising from such a structural outline. To launch the analysis, we need to establish the prologue and the two major divisions of the story.

The first thirteen verses of Mark form the prologue to the whole narrative.[37] Besides introducing Jesus and confirming his identity and authority by scriptural quotation (Mark 1:2–3), prophetic announcement (1:7–8), voice from heaven (1:10–11), and cosmic, apocalyptic signs (1:12–13), the prologue is carefully organized rhetorically into four sections by patterns of word repetition. After the opening three verses, an anaphoric[38] use of the impersonal ἐγένετο begins each of the sections:

---

37. The first person to argue that the prologue to Mark consists of vv. 1–13 was R. H. Lightfoot, *The Gospel Message of St. Mark* (London: Oxford University Press, 1950), 15–20. For the view that the prologue consists of vv. 1–15, see, e.g., L. E. Keck, "The Introduction to Mark's Gospel," *NTS* 12 (1966): 352–70; and R. Pesch, *Das Markusevangelium* (2 vols.; HTKNT 2; Freiburg/Basel/Wien: Herder, 1976–77), 1:71–73. As will become clear later, Mark 1:14–15 is indeed introductory but not a part of the prologue to the entire Gospel. Verses 14–15 introduce the first major division, Mark 1:16—10:52.

38. Anaphora (or epanaphora) is the repetition of the same word or phrase at the beginning of successive clauses, sentences, or sections. See, e.g., Demetrius, *On Style* 59–62; and *Rhetorica ad Herennium* 4.13.19.

Section 1—vv. 1–3: Ἀρχή . . . (scriptural quotation)
Section 2—vv. 4–8: ἐγένετο . . . (John the Baptist)
Section 3—vv. 9–10: καὶ ἐγένετο . . . (Jesus is baptized)
Section 4—vv. 11–13: καὶ φωνὴ ἐγένετο . . . (voice from heaven; Jesus in the wilderness)

Moreover, the four sections are related to one another by a loose anastrophe, in which a keyword or hook word[39] near the end of each section is repeated near the beginning of the next:

Section 1—v. 3: voice crying *in the wilderness* (ἐν τῇ ἐρήμῳ)
Section 2—v. 4: baptizing *in the wilderness* (ἐν τῇ ἐρήμῳ)

Section 2—v. 8: I *baptize* (ἐβάπτισα) you . . . but he will *baptize* (βαπτίσει) you
Section 3—v. 9: Jesus came . . . and was *baptized* (ἐβαπτίσθη)

Section 3—v. 10: the *heavens* (οὐρανοὺς) opened and *the spirit* (τὸ πνεῦμα) descending
Section 4—vv. 11–12: voice from *heaven* (οὐρανῶν) . . . and immediately *the spirit* (τὸ πνεῦμα) drove him

Thus the four sections, while separated from one another by word repetition (anaphora), are also linked by hook words (anastrophe) to form a unified rhetorical whole. The tendency to supply linking words or phrases, often but not always indicative of major themes, close to the end of one division and near the beginning of the next is a very common rhetorical practice. It serves to alert the reader to the shift in material while at the same time smoothing the transition. This type of stylistic feature is what Lucian had in mind on a grander scale in recommending that the historian adopt a smooth, even style of narration: "Only when the first point has been completed should it lead on to the next, which should be, as it were, the next link of the chain. There must be no sharp break, no multiplicity of juxtaposed narratives. One thing should not only lie adjacent to the next, but be related to it and overlap it at the edges."[40] While each of the four sections of the prologue is distinct, they "overlap" one another "at the edges."

Moreover, a further pattern of repetition establishes the relationship of the four sections to one another, for both in exact word repetition and in general content, sections 2 and 3 and sections 1 and 4 evince close connec-

39. I agree with Dewey (*Markan Public Debate,* 32) that "hook word" is probably a better, because more neutral, term for this type of repetition. See also H. Parunak, "Oral Typesetting: Some Uses of Biblical Structure," *Biblica* 62 (1981): 153–68.
40. Lucian, *De conscribenda historia* 55 (as translated by D. A. Russell in *Ancient Literary Criticism: The Principal Texts in New Translations,* ed. D. A. Russell and M. Winterbottom [Oxford: Clarendon Press, 1972], 545). Lucian wrote about 165 C.E.

tions with each other. In section 2 (Mark 1:4–8), we are told of John, who is baptizing all who come from Judea and Jerusalem in the Jordan River, and in section 3 (1:9–10) we are introduced to Jesus, who comes from Nazareth of Galilee and is baptized in the Jordan by John. Although section 2 is longer (containing a narrative description of John and an account of his preaching linked by references to clothing), the two central sections of the prologue are remarkably similar in vocabulary, theme, and characters. In addition, both end with an allusion to the Spirit: John announces a future baptism with the Holy Spirit in section 2 (v. 8), and the Spirit descends as a dove at the moment of Jesus' baptism in section 3 (v. 10). Indeed, the words of John in section 2, the first instance of second degree narrative in the Gospel, and their apparent fulfillment in section 3 also present the narrator with the first opportunity to develop situational irony at John's expense. John says that he is not worthy to untie the sandal thong of the one coming after him, but the narrator has him baptize Jesus; John says the one coming after him will baptize people with the Holy Spirit, but the narrator has Jesus himself experience Spirit baptism.[41] The narrator is already strengthening ties with the audience and at the same time making sure that no figure rivals Jesus. John may be a prophet in the clothing of Elijah (compare Mark 1:6 to 2 Kings 1:8), but his perceptions come through a "glass darkly," while Jesus is "face to face."[42]

If sections 2 and 3 display clear parallels, so also do sections 1 and 4. Again, exact vocabulary repetitions are present. Section 1 (1:1–3) speaks of the messenger (ἄγγελόν) and the voice crying in the wilderness, confirming the gospel of Jesus Christ, Son of God.[43] Section 4 (1:11–13) recounts the voice from heaven, naming Jesus as the beloved Son, and Jesus' temptation in the wilderness where he is served by angels (ἄγγελοι, messengers). In content, both sections present the witness of reliable commentary to the identity of Jesus. The narrator and the scriptural quotation from Isaiah[44]

41. I owe the recognition of situational irony in this scene to David Jacobsen, a ministerial student at Vanderbilt Divinity School.

42. Cf. 1 Cor 13:12.

43. The presence or absence of υἱοῦ θεοῦ in the original version of Mark 1:1 presents a difficult textual problem. Even though the 26th edition of Nestle includes it (although Nestle 25 did not), the external evidence is quite divided (see the discussion in B. Metzger, *A Textual Commentary on the Greek New Testament* [New York: United Bible Societies, 1971], 73). If the chiastic structure I am developing is persuasive, the presence of ὁ υἱός μου in Mark 1:11 might be seen as some internal evidence for the inclusion of υἱοῦ θεοῦ in the original of Mark 1:1.

44. Mark 1:2 is, of course, *not* from Isaiah, nor can it be found in any other text from the Hebrew Scriptures. It *may* be a composite text made up of a combination of Exod. 23:20 (LXX) and Mal. 3:1 (MT), further altered to serve the narrator's purpose. The narrator's purpose with this verse will be the subject of considerable discussion in a later section of the study, pp. 239–48. At the very least, one could suggest that

announce Jesus' role in section 1, and the voice from heaven affirms it in section 4. Moreover, in contrast to sections 2 and 3, sections 1 and 4 refer to cosmic events. In Mark 1:1–3, Jesus is named as the Christ, the Son of God, and the Scripture verses resonate with apocalyptic undertones in their references to the messenger sent by God and the voice crying out in the wilderness the command to be prepared. Moreover, the whole unit is given stately, liturgical tone through the use of rhyming devices. The first line, "The beginning of the gospel of Jesus Christ, the Son of God" ('Αρχὴ τοῦ εὐαγγελίου 'Ιησοῦ Χριστοῦ υἱοῦ θεοῦ), manifests an excellent example of parechesis, the repetition of the same sound in immediately succeeding words. That identical sound is then further developed by being used to begin the scriptural quotation in Mark 1:2–3, 'Ιδού, and then to rhyme the closing words of each clause in the quotation . . . σου, . . . σου, . . . ἐρήμῳ, . . . κυρίου, . . . αὐτοῦ.[45] Such rhyming enhances the formality of the narrator's opening address to the reader and intensifies the distanced, authoritative weight of the words themselves. Not only in *what* the verses say but also in *how* they say it is the importance of this announcement for all humanity conveyed.

The voice from heaven, the wilderness, Satan, wild beasts, and angels clearly connect the actions of section 4 (1:11–13) to cosmic forces and events. Furthermore, the forty days of temptation in the wilderness, while alluding to the Hebrew Bible characters Moses and Elijah (both of whom appear at the second advent of the heavenly voice in 9:4–8), may also prefigure the apocalyptic times of tribulation that Jesus will later foresee befalling his followers (13:5–27). Those terrible times, too, will be ended only by sending out the angels to gather the elect (13:27). As the angels will later preserve those who endure to the end (13:13b), they now serve Jesus in his period of testing. Thus, in exact word repetition and in general themes, sections 2 and 3 and sections 1 and 4 are paralleled, providing an overall chiastic structure to the prologue, A B B′ A′:

beginning the Gospel with a misplaced scriptural citation evidently did not disturb the narrator or, one supposes, the authorial audience.

45. Such end rhymes in clauses or verses is generally called homoioteleuton (the special situation of similar endings because of case, as in Mark 1:2–3, was sometimes designated as homoioptoton; see *Rhetorica ad Herennium* 4.20.28). Only the ἐρήμῳ of v. 3 is slightly out of rhyme. It should be further noted that two of the end rhymes, the second σου in v. 2 and the final αὐτοῦ, are alterations of the scriptural text, probably by the author.

While I am arguing for the integrity of Mark 1:1–3 primarily on rhetorical grounds, a strong case can also be made grammatically to connect 1:1 with 1:2–3 as a unified sequence. For an excellent argument from grammar and typical word usage, see R. Guelich, "'The Beginning of the Gospel'—Mark 1:1–15," *Biblical Research* 27 (1982): 6–8.

A   Section 1—vv. 1–3: Jesus, Son of God, messenger, voice, in the
                wilderness
   B   Section 2—vv. 4–8: John, baptizing, Jordan
   B'   Section 3—vv. 9–10: Jesus, baptized, John, Jordan
A' Section 4—vv. 11–13: Jesus, beloved Son, voice, in the wilderness,
                angels

The Markan prologue, like the prooemium of the epic, drama, or history,
functions to introduce major elements in the story to the reader.[46] Most
important, it establishes Jesus, through a series of reliable witnesses, to be
the evaluative center of the story to come. In addition, by means of its
chiastic structure, it emphasizes the two levels of the plot, the human and
the divine or cosmic. The Homeric epic and most of the ancient erotic
novels also develop this dual perspective on the action of their stories.[47]
While human actions remain human actions motivated by human aims,
they are at the same time irrevocably linked to the divine world. In the
ancient novels the divine realm, though omnipresent, rarely concretely
erupts into the story. Only at crucial moments are the gods appealed to or
through dreams and oracles make their presence and requirements known.
Nevertheless, to understand the story, one must constantly reckon with
their power and activity. Similarly, in the Gospel of Mark the evidence of
divine activity or purpose is often indirect, but at the same time it is all-
pervasive.[48] Only at the baptism (1:11) and the transfiguration (9:7) do the
words of God, as a speaking character, enter the narrative. Jesus' prayer
periods and blessings (e.g., 1:35; 6:41, 46; 8:6; 14:35–36) furnish reminders of God's presence, and certainly the resurrection announcement
by the young man at the tomb (16:6–7) by strong implication displays
God's triumphant power, but these few references are sufficient to indicate
the motivation for the ministry of Jesus in the divine plan. Moreover, Jesus'
recognition by and power over emanations from the cosmic level are complete. All of the demons immediately recognize his authority and identity,
and unlike some of his human followers, when he tells the demons to be
silent, they obey. From the prologue through the entire narrative, the audience is never given cause to question the inevitability of the cosmic triumph
over Satan and ultimately over death itself.

The human level of the story is, however, rather a different matter.

---

46. Aristotle defined the purpose of the prooemium (also called the exordium) this
way: "In prologues [of plays] and in epic there is an indication of what is to be said, so
that the hearers can know beforehand what the work is about and the mind not be kept
in suspense, since what is undefined makes the attention wander" (*Rhetoric* 3.1415a, as
translated by M. E. Hubbard in *Ancient Literary Criticism*, ed. Russell and Winterbottom, 159).

47. Hägg, *The Novel in Antiquity*, 6, 102–3.

48. See the fine discussion of the role of God in Mark in J. R. Donahue, "A
Neglected Factor in the Theology of Mark," *JBL* 101 (1982): 563–94.

Sections 2 and 3 (B B'), despite the hyperbole represented by *"all* the country of Judea" and *"all* the people of Jerusalem" (1:5),[49] emphasize very human elements. Although they also serve as an allusion to the prophet Elijah, the descriptions of John's clothing and food heighten the human focus, and his evident humility confirms it: he wears camel's hair and a leather girdle, eats locusts and wild honey, and feels unworthy to stoop down and untie the sandals of one who comes after him. Even the Spirit takes the form of a natural creature, a dove (1:10). Furthermore, the slightly ironic difference between what John says will happen and what the narrator shows actually to have happened foreshadows the ambiguity and uncertainty that will dominate the human level of the story. Jesus can exorcise demons, calm the waters and the winds, and overcome death, but he cannot force those he heals to obey his admonitions or give faith and understanding to his disciples. Perhaps the greatest irony of the Gospel of Mark is this constant, frustrating human failure in the face of cosmic victory. That the chiastic pattern of the prologue surrounds the human (B B') with the divine (A A') suggests some basis for describing the story as "good news" ($\epsilon\dot{\upsilon}\alpha\gamma\gamma\dot{\epsilon}\lambda\iota o\nu$), for the beginning and the ending rely on the authority of Jesus and the One who sent him.

The prologue of the Gospel of Mark anticipates a number of other aspects of the story that will become evident as we proceed through the text. Indeed, in a classic essay on stylistics, Ian Watt demonstrated that all of the major themes in Henry James's *The Ambassadors* could be found in its first paragraph alone, but as many commentators have pointed out, finding the themes depended on knowing what to look for, and knowing what to look for depended upon having read all of *The Ambassadors* and not just the first paragraph.[50] So it is also with the Markan prologue. As our study develops, the prologue's importance in foreshadowing much of the Gospel will increase as well, but we need to learn more of the story before seeing all the connections. After the prologue comes the brief two-verse introduction to the first half of the Gospel, so the reasons for positing two parts to the story need now to be examined.

Major Rhetorical Divisions—Two Parts

The major geographical divide in the Gospel of Mark has long been recognized as an important element of its organization and theology.[51] All

49. For a discussion of the importance of this hyperbole for establishing Mark's use of John the Baptist as the "restorer of Israel," see below, pp. 208–9, 246.

50. I. Watt, "The First Paragraph of *The Ambassadors:* An Explication," in *Contemporary Essays on Style: Rhetoric, Linguistics, and Criticism,* ed. G. Love and M. Payne (Glenview, Ill.: Scott, Foresman and Co., 1969), 266–83.

51. The classic statement of the view can be found in R. H. Lightfoot, *Locality and*

of the action in the first ten chapters of the Gospel takes place in and around Galilee, while all of the action in the last six chapters takes place in and around Jerusalem. As with so many other things, the first mention of the two geographical poles is provided by the prologue: as the people of *Jerusalem* go to John to be baptized (1:5), so Jesus comes from *Galilee* to be baptized (1:9). Moreover, since John's activities at the Jordan River are situated in Judea near Jerusalem, Jesus' journey from Nazareth of Galilee to John rehearses in miniature the geographical shift from the first part to the second part of the Gospel. In the story itself, the movement from Galilee to Jerusalem is emphasized by repeated anticipations that connect the coming events of arrest, death, and resurrection to the geographical destination of Jerusalem (e.g., 10:32–34). Since those anticipations of the Passion (e.g., 8:31; 9:31; 10:32–34) begin immediately after the incident at Caesarea Philippi where Peter identifies Jesus as "the Christ" (8:27–30), that incident, occurring so near the physical center of the narrative, easily qualifies as the central turning point of the story *(peripeteia)*, because at that point the momentum turns in a different direction.[52] Not until Jesus enters Jerusalem, however, does anticipation give way to action. Thus the shift from Galilee to Jerusalem heralds a shift from one phase of the story to the anticipated next phase, and each phase is associated not only with a specific geographical area but also with a dominant type of action.

The predominant kind of activity that characterizes each of the two major divisions of the story is announced clearly in the individual introductions, Mark 1:14–15 and 11:1–11, and thus the audience, in good epic or ancient novelistic style, is informed beforehand "what the work is about."[53] In

Doctrine in the Gospels (London: Hodder & Stoughton, 1938). For a survey of the debate over the significance of geography, see E. S. Malbon, "Galilee and Jerusalem: History and Literature in Marcan Interpretation," *CBQ* 44 (1982): 242–48.

52. If Mark 8:27–30 marks the *peripeteia* of the Gospel, it is not the surprising shift in fortune characteristic of tragedy but rather a change in momentum. From the apparently random journeying of the early chapters, Jesus and the disciples now have a definite, announced, and anticipated goal. J. D. Kingsbury in his helpful study of Markan Christology, determines that after the prologue the Gospel falls into two major parts: 1:14—8:26 and 8:27—16:8 (*The Christology of Mark's Gospel* [Philadelphia: Fortress Press, 1983], 50–51). That way of dividing the Gospel is based solely on the flow of dramatic momentum, and studies that have compared Mark with Greek drama usually emphasize the same shift (see, e.g., G. Bilezikian, *The Liberated Gospel: A Comparison of the Gospel and Greek Tragedy* [Grand Rapids: Baker Book House, 1977], 54–58; and B. Standaert, *L'Evangile selon Marc: Composition et genre littéraire* [Nijmegen: Stichting Studentenpers Nijmegen, 1978], 64–106). However, just as in tragedy *peripeteia* rarely coincides with the structural divisions of acts and scenes, so also the structure of Mark encompasses the dramatic flow from anticipation to result in its own pattern of divisions and segments.

53. Aristotle, *Rhetoric* 3.1415a. Many scholars who have argued that the Markan prologue continues through Mark 1:14–15 have argued for its summarizing, anticipatory, or introductory nature. I agree with that analysis but understand the verses to

Mark 1:14–15, the narrator declares the location and role of Jesus and then allows Jesus, speaking for the first time in his own voice, to give a programmatic summary of his message: "Jesus came into Galilee, preaching the gospel of God, and saying, 'The time is fulfilled, and the kingdom of God is at hand (ἤγγικεν); repent, and believe (πιστεύετε) in the gospel.'" In Galilee, Jesus is primarily the preacher, spreading the word that the kingdom of God has come and commanding repentance and faith. In Mark 11:1–11, the narrator indicates the location, "they drew near to (ἐγγίζουσιν) Jerusalem," but the role of Jesus is proclaimed by the crowds: "Hosanna! Blessed is he who comes in the name of the Lord! Blessed is the kingdom of our father David that is coming!" In Jerusalem, Jesus is primarily the openly proclaimed Messiah-King, Son of David coming into his city, temple, and kingdom and suffering the inevitable consequences of his identity. In Galilee, the emphasis is on the message and how people should respond to it; thus the introduction is mainly direct quotation, the words of Jesus. In Jerusalem, the emphasis is on the true role of Jesus and the persecutions its open announcement necessarily draw; thus its introduction is an episode illustrating the kingly function of Jesus and the first enthusiastic recognition of it. Both these elements, however, are part of the *same*, interconnected and interwoven story, for the preacher of God's good news[54] is the heir of David's throne in a world deeply gone awry.

Both introductions are rhetorically set apart from preceding and succeeding material but also attempt smooth transitions by the use of "overlapping at the edges" strategies. In Mark 1:14–15, the words of Jesus themselves are nicely set off by a small *inclusio*[55] repeating the word "gospel" (εὐαγγέλιον): "preaching τὸ εὐαγγέλιον . . . believe ἐν τῷ εὐαγγελίῳ." This stress on "gospel" additionally serves to recall the first line of the narrative as a

parallel Mark 11:1–11 *in function,* as introductions to the main concerns (though certainly not the *only* concerns) of the two major divisions. See Keck, "The Introduction to Mark's Gospel," 538–68; and Guelich, "'The Beginning of the Gospel'— Mark 1:1–15," 8–11; see also H. Weder, "'Evangelium Jesu Christi' (MK 1:1) und 'Evangelium Gottes' (MK 1:14)," in *Die Mitte des Neuen Testaments: Einheit und Vielfalt Neutestamentlicher Theologie* (Festschrift für Eduard Schweizer zum 70. Geburtstag), ed. U. Luz and H. Weder (Göttingen: Vandenhoeck & Ruprecht, 1983), 399–411; for a fine discussion of 1:14–15 as the "second introduction," see J. M. Robinson, *The Problem of History in Mark and Other Markan Studies* (Philadelphia: Fortress Press, 1982), 71–72. Also see Robbins, *Jesus the Teacher,* 82–83; and Lang, "Kompositionsanalyse des Markusevangeliums," 18–24.

54. Although I seem to be interpreting τὸ εὐαγγέλιον τοῦ θεοῦ (Mark 1:14) here as a subjective genitive, at other times I will use it as an objective genitive (gospel *about* God), for I think the grammatical ambiguity is part of the point.

55. Word repetition at the beginning and ending of a semantic-syntactic unit was most commonly designated by classical rhetoricians as *inclusio, prosapodosis,* or *redditio.* Quintilian defined the figure as "respondent primis et ultima" (*Institutio oratoria* 9.3.34); see also H. Lausberg, *Handbuch der literarischen Rhetorik* (2 vols.; Munich: Max Hueber Verlag, 1960), 1:236–39, 317.

whole: "Beginning of the gospel of Jesus Christ, the Son of God." At the outset, the narrator had informed the reader concerning the nature of the story to come and hence had represented the first degree narrative, which encompasses the whole story, to be "the gospel of Jesus Christ." Now, in Mark 1:14–15 the audience hears that Jesus is preaching "the gospel of God," and hence the second degree narrative, in which the character Jesus speaks to other characters, is to be devoted to a related but distinct communication. Jesus' message in the second degree narrative is not one of self-glorification but one of preaching God's good news. It is the narrator's perspective that transforms Jesus' message, life, and death into "the gospel" for the audience. This play on the word "gospel," then, hints to the audience of the fundamental parallel between the work of the character Jesus and the work of the narrator: what Jesus attempts to proclaim about God to other characters in the story, the narrator, on a different, encompassing level, is attempting to proclaim about Jesus to the audience.

Mark 1:14–15 is separated from the prologue by both grammatical break and geographical shift. Most of the sentences and clauses following the scriptural quotation in 1:2–3 evince the καὶ-paratactic style that will dominate the narrative. At Mark 1:14, that style is broken by beginning the sentence, Μετὰ δὲ (but, after). This disjunction functions both grammatically and rhetorically. Moreover, Mark 1:4–13 was set in the vicinity of the Jordan River and the wilderness beyond, but 1:14 reports that "Jesus came into Galilee." After the introductory verses, Mark 1:16ff. signals that the action of the first division has begun in earnest by a further geographical reference: "And passing along by the Sea of Galilee." Although Mark 1:14–15 is set apart from the prologue, the abruptness of the transition is smoothed greatly by beginning with an announcement of the fate of John: "Now after John was arrested, Jesus came into Galilee." Rhetorically, the advertence to John serves as a hook or link with the prologue; it permits the introduction of the first division and the prologue to "overlap" each other "at the edges." It also produces two other important effects by recalling the brief ministry of John. The narrator indicated that *all* the people of Judea and Jerusalem[56] had confessed their sins and been baptized by John (1:5). The report of John's arrest, then, comes as a sad and rather frightening commentary on the efficacy and endurance of those repentances. That *all* could confess their sins at one moment and John be arrested at the next is foreboding information. Furthermore, the narrator said that John preached a baptism of repentance (κηρύσσων βάπτισμα μετανοίας, 1:4). Jesus is also

56. The totality of this group is emphasized in the prologue by repetition: "*all* (πᾶσα) the country of Judea, and *all* (πάντες) the people of Jerusalem" (1:5). In Greek, the repeated terms form a small *inclusio* around the geographical references.

preaching (κηρύσσων, 1:14) repentance, but his message contains the additional element of faith, "Repent, and believe in the gospel" (μετανοεῖτε καὶ πιστεύετε ἐν τῷ εὐαγγελίῳ, 1:15). Faith in the gospel appears to be a distinctive mark of Jesus' ministry.

In the Gospel of Mark, John is not portrayed as an apocalyptic preacher, as he is in both Matthew (Matt. 3:7–12) and Luke (Luke 3:7–9). He baptizes people who have repented and witnesses to the one coming after him who is stronger than he, but he does not proclaim the coming kingdom or judgment. That message in Mark is reserved for Jesus. Although most translations render Jesus' words about the kingdom of God in Mark 1:15 in the present tense, "The time *is fulfilled,* and the kingdom of God *is at hand,*" in Greek both main verbs are in the perfect tense: the time *has been fulfilled* (πεπλήρωται), the kingdom *has come near* (ἤγγικεν). The force of the perfect tense is to represent an action begun in the past and continuing to the present.[57] Before his ministry itself starts, Jesus seems to be speaking about an event already well in process and on the verge of completion. The verb ἐγγίζω ("to come near") occurs only three times in Mark: here in the introduction of the first division, at Mark 11:1 in the introduction of the second division, and at Mark 14:42 as Judas arrives with the crowd to arrest Jesus. In the last instance, the use of the perfect tense is unsurprising, because Jesus' preaching and healing have led to that moment of arrest. However, to begin the ministry with such an assertion casts an atmosphere of urgency over everything: the second degree narrative opens with the acknowledgment that the time is already, almost past. The Markan narrative has no time; all is rushing to imminent conclusion.

That the narrator intends to interject a sense of immediacy into the story by fashioning Jesus' introductory words in this manner is confirmed by the pace of the succeeding narrative. Everything happens "immediately" in the Gospel, for εὐθύς ("immediately") is one of Mark's favorite words, appearing over forty times in the story, more than twice the occurrences found in any other Gospel. The καί-paratactic style itself, coupled especially with Mark's fondness for using participles, drives the narrative at a relentless rate, as if events were taking place so fast that one had no leisure to fashion full sentences but had, instead, to tumble phrases out on top of each other. Another common Markan feature, undetectable in most translations, imposes pace and presence on the narrative: the use of the historic present. Although the narrator is telling the story from some point *after* the events of the fictional world take place and thus reports them primarily in the past

---

57. J. H. Moulton, *A Grammar of New Testament Greek* (2 vols.; 3d ed.; Edinburgh: T. & T. Clark, 1908), 1:109.

tense, quite often, especially in exchanges of dialogue, the past tense is replaced by the present,[58] giving the effect of dramatic directness. Mark 2:14 offers a typical example of this narrational technique: And passing along, he *saw* Levi, son of Alphaeus, sitting in the tax office, and he *says* to him. . . . All of these stylistic devices contribute to the fast pace and immediacy of the narrative, but more important, they undergird at a formal level the urgency of Jesus' message and the lateness of the hour that are suggested in the introduction to the first major division, Mark 1:14–15.

The introduction to the second major division, Mark 11:1–11, is also set apart from surrounding material by an *inclusio,* repeating prepositions and geographical locations:

11:1— "They drew near (ἐγγίζουσιν) *to Jerusalem, to* Bethphage and *Bethany* (εἰς ʿΙεροσόλυμα εἰς . . . Βηθανίαν)."

11:11— "And he entered *into Jerusalem,* and . . . he went out *to Bethany* with the twelve (εἰς ʿΙεροσόλυμα . . . εἰς Βηθανίαν)."

Although Mark 11:1–11 is separated from the fig tree episode which immediately follows it by time markers (v. 11: "as it was already late"; v. 12: "on the following day"), mention of Bethany as the place where Mark 11:1–11 ends and the place where Mark 11:12–25 begins allows the material to overlap at the edges. Moreover, the transition from Galilee to Jerusalem and the next major phase of the story has been heavily anticipated in the preceding chapters and especially in Mark 10. Mark 10:32 places them "on the road, going up to Jerusalem," and as Jesus presents the third and most detailed prediction of the troubles to come, he explicitly connects them with Jerusalem: "Behold, we are going up to Jerusalem; and the Son of man will be delivered to the chief priests and the scribes, and they will condemn him to death, and deliver him to the Gentiles; and they will mock him, and spit upon him, and scourge him, and kill him; and after three days he will rise" (10:33–34). In the last episode before Jerusalem, which also happens to be the last healing miracle in the Gospel, Jesus for the first time is repeatedly called "Son of David," a clear foreshadowing of the major theme of the second division (10:47–48). Hence, the close of the first division overlaps at the edges with the opening of the second division.

While repetitions and anticipations smooth the transition from one division to the next, Mark 11:1–11 also clearly introduces some of the major

---

58. By one count, Mark uses the historic present 151 times to Matthew's 93 times and Luke's 8 times (13 times in Acts). See, e.g., Moulton, *A Grammar of New Testament Greek,* 1:120–22.

Cf. Longinus, *On Sublimity* 25.1: "To represent past events as present is to turn a narrative into a thing of immediate urgency" (as translated by Russell in *Ancient Literary Criticism,* ed. Russell and Winterbottom, 486).

shifts in emphasis that characterize the second part. Prior to Mark 11:1–11, Jesus' predictions concerning events had been limited to anticipations of the Passion (8:31; 9:31; 10:32–34) and oblique allusions to the future coming-in-power of the kingdom of God (e.g., 9:1; 10:29–30); for the first time Mark 11:2–6 portrays Jesus exercising prescience of an immediate physical situation. The detailed instructions to the two disciples concerning where to find the colt, what to do with it, and what to say (vv. 2–3) and the narrated confirmation of every element (vv. 4–6) are reminiscent of scenes from the Hebrew Scriptures in which God has given explicit instructions to an individual that are then meticulously followed (e.g., Exod. 4:1–31; 7:8–13, 14–24; 8:1–7, 16–19; Gen. 24:10–21; 35:1–4). From Mark 11 until the end, all of Jesus' predictions become focused on closely impending or immediate events and are matched by scenes indicating exact fulfillment (e.g., 14:13–16; 14:30, 72). The major exception to the observation concerning fulfillment is the apocalyptic discourse of Mark 13:5–37; however, Jesus' warnings about the coming judgment gain stronger authority within the context of this revelation of his prescient abilities. Thus the initial prediction-fulfillment sequence in the introduction foreshadows the increasing importance and prominence of Jesus' predictions in the second part of the Gospel as a whole.

Mark 11:1–11 displays another striking difference from earlier material: Jesus' willingness to receive, indeed his encouragement of, public recognition. From his earliest healing miracles (e.g., 1:43–45) through his most recent teaching sessions with the disciples on the road to Jerusalem (e.g., 7:24; 9:30–31), Jesus has consistently attempted to hide his actions, silence those who realize who he is, and in general cut a very low profile. While his efforts in this regard have usually been foiled, his intention has remained constant. Now, *he initiates* public celebration and recognition. He sends for the colt upon which he will ride into the city and to the temple, and by embodying messianic prophecies (cf. Zech. 9:9) he publicly claims his rightful identity and provokes equally public response. Beginning with Mark 11, secrecy, hiddenness, lonely places, and commands to silence are all things of the past. Jesus drives money-changers out of the temple, openly contests with scribes and Jewish leaders, and forthrightly declares that he is the Son of God when pressed by the chief priest. Jerusalem is not only a different location for Jesus' action, it is also the location for a different kind of action.

Thus, both Mark 1:14–15 and 11:1–11 function as introductions to the major divisions composing the Gospel. These divisions, while distinguished by separate geographical locations, are more importantly divided by varying emphases and different predominant concerns. Moreover, each division is further subdivided into roughly equal segments of material to allow breaks and resting places for the audience. With the exception of the first subdivision, the segments are set off from one another by paralleled episodes or images at their beginnings and endings, the parallels being established by repetition with variation. In addition, the material encompassed by these "episodic" *inclusios* often exhibits thematic or formal similarities or evinces some other reason why the included scenes need to be read together. Occasionally in the first part and consistently in the second, temporal indicators are used to tie incidents together or indicate separation. A schematic representation of the rhetorical structure of the Gospel of Mark would look as follows:

I. PROLOGUE—Mark 1:1–13
II. DIVISION ONE—Mark 1:14—10:52
   A. Introduction—1:14–15
   B. 1:16—3:6
      1. Opens 1:16–20—calls Simon, Andrew, James, John to follow him
      2. Ends 3:1–6—teaching and healing in synagogue
   C. 3:7—6:34
      1. Opens 3:7–35
         a. 3:7–12—by sea, teaching crowds, boat
         b. 3:13–19a—appoints 12 disciples
         c. 3:19b–35—controversy with relatives and rejection of family
      2. Ends 6:1–34
         c'. 6:1–6—rejection by his own country and kin
         b'. 6:7–13, 30—sends out 12 disciples
         a'. 6:31–34—boat, teaching crowds
   D. 6:35—8:21
      1. Opens 6:35–52—feeding multitude, boat trip
      2. Ends 8:1–21—feeding multitude, boat trip
   E. 8:22—10:52
      1. Opens 8:22–26—healing of blind man
      2. Ends 10:46–52—healing of blind Bartimaeus, who follows him
III. DIVISION TWO—Mark 11:1—16:8
   A. Introduction—11:1–11
   B. 11:12—13:37
      1. Opens 11:12–25—fig tree and purge of temple
      2. Ends 13:28–37—parable of fig tree and warnings of the end
   C. 14:1—16:8
      1. Opens 14:1–9—temporal transition, woman anoints Jesus with oil
      2. Ends 16:1–8—temporal transition, women go to tomb to anoint him

While full analysis of this structure will occur gradually throughout the rest of our study, several aspects should be noted at this point. Although Division Two is shorter than Division One, like the recognition sequences in the ancient novel, it is far more carefully organized over day and night periods. Mark 11:1—13:37 appears to take place over three days, with the final day heavily overloaded with material (viz., 11:11, 12, 19, 20). Since the temporal references are intended as guides for the hearers rather than accurate chronology, such overloading is not at all unusual. A second time sequence, referenced to the Passover and the Feast of Unleavened Bread, begins at Mark 14:1 and continues until the end of the Gospel, slowing down to an hourly count during the crucifixion itself (viz., 14:1, 12, 17, 26; 15:1, 25, 33, 34, 42; 16:1).

Division One evinces a few isolated temporal references (e.g., Mark 2:1; 8:1; 9:2) apparently designed simply to indicate the passage of time; however, there is one important exception at Mark 4:35. In Mark 4, Jesus has been teaching the crowds and the disciples in parables, but at 4:35 he and the disciples travel across the lake in the boat. Verse 35 begins with a remarkably pronounced and specific temporal reference that obviously ties it to the preceding teaching session: "On that day when evening had come." Jesus' explanations to the disciples about the kingdom and their fears for their own safety in the boat occur on the very same day. In this case, the temporal reference underlines the situational irony. Moreover, the travel across the sea also connects the next three healing miracles with the story and the teaching in parables. At Mark 5:1, Jesus and the disciples reach the other side, and later when they are asked to leave the country by the frightened townspeople (5:17), their trip back is met by Jairus (5:21–22), who asks Jesus to heal his daughter. On the way to the daughter, Jesus is touched by the woman with the flow of blood (5:24–30). Consequently, in a practice rather unusual for Division One, all of the material in Mark 4:1— 5:43 is sequentially linked. Indeed, the unit is the longest and most complex in Division One, being bounded on either side by chiastically arranged episodes. The beginning of the unit and that out of which everything else develops is the parable of the Sower. Hence, the rhetorical structure of Division One supplies yet another verification of the significance of the Sower.

The Parables of the Sower and the Tenants

One could argue for the importance of the parable of the Sower for understanding the Gospel on the basis of its distinctive narrative level, or on the basis of its introductory position in the unit from Mark 4:1 to 5:43, or on the basis of its possible functional similarity to the oracle in Xenophon's *An Ephesian Tale,* but one need not appeal to any of those arguments, for the clearest evidence of the centrality of the parable of the Sower comes in the words of the character Jesus himself: "Do you not understand this parable? How then will you understand all the parables?" (4:13). The rhetorical outline shows that a major parable appears near the opening of each of the two divisions, the parable of the Sower for Division One and the parable of the Tenants for Division Two. The Sower tells the story of a man who sows seed on different qualities of earth and, consequently, sees different results from total failure to great success. And the seed is the Word. The Tenants tells of a faraway vineyard owner who is denied the fruits of the vineyard by his tenants. After sending many servants, he sends one last emissary, his beloved son, the heir of the vineyard, but the tenants kill him, hoping to secure the vineyard for themselves, while actually only bringing judgment on their heads. And the tenants are the Jerusalem Jewish leaders. Each of these parables, then, appears to reflect the basic actions of Jesus and the other characters in its respective division.

The introduction to Division One (1:14–15) presents Jesus as the preacher of the gospel, and the parable of the Sower shows a man spreading the word with uneven results. The introduction to Division Two portrays Jesus as the public messiah-king, claiming his city, temple and kingdom, and the parable of the Tenants pictures the arrival and death of the heir of the vineyard. Since the significance of the two introductory passages may become clear to an audience only as the material progresses, the author of Mark has attempted to ensure the accessibility of the story by fashioning a plot synopsis near the beginning of each major division. The synopses, like Xenophon's oracle, are located far enough into the story for their elements to be identified but near enough to the beginning to function as guides for how everything is to be understood. Also like Xenophon's oracle, the parables are set off from surrounding material and designed to attract the audience's attention. Mark, as we noted, actually has Jesus tell the disciples (and thus the audience) to take special note of the Sower. Moreover, the parables as brief stories and Xenophon's oracle as poetry are fashioned in especially memorable forms, so that an audience can easily keep them in mind as the overall plot develops and use them to follow the unfolding story. The two parables in Mark present in concise, summary form the Gospel's view of Jesus: he is the Sower of the Word and the Heir of the Vineyard. The first emphasizes his task and the second his identity; together they make up the Gospel's basic narrative Christology.[59]

59. Discussions of the Christology (i.e., views of the nature and function of Christ) present in each of the canonical Gospels have focused in past New Testament research on the so-called "titles" used for Jesus (e.g., Son of God, Son of man, Son of David, Christ). Attempts have been made to establish a distinctive tradition for each "title"

In addition, as plot synopses, the parables do more than clarify Jesus' role in the story; they also define the roles of other characters and actions. The parable of the Sower, since it is the first and the one necessary for understanding the other parables (4:13), carries the greater responsibility for orienting the audience. The repetition and expansion provided by the parable of the Sower's full interpretation in Mark 4:14–20 witness to this importance. Not only does the interpretation supply additional information, it also aids the audience's memory by retelling the parable. The parable of the Sower as a plot synopsis of Division One is fairly forthright: Jesus, as the sower spreading the word everywhere, encounters four types of responses to that word. The first type is represented by the hardened ground of the path which seeds cannot even enter before the birds eat them (4:4) or the word cannot be heard because Satan removes it (4:15). The second type of response is a complex reaction that begins with immediate joy, endures for a while, but falters and disappears under persecution. The ground here is described as rocky (πετρῶδες) with little soil to support roots, so that the sun withers the plants (4:5–6, 16–17). Of the four kinds of responses, this second one is emphasized slightly by being given the longest explication of all in both the parable itself and the interpretation. The third type of response to the word is illustrated by seed thrown onto earth already covered by weeds (4:7). The weeds, interpreted as "the cares of the world and the delight in riches" (4:19), choke the seed and prevent it from producing fruit. Finally, after three types of responses to hearing the word that end in failure, the fourth response is one of remarkable success, for the

that influences its use by the Gospel writer. Indeed, one of the most creative hypotheses about the production of the Gospel of Mark related it to a christological controversy in the Markan community over whether Jesus was a suffering Messiah (Son of man) or a miracle-working Messiah (Son of God) (see T. J. Weeden, *Mark—Traditions in Conflict* [Philadelphia: Fortress Press, 1971]). Recently, the practice of looking at "titles" has come under increasing attack as the difficulty of establishing with certainty a fixed tradition of usage and meaning behind any of the "titles" has become increasingly clear. Whether they should be called "titles" at all is highly debatable. (See L. Hurtado, "New Testament Christology: A Critique of Bousset's Influence," *TS* 40 [1979]: 306–17; J. D. G. Dunn, *Christology in the Making: A New Testament Inquiry Into the Origins of the Doctrine of the Incarnation* [Philadelphia: Westminster Press, 1980], 12–97; H. C. Kee, "Christology and Ecclesiology: Titles of Christ and Models of Community," in *SBL Seminar Papers 1982*, ed. K. Richards [SBLSP 21; Chico, Calif.: Scholars Press, 1982], 227–42; and L. E. Keck, "Toward the Renewal of New Testament Christology," *NTS* 32 [1986]: 362–77.)

In order to discover the specific understanding of Jesus guiding each of the canonical Gospels, instead of studying "titles," a truly narrative Christology must be developed that attempts to perceive the distinctive function and depiction of the character Jesus within the dynamics of each story. For Mark, understanding Jesus as the Sower and the Heir of the Vineyard becomes the context for determining how any other "titles" are being used. Thus, the Christology of Mark is not established by looking at "titles" provided for Jesus; rather, the meaning of the "titles" is defined by the narrative itself.

good earth accepts the seed and bears fruit in a thirtyfold, sixtyfold, and hundredfold harvest (4:8, 20).

The characters, groups, and events of Division One are all portrayed as the concrete illustrations of these four fundamental kinds of responses to Jesus' word. Every episode and every character or group can be understood by the audience as an example of one of these four alternatives: the instant rejection of Jesus by the scribes and the Pharisees illustrates the first response; the immediate joy but ultimate failure of the disciples, the second; the wealth, too great to give up, of the rich man (10:17–22), the third; but what of the fourth type? The task of the material following the parable of the Sower, Mark 4:21—5:43, is to clarify the nature of the good earth that produces fruit. Thus the announcement of the threefold harvest from the good earth is closely followed by three healing stories in which faith produces results for all the world to see, for the fruits of the good earth can be most openly perceived in those, like the woman with the flow of blood, to whom Jesus says, Your faith has saved you (ἡ πίστις σου σέσωκέν σε, 5:34). The Pharisees, the disciples, the rich, the ones healed—all are illustrations of the four basic responses encountered by sowing the word, but since the Pharisees and the scribes are also the evil tenants, dominating the vineyard by force, the sower, who is the true heir to the vineyard, and all who follow him, can expect only violence, persecutions, and death in this world.

Summary

Like the ancient novels, epics, and dramas of the Greco-Roman world, the Gospel of Mark is replete with introductions, summaries, anticipations, and plot synopses to assist its audience in following its aural narrative. Mark's authorial audience and the authorial audiences of the ancient erotic novel would have expected such conventions and would have readily understood how to interpret and use them. Moreover, they would have expected the stories themselves to illustrate fundamental truths about the universe and human existence in it rather than simply to represent the surface exchanges and interactions of daily life. Modern audiences, however, raised on "realism," historical accuracy, psychological character development, and an abhorrence of "repetitious" writing, find such conventions puzzling and the narratives they dominate opaque and impenetrable. Yet it is possible by the use of both modern literary techniques and ancient rhetorical comparisons and information for contemporary readers to begin to enter imaginatively the ranks of the authorial audience of the Gospel of Mark and hence hear the Gospel with ears slightly more attuned to its own language.

An analysis of narrative levels in Mark reveals a remarkably consistent and dominant point of view shared by the implied author/narrator, the implied reader/narratee, and Jesus. Furthermore, by allowing Jesus, a character of the second degree narrative, to function with abilities reserved normally for public narrators alone, the story portrays Jesus' divine-human status in form as well as in content. What other characters do and say and the way they respond to Jesus are all judged by the reader from the single dominant perspective established by the narrator-Jesus alliance. Consequently, when Jesus presents the parables, the only third degree narratives in the Gospel, the reader immediately accepts them as authoritative and important. As third degree narratives the parables are heard not only by the audience but also by the other characters in the second degree narration. While the parables, like Xenophon's oracle, are primarily helps for the reader, the failure of the disciples to understand the parable of the Sower (4:10) allows the author both an excuse for repeating it and an opportunity to reveal the distance between the audience and the disciples. That the scribes and the Jerusalem leaders, on the other hand, do recognize that the parable of the Tenants was told against them (12:12) offers the author both a means of ensuring the audience's comprehension and an effective way of increasing the atmosphere of threat and foreboding that permeates Jesus' visit to Jerusalem.

As primarily mimetic narratives, the parables are designed to show in concise format the general principles organizing the story as a whole. Along with the prologue and the introductions to the two major divisions of the Gospel, the parables function, similarly to the prooemium of an epic, drama, or history, to inform the audience "beforehand what the work is about" in order to relieve any suspense they might have "since what is undefined makes the attention wander."[60] Moreover, "what the work is about" entails more than vague description, for Xenophon's oracle presents a relatively complete synopsis of the plot of *An Ephesian Tale*. So, if the parables of the Sower and the Tenants also function as plot synopses and if the rhetorical structure of two major divisions with their own introductions and predominant activities is generally correct—that is, if we have actually uncovered and properly understood several basic conventions governing the Gospel—then, using these conventions as guides, we should be able to explore in much greater detail how the various parts of the narrative merge together to present a unified, consistent, and peculiarly Markan story. To that task, the next four chapters of our study are devoted. Chapter 8: Jesus, the Sower of the Word will investigate Mark 4 and the material before and after it to develop more thoroughly the ramifications of the parable of the Sower for understanding Jesus and the other characters. Chapter 9: The

60. Aristotle, *Rhetoric* 3.1415a.

Good Earth and the Rocky Ground will deal with the ways in which the Gospel presents the healing miracles and the disciples. Chapter 10: Jesus, the Heir of the Vineyard will discuss the parable of the Tenants and the dominant portrayal of Jesus in Division Two as the true heir, the Son of David, the authoritative interpreter of Jewish Scripture and tradition. And Chapter 11: The Death of the Heir will explicate the Passion narrative or recognition sequence proper and try to reflect on the rhetorical force of the whole presentation of Jesus, the disciples, the miracles, the Jews, and the death at the hands of Romans for the audience.

8

Jesus,
the Sower
of the Word

That the parable of the Sower in Mark 4:3–9 displays a special status and performs a special function for the Gospel has been recognized by many commentators.[1] It is clearly "a part with a relation of particular privilege to the whole,"[2] but specifying the precise nature of this privileged relationship has been fraught with difficulties. The thorough rehabilitation of the disciples, effected by the Gospels of Matthew and Luke as well as by the increasingly reverential regard of two thousand years of Christian piety, makes Mark's predominant negative and ironic portrayal seem strange or even abhorrent and thus hard to see or accept. Consequently, the identity of the disciples as the group illustrating the second typical response to the word, that of initial acceptance, endurance for a time, and failure under

1. E.g., J. G. Williams, in *Gospel Against Parable: Mark's Language of Mystery* (Bible and Literature Series 12; Sheffield: JSOT Press, 1985), comments on "the close relation of the theme and images of the parables in ch. 4 to the plot of the gospel" (p. 180). See also E. Trocmé: "Why Parables? A Study of Mark IV," *Bulletin of the John Rylands Library* 59 (1977): 458–60; P. J. Achtemeier, "Mark as Interpreter of the Jesus Traditions," *Interpretation* 32 (1978): 345–46, 351; Rhoads and Michie, *Mark as Story,* 56, 119, 128; D. O. Via, Jr., *The Ethics of Mark's Gospel—In the Middle of Time* (Philadelphia: Fortress Press, 1985), 181–88; J. M. Robinson, "Gnosticism and the New Testament," in *The Problem of History in Mark and Other Markan Studies,* 43–47, 50; and W. S. Vorster, "Meaning and Reference: The Parables of Jesus in Mark 4," in *Text and Reality: Aspects of Reference in Biblical Texts,* ed. W. S. Vorster and B. C. Lategan (Atlanta: Scholars Press, 1985), 27–65.

2. Kermode, *The Genesis of Secrecy,* 16.

persecution, a role they rather obviously fit, has been obscured.[3] Further-more, the denigration of allegory as an appropriate description for parables by much parable scholarship of the last century[4] discouraged a close reading of the Sower and the Tenants in relation to the sections of the Gospel in which they stand.[5] Moreover, the primary interest of that scholarship in parables as *parables of Jesus* rather than as *parables of the Gospels* inhibited perceiving how each Gospel writer was employing the material.[6] Approach-ing the Gospel of Mark from a different direction, that of its similarities to the popular and rhetorical traditions of Hellenistic literature, and analyzing its structure with somewhat different tools, those of modern narrative theory and ancient rhetorical practice, allow a reassessment of the function and status of these particularly privileged parabolic parts for the whole of Mark's Gospel.

Like the oracle in Xenophon's *An Ephesian Tale* or the prooemium of the epic, drama, or history, the parables of the Sower and the Tenants provide the audience of the Gospel with summaries or synopses of the main action of surrounding material. By recalling these brief and highly mnemonic stories told by Jesus, the audience can interpret correctly the general point being illustrated in each episode or by each group of characters as the story progresses. The parables are meant to function, then, as sources of con-tinual orientation for readers, and the narrative of the Gospel as a whole embodies and expands the typologies established by them. Hence, Mark

3. For example, Trocmé, who wishes to see the disciples as positive characters in Mark, analyzes the second response to the word as representing Jesus' relatives and natural friends "who were bound to be well disposed towards him in the first place but then became frightened and hostile (3:20–21 and 3:31–35)" ("Why Parables? A Study of Mark IV," 466). The problem with Trocmé's argument is that the Markan narrative never portrays the relatives and friends of Jesus as initially positive; thus Trocmé argues from silence that they "were bound to be well disposed." The only group actually presented as moving from acceptance to failure when persecution arrives is the disciples. Indeed, as Mark 6:1–6 suggests, the very fact that kinspeople and friends knew Jesus in a different context prevented their acceptance of his words; their personal connection from the beginning prohibited faith.

4. See, e.g., Jeremias, *The Parables of Jesus*, 66–89; D. O. Via, Jr., *The Parables: Their Literary and Existential Dimension* (Philadelphia: Fortress Press, 1974), 4–10; J. D. Crossan, *In Parables: The Challenge of the Historical Jesus* (New York: Harper & Row, 1983), 8–15.

5. For a good study of the way a Lukan parable functions to illustrate and interpret its immediate context in the Gospel of Luke, see L. T. Johnson, "The Lukan Kingship Parable (LK 19:11–27)," *Novum Testamentum* 24 (1982): 139–59. Also R. Tannehill in his recent literary analysis of the Gospel of Luke (*The Narrative Unity of Luke-Acts: A Literary Interpretation,* vol. 1: *The Gospel According to Luke* [Foundations and Facets: New Testament; Philadelphia: Fortress Press, 1986]) recognizes that Luke uses the parable of the Sower "to suggest norms by which to evaluate characters in the story, especially the behavior of the disciples" (p. 212).

6. For a delineation of the major streams of parable research, see Tolbert, *Perspectives on the Parables,* 18–30.

stands in the basic tradition of most Greco-Roman literature as a typological or figurative writing. Indeed, it requires only a small amount of poetic license to describe the Gospel of Mark as a "concrete universal,"[7] in which the universal types supplied by the parables are concretized by the characters and plot of the overall narrative. In ancient thought, the moral significance of literature was derived from its ability to indicate the universality of the types of events, responses, or experiences depicted in it. Thus Aristotle, for example, argued that poetry was closely related to philosophy in its presentation of the probable and necessary in accordance with universal laws.[8] And although Plato himself ultimately decided to banish poets from the ideal republic, the force of the Platonic view that the tactile world was only a pale copy of the spiritual realm of essences, which alone was real, was to define the serious didactic task of the writer as the revelation of universal, spiritual reality in seemingly particularized, individual experience.[9] Such philosophical conceptions encouraged the production of illustrative literature that was heavily dependent on typology.

For the Gospel of Mark, the parables of the Sower and the Tenants are intended to reveal the fundamental typologies underlying the story, and the typologies they develop, while different, are deeply interwoven. The Sower, coming first in the narrative and additionally tagged by the character Jesus as the guide to understanding all the other parables (4:13), offers a fairly generalized and universal typology of four different possible responses to hearing the word. The Tenants, on the other hand, presents a more limited, quasi-historical typology to detail God's continually unfruitful relationship with the Jews which finally results in the vineyard being given to others. Yet the explanation of the Jews' unfruitfulness is to be found in their portrayal as the group illustrating the first response to the word, in which the seed is

7. While discussed at length by some New Critics (e.g., W. K. Wimsatt, "The Concrete Universal," in *The Verbal Icon: Studies in the Meaning of Poetry* [Lexington, Ky.: University of Kentucky Press, 1967], 69–83), the idea of literature as a "concrete universal" has a long history in both criticism and philosophy. Wimsatt traces it back to Aristotle's dual views that poetry imitates an action and is also an expression of universals. Sir Philip Sidney argued that "the poet coupleth the general notion with the particular example," and centuries later Coleridge praised Shakespeare for his excellent "union and interpenetration of the universal and the particular." The idealist philosophy of Hegel used the concept of "concrete universal" as a way of dealing with nature and the reality of universals. In this spectrum of views of "concrete universal," Mark not surprisingly would stand closest to Wimsatt's arguments about Aristotle: the particular action with agents that forms the story line of the Gospel illustrates universal principles.

8. See *Poetics* 1451b.

9. For Plato, the problem of the writer was that the process of depicting particularized experience inevitably entailed producing some kind of literary copy of the tactile world, which was itself only a copy of the real world of forms. Thus the writer, far from being able to reveal universal reality, by necessarily presenting a copy of a copy moved one further step *away* from reality. See *Republic* 10.595–607.

removed by Satan before it can even enter the ground (4:4, 15). Similarly, while the disciples show signs of incomprehension throughout the first part of the Gospel, it is only when active persecution occurs, typified by the last section of the parable of the Tenants (12:7–8), that their lack of roots (4:6, 17) is fully exposed, and they flee (14:50). Thus, although each parable presents a different kind of typology and dominates especially the action of its own section of the Gospel, they are thoroughly interrelated to produce a continuous, consistent story line.

Moreover, if Mark is an example of popular literature, as we have hypothesized, the typologies disclosed by the parables should be presented in a clear and accessible manner. In other words, what is required for understanding the typologies and for perceiving the role of the parables as guides to them ought to be readily apparent in the narrative itself, for the very nature of popular literature is to be available to a broad spectrum of readers with greatly varying degrees of knowledge or sophistication. If the identification of the typologies requires specialized or secret information absent from the narrative, then Mark becomes an esoteric[10] text accessible only to the initiated few.[11] Popular literature or "mass" literature by definition

10. Using the definition of genre as the expectations and conventions shared by authors and their audiences, which we developed earlier, we can posit a more sociological rather than wholly descriptive definition of esoteric texts. Esoteric texts are texts constructed under idiosyncratic conventions shared only by a specially initiated community, as opposed to exoteric texts which are constructed under conventions widely shared by the historical culture at large. The presence of symbolism, mystical numbers, allusions to other texts, pseudonymity, and the like, may or may not characterize esoteric texts; the definitive factor is the lack of accessibility of the conventions governing the work to those outside the initiated community but within the same general cultural milieu.

11. J. G. Williams's analysis of the Gospel of Mark, developed out of his identification of the elements in the parable of the Sower, provides an excellent example of a basically esoteric reading of Mark. By positing the suffering servant material in Isaiah 40—55 as "one of the main sources" of the Markan narrative, Williams finds the key to identifying the seed planted in the good earth of the parable of the Sower in Isa. 53:10. Thus, "what is sown is the sacrifice of the Son of Man, which will break the hold of the worldly quest for security for those who are able to see" (Williams, *Gospel Against Parable*, 44–47). That the seed falling on good earth should be interpreted as the Suffering Servant being crucified as a sacrifice for all is clearly *not* suggested by the interpretation of the parable in Mark 4:14–20 or by anything in the context of Mark 3 and 4. Indeed, allusions to the suffering servant material in Isaiah can be glimpsed only at three places in Mark (9:12; 10:45; 14:61), as Williams himself admits (pp. 44–45), and many scholars would deny that even these verses allude to Isaiah (see, e.g., H. C. Kee, *Community of the New Age: Studies in Mark's Gospel* [Philadelphia: Westminster Press, 1977], 45–48). Consequently, *nothing in the narrative of Mark* suggests Williams's reading. Such a reading can be arrived at only by the use of specialized or "secret" information supplied not by the text but by the initiated reader from his or her idiosyncratic and specialized pool of resources.

Williams's study illustrates well one of the difficulties inherent in studying ancient texts. Texts written using conventions generally recognized and understood within their own historical and cultural milieu *may appear esoteric* to later audiences who no

must supply most, although certainly not all,[12] of the information neccs-sary for its understanding and employ conventional patterns widely recog-nizable from their presence in similar texts within the cultural milieu. In order to see whether or not Mark fulfills this requirement of popular liter-ature we must, first, look at the two sections of material leading up to the parable of the Sower in Mark 4 to determine how the authorial audience is led to identify correctly the typology suggested by the parable. Second, we must look in some detail at Mark 4 itself to examine how the parable of the Sower and the other parables and sayings of that chapter are all related, and third, we must look briefly at the material following Mark 4 to gain some notion of how the plot and characters of the Gospel embody the typology revealed by the parable. Finally, before turning to a closer analysis of the disciples and the ones healed in the next chapter of our study, we can reflect briefly on what light is shed on the traditional issue of Mark's view of the kingdom of God by viewing the parable of the Sower as a plot synopsis.

Mark 1:16—3:6

After the introduction to the first section in Mark 1:14–15, the action of the Galilean ministry of Jesus opens in 1:16 with a geographical reference to the Sea of Galilee: "And passing along by the Sea of Galilee" (Καὶ παράγων παρὰ τὴν θάλασσαν τῆς Γαλιλαίας). This same reference with some variation is repeated at 2:13, where Jesus "again" goes out beside the sea and later "passes along" by it (πάλιν παρὰ τὴν θάλασσαν . . . παράγων); at 3:7, where Jesus and the disciples withdraw to the sea (πρὸς τὴν θάλασσαν); and at 4:1, where Jesus "again" teaches the crowds beside the sea (πάλιν . . . παρὰ τὴν θάλασσαν). These four locational references to the Sea of Galilee act as signposts to the audience, indicating the presence of divisions within the material: 1:16—2:12; 2:13—3:6; 3:7–35; and 4:1ff. Moreover, the use of "again" (πάλιν) in the second and fourth occurrences of the reference serves

---

longer read texts using those earlier conventions. All ancient texts, then, require some degree of literary-historical analysis in order to be understood in terms similar to (though not the same as) the way their authorial audiences would have understood them.

12. Demetrius's instructions on leaving gaps in narratives should be taken seriously: "Not everything should be given lengthy treatment with full details but some points should be left for our hearer to grasp and infer for himself. If he infers what you have omitted, he no longer just listens to you but acts as your witness, one too who is predisposed in your favour since he feels he has been intelligent and you are the person who has given him this opportunity to exercise his intelligence. In fact, to tell your hearer everything as if he were a fool is to reveal that you think him one" (*On Style* 222).

A reader or hearer becomes actively engaged in the narrative only when she or he must fill in or explain elements in the story; so, persuasive and engaging stories will never be thoroughly explicated.

to remind the audience that they have heard similar material before and encourages them to remember the earlier episode while hearing this new one. Indeed, the "again" in 2:13 by recalling the first time Jesus passed along beside the sea, in which he called his first disciples, helps the audience perceive in this second instance, also followed by the calling of a disciple, the establishment of a parallel pattern. The first calling of disciples in 1:16–20 is followed by four healing stories, 1:21–28; 1:29–34; 1:40–45; and 2:1–12, the last of which is a combination of healing story and controversy story. In parallel fashion, the second calling of a disciple in 2:13–14 is followed by four controversy stories, 2:15–17; 2:18–22; 2:23–28; and 3:1–6, the last of which is a combination of controversy and healing. Thus the opening segment of the first major division of the Gospel is composed of two rhetorically paralleled units[13] and may be outlined in the following way (for the full rhetorical structure, see Appendix A):

I. Prologue—Mark 1:1–13
II. Division One—Jesus, the Sower of the Word
   A. Introduction—1:14–15
   B. 1:16—3:6
      1. 1:16–20—passing along beside the sea, calls Simon, Andrew, James, John to follow him
         a. 1:21–28—healing in synagogue
         b. 1:29–34—healing of Simon's mother-in-law and crowds [1:35–39—prayer alone]
         c. 1:40–45—healing of leper
         d. 2:1–12—healing of paralytic/controversy with scribes
      2. 2:13–14—again beside the sea, calls Levi to follow him
         a. 2:15–17—controversy over eating with sinners
         b. 2:18–22—controversy over fasting
         c. 2:23–28—controversy over Sabbath observance
         d. 3:1–6—controversy over Sabbath/healing "again" in synagogue

The final episode in the whole section, Mark 3:1–6, in addition to formally paralleling the last episode in the first half of the unit by being a combined healing/controversy story, also forms a nice *inclusio* with the very first healing story by being set "again" in the synagogue on a Sabbath (1:21 = 3:1–2), thus rounding out the whole section rhetorically. The first half, 1:16—2:12, also contains a brief story about Jesus going early in the morning to a lonely place (εἰς ἔρημον τόπον) to pray (1:35–39). This episode is located right in the middle of the four healing stories and appears to

13. Structural outlines of this material, different from the one being proposed, may be found in, e.g., Robbins, *Jesus the Teacher,* 25–34; and Dewey, *Markan Public Debate,* 65–129.

have no parallel in the second half of the unit. Such a break in a rhetorical pattern is common, for these patterns are not rigid grids but fluid organizing structures. There is some evidence, in fact, in both Jewish and Greek literature that too balanced or symmetrical a structure was perceived as artificial and contrived.[14]

The four—or in the case of the first half, five—episodes that follow the call stories in each subsection evince remarkably similar themes and patterns. This connection is especially clear in the second half, for the three controversy stories in Mark 2:15–28 involve debates over rules governing eating practices: Should one eat with sinners (2:15–17)? Should Jesus' disciples fast as others do (2:18–22)? Should the disciples pick grain to eat on the Sabbath (2:23–28)? Furthermore, each of these controversies is closed by one or more proverbial sayings of Jesus: "Those who are well have no need of a physician, but those who are sick; I came not to call the righteous, but sinners" (2:17); "And no one puts new wine into old wineskins; if he does, the wine will burst the skins, and the wine is lost, and so are the skins; but new wine is for fresh skins" (2:22); "The sabbath was made for man, not man for the sabbath; so the Son of man is lord even of the sabbath" (2:27–28).

Indeed, all three of these controversy stories appear to be variations on a theme, and from a rhetorical standpoint what becomes significant about these episodes is their general similarities rather than their particular differences. In each case, Jesus seems to be making the same point, that the distinct needs of human beings in every special moment in time always take precedence over the established rules, rituals, and customs dictated by tradition. Just as a physician cannot treat the sick if custom prevents his or her contact with them, so Jesus cannot fulfill his mission to preach the gospel to sinners if he does not share table fellowship with them. The requirements of people and of Jesus' own task determine what is or is not permissible, not religious custom. This remarkably "situational ethic" does not constitute an outright rejection of traditional ritual or law, as the second controversy story indicates. Fasting is proper when the bridegroom

14. For an excellent general discussion of the importance of symmetry, balance, parallelism, and harmony in the stylistics of both Greco-Roman and Israelite-Jewish literature and art, see C. H. Talbert, *Literary Patterns, Theological Themes, and the Genre of Luke-Acts* (SBLMS 20; Missoula, Mont.: Scholars Press, 1974), 67–75.

For the importance of breaks in symmetry—or "symmetrophobia"—in Hebrew literature, see G. A. Smith, *The Early Poetry of Israel in Its Physical and Social Origins* (London: Oxford University Press, 1927), 17–20; and more recently, W. L. Holladay, "The Recovery of Poetic Passages of Jeremiah," *JBL* 85 (1966): 432–35, and P. Trible, "Wisdom Builds a Poem: The Architecture of Proverbs 1:20–33," *JBL* 94 (1975): 513–14.

For the caution that too balanced a piece appears artificial and contrived, see Aristotle, *Rhetoric* 3.2.4–5 (1404b), and Demetrius, *On Style* 15.

has been taken *away,* just as old cloth, not new, unshrunk cloth, is the proper material to use in patching old garments; however, fasting is *not* appropriate when the bridegroom is still with the guests, just as new wine-skins, not old ones, are necessary for new wine. Traditional rituals are suitable for traditional situations, but new situations require new responses. Custom, law, and ritual are not condemned, but they are sub-ordinated to the changing requirements of people in ever-new situations.

The last two controversies in the subsection bear out this general point. The hunger of the disciples, not the customs of Sabbath observance, takes precedence in Mark 2:23–28, and Jesus points out to the Pharisees, who have protested the unlawfulness of the disciples' action of picking grain on the Sabbath, that Scripture affirms that David himself understood human welfare to be a higher good than legal codes. The view is not new or original; people of religious insight like David have always known it. The gnomic saying of Mark 2:27–28 states the point concisely: rituals, laws, and customs were created to benefit and serve human needs; human beings were not created to serve ritual.[15]

Although the last of the four controversy stories does not raise the theme of eating, it is connected to the story immediately preceding it by the issue of Sabbath observance. This time the question is whether or not Jesus should heal a man with a withered hand on the Sabbath. It was, of course, legally possible to break the Sabbath to save life, but this man's life was not endangered. Nevertheless, Jesus' action in healing the man is completely in line with the general point being developed by all four of the controversies: human welfare, to do good, always takes priority over ritual observance or custom.[16] In addition, the narrator has crafted an ironic fillip to end this final controversy/healing story. The gnomic ending typical of the other stories is replaced by the narrator's report that "the Pharisees went out, and immediately held counsel with the Herodians against him, how to destroy

15. Whether "Son of man" in Mark 2:28 refers to Jesus as a title, apocalyptic or not, or is only being used here as a synonym for "human being," which is its general function in Hebrew and Aramaic, is a difficult issue to decide. Clearly, the phrase "sons of men" in Mark 3:28 is being used in the general sense, while the earlier singular usage of "Son of man" in 2:10 appears to refer definitely to Jesus with no apocalyptic overtones. Given the repeated gnomic type of conclusions to these controversies and the general point they are all making, I am inclined to view "son of man" in 2:28 as a general reference to humanity and "Lord" ($\kappa\acute{\upsilon}\rho\iota\sigma$) as meaning master or director; so human beings are directors even of the Sabbath. For a similar conclusion, see L. S. Hay, "The Son of Man in Mark 2:10 and 2:28," *JBL* 89 (1970): 73–75.

16. The three healing stories in Mark 5:1–43 actually allude to the same issue. The demoniac living among the tombs with pigs nearby, the woman with the flow of blood, and the dead child would in Jewish law all be considered ritually unclean and therefore untouchable. Yet Jesus *does* touch them and heal them. Ritual observance cannot be allowed to stand in the way of human welfare. On these stories, see M. J. Selvidge, "Mark 5:25–34 and Leviticus 15:19–20: A Reaction to Restrictive Purity Regulations," *JBL* 103 (1984): 619–23.

him" (3:6). Mark's favorite word "immediately" (εὐθὺς), while common in the earlier healings subsection of this unit, has not been used at all in these controversy stories until this final verse. Here it is not narrative pace that is at issue but irony. The Pharisees condemned Jesus' doing good on the Sabbath, and then they "immediately"—*still on the Sabbath*—plot to kill him. If Jesus' act of healing broke the Sabbath commandment, how much more does their act of destroying. Their hardness of heart not only prevents them from acknowledging the rightness of Jesus' position, it forces them to violate the spirit, if not the letter, of their own rules.

If the four controversy stories in the second subsection of this opening unit betray similar motifs, styles of ending, and general points at issue—all features to be expected, given the requirements of rhetorical amplification—what of the parallel healing stories in the first half of the unit (1:21—2:12)? All four of the healing stories, along with the calling of disciples that they follow, are dominated by speed. Everything happens "immediately," and the narrative pace of the entire subsection hardly allows an auditor time to assimilate the separate actions. Not only does this fast progress reinforce the claim of the introductory verses that the time has been fulfilled (1:15), it also lessens the impact of the miracles themselves. The actual act of healing passes so quickly that the audience is more affected by its initiation and result than by its miraculous quality. Indeed, all four of these healings evince a pattern that characterizes all the Markan healing stories throughout the Gospel: Jesus does not initiate healings; the persons to be healed must come to him, be brought to him, appeal to him, or otherwise inaugurate the action. Jesus heals as a response to the initiative of others. For example, in the first healing episode of the Gospel (1:21–28), Jesus is teaching "with authority" in the synagogue when a man with an evil spirit confronts him, loudly announcing Jesus' identity as the "Holy One of God." In silencing the evil spirit, Jesus commands it to come out of the man. Likewise, "they" must tell Jesus of Simon's mother-in-law's illness before he acts (1:30–31); the leper must come and request Jesus' help (1:40); and the paralytic must be brought by friends who have to remove the roof of the house to get the sick man to Jesus' attention (2:3–4). In this last instance, the narrator identifies the motivation of these people in bringing the paralytic to Jesus as "their faith" (2:5), and it is perceiving "their faith" (τὴν πίστιν αὐτῶν) that moves Jesus to act. Jesus' miraculous power, then, is a response to the initiative of others and not itself the focus of attention. The fast pace of the narrative, which minimizes the miraculous quality of the healing stories, conforms to this position. Jesus, as the divine Son, clearly has the power to exorcise demons and miraculously heal, but the narrator emphasizes the inauguration and result of these healings more than their miraculous quality per se.

The first and the last of the four healing stories explicitly relate the healings[17] to Jesus' "authority" (ἐξουσία). This "authority" is not simply a matter of status or knowledge, which the scribes would also have, but rather a matter of power. Jesus has the power to act; his words can effect changes. In the first healing story, the dialogue between Jesus and the evil spirit is surrounded by references to the amazement of the people at the authority of Jesus' teaching, reported first by the narrator (1:22) and finally by direct speech of the people (1:27). In the last healing story (2:1–12), which incorporates a controversy with scribes as well, Jesus himself interprets his ability to heal the paralytic as an illustration "that the Son of man has authority on earth to forgive sins" (2:10).[18] In both cases, Jesus' ἐξουσία is demonstrated in the power of his words to effect healing. In the parlance of contemporary speech-act theory, Jesus' teaching with authority constitutes performative utterance: what he says, happens; his word performs an act. For the Gospel of Mark, as these two stories indicate, Jesus' teaching is identified with his actions; his words and his deeds are one. Thus the new teaching of Jesus with authority that exorcises demons and heals the sick is his message.[19]

17. Exorcisms and healings are treated in much the same manner by the narrator, and it appears to make little sense to try to distinguish sharply between them. The only major difference is that the evil spirits who must be exorcised often attempt, though not always, to speak with Jesus and in so doing remind the audience of Jesus' divine identity. These evil spirits are also reminders of the cosmic level of the story.

18. The anacoluthon (or grammatical irregularity) in 2:10, caused by the shift in pronouns from second person plural, "that you may know . . . ," to third person singular, "he said to the paralytic . . . ," has generated considerable scholarly debate, primarily because it contains the first use in the Gospel of "Son of man." Some scholars, following the hypothesis of G. H. Boobyer ("Mark II, 10a and the Interpretation of the Healing of the Paralytic," *HTR* 47 [1954]: 115–20), have tried to argue that the phrase, "But that you may know that the Son of man has authority on earth to forgive sins," should be understood like 13:14 as a direct address of author to reader, thereby making "Son of man" a title used by the Markan community for Jesus rather than only Jesus' self-reference; for this view, see, e.g., C. E. B. Cranfield, *The Gospel According to St. Mark: An Introduction and Commentary* (Cambridge Univ. Press, 1979), 100; C. Ceroke, "Is Mark 2, 10 a Saying of Jesus?" *CBQ* 22 (1960): 369–90; and L. S. Hay, "The Son of Man in Mark 2:10 and 2:28," *JBL* 89 (1970): 69–75. Since no one argues that Mark 2:8–9 is anything other than Jesus' direct address to the (second person plural) scribes, there seems no grammatical or textual justification for positing a break between v. 9 and v. 10a. Verse 10a, then, is simply the continuation of Jesus' address to the scribes that began in v. 8 or, in our terminology, the continuation of second degree discourse. The break comes between v. 10a and v. 10b. Analyzing the verse by levels of narration clarifies what is going on. Verse 10a is a continuation of the second degree narration of the character Jesus talking to other characters, which indeed continues into v. 11; in v. 10b the narrator interrupts in first degree narration to indicate to the narratee that Jesus' addressee changes from the scribes to the paralytic. The anacoluthon is simply a shift in narrative levels, not at all the exit from the story line found at Mark 13:14.

19. In the Gospel of Matthew, especially, the situation is quite different. Matthew separates long blocks of teaching material (e.g., the Sermon on the Mount in Matthew 5—7) from sections of the text that present Jesus healing the sick or performing

However, as the last healing/controversy suggests, Jesus' words cannot effect change in everyone, for the scribes are offended by his performative teaching. Jesus' words hold the power for healing only for those who come seeking it from him. The healing of the leper (1:40–45), the third of the four healing stories in this subsection, while not explicitly referring to "authority," reflects strikingly on this issue of the kind of person Jesus' ἐξουσία can affect. The leper comes beseechingly to Jesus, kneels, and speaks: "If you will, you can make me clean." The leper expresses absolute confidence in Jesus' ability to act in his behalf *prior to* Jesus' actually doing anything. Reaching out and touching the leper, Jesus responds, using the leper's own words: "I will; be clean," and his words accomplish the act immediately. Fashioning this exchange in direct discourse increases the dramatic effect of the episode on the audience, while further identifying Jesus' actions with his speaking. In the final healing story of the section, confidence like that of the leper is designated by the narrator as "faith" (2:5), and such faith exists prior to Jesus' healing words to the paralytic just as it did for the leper. Hence all four of these opening healing stories reflect the fast pace of the narrative, and three of the four share two additional concerns: the identification of Jesus' authoritative new teaching with healing, in which his words perform deeds, and the responsibility for inaugurating the healing act falling on those seeking it and not Jesus. The evil spirit in the first healing episode confronts Jesus out of sure knowledge of who he is, while the leper and those bringing the paralytic act out of confidence or faith in Jesus' power, prior to experiencing it themselves.

All four of the healing stories, and indeed even the prayer episode of Mark 1:35–39, display another dominant similarity: the spread of Jesus' fame despite all his efforts to the contrary. Just as the controversy stories of the second half of this opening section ended with formally similar gnomic sayings, just so do all the healing stories of the first half end with reports of Jesus' fame extending throughout the land or with the attempts of Jesus to prevent his name from becoming known. After the crowds comment on the authority of Jesus' new teaching in exorcising the demon in the first healing story, the narrator relates that immediately "his fame spread everywhere throughout all the surrounding region of Galilee" (1:28). In the house of Simon and Andrew, Jesus heals Simon's mother-in-law[20] and later in the

---

miraculous deeds. For Mark, Jesus' teaching is acting and his acting, teaching. For Matthew, teaching is thoroughly distinct from acting. Not surprisingly, one of the few Markan stories that Matthew completely omits is this first healing episode in Mark 1:21–28, in which the narrator explicitly identifies Jesus' words with his power to exorcise and heal.

20. The RSV translates the mother-in-law's action after being healed as "and she served them" (Mark 1:31). The Greek of this phrase is καὶ διηκόνει αὐτοῖς. In Mark 1:13 the very same verb is used to describe the action of the angels, καὶ οἱ ἄγγελοι διηκόνουν

evening heals many from the whole city gathered at the door, but as the narrator reports, "he would not permit the demons to speak, because they knew him" (1:34). The audience understands what the demons' knowing him means, because in the immediately preceding episode, the evil spirit had said, "I know who you are, the Holy One of God," and that incident had resulted in the spread of his fame. Jesus evidently at this point does not wish who he is to be widely known. And the audience must wonder why he does not. The prayer episode and the healing of the leper begin to suggest a reason for Jesus' attitude.

Jesus' identity becoming known or his fame spreading leads inevitably to the drawing together of huge crowds, seeking Jesus, trying to touch him or follow him. In the morning after his evening of healing the whole city, Jesus retreats to a "lonely place" (ϵἰς ἔρημον τόπον) to pray, as he will try to do occasionally in the Gospel (e.g., 6:31, 35, 46–47; 8:3–4), but Simon "pursued him." The Greek word καταδιώκω carries a very strong, often hostile sense: Simon and the others harassed him or hunted him down. Their message is that everybody is searching for him, and Jesus accedes to their needs, for that is his mission (1:37–39). This brief interlude in the midst of the healing stories focuses the attention of the audience on the growing demands that Jesus' actions necessarily inspire, whatever his own wishes might be. The conclusion of the healing of the leper confirms and increases this dilemma. Jesus commands the leper to "say nothing to any one" about what has happened to him but to go to the priest to make the customary offering for his healing. Instead, the leper begins to preach (κηρύσσειν) and spread the word everywhere, with the result that Jesus can "no longer openly enter a town" but must stay out in a lonely place (ἔξω ἐπ' ἐρήμοις τόποις), and even then people come to him from all around (1:43–45).

Jesus' name and fame spread despite his best efforts, and the crowds grow to the point of blocking his free movement. Because of the repetition at the conclusion of each of these healings of the related motifs of Jesus' name and fame spreading, the crowds growing, and his attempts to stem that tide, the audience is clearly aware that Jesus is not trying to win fame for himself or to attract large crowds; indeed, he is actively trying to suppress knowledge about himself. Moreover, the audience is also aware that his very mission, the preaching of the good news with authority that effects changes in people's lives, cannot be hidden; people will come to him in increasing numbers as they hear. Thus the result of Jesus' healing is the spread of his fame and the growth of crowds, but Jesus himself does not seek this fame or

αὐτῷ; the RSV, however, chooses to translate this as "and the angels ministered to him." The same word in such close proximity ought to be given the same translation, or it is misleading to non-Greek readers. In this case, of course, it also encourages sexism.

encourage these crowds; instead, he is harassed and burdened by the crowds and increasingly unable to escape them.

The final healing story of the section, which is also a controversy story, marking the first appearance in the narrative of the scribes, does not end with an explicit report of the spread of Jesus' fame but rather with a direct discourse exclamation by the people, amazed and glorifying God: "We never saw anything like this!" (2:12). However, that the people were *glorifying God and not Jesus* is a significant minor acknowledgment of Jesus' attempts to suppress his growing reputation. Moreover, since this last episode in the first subsection is formally parallel to the last episode in the second half, as combined healing/controversy stories, the ending poses a sharp contrast to the ending of its counterpart in Mark 3:1–6. There, the narrator reports the plot to destroy Jesus by the Pharisees and the Herodians (3:6); here, the crowd expresses its amazement and affirmation of Jesus' teaching with authority. The parallel structure of the entire opening unit stresses the radically different responses to Jesus' word of those healed and the crowds in the first half and of the scribes, Pharisees, and Herodians in the second. In the latter stories, furthermore, no particular distinctions are drawn between scribes, Pharisees, and Herodians, whatever their historical differences might have been.[21] First the scribes appear (2:6), then the peculiar "scribes of the Pharisees"[22] (2:16), then the Pharisees alone (2:24), and finally the Pharisees and the Herodians (3:6). In all cases, the point of the narrative is simply that they oppose Jesus; their particular historical beliefs or actions are of no concern unless these actually become the subjects of the controversy (e.g., 7:1–5; 12:18–27). In addition, the very first response of the scribes in this, their very first appearance in the narrative, is to accuse Jesus of blasphemy in their hearts (2:6), and it is with this same

21. See the excellent study by M. Cook, *Mark's Treatment of the Jewish Leaders* (Leiden: E. J. Brill, 1978), in which he argues that the author of Mark knew little or nothing about Jewish leadership groups actually functioning during Jesus' lifetime; he simply drew upon and combined information in his source materials to produce the scribes, Pharisees, chief priests, Herodians, and elders. Indeed, Cook argues persuasively that "some of the group titles ('chief priests,' 'Herodians,' 'elders') are merely general constructs, i.e., literary devices serving the convenience of the Synoptists . . . [and] not reflective of leadership groups actually functioning in Jesus' time or later" (p. 1). For Cook, the "Jewish leaders functioned here merely as a foil for Jesus: conflict, or at least contrast, with Jesus was stressed; possible commonality . . . was downplayed virtually altogether" (p. 79).

22. A textual problem exists here. Some manuscripts read "scribes and the Pharisees," which is the more common expression. The more difficult reading of "scribes of the Pharisees" is probably to be preferred and again suggests Mark's use of these groups as illustrative of the underlying typology and not as representing historical situations. Indeed, Cook argues that "scribes" and "Pharisees" historically may have been terms for the *same* group which Mark has mistakenly divided (see *Mark's Treatment of the Jewish Leaders*, 5, 58–67, 83–91).

charge of blasphemy that the high priest and the Jewish leaders later condemn Jesus to death (14:63–64). From first to last, the response of the Jewish groups to Jesus never wavers or changes.

The parallel structure of the opening segment of the Gospel encourages generalized, as well as specialized, comparisons between the two subdivisions:

1:16–20—passing along beside the Sea of Galilee —calls Simon, Andrew, James, John to follow	2:13–14—again beside the sea, passing along, crowds gather —calls Levi to follow
1. 1:21–28—synagogue on Sabbath —teaches with authority; exorcises —fame spreads everywhere	1. 2:15–17—Levi's house; many followed —eating with sinners —came to call not righteous but sinners
2. 1:29–34—Simon's house —heals mother-in-law and whole city —prohibited demons from speaking because they knew him	2. 2:18–22—should his disciples fast? —wedding guests do not fast when bridegroom is with them —old cloth to patch old garment —new wineskins for new wine
[1:35–39—lonely place to pray —hunted down by Simon and others —goes throughout Galilee preaching and exorcising]	
3. 1:40–45—leper asks for healing —Jesus charges him to tell no one —leper preaches —Jesus cannot enter towns, must stay in lonely place; people come	3. 2:23–28—picking grain on Sabbath to eat —David violated the law for his own welfare —Sabbath made for people, not people for Sabbath
4. 2:1–12—paralytic brought —Jesus sees their faith; shows authority —scribes think blasphemy in their hearts —people amazed and glorified God, "We never saw anything like this!"	4. 3:1–6—again in synagogue on Sabbath —should he heal man on Sabbath? —anger at their hardened hearts —Pharisees and Herodians "immediately" plot to destroy him

Overall, the two subsections portray two drastically different responses to Jesus. The fast-paced first half emphasizes the growing crowds of people flocking to Jesus, the confidence or faith of those that come to be healed, the performative power of Jesus' new teaching, and the spread of Jesus' fame despite his strenuous efforts to prevent it. The slower second half concentrates on opposition to Jesus' (or the disciples') actions by scribes or Pharisees, Jesus' proverbial type of responses, and Jesus' insistence on human well-being as a higher priority than ritual, law, or custom. The first half ends in amazement, glory to God, and the people exclaiming, "We never saw anything like this!" The second half ends with the plot of the Pharisees and the Herodians to destroy Jesus. The transition between the two halves is smoothed by some overlapping at the edges, for the last healing story introduces controversy with the scribes, and the first controversy story (and the call of Levi as well) mentions the crowds and many who followed Jesus. Controversy is not a part of any of the earlier healings, and crowds are not reported in any of the later controversy stories. In addition to depicting Jesus as the powerful speaker of a new word that can heal and as a purveyor of wisdom, these two subsections introduce two other major Gospel groups, those seeking healing and the scribes, Pharisees, and Jewish leaders, along with the typical, and repeated, responses of each group to Jesus.

Moreover, each of the subsections begins with the calling of disciples to follow Jesus; so the opening unit also introduces a third major group, the disciples. The first call story is considerably longer than the second and presents four disciples, three of whom become the major representatives of the disciples throughout the Gospel: Simon, James, and John. Both the call stories, in contrast to the healing episodes,[23] emphasize the initiative of Jesus in commanding the disciples to follow. Jesus sees them and tells them to follow (1:16–17, 19; 2:14). Their action is wholly responsive, and in the first case at least, the alacrity of their response is emphasized by εὐθὺς ("immediately," 1:18, 20). Although one healing episode takes place in Simon's house (1:29–34) and one controversy takes place in Levi's house (2:15–17), the disciples in general play little part in the episodes of this opening unit. When they do appear, it is often in marginally negative contexts: Simon and the others hunt Jesus down (1:36–37); Jesus' disciples do not fast (2:18); Jesus' disciples pluck grain in violation of the law (2:23). Nevertheless, the strength of their positive responses to Jesus' calls ensures

---

23. The final combined controversy/healing episode of the unit, Mark 3:1–6, portrays Jesus taking much more initiative in a healing situation than he typically does in the Gospel. Since that healing is for the sake of making a controversial point against the Pharisees, the healing pattern is eclipsed by the needs of the controversy story.

the audience's favorable regard for them in these beginning stories. Now, to be sure that these three groups and their characteristics are clearly understood by the audience, following the next geographical reference to the sea in Mark 3:7, the narrator summarizes and further defines each group before presenting, after the final reference to the sea in 4:1, the plot synopsis of the parable of the Sower.

Mark 3:7–35

In Mark 3:7, Jesus and the disciples withdraw to the sea and a great crowd from Galilee follows. After the sea reference, denoting the start of a new section, the material falls into three sharply divided episodes, each dealing with one of the major groups introduced in the preceding section: 3:7–12, those healed and the crowds; 3:13–19a, the disciples; and 3:19b–35, the scribes and their controversies. The episodes are separated from one another by locational shifts: 3:13, "he went up on the mountain"; 3:19b, "he went home." Moreover, the last episode is in two parts, vv. 19b–30 and vv. 31–34, with different but related groups involved. The rhetorical purpose of the section as a whole is to repeat, summarize, and further delineate the groups, motifs, and issues already established by 1:16—3:6. Such summaries and repetitions, as we have seen, are characteristic of aural narratives and quite common in the ancient erotic novels.

Mark 3:7–12 begins with impressive evidence that Jesus' fame has spread far and wide, for crowds come to him "from Judea and Jerusalem and Idumea and from beyond the Jordan and from about Tyre and Sidon" (3:7–8). These people come because they have heard what he has done (ἀκούοντες ὅσα ἐποίει); *hearing* is the crucial element in eliciting their response. Yet these crowds press against Jesus to such a degree that he tells the disciples "to have a boat ready for him because of the crowd, lest they should crush him" (3:9). As in the first half of the opening unit, news of Jesus' healing activity brings masses of people to him, whose very numbers and urgency threaten his movements and safety. This summary episode closes with a definite indication to the audience that this situation is not what Jesus desires, for he orders the unclean spirits who cry out, "You are the Son of God," not to make him known (3:11–12). The brief episode, then, has reminded the audience of the overwhelming success of Jesus' healing ministry, the growth of crowds of followers that pose problems even for Jesus' own well-being, the sure knowledge of the evil spirits from the cosmic realm of who Jesus is, and Jesus' own strenuous, but apparently futile, efforts to keep himself from being known.

In Mark 3:13, Jesus goes up on the mountain and calls to him those he wishes. While in the beginning episodes of each subsection of the first unit

Jesus had addressed characters by name and told them to follow him, prior to this episode in 3:13–19a, those following Jesus seemed to be a large and diffuse group. Mark 2:15 reports that "there were many who followed him," and earlier we heard of "Simon and those who were with him" (1:36). Only at this point does a definitive group of twelve emerge as those appointed to be "with him" ($\mu\epsilon\tau$ ' $a\dot{v}\tau o\hat{v}$) and "to be sent out to preach and have authority ($\dot{\epsilon}\xi ov\sigma\acute{\iota}a$) to cast out demons" (3:14–15). Both the number of disciples chosen and the location on the mountain have strong symbolic overtones from Jewish tradition: the twelve tribes of Israel, the mountain of the covenant, or the mountain of divine revelation, and so forth.[24] Mark, however, makes very little use of these allusions either here or later in the text.[25] Only four of the twelve play any individual role in the story: Simon, James, John, and Judas;[26] and "the twelve" as a group still apparently continues to be mixed with a larger following of disciples (e.g., "those who were about him with the twelve," 4:10). Besides this appointing of the Twelve, the sole remaining episode related completely to them is the sending out of the Twelve in Mark 6:7–13, 30. That latter episode repeats much of the vocabulary of 3:13–19a, clearly reminding the audience of the initial appointment and task of the Twelve. Indeed, all three of the episodes in 3:7–35 have fairly evident parallels in 6:1–34.

a. 3:7–12—by the sea; crowd from many (named) towns; boat ready so as not to be crushed; heals many

a'. 6:31–34—go to lonely place by boat; crowd from all the towns; teaches them

b. 3:13–19a—calls and appoints twelve to be sent out to preach and have authority over demons; names them

b'. 6:7–13,30—calls and sends out twelve and gives them authority over unclean spirits; instructions for mission; they preach repentance

c. 3:19b–35—seized by those "near him" as "beside

c'. 6:1–6—teaches in his native place; rejected by relatives

24. For various theories on the symbolism of "the twelve," see G. Schmahl, *Die Zwölf im Markusevangelium* (Trier: Paulinus Verlag, 1974), 1–15; also E. Best, "Mark's Use of the Twelve," *ZNW* 69 (1978): 11–35; and R. P. Meye, *Jesus and the Twelve: Discipleship and Revelation in Mark's Gospel* (Grand Rapids: Wm. B. Eerdmans, 1968). On the associations of the mountain, see K. Stock, *Die Boten aus dem Mit-Ihm-Sein* (AnBib 70; Rome: Biblical Institute, 1975), 10f.; and W. Burgers, "De instelling van de Twaalf in het evalgelie van Marcus," *ETL* 36 (1960): 625–54.

25. J. R. Donahue, *The Theology and Setting of Discipleship in the Gospel of Mark* (Milwaukee, Wisc.: Marquette University Press, 1983), 7–10.

26. Andrew, although one of the first four called along with Simon, James, and John, is absent from most of the story. He appears with the other three only in Mark 13:3. Levi, called in the second calling story of the opening unit, does not even appear in the list of the Twelve. Again, Mark's concern is figurative, not historical.

himself"; controversy with   and neighbors; he marvels
scribes; rejects his old family,   at their lack of faith
establishes rule for new family

The paralleled episodes are in inverted order, thus forming a chiastic pattern that extends from 3:7 to 6:34 with Mark 4 and 5 at its center; the rhetorical structure can be outlined as follows (for the full rhetorical structure, see Appendix A):

I. Prologue—Mark 1:1–13
II. Division One—Jesus, the Sower of the Word
   A. Introduction—1:14–15
   B. 1:16—3:6
      1. 1:16—2:12—calls disciples; four healing stories
      2. 2:13—3:6—calls disciple; four controversy stories
   C. 3:7—6:34
      1. 3:7–35
         a. 3:7–12—by sea, crowds from many towns, boat, healing
         b. 3:13—19a—calls and appoints the Twelve
         c. 3:19b–35—controversy with those "near him" and scribes; rejects old family
      2. 4:1—5:43
      3. 6:1–34
         c'. 6:1–6—rejected by neighbors; family named
         b'. 6:7–13, 30—calls and sends out the Twelve
           [6:14–29—death of John the Baptist by Herod]
         a'. 6:31–34—by boat to lonely place, crowds from all towns, teaching

For the audience listening to the Gospel, the primary point of the repetitions in 6:1–34 would be to recall some of the major themes and issues that had been introduced earlier in the story which now take on a somewhat different complexion after the plot synopsis provided by the parable of the Sower. When Jesus initially calls and appoints the Twelve in Mark 3:13–19a, the audience should regard the disciples in a generally favorable light because of their positive response to Jesus, even though the narrator clouds that positive response with foreshadowings of death by revealing that Judas Iscariot also "betrayed him." However, by Mark 6:7–13 the audience should realize that the incipient acceptance of the disciples is destined to change to failure and rejection because they are the main group illustrating the second possible response to the word, that of initial joy, endurance for a time, and failure under persecution. That knowledge on the part of the audience can be used by the narrator to shape their understanding of the disciples' actions in all future episodes. Because they know that the disciples will eventually fail, the audience can begin to look for evidences or forewarnings of that result. The central tension in the Gospel of Mark, as in Xenophon's *An Ephesian Tale*, Chariton's *Chaereas and Callirhoe*, Homer's *Odyssey,* or Greek epic and drama generally, is not *what* is going to happen, but *how it will happen.* By the end of Mark 4, any ancient audience, even one without much prior information concerning the Christian story, should recognize the basic outline of the plot: the scribes, Pharisees, and Jewish leaders will oppose and finally destroy Jesus, Judas will betray him, the disciples will flee under persecution, but some people will be healed, go out, and produce great fruit. After Mark 4, the only real question is *how* all of these events will come about. Thus, although Mark 6:1–34 does repeat some of the words, themes, and groups found in 3:7–35, it is repetition with a difference, and the difference in this case rests in the clarity with which the audience will be following the unfolding story, as we shall see.

Although the basic attitude of the audience to the disciples at the time of the appointment of the Twelve in Mark 3:13–19a is favorable, that episode provides one of the major correspondences that will assist the audience in identifying the disciples as types of the second response to the word. In reporting the names of the Twelve, the narrator separates the first three from all the rest by indicating that Jesus supplied them with special "nicknames." James and John, the second and third disciples mentioned, are called by Jesus "Boanerges," which the narrator explains means "sons of thunder" (3:17). The first disciple listed, Simon, whose name is additionally set off from the rest grammatically,[27] is nicknamed "Peter" (Πέτρος) by Jesus, but the narrator offers no further elaboration. The explanation of the nickname will come in the parable of the Sower when the second type of ground upon which the seed is sown is described as πετρώδης (καὶ ἄλλο ἔπεσεν ἐπὶ τὸ πετρῶδες, 4:5). Simon Πέτρος, Simon the "Rock," signals the basic relationship of the disciples to the πετρώδης, the "rocky ground." Unlike Matthew and Luke, who identify the leading disciple as Simon Peter very early in their narratives, thus obscuring the correspondence between Simon's nickname and the second type of ground in the parable,[28] Mark has unfailingly and with utter consistency referred to the

---

27. Simon is in the dative case rather than the expected accusative case used for all the other names of disciples. See the discussion in E. Best, *Following Jesus: Discipleship in the Gospel of Mark* (JSNTSup 4; Sheffield: JSOT Press, 1981), 180–81.

28. Matthew uses the double name the very first time he introduces Simon Peter (Matt. 4:18), while Luke uses it in the second episode involving Simon Peter (Luke 5:8). Matthew, furthermore, does not suggest that the name was given by Jesus (Matt. 10:2). Although both Matthew and Luke refer to the second type of ground as rocky (Matthew: ἐπὶ τὰ πετρώδη; Luke: ἐπὶ τὴν πέτραν), these references, in Matt. 13:5 and Luke 8:6, respectively, appear in the text so far removed from the first instance of Simon Peter's name that any possible connection is thoroughly discouraged. For an example of commentators who see this connection in Mark but at the same time do not see it, see Rhoads and Michie, *Mark as Story,* 128.

leading disciple simply as Simon up to Mark 3:16. From 3:16 to the end of the Gospel, he is just as consistently called Πέτρος.[29] This striking change of name is then followed in close proximity by the description of the "rocky ground" in Mark 4:5, and the resulting rhetorical paronomasia, or wordplay, establishes the bond between Πέτρος and πετρώδης, the "Rock" and "rocky ground."[30]

In fashioning such a play on words, Mark has also implicitly developed a kind of etiological legend for the origin of Simon's nickname: Jesus names him "Rock" because of his hardness; he typifies hard and rocky ground, where seed has little chance of growing deep roots. For the Gospel of Mark, hardness, especially hardness of heart, signifies the rejection of Jesus' word (e.g., 3:5; 6:52; 8:17).[31] For the Gospel of Matthew, the hardness of rock suggests a different image altogether. Matthew, besides suppressing the link between Simon's nickname and the rocky ground of the parable of the Sower, counters Mark's implicit etiology with a radically different explicit etiological legend of its own, also founded on paronomasia: "And I tell you, you are Peter (Πέτρος), and on this rock (πέτρᾳ) I will build my church, and the powers of death shall not prevail against it" (Matt. 16:18). Mark's hard-hearted disciple has become in Matthew the sure foundation of the church; yet both authors establish their opposite typologies for the leading disciple by exploiting various connotations of Simon's nickname.[32]

Closing the list of the Twelve by reference to Judas's coming betrayal, as we have discussed earlier,[33] creates a double entendre in Jesus' controversy with the scribes from Jerusalem and "those near him" (οἱ παρ' αὐτοῦ) in 3:19b–30. From the standpoint of first degree narrative, knowing that one

29. The only slight exception is Mark 14:37, where both Peter and Simon appear together. The possible significance of that incidence will be discussed in the next chapter, pp. 216–17.

30. Since Simon's nickname is usually transliterated as Peter rather than translated as "Rock," this important rhetorical play on words is completely lost in English translations of the Gospel of Mark. For an ancient rhetorical discussion of the various forms and usages of paronomasia, see *Rhetorica ad Herennium* 4.21.29–32.

31. D. O. Via, in *The Ethics of Mark's Gospel*, 115–24, presents an insightful study of the "hardening of hearts" motif in Mark. For Mark, Via argues, hardness of heart is the opposite of faith: "Heart in Mark, as in the Old Testament, is the hidden inner core of the human being, and hardness of heart is its religious and moral deformation" (p. 119).

32. That Simon actually was nicknamed "Rock," whatever the name's possible origin might have been, seems quite likely from Paul's use of the Aramaic word for "rock," Cephas, as Simon's name. See 1 Cor. 1:12; 3:22; 9:5; Gal. 1:18; 2:9, 11, 14.

That Matthew develops its own etiological legend to support Peter's name might be taken as some evidence that the author of Matthew, at least, was clearly aware of the significance of the wordplay between Peter's name and the rocky ground in Mark and wished to counter it in a forthright and striking manner.

33. See chapter 7, pp. 99–101.

of Jesus' own "house" of disciples will betray him allows the audience to hear Jesus' response to the scribes concerning the inevitable fall of a house divided against itself, as a foreshadowing of the future of Jesus' disciples as well as a cogent defense against the charge of collusion with the forces of Satan. The effect of such a warning about the future of the disciples at this juncture in the story is to pave the way further for the audience's coming identification of their typical role in the parable of the Sower. From the standpoint of second degree narrative, Mark 3:19b–30 presents another example of the opposition of Jewish authorities to Jesus, and this time the scribes come from Jerusalem and attack, not his subordination of law to human welfare, but the very source of his authoritative teaching that heals. They assert that the power of Jesus' healing words comes from Satan, but Jesus rigorously denies that such a possibility even exists, for "how can Satan cast out Satan?"

In the course of his response, Jesus also refers to the issue of blasphemy; most blasphemies can be forgiven but not blasphemy against the Holy Spirit (3:28–29). The assertion is a warning to the scribes and is indeed well deserved. In the first appearance of the scribes they accused Jesus of blasphemy in their hearts (2:6–7); later, Jesus was both angered and grieved at the Pharisees' hardness of heart (3:5); now blasphemy again is the path chosen by scribes from Jerusalem. This consistent, almost monolithic, stance of the Jewish groups toward Jesus will extend throughout the Gospel to culminate in the high priest's charge of blasphemy at Jesus' trial (14:64), but in charging Jesus, the divine Son, with blasphemy they themselves commit the unforgivable blasphemy, for "whoever blasphemes against the Holy Spirit never has forgiveness, but is guilty of an eternal sin" (3:29). Jesus' dire warning of the consequences of calling evil and unholy that which is truly holy permeates the entire monolithic depiction of the Jewish authorities in the Gospel.

The second part of the controversy section, Mark 3:31–35, is connected to the first part by similarity in the groups involved. The arrival of Jesus' mother and brothers to call for him in Mark 3:31 creates the opportunity for Jesus to discuss the true nature of family. Earlier, in 3:20–21, the pressure of the demanding crowd, which prevents Jesus even from eating, draws out "those near him" (οἱ παρ᾽ αὐτοῦ), a group that may have included some of his followers as well as relatives and family, to seize him because people were saying that he was insane. The action of this group might be seen as protective rather than totally negative, but the problem is that it also represents a complete lack of confidence or understanding about Jesus. Correspondingly, there is nothing threatening or necessarily negative about the arrival of Jesus' mother and brothers "outside" where he is teaching.

The problem is that they evidently expect him to respond to traditional or customary relationships. That is, like the earlier group, who may have been attempting to rescue Jesus from the crowd, his mother and brothers have not comprehended the totally new nature of the situation. Jesus is no longer their son or brother, friend or relative, automatically by birth or custom. He is the divine Son, whose authority, his power to act, comes from God. Traditional relationships no longer apply. However, Jesus uses the occasion to define the kind of family suitable to this new age: "And looking around on those who sat about him, he said, 'Here are my mother and my brothers! Whoever does the will of God is my brother, and sister, and mother'" (3:34–35). As in the four controversy stories in Mark 2:15—3:6, old laws and customs, old relationships no longer suffice for this new moment. Jesus' family now consists of all who do the will of God. His natural family need not remain "outside" (3:31–32), for the new criterion of family membership can also include them, if they hear the word and do it. This final episode before the plot synopsis of the parable of the Sower provides the fundamental perspective needed by the audience to determine who is with Jesus and who is not, who is inside and who is outside. Traditional roles, customary relationships, established laws no longer obtain; the sole criterion of the new age is to do the will of God.

Mark 4:1–34—Parable of the Sower and Its Interpretations

Both Mark 4 and 5 are enclosed by the chiastic *inclusio* of Mark 3:7–35 and 6:1–34, but those two chapters easily divide into two major segments: 4:1–34 and 4:35—5:43. In 4:1, Jesus begins "again" to teach beside the sea. The sea reference signals the audience that another new section has begun. The material in vv. 2–34 which follows is set off by a small *inclusio* of its own formed by the varied repetitions of "many things in parables" (ἐν παραβολαῖς πολλά, 4:2) and "with many such parables" (τοιαύταις παραβολαῖς πολλαῖς, 4:33), and itself contains three units. Mark 4:35 begins a series of sea crossings, from one side to the other, that connects all four episodes in 4:35—5:43. Moreover, the two major segments, while separate, are firmly linked by the definite time notice in v. 35: "On that day, when evening had come." The incidents of the sea crossings occur on the same day as the teaching in parables; hence the rhetorical structure of the section[34] can be outlined as follows:

34. For an excellent review and comparison of the views of many other scholars on the structure or composition of this section of the Gospel of Mark, see Petersen, "The Composition of Mark 4:1—8:26," 185–217. For an analysis of the rhetorical structure of Mark 3—6 that is remarkably similar to my own, see K. Fisher and U. C. von

1. 3:7–35
2. 4:1—5:43
   a. 4:1–34—parables
      1. 4:1–2—introduction
      2. 4:3–32—teaching in parables
         a. vv. 3–9—parable of the Sower
         b. vv. 10–23—first interpretation
         c. vv. 24–32—-second interpretation
      3. 4:33–34—close
   b. 4:35—5:43—sea crossings to "other side"
      1. 4:35–41—calming the sea storm
      2. 5:1–20—healing the demoniac
      3. 5:[21–24a] 24b–34—healing of woman with flow of blood
      4. 5:21–24a, 35–43—healing of Jairus's daughter
3. 6:1–34

In addition to opening with a geographical reference to Jesus' "again" beginning to teach beside the sea, by this point a quite familiar signpost for the audience, Mark 4:1 displays rather unusual care in setting the scene for the teaching session: "And a very large crowd gathered about him, so that he got into a boat and sat in it on the sea; and the whole crowd was beside the sea on the land." Three repetitions of Jesus' link with the sea in so few words suggest that the relative positions of Jesus and the crowd are important for the audience to note. Jesus teaches from a boat on the sea and the massive crowd is by the sea on the earth ($\dot{\epsilon}\pi\grave{\iota}$ $\tau\hat{\eta}s$ $\gamma\hat{\eta}s$). It is typology, not geography or history, that stands behind this setting. In the parables that follow, those who hear the word that Jesus speaks may respond in one of the same four ways in which the four different types of earth ($\gamma\hat{\eta}$) respond to the seed sown in them. The huge crowds who listen to Jesus "on the land" are types of the parabolic "earths" about to be expounded.

Three parables about seeds and earth—the Sower (4:3–8), the Seed Growing Secretly (4:26–29), and the Mustard Seed (4:30–32)—and a number of proverbial sayings succeed this introductory stage setting. As the traditional scholarly names given to the parables suggest, most studies of them have assumed that the important, significant, or emphasized element in all of these parables is the seed. *In the context of the Gospel of Mark, however, it is not the seed but the earth that is the focus of attention.* They are not, for Mark, seed parables but earth parables, and it is multiple references to "earth" that bind them together. The pervasive tendency of form criticism to remove these parables from their Gospel contexts, separate

Wahlde, "The Miracles of Mark 4:35—5:43: Their Meaning and Function in the Gospel Framework," *Biblical Theology Bulletin* 11 (1981): 13–16.

them from one another, and try to fit them into the historical ministry of Jesus has in the past and continues in the present to obscure what Mark is doing with them.[35] For Mark, they are not simply joined by a similar theme, "seed," nor are they randomly thrown together for lack of a better place to put them in the text. They are, instead, purposely arranged to expound and then further refine the basic typology of hearing-response (sowing-earth) fundamental to the plot of the entire Gospel. And the stylized setting of Jesus on the sea with all the crowds on the earth in Mark 4:1 is the first indication of that emphasis.

Along with "earth," the vital role of hearing for the whole process is stressed by constant repetition. Forms of the verb "to hear" (ἀκούειν) appear thirteen times in Mark 4:1–34, four of these in the interpretation of the parable of the Sower (vv. 14–20) alone. Indeed, the entire teaching session begins with Jesus commanding the people to hear ('Ακούετε, 4:3)[36] and ends with the narrator commenting: "With many such parables he spoke the word to them, as they were able to hear it" (ἀκούειν, 4:33). Moreover, the proverbial saying, Let the one with ears to hear, hear (ὃς ἔχει ὦτα ἀκούειν ἀκουέτω), occurs with slight variation twice in these verses (4:9, 23) both to stress the crucial role of hearing[37] and to mark out divisions within the material. The parable of the Sower begins with the command to hear (v. 3) and ends with the first proverbial admonition (v. 9). The second proverbial warning, in 4:23, ends a unit of material providing general comment on and interpretation of the Sower, 4:10–23; the remainder of the verses,

---

35. For the long history of viewing these parables as "seed parables" see, e.g., Jeremias, *The Parables of Jesus,* 146–53; C. H. Dodd, *The Parables of the Kingdom,* rev. ed. (New York: Scribner's, 1961), 140–56; Crossan, *In Parables,* 39–52. For an interpretation of the parable of the Sower that begins to appreciate the importance of the earth, see J. D. Crossan, *Cliffs of Fall: Paradox and Polyvalence in the Parables of Jesus* (New York: Seabury Press, 1980), 25–64.

J. G. Williams's interpretations of the parables in Mark, by focusing on the seed rather than on the earth, demonstrate the difficulty of understanding Mark's use of the parables if the seed is the major element. For Williams, mysterious, esoteric, and elusive meanings result from these parables (*Gospel Against Parable,* 93–97, 156–78). Occasionally Williams himself notices the problem, as, e.g., on p. 172: "Of course, such an interpretation of the parable may seem far-fetched."

For a review of various positions on the interpretation of these parables as seed parables, see P. R. Jones, "The Seed Parables of Mark," *Review and Expositor* 75 (1978): 519–38.

36. The parable in Mark actually begins ἀκούετε ἰδοὺ ("hear, see"). The doubling of imperatives underlines the importance of what is coming as well as emphasizing the need to hear. Matthew drops the ἀκούετε, keeping only the command to "see," and Luke drops both (Matt. 13:3; Luke 8:5). English translations vary greatly on which or how many of Mark's double imperatives they translate.

37. "The point is not so much that the function of an ear is to hear . . . as that the ear does not always listen carefully and give heed. The emphasis is on listening, not on mere hearing" (E. F. F. Bishop, "'Ακούειν ἀκουέτω Mark 4:9, 23," *The Bible Translator* 7 [1956]: 39).

4:24–32, beginning with an exhortation to heed what is heard (βλέπετε τί ἀκούετε), further detail the nature of the kingdom of God, or, as the parable of the Sower symbolizes it, "the good earth." The three divisions of the teaching in parables, then, are 4:3–9, 10–23, and 24–32, and all are delineated by references to hearing.

Mark 4:3–9, 14–20

The parable of the Sower itself, beginning with a command to hear and ending with a gnomic warning to attune one's ear to hear clearly, bristles with flags to the audience indicating its importance. Moreover, if auditors miss some of the elements the first time through, the whole parable, expanded into its typological construction, is repeated (vv. 14–20) following another, even more blatant, signal of its significance: "And he *says*[38] to them, 'Do you not understand this parable? How then will you understand all the parables?'" (4:13). The parable in vv. 3–9 depicts a sower going out to sow, scattering seed on four types of earth, three of which for different reasons eventually fail, while the fourth bears fruit in a triple abundance:[39]

Hear! See! The sower went out to sow (ὁ σπείρων σπεῖραι). And it happened (ἐγένετο) as he sowed:

1) Some fell (ὃ μὲν ἔπεσεν) along the way, and birds came and devoured it;

2) and other fell (ἄλλο ἔπεσεν) on rocky ground (πετρῶδες), where it had not much earth (γῆν), and immediately (εὐθὺς) it sprang up, since it had no depth of earth (γῆς), and when the sun rose it was scorched, and since it had no root, it withered away;

---

38. Mark's use of the historic present at this moment further dramatizes Jesus' words of explanation. English translations generally do not indicate the shift to historic present.

39. A full bibliography of studies of this parable would be massive. The major classic or recent positions on the parable can be found in the following works: Jeremias, *The Parables of Jesus*, 149–51; Crossan, *Cliffs of Fall*, 25–64; R. Bultmann, "Die Interpretation von MK 4, 3–9 seit Jülicher," in *Jesus und Paulus*, ed. E. E. Ellis and E. Grässer (Göttingen: Vandenhoeck & Ruprecht, 1975), 30–34; J. Lambrecht, "Redaction and Theology in Mk. IV," in *L'Evangile selon Marc: Tradition et rédaction*, ed. M. Sabbe (Gembloux: J. Duculot, 1974), 269–307; C. F. D. Moule, "Mark 4:1–20 Yet Once More," in *Neotestamentica et Semitica: Studies in Honour of Matthew Black*, ed. E. E. Ellis and M. Wilcox (Edinburgh: T. & T. Clark, 1969), 95–113; D. Wenham, "The Interpretation of the Parable of the Sower," *NTS* 20 (1974): 299–319; Drury, "The Sower, the Vineyard, and the Place of Allegory in the Interpretation of Mark's Parables," 367–79; Boucher, *The Mysterious Parable*, 45–53; B. Gerhardson, "The Parable of the Sower and Its Interpretation," *NTS* 14 (1968): 165–93; A. N. Wilder, "The Parable of the Sower," *Semeia* 2 (1974): 134–51; P. B. Payne, "The Seeming Inconsistency of the Interpretation of the Parable of the Sower," *NTS* 26 (1980): 564–68; and idem, "The Order of Sowing and Ploughing in the Parable of the Sower," *NTS* 25 (1978): 123–29.

3) and other fell (ἄλλο ἔπεσεν) among thorns and the thorns grew up and choked it and it gave no fruit (καρπὸν);

4) and others fell (ἄλλα ἔπεσεν) into the good earth (εἰς τὴν γῆν τὴν καλὴν) and gave fruit (καρπὸν), growing up and increasing and yielding thirtyfold and sixtyfold and a hundredfold.

Let the one who has ears to hear, hear (ἀκούειν ἀκουέτω).

The careful rhetorical patterning of the parable is easy to see and even easier to hear. Each of the four situations into which the seed falls is opened with almost identical words; however, the last presents a plural seed rather than the singular seed of the other three and balances the three failures by its triple growth and result: "growing up and increasing and yielding thirty-fold and sixtyfold and a hundredfold."[40]

Having "those who were about him with the twelve" question Jesus about the parable[41] allows the author to repeat it with its typological explanation in vv. 14–20:

The sower sows the word.

1) Then these are (οὗτοι . . . εἰσιν) the ones along the way, where the word is sown,
   and when they hear (ὅταν ἀκούσωσιν)
      immediately Satan comes and takes away the word that is sown in them;

2) and these are (οὗτοί εἰσιν) the ones sown in rocky ground (πετρῶδη), who, when they hear (ὅταν ἀκούσωσιν) the word,

---

40. Since a fivefold to tenfold harvest was about normal for Palestine in the first century, a thirtyfold, sixtyfold, or hundredfold harvest suggests abundance beyond imagination. However, some scholars have argued that the numbers refer to individual ears of corn rather than to the entire harvest and hence are more normal figures for a realistic harvest. For the various sides of the debate, see Jeremias, *The Parables of Jesus,* 150–51; Crossan, *Cliffs of Fall,* 41–45; and E. Linnemann, *Jesus of the Parables,* trans. J. Sturdy (New York: Harper & Row; London: SPCK, 1966), 116–19.

Such a debate really misses the point, for what is at stake is typology, not agricultural practice. The threefold increasing result of the seed sown in good earth balances the three failures of the earlier types of ground. As with Xenophan's oracle, the audience is intended to relate this to the present story, not to farming.

41. Having the disciples ask Jesus to explain something he has said is an excellent narrative strategy to allow the Markan author to repeat and expand upon particularly important material. Presenting much the same information twice in brief compass assures that the audience will hear it clearly. Besides here in Mark 4:10, examples of this rhetorical strategy can be found at Mark 7:17; 9:28; 10:10; 13:3–4.

In Xenophon's *An Ephesian Tale,* the major elements in Apollo's summarizing oracle are repeated in prose immediately after the oracle itself by the narrator with the excuse that the parents of the couple deliberated without much insight on the meaning of those elements in the oracle (1.6.2–3). Again from the standpoint of narrative strategy, the purpose of these immediate repetitions is to fix the material in the mind of the auditor or stress its importance.

immediately with joy they receive it, and they have no root in themselves but endure for a time; when tribulation or persecution arises on account of the word, immediately they fall away (σκανδαλίζονται).

3) And others are (ἄλλοι εἰσὶν) the ones sown among thorns;
   these are the ones who hear (ἀκούσαντες) the word,
      but the cares of the world and delight in riches and desire for other things, entering into them, choke the word and it is unfruitful;

4) and those are (ἐκεῖνοί εἰσιν) the ones sown in the good earth
   who hear (ἀκούουσιν) the word
      and accept it and bear fruit thirtyfold and sixtyfold and a hundredfold.

The pattern for each kind of earth is the same throughout the Interpretation: first, the type of earth from the parable is identified; second, the requirement of hearing the word is emphasized; and finally, the result of the sown seed[42] in each type of earth is related. While the sower sows the word, the focus of the Interpretation, highlighted by the quadruple repetition of "when they hear the word," is the response to hearing rendered by each type of earth. Moreover, each type of response, each type of ground, is from the outset clearly identified as a *group of people*. The first two groups are referred to as "these" (οὗτοι), the third as "others" (ἄλλοι), and the fourth as "those" (ἐκεῖνοι). The contrast should suggest to the audience that "these" are groups nearby, recently discussed; "others" and "those" are not yet fully explicated.

Ground Along the Way

Recognizing the two groups in the story most closely related to the first two types of earth, the earth along the way and the rocky ground, ought by this point to be a reasonably easy task for the audience. The parable pictures the seed along the way or path to be eaten by birds, interpreted as Satan immediately removing the word. The seed never has a chance of entering the earth or taking root; the word is removed at once before any possible positive response can occur. Only one group of characters in the Gospel has been portrayed as utterly opposed to Jesus from the beginning. Indeed,

42. The slight grammatical problem in Mark 4:16, 18, 20 posed by the use of σπειρόμενοι (vv. 16, 18) and σπαρέντες (v. 20), which, technically speaking, identifies the groups with the seed sown rather than with the earth into which they are sown, has no chance of confusing the audience because of the clarity of the context. The seed is the word; the types of ground are groups of people, but what the author is trying to communicate is the merging of seed and ground or sown seed. See Payne, "The Seeming Inconsistency of the Interpretation of the Parable of the Sower," 568.

already in the early stages of his ministry they have hardened their hearts and begun to plot together on how to destroy him. These, the ones along the way, are the scribes, the Pharisees, the Herodians, and the Jerusalem Jews. From their first appearance in the story to their last, they oppose Jesus and they calumniate his powerful word as blasphemy. For them, to hear is to disaffirm. Such a response, as the Interpretation indicates, can only arise from the work of Satan. Far from Jesus being in collusion with Satan, as the scribes alleged (3:22), they themselves are Satan's feeding ground, the hard earth which the seed cannot enter.

Rocky Ground

Because there is a little earth covering the rock, the seed springs up immediately in rocky ground, but since the rock blocks the growth of roots, when the sun comes up the plant quickly withers. This action constitutes a considerably more complex response than any of the others, and in both the parable and the Interpretation the space devoted to detailing the problem is greater than for any of the other types of ground. The Interpretation defines "these" sown in rocky ground as people who respond immediately to hearing the word but have no ability to last. For a season ($\pi\rho\acute{o}\sigma\kappa\alpha\iota\rho\sigma\varsigma$, v. 17) they remain committed, but as soon as difficulty or persecution arises because of the word, they collapse. So far in the narrative only two groups have been depicted as accepting or believing immediately in Jesus' performative word: the disciples and those healed. The call of the four disciples in Mark 1:16–20, liberally sprinkled with $\epsilon\vartheta\vartheta\grave{v}\varsigma$, emphasizes the sudden and complete response of Simon, Andrew, James, and John. The first two "immediately" follow Jesus, and the latter two are in such a hurry that they desert their father in the boat (1:20).[43] They "immediately" respond. On the other hand, the wordplay on Peter's name, the indication of Judas's coming betrayal, and the ominous—to the audience—discussion by Jesus of the ultimate failure of divided houses (3:16–26), all strongly nominate the disciples as the group representing "these" sown in rocky ground.

The succeeding chapters of the Gospel of Mark will quickly and thoroughly remove any possible doubt about the disciples' election to that ignominious status, as we shall discuss in detail in the next chapter. For now, it is sufficient to note that the disciples do, in fact, fail Jesus at precisely the moment his persecutions in Jerusalem begin (see 14:43–50). Furthermore, Jesus predicts their failure (and they deny it) in language echoing the Interpretation: "And Jesus said to them, 'You will all fall away ($\sigma\kappa\alpha\nu\delta\alpha\lambda\iota\sigma\vartheta\acute{\eta}\sigma\epsilon\sigma\vartheta\epsilon$). . . .' Peter said to him, 'Even though they all fall away ($\sigma\kappa\alpha\nu\delta\alpha\lambda\iota\sigma\vartheta\acute{\eta}\sigma\sigma\nu\tau\alpha\iota$), I will not'" (14:27, 29). The Interpretation of the

43. James and John $\dot{\alpha}\phi\acute{\epsilon}\nu\tau\epsilon\varsigma$ $\tau\grave{o}\nu$ $\pi\alpha\tau\acute{\epsilon}\rho\alpha$ (Mark 1:20) in order to follow Jesus. In a sadly ironic twist, that action is also precisely what they and the other disciples do to Jesus during the arrest: deserting him ($\dot{\alpha}\phi\acute{\epsilon}\nu\tau\epsilon\varsigma$ $\alpha\dot{v}\tau\grave{o}\nu$), they all fled (14:50).

parable of the Sower foretells that "when tribulation or persecution arises on account of the word, immediately they fall away (σκανδαλίζονται)" (4:17). All too painfully like sheep, the disciples in Mark are quick to join and just as quick to flee, betray, and deny when danger threatens.

For a modern reader of the Gospel, influenced by centuries of Christian piety, the use of the disciples, and particularly Peter the "Rock," to typify fickle, "fair-weather friends" may seem an unbelievable abuse and for that reason an impossible identification for the second kind of ground. If it were equally impossible, or at least implausible, to the authorial audience, our understanding of the parable of the Sower as a plot synopsis would be seriously compromised, since the Markan portrayal of the disciples fits the pattern of the rocky ground so well. However, although Matthew and Luke construct considerably stronger pictures of the disciples than Mark,[44] one other very early New Testament witness stands strikingly close to Mark's portrait: Paul. Indeed, Paul, in writing and evidently in person before Christians in Antioch, denounced Peter as a hypocrite (Gal. 2:11–14). Paul relates to the Galatians the agreement he reached with those "of repute" in Jerusalem, including Peter (Gal. 2:6), concerning the full status of uncircumcised Gentile Christians within the movement. Later, Peter visited Antioch and ate with Gentile Christians openly until a group from James arrived whom, Paul says, Peter feared (Gal. 2:12). Then Peter withdrew from his Gentile Christian brothers and refused to eat with them, thus infuriating Paul, who condemned Peter to his face for such dishonesty. Paul's view of Peter in this instance, reported to the Galatians and possibly shared by many in Antioch, could hardly be categorized as respectful, much less adulatory. Peter is portrayed by Paul to be all too willing to let his principles fluctuate with his audience. Whether or not such a description is historically accurate or even fair is completely irrelevant. All that matters for our purposes is that Paul's statements to the Galatians confirm the possibility of adopting a negative or at least unimpressed opinion concerning those "of repute" in Jerusalem and especially Peter.[45] Nor is it

44. While Matthew and Luke do present more positive portrayals of the disciples than Mark, this issue may be one place in which reading the three synoptics together tends to distort Matthew and Luke. Both Matthew and Luke show the disciples during the ministry of Jesus to be flawed in understanding. For Matthew, the disciples are learners who do not fully understand who Jesus is until the resurrection, at which point they finally qualify as teachers (see Matt. 28:18–20). For Luke, even after the resurrection the disciples need special teaching by Jesus *and* the descent of the Holy Spirit at Pentecost before their faith is complete and firm (see Luke 24:25–27, 44–49; Acts 1:3; 2:1–5). Mark's view of the disciples is so negative that Matthew's and Luke's descriptions seem positive by comparison. However, if they are read on their own, neither Matthew nor Luke establishes the disciples as insightful followers or faithful models of Christian discipleship during Jesus' ministry.

45. In referring to the Jerusalem leaders he spoke with, Paul describes them as "those who were reputed to be something," and then he continues in an aside, "What

necessary, moreover, to argue that Paul *directly* influenced Mark or Mark's authorial audience; rather, Paul's evidence makes plausible the claim that there were some within the Christian community who would have had no compunction about identifying the disciples with "these" sown on rocky ground.[46]

Thorny Ground

Hence, by Mark 4, the authorial audience should have no great difficulty in recognizing the character groups who illustrate the first two possible responses in the hearing-response typology:

Parable of Sower		*Interpretation*		*Gospel Group*
1. seed sown along the way; eaten by birds	=	these in whom the word is immediately removed by Satan	=	scribes, Pharisees, Jerusalem Jewish leaders
2. seed sown in rocky ground; comes up quickly but has no root; withers with the sun	=	these who accept the word immediately; endure for a time, but fall away when tribulation or persecution comes	=	disciples, especially Peter, James, and John

But what of the third unfruitful ground, the "others" in whom the word is sown among thorns or weeds? As the initial "others" (ἄλλοι) suggests, this group has not yet made an appearance in the Gospel, but its characteristics are quite clear. Unlike either of the first two groups, the ground here is actually fertile, and there is a possibility of growth and fruit. The problem is that too many noxious plants are already growing in the ground, and they choke out the seed, rendering it unfruitful. The Interpretation defines these noxious growths as "the cares of the world, and the delight in riches, and the desire for other things" (4:19). That the implied author has not introduced this group in the chapters preceding the parable of the Sower and, in fact, only presents a few illustrations of the type throughout the first major

---

they were makes no difference to me; God shows no partiality" (Gal. 2:6). For an insightful discussion of Paul's understanding of God's impartiality, see D. Patte, *Paul's Faith and the Power of the Gospel* (Philadelphia: Fortress Press, 1983), 128–47, 169–89.

46. The *Epistle of Barnabas* suggests a continuation of a somewhat negative view of the disciples to later periods, now integrated into Christian piety: "But when He chose His own apostles who were to preach His Gospel, [He did so from among those] who were sinners above all sin, that He might show He came 'not to call the righteous, but sinners to repentance'" (5:9).

Luke presents a much more harmonious version of the Jerusalem conference between Paul and Peter and their later interactions (Acts 15) than Paul's own account in Galatians suggests. Consequently, in Luke's version, Peter appears in a much better light than Paul portrays him to the Galatians.

division of the Gospel which the parable of the Sower summarizes, may indicate that the response was not overly interesting or relevant to the author or, one assumes, the authorial audience, but since it did constitute one possible response to the word, it needed to be depicted, if only minimally.

The most conspicuous example of this type is the meeting between Jesus and the rich man in Mark 10:17–22. The episode is remarkable for the degree to which it matches the parabolic type. The rich man runs up to Jesus, kneels, and asks, "What must I do to inherit eternal life?" Jesus queries him on his life up to this point and learns that he has observed all the commandments from his youth. The man obviously represents fertile ground: he recognizes Jesus' authority; he wants to learn; and he has already established his religious zeal by his obedience to the law. In an extraordinary phrase, the narrator notes that "Jesus looking upon him loved him." Jesus responds to the quality of the man; surely, he is the "good earth." Moreover, Jesus formally calls the man to follow him, as he did with Simon, Andrew, James, and John earlier, but, first, the man must sell what he owns and give it to the poor. Yet this act he cannot do: "At that saying his countenance fell, and he went away sorrowful; for he had great possessions." The rich man typifies fertile ground in which the seed is sown but no fruit can be produced, for growth of the word is choked off by "the delight in riches."

In a less pronounced but rather fascinating way, one other episode appears to be molded around this same typology: the death of John the Baptist in the court of Herod in Mark 6:14–29. Both the bizarre nature of the story and its position as a break in the formal chiastic pattern established by Mark 3:7–35 and 6:1–34 set it apart for special attention. With its transition from the preceding episode concerning the Twelve provided by the motif of Jesus' name becoming known (6:14) and its closing reference to the burial of John by his disciples (6:29), the passage relates both to the increasing spread of Jesus' fame and the coming failure of Jesus' own disciples. Yet it is the interaction between Herod and John that illustrates the thorny ground response. Herod had John arrested because of John's denunciation of his marriage to Herodias, Philip's wife (6:17–18).[47] Herodias wanted to kill John, but Herod "feared John, knowing that he was a righteous and holy man, and kept him safe" (6:20). The narrator then characterizes the relationship that developed between the two men in a brief *inclusio* formed by the verb "to hear": *When he heard* (ἀκούσας) him, he was much perplexed but gladly did him *he hear* (ἤκουεν). While he did not

---

47. That Herod did indeed kill John the Baptist is supported by Josephus. Although Josephus reports John's criticism of Herodias, he indicates that Herod killed him because he feared John would lead a popular insurrection, not because he received a request from Herodias's daughter after her dance. See *Antiquities* 18.5.2.

necessarily understand John, Herod recognized his righteousness, kept him safe, and heard him gladly.

So the situation remained until the fatal birthday banquet.[48] Besides supplying marvelous material for innumerable paintings, dances, operas, and plays, the dance of Herod's daughter and her request, at her mother's prompting, for the head of John the Baptist is a scene that would be completely at home in Xenophon's *An Ephesian Tale* or Chariton's *Chaereas and Callirhoe*. Because of her splendid dancing, the king before all his assembled guests swears an oath to give her whatever she wants, "even half of my kingdom" (6:23). At Herodias's instigation, the girl asks for the head of John the Baptist. The narrator reports Herod's response: "And the king was exceedingly sorry; but because of his oaths and his guests he did not want to break his word to her" (6:26). Like the rich man, Herod is very sorry about what he is asked to do; also like the rich man, Herod is prevented from acting on his better instincts by his concern for other things—in this case, his reputation and word before his guests. Herod is not portrayed as either evil or weak. He has been protecting John and even hearing him gladly, but the word sown in him cannot grow or produce fruit, for "the cares of the world . . . and the desire for other things, enter in and choke the word" (4:19). Herod values his position, his reputation, and his oath more highly than what he has been hearing gladly. Riches, worldly power, and concern about the regard of others are all noxious weeds that kill the word. Consequently, both Herod the ruler in Mark 6:14–29, within the same overall rhetorical unit as the parable of the Sower, and the rich man of 10:17–22 illustrate the fatal effect of worldly power and wealth on the word and fill out the third response in the typology of the parable of the Sower:

	Parable of Sower		*Interpretation*		*Gospel Group*
3.	seed sown among thorns; choke it and it produces no fruit	=	others in whom the word is choked by cares of the world, delight in riches, desire for other things	=	Herod; rich man of 10:17–22

Value of Failure

That three out of four responses to the word, taking up the vast majority of both the parable of the Sower and its Interpretation, detail failure strongly suggests that what interests Mark and Mark's authorial audience most is why the word does not bear fruit. In our modern context, we most often want to know how to succeed or why someone has become a success,

48. For a very interesting treatment of this material, see R. Girard, "Scandal and the Dance: Salome in the Gospel of Mark," *New Literary History* 15 (1984): 311–24.

perhaps in order to imitate that pattern. We assume that success is somewhat unnatural and must be won by purposeful effort and a bit of luck.
However, for the Gospel of Mark, seed planted in the earth *should* produce
fruit; success is the natural, expected result. Why some seed does not grow
requires explanation, reflection, and illustration.[49] To employ the image
the parable furnishes, a farmer sowing seed expects it to grow; when it does
not, the farmer wants to know why. Not only are most of the parable of the
Sower and its Interpretation given over to failure, in illustrating the typology, most of the Gospel is as well. Yet, constructing symbolic groups to act
out each of the types permits the author to probe the human faults that may
lie behind each unfruitful response. Such a process is, indeed, the whole
point of typological or figurative narrative. An audience sees a universal
principle with a human mask but in so doing is encouraged to perceive that
same principle in the real faces around it.

By Mark 4, or very soon thereafter, the authorial audience should not
only understand the fundamental typology of hearing-response but also be
well able to identify the groups in the Gospel that illustrate each type. The
audience's questions then become *how* each group typifies the response and
why it does. As the characters interact and the plot moves toward its inevitable climax, the audience can begin to understand the "fatal flaws" that
propel the scribes and the Pharisees, the disciples, Herod, and the rich man
to their various unproductive ends. Such an effect on the audience might
well be described as a popularized, diminished form of catharsis, the clarification of the pitiable and fearful experiences of failure to bear fruit.[50] Since
the typology is a *universal* pattern of response, it precedes Jesus (as the
Herod–John the Baptist episode illustrates) and—a crucial point for the
audience—it succeeds him as well. The same possible responses of failure
tempt the authorial audience hearing the word as affect the characters in the
story. This overall effect of typological narrative on its hearers is an issue to
which we must return in the final chapter of our study.

---

49. Crossan, noting the discrepancy between the detailed descriptions of failure and
the rapid, generalized presentation of success in the parable of the Sower, relates it to
the fact that it is easy to say why something fails but not so easy to say why it succeeds
(see *Cliffs of Fall,* 50–51). I am pointing to the same discrepancy but explain it in the
context of Mark's narrative somewhat differently.

50. For Aristotle, the catharsis of pity and fear was the desired effect of tragedy on
an audience (see *Poetics* 1449b). That catharsis was an intellectual experience, a mental
clarification, rather than an emotional purging seems strongly indicated by Aristotle's
entire discussion. See the insightful analysis in L. Golden and O. B. Hardison,
Aristotle's Poetics: A Translation and Commentary for Students of Literature (Englewood
Cliffs, N.J.: Prentice-Hall, 1968), 114–20, 133–37.

I am not claiming tragic catharsis for the Gospel of Mark; I am suggesting only that
the effect on the audience of seeing these types of failure played out in narrative form
might be described as a kind of mini-catharsis or diluted catharsis, suitable to popular
consumption. The Gospel of Mark is not high tragedy.

Mark 4:10–12, 21–23

Before we discuss the nature of the good earth, which is developed and refined further in the second unit of interpretational material following the parable of the Sower, Mark 4:24–32, we need to comment briefly on the verses in the first unit that surround the Interpretation itself, Mark 4:10–12 and 21–23. Verses 10–12 have probably elicited more scholarly debate than any two similar verses in all of the New Testament.[51] The problem is that the verses suggest that Jesus is teaching in parables *so that* "those outside" will not understand what he is saying: "And he said to them [those about him with the Twelve], 'To you has been given the secret of the kingdom of God, but for those outside everything is in parables; so that (ἵνα) they may indeed see but not perceive, and may indeed hear but not understand; lest they should turn again and be forgiven" (4:11–12). Since our concern is how this material is understood within the context of the Gospel and not whether or not the historical Jesus may have said it, we are relieved of much of the scholarly debate. Nevertheless, a literary analysis of these verses within their specific context reveals several important points: (1) Those outside (ἐκείνοις . . . τοῖς ἔξω) should not be identified with the crowd to whom Jesus is speaking, for in the immediately preceding episode "those outside" denoted Jesus' natural family, while those inside were his new family, people who do the will of God (3:31–35). "Those outside" in 4:11, then, corresponds to that class of people who, for whatever reasons, do *not* do the will of God. (2) The "you" to whom the mystery of the kingdom of God is given are not solely the Twelve, for "those who were about him with the twelve" indicates a considerably larger group.[52] Thus the division between those who are given the mystery, the insiders, and those who hear riddles, the outsiders, is not a simple opposition of disciples versus crowds; instead, it is an opposition of categories: those who do the will of God and those who do not, those who have ears to hear and those who have not. The same parable will be heard differently by these two groups, for outsiders *will not* understand, *because they are outsiders,* and insiders *will* understand, *because they are insiders.* The parables, like Jesus' healing and preaching ministry in general, do not force people outside or pull people inside; they

---

51. See, e.g., Jeremias, *The Parables of Jesus,* 12–18. For a review of various positions on these verses, see C. Evans, "The Function of Isaiah 6:9–10 in Mark and John," *Novum Testamentum* 24 (1982): 124–38; and S. Brown, "'The Secret of the Kingdom of God' (Mark 4:11)," *JBL* 92 (1973): 60–74.

52. Since the aim of figurative narrative is to communicate its general or universal points with only some covering of verisimilitude, the guiding concern is always the illustration of principles, not the depiction of "realistic" action. Consequently, Mark's authorial audience would have been very little bothered by the shift of Jesus from the crowds (Mark 4:1) to a session alone with followers (4:10) and evidently back to the crowds again at some point (4:33–34), as some modern scholars have been. The problem is neither "sources" nor history but typology.

simply reveal the type of ground already present. (3) Since the audience of the Gospel, from their privileged position of first degree narrative, not only perceive the parables as unconfusing but, even more, understand them as guides for appreciating the entire plot, Jesus' comment designates the audience as the greatest insider of all. Whatever the characters in the second degree narrative may or may not be portrayed as realizing, the audience stands with the narrator (and Jesus) in full knowledge of the implications of the parables. (4) Although the insiders do not hear riddles, they are still faced with a mystery. The kingdom of God is a secret, but a secret that cannot be hidden. Mark 4:10–12 is balanced by 4:21–22: "Is a lamp brought in to be put under a bushel, or under a bed, and not on a stand? For there is nothing hid, except to be made manifest; nor is anything secret, except to come to light." The secret of the kingdom of God, given to insiders who do the will of God, can remain a secret only for a brief time, for nothing is "secret except to come to light." Neither Jesus himself, nor his powerful healing word, nor those of the good earth who bear fruit can remain secret or be hidden, for secrecy is only for the purpose of bringing to light. All the apparent secrets in the Gospel—Jesus' identity, his healing miracles, his control over evil spirits—have as their goal the revelation of the kingdom, but only those with the ears to hear it will hear it.

The Good Earth and Mark 4:24–32

The kingdom of God is a mystery ($\tau\grave{o}$ $\mu\nu\sigma\tau\acute{\eta}\rho\iota o\nu$, 4:11), and as such, it cannot be defined or explained in propositional language. It can, however, be illustrated by comparison with actions more commonly experienced, like the growth of seeds in the earth. The fourth response of the parable of the Sower is that of productive, good earth. The good earth that produces a triple abundance are those "who hear the word and accept it and bear fruit" (4:20). By employing two more parables about seeds and earth, the second interpretational unit following the parable of the Sower, 4:24–32, provides an imagistic clarification of this productive good earth, which is, indeed, the kingdom of God for the Gospel of Mark. The first image, the parable of the Seed Growing Secretly (vv. 26–29), which might be better titled the parable of the Earth Producing of Itself, depicts a sower scattering seed upon the ground and sleeping and waking, night and day. The seed meanwhile sprouts and grows, "he knows not how. The earth produces of itself ($\alpha\grave{v}\tau o\mu\acute{\alpha}\tau\eta$), first the blade, then the ear, then the full grain in the ear" (4:27–28). Productive earth, the good earth, produces on its own, as the repetitions of seed ($\sigma\pi\acute{o}\rho o\varsigma$, vv. 26 and 27) and earth ($\gamma\hat{\eta}$, vv. 26 and 28) emphasize. The sower does not dominate the production and does not make it happen; the sower only sows and goes about life, while the earth brings forth the harvest out of itself. Furthermore, the sower does not know *how* the earth accomplishes this act, only *that* it does, and knowing how is of little value when the aim is to harvest ripened grain (v. 29). How some people, upon hearing the word, can accept it and bring forth fruit is unknown. They produce the yield out of themselves because of who they are, and it is precisely by bearing fruit that their membership in the good earth type is demonstrated.

The second image, the parable of the Mustard Seed (4:30–32), which might be better called the parable of the Transforming Earth, tells of the smallest seed which becomes the greatest shrub. The emphasis of this parable, too, can be determined by its repetitions: It is like a grain of mustard, which, *when sown upon the earth* (ὅταν σπαρῇ ἐπὶ τῆς γῆς), is the smallest of all the seeds *upon the earth* (ἐπὶ τῆς γῆς), but *when sown* (ὅταν σπαρῇ), it grows up and becomes the greatest of all shrubs. The repetitions of "earth" and "when sown" stress the vital factors that transform the smallest seed into the largest shrub. How does the mustard seed become the bushy refuge of the birds of heaven? *By being sown in the earth.* The power of the earth makes the difference. The parable, as Mark is using it, is neither about the small beginning nor the large ending,[53] but rather it underscores the *cause* of the amazing transfiguration, the earth itself. Like the thirtyfold, sixtyfold, and hundredfold abundance of the seeds sown in the good earth of the parable of the Sower, the tiny mustard seed is metamorphosed into the great bush by the creative power of the earth. Such powerful earth is the kingdom of God, and those who hear the word, accept it, and bear fruit are its human manifestations. They are the ground of God. Jesus, in preaching the word, does not create them or convert them; he *reveals* them. Those who hear his word, accept it, and bear incredible, amazing fruit show themselves to be God's good earth:

Parable the Sower		Interpretation		Second Interpretation		Gospel Group
4. seed sown on good earth brings forth grain in triple abundance	=	those who hear the word, accept it, and bear fruit in triple abundance	=	—earth produces of itself, we know know not how —earth can transform small seed into great plant —such earth is the kingdom of God	=	?

The proverbial sayings that open this small unit also become clear in the context of the parable of the Sower: Heed what you hear; by the measure

---

53. Most interpretations of the parable of the Mustard Seed have emphasized one end or the other of the process, not the cause of the growth. See, e.g., Dodd, *The Parables of the Kingdom,* 140–56; and Jeremias, *The Parables of Jesus,* 146–53.

you measure, it will be measured to you, and even more will be given to you, for whoever has will be given more and whoever has not, even what he or she has will be taken away (4:24–25). Hearing the word is the crucial moment of revelation, and then how one responds to that hearing determines the result. Those who are the good earth and respond with acceptance will bear fruit in profusion—whoever has will be given more. Those who fail to hear the word or to respond to the seed that has been sown in them will be infertile—whoever has not, even what he or she has will be taken away. The good earth, because it is already good before the seed is sown, is able to transform the seed to glorious benefit; the unproductive earth, because it is already bad before the seed is sown, allows it to be taken away, wither, or be choked out. The consequent loss is great, and if it is recognized at all, it brings sadness (e.g., 6:26; 10:22; 14:72).

The seed itself does not create good or bad earth; although we can describe some of the traits and observe the end results, why some earth is productive and some not we ultimately do not know (cf. 4:27). For the Gospel of Mark, it is simply the hard and painful truth that some people are in essence good and others are not. Those who are reveal their affiliation with God's good earth by the abundant fruit they bear; those who are far from God's kingdom risk becoming prey to Satan in their hard-hearted unfruitfulness. The seed, the word Jesus preaches, acts as the necessary catalyst to the process of transformation, but it can elicit growth only from good ground. Jesus does not bring the kingdom of God, for the good earth already exists, at least in potential, just as the unproductive earth, Satan's feeding ground, already exists. Hearing Jesus' performative word releases that potential into powerful, transforming activity. The seed and the good earth, the two necessary elements, must combine to bring the kingdom in power. Either element without the other remains dormant. Hence, the sowing-earth or hearing-response typology, as the Gospel of Mark defines it, is a *typology of disclosure and interaction* rather than conversion and dominance. But sowing the word not only uncovers the good earth, it also exposes the bad: righteous, law-abiding Jews plot murder, and hard-working fishermen desert and deny their teacher. Satan's ground as well as God's ground is revealed in the hearing of the word. If the kingdom comes in power through the fusion of the word and the good earth, the forces of evil are similarly aroused to oppose it.

Mark 4:1–34 supplies the audience with the fundamental typology of hearing-response that organizes the entire plot of the Gospel. However, the parable of the Sower (or, better, the parable of the Four Types of Earth) and its two following sections of interpretational material do more than provide a general plot synopsis; they also develop in imagistic or symbolic terms a theological vision of the world and Jesus' mission in it. The earth is divided between Satan's realm and God's, but those who are of God's kingdom are unaware of their position and are, consequently, often controlled unnecessarily by the forces of Satan. Jesus' task is to sow the good news throughout the nations, and that good news is the announcement that the kingdom of God has already come (Mark 1:15). Those who hear this gospel and believe it reveal themselves to be part of the kingdom and, further, are transformed by such a disclosure into producing abundant fruit. While Mark 4:1–34 reflects this theological vision in the symbolic or parabolic categories of nature, such as sown seed and productive or unproductive earth, the purpose of the Gospel narrative as a whole is to portray it in human form. What human traits or characteristics accompany each typical group? What are their flaws or strengths? Mark 4:35—5:43 begins to answer such questions by initiating the basic emotional opposition that divides those illustrating the good earth from those of the unproductive earths, faith versus fear, and in so doing, this material also identifies the Gospel group typifying the good earth.

Mark 4:35—5:43—Faith or Fear

The function of a plot synopsis, or prooemium, in Greek literature was primarily to orient the audience to the material that *followed* the synopsis. In Mark, we have seen that the episodes leading up to the parable of the Sower establish basic patterns and themes that aid the audience in identifying the Gospel groups typifying each kind of response to the word, but even so, for Mark as well, the primary focus of the plot synopsis is on the material following it. From Mark 4:35 through the remainder of the Gospel, but especially for the rest of Division One, the audience's perception of each succeeding episode is structured by the hearing-response typology developed by the parable of the Sower. As the material immediately after the parables section, Mark 4:35—5:43 is sharply illuminated by this orienting perspective. Moreover, the narrator stresses the link between the two sections by the use of an uncharacteristically definite time reference: "On that day, when evening had come" (4:35).

Three of the four episodes in Mark 4:35—5:43, the stilling of the storm (4:35–41), the healing of the demoniac (5:1–20), and the healing of Jairus's daughter (5:21–24a, 35–43), are explicitly connected to one another by references to crossing the sea from one side to the other (4:35–36; 5:1, 18, 21). The fourth episode, the healing of the woman (5:24b–34), is related to the group by a common Markan narrative technique called "intercalation" or "insertion".[54] The story of Jairus's request for his

---

54. For a catalogue of Markan insertions, see J. R. Donahue, *Are You the Christ? The Trial Narrative in the Gospel of Mark* (SBLDS 10; Missoula, Mont.: Scholars Press,

daughter's healing is begun, and then into the midst of it a separate healing story is inserted before Jairus's episode is concluded. Hence all four of these stories are carefully joined to one another. Although all the stories relate miracles, the first is a nature miracle involving the interaction of Jesus and the disciples, while the others are healing miracles initiated by people seeking Jesus' help in much the same pattern observed in the four healing episodes of Mark 1:21—2:12. Unlike those earlier healings, however, the three episodes in Mark 5 provide considerably more information about the people who come and about the circumstances of the healings themselves. Such detail, besides carrying a certain entertainment value after the serious teachings of the parables, also draws the audience's attention to these stories individually in a way not evident before. In our discussion of the audience's possible identification of the group illustrating the rocky ground response, we noted that only two groups in the Gospel had been portrayed as responding immediately and positively to Jesus prior to Mark 4, the disciples and the people healed. These four episodes, by contrasting the disciples to three people seeking healing, distinguish the rocky ground from the good earth and the human response of fear from the healing one of faith.[55]

Yet the disciples appear to enter the contest with a clear advantage, for the narrator reports at the close of the parables section that "privately to his own disciples he explained everything (πάντα)" (4:34b). Earlier in the parables section, having the disciples and others question Jesus privately about the parable of the Sower permitted the author to repeat the parable, expanded into its typology, for the benefit of the audience's memory (4:10–20). Since this ending allusion to private teaching bestows no similar functional benefit, its importance must reside in the information it conveys: Jesus has just explained *all* to the disciples. They have evidently been supplied with a private teaching that should raise their level of knowledge much above other second degree characters not privy to such instruction, or at least so the narrator implies to the audience. Consequently, the subsequent behavior of the disciples will be judged by the audience in the light of this advanced preparation.

The episode of Jesus and the disciples crossing the sea in a storm (4:35–41) is relatively brief. Since the narrator describes the general situation, the dramatic emphasis in the story falls on the direct discourse exchange between the disciples and Jesus. They are in a boat with other boats around,

---

1973), 58–63. For a discussion of the effects of intercalation in Mark, see Kermode, *The Genesis of Secrecy*, 133–40.

55. For an insightful discussion of fear versus faith in the Gospel of Mark that bears strong similarities to the position I am developing, see Robinson, *The Problem of History in Mark and Other Markan Studies*, 116–26.

when a storm arises. Jesus sleeps as the storm waves begin to fill the boat with water, until the disciples call him, "Teacher, do you not care if we perish?" Jesus awakes, rebukes the wind, and tells the sea to be silent. After the elements of nature obey his commands, he turns to the disciples and says, "Why are you afraid? Have you no faith?" Jesus has presented in these two questions the two basic alternatives for human response to the word: fear or faith. Fear comes from lack of faith, but faith can drive out fear. The disciples do not directly answer Jesus, but the narrator reports their reaction in a remarkably damning phrase: and they feared a great fear (ἐφοβήθησαν φόβον μέγαν).[56] In the context of Jesus' question, "fearing a great fear" is not an attitude of worshipful adoration or awe but an admission of faithlessness. They must ask one another, "Who then is this, that even wind and sea obey him?" (4:41). Since the audience was informed immediately prior to this episode that Jesus had explained everything to the disciples, their evidently utter incomprehension at Jesus' authority seems all the more damaging. Such fear and lack of understanding from those who have had greater opportunities to hear Jesus' powerful words and see their amazing results than any other group confirm the hardness beneath the accepting surface of the disciples. They are rocky ground. But if Jesus' disciples do not constitute the good earth, who does?

The abundant triple yield of the good earth in the parable of the Sower is now matched by a series of three healings, more difficult than any Jesus has attempted before and thus more remarkable in their thorough success: the healing of a man with many demons, the healing of a woman without even his conscious assent, and the raising of a child from death. Yet, with these healings as with ones earlier in the narrative, Jesus is passive; those desiring healing must initiate the action, come to him, entreat him, and believe in his powerful word. As the seed must be sown in the earth to produce fruit, so healing is also the result of an interaction between the one healed and Jesus. Jesus does not dominate the event as much as participate in it. The first of the three, the healing of the demoniac (5:1–20), like the story of the death of John the Baptist at Herod's court, is full of entertaining and rather bizarre details. While developing a serious theme, it also adds a touch of lightness to the narrative which effectively relieves some of the tension and somberness of the preceding teaching section.[57]

56. The RSV translates this Greek phrase reasonably, but perhaps a little too kindly, as "they were filled with awe." The Greek phrase and a literal translation of it may lack elegance but certainly demonstrate the dramatic emphasis given to *fear*.

57. For an interesting structural analysis of this story that emphasizes a number of its literary features, see J. Starobinski, "The Gerasene Demoniac: Literary Analysis of MK 5:1–20," *New Literary History* 4 (1973): 331–56; also F.-J. Leenhardt, "An Exegetical Essay: Mark 5:1–20: 'The Madman Reveals the Final Truth' (M. Foucault)," in *Structural Analysis and Biblical Exegesis: Interpretational Essays,* by R. Barthes, F.

The possessed man's horrible condition is described in grisly detail for three verses (5:3–5), painting an unmistakable picture of someone completely out of control. Yet this man whom no one had the strength to subdue, who roamed day and night among the tombs crying out and hitting himself with stones, "when he saw Jesus from afar, he ran and worshiped him" (5:6). That immediate, positive recognition of Jesus' authority by the possessed man is followed by a conversation between Jesus and the demons inhabiting the man. As with the demons Jesus has exorcised previously, these too know and name him and respect his power over them: "What have you to do with me, Jesus, Son of the Most High God? I adjure you by God, do not torment me" (5:7). The words of the possessed man, besides heightening the drama of the situation, also serve to remind the audience of Jesus' identity and his confident authority over the cosmic realm. The name of the demon is Legion, "for we are many," and it begs Jesus not to send it (them) away but to allow it to enter a nearby herd of two thousand swine, which is not, as it turns out, a particularly good idea. Jesus grants the request, and the demon leaves the man for the swine, who react to this invasion by running into the sea and drowning themselves. The herdsmen, having watched their maddened swine drown, flee into the town to tell what has happened. The humor in the story is thoroughly evident, and it compares well with similar miraculous escapes in the ancient erotic novels.

The more serious aspect of the story concerns the differing responses to Jesus of the man healed and the townspeople who come out to see what has happened. The people, when they see the former demoniac, clothed and in his right mind, *are afraid* (καὶ ἐφοβήθησαν, 5:15) and beg Jesus to leave, thus forestalling any further healing or powerful act he might do for them. The man, on the other hand, begs Jesus to let him "be with him" (μετ' αὐτοῦ). Jesus refuses the request and instead commands the man to go to his own land and his own people and "tell them how much the Lord has done" for him (5:19). The narrator reports that the man went and preached (κηρύσσειν) in the Decapolis what Jesus had done for him, and everyone was amazed. The healed man clearly produces abundant fruit for everyone to see; he is an example of the good earth that yields a rich harvest.

Moreover, the man's request and Jesus' reply manifest an interesting contrast with former situations in the Gospel. Prior to this episode, Jesus has usually charged those he heals with silence, as he did the leper in Mark 1:44–45. Here, surprisingly, he commands the healed man to go and tell. Of course, the all-pervasive, harassing crowd has been left behind (4:36), so

Bovon, F.-J. Leenhardt, R. Martin-Achard, and J. Starobinski, trans. A. Johnson (Pittsburgh: Pickwick Press, 1974), 85–109.

Jesus need have no immediate concern about attracting more attention, but that explanation alone for this shift in behavior is not sufficient. When Jesus called the Twelve in Mark 3:13–19a, he appointed them "to be with him (μετ᾽ αὐτοῦ), and to be sent out to preach (κηρύσσειν) and have authority to cast out demons" (3:14–15). Now a man whose demons have been cast out is refused permission "to be with him" but is directed to go and preach. The instruction to go (ὕπαγε) is a characteristic feature of healings (e.g., 1:44; 2:11; 5:19, 34; 7:29; 10:52) both before and after this one. In the story of the demoniac, however, its opposite action is presented, "to be with him." The disciples were appointed to be with Jesus and to preach and cast out demons. Since the former demoniac is also commissioned by Jesus to preach, being with Jesus is not a requirement for preaching, nor is it for casting out demons, as a later episode will illustrate (9:38–40). Why are the disciples allowed "to be with him," while the ones healed are generally commanded to "go"? The typology of the seed sown in good ground suggests an answer. In the parable of the Earth Producing Of Itself (4:26–29), the seed planted in the good earth of the kingdom of God *produced of itself without the constant nurture or attention of the farmer;* the farmer needed only to sow the seed and then the earth grew the ripened fruit which the farmer could harvest. Analogously, those of the good earth who hear the word, accept it, and bear fruit do not require the further nurture or care of Jesus; once the seed is sown, they can produce of themselves. For the former demoniac "to be with" Jesus would only slow the harvest, for he needs no more instruction or understanding than he now has to bear abundant fruit. Not so, the disciples. The disciples, the rocky ground, demand continuous cultivation, if any positive growth at all is to result. But, as becomes increasingly evident, even the divine Sower can do only so much.

Although the response of faith as the opposite of fear is not raised in the healing of the demoniac, probably because the demons knew positively who Jesus was and acknowledged his cosmic power, the last two of the three healings are very much involved with faith versus fear. In addition, not only is one intercalated into the other, but both involve the healing of females, one with a twelve-year illness and the other twelve years old.[58] While the

58. Numerology was extremely important in the Hellenistic world, and I am convinced that there was some significance to the Gospel's remarkable love of 3s and multiples of 3 (6, 12, thirtyfold, sixtyfold, etc.). Unfortunately, very little has been done on early Christian numerology, and that lacuna serves to encourage all sorts of speculative theories. In the case of the twelve-year-old child and the woman with a twelve-year illness, it is very tempting to note that the only use of twelve prior to their appearance is related to the disciples, the Twelve. That those twelve turn out to be rocky ground, while these two healed ones demonstrate the fruitfulness of faith raises the possibility of seeing this use of twelve as a subtle clue to the identity of Jesus' true family.

story of the healing of Jairus's daughter opens the unit (5:21–22) with the arrival of Jairus, "one of the rulers of the synagogue," to fall at Jesus' feet and request healing for his little daughter who is near death, the healing of the woman with the flow of blood is actually completed first. The woman is in the crowd following Jesus to Jairus's house (5:24b–25), and the narrator says that she had *heard* about him (v. 27) and wanted to touch his garments, for as she herself says, If I touch even his garments, I shall be saved (5:28).[59] Her confidence comes from what she has *heard,* not from contact with Jesus himself. So she touches him from behind without his assent or knowledge, and "immediately the hemorrhage ceased," and she knew she was healed. It is important to note that this whole healing occurs without Jesus' compliance in any way. The woman has heard; she comes; she believes that she will be healed if she touches his garment; she does so; and she is healed. Only afterward does Jesus respond actively to the situation by asking the crowd who it was who touched his garments. The woman, recognizing her healing, comes to Jesus "in fear and trembling" (φοβηθεῖσα καὶ τρέμουσα), falls down before him, and tells him what she did. He responds, Daughter, your faith has saved you (ἡ πίστις σου σέσωκέν σε); go (ὕπαγε) in peace and be healed of your disease (5:34).

The woman is not courageous; when she must confess, she does so "in fear and trembling." But faith can drive out fear. Her faith in Jesus' power is so great that she can touch him and be saved. Faith is not solely the domain of the strong, the powerful, and the confident, but even the weak, the lowly, and the cowardly can respond with faith that drives out fear and thus saves. When Jesus asks who touched his garments, the disciples reply in amazement that the crowds are constantly pressing around him (5:31), and their comment is significant because it indicates that simply touching Jesus was not sufficient to release his power (δύναμις, v. 30). The woman touched him with absolute faith that she would be saved; that faith was the crucial factor. *Faith, then, is the prerequisite of healing for the Gospel of Mark, not its result.* One does not have faith *because* one was healed; one has faith *so that* one can be healed. The miracles in Mark are not intended as signs to induce belief; they are, instead, the visible, tangible fruits of faith. Jesus did not himself heal the woman, for as he rightly points out to her, "Your faith has made you well." Jesus is the catalyst of the healing process, but the woman's faith is the essential prerequisite, because seed yields fruit solely in the good

---

59. The Greek verb σῴζω, used by the woman here and repeated by Jesus in Mark 5:34, refers both to physical healing *and* to spiritual salvation. The double reference is extremely important for Mark's sense of the underlying meaning of these healings. Healing and being saved for the Gospel are essentially identical. Cf. D. E. Nineham, *The Gospel of St. Mark* (Harmondsworth: Penguin Books, 1964), 158–59; and E. Schweizer, *The Good News According to Mark,* trans. D. Madvig (Richmond: John Knox Press, 1970), 118.

earth. Nor did Jesus create faith in her or bring faith to her; faith was her response to hearing. Yet only in the presence of such faith can Jesus' power be released.

Faith, then, is the human manifestation of the good earth, the kingdom of God. If faith is the response to hearing the word, the kingdom of God is revealed in transforming power that produces incredible results. If faith is not the response, then little can be done, as the episode of Jesus' rejection by his hometown, the episode immediately following these three healings, clearly illustrates (6:1–6). When Jesus teaches in his own country, the people who knew him and still know his family, influenced by past roles, customs, and relationships, take offense at him. While able to do a few things, the narrator reports that "he could do no mighty work there. . . . And he marveled because of their unbelief (ἀπιστίαν)" (6:5–6). Jesus' mighty works depend upon the presence of faith; without faith, Jesus can do practically nothing. Faith, for Mark, precedes and is the prerequisite of mighty works, just as the good earth precedes and is the prerequisite of abundant fruit. Jesus sows the seed, but the good earth produces the crop. Both elements are necessary for the kingdom to be manifested in power.

While Jesus is still talking to the woman, messengers arrive to tell Jairus that his little daughter is dead (5:35). Jairus had originally come to Jesus in the firm belief that he could save her (5:23). Now that she is dead, will he lose that faith? Jesus quickly exhorts him, "Do not fear (φοβοῦ), only believe (πίστευε)" (5:36). As with the disciples in the boat, Jesus again defines fear as the enemy and opposite of faith. Although Jairus is allowed no verbal reply, the narrator indicates that the journey to Jairus's house continues; however, Jesus is accompanied only by Peter, James, and John, not all the others. The crowds and the mourners are left aside, as Jesus enters the child's room with her parents and his three disciples, takes her by the hand, and commands her to arise. Immediately she does, to the amazement of all, and Jesus, once again being trailed by a crowd, charges them to tell no one about what has happened. That the child is really alive and not just an apparition or spirit, Jesus confirms by ordering food for her. Faith, it seems, can overcome not only fear, it can overcome death as well.

These three healings, like the thirtyfold, sixtyfold, and hundredfold harvest of the parable of the Sower, depict miraculous results when the word is accepted in faith rather than fear. The good earth, the faithful earth produces abundantly. Furthermore, that a man whose home is in the Greek cities of the Decapolis (5:20), a poor woman (5:26), and a leader of a Jewish synagogue (5:22) should all prove themselves to be good earth with faith capable of producing fruit indicates the universal nature of the kingdom of God. Whether Greek or Jew, male or female, powerful or weak, all can be part of God's ground if faith is their response to hearing the word. By the close of this section the audience ought to have identified the Gospel groups representing each hearing-response type in the parable of the Sower.

Parable of Sower		*Interpretation*		*Gospel Group*
1. seed sown along the way; eaten by birds	=	these in whom the word is immediately removed by Satan	=	scribes, Pharisees, Jerusalem Jewish leaders
2. seed sown in rocky ground; comes up quickly but has no root; withers with the sun	=	these who accept the word immediately; endure for a time, but fall away when tribulation or persecution comes	=	disciples, especially Peter, James, and John
3. seed sown among thorns; thorns choke it and it produces no fruit	=	others in whom the word is choked by the cares of the world, delight in riches, and desire for other things	=	Herod; rich man of 10:17–22[60]
4. seed sown on the good earth; brings forth grain in triple abundance	=	those who hear the word, accept it, and bear fruit in triple abundance	=	ones healed (or saved) by their faith

The four episodes of Mark 4:35—5:43 are designed primarily to clarify the distinction between the rocky ground and the good earth. In so doing, the stories introduce oppositions that characterize each group: faith versus fear; go versus be with him. These oppositions join those the Gospel has already posed: insider versus outsider; doing the will of God versus not doing God's will; hearing the mystery of the kingdom versus hearing riddles; having the ears to hear versus not having them; and productive earth versus unproductive earths. Moreover, the chapters that follow will add further oppositions, such as last versus first and least versus greatest, all of which converge to characterize those of God's ground versus those hardened into Satan's prey. Since the basic typology is established and identified by Mark 6, Mark 7—10 can develop and amplify the fundamental patterns for the sake of the audience's greater appreciation. By

60. While the story of Herod is located in the chiastic section surrounding Mark 4 and 5, it follows close enough for identification. The rich man in Mark 10:17–22 is such a dramatic example of the type that the audience should have no difficulty understanding what he illustrates.

looking carefully at the four episodes following the teaching in parables, we have been able to perceive the growing typologies distinctly; however, for the authorial audience, many of whom were probably auditors, considerable repetition would be necessary for full understanding to occur, and that repetition with variation and elaboration is found in Mark 6:35—10:52. But before moving on to study the typological development of the rocky ground and the good earth in the remainder of Division One, we need to reflect briefly on what our analysis of the parable of the Sower suggests about the concept of the kingdom of God in Mark.

Kingdom of God

Because of the desire to focus on the historical Jesus' possible understanding of the kingdom of God with its connections to apocalyptic Judaism of the first century, most scholarly studies of the concept begin by defining the Greek word for kingdom, βασιλεία, primarily in terms of its Aramaic parallel *malkuth*.[61] The two terms differ not so much in basic reference as in connotation: the Aramaic bears a stronger verbal sense, the rule of God, and the Greek a stronger spatial perspective, the domain of God's rule. By explicating the kingdom of God through the metaphor of good earth, Mark appears to be developing the concept in its Greek form rather than the earlier Aramaic. For Mark, the kingdom of God is God's ground which produces of itself and in transforming abundance. It is not so much God's reign that is at issue but the land over which God legitimately rules, a land that has at least in part been usurped by evil powers.

The parables of the Four Types of Earth, the Earth Producing of Itself, and the Transforming Earth in Mark 4:3–32, along with the parable of the Vineyard and the Tenants in Mark 12:1–11, demonstrate a remarkable confluence of ground imagery for the kingdom of God: It is the good earth that yields fruit; the earth that, once sown, produces of itself; the earth that can transform a tiny seed into a magnificent bush; and a lovingly created and planted vineyard now in the hands of tenants who refuse to provide fruit to the lord of the vineyard. This pervasive use of land or earth as the metaphor for the kingdom of God coincides with Mark's primarily spatial language for participation in the kingdom: "It is better for you *to enter* the kingdom of God with one eye" (9:47); "Whoever does not receive the kingdom of God like a child *shall not enter it*" (10:15); "How hard it will be

61. For a general discussion of the kingdom of God in the teaching of Jesus, see Perrin, *Jesus and the Language of the Kingdom,* 1–88. For different views on the kingdom of God in Mark, see W. Kelber, *The Kingdom in Mark: A New Place and a New Time* (Philadelphia: Fortress Press, 1974); Kee, *Community of the New Age: Studies in Mark's Gospel,* 107–9; and Taylor, *The Gospel According to St. Mark,* 114–17.

for those who have riches *to enter* the kingdom of God! . . . Children, how hard it is *to enter* the kingdom of God!" (10:23–24); "You are *not far* from the kingdom of God" (12:34). Hence the Gospel manifests a fairly consistent imagistic pattern for representing the kingdom metaphorically.

Furthermore, the agricultural pattern clarifies the role of Jesus in relation to the kingdom. Jesus does not bring the kingdom, for the kingdom, like the good earth, already exists before the sower begins to sow. The use of the perfect tense in Mark 1:15 (the time *has been fulfilled,* the kingdom of God *has come near*) reflects this sense that the kingdom began in the past and continues into the present. However, although the kingdom, the good earth, existed prior to the coming of Jesus, it was fallow ground, unseeded, and consequently dormant and unproductive. Jesus sows the seed that activates the good earth into dramatic production. Such sowing both reveals what is good earth and what is not and also acts as the catalyst of abundant growth when good earth is present. It is the interaction of Jesus and the newly disclosed good earth that results in powerful transformations. Jesus' power, then, is circumscribed by the type of ground he discovers; without good earth his sowing brings little return, but with good earth it brings miraculous fruit. Thus, for the Gospel of Mark, while God's good ground antedates Jesus, Jesus' sowing brings it with power. Before Jesus, the kingdom is present in potential; with Jesus, it is revealed with power. Jesus' saying to the crowds and the disciples in Mark 9:1 functions perfectly well on the level of second degree narrative: "Truly, I say to you, there are some standing here who will not taste death before they see that the kingdom of God has come with power (ἐν δυνάμει)." The character Jesus speaking to other characters insists that some of them will not die before realizing that the kingdom has already come in power. The audience, on the level of first degree narrative, affirms the truth of Jesus' saying, because it knows that Jesus himself has inaugurated that state.

Though the Gospel uses the concrete metaphor of earth to represent the kingdom of God, the mystery of the kingdom is not agricultural but human. It is the human heart, not land, that is the seat of God's domain.[62] While the third degree narrative of the parables reflects the metaphorical, agricultural explication of the kingdom, the second degree narrative of Jesus and the other characters typifies the human explication of the kingdom. Jesus is the messenger of God's good news that the kingdom of God has already come. Those who believe what he says reveal God's rule in their own hearts; that is, *for those who have faith that the kingdom has come, it has come in them.* And such faith transforms their lives, an event that the Gospel often graphically represents as miraculous healings. Faith that they will be

---

62. See Via, *The Ethics of Mark's Gospel,* 116–21.

healed heals them. Hearing Jesus' good news and responding in faith converts potential into power. The fearless, trusting confidence of children
supplies an analogy for this faith (10:14–16), but faith is an adult response
and responsibility, as the Gospel makes clear by emphasizing the role of the
parent's faith for healing the child (5:35–43; 7:25–30; 9:14–27).

Moreover, the response of faith breaks across all the traditional social,
cultural, and religious boundaries: Jews, Greeks, males, females, powerful,
and powerless by their faith join together to form a new family, Jesus' true
family, composed of those who do the will of God (3:34–35). As Jesus tells
the disciples, anyone who has broken away from old relationships and
possessions because of his message will "receive a hundredfold now in this
time, houses and brothers and sisters and mothers and children and lands,
with persecutions, and in the age to come eternal life" (10:30). This new
family is God's domain, God's kingdom come in power at the instigation of
Jesus. Consequently, the kingdom of God, God's metaphorical good earth,
are those whose response to the word is characterized by faith and manifested in mighty works, resulting in a new universal family now and eternal
life in the age to come.

Yet the universal family now is beset by persecutions because Jesus'
message reveals not only God's good earth but the bad earth now usurped
by Satan, and unfortunately, as the parable of the Vineyard and the Tenants
indicates, those who presently control the vineyard are evil and destructive.
As long as that control continues, as long as this present age lasts, God's
powerful domain will be harassed and plundered. The inevitability of such
tribulation explains why the opposite of faith for the Gospel of Mark is not
doubt but fear. Indeed, doubt may well accompany faith (e.g., 9:22–24);
however, fear can defy it. So the metaphorical bad earths are those whose
response to the word is characterized by fear and manifested in hardness of
heart, resulting in betrayal, denial, and death. But the lord of the vineyard
will not allow this state of affairs to last forever. Instead, "he will come and
destroy the tenants, and give the vineyard to others" (12:9). There is, then,
a third stage in the progress of God's kingdom, marked by the end of this
present age and the beginning of a new order entirely. When God comes in
glory with the Son and holy angels (e.g., 8:38; 14:62) to remove this world
order and establish a new one, eternal life will be granted to those faithful
ones who endured. Hence the Gospel of Mark suggests three periods in the
development of the kingdom of God: it existed in potential before the
coming of Jesus; with Jesus' message, it is revealed and empowered to
produce abundant fruit, but it is still opposed by the evil authorities of this
age; and soon—though we know not the day or the hour (13:32)—the
kingdom of God will arrive in all its glory as the present age is wiped away

by the apocalypse and eternal life for God's elect begins. Further explication of this final stage must wait until we reach Division Two of the Gospel.

Summary

The parable of the Sower (or the parable of the Four Types of Earth) and the interpretational material following it in Mark 4:3–32 function as a plot synopsis, or prooemium, a conventional feature of Greek literature, for the Gospel of Mark. The material that precedes the parable introduces the audience to the habits and responses of several major groups in the Gospel: the disciples, those healed, and the scribes, Pharisees, and other Jewish opponents. That initial perspective then assists the audience in identifying the Gospel groups that illustrate each of the four basic types of responses to the word outlined by the parable. The stories immediately succeeding the parables distinguish sharply between those representing the rocky ground and the good earth, the two responses most easily confused because of the positive beginning of the rocky ground type. While the parables, examples of third degree narrative, develop the hearing-response typology using agricultural metaphors of sowing seed and earth, the characters in second degree narrative illustrate the typology in human terms. The fundamental human responses that differentiate the good earth from the bad earths are faith versus fear, and they are illustrated by the healed ones versus the disciples.

Since an aural narrative must always be concerned with the requirements of rhetorical amplification, the remaining chapters of Division One, Mark 6 to 10, repeat, refine, vary, and illustrate the points already made. In so doing, additional human traits distinguishing the faithful from the fearful are developed, and the nature and the power of faith are contrasted with the faults that underlie fear. To trace that explication, we must now turn to the rest of Division One and "The Good Earth and the Rocky Ground."

9

The Good Earth
and the
Rocky Ground

Although the anomalous role of the disciples in Mark has become the centerpiece of much recent research on the Gospel,[1] the miracle stories, occupying nearly a fourth of the length of the Gospel of Mark, as much as the Passion narrative and the controversies,[2] have received considerably less attention as integral elements in the Markan story.[3] While modern readers

1. See, e.g., Weeden, *Mark—Traditions in Conflict;* Best, *Following Jesus: Discipleship in the Gospel of Mark;* Donahue, *The Theology and Setting of Discipleship in the Gospel of Mark;* Tannehill, "The Disciples in Mark," 386–405; J. B. Tyson, "The Blindness of the Disciples in Mark," *JBL* 80 (1961): 261–68; D. J. Hawkin, "The Incomprehension of the Disciples in the Markan Redaction," *JBL* 91 (1972): 491–500; C. Focant, "L'incompréhension des disciples dans le deuxième évangile: Tradition et rédaction," *Revue Biblique* 82 (1975): 161–85; and Robbins, *Jesus the Teacher.*

2. E. Best, "The Miracles in Mark," *Review and Expositor* 75 (1978): 541; and Trocmé, *The Formation of the Gospel According to Mark,* 45–47.

3. For general studies of miracles in the early Christian tradition, see R. Bultmann, *The History of the Synoptic Tradition,* trans. J. Marsh (New York: Harper & Row, 1963), 218–44; M. Dibelius, *From Tradition to Gospel,* trans. B. L. Woolf (New York: Charles Scribner's Sons, 1935), 70–103; and more recently, G. Theissen, *Urchristliche Wundergeschichten: Ein Beitrag zur formgeschichtlichen Erforschung der synoptischen Evangelien* (SNT 8; Gütersloh: Gerd Mohn, 1974).

For hypotheses about the sources of Mark's miracle stories, see P. J. Achtemeier, "Towards the Isolation of Pre-Markan Miracle Catenae," *JBL* 89 (1970): 265–91; and idem, "The Origin and Function of the Pre-Markan Miracle Catenae," *JBL* 91 (1972): 198–221.

For studies of the miracles in Mark, see Best, "The Miracles in Mark," 539–54; L. Schenke, *Die Wundererzählungen des Markusevangeliums* (Stuttgart: Katholisches Bibelwerk, 1974); T. Snoy, "Les miracles dans l'évangile de Marc," *Revue Théologique de Louvain* 3 and 4 (1973): 58–101; and D.-A. Koch, *Die Bedeutung der Wunderer-*

may experience some discomfort or embarrassment in encountering these episodes, desiring either to rationalize them away or to view them as the objectives of Markan polemic,[4] such stories were enormously popular in the Hellenistic world.[5] That Mark should abound with them suggests again its function as a popular text, accessible and attractive to a wide spectrum of ancient society. Yet these stories are more than seductive trappings, for Mark adapts and uses miracle stories to illustrate a theological program. The miraculous physical transformations of the healings are only the outward manifestations of a condition of the heart characterized as faith in the gospel. And faith, as the parable of the Sower (or the parable of the Four Types of Earth) indicates, is an immediate response to hearing the word which results in mighty works. When faith is the response, nothing further is required—no extra teachings, no special regulations, no formative discipline. Faith in the gospel reveals the kingdom of God, God's good earth, in the faithful heart. Such a theological position is profoundly charismatic, depending on the experience and inspiration of the moment, rather than tradition, training, or instruction, to secure commitment and effect change.

Though the good earth produces abundantly, it is faced with the triple failure of the three types of unproductive ground: the ground along the way that never even receives the seed (the scribes, the Pharisees, and the Jewish opponents); the rocky ground that grows at first but withers away under tribulation (the disciples); and the thorny ground which chokes out growth by worldly possessions and cares (Herod and the rich man). Furthermore, these failures and the possible human faults behind them are the main concerns of the Gospel, for, after all, those who are the good earth need

---

zählungen für die Christologie des Markusevangeliums (BZNW 42; Berlin: Walter de Gruyter, 1975). Most of the recent study of the miracles in Mark have concerned whether or not Mark presents (or attacks) a *theios anēr* ("Divine Man") Christology. For a review of the various sides of the debate, see J. D. Kingsbury, "The 'Divine Man' as the Key to Mark's Christology—The End of an Era?" *Interpretation* 35 (1981): 243–57.

One attempt to understand the role of the supplicants for healing in relation to other character groups in the Gospel from a literary standpoint can be found in R. Tannehill, "The Gospel of Mark as Narrative Christology," *Semeia* 16 (1979): 57–95.

4. The argument that Mark attacks a *theios anēr* Christology, exalting Jesus as a miracle-worker, by placing it on the lips of the disciples and then having Jesus reject it in favor of suffering (see, e.g., Weeden, *Mark—Traditions in Conflict*), besides the historical problems related to it, faces one major narrative objection: the disciples never seem to understand Jesus' miracles (e.g., Mark 6:51–52; 8:17–21; 9:10).

5. After indicating the widespread evidence for miracle stories in the Jewish, Greek, and Egyptian strands of Hellenistic culture as well as in Buddhist traditions, Trocmé concludes, deprecatingly but quite significantly for our hypothesis of Mark's popular origins, that the miracles are "anonymous tales told with rudimentary means and consequently subject to the influence of the degenerate literary themes that formed the common fund of popular culture in the Middle East of two thousand years ago" (*The Formation of the Gospel According to Mark*, 48).

only to realize who they are to bear fruit; it is the ones "not far" from the kingdom who need to be warned and exhorted, who need the continual sowing of the word. Of the three failing types, the first, the Jewish opponents, already a significant element in the story, will dominate Division Two with their absolute rejection of Jesus, leading to his death. The other two types, and especially the disciples, organize the remaining two sections of Division One, Mark 6:35—8:21 and 8:22—10:52. Surrounded by the two stories of the feeding of the multitudes with their boat trip conclusions, Mark 6:35—8:21 depicts the shift of the disciples from acceptance to hardheartedness, from possible faith to fear, while Mark 8:22—10:52, enclosed by Jesus' successful healing of the blind and structured by three Passion prediction units, amplifies and specifies the human desires of the disciples that prevent them from fully hearing what Jesus is trying to tell them. The rhetorical organization of these two sections may be outlined as follows (for the full structure, see Appendix A):

D. 6:35—8:21
  1. 6:35–52
     a. 6:35–44—feeding of five thousand
     b. 6:45–52—walking on water; disciples' hearts hardened
  2. 6:53—7:37
     a. 6.53–56—general healing; immediately recognized
     b. 7:1–23—inner heart versus outer tradition
        1. vv. 1–13—controversy with scribes over heart versus show
        2. vv. 14–15—teaching to crowd on inner versus outer uncleanness
        3. vv. 17–23—repetition to disciples of inner versus outer
     c. 7:24–30—healing of Syrophoenician woman's daughter
     d. 7:31–37—healing of deaf mute
  3. 8:1–21
     a. 8:1–10—feeding of four thousand
     b. 8:11–21
        1. vv. 11–13—Pharisees demand a sign
        2. vv. 14–21—boat trip; disciples do not understand

E. 8:22—10:52
  1. 8:22–26—healing of a blind man
  2. 8:27—9:29—first Passion prediction unit
     a. 8:27–30—Peter identifies Jesus as Christ
     b. 8:31—first Passion prediction
     c. 8:32–33—Peter rebukes Jesus and Jesus rebukes Peter
     d. 8:34—9:13—Jesus teaches: save life/lose life
        1. 8:34—9:1—save/lose; shame/glory
        2. 9:2–13—transfiguration

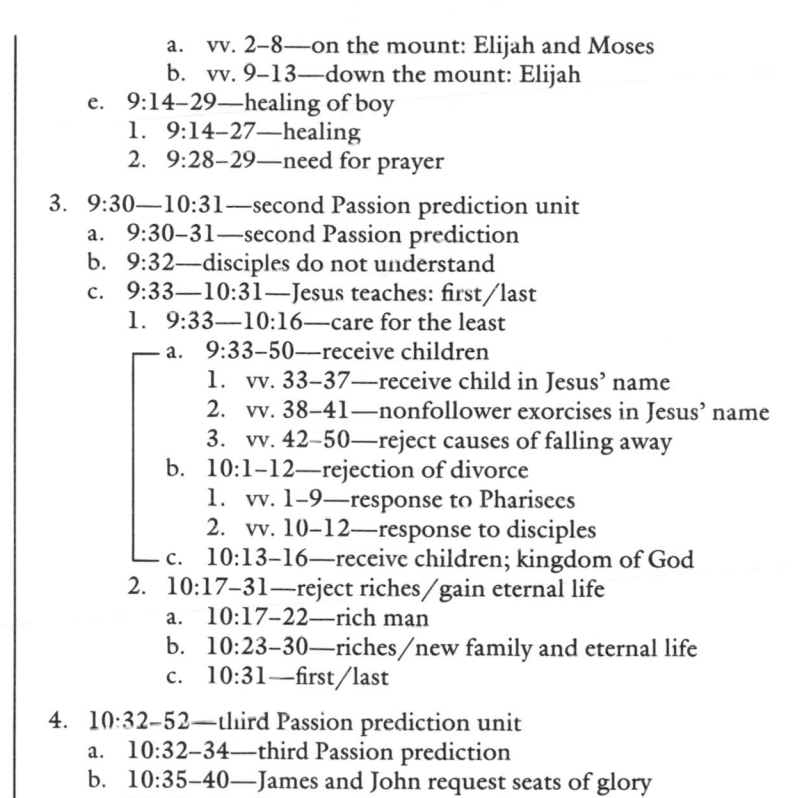

            a. vv. 2–8—on the mount: Elijah and Moses
            b. vv. 9–13—down the mount: Elijah
        e. 9:14–29—healing of boy
            1. 9:14–27—healing
            2. 9:28–29—need for prayer

    3. 9:30—10:31—second Passion prediction unit
        a. 9:30–31—second Passion prediction
        b. 9:32—disciples do not understand
        c. 9:33—10:31—Jesus teaches: first/last
            1. 9:33—10:16—care for the least
                a. 9:33–50—receive children
                    1. vv. 33–37—receive child in Jesus' name
                    2. vv. 38–41—nonfollower exorcises in Jesus' name
                    3. vv. 42–50—reject causes of falling away
                b. 10:1–12—rejection of divorce
                    1. vv. 1–9—response to Pharisees
                    2. vv. 10–12—response to disciples
                c. 10:13–16—receive children; kingdom of God
            2. 10:17–31—reject riches/gain eternal life
                a. 10:17–22—rich man
                b. 10:23–30—riches/new family and eternal life
                c. 10:31—first/last

    4. 10:32–52—third Passion prediction unit
        a. 10:32–34—third Passion prediction
        b. 10:35–40—James and John request seats of glory
        c. 10:41–45—Jesus teaches: greatest/servant
  [5.] d. 10:46–52—calls and heals blind Bartimaeus, who follows him
        on the way

A few healing stories and exhortations to faith are interwoven into the unraveling of the disciples' failure. In Mark 6:35—8:21, healing miracles with warnings of Jesus' growing fame included in them (6:53–56; 7:24–37) surround the long teaching section on the inner state of the heart versus the outer appearance of custom and tradition in Mark 7:1–23, a theme already familiar to the audience. In addition, the three Passion prediction units of Mark 8:27—10:52 are enclosed by two stories of the healing of the blind. As many commentators have pointed out about this section, Jesus can open the eyes of the blind, but he cannot make his disciples see.[6] Moreover, the first and last Passion prediction units end with healing stories, while the long, central unit focuses solely on teaching. The healing of blind Bartimaeus in Mark 10:46–52 thus performs a triple rhetorical

---

6. See, e.g., Perrin, *The New Testament: An Introduction*, 155; and Rhoads and Michie, *Mark as Story*, 126–27.

function: it closes the third Passion prediction unit; it closes the last section of Division One; and it closes Division One. A story with such strategic functions will have to be considered carefully. However, the interrelationship of the disciples' problems with the healing stories involves more than simple variation or location; the two have a direct thematic bearing on each other. The ability of Jesus to heal those who seek it from him highlights his inability to open the hearts of the disciples. Since for the audience Jesus cannot be at fault, the blame for their opacity falls squarely on the disciples themselves.[7] That others without their advantages of private and constant instruction can respond in faith to Jesus not only exacerbates their dullness but also calls into question the *necessity* of instruction for faith, a point already raised by the preaching of the former demoniac.

Alternatively, the increasing revelation of the disciples' hardness of heart coincides with the increasing difficulty Jesus finds in healing those who come to him or in performing miracles of any kind in Mark 6 to 10.[8] While the miracles of Mark 1 through 5 are concluded easily, once even without Jesus' conscious participation (5:27–29), the later miracles require elaborate preparation (7:33; 8:23), sighs and groans (7:34; 9:19), prayer (9:29), and occasionally a second try at it (8:24–25). As the story of Jesus' rejection by his hometown and consequent inability to accomplish mighty works (6:1–6) makes clear, miracles in the Gospel are not signs to induce faith in unbelievers; they are, instead, the fruits of faith. Since faith is the prerequisite of miracle, as the disciples manifest deeper degrees of unfaith, Jesus encounters greater difficulty in performing mighty works. When opposition from the Jewish authorities and misunderstanding, betrayal, and denial from the disciples dominate the scene, as they do in Division Two, no miracles at all can occur. The restored sight of blind Bartimaeus is the last healing of the Gospel, and the final miracle of any kind, the cursing of the fig tree (11:12–14), accompanies the Gospel's concluding teaching by Jesus on the nature of faith (11:20–25). As faithlessness extrudes, miracles disappear.

7. Attempts to redeem the disciples by claims that Jesus has not explained enough to them or given them sufficient interpretation of events violates the basic ideological and evaluative dynamic of the Gospel. Jesus is the completely positive pole of the story with whom the audience identifies. He cannot be in the wrong. Besides, the narrator goes to some pains to assure the audience of the fullness of Jesus' instruction to the disciples (e.g., Mark 4:34; 8:32a). For such a suggestion about Jesus and the disciples, see Rhoads and Michie, *Mark as Story*, 89–96.

8. The decline in numbers at the two feedings and the increasing difficulty of the healings have been noted by a number of commentators; see, e.g., A. Farrer, *A Study in St. Mark* (New York: Oxford University Press, 1952), 290–304. The connection of faith or rather lack of faith with this decline is superbly argued by L. W. Countryman, "How Many Baskets Full? Mark 8:14–21: The Value of Miracles in Mark," *CBQ* 47 (1985): 643–55.

As deeply interrelated as these two groups are, in order to trace the progress of the good earth and the decline of the rocky ground clearly, we will need to discuss each of them separately. We will look first at those healed and follow the development of faith through the Gospel. Second, we will briefly survey the depiction of the disciples until their flight in Mark 14:50–52, paying special attention to the striking scenes of the transfiguration and Gethsemane. Based on this analysis of their narrative roles, finally, we must ask why the disciples of Jesus were chosen to illustrate the rocky ground type for the Gospel of Mark and why the nameless masses who came forth for healing were depicted as the human representatives of the fruitful ground of God's kingdom.

The Good Earth—Miracles and Faith

After the three healings of Mark 5:1–43, the audience should have identified the Gospel group illustrating the good earth type as those who are healed. In addition, the contrast between faith and fear has twice been placed on the lips of Jesus (4:40; 5:36), and the presence of faith as the prior requirement of healing has been soundly emphasized in the healing of the woman (5:24b–34). Three of the episodes in Mark 6:1–34 reprise in inverted order the three episodes of Mark 3:7–35, with the story of John the Baptist's death (6:14–29) interrupting the chiastic plan in order to illustrate, among other things, the third failing response to the word fairly soon after the parable. Although vocabulary and themes in the three stories are similar to Mark 3:7–35, the critical difference is the orientation to the entire narrative the audience now possesses, which serves to stress aspects of the episodes possibly missed otherwise.[9] The first story in Mark 6, while again demonstrating the inappropriateness of past roles and customary relationships, clarifies fully the connection between faith and Jesus' mighty works. Because the people of his hometown rejected him as Mary's son and the brother of James and Joses and the others, they lacked faith (6:6), and Jesus "could do no mighty work there" (6:5a). Mighty works are the result of the interaction of Jesus and people of faith. Without the faith of the people, Jesus cannot bring forth fruit.

This understanding of the correlation between faith and mighty works

9. A good illustration of this process would be a "youth symphony" in which schoolchildren are brought to hear a symphony orchestra play and before each piece the conductor explains what to listen for—when the woodwinds will carry the melody or the brass or the strings. With such an orientation, what would otherwise be simply a pleasant tune to children can become a complex and surprising experience in orchestral harmony and movement. The key, however, is to know what to listen for. Similarly, the point of a prooemium in ancient literature was to assist the audience in following an aural narrative by presenting in advance what to listen for.

illuminates two other passages in the Gospel: the Pharisees' request for a sign (8:11–13) and the mocking of Jesus on the cross (15:29–32). In order to test him the Pharisees request a sign (σημεῖον) from heaven, but Jesus refuses, saying, "No sign shall be given to this generation (τῇ γενεᾷ ταύτῃ)" (8:12). Though the exchange directly follows the second feeding of the multitudes, which one might think would be sign enough for anyone, the effect of the episode is to reconfirm that miracles in Mark do not function as signs to persuade people to believe. "This generation," a phrase used consistently in Mark to portray the unbelieving, evil, and destructive people of the world (e.g., 8:38; 9:19), will receive no sign, because they have not the eyes and ears of faith. Their lack of faith utterly prohibits mighty works. The Pharisees want it the wrong way around: they want to be shown a sign so that they can believe; in truth, only when people believe can miracles occur.[10]

The irony of the mocking of Jesus on the cross, which we have already discussed,[11] reveals again the tragic misunderstanding of the nature of miracles held by Jesus' Jewish opponents. As he is hanging from the cross, the scribes and the chief priests deride him with, "He saved others; he cannot save himself. Let the Christ, the King of Israel, come down now from the cross, that we may see and believe" (15:31–32). They demand a miracle, a sign, upon which to found their faith, but faith is not something an action of Jesus can give to them; faith is something within them that responds to Jesus. Indeed, when Jesus interacts with those of faith, they are saved, not by Jesus, but by their faith. Jesus truly cannot save himself, not only because it may violate God's will, but more directly because his power depends upon faithful response. Miracles will not come to those who seek them *in order to* believe; for the Gospel of Mark, *miracles occur as the fruit, not the cause, of faith.* In mocking Jesus as "the Christ, the King of Israel," the Jewish opponents ironically bring scorn upon their own heads, for he is in fact "the Christ, the King of Israel." In demanding that he save himself by coming down from the cross so that they can see and believe, they reveal their profound ignorance of the nature of faith and the nature of God's kingdom. They are Satan's feeding ground most surely.

10. The calling of the disciples in the Gospel of Luke illustrates the Pharisees' position. In Luke 5:1–11, Simon and James and John have been fishing all night, with nothing to show for it. Jesus orders Simon to put out his net again, and when he obeys, he catches a great shoal of fish to the point of breaking the nets and sinking the boats. When Peter sees this miracle, he falls at Jesus' feet in belief and worship. The miracle here induces belief in Jesus, but such a pattern is rejected by the Gospel of Mark. As Best says ("The Miracles in Mark," 545), "In contrast to many miracles from the contemporary religious world, faith is the presupposition of miracle and not its result."

11. See above, p. 99.

Mark 6:35—8:21

The dominance of faithlessness in the second half of the Gospel, so well illustrated by the mocking of Jesus on the cross, creates an atmosphere in which miracles become impossible, but the narrative focus on the shift of the disciples from acceptance to hardness of heart burdens Jesus' miraculous activities much earlier in the story. The second feeding of the multitudes episode, which ends the unit of Mark 6:35—8:21, discloses in its numbers a decrease in miraculous activity. In Mark 8:1–10, Jesus feeds fewer people (four thousand as opposed to five thousand in 6:35–44), with more food (seven loaves and a few fish as opposed to five loaves and two fish earlier) and gets fewer leftovers (seven baskets as opposed to twelve baskets earlier).[12] In the boat trip immediately following this feeding (8:14–21), Jesus prods the disciples' memories and challenges their continual misunderstanding by repeating the *numbers:* "'When I broke the five loaves for the five thousand, how many baskets full of broken pieces did you take up?' They said to him, 'Twelve.' 'And the seven for the four thousand, how many baskets full of broken pieces did you take up?' And they said to him, 'Seven'" (8:19–20). These questions and the disciples' answers not only graphically demonstrate that the participation and memory of the disciples in both feedings was and continues to be without understanding, but they also document numerically the decline in Jesus' ability.[13] That decline has not to do with Jesus but with the increasing faithlessness he encounters.

Between the two feeding stories, three healing episodes are recounted.

12. Countryman, "How Many Baskets Full?" 647–50.

13. Some scholars argue for a symbolic significance to these numbers. In a presentation to the Cambridge (U.K.) New Testament Seminar on May 13, 1986, John Drury argued that the 5 loaves for 5,000 with 12 baskets of fragments and the 7 loaves for 4,000 with 7 baskets of fragments was based on the story of David's eating the bread of the Presence in 1 Sam. 21:1–7, which Mark alludes to in Mark 2:25–26. David found 12 loaves (Lev. 24:5–9) and took 5, leaving 7. The 5 loaves, then, represent Judaism, and the 7 left loaves represent the Gentile world. Drury is among a number of scholars who argue that the first feeding represents the Jewish world and the second the Gentile (see, e.g., Farrer, *A Study in St. Mark,* 297–301; and Kelber, *The Kingdom in Mark,* 55–61). Basing this division solely on the location of the two feedings is problematic, since the narrative itself barely hints at the location of either feeding.

That these numbers, and most of the others in the Gospel, carry symbolic significance seems highly likely, given the habits of Hellenistic culture. Just what they might symbolize is difficult to specify on the basis of our present lack of information concerning early Christian numerology. Drury may well be correct in seeing 1 Sam. 21:1–7 behind the numbers in these stories. Whether or not his conclusions about Jewish and Gentile allusions are correct is another matter. Popular literature must be broadly accessible; so, its main points ought to be obvious and repeated. On the other hand, to be attractive to the better-educated portion of its audience, popular literature, then and now, can contain little subtleties and allusions to challenge and gratify the careful or learned reader.

The first, Mark 6:53–56, is the narrator's summary of many healings; it stresses in its opening lines the degree to which Jesus is now known. When he gets out of the boat "immediately the people recognized him." Everywhere he goes, crowds gather, and the sick are brought to him, begging simply to touch the fringe of his garment and "as many as touched it were made well" (6:56). Earlier, in Mark 6:14, the audience learned that Jesus' fame had even reached Herod's ears; now, everywhere he goes he is recognized, sought after, and crowded. Moreover, in this healing summary, as in earlier healings, those who have faith in his power are still healed with ease.

Following the summary is a long, repetitious controversy/teaching episode (7:1–23). The fundamental point of the proceedings is that the heart is the basis of good or evil, not outward custom, appearance, or ritual, a point that quotes the prophet Isaiah and is strongly reminiscent of the prophet Jeremiah's call for "circumcision of the heart" (Jer. 4:3–4; 9:23–26) centuries before and also a point that is totally in harmony with the general principle expressed in the controversies of Mark 2:15—3:6 that law, custom, and ritual must be adapted to the needs of people in every new situation. Established tradition, custom, prescribed rituals are, for the Gospel of Mark, secondary values *at best.* The welfare of human beings, especially the weak and oppressed, and the disposition of the heart are the primary demands of religious life. Jesus makes this argument, first, in a diatribe against the hypocrisy of the Pharisees and scribes (7:1–13) who "leave the commandment of God, and hold fast the tradition of men" (7:8). Next, he calls the crowds to "Hear me, all of you, and understand," telling them that human defilement arises from within, not from the outside. Finally, in a third repetition to the disciples who ask him privately to explain, as they did with the parable of the Sower in Mark 4:10, Jesus amplifies and concretely illustrates the same point once more.

Since the position that Jesus is championing holds a hallowed place in Hebrew thought and, besides, is not particularly difficult to grasp, especially with the preparation of Mark 2:15—3:6, the triple repetition seems to be too much of a good thing. If the examples from Jewish practice might be confusing to the audience, as the narrator's less than clear explanations (7:1–4, 11) appear to suggest, surely the statement to the crowds (7:14–15) is obvious enough. The third repetition privately to the disciples must have a function different from simply that of clarity or mnemonics. Actually, it has two functions. First, since the audience probably does understand the issue, the fact that the disciples do not augments the distance between the audience and the disciples and provides the narrator with an opportunity for Jesus to underline that distance with, "Then are you also without understanding?" (7:17). Second, the fuller explanation to the disciples can forgo Jewish custom and discuss instead the ramifications of the position for an explosive issue in the early Christian community: dietary regulations. As the narrator remarks in an aside, Jesus' words declare all foods clean (7:19). From Paul's letters and from Acts, it is evident that the early communities were plagued by problems of table fellowship and eating regulations. That the three controversies in Mark 2:15–28 all have to do with eating, as does this third repetition of the heart versus the outside in Mark 7:17–23, implies the critical nature of that issue for the Markan author and authorial audience as well. For Mark, freedom from dietary laws, oppressive customs, or outdated rituals springs from the same source: the insight that the heart, not external activities, is the ground of good and evil, God or Satan, faith or fear.[14] If the heart is God's ground, nothing else is required; if the heart is not God's ground, nothing else will suffice.

The story of the healing of the Syrophoenician woman's daughter, the second of the three healings between the feeding stories, dramatizes the principle behind the controversy/teaching session. The story begins, as did the healing immediately preceding the teaching episode, with another reminder of Jesus' fame and his attempts to avoid it. He goes to Tyre and Sidon, trying not to let anyone know of his presence, but "he could not be hid" (7:24). This healing follows the pattern of the healings in Mark 5:1–43. The Greek woman *hears* about him, comes and falls down at his feet, begging him to heal her daughter (cf. 5:6, 22–23). Jesus, in an apparent reversal of position from the just concluded teaching session, expresses his reluctance to help her in a highly disparaging metaphor, likening her to a dog. Her nationality, an external factor over which she has no control, prevents her from sharing "the children's bread." Since he has healed non-Jews before (e.g., the demoniac from the Decapolis), nationality cannot be the real issue. His rebuff provides the opportunity for her faith to be fully revealed, for she takes his metaphor and turns it back on him: "Yes, Lord; yet even the dogs under the table eat the children's crumbs" (7:28).[15] He agrees and tells her to "go" ($\H{v}\pi\alpha\gamma\epsilon$), for her daughter is healed. By faith, Greeks too can share "the children's bread." Table fellowship is not related to nationality, sex, or religious tradition; all those who respond in faith share "the children's bread."

---

14. See the excellent discussion of Mark's rejection of the validity of cultic forms and moral rules in the light of the inclination of the heart toward love or evil in Via, *The Ethics of Mark's Gospel,* 88–98, 116–21.

15. In likening the Gentile woman to a little dog ($\kappa\upsilon\nu\alpha\rho\iota\upsilon\nu$), the author may be playing on another common type in Hellenistic society: the Cynic philosopher. Cynics were distinguished, not so much for their philosophical views as for their impudent, argumentative style. Diogenes of Sinope, the founder (fourth century B.C.E.), was called "the dog" ($\kappa\upsilon\omega\nu$) for his rudeness and impudence, thus naming the $\kappa\upsilon\nu\iota\kappa\H{\eta}$ $\phi\iota\lambda\omega\sigma\omega\phi\iota\alpha$ (Cynic philosophy) school. The woman's response to Jesus' initial rejection displays a certain impudent challenge worthy of a "little dog." For a brief discussion of Cynicism and Christianity, see H. Koester, *Introduction to the New Testament* (Philadelphia: Fortress Press; Berlin and New York: Walter de Gruyter, 1982), 1:153–54.

Jesus' reluctance to heal the woman's daughter, however, is the first sign of the increasingly evident burden that healings and miracles are becoming. In the boat story that concluded the first feeding of the multitudes in Mark 6:35–52, the narrator bluntly closes the episode with this report concerning the disciples: "And they were utterly astounded, for they did not understand (συνῆκαν) about the loaves, but their hearts were hardened" (6:51b–52). Like the scribes and Pharisees earlier (3:5), the disciples now also have hardened hearts. It is that hardening which is again emphasized in the third repetition of the teaching session when Jesus asks them, "Then are you also without understanding (ἀσύνετοί)?" (7:18). That those with him and following him have shifted to the "heart-set" of the Jewish opponents drains the ground of the faith so essential to mighty works.

In the third of the three healings, that of the deaf mute (7:31–37), Jesus' own weariness is accompanied by elaborate rituals, required for the first time in his healings: "And taking him aside from the multitude privately, he put his fingers into his ears, and he spat and touched his tongue; and looking up to heaven, he sighed, and said to him, 'Ephphatha,' that is, 'Be opened'" (7:33–34).[16] The narrator closes this healing with a general observation the audience by now expects and understands, for it has been dramatized many times: "And he charged them to tell no one; but the more he charged them, the more zealously they proclaimed it (ἐκήρυσσον). And they were astonished beyond measure, saying, 'He has done all things well; he even makes the deaf hear and the dumb speak'" (7:36–37). Jesus' attempts to hide himself, prevent his name from becoming known, and avoid crowds are all doomed to failure; yet such failure is precisely what the proverbial sayings after the parable of the Sower posited as the purpose of secrets: "For there is nothing hid, except to be made manifest; nor is anything secret, except to come to light" (4:22). Jesus' commands to silence, his evasions of crowds, and his private teachings—whatever other purposes they may serve—are not finally intended to prevent the spread of his word or knowledge of who he is from reaching the people. These two statements, that nothing is secret except to come to light and "the more he charged them, the more zealously they proclaimed it," are two levels of the same issue, one proverbial and the other human. Secrets come to light, and commands to silence provoke preaching, but that light and that preaching also bring with them an inevitable increase in opposition and hostility: faithlessness rises to confront faith.

16. Once before Mark has Jesus use an Aramaic phrase in healing (the raising of Jairus's daughter, Mark 5:41). The use of strange words or sounds, perceived to have magical power, was a common motif of Hellenistic miracles (see, e.g., J. Hull, *Hellenistic Magic and the Synoptic Tradition* [SBT 28; London: SCM Press, 1974], 82–86; and M. Smith, *Jesus the Magician* [San Francisco: Harper & Row, 1978], 94–96). These Aramaic words may well have seemed esoteric and magical to Mark's Greek-speaking audience.

The episode of the deaf mute is followed by the concluding feeding story of the section with its reduced level of effectiveness and its painful boat trip, in which the disciples, interpreting Jesus' metaphor concerning "the leaven of the Pharisees" literally, worry about having so little bread with them in the boat, provoking Jesus into a condemning series of rhetorical questions about their lack of understanding and hardness of heart (8:1–21). The healing of the blind man subsequent to this disheartening scene begins the final section of Division One and demonstrates the continuing downward cycle of the miracles. Not only must Jesus take the man aside and use elaborate procedures, as he did with the deaf mute, but his first attempt fails, and he must try a second time to effect the healing: "And when he had spit on his eyes and laid his hands upon him, he asked him, 'Do you see anything?' And he looked up and said, 'I see men; but they look like trees, walking.' Then again he laid his hands upon his eyes; and he looked intently and was restored, and saw everything clearly" (8:23b–25). Since, as the audience fully realizes, Jesus' power depends upon faithful response, the difficulties of these healings indicate the proliferation of unfruitful ground around Jesus.[17] And, indeed, although the Gospel is barely halfway through, only two more healings and one nature miracle remain to be presented. Hardness of heart, betrayal, and death are on the advance, as the three Passion predictions that structure this final section make abundantly clear. Yet, as if in reply to this assault, all three of the final miracles reiterate in the strongest way the nature and power of faith.

Mark 8:27—10:52

The first Passion prediction unit, Mark 8:27—9:29, like the last Passion prediction unit (10:35–52), ends with a healing miracle. In Mark 9:14–29, Jesus and his three major disciples, Peter, James, and John, have just come down from the mountain of transfiguration to find the other disciples surrounded by an argumentative crowd. The crowd runs to Jesus when he appears, and he is informed that his disciples have been unable to exorcise a demon from a young boy who had been brought by his father for healing. Upon hearing of that failure, Jesus expresses his greatest frustration yet in the narrative: "O faithless generation (γενεὰ ἄπιστος), how long am I to be with you? How long am I to bear with you?" (9:19). While "faithless generation" may be a general condemnation of the scribes, crowds, father,

---

17. If miracles are intended to be signs of Jesus' authority and power or elements used to convert unbelievers to faith, such episodes as the healing of the deaf mute (Mark 7:31–37) and the healing of the blind man (8:22–26) would serve to undermine the vigor of Jesus' abilities. Some such worry about these stories may lie behind the fact that *both* Matthew and Luke omit them from their Gospels. Since Mark's view of the purpose of miracles is quite different, in the Gospel of Mark these episodes illustrate the hardening of opposition, not the weakening of Jesus.

and others at the scene, since it immediately follows the news of the disciples' problem, they must certainly be included in its lament. Jesus inquires after the state of the boy's illness, and the father ends his explanation to Jesus with the plea, "If you can do anything, have pity on us and help us." That the father is unsure of Jesus' ability is understandable after the failure of his disciples, but since Jesus' power is dependent upon the faith of the petitioner, doubt necessarily impels exhortation from Jesus: "If you can! All things are possible to him who believes" (9:23). The father's reply, justly celebrated through the centuries as the condition of most of humanity, is, "I believe; help my unbelief!" (9:24). Both Jesus' frustrated exclamation and the exchange between Jesus and the boy's father are presented in direct discourse, heightening the drama of the scene for the audience and indicating the emphasis of the story.

The boy's father, another parent responsible for his child (cf. 5:22–23; 7:25–26), is both part of and not part of the present "faithless" (ἄπιστος) generation," for as he says, "I believe (πιστεύω); help my unbelief (ἀπιστία)." He does not have the confident faith of the earlier supplicants for healing, but on the other hand he is not totally hardened against Jesus either. He is on the borderline of the good earth, one, like the later scribe who answers Jesus wisely (12:28–34), who is "not far from the kingdom of God." For such as he, Jesus exhorts and instructs, telling him—and the audience—that all things are possible to one who believes. That instruction again demonstrates the link between faith[18] and mighty works: faith is the necessary precondition of the ability to do all things. In addition, because he is faithless as well as faithful, Jesus must exert special effort to effect the healing. As he informs the disciples privately, "This kind cannot be driven out by anything but prayer" (9:29).

The reference to prayer, a rare topic for Mark, functions not only to stress the difficulty of healing on the boundary between faith and unfaith but, since the statement comes as the reply to the disciples' query about why they could not exorcise the demon, it also functions to reflect negatively on the behavior of the disciples once again. If such exorcisms require prayer, and the disciples failed, the obvious implication is that the disciples do not pray.[19] In fact, the Gospel narrative bears out this implication. Besides the

---

18. The noun sometimes translated as "belief" and sometimes as "faith" is precisely the same word in Greek, πίστις. Similarly, the verb sometimes translated as "to believe" and sometimes as "to have faith" is also the same Greek verb, πιστεύω. Mark does not make the kind of distinction found in some modern theology of belief in dogmas but faith as a quality of life.

19. The relation of the disciples to prayer was first pointed out to me by Edgar Peters, a Ph.D. student in Vanderbilt's Graduate Department of Religion. See also, S. E. Dowd, *Prayer, Power, and the Problem of Suffering* (SBLDS 105; Atlanta: Scholars Press, 1988).

customary blessings of food or children, on a number of occasions throughout the story Jesus has gone aside especially to pray. These times are
characterized by isolation: he always goes alone, and he goes to a lonely
place (1:35; 6:45–46). During the periods of withdrawal, the disciples
either are in difficulty (6:48) or are harassing him (1:36). Even in the blessings, the disciples often miss the point (6:41; 8:6) or actually obstruct
Jesus' action (10:13–16). With such a background, the audience should be
surprised neither at the disciples' failure to exorcise a demon that requires
prayer nor at their coming utter incapacity to watch and pray with Jesus in
Gethsemane (14:37–40). Prayer in the Gospel of Mark is consistently outside the disciples' range of understanding or participation.

Mark 10:46–52

The final healing miracle of the Gospel closes the third Passion prediction
unit, the last section of Division One, and Division One itself. This strategic placement of the healing of blind Bartimaeus (10:46–52) is matched
by a number of unusual features in the episode itself.[20] First, with the single
exception of Jairus in Mark 5:22–23, unlike the disciples, all the ones
requesting healing have been unnamed until now. "Bartimaeus" is the
Aramaic equivalent of "son of Timaeus,"[21] and the use of both references
within the text is another indication of Mark's attempt at broad accessibility. Second, the healing of Bartimaeus epitomizes the faith-empowered

20. For a discussion of the relation of this story both to the Galilean ministry and
to the coming Jerusalem period, see V. Robbins, "The Healing of Blind Bartimaeus
(10:46–52) in the Marcan Theology," *JBL* 92 (1973): 224–43. For the relation of the
episode to discipleship in the Gospel, see E. S. Johnson, "Mark 10:46–52: Blind
Bartimaeus," *CBQ* 40 (1978): 191–204; and P. J. Achtemeier, "'And He Followed
Him': Miracles and Discipleship in Mark 10:46–52," *Semeia* 11 (1978): 115–45.
    Moreover, Via's discussion of Mark 10 as the middle of the Gospel, reflecting the
beginning and foreshadowing the ending, augments my analysis of the crucial position
of the Bartimaeus episode (see *The Ethics of Mark's Gospel,* 76–79). Via, however, while
seeing Bartimaeus as the epitomy of true discipleship for the Gospel, fails to recognize
the significance of having one of the healed represent ideal following rather than one
of the Twelve (see esp. 160–63).
    21. Some scholars argue, simply on the basis of finding a name in stories where
names do not usually appear, that Bartimaeus must have been a historical person
known to the Markan community (see, e.g., E. S. Johnson, "Mark 10:46–52: Blind
Bartimaeus," 193–94; Taylor, *The Gospel According to St. Mark,* 448). Such arguments
lose whatever slight credibility they have, if, as I will argue, there is a pressing *narrative*
explanation for a name at this point. The name Timaeus has, of course, a strong
symbolic overtone in Greek tradition, for the narrator of Plato's most important
theological treatise was the fictional Timaeus (see the discussion in Plato, *Timaeus and
Critias,* trans. with introduction by H. D. P. Lee [Harmondsworth: Penguin Books,
1965], 7–12, 22–25, 28). Given Mark's tendency toward figurative or typological
narrative, a symbolic rather than historical basis for the name itself is probably
preferable. Moreover, both Matthew and Luke omit the name and the figurative
significance of the story.

healings of Mark 1 through 5 rather than the declining cycle of Mark 6 through 10. As with the earlier healings, Bartimaeus *hears* of Jesus' presence and cries out for his aid (10:47). When Jesus asks what he wants, like the leper of Mark 1:40–42, he confidently requests healing, the return of his sight. Jesus responds, as he has with others seeking healing, Go (ὕπαγε, cf. 1:44; 2:11; 5:19, 34; 7:29), your faith has saved you (ἡ πίστις σου σέσωκέν σε; cf. 5:34). Hence all the positive motifs associated with healing in Mark, that is, associated with the fruitfulness of faith, reach their climax in Bartimaeus. He typifies the good earth.

However, Bartimaeus typifies more than that, for, third, the episode also contains a number of elements connected, not with those healed, but with the disciples. Besides being named as are the disciples, Bartimaeus is called by Jesus: "And Jesus stopped and cried, 'Call him.' And they *called* the blind man, saying to him, 'Take heart; rise, he is *calling* you'" (10:49).[22] The pervasive pattern of healings, as we have seen time and again, is for the supplicant for healing to initiate the action with Jesus responding, while the pervasive pattern of discipleship is for Jesus to initiate the call with the person responding by following or not (1:16–20; 2:14; 10:17–22). Bartimaeus has initiated the situation by crying out to the passing Jesus (10:47–48), but the threefold repetition of "call" in v. 49 accentuates Jesus' initiative in calling Bartimaeus. Moreover, although Jesus delivers the normal command for the healed, "Go," the narrator reports that Bartimaeus "followed him on the way (ἠκολούθει αὐτῷ ἐν τῇ ὁδῷ)" (10:52). Following Jesus on the way, though often with fear rather than faith, has been the function of the disciples (e.g., 1:18, 20; 2:14; 6:1; 10:28, 32). Further, except for the demons, the only ones so far to announce Jesus' divine identity have been the disciples in the voice of Peter (8:29), but here Bartimaeus cries out Jesus' name with a royal messianic title: "Jesus, Son of David, have mercy on me!" (10:47). When Peter identifies Jesus as "Christ," Jesus rebukes (ἐπετίμησεν, 8:30) the disciples to tell no one. When Bartimaeus identifies Jesus as "Son of David," many rebuke (ἐπετίμων, 10:48) him, telling him to be silent. Unlike the disciples, who generally obey Jesus' commands to silence, in part because they do not understand the issue anyway (e.g., 9:9–10), but like the ones healed and the proverbial prescription about the purpose of secrets (4:22), Bartimaeus rejects silence and instead cries out "all the more." Secrets are meant to come to light.

Consequently, the episode of the healing of blind Bartimaeus has been carefully composed to combine elements related to the healed with ele-

22. For an argument supporting the call story nature of the Bartimaeus episode by comparing it with call stories in the Hebrew Bible, see M. G. Steinhauser, "The Form of the Bartimaeus Narrative (Mark 10:46–52)," *NTS* 32 (1986): 583–95.

ments related to the disciples. Bartimaeus not only typifies the fruitfulness of faith but also the faithfulness of the ideal follower of Jesus. As an example of the common folkloric strategy of end stress,[23] the last one healed in the Gospel is the symbolic ideal. The rhetorical placement of the story at the end of three structural units—the third Passion prediction unit, the last section of Division One, and Division One itself—confirms this status. The last section of Division One begins with Jesus' two attempts to heal a blind man (8:22–26). The healing of Bartimaeus is parallel to but much better than that opening healing. The audience, when hearing the story of Bartimaeus and remembering the earlier blind man, should understand again the importance of faith for ease of healing. Additionally, this last section is organized by three Passion prediction units, the first and last of which close with healings. In the first unit, Jesus tells the disciples and the crowds, If anyone wishes to follow after me, let that one deny himself or herself and take up her or his cross and follow me (8:34). The three Passion predictions themselves reveal that such cross-bearing will not be just the metaphorical but also the literal experience of Jesus' followers, and Jesus' arrival in Jerusalem will start the process. The third Passion prediction unit, which is ended by the healing of Bartimaeus, opens with the report that they were on the way (ἐν τῇ ὁδῷ) up to Jerusalem, and Jesus was going ahead of them and "those who followed were afraid (οἱ . . . ἀκολουθοῦντες ἐφοβοῦντο)" (10:32). The disciples follow on the way with fear. In contrast, the unit ends with Bartimaeus, saved by his faith, following on the way. The true follower who can take up the cross and follow Jesus into persecutions is one who responds in faith, not fear.[24]

The middle Passion prediction unit (9:30—10:31) ends not with a healing but with the story of the rich man's encounter with Jesus and Jesus' subsequent teaching to the disciples. After the rich man departs in sorrow, Jesus comments on the difficulty those with riches face in entering the kingdom of God (10:23–25). The disciples in amazement ask, "Then who can be *saved* (σωθῆναι)?" (10:26). While Jesus indirectly answers their question in his teaching on discipleship, the real answer is illustrated dramatically in the Bartimaeus episode, for Jesus says to Bartimaeus, your faith has *saved* you (ἡ πίστις σου σέσωκέν σε). Those who respond with faith can be

---

23. A. Olrik, "Epic Laws of Folk Narrative," in *The Study of Folklore,* ed. A. Dundes (Englewood Cliffs, N.J.: Prentice-Hall, 1965), 136–37.

24. The realization that the Gospel of Mark is an ancient figurative or typological narrative and not a modern realistic one is important here. Realism would decree that Bartimaeus appear faithfully championing Jesus' cause all the way through the Passion story. But for Mark, Bartimaeus epitomizes the true follower of faith in an ideal or symbolic fashion. He is the *type* that all Jesus' followers ought to be; he is not a character who must now become involved in the working out of the story.

saved and are thereby part of God's kingdom. Moreover, the middle Passion prediction unit is surrounded by repetitions of the proverbial saying of Jesus that "the first will be last and the last first" (9:35; 10:31). On both occasions the sayings are directed to the disciples, and indeed the very first episode in all of Division One concerned the calling of disciples to follow Jesus (1:16–20). The Bartimaeus episode, the very last episode in Division One, concerns the calling of one who is healed by his faith and follows Jesus on the way. The first called are the hard-hearted disciples (e.g., 6:52; 8:17–18), the rocky ground, who accept at first, endure for a time, and then fall away when opposition threatens. The last called is the supplicant for healing whose faith saves him, the good earth that bears abundant fruit. The first will be last and the last first—that proverb not only indicates the paradoxical quality of the kingdom of God, it also describes the narrative plan of Division One. Like the disciples, Bartimaeus is named, called, and follows Jesus on the way; like the ones healed, he initiates the action, expresses confident belief, is commanded to go, for his faith has saved him. He is the last who has become the first, the epitome of the good earth and the faithful follower. He is what the Twelve are not, the fruitful ground, not the rocky ground. With this example of the ideal type of Jesus' follower, Division One ends, and the period of open persecution in Jerusalem begins.

Mark 11:12–25

In discussing the shift between Division One—Jesus, the Sower of the Word and Division Two—Jesus, the Heir of the Vineyard,[25] we pointed out that the transition was smoothed in the accepted rhetorical style of the time by an "overlapping at the edges" technique. Division One foreshadows Division Two in the three Passion predictions, the association of Jerusalem with these sufferings, and in Bartimaeus's identification of Jesus as "Son of David,"[26] an identification that is taken up in the introduction to Division Two (11:9–10). Division Two is linked to Division One by presenting as its first episode following the introduction the last miracle of the Gospel and the final—and most openly didactic—teaching on faith, Mark 11:12–25. The cursing of the fig tree, with the story of Jesus' cleansing of the temple inserted in the midst of it (11:15–19), is a miracle illustrative of the unfruitfulness, hard-heartedness, and opposition now poised to engulf Jesus. It is not a miracle of healing, of triumph over the

25. See above, pp. 118–19.
26. For a more traditional discussion of "Son of David" as a title for Jesus, see, e.g., C. Burger, *Jesus als Davidssohn* (FRLANT 98; Göttingen: Vandenhoeck & Ruprecht, 1970).

demonic world, or of controlling the destructive chaos of nature, typical of the miracles in Division One. It is, instead, the symbolic cursing of unfruitfulness.

To Jesus' hunger the fig tree offers nothing except leaves (11:12–13), just as for the spiritual hunger of the nations the temple offers not a "house of prayer" but a "den of robbers" (11:17). Whether the perpetually fruitful apocalyptic tree of Ezek. 47:12 stands behind Mark's fig tree or not, Jesus' cursing of the tree is not a fretful attack on the seasonal cycles of nature but a symbolic cursing of all fruitless, faithless responses to human need. The narrator's explanation that it was not the season for figs (11:13) encourages the audience to perceive the symbolic rather than mundane character of Jesus' action, and the ominous finality of Jesus' words to the tree, "May no one ever eat fruit from you again," suggests that time can, indeed, run out for fruitless trees, prayerless temples, and perhaps faithless disciples.[27] The image of the eternal death of the fruitless tree appropriately dominates this opening of the second part of the Gospel, for it is the story of failure, death, and judgment that must now be narrated. That the final miracle of the Gospel should be one of destruction rather than growth is typical of Mark's overall interest in unfruitful grounds and their fearful responses to Jesus' performative words, and it also signifies the pervasiveness of hard-hearted, fruitless responses now surrounding Jesus in Jerusalem.

As many commentators have pointed out, the insertion of the temple-cleansing episode between the two parts of the fig tree story serves to associate the barrenness of the fig tree with the corruption of the temple,[28] introducing a series of explicit and implicit attacks on the temple that form an anti-temple polemic throughout the final chapters of the Gospel. That polemic and Jesus' authority to mount it will be explored further in chapter 10 of our study. For our present purposes, it is the connection of the miraculous cursing of the fig tree with Jesus' most explicit teaching on the nature of faith that is of concern.[29] While the disciples have often missed

27. While one does not wish to posit too great a subtlety to the Markan narrative, there is a remarkable similarity in vocabulary used to describe the tree not presently in the season (καιρὸς) for figs which will be forever (εἰς τὸν αἰῶνα) fruitless (Mark 11:13–14) and the description of Jesus' followers who will experience persecutions now in this season (ἐν τῷ καιρῷ τούτῳ) but eternal life in the coming age (ἐν τῷ αἰῶνι τῷ ἐρχομένῳ) in Mark 10:30. Fruitlessness now means fruitlessness for eternity, but fruitfulness now brings abundance with persecutions and life for eternity.

28. See, e.g., D. Juel, *Messiah and Temple: The Trial of Jesus in the Gospel of Mark* (SBLDS 31; Missoula, Mont.: Scholars Press, 1977), 127–36; and Donahue, *Are You the Christ?*, 113–22.

29. The tendency in past form- and redaction-critical scholarship to read the Gospel in small fragments has generally cloaked the connection between miracles and faith so consistently expressed in the narrative and consequently has led critics to miss the logic of this teaching on faith following the miracle of the fig tree. See, e.g., Taylor, *The Gospel According to St. Mark*, 458–59, 465–67.

the point or failed to understand past miracles in the Gospel (e.g., 4:41; 6:50–52; 8:17–21), this miracle of destruction and death is actually called to Jesus' attention by—most appropriately—the epitome of the rocky ground itself, Peter (11:21). Furthermore, the narrator heightens the association of the unfruitful tree with Peter and the disciples by describing the tree, "withered away to its roots (ἐξηραμμένην ἐκ ῥιζῶν)" (11:20), in words that echo the problem of the seed on rocky ground that withered away because it had no root (διὰ τὸ μὴ ἔχειν ῥίζαν ἐξηράνθη, 4:6).[30] This miracle, then, is clearly the kind that should be most recognizable to the disciples.

Jesus' response to Peter's exclamation concerning the death of the cursed tree is a teaching about faith in God. The audience has repeatedly heard the relationship between faith and miracles dramatized in the healings of the preceding chapters; now in the story of this final miracle, the Markan Jesus delineates the issue openly: "'Have faith in God. Truly, I say to you, whoever says to this mountain, "Be taken up and cast into the sea," and does not doubt in his heart, but believes that what he says will come to pass, it will be done for him'" (11:22–23). Faith is the prerequisite of miracles, for if one has faith that it will happen, then it will happen. Indeed, the Gospel of Mark presents a remarkably consistent view of faith: faith is the heartfelt conviction that something will be done *prior to* the event, and, moreover, it is that conviction itself which assures the result. Miracles, then, can never be the cause of faith; they can only be its result, as the author has demonstrated time and again. Jesus further extends this understanding of faith to prayer and forgiveness: "'Therefore I tell you, whatever you ask in prayer, believe that you have received it, and it will be yours. And whenever you stand praying, forgive, if you have anything against any one; so that your Father also who is in heaven may forgive you your trespasses'" (11:24–25). Prayer from the faith-filled heart receives its request, and prayer that forgives all others assures God's divine forgiveness. For Mark, the key to miracles, effective prayer, and divine forgiveness lies within the human heart. God does not manipulate the will by miraculous signs or entice the mind by unexpected gifts or induce a forgiving spirit through guilt. Instead, it is the human initiative of the faithful ground that produces the abundant fruits of the kingdom of God.

With this final explication of faith as the prerequisite of miracle and the corollary notions of faith as necessary for effective prayer and human forgiveness as necessary for divine forgiveness, the story of the fruitful

30. Since the distance between the description of the tree in Mark 11 and the rocky ground in Mark 4 is quite extended, this echo may well not have been clear to the general auditor of the Gospel. It functions, then, as another subtle connection for the appreciation of the careful or learned ranks of the authorial audience.

ground in the Gospel of Mark ends. No more miracles, no further requests for healing, no faithful responses to the word remain to be detailed during the days in Jerusalem leading up to Jesus' final victory over death itself. After Mark 11:12–25, unfruitful ground, fear, confrontation, betrayal, denial, and death rule the narrative, as indeed for the Gospel of Mark they symbolically rule the vineyard and actually rule the world as a whole. The workers in this evil kingdom are primarily the chief priests, the scribes, and the Jerusalem Jewish leaders whom the narrator now firmly connects with the unfruitful response of fear ("and the chief priests and scribes *heard* it and sought a way to destroy him; for they *feared* him," 11:18). Yet these characters have opposed Jesus from the beginning and their response, while terrible, is predictable and expected. The real tragedy of the Gospel on the human level is the failure of the disciples, the rocky ground that Jesus has worked so hard to cultivate. Although the authorial audience has known since the parable of the Sower that the disciples will eventually stumble when persecution arrives, how this change occurs and why supply the major dramatic tension of Division One and extend into Division Two for conclusion. Thus it is to the story of the Markan disciples that we must now turn.

The Rocky Ground—Failure and Fear

Because the story of the disciples in Mark supplies so much of the Gospel's dramatic impetus, being as they are the only character group to change state in the course of the narrative,[31] we have already had occasion to describe much of their portrayal in earlier sections of this study. We need only to reprise that material, focusing especially on their shift to hardheartedness and fear as dramatized in Peter's confession (8:27–33) and the transfiguration (9:2–13), and then to follow out their tale to its conclusion in Gethsemane (14:32–50) and the high priest's courtyard (14:66–72). As

---

31. The disciples' change of state from initial faith to fear and failure, illustrating on the human level the rocky ground response to hearing the word, has caused considerable confusion in Markan scholarship. Some scholars, emphasizing the deeply negative depiction of the disciples in the later chapters, have argued that for Mark the disciples are the opponents of Jesus or the object of the author's strongest polemic (see, e.g., Weeden, *Mark—Traditions in Conflict*, 26–51; and W. Kelber, *The Oral and the Written Gospel: The Hermeneutics of Speaking and Writing in the Synoptic Tradition, Mark, Paul, and Q* (Philadelphia: Fortress Press, 1983), 97–99, 125–29). Other scholars, weighting the earlier, more positive portrayal (often with more weight than it can reasonably bear), have argued that Mark is only presenting the disciples as fallible followers, indicating that discipleship is a difficult business and not easily accomplished (see, e.g., Tannehill, "The Disciples in Mark: The Function of a Narrative Role," 386–405; and Malbon, "Fallible Followers: Women and Men in the Gospel of Mark," 29–48). For the authorial audience, familiar with the ancient conventions of illustrative characterization, plot summaries, and typological narrative, such confusion would have been much less likely.

the second degree narrative representatives of the rocky ground type, the characterization of the disciples in Mark 6 through 10 holds special interest for illustrating the human traits behind their ultimate failure; so we must consider carefully how their concerns, views, and actions are portrayed in contrast to other characters.

Receiving the Word with Joy

In the Interpretation of the parable of the Sower, the rocky ground type is explained as that group "who, when they hear the word, immediately receive it with joy; and they have no root in themselves, but endure for a while; then, when tribulation or persecution rises on account of the word, immediately they fall away" (4:16–17). The disciples' initial response of acceptance and faith is depicted primarily in three (or four) episodes devoted to them in the first two sections of Division One (1:16—6:34): the calls (1:16–20; 2:13–14), the designation of the Twelve (3:13–19), and the sending out of the Twelve (6:7–13, 30). The alacrity of the disciples' response to Jesus' calls is emphasized both by the descriptions of their actions and by repetitions of εὐθὺs ("immediately," 1:18, 20). Simon and Andrew drop their net to follow; James and John desert their father in his boat; and Levi simply rises from his tax office seat and goes after Jesus. Since the reader views all characters by their response to Jesus, the powerful central hero of the story, the remarkable receptiveness and obedience of the disciples ensure their favorable regard at the outset of the narrative. The special status accorded the Twelve by being selected by Jesus to be with him and to be sent out to preach and cast out demons (3:14–15) and their successful completion of a teaching and healing mission (6:7, 12, 30) confirm and expand that favorable assessment.

However, it would be incorrect to suggest that in these opening events no negative elements appear. The narrator prepares the audience to accept the ultimate role of the disciples even in their initially positive presentation in both obvious and subtle ways. As we have already observed, the last verse in the designation of the Twelve (3:19) informs the reader that one of these twelve, Judas, will betray Jesus, a blatantly negative note. Moreover, in the immediately succeeding episode Jesus' teaching about the inevitable demise of divided houses and kingdoms (3:23–25) reflects ominously on the future of his own disciples.[32] By depicting Simon and the others as harassing (κατεδίωξεν, 1:36) Jesus and the actions of the disciples as the cause of some of Jesus' early controversies (e.g., 2:18, 23–24), the narrator almost inconspicuously begins associating the disciples with trouble for Jesus. The confusion of the disciples at Jesus' ability to calm the storm, just after he has

32. See above, pp. 99–101.

explained *all* to them (4:34–41), adds to their increasingly ambivalent portrait in these early chapters.

Furthermore, the successful mission of the Twelve (6:7–13, 30) which, next to the call stories, is easily the most positive representation of the disciples in the entire Gospel, is interrupted by the bizarre and frightening episode of John the Baptist's death in Herod's court. The insertion of this striking episode in the midst of the story of the mission begs for some explanation. The often-expressed view that Mark placed the story of John's death at this point to "fill the gap" between the sending out of the Twelve and their return[33] hardly does justice to the dramatic force of the ploy. The images of the birthday banquet, the girl's dance, and John's head served up on a platter completely overshadow the mission of the Twelve, and consequently the intercalation of this episode undercuts the positive action of the Twelve by stressing the negative action of Herod. The period of the disciples' mission of preaching,[34] casting out demons, and healing is dominated narratively by death and the whimsy of evil.

Yet, for the authorial audience the effect of the arrangement was probably even more profound. As in the case of the insertion of the cleansing of the temple in the midst of the fig tree episode (11:12–25), Mark characteristically uses this intercalation strategy[35] to forge a close symbolic, narrative, or chronological association between the inserted story and its encompassing episode. Some interweaving of interpretation always results. In this case, regardless of some commentators' desires, chronology alone is not the point.[36] The authorial audience has just been informed that those of the rocky ground type will stumble "when tribulation or persecution arises on

33. See, e.g., Taylor, *The Gospel According to St. Mark,* 307; Nineham, *Saint Mark,* 172; and C. E. B. Cranfield, *The Gospel According to Saint Mark,* 206.
The historicity of Mark's account of John's death faces great difficulties because of its strong differences from Josephus's record (*Antiquities* 18.5.2). In Josephus, Herod executes John summarily because he fears that John might incite a revolution among the people with whom he is extremely popular. Mark's portrayal of a sympathetic Herod who kills John only reluctantly because of his public promise to the girl is founded not on history but on typology.

34. The narrator reports that the disciples "preached that men should repent" (Mark 6:12). Jesus' preaching, reported in Mark 1:15, was that people should "*repent,* and *believe* in the gospel.*" Even in this most positive action of the disciples, it is fascinating to notice that the narrator refuses to associate them with faith. Their preaching is closer to that of John the Baptist (cf. 1:4) than that of Jesus, and having John's story immediately follow the narrator's report of the disciples' preaching may serve to remind the careful reader of that difference.

35. For studies of this rhetorical technique throughout Mark, see Donahue, *Are You the Christ?* 53–63; Kermode, *The Genesis of Secrecy,* 127–45.

36. Kermode rightly criticizes biblical scholars for narrative naiveté in suggesting that Mark needed to show the passage of time between the disciples' mission and return as the reason for placing the story of John's death at this point. See *The Genesis of Secrecy,* 130–31.

account of the word" (4:17). Although some future persecution of Jesus has already been foreshadowed in the plot of the Pharisees and the Herodians reported in Mark 3:6, the story of John's death in Herod's court is the most shocking, graphic, and frightening description of the deadly nature of tribulation on account of the word to be found anywhere in the Gospel except at the crucifixion itself. It is not only the grotesque image of John's head on a platter but also the pervasiveness and capriciousness of evil that make the episode so disturbing. Because of a girl's dance and a rash promise, Herod shifts from protecting John and hearing him gladly to ordering him beheaded and delivering his head on a platter like the final course of the banquet to the girl and her mother. A world in which "a righteous and holy man" (6:20) can be so wantonly destroyed is clearly a world glutted with evil, promising very real and very deadly tribulations and persecutions.

Hence, while John's death, just like his earlier ministry (1:4–8), obviously anticipates the death of Jesus,[37] its main function for the authorial audience is to emphasize in the most dreadful fashion the lethal omnipresence of evil. Tribulation and persecution in such a world as this are as inevitable as the rising of the sun (cf. 4:6). In the midst of the disciples' successful mission, the narrator confirms the implacable evil facing Jesus and his predecessors and followers. The rocky ground may receive the word with joy, but tribulation and persecution await just down the road. Indeed, the narrator links the Herod story to the disciples' mission by implying that the very success of their work was responsible for bringing them—and Jesus—to Herod's attention. Herod's view that Jesus was John, raised from the dead (6:16), carries sinister overtones for Jesus' future, for becoming known to Herod is manifestly a dangerous position to be in, as John's experience proves.

Thus, even in the opening sections of the Gospel the initial positive response of the disciples in accepting Jesus' call, being designated as his special companions, and being sent out to preach and heal, is tempered by both obvious and subtle anticipations of their later failures and a vivid depiction of the inevitable persecutions besetting the holy and righteous.

Enduring for a Time

Whatever positive portrayal the disciples receive in the first two sections of Division One is quickly and utterly dissipated by the final two sections (6:35—10:52). In the first of these (6:35—8:21), the two feeding stories with their boat trip conclusions disclose the hardened hearts of the disciples, while the final section (8:22—10:52) explores some of the human

---

37. It is a foreshadowing with a difference, though, for when John dies, his disciples come and take the body away for burial (Mark 6:29). At Jesus' death, his disciples having all fled, a stranger must take the body and bury it (15:42–46).

traits that may lie behind such hardening. The disciples' transition from acceptance to hard-heartedness does not follow the pattern of slow, internal, psychological development one expects and finds in modern literature.[38] Instead, after the disciples' terrified response to seeing Jesus walking on the sea and Jesus' repetitive admonition for them not to fear (6:49–51), the narrator bluntly informs the audience that the disciples did not understand, for "their hearts were hardened" (ἡ καρδία πεπωρωμένη, 6:52). The gravity of this description is increased by the fact that the same words were used to describe the Pharisees and the Herodians who were plotting to destroy Jesus (ἐπὶ τῇ πωρώσει τῆς καρδίας αὐτῶν, 3:5–6). The shift from the successful preaching mission of Mark 6:13, 30 to the hard-heartedness of Mark 6:52 seems sudden and inexplicable to modern readers schooled in the conventions of the contemporary novel. To an ancient audience, however, who were already aware of the ethical type of response being illustrated by the disciples, the change would have been anticipated and expected.[39] *Why* the disciples do not understand and have hardened hearts is still unclear; *that* they would at some point shift positions has been known since Mark 4 and 5. Now that the narrator has announced the change, the audience can begin to search for the "why" by comparing and contrasting the attitudes and actions of the disciples to Jesus, the ones healed, and the Jewish opponents.

The narrator's assessment of the disciples' altered heart-set is confirmed in the dramatic confrontation between them and Jesus in the boat trip following the second feeding story (8:1–21), when the disciples interpret literally Jesus' metaphorical warning about "the leaven of the Pharisees and the leaven of Herod"[40] (8:15) and worry about having too little bread. The possible significance of the repetition of the numbers involved in the feeding stories has already been addressed;[41] in order to emphasize the change

38. "The concept of the developing character who changes inwardly is quite a late arrival in narrative," so say R. Scholes and R. Kellogg, *The Nature of Narrative* (London: Oxford University Press, 1966), 165. See their discussion of the evolution of inward characterization on pp. 160–70.

39. With characters in ancient narrative, "we are not called upon to understand their motivation as if they were whole human beings but to understand the principles they illustrate through their actions in a narrative framework" (Scholes and Kellogg, *The Nature of Narrative*, 88).

40. Mark leaves Jesus' metaphor unexplained, assuming the audience will recognize it for what it is and thus again feel superior in understanding to the disciples, who so completely miss the point. Matthew in his version of the story explicitly explains the metaphor, so as to leave the audience (and the disciples) in no doubt: "Then they understood that he did not tell them to beware of the leaven of bread, but of the teaching of the Pharisees and Sadducees" (Matt. 16:12). Mark here seems to be closer than Matthew to Demetrius's advice to leave some points for your hearer to comprehend on his or her own; so, then, the hearer becomes witness and is not treated as though a fool (see *On Style* 222).

41. See above, p. 183.

in the disciples, the author has Jesus challenge them in words that repeat the Isaiah allusion of Mark 4:11–12. In that earlier passage, "those who were about him with the twelve" were evidently among the "you" to whom the secret of the kingdom of God was given, while "those outside" heard parables, "so that they may indeed see (βλέπωσιν) but not perceive, and may indeed hear (ἀκούωσιν) but not understand (συνιῶσιν); lest they should turn again, and be forgiven." Now it is the Twelve who embody the traits of the "outsiders," as Jesus queries, "Do you not yet perceive or understand (συνίετε)? Are your hearts hardened? Having eyes do you not see (βλέπετε), and having ears do you not hear (ἀκούετε)?" (Mark 8:17–18). What the narrator reported in 6:52, Jesus now dramatically reiterates: far from avoiding the leaven of the Pharisees and Herod, the disciples have become like the Pharisees and the Herodians before them by having hardened hearts, and such hardness, found both in the ground along the path and the rocky ground, prevents the seed from taking root and producing fruit. Those who seemed to be insiders now expose the underlying hardness of outsiders. But what are the human characteristics that accompany such hardness?

The last section of Division One (8:22—10:52) contrasts the teachings of Jesus with the actions, ideas, and desires of the Twelve to illustrate the human flaws that may block the hearing of the word. In each of the three Passion prediction units that organize this section (8:27—9:29; 9:30—10:31; 10:32–52) Jesus' teaching about his upcoming suffering in Jerusalem is either ignored, misunderstood, or rejected by his disciples. The first unit is particularly striking, for it contains not only Peter's confession of Jesus as the Christ (8:29) but also the amazing episode known as the transfiguration (9:2–8), all of which the narrator uses to begin to sketch the disciples' desire for very human glory, status, and power in contrast to the "glory" of suffering, the "status" of servanthood, and the "power" of new life associated with the kingdom of God as Jesus reveals it. That the whole of this last section is surrounded by two stories of Jesus giving sight to the blind (8:22–26 and 10:46–52) serves to stress the pervasive irony of the disciples' portrayal: Jesus can give sight to the physically blind who come to him in faith, but he cannot give insight to his fearful disciples; what would seem the harder task faith makes easier, while what would appear the easier task fear renders impossible.

Mark 8:27—9:1—Peter's Confession

Peter's confession that Jesus is the Christ in Mark 8:29 is the first time in the story that a human character rather than a demon or spirit confirms the narrator's initial introduction of Jesus as the Christ in Mark 1:1. Because of

Peter's earlier and immediately following misunderstandings concerning Jesus and because of the nature of Jesus' response to his confession (the word the narrator uses to "charge" the disciples, ἐπετιμάω, in 8:30 is the same word used for Peter's "rebuke" of Jesus in 8:32 and Jesus' "rebuke" of him in 8:33; it is also most often used in Mark for exorcisms; see 1:25; 3:12; 9:25), scholars have debated whether this confession by Peter is accepted or rejected by Jesus.[42] Is it a correct identification of Jesus or not? Approaching the story from the standpoint of narrative levels clarifies the dynamics of the episode greatly. The narrator announced Jesus as the Christ, the Son of God, in the opening line of the story. Further, the reader has been reassured of that identification by the voice from heaven (1:11) and by a number of spirits from the cosmic realm (e.g., 1:24; 3:11; 5:7) as well as by Jesus' own miraculous activities.[43]

Consequently, by Mark 8:29 the audience knows that Jesus is indeed ὁ Χριστός, the Son of God, and would recognize Peter's assertion as correct. Peter now understands what the audience has known from the beginning about Jesus. Given such knowledge, Peter's next actions in relation to Jesus are shocking in the extreme. When Jesus starts to teach the disciples about the inevitability of suffering, rejection, and death that he faces, Peter rebukes him (8:31–32). Peter evidently believes he knows better than the Messiah! What degree of pride or arrogance must exist to allow one to refute the Messiah? For the audience, knowing that Jesus is the Christ and seeing him characterized with powers very similar to those of the omniscient narrator have resulted in a thorough alignment of their views with those of Jesus. For Peter, confessing Jesus as the Christ gives rise to a blatant exhibition of pride and hardness of heart (and head). The authorial audience and Peter stand on opposite sides. As long as Peter or the disciples could be credited with a lack of knowledge concerning who Jesus was, their

---

42. See, e.g., Taylor, *The Gospel According to St. Mark*, 374–77; Nineham, *Saint Mark*, 224–27; and Weeden, *Mark—Traditions in Conflict*, 97–100.

43. The use of "Christ" as a name or title for Jesus is relatively rare in Mark. The narrator uses it in the opening line along with "Son of God" (see p. 110, n. 43 for our argument on internal evidence that "Son of God" should be part of the original text); Peter uses it here at Mark 8:29; Jesus uses it in teachings at 9:41 and 12:35; and the high priest uses it along with a periphrasis for Son of God at 14:61 and in mocking Jesus on the cross at 15:32. ὁ Χριστός is the Greek version of Messiah, a specifically Jewish designation for Jesus, and thus Mark quite appropriately places it on the lips of Jesus' Jewish disciples and Jewish opponents. The cosmic spirits and non-Jews (e.g., the centurion in 15:39) tend to use the broader, more Hellenistic designation Son of God. That the narrator employs both terms in the opening of the Gospel and has Jesus affirm both to the high priest (14:61–62) indicates their basic synonymity for the author and authorial audience. To be the Jewish Christ, for Mark, was to be Son of God.

failures might be at least partially excused on the basis of ignorance. No such excuse exists any longer, and the enormity of Peter's arrogance is justly condemned by Jesus in the rebuke, "Get behind me, Satan! For you are not on the side of God, but of men" (8:33).[44]

The teaching to which Peter has the presumption to object concerns the necessity (δεῖ, 8:31) of suffering not only for Jesus but, as Jesus explains to the multitude (8:34), for all who wish to follow him as well. Suffering, the cross, and death are the inevitable results of walking the way of Jesus "in this adulterous and sinful generation" (8:38), and the narrator imbues the entire episode with an atmosphere of evil at the very beginning, for the answers the disciples give to Jesus' opening question of who people say he is are almost an exact repetition of the options outlined for Herod at the beginning of the episode of John the Baptist's death in Mark 6:14–16. Herod believed that Jesus was John raised from the dead, but he also heard that Jesus was Elijah or one of the prophets. By repeating that same materials here, the author invokes the earlier story and thus reminds the audience of the pervasiveness and capriciousness of evil. That Jesus refers to "this generation" as an "adulterous" one (8:38) may additionally allude to the earlier Herod story.

Recalling Herod's treatment of John the Baptist as a background for Jesus' first prediction of his passion and the necessary suffering of his followers reminds the audience of just *how* sinful "this generation" really is and hence provides an important clue to why such suffering must be expected. By failing to note the connection between this first Passion prediction and the episode of Herod and John the Baptist, established narratively through exact repetition and allusion, many commentators have assumed that the Markan δεῖ, like δεῖ in much apocalyptic literature, refers primarily to *divine* necessity.[45] God, thus, ordains the suffering of Jesus and those who follow him. While for Mark, God is certainly sovereign over all creation, the direct cause of suffering for Jesus is the current dominance of "this adulterous and sinful generation." It is not God's will but the evil will of the present authorities and powers that makes suffering inevitable. As the parable of the Tenants and the Apocalyptic Discourse in Division Two of the Gospel will clarify and confirm, the creation of God is now in the hands of a

44. The command to Peter as Satan in Mark 8:33, Ὕπαγε ὀπίσω μου (Go [away] *behind me*), is played upon in 8:34 as Jesus states what is needful for those who θέλει ὀπίσω μου ἀκολουθεῖν (wish to follow *behind me*). That play might well remind the careful reader that Simon was originally called Δεῦτε ὀπίσω μου (come *behind me*) in Mark 1:17. One whom Jesus called to come has from his own hard-heartedness forced Jesus to command to go away.

45. See, e.g., Nineham, *Saint Mark*, 225–27; Rhoads and Michie, *Mark as Story*, 76–77; and Donahue, "A Neglected Factor in the Theology of Mark," 586–87.

murderous generation who will destroy anyone daring to challenge their privileges. However, it will not always be so, for the parable of the Tenants also indicates that God will come and put out the present group and give the vineyard to others. Yet, until that final judgment occurs, persecution, death, and suffering will of necessity plague God's servants. Although God may be held obliquely responsible for the suffering of Jesus and his followers by delaying that ultimate action, as the narrative link between the first Passion prediction unit and Herod's banquet suggests and Division Two will corroborate, for Mark the basic cause of Jesus' suffering is this evil generation presently controlling God's creation. Only by precipitate divine intervention could Jesus and his followers avoid persecutions and tribulations.

That divine intervention will come, as Jesus asserts in Mark 8:38, when the Son of man returns "in the glory of his Father with the holy angels," but the time is not yet. So, for the present, Jesus and anyone who wishes to follow him can expect to take up a cross and lose life, but that apparent loss is actually an incredible gain, for in losing one's life for Jesus' sake and the gospel's, one saves (σώσει) it (8:34–35). Since the audience has already heard of many healed who were saved by their faith, the miraculous efficacy of such salvation is clear, and Jesus' claim to the crowds in second degree narrative that some standing there will not die "before they see that the kingdom of God has come with power" (9:1) can be affirmed by the audience simply on the basis of what they have already seen of Jesus' ministry. For those who have faith in Jesus' performative word, the kingdom of God comes with the power to save. However, the disciples in the person of Peter reject Jesus' description of the way to be followed, just as they have earlier failed to understand the feedings and many of the healings; perhaps a more glorious vision of who Jesus is and what he is about will soften those hardened hearts that stymie Jesus' plain words. Just such a vision is now presented to the disciples in the episode often called the transfiguration.

46. On whether the transfiguration should be viewed as an epiphany or a vision (specifically an apocalyptic vision), see H. C. Kee, "The Transfiguration in Mark: Epiphany or Apocalyptic Vision?" *Understanding the Sacred Text: Essays in Honor of Morton S. Enslin on the Hebrew Bible and Christian Beginnings*, ed. J. Reumann (Valley Forge, Pa.: Judson Press, 1972), 137–52.

For a recent bibliographic survey of scholarship concerning the transfiguration, see T. F. Best, "The Transfiguration: A Select Bibliography," *Journal of the Evangelical Theological Society* 24 (1981): 157–61.

47. The continuing debate over whether or not the transfiguration is a misplaced (by Mark) resurrection appearance story can be found in, e.g., R. H. Stein, "Is the Transfiguration (Mark 9:2–8) a Misplaced Resurrection-Account?" *JBL* 95 (1976): 79–96; and M. Smith, "The Origin and History of the Transfiguration Story," *USQR* 36 (1980): 39–44.

Mark 9:2–13—The Transfiguration

While much of the scholarly debate concerning the correct formal designation for the story[46] and its possible sources[47] is tangential to our interest in how Mark is using the episode,[48] even within the Gospel the transfiguration is striking. Along with the baptism, it presents one of the few instances in which the divine basis of the story world takes concrete narrative form: a voice speaks from the clouds, and, what is more, former religious leaders of Israel, Elijah and Moses, appear alive talking with Jesus. The close connection of the passage with Jesus' comment about the future coming of the Son of man "in the glory of his Father with the holy angels" (8:38) clearly casts the episode as a foreshadowing of that impending event[49] and a confirmation of Jesus' prediction. Thus the transfiguration embraces both the opening of Jesus' ministry and its future cosmic culmination.

However, to the authorial audience the episode for all its dramatic force presents little new information: they already know that Jesus is God's beloved Son; they already know that he possesses miraculous powers—he can still the storm with a word, walk on water, and multiply loaves and fish; that his human form should momentarily be altered to a purer, brighter essence is not astounding. Only the living presence of Elijah and Moses expands the audience's understanding of Jesus by anticipating his role as the beloved son sent as the final messenger by the lord of the vineyard to the wicked tenants in the parabolic plot synopsis of Division Two of the Gospel. Jesus stands in the line of Elijah, Moses, and the new Elijah, John the Baptist (see 9:13), as a messenger to "this adulterous and sinful generation."

If the transfiguration serves mainly to remind the audience in first degree narration of what they already know, it communicates quite new perspectives to the characters in second degree narration. The disciples were not witnesses of Jesus' baptism, and although they have experienced most of his

48. If the transfiguration is playing upon a conventional type-scene, then the nature of that scene as epiphany, vision, or whatever would be important for us to ascertain, because the author might well be using the scene to produce some conventionalized responses in the authorial audience that we modern readers miss. On the importance of type-scenes in biblical literature, see R. Alter, "Biblical Type-Scenes and the Uses of Convention," in *The Art of Biblical Narrative* (New York: Basic Books, 1981), 47–62; and J. Darr, "'Glorified in the Presence of Kings': A Literary-Critical Study of Herod the Tetrarch in Luke-Acts" (Ph.D. diss., Vanderbilt University, 1987), 125–97. Such a search through Hellenistic literature is beyond the scope of this study but suggests an important channel for future research.

49. A number of scholars have argued that the nature of the story, along with the "after six days" of the introduction and the "he charged them to tell no one what they had seen, until the Son of man should have risen from the dead" of the conclusion, clearly indicate that the story is intended to be proleptic of the Parousia. See, e.g., Perrin, *The New Testament: An Introduction*, 148.

miracles, they have apparently understood little. The transfiguration of Jesus, then, on its manifest level is primarily *for their benefit*. While the audience can affirm the truth of Jesus' saying in Mark 9:1 that "there are some standing here who will not taste death before they see that the kingdom of God has come with power," for they have seen and heard those healed, the disciples still remain in darkness. Even Peter's affirmation that Jesus is the Messiah was immediately spoiled by his refutation of Jesus' words. But in witnessing the transfiguration, the disciples can no longer claim ignorance of just who Jesus is or the extent of his authority and power. They are given a dramatic demonstration of what the audience has known from the beginning of the Gospel. How they respond to that demonstration will mark their distance from or proximity to the views of the authorial audience.

The specific time reference in Mark 9:2, "after six days," both connects the transfiguration with the immediately preceding teaching session and separates it somewhat from it.[50] Jesus' ascent of the mountain with his three special disciples, the transfiguration itself, and the appearance of "Elijah with Moses" are all succinctly reported by the narrator, thus assuring the veracity of the account. The only direct discourse occurs in Peter's address to Jesus and the words of the voice from the cloud; yet the drama of the episode focuses on these statements. After seeing the transfigured Jesus and the appearance of Elijah and Moses, Peter responds to Jesus, "Rabbi, it is well that we are here; let us make three booths, one for you and one for Moses and one for Elijah" (9:5). Whether Peter means to construct three booths or "tabernacles" (Gk.: σκηνή) as permanent dwellings for these three "gods" or simply to erect temporary shelters for their comfort, his desire is clearly to commemorate and honor the occasion in some material way. In contrast to his utter rejection of Jesus the Messiah's words about the inevitability of suffering (8:31–33), this glorified Jesus in company with Elijah and Moses wins his approval ("it is well that we are here") and his esteem. He wants to honor what he has seen.

The foolishness of Peter's response and its source are immediately indicated by the narrator: "For he did not know what to say, for they were exceedingly afraid" (9:6). Peter's inappropriate response to the incident stems from fear, the human trait that blocks out faith. Because they are

---

50. The use of *six* days, another of Mark's multiples of three, has engendered considerable speculation. Those who hold that the story is a misplaced resurrection account, or a foretaste of the Parousia, point to the "after three days" of the Passion predictions (see, e.g., Mark 8:31) as a possible connection. For a somewhat different approach to the number, see F. R. McCurley, Jr., "'And After Six Days' (Mark 9:2): A Semitic Literary Device," *JBL* 93 (1974): 67–81.

From the perspective of a modern reader, a student of mine commented that it probably took Jesus at least six days to get over Peter's foolish outburst.

afraid, the disciples cannot see who Jesus really is, hear what he teaches, or understand the way he must go. Whether with words of suffering or visions of glory, fear prohibits understanding. But the episode does not end here. If the appearance of Elijah and Moses was not sufficient to demonstrate Jesus' authority, now a voice from the clouds, the same voice that spoke at Jesus' baptism, publicly confirms beyond all doubt the identity of Jesus: "This is my beloved Son; listen to him" (9:7). These words bring the scene to its climax and at the same time create its profound irony.

The final command of the voice from the clouds, Hear him! (ἀκούετε αὐτοῦ), forces the audience to reassess the apparent point of the episode. From its outset, the transfiguration has emphasized what is *seen:* the glow and color of Jesus' clothing (9:3), the appearance (ὤφθη) of Elijah with Moses (9:4), even the three booths Peter wished to build and the over-shadowing cloud (9:5, 7). Surely all of these "sights" must be what Jesus meant about *seeing* (ἴδωσιν, 9:1) the kingdom of God has come in power, and had the voice said, "Behold him," or "See him," or "Look upon him," this interpretation would go unchallenged. But in a passage where Jesus speaks not at all, where the emphasis is overwhelmingly on vision, the voice from the cloud incongruously commands, *Hear* him. Such incongruity is the hallmark of stable irony.[51] Being divinely required to listen to Jesus when he is not talking but glistening in the whitest of garments turns the whole episode on its head. It is not what it appears to be. The glorious vision of a transformed Jesus with Elijah and Moses that so impresses Peter is undercut by the words from heaven.[52]

What Jesus has been saying to Peter, the disciples, and the multitude, and what he will reiterate in the coming chapters is the way of suffering, the cross, and death, which he and any who would follow him must walk in this world. The glorious vision may be what Peter and many others want to see, but it is the message of suffering that all must hear. Moreover, it is hearing the words of Jesus that the author has stressed throughout Division One and symbolized by identifying the seed that the sower sows as the word. Indeed, one aspect that makes the transfiguration initially so striking is that it seems to substitute the image of a glorified deity for the hardworking and often unsuccessful sower.[53] However, by having the voice command that

51. W. Booth (*A Rhetoric of Irony,* 10–11) asserts that the first step in identifying stable irony is recognizing "either some incongruity among the words or between the words and something else."

52. For Booth, step two in reconstructing stable irony is discovering that alternative explanations, forced by recognizing the incongruity, "will all in some degree be incongruous with what the literal statement seems to say . . . in some sense a retraction, diminution, or undercutting" (*A Rhetoric of Irony,* 11).

53. Step three in reconstructing stable irony, according to Booth, is that "a decision must therefore be made about the author's knowledge or belief," for, as Booth asserts, "I must somehow determine whether what I reject is also rejected by the author, and whether he has reason to expect my concurrence" (*A Rhetoric of Irony,* 11).

we *hear* Jesus, the glorious image ironically becomes yet another confirmation of the word he preaches. Why the narrator demeans Peter's response to the scene as inappropriate becomes clearer when the essential irony of the entire episode is recognized. Peter is willing to be impressed by seeing a transformed Jesus but unwilling to accept the word he preaches, and *it is the word, not the image, that brings the kingdom of God in power.*[54] Thus the response of the disciples to the transfiguration episode in the person of Peter is doubly damning, for not only do they fear what they see, a state the audience recognizes as negative from many earlier incidents, but also they are impressed by the glorified image after rejecting the saving words. In contrast, the audience is brought into even closer alignment with the position of the narrator/implied author by perceiving the irony of scene.[55] The kingdom of God coming in power is not the result of seeing Jesus' shining garments or his communion with Elijah and Moses; it is the result of hearing his word and responding in faith. "This is my beloved Son; listen to him" (9:7). And quite appropriately after the voice commands all to hear, the vision disappears and the disciples are left with Jesus alone.

Attached to the transfiguration proper is a secondary interlude relating the conversation of Jesus and the three disciples as they descend the mountain (9:9–13). The brief scene is used both to lampoon again the opacity of the disciples and to remind the audience of the pervasive evil of the world. The narrator reports that Jesus orders the disciples to tell no one what they had seen "until the Son of man should have risen from the dead" (9:9). Rather than using the opportunity to query Jesus on just what they did see, the disciples question among themselves "what the rising from the dead meant" (9:10). Not only does their ignorance seriously compromise their ability to obey Jesus' instructions, it seems especially preposterous coming from these three disciples, for it was Peter, James, and John alone among all the disciples and the multitudes who were permitted to accompany Jesus to Jairus's house and see him *raise Jairus's daughter from death* (5:37–42). Why the narrator recounted the unusual detail of naming the special disciples allowed to witness that earlier miracle (5:37) now becomes evident. Of all of Jesus' followers, Peter, James, and John had better reason than anyone else to know "what the rising from the dead meant" (9:10). Furthermore, in the episode they had just witnessed, they had seen Elijah and Moses, two leaders who had died centuries earlier, *alive* and talking with Jesus. That these disciples should still be unsure after such outstanding

54. The fourth and final step in reconstructing stable irony for Booth is choosing a new meaning "in harmony with the unspoken beliefs that the reader has decided to attribute to . . . [the author]" (*A Rhetoric of Irony,* 12). That decision, of course, rests on the author's views seen elsewhere in the text.

55. For Booth, the most important effect of irony is "building amiable communities," for "often the predominant emotion when reading stable ironies is that of joining, of finding and communing with kindred spirits" (*A Rhetoric of Irony,* 28).

proofs underlines yet again their failure: they have eyes that do not see and ears that do not hear (see 8:18).

The interlude concludes with a direct discourse exchange between the disciples and Jesus concerning the role of Elijah in the apocalyptic drama. Since the disciples have just seen Elijah, their interest seems natural enough. They ask Jesus to explain the scribes' teaching that Elijah must come first. The allusion is to the prophecy found in Mal. 4:5–6 (LXX; MT: Mal. 3:23–24) which declares that Elijah will come before the great and illustrious day of the Lord. While the disciples' quest centers on sequence, Jesus accents function: "Elijah does come first to restore (ἀποκαθιστάνει) all things (πάντα)" (Mark 9:12a). Malachi defines Elijah's purpose as one of restoring the heart (ἀποκαταστήσει καρδίαν) of father to son and the heart of human being to neighbor (Mal. 4:6 LXX). The lack of such restored heart relations is precisely the problem Jesus has encountered in the hard-heartedness of the Pharisees and the Herodians (Mark 3:5) and now in the disciples. Yet Jesus affirms "that Elijah has come, and they did to him whatever they pleased" (9:13).

The authorial audience should have no difficulty identifying John the Baptist as the subject of Jesus' intimation, for John was initially described by the narrator in the prologue of the Gospel dressed in the garb of Elijah (Mark 1:6 = 2 Kings 1:8). Moreover, the seemingly exaggerated nature of John's accomplishment in which *"all* (πᾶσα) the country of Judea, and *all* (πάντες) the people of Jerusalem" were baptized in the Jordan, "confessing their sins" (Mark 1:5), fulfills Jesus' claim that Elijah's function is "to restore *all* things (πάντα)" (9:12a). That John the Baptist could be arrested soon after such a massive repentance (1:14a) and later beheaded as the consequence of banqueting and dancing anticipates the point Jesus is making: If Elijah is "to restore all things" and "Elijah has come," why must the Son of man suffer and be treated with contempt (9:12b)? As the audience has heard, the repentances John the Baptist inspired were not sufficient to protect him from the pervasive evil of "this generation,"[56] and thus Elijah's restoration, such as it is, must also fail to guard the Son of man from suffering and contempt. The heart of "this generation" is simply too hard to be restored to right relations by the preaching of Elijah; like Elijah/John the Baptist, the Son of man must face suffering and death in a world this evil. In the event that Elijah cannot restore the heart, Mal. 4:6 threatens that God will come and destroy the earth utterly (μὴ ἔλθω καὶ πατάξω τὴν γῆν ἄρδην). The hard ground that neither the predecessor of the sower nor

---

56. Notice that references to this evil and faithless generation surround the transfiguration episode:

8:38—"this adulterous and sinful generation"

9:19—"O faithless generation, how long am I to be with you?"

the sower himself can cultivate[57] risks the wrath to come, as Division Two will make very plain. As with the transfiguration itself, this interlude of descending the mountain reaches back to the Gospel's prologue and points forward to its climax.

The first Passion prediction unit closes with Jesus' healing of the boy whom the disciples could not help (9:14–29), accompanied by his further exhortations on the essential requirement of faith. This first unit of the last section of Division One portrays the disciples, represented especially by Peter, in overt conflict with the teachings of Jesus. While they openly acknowledge that Jesus is the Christ and later hear the voice from the clouds proclaim him the beloved Son, they still feel sure enough of themselves to rebuke his disagreeable words. They are impressed by visions of glory, but their fearful natures prohibit appropriate response just as they prevent any acceptance of the necessity of suffering. Their hearts are hardened; they have eyes that cannot see and ears that cannot hear. By observing the actions of the disciples in these episodes, what they accept and what they reject, the audience can begin to understand the human traits lying behind their fearful, unfruitful response to the word. The disciples desire glory, honor, and status; they think highly of themselves, more highly indeed than they occasionally think of the One who selected them to be with him. Like Jesus' kin and neighbors earlier, the disciples respond in traditional or customary ways (e.g., Peter's three booths) to the extraordinarily uncustomary events happening around them. Their values remain those of "this generation"; they are not on the side of God.

In good rhetorical fashion, the last two Passion prediction units (9:30—10:31 and 10:32–52) reiterate and expand this depiction of the disciples by constantly contrasting their actions and words with Jesus' teachings. After the second prediction of his passion to the disciples (9:31), the narrator reports pointedly that "they did not understand the saying, and they were afraid (ἐφοβοῦντο) to ask him" (9:32). Their bewilderment is not surprising, since they had been discussing which of them was the greatest (9:34) while Jesus was talking of suffering. Jesus perceives that the disciples want to be "first"—first in status, first in glory, first in authority, first in honor. Yet, to be first in the kingdom Jesus proclaims is to be last, least, and servant of all (9:35), a teaching the disciples quite evidently do not assimilate, for they delegate to themselves the authority to determine who can use Jesus' name (9:38–41) and who can approach him for blessing (10:13–16) in opposition to his wishes. Indeed, John's complaint about the man casting out demons in Jesus' name is that "he was not following *us*" (9:38). Although Jesus changes the "us" back to "my name" and "me" (9:39), the

57. The "heart" and "ground" metaphors found in the Septuagintal version of Mal. 4:5–6 bear striking affiliations with the language world of Mark's Gospel.

disciples, who had themselves just failed to exorcise a demon (9:14–29), stopped a successful healer mainly because he was not part of their group. Instead, for Jesus the performance of mighty works in his name demonstrates the healer's membership in the new family of those who do the will of God.

The central part of the second Passion prediction unit is composed of an *inclusio* about receiving children (9:36–37 and 10:13–16), surrounding three episodes that focus in different ways on the proper treatment of weak or disenfranchised people: the alien exorciser (9:38–41), the "little ones" (9:42–50), and the divorced wife (10:2–12).[58] The elements of the *inclusio* itself dramatize the disciples' continuing waywardness. In teaching them about first and last, Jesus takes a child in his arms and says, "Whoever receives one such child in my name receives me" (9:37). Shortly thereafter, the disciples, in manifest defiance of Jesus' words, rebuke and deter people trying to bring children to him for blessing (10:13–16). They do not receive children, just as they do not receive the kingdom of God (10:15). Given their acclaim of greatness, obviously for the disciples it is not children who should enter the kingdom of God but rather rich men, and when Jesus remarks that it is "easier for a camel to go through the eye of a needle than for a rich man to enter the kingdom" (10:25), they voice their complete incredulity in, "Then who can be saved?" (10:26).

Immediately after the last, longest, and most detailed prediction of his passion in Jerusalem, Jesus is approached by James and John with a thoroughly unseemly request: "Grant us to sit, one at your right hand and one at your left, in your glory" (10:37). No matter how often or plainly he teaches them about suffering, being the servant, the child, or the least, patently all that the disciples can think about is being the greatest, the first, the most glorious, the most powerful, the leader. They are as constant in error as Jesus is in sowing the word, and their fervent affirmation, "We are able," to Jesus' metaphorical questions about their ability to endure suffering (10:38–39) rings with hollow bravado rather than sober reflection, for they follow in fear (10:32), not in faith. One final time before the persecutions of Jerusalem begin, Jesus tries to teach them the ethics of the kingdom: "Whoever would be great among you must be your servant, and whoever would be first among you must be slave of all. For the Son of man also came not to be served but to serve, and to give his life as a ransom for many" (10:43–45). His values and theirs could not be more disparate.

---

58. This *inclusio* and the nature of the material it binds together were pointed out to me by Mark Roberts, a Ph.D. student in the Graduate Department of Religion at Vanderbilt University.

Falling Away When Persecution Arises

Unlike the good earth, whose story ends before the entry into Jerusalem with the healing of Bartimaeus, the ideal faithful follower, the disciples' denouement awaits the active persecution of the Passion because, as the Interpretation of the parable of the Sower explained, "When tribulation or persecution arises on account of the word, immediately they fall away (σκανδαλίζονται)" (4:17). Aside from Peter's brief role in pointing out the withered fig tree (11:20–21) and a disciple's homage to the temple buildings (13:1), the closing moments of the rocky ground are related primarily in the second section (14:1—16:8) of Division Two. Specifically, Mark 14:10–72 charts their triple failure: betrayal, flight, and denial. The climax of their journey comes in Gethsemane (14:32–50) with Peter's further downfall in the high priest's courtyard as a sad epilogue (14:54, 66–72).

The Jerusalem religious leaders wanted to arrest Jesus privately, for they feared the reaction of the crowds to the seizing of a popular teacher (12:12 and 14:1–2). Judas Iscariot, who the audience had been informed would betray Jesus early in the story at the choosing of the Twelve (3:19), offers the chief priests the opportunity they seek in return for money (14:10–11). *Why* Judas should betray Jesus is omitted in Mark's Gospel, and, in fact, the detailing of motivations of that kind is more a modern narrative convention than an ancient one.[59] Judas illustrates or symbolizes one possible consequence of a hardened heart: the betrayal of friends. That the narrator indicates he was promised money in return for his act serves to remind the audience of the disciples' high regard for riches in contrast to Jesus' disapproval (e.g., 10:25–26; 12:41–44). Moreover, the immediately preceding story (14:3–9) demonstrates the proper use of money to finance an act of love, ministry, and gentleness and thus provides a stark counterbalance to "Judas Iscariot, who was one of the twelve" (14:10). Although examining what factors cause Judas to betray his teacher is of no concern to the author of Mark, that such an act has chilling repercussions for the perpetrator is sharply emphasized in Jesus' direct discourse to the disciples at the Passover meal (14:18–21). While the nameless woman who anointed Jesus' head with nard will have her act of respect told "in memory of her" wherever the gospel is preached (14:9), for Judas the paid betrayer, "it would have been better for that man if he had not been born" (14:21).

Mark 14:17–31

As in the recognition sequences of the ancient erotic novels, the final events in Mark are carefully plotted over a definite, limited time, in which

59. See Scholes and Kellogg, *The Nature of Narrative,* 84–99.

all that the audience has anticipated since early in the story plays out to its conclusion. The events of Judas's betrayal, the disciples' flight, and Peter's denial all take place on one evening after the Passover meal and Jesus' prayer period in Gethsemane. As the two episodes leading up to these final actions, the supper and Gethsemane are especially heavily weighted with forebodings of failure. The four scenes composing the episodes alternate dialogue with monologue, confrontation with command to achieve a kind of interlocking crescendo:

Confrontational Dialogues   *Commanding Monologues*

14:17–21—"Is it I?"

                                        14:22–26a—"Take"

14:26b–31—"I will not"

                                        14:32–42—"remain here, and watch"

The two dialogues are both initiated by a prediction by Jesus concerning the upcoming behavior of the disciples and include the unusual report that each of the disciples individually replied in the same manner (14:19, 31b); so, though Judas and Peter are singled out for special onus, all of the Twelve are implicated in what takes place.

The responses of the disciples to Jesus' two forecasts, first that one of them would betray him (14:18) and second that they would all fall away (14:27), depict the disciples as transparent boasters, for in the first instance, each asks if he will be the one to betray while in the second they all swear to die rather than deny Jesus. If they are not sure whether or not they will betray him, how can they possibly swear faithfulness to death? Their first response undercuts the credibility of their second one. Furthermore, the second declaration made by Jesus is given additional verification by scriptural quotation: "You will all fall away (σκανδαλισθήσεσθε); for it is written, 'I will strike the shepherd, and the sheep will be scattered'" (14:27). Yet, with the same arrogance that marked his earlier rebuke of the just-confessed Messiah (8:29, 32), Peter vigorously refutes this doubly authoritative dictum, repeating again the key word "fall away" (σκανδαλισθήσονται, 14:29) to confirm the allusion to the parable of the Sower ("immediately they fall away," εὐθὺς σκανδαλίζονται, 4:17). In reproving Peter's brag this time, Jesus advances a highly ironic, individualized prediction for Peter alone: "Truly, I say to you, this very night, before the cock crows twice, you will deny me three times" (14:30). By vehemently rejecting Jesus' assertion a second time, Peter underscores the irony of the exchange: his strident contradictions are themselves denials of Jesus' words and authority. Already in this brief dialogue, Peter has twice disputed Jesus' (and Scripture's) solemn prophecies. Three more denials will only serve to continue a lamentably consistent pattern. Lost in Peter's eagerness to repel any reproach on his future actions is Jesus' promise, "But after I am raised up, I will go before you to Galilee" (14:28). Not only does Peter ignore the remark but the earlier confusion of the disciples concerning "what the rising from the dead meant" (9:10) bodes ill for their ability to share in this assurance.

The two monologue scenes (14:22–26a and 14:32–42) both contain Jesus' imperative instructions to the disciples, but the second scene in Gethsemane is longer and contains within it an interior monologue in the form of a prayer that is unique to the Gospel. Triple repetitions, the unique prayer revealing Jesus' inner struggle, and the announcement that the hour has come all disclose the Gethsemane scene as a climactic episode in the disciples' saga that we must consider carefully. The earlier "words of institution," as they are often called, at the supper are a monologue only in that Jesus alone speaks. His words are addressed to the disciples and indeed beyond the disciples to the "many" (v. 24), and the narrator reports that they obey his command to take the broken bread which signifies "my body" (v. 22). Bread and feeding have played a major role in previous episodes of the Gospel. Feeding the crowds in the wilderness implicitly connected Jesus' mission with Moses and the children of Israel, who were fed manna in the wilderness by a protecting deity. However, those feedings also served to reveal the hardness of heart of the disciples, for they did not understand about the bread (6:52). Here Jesus explicitly relates the broken bread to his body ($\sigma\hat{\omega}\mu\acute{a}$), which will be broken for their sakes and the gospel's. Whether the disciples will be nourished by the metaphorical as well as the literal bread is doubtful, given their past performance, but Jesus' words are also heard by the audience, and hearing him they too have the opportunity for metaphorical enrichment.

The play between literal and metaphorical meanings[60] is even more pronounced in reference to the cup ($\pi o\tau\acute{\eta}\rho\iota o\nu$). At the supper they all drink from a cup Jesus passes around. He then indicates that the wine in the cup is metaphorically his blood of testament and that he will not drink wine again until he drinks it in the kingdom of God, a clear indication to the listeners that the final moments of the story have arrived. The mention of all present drinking from the same cup should remind the audience of the inappropriate request of James and John following the third Passion prediction (10:35–40), because Jesus had asked them if they could "drink the cup that I drink" (10:38). Here they indeed drink from the literal cup Jesus uses. However, Jesus' question to them had not been literal but metaphorical. It is not the cup of wine at supper that Jesus insists they must drink; it is,

---

60. Playing literal meanings off against metaphorical meanings has been used to the disciples' detriment before in Mark 8:14–21.

instead, the "cup" he asks God in Gethsemane to remove from his future (14:36) that he and all his faithful followers must share. Yet, while Jesus is agonizing over that metaphorical cup, James and John along with Peter are fast asleep (14:37). That cup they will not prove able to drink.

Mark 14:32–72—Gethsemane and the Aftermath

The image of the cup links Jesus' "words of institution" at the supper with his pain-filled prayer in Gethsemane. If his disciples have failed to understand or respond fruitfully to his performative words and teachings formerly, their failure in Gethsemane is of both a more personal and a more unkind nature, for it is not his views or values they do not support but his very person, his agonized humanity. Leaving most of the disciples behind, to sit "while I pray" (14:32), Jesus takes Peter, James, and John on farther as the distress at what now awaits him presses his spirit. In words that echo the closing warnings of the Apocalyptic Discourse (13:35–37), Jesus commands the three to "remain here, and watch" (14:34). So seldom has the Gospel described Jesus' own emotions (see, e.g., 1:41; 3:5; 10:14, 21) that the piling up of adjectives by both the narrator and Jesus himself creates a potent gravity: "greatly distressed and troubled" (14:33); "very sorrowful, even to death" (14:34). The seriousness of Jesus' situation and the reality of his pain are unmistakably emphasized by the implied author as background both for his private prayer and for the disciples' nadir.

Jesus' prayer in Gethsemane, reported both in narrative summary ("he fell on the ground and prayed that, if it were possible, the hour [ἡ ὥρα] might pass [παρέλθῃ] from him," 14:35) and in direct discourse (Abba, father, all things are possible for you; take this cup from me; but not what I desire but what you desire, 14:36), is a superb example of what is technically called an "interior monologue," a narrative soliloquy used at a critical moment to dramatize internal struggle.[61] Interior monologue and stream of consciousness are commonly found combined in extended format in modern narrative, and thus we may not recognize the important but sparing use of interior monologue in ancient writings. Its earliest appearance can be found in Homer, but Apollonius Rhodius, Virgil, Ovid, and Xenophon of Ephesus also employed and developed the device.[62] For illuminating Mark's use of the convention for Jesus in Gethsemane,[63]

61. Much of the discussion that follows is dependent upon Scholes and Kellogg, *The Nature of Narrative,* 177–94.
62. Ibid., 178.
63. Arguments for the historical basis of the prayer have always been difficult to make for the simple reason that as Mark describes the scene, no one could have heard what Jesus says. For a fair review of the various positions in the historical debate, see Nineham, *Saint Mark,* 389–91.

Homer and Xenophon are especially helpful. Half of the interior monologues in the *Iliad* come at a crucial point when a character experiences fear on the verge of battle or some other risky venture and each of these repeats the same formulaic line: "but why does my own heart dispute with me thus?" (Odysseus in 11.402; Menelaus in 17.97; Agenor in 21.562; and Hector in 22.122).[64] For Homer, then, the interior monologue is particularly suited to those critical moments when "a character seems to be giving way to the promptings of his *thymos* [heart or mind] but pulls himself together in the formulaic line . . . and proceeds to do the right thing."[65]

While Homer's monologues are truly unspoken, that is, the character's internal dispute is not spoken aloud in the narrative, Xenophon of Ephesus and some other of the later writers tended to compose monologues in the form of prayers or laments spoken aloud, but in private, to god at a moment of crisis.[66] The emotion dividing the will for Homer was mainly fear, and the resolution, after internal debate, was always for the right or courageous action. Later writers like Xenophon applied the technique to a wider range of situations (e.g., love, honor, loyalty) but preserved the crisis nature of the scene. Although in all the ancient writers some concept of a divided psyche[67] must be assumed behind the development of interior monologues, ancient monologues, unlike their modern descendants, are not basically psychological but rather rhetorical.[68] They are "words artfully deployed so as to move the reader or audience."[69]

Jesus' prayer in Gethsemane clearly reflects the ancient convention. It comes at a moment of great crisis, for the hour is now upon him (14:41); the rhetorical play between the cup of testimony at the supper and the cup of suffering before him provides the audience with a profound sense of the sacrifice he is about to make "for many" (see 14:24); and the agony in his own psyche (14:34) is appropriately and heroically resolved in favor of God's will. Though internal dispute is a typical feature of these monologues, depicting Jesus as manifesting such division bonds him more firmly

64. Scholes and Kellogg, *The Nature of Narrative*, 179.

65. Ibid., 180.

66. For Xenophon, the god is generally Eros and Robert Scholes's translation of an early interior monologue/prayer by Habrocomes, the hero, is useful in comparison to Mark: "He spoke thus, but the god pressed him harder and harder, dragging him against his will to that torment which he wanted no part of. When he could stand it no longer, he threw himself on the ground, saying, You have beaten me, Eros, and deserve a great trophy for your victory over the chaste Habrocomes" (*An Ephesian Tale* 1.4.4, as cited in Scholes and Kellogg, *The Nature of Narrative*, 289–90).

67. Scholes and Kellogg explain: "The psyche has been divided into two parts which dispute for mastery, often in a manner hinting at a concept of the ego, which cares for its own preservation, and a superego which drives the individual toward acceptable action" (*The Nature of Narrative*, 180).

68. Ibid., 181, 185.

69. Ibid., 185.

in the audience's sympathy, for he is human, as we are, and allows his correct resolution of the struggle to stand as an example to be imitated. Moreover, that his human anguish should be ignored and unsupported by his sleeping disciples serves to separate those disciples even more strongly from the audience's approval. Since convention dictated that such monologues occur at critical junctures, finding one here would alert the authorial audience to the climactic nature of the Gethsemane episode, and hearing Jesus' prayer formulated in this familiar pattern would assure the audience not only of Jesus' full cognizance of what the future holds for him but also of his resolute willingness to face that future as God wills. He is neither a joyful martyr bent on self-destruction nor an unwilling pawn forced into sacrifice; rather, like Odysseus, Menelaus, or Hector, he is a courageous hero who knows what dangers lie ahead and resolves to do the will of God (see 3:35).

Yet, what of the disciples? After the conclusion of his monologue, Jesus returns to the trio and finds them asleep. His words to Peter are very significant: "Simon, are you asleep? Could you not watch one hour ($\mu\iota\alpha\nu$ $\omega\rho\alpha\nu$)? Watch and pray that you may not enter into temptation; the spirit indeed is willing, but the flesh is weak" (14:37–38). For the first and only time since Peter was nicknamed "Rock" in Mark 3:16, Jesus addresses him as "Simon." Reviving the name "Simon" reminds the audience that the rocky ground was initially fruitful and suggests the possibility of resurrecting that fruitfulness in this final hour. Since Jesus' prayer resolved his inner conflict, perhaps if the hardened Peter would similarly pray, the fruitful Simon might still succeed. The mention of hour and watching, alluding again to the warnings of the Apocalyptic Discourse (13:32–37), underscores the urgency of the moment. Jesus' closing observation that the spirit is eager ($\pi\rho\acute{o}\theta\upsilon\mu o\nu$) but the flesh is weak may well represent the implied author's basic view concerning why some people who hear the word receive it with joy, endure for a time, and then, when persecutions arise, fall away. They have eager and ready spirits, but they fear for their bodies; they are, indeed, divided in themselves between a willing enthusiasm and a practical desire for self-preservation and even self-enhancement.

However, the hope that "Simon" might emerge from the rock of Peter dies stillborn as Jesus leaves and returns a ritual three times to find only sleeping disciples who neither watch nor pray (14:39–41a). Their last chance has passed. Jesus pronounces the verdict in one word that has troubled translators of Mark[70] for years: $\dot{\alpha}\pi\acute{\epsilon}\chi\epsilon\iota$. The Greek word is an

---

70. For a review of the variety of translations suggested for this word, see Taylor, *The Gospel According to St. Mark,* 556–57; Nineham, *Saint Mark,* 392–93; and R.

impersonal verb that had wide use as a technical commercial term in receipting a bill. Written on a bill or a receipt, it meant "paid in full."[71] And so it quite appropriately means this as well for the disciples' role in the Gospel of Mark. Jesus, the sower, has taught, cajoled, threatened, exhorted, warned, admonished, and repeatedly explained to them what is necessary for entering the kingdom of God. Now in this climactic hour he has given them three final opportunities to watch and pray that they "may not enter into temptation." All has failed; their bill is paid in full; the account book on them is now closed; their fate is sealed. "The hour has come" (14:41).

Following Jesus' announcement of closure on the disciples' possibilities, the narrator relates their betrayal, flight, and denial in rapid succession. Each consequence of a hardened heart is typified in the actions of one character: Judas as betrayal (14:42b–45); the young man as flight (14:50–52);[72] and Peter as denial (14:54, 66–72). The emphasis in the betrayal scene, as witnessed by repetition and direct discourse, falls on the sign that Judas employs to identify Jesus for the crowd: a kiss. To be betrayed by a kiss—the symbol of intimacy, affection, and respect—is an incredibly apt image for the relation between the disciples and Jesus in the Gospel of Mark. Those who are closest, best known and cared for, fail most miserably. Turning a sign of love into a sign of death is the result of hard-heartedness and fear. Furthermore, the repetition of fleeing (ἔφυγον, 14:50; ἔφυγεν, v. 52) and naked (ἐπὶ γυμνοῦ, v. 51; γυμνὸς, v. 52) in the flight scene intimates that fleeing strips away the last remnants of respectability from the disciples, exposing them for the hard ground they really are.

Peter's triple denial, in fulfillment of Jesus' prediction (14:30), utilizes repetition and intercalation to stress the depth of his fall. As Jesus is led to the high priest and assembled Jerusalem leaders, Peter follows along at a distance, enters the courtyard, and sits warming himself by the fire (14:53–54). For the next eleven verses the scene shifts to Jesus' trial before the assembly (14:55–65) in which he publicly affirms that he is the Christ, the Son of God (14:61–62), resoundingly smashing any last remnants of secrecy. Mark 14:66 again picks up the story of Peter in the courtyard warming himself. The exact repetitions of Peter's location and action be-

Bratcher and E. Nida, *A Translator's Handbook on the Gospel of Mark* (London and New York: United Bible Societies, 1961), 452–53.

71. Taylor, *The Gospel According to St. Mark,* 556; and Bratcher and Nida, *A Translator's Handbook,* 452.

72. The excellent suggestion that the puzzling young man who runs away naked is the symbolic representation of flight comes from Kermode, *The Genesis of Secrecy,* 55–63, who is here developing a suggestion in the intriguing study of Mark by Farrer, *A Study in St. Mark,* 141. Such a typological understanding of the young man in the *sindon* accords well with the kind of characterization that this study argues Mark is presenting throughout.

tween v. 54 and vv. 66–67 indicate that this intercalation is being used to imply simultaneity, as many commentators have noted.[73] Peter's three denials of affiliation with Jesus—two in answer to assertions by a maid of the high priest and the last in answer to bystanders—occur *at the same time* as Jesus' affirmation of his identity. Jesus accepts recognition of who he really is while Peter rejects it. Mark's intercalation or insertion technique here allows linear, sequential narrative to dramatize simultaneously type and antitype of a recognition scene.

When Peter hears the cock crow the second time immediately after his third and most violent denial, he remembers Jesus' earlier words and repeats them aloud for the sake of the audience's memory as well: "Before the cock crows twice, you will deny me three times" (14:72//14:30). Then the narrator reports Peter's response: "And he broke down and wept" (14:72b).[74] At the realization of his utter failure, his sorrow is intense, but the Gospel gives us no grounds for supposing that Peter's lament signifies a change of heart, for sorrow has been experienced before by those who comprehend their failure (see, e.g., 6:26; 10:22). The saga of Peter and the disciples ends, as did that of the rich man (10:17–22), in grieving failure. Only once more are they even mentioned in the Gospel—by the young man at the tomb (16:7)—and the point of that final reference must wait until the last chapter of our study, when we explore the strange ending of Mark.

Typology and Characterization

If we accept that the Gospel of Mark develops a typology of hearing-response, expressed metaphorically in the parable of the Sower and its Interpretation and expressed in human terms by the character groups in the narrative, the intriguing question arises concerning why certain groups were selected to illustrate each type. This question is particularly provocative in the case of the disciples as the rocky ground, given the reverence accorded them by later centuries of Christian tradition. Why were the disciples of Jesus, his chosen twelve, fashioned by Mark to represent one of the unfruitful responses to hearing the word? However, raising the issue for the disciples similarly begs the question for the ones healed, the Pharisees

73. See, e.g., Kermode, *The Genesis of Secrecy,* 139–40; E. Best, *Mark: The Gospel as Story* (Edinburgh: T. & T. Clark, 1983), 131.
74. The precise sense of the participle ἐπιβαλὼν is difficult to determine. It may refer to the bursting out of sound in Peter's weeping or some action of throwing himself on the ground. At any rate, the violence of his final denial is matched by the violence of his sorrow. For various suggestions for translating the word, see, e.g., Taylor, *The Gospel According to St. Mark,* 576–77; and Bratcher and Nida, *A Translator's Handbook,* 472.

and the Jerusalem leaders, and indeed for the characterization of Jesus himself, for the same choice and composition that molded the depiction of the disciples cast the entire Gospel. Recent Markan scholarship has proposed some historical hypotheses for the negative depiction of the disciples. After briefly reviewing several of these hypotheses, we will develop some possible narrative and rhetorical reasons for characterizing these groups as they are, leading to a new construction for an old problem in Mark: the purpose of the secrecy motif.

Historical Hypotheses

Until the appearance of William Wrede's classic study *Das Messiasgeheimnis in den Evangelien* in 1901, the Gospel of Mark had been viewed as a simple and accurate account of the ministry, passion, and death of Jesus based primarily on memoirs of Peter. From that standpoint the failure of the disciples at Gethsemane, for example, was just a reflection of what happened. Indeed, the negativity of their portrayal was taken as a strong claim for authenticity because, as Vincent Taylor puts it, "Only as dependent on the testimony of Peter himself is a story so damaging to his reputation and that of all the disciples conceivable."[75] Wrede's insistence that the Gospel's many commands to secrecy and that the blindness characteristic of the disciples were formulations either of the early church or of the author himself destroyed the foundations of that earlier position.

Wrede's own explanation of these elements in Mark involved a reconstruction of the history of Christian dogma. For Wrede, the earliest traditions of the sayings of Jesus were completely nonmessianic, implying of course that Jesus himself made no claim to be the Messiah. Only after the resurrection experience did followers of Jesus proclaim him to be the promised Messiah. The later church tradition and Mark, then, tried to harmonize the initial lack with the later claim by devising the idea that Jesus actually did acknowledge his messianic identity but commanded secrecy about it during his lifetime and further that the disciples did not understand until after the resurrection who Jesus really was or what he taught. While Wrede was generally successful in removing the patina of simple history from the Markan narrative, his reconstruction left much to be desired.[76] How, for

75. *The Gospel According to St. Mark,* 551. Although Taylor's commentary was produced almost fifty years *after* Wrede, his generally conservative stance often forces him back to considerably older positions.

76. An excellent review of Wrede's position, its strengths and its problems, can be found in W. C. Robinson, "The Quest for Wrede's Secret Messiah," *Interpretation* 27 (1973): 10–30. Some of the classic articles analyzing the secrecy issue and the disciples' blindness in line with Wrede's concerns have been collected together in C. Tuckett, ed., *The Messianic Secret* (IRT 1; Philadelphia: Fortress Press, 1983).

instance, are Jesus' triumphal entry into Jerusalem and his affirmation that he is "the Christ, the Son of the Blessed" (14:61–62) to the high priest to be united with the secrecy apologetic?

Though Wrede's own reconstruction was challenged, his decision to explain narrative configurations on the basis of hypothetical reconstructions of early Christian history has had a host of followers. One fascinating proposal, suggested by T. J. Weeden, Sr.,[77] draws parallels between the situation of the Gospel of Mark and some of the problems Paul faced at Corinth. One theory about Paul's correspondence with the Corinthians argues that Paul's enemies there adopted a *"theios anēr* Christology" and thus a *"theios anēr* discipleship," which emphasized miracle-working, power, and spiritually glorified experiences to the exclusion of all else.[78] Weeden posits a similar group in the community out of which the Gospel arose. The author of Mark wished to counter a "false" view of Christ as mainly a miracle-working "divine man" by emphasizing the suffering servanthood of Jesus. To accomplish this end, according to Weeden, the author placed the false *theios anēr* portrait of discipleship on the lips of the Twelve and dramatized their constant conflict with Jesus' true suffering servant view of discipleship. Thus the negative depiction of the Markan disciples is explained as a result of a christological controversy within the community producing the text. Although Weeden's hypothesis continues to attract adherents, it, like Wrede's, faces a few snags in the Gospel narrative. If the disciples are supposed to be championing a *"theios anēr* Christology" that glorifies miracle-working, why are they depicted so often as failing to understand, accept, or acknowledge Jesus' miracles (e.g., 4:41; 6:49–52; 8:14–21; 9:6, 28–29)?

Another creative proposal that also looks to the special situation of the community producing the Gospel as the key to its negative view of the disciples is that of Werner Kelber.[79] For Kelber, it is not christological disputes that occasioned the Gospel but rather the need to justify the demise of Jerusalem and the Jerusalem Christian community as the center of Christianity after the Jewish War against Rome in 66–70 C.E. Kelber points out that Paul's letter to the Galatians indicates the existence of an authoritative Jewish-Christian church in Jerusalem under the leadership of Peter, James (the brother of Jesus, not the son of Zebedee), and John (Gal. 2:9) in the decades following the death and resurrection of Jesus. When the Roman armies destroyed Jerusalem and the temple in 70 C.E., that church too undoubtedly fell. How were Christians to understand such a harsh judgment on their central community?

77. Weeden, *Mark—Traditions in Conflict.*
78. Ibid., 59–61.
79. W. Kelber, *Mark's Story of Jesus* (Philadelphia: Fortress Press, 1979), 88–95.

Mark's solution, according to Kelber, was to mount an anti-Jerusalem and anti-disciple polemic. Jesus' command was for the disciples to return to Galilee (14:28; 16:7), but because of Peter's failure to listen and the women's failure to speak, that command was disobeyed, and the church established itself in Jerusalem under Peter's leadership. Its fall was a judgment on disobedience. Kelber's reconstruction has the added benefit of suggesting a reason for fashioning a story about Jesus' ministry and passion. In order to defend the collapse of the Jerusalem church, Mark had to undermine thoroughly the credibility of Peter and the others. Yet, if they were no longer authoritative disseminators of the tradition, how could one learn about it? The answer was to write a narrative telling the story that all could read for themselves: the gospel genre was born.

All of these historical reconstructions have elements to recommend them. They attempt to make sense of Mark while at the same time refining our image of early Christianity. From the perspective of this study of the Gospel of Mark, however, their main problem lies in the rapidity with which they move from the text to speculations about its production. Usually, only one or two aspects of the whole narrative provide the foundation for the reconstruction, and other aspects are ignored. Hence, Weeden emphasizes the failure of the disciples and the dominance of miracles, while Kelber focuses on the failure of the disciples and the anti-temple polemic. Though selectivity is legitimately a part of any process of interpretation, be it literary or historical, we must first be sure to establish, in Wrede's words (though not in his actions), "the thorough illumination of the accounts in the spirit of those accounts themselves, to ask what the narrator in his own time wanted to say to his readers."[80] To a fuller exploration of possible narrative and rhetorical purposes for the range of characterizations found in Mark, we now turn.

Narrative Strategies

The most obvious functional benefit bestowed upon the narrative by the disciples' lack of comprehension is the opportunity it provides the author through both the narrator and the character Jesus to explain, repeat, and elaborate upon important teachings and issues. Because the disciples do not understand and because, next to Jesus, they are the most constantly present character group in the Gospel, they can become springboards for Jesus' teaching. Often they ask him privately to explain what he has already said (e.g., 4:10; 7:17; 9:28; 10:10), permitting the repetition or expansion of material for the sake of the memory or clarification of the audience. In the

---

80. W. Wrede, *Das Messiasgeheimnis in den Evangelien* (Göttingen: Vandenhoeck & Ruprecht, 1901), 5–6.

last section of Division One (8:22—10:52) especially, their blindness and opposition to Jesus' words spark extended comments by Jesus on the nature of discipleship. If the disciples were in harmony with Jesus on every point, much of this message would be difficult, if not impossible, to incorporate into the narrative. The value of fashioning dull or contentious discussion partners was well known in antiquity, as Plato's Socratic dialogues amply demonstrate. Socrates always makes his case either by inspiring proper responses in an eager but uneducated student or by exposing the errors of arrogant opponents. That the "socratic method" is most effective as a *narrative* technique, in which an author controls all the questions and all the answers, will be evident to anyone who has made the mistake of trying to use it in an actual classroom situation, where the teacher may control the questions but no one controls the answers.

The disciples not only supply an opening for teaching but by speaking and acting in ways contrary to Jesus, they function as foils for him. He says children should be received (9:37) and he receives them (10:14–16), while the disciples do not (10:13); he says no one knows when the hour will come, so all must watch (13:32–37) and he watches and prays as the hour draws near (14:32–36), while the disciples sleep (14:37–41); he says that anyone who follows his way must suffer, take up a cross, and die (8:31–35) and he does just that, while the disciples betray, flee, and deny. The use of contrasting examples to prove an argument or enhance the distinctive characteristics of a favored position was a recommended procedure in ancient rhetoric.[81] As constant foils to Jesus' words and actions, the disciples allow the author to emphasize the special nature of Jesus' outlook and his faithfulness in following its consequences through to the end.

Moreover, that the constant, primary foils to Jesus should be his specially chosen disciples makes the contrast all the more striking. In ancient writing, although it was not impossible for disciples to prove faithless, conventionally a teacher's disciples, even if slow at first, generally supported their master.[82] Mark's use of disciples to illustrate the rocky ground thwarts conventional expectations. This defamiliarizing of normal patterns presses the reader to see something new happening in the text. Wolfgang Iser terms the strategy "coherent deformation," and its special grace is to force the reader into intense activity, seeking the cause of the deformation.[83] Texts that confirm customary norms allow readers to remain basically passive,

81. See, e.g., Aristotle, *Rhetoric* 2.20.2–4 (1393a–1393b); *Rhetorica ad Herennium* 4.28.25–26.

82. For many examples of disciples who learn from their teachers in both the Hebrew Scriptures and Greco-Roman literature, see Robbins, *Jesus the Teacher,* 125–96.

83. W. Iser, *The Act of Reading: A Theory of Aesthetic Response* (Baltimore: Johns Hopkins University Press, 1978), 81–85, 227–29.

whereas texts that cut away common ground propel readers into active engagement.[84] It is not necessarily the case that incidents of failure, suffering, and evil in a text are intended as "simply copies of a depraved world"; rather, "failure and deformation are surface signs that indicate a hidden cause," a cause that the reader must consciously work out.[85]

In the Gospel of Mark that cause has to do with the clash of worldviews held by participants in the kingdom of God and the members of this sinful, adulterous, and faithless generation. By coherent deformation of conventional expectations, Mark assures the active involvement of its audience in trying to understand the nature and ramifications of that clash. Though the characters in good stories and certainly in the Gospel of Mark seem to audiences to take on a certain independence of thought and action, that autonomy is the singular illusion of narrative.[86] All the characters, their words, and their actions have been molded as they are to communicate to or have an effect upon an audience. They are not copies of the world; they are, instead, a world of their own, created especially to persuade. Thus, exploring the narrative strategies attendant on Mark's negative portrayal of the disciples leads directly to a consideration of the rhetorical aims involved: how does this characterization affect an audience?

Rhetorical Aims

Certainly for ancient writing, if not for modern, distinguishing between narrative strategies and rhetorical aims suggests a false separation, for narrative was composed mainly to affect its audience, and thus ignoring the possible effects on the audience produced by the typological characterization of the Gospel of Mark would jeopardize any attempt to understand it within its own literary-historical milieu, a milieu that was, above all else, rhetorical. The negative characterization of the disciples has at least two related effects on readers. In the first place, because, as we have seen, irony is one of the most common devices used against the disciples in Mark, the audience is made to feel superior to the disciples in knowledge and understanding time and again. The audience shares the views of Jesus and the narrator in opposition to the actions of Peter, James, John, Judas, and the others. For example, while the disciples cannot fathom how Jesus will be able to feed the four thousand in the desert (8:3–4), the audience knows he will do it, just as he earlier fed the five thousand (6:35–44); and while the disciples sleep in Gethsemane, the audience hears Jesus' prayer and shares his pain. These incidents and many others contribute to making the audi-

84. Ibid., 84–85.
85. Ibid., 227–28.
86. For a discussion of the development of illusory autonomy in narrative, see Lanser, *The Narrative Act,* 146.

ence *better than* the disciples, but the effect is actually even greater, for portraying the *disciples* as failing foils to Jesus manipulates the reader to respond by becoming a *better disciple*. In rejecting the views and actions of the Twelve and affirming the words and work of Jesus, the reader herself or himself becomes a faithful disciple. We will need to explore this rhetorical effect of Mark's story further when we discuss the ending of the Gospel in the last chapter.

In addition to making faithful readers into faithful disciples, in the second place, the negative depiction of the Twelve encourages the audience to search for the flaws that make initially fertile ground into rocky ground. The gradual clarification of what it is about this group that transforms disciples into betrayers, fleers, and deniers might be termed a popularized form of catharsis (κάθαρσις). For Aristotle, the special pleasure involved in literature is a kind of learning about the universal truths of existence that actual daily life often obscures.[87] The end effect on an audience of this learning experience is a catharsis of whatever emotions are aroused by perceiving those truths in the plot.[88] Exactly what Aristotle meant by catharsis has been the subject of considerable debate, but given his emphasis on learning, catharsis is probably best understood as a process of clarification, the action of the will or mind, rather than a purging or purifying of feelings.[89] Achieving greater clarity on why some ground proves fertile and other ground proves unfruitful is manifestly a large element in the organizing intention governing the Gospel of Mark. Consequently, observing the character traits associated with the varying fates of all groups and individuals in the Gospel is a major part of an audience's experience of it.

However, while the audience is concerned with all groups, the coherent deformation provided by unsuccessful disciples draws particular attention to their situation. That personally selected disciples with greater opportunities to hear and learn than any others could still utterly fail their master raises for the audience a frightening prospect which they must consider for themselves. What flaws or faults or weaknesses can cause initially eager spirits to fall away? Because the typology the disciples illustrate is a universal truth, those same weaknesses may plague the reader—or people the reader knows—as well. Character in ancient literature was revealed by choices: what one wills to do or avoids doing.[90] Aristotle's moral flaw[91] or Mark's sin (1:4, 5; 2:5, 7, 9–10), both ethical senses of the Greek ἁμαρτία, a

87. See Aristotle, *Poetics* 4.5 (1448b); 9.1–4 (1451a–1451b).
88. *Poetics* 6.2–3 (1449b).
89. See the excellent discussion of this view of catharsis in O. B. Hardison's commentary on the *Poetics* in Golden and Hardison, *Aristotle's Poetics,* 113–20, 133–37.
90. See Aristotle, *Poetics* 6.24 (1450b).
91. See *Poetics* 13.5 (1453a).

"missing the mark," will, then, be disclosed in what the disciples do and what they avoid doing.

What the disciples avoid doing is quite obvious in their actions of betraying, fleeing, and denying and in their earlier rejection of Jesus' passion predictions: they avoid taking up their crosses and losing their lives for the sake of the gospel. Moreover, the parable of the Sower indicated that their "falling away" would come in relation to persecutions and tribulations "on account of the word" (4:17), and throughout the rest of the narrative they are firmly associated with the response of fear (e.g., 4:40–41; 6:50; 9:6, 32; 10:32). Their fearful natures prevent them from enduring the inevitable sufferings involved in following the way of Jesus. Nor are they capable of watching and praying in order to survive their hour of trial or of accepting Jesus' (and Scripture's) warning about their impending behavior and future assurance (14:27–31). All of these actions the disciples evade.

What the disciples do or want to do, on the other hand, is less obvious, for it must be derived from their conflicts with Jesus and occasional independent actions, but it is equally important. The disciples want to be great (9:34); they want to be first (9:35); they want to determine who can be part of their group (9:38) and who can approach Jesus (10:13), or, in other words, they want to rule over others (10:42–43); they want either riches to qualify one for the kingdom or leaving everything to be all that is required (10:26–28); they want glory (10:37) and admire concrete honors (9:5; 13:1); they want their physical needs satisfied before considering the needs of their hearts, minds, or spirits (2:23; 8:14–17; 14:37–41); and they want their words and views to supplant those of the Messiah (8:31–33; 14:29–31). They want the things of this world: fame, comfort, wealth, high reputation, authority, and glory. Furthermore, many of these same concerns may be found among the other groups illustrating unfruitful grounds. Herod has John the Baptist beheaded to protect his reputation before his guests (6:26); the rich man values his wealth more than eternal life (10:21–22). The Pharisees, the scribes, and the Jerusalem leaders challenge the authority of Jesus' words (2:6–7; 11:27–28); want recognition, honor, and first places in synagogues and at feasts (12:38–40); value appearances and the performance of rules and rituals regardless of human needs (3:2–5; 7:5–8; 12:38); and want their traditions to supplant those of God (7:9–13; 10:2–9).

In contrast to this remarkably consistent set of traits found among the various unfruitful earths is the depiction of the ones healed. They generally come out of anonymity and fade back into it. With only two exceptions they are unnamed, and even the woman whose story will be told wherever the gospel is preached "in memory of her" (14:9) will be remembered only as a loving action, not as a specific, named individual. When they spread the word or heal, it is Jesus who is praised and becomes known, not they themselves (1:45; 5:20; 9:38–41). What money they have is given freely in devotion to God or Jesus (12:41–44; 14:3–9). They gladly serve the needs of others (1:31; 2:3–5; 5:18; 14:8–9), and they do not allow conventional practices or rules to stand in the way of their faith or love (2:4; 5:27–34; 7:25–30; 10:48; 14:3–5). They do not seek fame, wealth, personal glory, reputation, or honor. Instead, they hear the word that Jesus sows, emerge from the collective masses to respond in faith, are saved, and then go—all in anonymity. They are the last and the least of this world who have become the first in the kingdom of God.

As the audience begins to discern the actions and desires of the disciples and to perceive the disciples' similarities with the other unfruitful grounds and their contrasts with the persons who are healed, it should become clear that the flaw upon which the disciples' originally eager spirits founder is their craving for self-enhancement. They want to be known, respected, honored, obeyed, and generally held in high repute as the greatest and the first. If we take Peter's rebuke of the Messiah, the disciples' concern with who is the greatest, and James and John's request to have the first places in glory as incidents indicative of their character, that is, the actions they choose, the disciples are portrayed as following Jesus in hopes of gaining high repute or renown. Not only is this drive the antithesis of that embodied by the anonymous, faithful ones who are healed, it also stands in stark contrast to the depiction of Jesus himself, who throughout Division One actively strives to suppress his reputation and keep his name from becoming known.[92] Recognizing that the disciples' desire for honors is an-

---

92. Although I do not develop this terminology in the following discussion, the clash of worldviews being suggested here could be very appropriately and quite insightfully analyzed in terms of competing systems of honor/shame, the social value system that cultural anthropologists argue was and is pivotal for understanding the Mediterranean world. The disciples espouse a view of honor as power, reputation, fame, and wealth which was probably conventionally dominant in ancient Greco-Roman culture; they then represent the values of this faithless generation, the values of the kingdom of Satan. Jesus challenges that dominant system with a view of honor as anonymity, selflessness, service to others regardless of status, giving up of power and all claims to high reputation, a system in fact that turns the conventional contest of honor on its head. For Jesus, honor does not come from blood or kinship ties, traditional religious observances, or the approval of peers; it comes only from God and by doing God's will faithfully and courageously. What this generation calls honor is actually shameful, and it may be that Peter's weeping after his triple denial should be understood as his realization that in the system of honor that governs the kingdom of God, he has been shamed. For studies of the honor/shame matrix in the Mediterranean, see, e.g., B. Malina, *The New Testament World: Insights from Cultural Anthropology* (Atlanta: John Knox Press, 1981), 25–50; and D. Gilmore, ed., *Honor and Shame and the Unity of the Mediterranean* (AAA 22; Washington, D.C.: American Anthropological Association, 1987).

other way in which they function as foils to Jesus leads us to a reconsideration of an old problem in Mark: the secrecy motif.

Secrecy

Wrede's argument that secrecy in Mark is related to Jesus' messianic identity has long been rejected on basically two grounds. First, Jesus' commands to secrecy and the narrator's comments on Jesus' attempts to stay hidden often occur in contexts that have nothing to do with claims about Messiahship (e.g., 1:44–45; 7:24; 9:30). Second, it is hard to locate any for whom Jesus' claim of messianic identity is a secret: the audience learns of it in the first line (1:1), Peter confesses it (8:29), the demons all know, and the scribes and the Jerusalem leaders know (12:12; 14:61–62). Jesus as the Messiah, then, is demonstrably not the concern motivating the references to secrecy. Moreover, as many scholars have pointed out, those references appear to be inconsistent: while most demons and many who are healed are commanded to keep silent, the demoniac in Mark 5:1–20 is actually instructed to go and tell, and any attempt at secrecy is dropped when Jesus arrives in Jerusalem.

Understanding the disciples' desire for glory and renown as a foil to Jesus' actions suggests a different construction for secrecy: Jesus' commands for silence and his attempts to stay hidden define his steadfast rejection of personal renown and glory. Closely related to this rejection is his attempt to avoid drawing crowds.[93] We noted in the last chapter that the first four healing stories in the Gospel (1:21—2:12) all ended in reports of Jesus' fame spreading, crowds growing, and his constant efforts to stem that tide.[94] His consistent point is to keep from becoming known (1:34; 3:12; 5:43; 7:24). Yet it is inevitable that he will become known and attract crowds, for secrets are for the purpose of coming to light (4:22), and besides, "the more he charged them [to tell no one], the more zealously they proclaimed it" (7:36). Hence the author's intention in fashioning the secrecy passages is *not* to propose that Jesus remained unknown and did not attract crowds but rather to verify that Jesus did not seek for himself renown

93. The crowds in Mark do not function as a character group, although they are the collective out of which many individuals come to be healed. The crowds, rather, are used to reflect whatever is happening at that moment in the story. They may be amazed, praise God, be hungry, or call for crucifixion—in all cases they are commenting upon the current action of the plot. Their role, then, is similar to that of the chorus in Greek drama, and a comparable "observing and commenting collective" may be found in the ancient novel as, for example, Xenophon's "people of Ephesus." Hägg suggests that these groups in the ancient novel become "a kind of intermediary between the individual characters and the reader." See Hägg, *Narrative Technique in Ancient Greek Romances*, 123.

94. See above, pp. 135–40.

or glory,[95] although the spread of his fame and the growth of multitudes around him was inescapable, given who he was and what he did. It was not his desire but his fate.

Besides stressing the harmony between Jesus' attitude and the anonymity of the persons healed, the fruitful ground of God's kingdom, Jesus' rejection of personal glory in trying to keep his activities secret, himself hidden, and all credit directed toward God (e.g., 2:12; 5:19; 10:18) and his efforts to avoid crowds (e.g., 1:45; 3:9; 4:36; 6:31–34) produce several other important yields for the story as a whole. First, when Pilate asks Jesus whether he is "the King of the Jews" (15:2–5), as the chief priests and others have evidently charged, even though Jesus answers ambiguously with "You have said so," the audience knows beyond all doubt that Jesus has not campaigned for crowds to overthrow Roman rule. Jesus need not defend himself against the charge of insurrection, for the author has repeatedly shown him trying to escape harassing crowds and restrain his popularity. For the authorial audience, this evidence may have been especially significant, for Rome looked with distrust on religious leaders gathering large crowds, and those who governed at Rome's consent were similarly inclined, since, according to Josephus, Herod had John the Baptist killed precisely because he feared that John's fame with the masses would lead to insurrection.[96] Mark demonstrates constantly that such aims were not part of Jesus' mission; Rome had nothing to fear from him.

Second, the authorial audience may also have perceived Jesus' rejection of personal glory as an indication of the legitimacy of his message, for there appears to have been a fairly widespread commonplace that false teachers and religious figures were devoted primarily to building reputations for themselves. Just such a glory-seeking pseudo-philosopher, who goes to the extreme of self-immolation for the sake of "notoriety" (δόξα),[97] is satirized in Lucian's *The Passing of Peregrinus*. The desire to be famous, to be of high repute, was a common one throughout the Greco-Roman period. To be remembered for spectacular deeds or great thoughts was a kind of immortality greatly prized.[98] Yet true philosophers and religious teachers eschewed such love of glory or fame as fallacious goals in the quest for

---

95. Even in the case of the demoniac of Mark 5:1–20, Jesus orders him to tell "how much the Lord has done for you" (5:19), but what he decides to tell is "how much *Jesus* had done for him" (5:20). Also, the crowd is absent when Jesus commands him to go and tell, and he is going to a different region.

96. See *Antiquities* 18.5.2.

97. In *The Passing of Peregrinus* 1, Lucian asserts that it was not the love of wisdom but the love of glory (ἔρωτι τῆς δόκης) that motivated Peregrinus's actions.

98. See the interesting discussion in A. D. Nock, *Conversion: The Old and New in Religion from Alexander the Great to Augustine of Hippo* (London: Oxford University Press, 1961), 200–202.

wisdom or God.[99] The Cynic Crates in a letter "To Diogenes" speaks of his struggle with fame: "We are indeed already free from wealth, but fame (δόξα) has up to this point not yet released us from bondage to her, although, by Heracles, we have done everything to be set free from her."[100] The "glory" (δόξα, Mark 10:37) that James and John seek may communicate to the audience some connotation of this sort of fame rather than solely the rightful apocalyptic "glory" of the Father, which will surround the return of the Son of man (8:38; 13:26). Their path to eternal life in the kingdom has gone astray through desire for self-aggrandizement. Jesus, however, actively struggles to avoid such "notoriety." Praise comes to him but not because he seeks it or desires it.

Finally, and perhaps most profoundly, Jesus' pursuit of secrecy is a bid to buy time from the inevitable. In the parable of the Tenants, which we will discuss in more detail in the next chapter, as soon as the tenants recognize the final messenger as "the heir," they decide to kill him to keep "the inheritance" (12:7). Whether such a decision makes legal sense or not, it makes excellent typological sense. That Jesus' name would become known was inescapable; indeed, by Mark 6:14, Jesus' name had become known to Herod, a chillingly foreboding fact in the light of Herod's treatment of John the Baptist. That such knowledge would launch attempts to destroy him by the minions of Satan's kingdom was equally inescapable. Once Jesus' identity is known, once he is recognized as the true heir, the result is a foregone conclusion: death.

Thus Jesus' efforts to prevent his name from becoming known throughout the first part of the Gospel are ultimately efforts to hold back the denouement, to create time where time no longer exists. In other words, *he tries to buy time for sowing the word.* Only when all the various grounds have had an opportunity to hear and, in hearing, to display their affinity with God's kingdom or Satan's, does Jesus' urge for secrecy end. By the entry into Jerusalem in Mark 11, the shift is taking place, but his public declaration of identity (14:62) delays until the disciples have had their final chances to prove fruitful, until the account book on them is closed (14:41). Time has run out and the hour has come—at least for all the characters in the story. Silence need be kept no longer. Of course, from the beginning silence could not be kept anyway, which is why Jesus had so little time. The hour was near as soon as he started (1:14–15), for something is hidden only for the purpose of coming to light (4:22).

The final irony for the disciples resides in the realization that what they

---

99. See Paul's comments in Gal. 2:6 on God's lack of partiality for those "of repute."

100. A. Malherbe, *The Cynic Epistles: A Study Edition* (SBLSBS 12; Missoula, Mont.: Scholars Press, 1977), 58–59.

most desired—greatness, repute, renown, power—was the very thing that would ineluctably bring upon them what they most wanted to avoid—suffering, the cross, and death. When the moment of recognition comes, they flee, too fearful and too concerned with self-preservation to endure through persecutions to resurrection and eternal life. They illustrate the truth that when name, reputation, glory, and greatness become ends in themselves, betrayal, flight, and denial inevitably follow. Jesus and the anonymous faithful who are healed spurn renown and personal praise for the greater glory of the kingdom of God. Nevertheless, their words and acts do become known, and the result, in this evil and faithless generation, will always be death. Let us now follow Jesus through that final conflict, for the time of sowing is over.

10

Jesus,
the Heir
of the Vineyard

If the first part of the Gospel of Mark (Division One—Mark 1:14—10:52) is concerned primarily with Jesus' mission, that is, with the sowing of the word and the responses of the various types of ground, the action of the second part (Division Two—Mark 11:1—16:8) is dominated by the issue of Jesus' true identity and the inevitable result its publication draws. Appropriately, no healing miracles occur during the days in Jerusalem, for the faith upon which such miracles depend is absent in those people now surrounding Jesus. After the introductory scene of the triumphal entry (11:1–11),[1] the Jerusalem section begins with the final miracle of any kind in the Gospel: the cursing of the fig tree (11:12–14, 20–25), a miracle of destruction and death, the symbolic cursing of all unfruitfulness.[2] The first of the two rhetorical subsections composing Division Two is surrounded by the image and lesson of the fig tree and is temporally and geographically organized over two full days in and around the temple precincts in Jerusalem. Its rhetorical outline is as follows (for the full rhetorical structure, see Appendix A):

III: Division Two—Jesus, the Heir of the Vineyard—Mark 11:1—16:8
    A. Introduction—11:1-11
    B. 11:12—13:37
        1. 11:12–25—unfruitfulness and fig tree

---

1. See above, pp. 118–9.
2. See above, pp. 192–5.

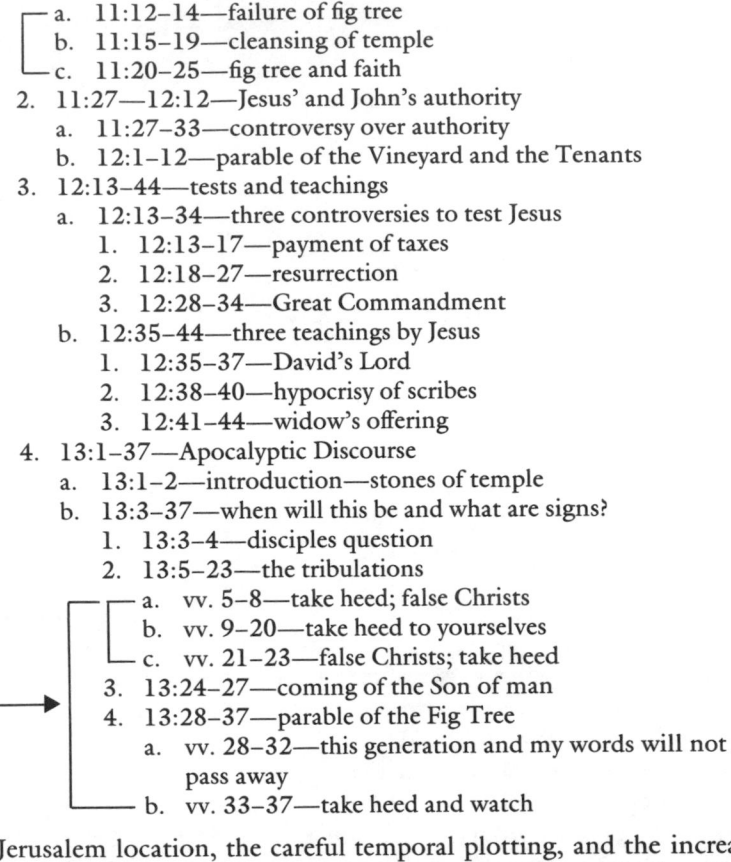

       a. 11:12–14—failure of fig tree
       b. 11:15–19—cleansing of temple
       c. 11:20–25—fig tree and faith
   2. 11:27—12:12—Jesus' and John's authority
       a. 11:27–33—controversy over authority
       b. 12:1–12—parable of the Vineyard and the Tenants
   3. 12:13–44—tests and teachings
       a. 12:13–34—three controversies to test Jesus
          1. 12:13–17—payment of taxes
          2. 12:18–27—resurrection
          3. 12:28–34—Great Commandment
       b. 12:35–44—three teachings by Jesus
          1. 12:35–37—David's Lord
          2. 12:38–40—hypocrisy of scribes
          3. 12:41–44—widow's offering
 4. 13:1–37—Apocalyptic Discourse
       a. 13:1–2—introduction—stones of temple
       b. 13:3–37—when will this be and what are signs?
          1. 13:3–4—disciples question
          2. 13:5–23—the tribulations
             a. vv. 5–8—take heed; false Christs
             b. vv. 9–20—take heed to yourselves
             c. vv. 21–23—false Christs; take heed
          3. 13:24–27—coming of the Son of man
          4. 13:28–37—parable of the Fig Tree
             a. vv. 28–32—this generation and my words will not
                pass away
             b. vv. 33–37—take heed and watch

The Jerusalem location, the careful temporal plotting, and the increasingly public nature of Jesus' assertion of authority all set Division Two apart from the earlier sections of the Gospel as the climactic recognition sequence. To guide the audience through the material, another parabolic plot synopsis is supplied close to the beginning of the segment: the parable of the Vineyard and the Tenants (Mark 12:1–12). Our study of the final the chapters of Mark, then, will also need to be directed by reference to this parable. We must explore the controversy on authority (11:27–33) that introduces the parable, the insight the parable provides on the relationship of Jesus to John the Baptist and earlier prophets, the manner in which the author proves Jesus to be the true heir of the vineyard, the future judgment on the stones of the temple for rejecting the cornerstone, and the death of the heir at the hands of the present tenants. After allowing the parable to chart our course through the Markan Passion narrative, we must finally confront the peculiar ending of the Gospel and in so doing evaluate the effect of the whole story on its audience, then and now.

Mark 11:27—12:12—The Passion in the Light of the Parable

In the triumphal entry (11:1–11) and the cleansing of the temple (11:15–19) Jesus acts with a provocative openness that contrasts sharply with his earlier attempts to stay hidden in Galilee and on the road to Jerusalem. This shift in manner, along with the shift in geography, signals to the audience that a new phase of the story has begun. However, to smooth what is otherwise a fairly abrupt transition, the final miracle, accompanying the final and most explicit discussion of faith in the Gospel, follows (and surrounds) these seemingly uncharacteristic actions. As soon as this easing of the transition has been accomplished, the author introduces the second—and last—parabolic plot synopsis to aid the audience's understanding and assimilation of the upcoming final events.

The parable of the Tenants is introduced by a controversy between Jesus and the scribes, the chief priests, and the elders in the temple concerning Jesus' authority (ἐξουσία) to do what he does (11:27–33). The controversy opens with a locational reference, "And they came again to Jerusalem" (11:27), in which the "again" (πάλιν) reminds the audience of Jesus' visit to the Jerusalem temple the day before (11:15–19). Since during that earlier trip Jesus had driven out the money-changers and taught what the purpose of the temple should be ("a house of prayer for all nations," 11:17) to the astonishment of the crowds and the growing fear of the Jerusalem hierarchy (11:18), the audience can understand the specific "things" alluded to by the Jerusalem leaders for which they demand to know Jesus' authority (11:28).

In addition, more generally the question of Jesus' authority echoes both the very first healing miracle of the Gospel (1:21–28), in which the authority of his performative word was contrasted to the teaching of the scribes (1:22, 27), and also the very first controversy of the Gospel (2:1–12), in which Jesus demonstrated to hostile scribes his "authority on earth to forgive sins" (2:10). Thus the issue of Jesus' authority to do and say what he does has been at the center of his conflict with the scribes, the Pharisees, and other leaders from the beginning of the story. Moreover, that conflict has so consistently emphasized the distinction between Jesus' teaching with authority and the teaching of the scribes that the audience should not be surprised when Pilate identifies as envy the motive behind their action in seeking Jesus' death (15:10). It is less his popularity with the multitude and more the power of his performative words that excites their wrath and opposition, for he speaks and acts as they cannot.

In the temple, the Jerusalem leaders now confront Jesus openly with the question of his authority, but Jesus returns question with question to elucidate the craven vacillation of their views. He will answer their question, if they will answer his: "Was the baptism of John from heaven or from men?"

(11:30). The argument that Jesus' question engenders among the Jerusalem hierarchy exposes the actual basis of their teachings: self-interest and popular opinion. They do not search Scripture, employ logic, or voice deeply held convictions to determine their response. Instead, they fear looking foolish or provoking the crowd, and hence they conclude that no answer is the best answer: "We do not know" (11:33). By formulating their dispute in direct discourse, the author dramatizes for the audience the *lack* of authority behind their teachings, which is the reason that what they say always compares so negatively to the words of Jesus. Even here, although Jesus nominally refuses to answer their question as well, he actually proceeds to show the source of his authority through the figurative language of a third degree narrative, the parable of the Tenants. Jesus' initial refusal, followed immediately by his indirect articulation, is a narrative example of paraleipsis, a common rhetorical ploy of saying "that we are passing by, or do not know, or refuse to say that which precisely now we are saying."[3] What he says he will not tell them (11:33b), he now tells them "in parables" (12:1a), and his opponents' recognition of the maneuver is clear from their response, "for they perceived that he had told the parable against them" (12:12).

Not only does the controversy recall the opening episodes of the Gospel through its focus on authority, but Jesus' question concerning the source of John's baptism also summons to mind the Markan prologue (1:1–13) and indeed the references to John's life (e.g., 1:14; 2:18), death (6:14–29), and role (9:11–13) throughout the Gospel. This recollection is helpful in the proper identification of the parabolic types about to be narrated, for the parable of the Tenants indicates not only the basis of Jesus' authority but that of John too. Both Jesus and John stand in a long line of prophetic messengers sent by the lord of the vineyard to demand the rightful fruit from the tenants. Other than this reminder about John the Baptist and the broad clue provided by the narrator's report at the end that the Jerusalem leaders realized the parable was spoken "against them" (i.e., tenants = scribes, chief priests, elders, etc.), the audience requires no further assistance in interpreting the parable, because the images it employs—land, fruit, beloved son—are thoroughly familiar from the preceding episodes of the Gospel. Thus, unlike the parable of the Sower, no point-by-point interpretation is given or is necessary, for the Markan narrative itself provides the illuminating context.

The parable (Mark 12:1–11) begins and ends with scriptural allusion (Mark 12:1≈Isa. 5:1–2) and quotation (Mark 12:10–11 = Ps. 118:22–23) and is divided into two parts: the current situation of the vineyard, enclosed

3. *Rhetorica ad Herennium* 4.27.37.

in an *inclusio* formed by ἀμπελών ("vineyard") in 12:1 and 12:8, and the future judgment on the vineyard, signaled by the shift to an interrogative construction at 12:9. The first part is internally structured by four acts of sending out by the lord of the vineyard, the last of which being additionally stressed by the presence of direct discourse. Each sending out is met by the tenants in an escalating pattern of violent rejection:

> (12:1) A <u>vineyard</u> (ἀμπελῶνα) a person planted and placed a hedge around it and dug a pit for a winepress and built a tower and gave it out to tenants and went abroad.

1. SENDING (12:2): And <u>he sent out</u>^a (ἀπέστειλεν) to the tenants at the proper season a servant <u>to take</u>^b (λάβῃ) from the tenants of the fruit of the vineyard,

   RESPONSE (12:3): and <u>taking</u>^{b'} (λαβόντες) him they beat him and <u>sent him out</u>^{a'} (ἀπέστειλαν) empty.

2. SENDING (12:4a): And again <u>he sent out</u> (ἀπέστειλεν) to them another servant,

   RESPONSE (12:4b): and they wounded him in the head and dishonored him.

3. SENDING (12:5a): And another <u>he sent out</u> (ἀπέστειλεν), and

   RESPONSE (12:5a): and they killed him;

   [SENDING] (12:5b): and many others,

   [RESPONSE] (12:5b): some on the one hand they beat, some on the other hand they killed.

4. SENDING (12:6): Still he had one, a beloved son; <u>he sent out</u> (ἀπέστειλεν) him last, saying, "They will revere my son."

   RESPONSE (12:7–8): But those tenants said to each other, "This one is the heir; come, let us kill him and ours will be the inheritance." And taking him, they killed him and threw him out of the <u>vineyard</u> (ἀμπελῶνος).

The first sending out exhibits a chiastic repetition (a b b' a') that underscores the defiance of the tenants: while the vineyard owner (a) <u>sends out</u> the servant (b) <u>to take</u> the fruit, the tenants, instead, (b') <u>take</u> the servant and (a') <u>send him out</u>. Moreover, the third action of sending out by the owner contains an additional report of many others going to the tenants, demonstrating the patience and good faith of the owner in the face of the intensifying enmity of the tenants, which progresses from beating to wounding in the head and dishonoring to, finally, killing. The decision to send a fourth emissary, the one left, a beloved son, thoroughly divests the story of any hint of verisimilitude, for what owner could possibly be so foolhardy as to risk a beloved son after such a show of violence.[4] What the decision attests, rather, is the graciousness and slowness to anger of the owner, now clearly representing God sending out the beloved Son, Jesus. Every opportunity is to be offered these tenants to repent of their lawless actions, even if it means imperiling a precious child. For modern readers, centuries of familiarity with this image may have dulled the absurd charity of endangering a loved relative in order to give murderers a final chance to turn around, but multiplying the servants in the third instance of sending out purposely emphasizes the preposterous nature of the owner's fourth dispatch. This act defies common sense and surpasses human compassion.

By comparing and contrasting the first three missions with the last, the audience can grasp with clarity and economy the similarity and distinctiveness of Jesus' ministry, as the author of Mark portrays it. The task entrusted to Jesus is precisely the same task motivating all the prophets and John the Baptist: to demand the fruit of the vineyard for its rightful owner and creator. John called for repentance and baptized the whole country (1:4–5); yet he was still arrested, imprisoned, and eventually beheaded. The vineyard's fruit remained in bondage. Jesus also came calling for repentance and faith in the good news that the kingdom of God has drawn near. Both his mission and John's are to demand a change of heart and the release of the fruit from the vineyard. John's mission failed to restore all things (cf. 9:12–13), but what of Jesus' mission? According to the parable it too apparently fails, for the son is killed by the tenants and thrown out of the vineyard. However, this failure is failure with a difference, and the difference has to do with the distinctive features of Jesus' ministry.

Although his mission is the same as that of his predecessors, the identity and position of the fourth emissary are quite distinct. He is not a slave like the others but a beloved son, and he is not one of a continuous stream of messengers but the last ($\H{\epsilon}\sigma\chi\alpha\tau\text{o}\nu$, 12:6). Moreover, it is the tenants' realization of that identity that precipitates his death, for they want what he legally

---

4. Attempts to argue for a real-life basis for the parable of the Tenants have always had to strain mightily to explain the apparent absurdity of the owner's action in sending his beloved son and also the equally peculiar reasoning of the tenants in thinking that killing the heir would give them the inheritance. See, e.g., Dodd, *The Parables of the Kingdom*, 96–102; and Jeremias, *The Parables of Jesus*, 70–77.

possesses, his inheritance (12:7). While the owner hoped the tenants would revere his son, they respond instead by killing him because they desperately desire what is rightfully his—because they "envy" him, as Pilate recognizes (15:10). Not only is his identity different from that of the earlier group but his position is as well, and consequently the reaction of the owner of the vineyard to the failure of his final messenger is not to send another but to come himself in wrath and destruction.

The second part of the parable of the Tenants, delineating this future judgment, is composed of a question Jesus asks and answers himself with the support of Scripture: What will the lord (ὁ κύριος) of the vineyard do? He will come and destroy the tenants and give the vineyard to others. Now have you not read this Scripture, "The stone which the builders rejected has become the head of the corner; by the Lord (παρὰ κυρίου) this was done and it is marvelous in our eyes" (12:9–11). The proximity of the references to the "lord" of the vineyard and to the "lord" of Scripture confirms for the audience, if such confirmation is needed, that they are one and the same. Since Jesus is the last messenger sent by the lord of the vineyard, his death at the hands of the tenants inevitably leads to their destruction and the giving of the vineyard to others, who, one assumes, will provide the lord with abundant fruit. Since the parable of the Sower, and indeed the entire Gospel narrative up to this point, have contrasted fruitful with unfruitful grounds, the "others" to whom the vineyard will be given suggest those whose faith has already made them fruitful.

When and how the old tenants will be evicted and the new ones installed or the rejected stone will become the headpiece is not detailed in the parable itself, but the parable's closing stress on the stone (λίθον) rejected by the builders (οἱ οἰκοδομοῦντες) in Mark 12:10 will guide the audience's understanding of Jesus' extended response to the disciple who marvels at the "wonderful stones" (λίθοι) and "wonderful buildings" (οἰκοδομαί) of the temple in Mark 13:1–2, which is often called the Apocalyptic Discourse. In that discourse, Jesus indicates the signs that portend the coming end and what human and cosmic trials his followers will be subjected to during the event, promising that those who endure to completion will be saved (13:13). In the Gospel narrative, the discussion of the end time is placed prior to Jesus' death, while in the parable of the Tenants the coming of the lord in wrath and destruction is the direct result of the killing of the beloved son. Thus the Apocalyptic Discourse is displaced from its parabolic order and, in fact, is the only major narrative displacement from the order fixed by either of the parabolic plot synopses. The author has Jesus present the material as a prediction of future events, but by reference to the parable of the Tenants the audience understands that these future events are the consequences of killing Jesus, not simply the ineluctable working out of some cosmic plan set from the origins of the universe. Unrepentant human evil, climaxing in the murder of the heir, provokes the ultimate tribulation to come.

Even from this brief analysis of the parable of the Tenants, it is quite evident how crucial its typology is for comprehending the dominant themes of the recognition sequence or Passion narrative: the sending of the beloved son, the true heir, who will be murdered by the tenants as soon as his identity is openly perceived, and the consequences that murder will inevitably produce. Although grasping the allusion to Isaiah's song of Israel as the unfruitful vineyard of God (Isa. 5:1–7) in the opening verse of the parable of the Tenants (Mark 12:1) might enrich an audience's appreciation of the plot, the author has so filled the parable with material drawn from preceding episodes that members of the authorial audience unfamiliar with Isaiah should have little difficulty discerning the typology. The details of the watchtower and the pit for the winepress stress, as they do also in Isaiah, the care and thoroughness of the vineyard's planter and creator. This vineyard is important to the owner. Indeed, connecting the parable too closely with Isaiah's vineyard might mislead the audience into an overly rigid historical interpretation of the parable's typology, for while the vineyard certainly does refer to Judaism with the Jerusalem leaders as the evil tenants opposing Jesus in Mark's narrative, typology by its very nature encourages a more generalized application: any group in power that obstructs the fruitfulness of God's good earth is a manifestation of the evil tenants in the vineyard. It may be to avoid such rigidity that the Isaiah passage is not directly quoted or referenced (unlike the quotation from Psalm 118 that closes the parable) but only alluded to indirectly.

Moreover, the procession of servants sent to the tenants and their progressively hostile reception are also types, which the prophets, John the Baptist, and Jesus illustrate concretely. Hence, though John is "wounded in the head" (12:4), he is also "killed" (12:5). He does not embody any particular sending out but is one of the procession. Jesus, of course, does exemplify one special emissary, the last, and that position is part of his distinctiveness. In addition, although the parable reports solely that the beloved son is killed and cast out of the vineyard (12:8), Mark portrays Jesus' passion as a summation of all the violence perpetrated against God's messengers: he is beaten (14:65); he is wounded in the head (15:17–19); he is dishonored (14:65; 15:17–20, 29–32); and he is killed (15:37). That this cacophony of violence will descend upon Jesus is already known by the audience from the three Passion predictions in the last section of Division One (8:31; 9:31; 10:33–34), and consequently they should have no difficulty positing both Jesus and John as messenger types. However, the description of the heir as "a beloved son" (12:6) recalls Jesus alone, for the voice from heaven has twice called him beloved son (1:11; 9:7). Thus, both his position and his identity distinguish him from all the previous messengers, including John the Baptist. He is one of the types but at the same time different from the rest.

Because the last emissary, the beloved son, can refer only to Jesus, the typology of the parable of the Tenants is not truly universal, as is the typology of the parable of the Sower. Yet it is not thoroughly historical or narratively limited either, as the ambiguous placement of John the Baptist in the parable demonstrates. The parable of the Tenants is probably best described as a semihistorical typology, which has some unique equivalences (the lord of the vineyard sending his beloved son last solely refers to God sending Jesus), some historically suggestive equivalences (the allusion to Isaiah's vineyard of Israel in the opening verse), and some generalized or typical equivalences (the servants represent any who have been or will be sent to demand fruit, and the wicked tenants are any who obstruct the rightful distribution of fruit). This mixed nature of the typology of the parable of the Tenants corresponds to its function as a plot synopsis for the final episodes of the Gospel, for it is not intended to illuminate the whole action as is the parable of the Sower but only the particular working out of the recognition sequence. Its more restricted reference demands and allows more narrative specificity. The basic relationship of the Jewish leaders, the scribes, and the Pharisees to Jesus, like that of the disciples, has already been defined by the parable of the Sower. The task of the parable of the Tenants is confined to alerting the audience to the important features of the closing scenes of the Gospel.

However, before we employ the parable of the Tenants for its designed purpose in exploring the final episodes of Mark, we must first investigate what it suggests about the very beginning verses of the Gospel and the relationship of Jesus to John the Baptist.

Mark 1:1–3—Jesus and John as Messengers of the Lord

In the earlier discussion of the Markan prologue (1:1–13), we demonstrated that the prologue is rhetorically divided into four units: 1:1–3, 4–8, 9–10, and 11–13.[5] The first unit, Mark 1:1–3, introduces Jesus Christ, Son of God (v. 1), and then continues with a scriptural quotation from Isaiah (vv. 2–3): Behold I send out (ἀποστέλλω) my messenger (ἄγγελόν) before your face, who will build your way (ὁδόν); a voice of one calling out in the wilderness (ἐν τῇ ἐρήμῳ), "Prepare the Lord's way (τὴν ὁδὸν κυρίου), make level his paths." The second unit begins at Mark 1:4 with the report of John

5. See above, pp. 108–13.

baptizing "in the wilderness" (ἐν τῇ ἐρήμῳ). Probably under the influence of John's location "in the wilderness" and the recrafting of the scene by both Matthew and Luke, scholars have almost universally understood the Isaiah quotation in Mark 1:2–3 to refer to John the Baptist alone.[6] Nevertheless, based on the parable of the Tenants and indeed on the whole narrative portrayal of Jesus in the Gospel of Mark, we wish to argue that the scriptural quotation is intended to describe primarily Jesus, its most natural grammatical and rhetorical referent, and secondarily, John, since they both share the same mission.

From the standpoint of narrative sequence, the only character in Mark introduced to the audience to whom the Scripture could refer is Jesus: Jesus is named in 1:1, then comes the Isaiah passage in vv. 2–3, and only afterward is John presented in v. 4. This sequence alone makes the object of the scriptural passage ambiguous at best. Both Matthew and Luke remove the ambiguity completely by ushering Jesus on the scene through extended, though quite different, birth narratives and then introducing John the Baptist and describing his preaching *before* quoting the Isaiah passage (Matt. 3:1–3; Luke 3:1–6). The passage is thoroughly separated from Jesus, and John is presented immediately before it as its sole referent. Their rearrangement of Markan material has, unfortunately, been consistently read back into Mark, although their additions of elaborate birth narratives ought to have suggested that their understandings of who Jesus was and what he was to do must be rather different from Mark's.

Moreover, the first verse of Mark's Isaiah quotation (Behold, I send out my messenger before your face, who will build your way) does not appear anywhere in Isaiah. In fact, it does not appear in any extant versions of the Hebrew Scriptures or the Septuagint. Mark 1:2 is a hybrid which seems to be a combination of Exod. 23:20 (LXX) and Mal. 3:1 (MT), although the latter ascription is rather uncertain. Whether Mark found the verse already combined or created it himself, it is a remarkably apt summation of several major themes Mark consistently associates with Jesus: Jesus is sent out by God on his mission (e.g., 1:38; 9:37; 12:6); he is the messenger, the sower of the word (1:14–15; 4:14, 33; 8:38; passim); he is on the way (8:3, 27; 9:33, 34; 10:32, 52); and to follow him on that way one must do as he does and teaches (8:34; 10:21, 28–31, 38–39). For Mark, Jesus, not John, is the one sent by God to show everyone the way that must be followed for salvation and eternal life, a way that involves suffering persecutions, the cross, death, and then resurrection.

6. See, e.g., W. Marxsen, *Mark the Evangelist* (Nashville: Abingdon Press, 1969), 30–53; Lightfoot, *The Gospel Message of St. Mark,* 15–20; E. Lohmeyer, *Das Evangelium des Markus* (Göttingen: Vandenhoeck & Ruprecht, 1953), 10–13; Pesch, *Das Markusevangelium,* 1:77–78; Taylor, *The Gospel According to St. Mark,* 152–57; and Rhoads and Michie, *Mark as Story,* 64–65.

Although the faulty attribution of a verse to Isaiah at the beginning of the story manifestly bothered neither the author of Mark nor the audience as the author conceived it, both Matthew and Luke are considerably more fastidious. In their initial presentations of John the Baptist, Matthew and Luke, drop the offending verse and quote only the legitimate verse(s) of Isaiah. However, in strikingly similar passages, which imply a Q origin (assuming the two-source hypothesis), they both apply the hybrid verse to John the Baptist without mentioning Isaiah (Matt 11:7-11; Luke 7:24–28).[7] In order to posit that this verse describes only John in Mark's Gospel as well, scholars must accept some odd assumptions. First, if John is the messenger, the one he is sent out before must be Jesus; however, since the quotation is fashioned as a first person to second person address ("I" to "you"), it means that the prophet, speaking for God, is addressing, not the audience or the people, but Jesus alone: I, God, send out my messenger before you, Jesus.[8] So, we must presume that the Gospel narrator begins by proclaiming to the audience the good news of Jesus Christ (1:1) and then supports that proclamation by quoting a Scripture directed not to the audience but to Jesus. The audience simply overhears God's words to Jesus. Such switching of narratees (from the reader to Jesus, a character) almost in mid-breath is strained and confusing, to say the least. It is also an unusual interpretation of prophetic writing. Prophets generally speak for God to the people or the leaders of the people, not for God to God's son (e.g., 7:6–7; 14:27).[9]

How much more natural it would be to understand the entire prologue

---

7. The similarity of Matt. 11:7–11 and Luke 7:24–28, along with the similarity of their baptism sequences (Matt. 3:7–12 and Luke 3:7–17), strongly suggests that they are drawing from a Q tradition concerning John to supplement Mark. It seems reasonable to hypothesize that Matthew and Luke did not independently make the same alterations on Mark but rather had another source, Q, which ascribed the scriptural quotations in Mark 1:2–3 to John the Baptist. Matthew and Luke, then, were faced with two alternate views of the role of Jesus and the role of John supported by the same scriptural passages. The "low" Christology inherent in identifying Jesus as a messenger of God sent to make the way for others to follow which Mark presented was less amenable to the theological perspectives of Matthew and Luke than was the apocalyptic coloring of John's message obtained by connecting the verses with him; thus, Q was favored.

If Mark and Q use the same hybrid verse for different purposes, it suggests the possibility that both were drawing from a *Testimonia*. The evidence of a *Testimonia* in the Qumran community (4QTestim), which listed messianic proof texts culled from Scripture, raises the probability of the same kind of document in early Christian circles.

8. For a careful analysis of Mark 1:2–3 along these lines, see Kingsbury, *The Christology of Mark's Gospel*, 56–60.

9. Mark 12:35–37 might be seen as an exception to this general principle, for Jesus quotes David talking about what "The Lord said to my Lord" or, i.e., God speaking to the Christ. In this case, however, the "overheard" conversation permitted "by the Holy Spirit" (12:36) is carefully prepared for and made the point of Jesus' proof. Hence, no audience confusion would arise. It is the lack of such preparation and clarity that makes viewing Mark 1:2–3 also as an overheard conversation so difficult to support.

up to Mark 1:7, including the scriptural quotation, as the narrator speaking to the narratee in first degree narration. The quotation itself, of course, is technically a second degree narrative of Isaiah speaking to the people of Isaiah's time about a future event, being used by the Markan narrator for the authorial audience. Then, the messenger is Jesus, who is introduced immediately before the Scripture, and the prophet is speaking for God to the people in the normal manner. No as yet unidentified character (i.e., John) is being discussed. It might be objected that the "you" to whom the messenger is sent is in the singular (σου), not the plural we might expect, if the people as a whole or the audience were being addressed. That objection is based on an assumption concerning how the author conceived the authorial audience. The only possible evidence available to decide the issue is the unusual "wink" to the reader by the author at Mark 13:14. In the midst of Jesus' speech to the disciples, the author suddenly interrupts to address the reader of the Gospel directly: "let the reader understand (ὁ ἀναγινώσκων νοείτω)." The reader addressed is in the singular. Whether the author imagined the gospel message to be aimed at individuals, an issue we will pursue later, or whether the authorial audience is taken as a corporate personality, a communal singularity in which the part represents the whole (synecdoche), from what little indication exists it seems that the author of Mark invokes a singular audience.[10]

Second, if John is the referent of the Isaiah quotation, the grammatical relation of the quotation in vv. 2–3 with the introduction of John in v. 4 poses a problem. To connect it with John, Mark 1:1 must be separated from vv. 2–3, making καθὼς γέγραπται ("As it is written") the start of a new sentence. It is possible for καθὼς ("as") to begin a sentence but usually only in a καθὼς . . . οὕτως ("as" . . . "so") construction,[11] and by a major extension of grammatical latitude, one might construe καθὼς . . . ἐγένετο ("as" . . . "it happened," v. 4) as a passable substitute for καθὼς . . . οὕτως. The problem still remains, however, for when used as an introductory formula for a scriptural quotation, either in the Septuagint or in the New Testament, καθὼς γέγραπται ("as it is written") "*never* appears at the start of a new sentence."[12] As Robert Guelich points out in his study of the phrase, "The very function of the words 'as has been written,' when used as an introductory formula, consists in forming a bridge between what has preceded and the quotation that follows. The formula and quotation *always refer*

---

10. It is interesting to note that Luke addresses his narrative to an individual as well, whether actual or symbolic. See Luke 1:3 and Acts 1:1.

11. So argues Taylor, *The Gospel According to St. Mark*, 153. See, e.g., Luke 9:30; 17:26; John 3:14.

12. Guelich, "'The Beginning of the Gospel'—Mark 1:1–15," 6, emphasis his.

back and never forward in the context."[13] In back of Mark's initial "as has been written" stands Jesus (1:1), not John.

Third, the separation of Mark 1:1 from 1:2ff. raises the issue of how v. 1 functions. Some scholars have suggested that "Beginning the gospel of Jesus Christ, Son of God" forms a title for the text and is not a part of the story itself.[14] Others dispute that position on the grounds that the phrase reports essential information to the audience, required in understanding much of the rest of the story.[15] Furthermore, to what does ἀρχή ("beginning") refer? Few scholars support the view that "the beginning of the gospel of Jesus Christ" is to be found in the coming of John the Baptist, for even John's direct discourse concerns the stronger one who will come after him (1:7), pointing to Jesus; thus Jesus, not John, is the focus of the prologue. Some have argued that the "gospel of Jesus Christ" is the entire story, reaching on into the life of the early church, and the coming of Jesus, then, is just the beginning of this longer Christian story.[16] However, an analysis of similar uses of ἀρχή in headings of extrabiblical works indicates that it "always pertains either to the immediate introduction of a literary work or the actual beginning of the main section" and consequently, in its own literary milieu, "the beginning of the gospel of Jesus Christ" was unlikely to be intended to encompass the whole narrative.[17]

If the formula "as it is written" always corresponds to what precedes it (e.g., 7:6–7; 9:13; 14:21) and "beginning" in a heading always refers to its immediate context, how much simpler it is to recognize that Jesus Christ, Son of God (1:1), is the messenger sent by God to show the way we are to follow (1:2) and that the beginning of this good news is found in the prophecy of Isaiah, for God in Isaiah's time foretold the sending of his special emissary into the world. Although contemporary biblical scholarship can never be accused of slavish obedience to the dictates of Occam's Razor,[18] in this case with the support of the parable of the Tenants and the

13. Ibid., emphasis mine. Also note the rhetorical rhyming connections between Mark 1:1 and vv. 2–3 that we developed above, pp. 111. Both grammatically and rhetorically, vv. 1–3 belong together.

14. So, e.g., Taylor, *The Gospel According to St. Mark,* 152; and Pesch, *Das Markusevangelium,* 1:74–75.

15. See, e.g., J. Gnilka, *Das Evangelium nach Markus* (EKKNT 2; 2 parts; Zurich: Benziger Verlag, 1978–79), 1:42–43; and Kingsbury, *The Christology of Mark's Gospel,* 55–56.

16. For an interesting development of this view, see Keck, "The Introduction to Mark's Gospel," 365–68.

17. Guelich, "'The Beginning of the Gospel,'" 8; see also D. E. Aune, *The New Testament in Its Literary Environment* (LEC; Philadelphia: Westminster Press, 1987), 17.

18. The law of parsimony devised by the English philosopher William of Occam states that elements should not be multiplied beyond the necessary. In cases where a number of theories fits the known evidence, the simplest is best.

overall narrative portrayal of Jesus in Mark, the simplest reading of Mark 1:1–2 may be the best. If Mark 1:3 ("the voice of one crying in the wilderness: Prepare the way of the Lord, make his paths straight"), the verse actually derived from Isaiah and the one used by both Matthew and Luke to identify John alone, also fits this simpler interpretation, then the connection of the scriptural quotation in Mark with Jesus as well as with John will constitute a strong alternative.

Since John the Baptist is not named until *after* the Isaiah quotation in Mark, for an audience free of the influence of Matthew and Luke the only point of connection between John and the Scripture would be the anastrophic use of "in the wilderness" that links the close of the first unit of the prologue with the opening of the second unit:[19] a voice cries in the wilderness and John baptizes and preaches in the wilderness. By recalling John's baptizing activity just prior to presenting the parable of the Tenants (11:30–33), the author indicates to the audience John's role as one of the servants sent by the owner of the vineyard to the tenants. In the Markan prologue, John is depicted in precisely that manner, for he preaches and baptizes for repentance, a turning around of the people. He also informs the people that a mightier one will come after him (1:7–8) and then baptizes Jesus, whom the voice from heaven addresses as "my beloved Son" (1:9–11). This action accords with the final sending of the beloved son in the parable of the Tenants, after all the other messengers have delivered their messages to no avail. The last emissary is stronger, for he is son, not servant, and he is the heir to the vineyard; thus, while John preaches repentance, Jesus preaches repentance and faith and the coming of God's kingdom (1:15). The audience should see John as a lesser messenger of God, one of those many prophets sent on the mission before the mightier son and heir; thus some secondary connection of John to the Isaiah prediction is appropriate.

Yet John's association with the wilderness begins and ends in Mark 1:4, while Jesus' bond with the wilderness or wilderness places begins in the prologue and extends throughout the sowing time in Galilee.[20] Immediately after his baptism, Jesus is driven by the Spirit "into the wilderness" (1:12), and he stays "in the wilderness" for forty days (1:13). So, the

19. See the discussion of the rhetorical organization of the prologue above, pp. 108–13.

20. For an interpretation of the wilderness theme in Mark that emphasizes its roots in the Hebrew Scriptures and its relation to the defeat of Satanic forces, see U. Mauser, *Christ in the Wilderness: The Wilderness Theme in the Second Gospel and Its Basis in the Biblical Tradition* (Naperville, Ill.: Alec R. Allenson, 1963).

For a structural interpretation of the wilderness—and indeed of all other spatial references in Mark—that attempts to develop their mythic signification, see E. S. Malbon, *Narrative Space and Mythic Meaning in Mark* (NVBS; San Francisco: Harper & Row, 1986), for wilderness, esp. 72–79.

Markan prologue opens with a prophecy about a voice "in the wilderness" (v. 3), places John "in the wilderness" (v. 4), and then closes with two references to Jesus "in the wilderness" (vv. 12–13). The chiastic pattern of the prologue[21] additionally stresses the relation of the prophecy to Jesus' wilderness sojourn (A: vv.1–3 to A': vv. 11–13). Moreover, Jesus' preaching mission in Galilee is often linked with wilderness places (ἔρημος τόπος): soon after the start of his ministry, he goes out to a wilderness place to pray (1:35); then, as his fame spreads, he can no longer enter towns openly and so stays out in a wilderness place but people still come to him from everywhere (1:45);[22] and both the incidents in which Jesus feeds the multitudes after teaching and preaching to them for days occur in wilderness areas (6:31, 32, 35; 8:4). Throughout the sowing of the word, Jesus repeatedly embodies "the voice of one crying in the wilderness" (1:3).

According to the Isaiah quotation, what the voice in the wilderness commands of the people is, "Prepare the way of the Lord, make his paths straight" (1:3).[23] Those who argue that the Isaiah prophecy refers only to John the Baptist identify "the Lord" as Jesus rather than God,[24] another odd assumption in the context of Mark's Gospel, for in every other scriptural quotation that employs κύριος ("Lord") in the Gospel, the referent is clearly God in distinction from Jesus (e.g., 11:9; 12:11, 29, 30, 36, 37). Jesus himself calls God κύριος in Mark 5:19 and 13:20, and the conventional nature of its association with God is demonstrated by its presence in symbolic phrases like the lord of the vineyard (12:9) and the lord of the house (13:35). Only when manifestly functioning as a title of respect (sir or master) is κύριος connected to Jesus (7:28; 11:3).[25] To assume that Mark begins the story with a scriptural quotation in which the audience is expected to recognize that κύριος represents someone it never represents anywhere else in the Gospel is strange, indeed.

Moreover, the message the voice delivers, "Prepare the way of the Lord,"

21. See above, pp. 111–13.
22. Most translations render ἔρημος τόπος at Mark 1:35 and 1:45 as "a lonely place" or "the country," because, as many commentators have pointed out, there was no wilderness anywhere around Capernaum (see, e.g., Taylor, *The Gospel According to St. Mark,* 183). Whether Mark knew the correct geography or not, the point here is Jesus as the fulfillment of prophecy, not the cultivation or lack thereof of land around Capernaum.
23. Mark is using here—as he does almost exclusively throughout the Gospel—the LXX rendering of Isa. 40:3 rather than the Hebrew version. In the LXX, the voice is in the wilderness, but in Hebrew it is the way of the Lord that is in the wilderness, not the voice.

Mark alters the close of the quotation, substituting αὐτοῦ for τοῦ θεοῦ ἡμῶν, probably to preserve the end rhyme of each clause. See above, p. 111.
24. See, e.g., Taylor, *The Gospel According to St. Mark,* 153–54; and Kingsbury, *The Christology of Mark's Gospel,* 110–11.
25. The "my Lord" of the Scripture quotation at Mark 12:36 should probably be understood in this respectful manner to distinguish it from "the Lord": so, The Lord said to my master.

is fundamentally an apocalyptic enterprise. The coming that the people must prepare for, like the coming of the lord of the vineyard in the parable of the Tenants, is a coming in wrath, judgment, power, and glory. Isaiah 40:3, which Mark is quoting in v. 3, was already an apocalyptic proof text before the time of the Gospel of Mark. In its *Manual of Discipline,* the Qumran community had applied the verse to their efforts in the Judean wilderness to encourage the eschaton by study of the law perhaps as much as two centuries prior to Mark.[26] Further, Matthew and Luke, both of whom connect Isa. 40:3 solely with John the Baptist, also depict John as an apocalyptic preacher, warning of the ax now poised over the root (Matt. 3:7–12/Luke 3:7–9, 16–17); however, such a portrayal of John is conspicuously absent from Mark. In Mark, John's function, as dramatized in the prologue and interpreted by Jesus later, is "to restore all things" (Mark 9:12; cf. 1:5). Since the restoration by Elijah redivivus fails, as Mark indicates (1:14; 9:12–13), the Son of man who follows him can expect to suffer many things. In the parable of the Tenants, the rejection encountered by all of the servants leads directly to the vineyard owner's decision to send the last one, his beloved son; only at the son's rejection is the lord's wrath finally provoked (12:9–11). Hence, for Mark, John the Baptist unsuccessfully attempts to restore the hearts of the people (cf. Mal. 4:6 LXX) and announces that a mightier one will follow him, but he does not admonish the people concerning impending judgment, for that is the distinctive task of the son, the last one.

Jesus, not John, is the apocalyptic preacher in Mark's Gospel. Though John's downfall results in the coming of Jesus, Jesus' death will prompt the coming of the Son of man "in the glory of his Father with the holy angels" (8:38). Jesus describes this event at length (13:14–27) and exhorts all to watch for its coming (13:32–37), promising that those who endure all the persecutions and tribulations will be saved (13:9–13). While Jesus confesses that no one knows exactly when this coming will take place except God (13:32), evidently for Mark it looms closely on the horizon, for the death of the son is its trigger. The imminence of the eschaton is mitigated in the Gospels of Matthew and Luke, and they both work to disassociate Jesus from the predominantly apocalyptic role that Mark fashions for him; so, for them, Isa. 40:3 is not an appropriate description of Jesus' message. For Mark, it is. Jesus is the messenger sent by God to proclaim the coming near of God's kingdom. In addition, by the way he goes through persecutions, suffering, and death, he exemplifies what all who seek salvation must do to be prepared for the Lord's coming. Jesus and John are messengers of the lord of the vineyard, but it is only Jesus, as the last messenger, who can proclaim to the faithful the good news that God's kingdom has come in

26. See 1QS 8.14–18.

power and will soon come in all its glory, wiping away the domination of the vineyard by this evil generation. Granted that between the present state and that future resolution, while the gospel is being preached to every nation, tribulation, suffering, and death will fall upon the elect; nevertheless, the destruction of the evil tenants is inevitable and rapidly approaching and that is good news indeed.

For Mark, the good news about Jesus Christ, Son of God, begins in God's promise through the words of the prophet to send out a messenger to forge the way we must follow to salvation and eternal life in the light of the imminent apocalyptic coming of the Lord. Since the function of a prologue or prooemium in Greco-Roman writing was to introduce the reader in summary fashion to the major themes of the forthcoming story, Mark's use of this scriptural quotation is quite appropriate, for it suggests Jesus' role and message. Combined with the opening line of the Gospel, which announces Jesus' identity as Christ and Son of God, Mark 1:1–3 orients the reader to all that follows:

> The beginning of the good news about Jesus Christ, Son of God, as it has been recorded by the prophet Isaiah:
> Behold I am sending out my messenger before your face
> who will build your way;
> The voice of one calling out in the wilderness,
> Prepare the way of the Lord,
> Make his paths level.

The linking by location of John the Baptist in Mark 1:4 to the Isaiah passage, implying his role as messenger too, prepares the reader to understand John's arrest and later death as a grim foreshadowing of Jesus' fate: It happened that John was baptizing in the wilderness and preaching a baptism of repentance for the forgiveness of sins. When John's baptisms of repentance fail to protect him from being delivered up to his enemies (1:14), the lord of the vineyard sends out another messenger, a final one, who is not servant but son and who preaches not only repentance but also faith in the coming near of God's kingdom (1:14–15).

In order to recognize the application of Mark's opening scriptural citation to Jesus primarily and to John secondarily, we have had to work backward from the parable of the Tenants and the general portrayal of Jesus in the Gospel of Mark to the prologue. For the authorial audience who were—in this instance at least—blessedly free of the influence of Matthew's and Luke's versions of the story and the heavy burden of later scholarship, the prologue could be employed in its intended manner as a guide to the depiction of Jesus and the interpretation of the parables in the succeeding narrative. After these many centuries from the creation of the Gospel of Mark, attempting to enter the ranks of its authorial audience can be a laborious and sometimes impossible enterprise, but the attempt itself is worthwhile if it helps us to hear the Gospel anew with ears a little more in tune with Mark's own narrative rhythms. Having permitted the parable of the Tenants to illuminate the beginning of the gospel of Jesus Christ, let us now turn its focus onto the closing episodes of the story to see how Mark demonstrates that Jesus is truly the heir of the vineyard.

Mark 12:13–44—Jesus as Heir

The tenants who control the vineyard recognize the last messenger sent, the beloved son, as "the heir" (ὁ κληρονόμος) and decide, mistakenly as it turns out, that by killing him "the inheritance" (ἡ κληρονομία) will belong fully to them (12:7). The emphasis on "heir" and "inheritance" in the tenants' direct discourse, caused by the lexical similarity of the two terms in such close proximity (a form of polyptoton), should alert the audience to the importance of this new perspective on Jesus' identity. The audience has known from the beginning of the story that Jesus is the son (1:1), indeed the beloved son (1:11; 9:7), but what does it mean that he is additionally the heir and that the vineyard is his inheritance? The first hint of this expanded identity occurs in Bartimaeus's address to Jesus as "Son of David" (10:47), which links the end of Division One with the opening of Division Two by anticipating a major theme of Division Two, the relationship of Jesus to the traditions of Israel. The triumphal entry (11:1–11), functioning as the prologue of Division Two, trumpets this identity abroad in the cries of the multitudes, "Hosanna! Blessed is he who comes in the name of the Lord! Blessed is the kingdom of our father David that is coming! Hosanna in the highest!" (11:9–10).

That Jesus is identified just outside Jerusalem as "Son of David" and the Jerusalem crowds welcome him with rejoicing over the coming kingdom of "our father David" firmly establishes Jesus as a true Jew, one of the family of David's descendants. Furthermore, by stocking the episode of the triumphal entry with allusions to messianic and kingship texts (e.g., the king's prerogative to take animals, Mark 11:2–3, in 1 Sam. 8:10–11, 17; the messiah riding a colt, Mark 11:7, in Zech. 9:9; the spreading of garments before the king, Mark 11:8, in 2 Kings 9:13), Mark presents Jesus as the Davidic Messiah-King.[27] However, the parable of the Tenants and Jesus' later teachings in Jerusalem (12:35–37) clarify Mark's particular concept of Jesus as David's son. Although Jesus is a Jew of David's lineage, his authority is not derived from David's political or military prerogatives. Jesus does

27. For a careful discussion of Mark's view of Jesus as Son of David that reaches conclusions similar to mine but by a different route, see Kingsbury, *The Christology of Mark's Gospel*, 102–14.

not relate to Israel as king to country, for Jesus' source of authority is far greater than a king's. Jesus is the son of the creator; he is the true heir, and the whole of the vineyard, its traditions, people, temple, land—heart and soul—*belong* to him, for they are his inheritance. It is appropriate to view Jesus as Son of David, if one recognizes that David's son is also David's lord and master (12:36–37). Jesus' rights, authority, and power far exceed those of a king, even King David, because they are bestowed by reason of his divine sonship, not his Jewish ancestry. Thus, Son of David is only one aspect of Jesus' wider role as heir of the vineyard.

Even before narrating the parable of the Tenants, the author depicts this wider role in the affair of the cleansing of the temple (11:15–19), the little episode intercalated into the cursing of the fig tree (11:12–14, 20–25).[28] In driving out the merchants and money-changers, Jesus publicly asserts his jurisdiction over the center of Jewish religion, the temple. Quoting a verse from Isaiah, he defines the proper function of the temple in religious life and contrasts it with the current situation: "Is it not written, 'My house shall be called a house of prayer for all the nations'? But you have made it a den of robbers" (11:17). In Jesus' renewed profile, God's house is not for the Jews alone but for all people, and it is not a commercial venture but a "house of prayer." His right to effect such a realignment demonstrates that his power extends beyond the nationalistic boundaries of a Davidic Messiah-King with military and political sway into the universal religious domain of priest and scribe. As the parable of the Tenants will confirm for the audience, Jesus is the heir of the entire vineyard, and the two "uncharacteristic" actions (the triumphal entry and the cleansing of the temple) that open Division Two begin to sketch the outlines of this heir's true inheritance.

That the crowds quote Psalm 118 in welcoming Jesus into Jerusalem (Mark 11:9) and that Jesus himself quotes from Isaiah in cleansing the temple (11:17) introduce another aspect of Jesus' identity as heir: he is heir to the scriptural traditions of Israel and indeed is presented as the authoritative interpreter and arbitrator of those traditions in contrast to the scribes, the chief priests, and the Pharisees. Although Jesus has quoted or alluded to Scripture before the recognition sequence (see, e.g., 2:25–26; 4:12; 7:6–7), from Mark 11 to the end of the Gospel "the number of quotations from and allusions to scripture increases sharply as compared with the first ten chapters of the book."[29] Moreover, while Jesus has in the past occasionally used Scripture to defend his practices (e.g., 2:25–26) or correct deficient moral positions (e.g., 7:9–13; 10:2–9), in the three controversies and the three

28. See above, pp. 192–95.
29. H. C. Kee, "The Function of Scriptural Quotations and Allusions in Mark 11–16," in *Jesus and Paulus,* ed. Ellis and Grässer, 166.

teachings that compose Mark 12:13–44, Jesus defines the proper relation of religion to the state (12:13–17) and the proper interpretation of tradition (12:18–27, 28–34, 35–37) all by allusion to or quotation of Scripture before concluding with examples of improper and proper cultic participation (12:38–40, 41–44). Mark thus portrays Jesus as the true heir of the vineyard by demonstrating his mastery over the traditions of Israel and his authority over its cultic practices; Jesus is a greater scribe than the scribes, a more knowledgeable lawyer than the lawyers, and a better priest than the chief priests.

Though the content of Jesus' controversies and teachings mostly deal with Jewish belief and practice, the form of his arguments is thoroughly Hellenistic. In Greco-Roman rhetoric, the two primary modes of proving an argument against an opponent were the enthymeme and the example. For Aristotle, the enthymeme and the example in rhetoric corresponded respectively to the syllogism and the induction in dialectic.[30] Deductive argumentation, positing universally or generally acceptable premises and deriving specific conclusions from them, appears in rhetoric as enthymemes, while inductive argumentation, citing specific instances and drawing general conclusions from them, appears as examples. In the six episodes of Mark 12:13–44, the first two tests (12:13–17, 18–27) and the first teaching (12:35–37) depict Jesus speaking enthymematically and the last two teachings (12:38–40, 41–44) rely upon examples to establish their point. The third test (12:28–34), after which "no one dared to ask him any question" (12:34), uses repetition to assert Jesus' higher authority over the wise scribe.

A logical syllogism usually proceeds by stating a major premise, which must be universal and acceptable by definition, a minor premise, which is more specific but still generally acceptable, and a conclusion reached by combining the major and minor premises, which is unavoidable, given the truth of the two premises. In rhetoric such full syllogisms rarely appear;[31] instead, some of the elements of the syllogism are assumed, implied, or just suppressed. This abbreviated syllogism is the enthymeme and may occur simply as a statement with an accompanying reason. Moreover, the enthymeme often substitutes common opinion, folk wisdom, or probable truths for the necessary universals of the syllogism.[32] In the enthymemes of Mark 12, allusions to or citations from Scripture, since they are assumed to be valid for all parties, usually occupy the positions of major or minor prem-

---

30. *Rhetoric* 1.2.8 (1356b); see also Demetrius, *On Style* 30–33.

31. A full syllogism in rhetoric is called an epicheireme. The discussion of the enthymeme that follows is based in part on Kennedy, *Rhetorical Criticism*, 15–18.

32. Aristotle, *Rhetoric* 1.2.14 (1357a).

ises. In order for modern readers to follow the full argument of a rhetorical enthymeme, it is helpful to reconstruct the syllogism that stands behind it; however, such measures would have been unnecessary for the authorial audience because of the conventional and widespread use of the form in the Greco-Roman world.

The question of whether or not taxes should be paid to Caesar (12:13–17) is the first test directed at Jesus by the Jerusalem leaders in an attempt to trap him into saying something that could be used against him, after his indirect attack on their authority in the parable of the Tenants. Although paying taxes was unpopular with the crowds, encouraging people to withhold their taxes was even more unpopular with the Roman overlords. Thus the question was intended to bring Jesus into disfavor with one group or the other. Jesus responds by enunciating two enthymemes, one overt and one implied, derived from the same suppressed major premise:

Major premise:
Whatever bears the image and inscription
of someone belongs to that one.

Overt minor premise: *Implied minor premise:*
A denarius carries Caesar's   Human beings are in the image
image and words (Mark 12:16).   of God (see Gen. 1:26–28).

Conclusion: *Conclusion:*
"Render to Caesar the things   "and to God the things
that are Caesar's" (Mark 12:17).   that are God's" (Mark 12:17).

The double conclusion of the enthymemes (the things of Caesar give to Caesar and the things of God to God, 12:17) is articulated with the balanced members characteristic of the Greek period[33] and contrasts sufficiently with the dominant disjointed sentence style of the Gospel to sound like a proverb or maxim from the lips of Jesus. Since enthymemes in rhetoric, unlike syllogisms in logic, can appeal to common opinion or folk wisdom, Aristotle stresses that gnomic sayings or maxims are especially appropriate as either premises or conclusions for enthymematic arguments.[34] As in the three controversies concerning eating practices with their gnomic conclusions found earlier in Mark 2:15–28,[35] the maxim-like con-

---

33. For a good discussion of the uses and charm of the balanced symmetry found in the periodic type of sentence structure in Greek as opposed to the disjointed style (which dominates the Gospel of Mark), see Demetrius, *On Style* 12–35.

34. *Rhetoric* 2.21.1–16 (1394a–1395b).

35. See above, pp. 133–35.

clusion of this dispute with the Pharisees and the Herodians gains the amazement and implicit concurrence of Jesus' opponents by its seeming appeal to common sense or traditional wisdom.

The Sadducees pose the second test for Jesus (12:18–27), and the narrator identifies the group for the information of the authorial audience as those "who say that there is no resurrection" (12:18), a fact needed to understand the question they raise. This episode dramatizes a confrontation of beliefs by a confrontation of rhetorical modes of proof, the example versus the enthymeme. The Sadducees challenge Jesus with an extended example of seven brothers and one wife based on the tradition of levirate marriage (see Gen. 38:8–11 and Deut. 25:5–10) that is designed to display the silliness of any belief in the resurrection of the dead. Each of the seven brothers takes the same wife and dies before children are conceived, and then the woman finally dies; so, whose wife will she be in the resurrection (12:20–23)? While examples in rhetoric can be persuasive, because by their very nature they must be specific and limited, they often meet with less approval from the audience than enthymemes, as Aristotle points out.[36] Thus, by fashioning the heart of Jesus' reply to this example in enthymematic form, Mark has assured the greater persuasiveness of Jesus' position against that of the Sadducees.

Jesus' response (12:24–27) must deal with two issues: the character of resurrected life and the truth of resurrection itself. Taking the less important point first, Jesus contends that human institutions like marriage are absent from life after death; instead, those resurrected will be like "angels in heaven" (12:25).[37] However, Jesus' description of what life after death will be like is dependent upon the reality of resurrection itself; hence the more crucial issue is the truth of a belief in resurrection. This proof is formulated as an enthymeme founded on Scripture. The full syllogism would appear this way:

> *Major premise:* God is not God of the dead but of the living (12:27).
> *Minor premise:* God said to Moses, "I am the God of Abraham, and the God of Isaac, and the God of Jacob" (12:26).
> *Suppressed minor premise:* Moses lived after the deaths of Abraham, Isaac, and Jacob.
> *Conclusion:* The dead are alive and thus resurrection exists.

Surrounding Jesus' argument with assertions about the wrongness of the Sadducees' position (12:24a and 27b) and composing the major premise as

---

36. *Rhetoric* 1.2.10–11 (1356b).
37. Compare Paul's rather similar arguments for a "spiritual" rather than physical resurrection existence in 1 Cor. 15:35–50.

a closing asyndeton[38] (12:27) add to the rhetorical force of the unit. Since God is God of the living and spoke in the present tense to Moses about people who had died generations earlier, Scripture proves the dead are raised to life, and the Sadducees are wrong about Scripture and about God's power to raise the dead.

In Mark's narrative, the Sadducees are not alone in questioning the meaning or reality of rising from the dead. Jesus has predicted or alluded to his own resurrection to the confusion of the disciples on a number of occasions (8:31–32; 9:9–10, 31–32; 10:33–34). Even though Peter, James, and John had witnessed Jesus' raising of Jairus's daughter from the dead (5:37–42), they do not later understand "what the rising from the dead meant" (9:10). However, the disciples' mystification and the Sadducees' disbelief reveal the error of their own thinking and not the standard opinion displayed by other figures in the story world. In suspecting that Jesus was John the Baptist raised from the dead, Herod is clearly depicted as accepting the reality of resurrection (6:14). Moreover, in testifying that people considered Jesus to be Elijah or John the Baptist (8:27–28), the disciples imply a widespread belief in resurrection among the society of Galilee. For the reader, who has heard the words and witnessed the activities of Jesus along with the disciples, the evidence for resurrection is extremely strong: Jairus's daughter is raised from the dead (5:35–43); Elijah and Moses appear alive, talking with Jesus (9:4); Jesus implies that John the Baptist is Elijah redivivus (9:12–13); the exorcised boy who looks "like" he is dead is lifted up by Jesus[39] (9:26–27); and Jesus refutes the Sadducees with scriptural evidence for the continued existence of Abraham, Isaac, and Jacob (12:26–27).[40] All of these incidents assure the reader of the veracity of both Jesus' predictions concerning his own resurrection (8:31; 9:31; 10:34; 14:28) and his promise of eternal life for his followers (10:30).

For the Gospel of Mark, then, resurrection is presented as a normally

---

38. The omission of connectives with surrounding material. See *Rhetorica ad Herennium* 4.30.41.

39. The similarity in vocabulary between the boy who is "like a corpse" (Mark 9:26–27) and the daughter of Jairus (5:39–41) is probably intended to remind the audience of Jesus' earlier act of raising the girl from the dead as a counter to the disciples' most recent expression of confusion over what rising from the dead means (9:10).

40. The Gospel makes no attempt to develop a systematic view of resurrection, but it appears that although "when they rise from the dead" they "are like angels in heaven" (Mark 12:25), when those risen appear on earth, they appear in their normal human form (thus Peter can recognize Elijah and Moses; the girl is still the daughter of Jairus; etc.). It would probably be a mistake to attempt to push Mark's narrative portrayal of rising from the dead too far into the conceptual or consistent ideational realm.

accepted view, and the denial or confusion of the Sadducees and the disciples functions as another indication of the blindness that accompanies unfruitful ground. Further, unlike Paul's conviction that Jesus' resurrection was the first fruit and proof of a general resurrection to come (1 Cor. 15:12–24), in Mark God's activity of raising the dead extends back at least to Abraham, Isaac, Jacob, Moses, and Elijah, is currently visible through Jesus in Jairus's daughter, and will continue in the future for Jesus and his followers. Hence Jesus' resurrection is not a unique event, nor does it really distinguish him from messengers God has sent to the vineyard in the past. For the Gospel of Mark, Jesus' *death,* as the death of the final messenger, the son, which provokes the coming of the lord of the vineyard, *is what makes Jesus distinctive and vitally important,* while his resurrection is depicted as simply an assured aspect of God's abiding practice. That Mark ends with just an announcement that Jesus has risen and an empty tomb (16:1–8), rather than the glorious appearances of the resurrected Jesus that close the Gospels of Matthew and Luke, accords well with this understanding. It is not Jesus' resurrection but his death—and what that death inevitably stimulates—that makes Jesus unique. Resurrection is a part of God's longstanding procedure, as proved by Scripture and argued enthymematically by Jesus to the detriment of the Sadducees.

The final test that Jesus must face (12:28–34) on this long day of teaching in the temple is different from the two preceding disputes. Although the Pharisees and the Herodians had begun their attack on Jesus with compliments (12:14–15a), the narrator (12:13, 15b) clearly indicated their malicious intent, and the stated belief of the Sadducees (12:18) obviously conflicted with Jesus' position. Consequently, both earlier episodes pitted Jesus against overt opponents, and employing enthymematic proofs in such situations was thoroughly appropriate. In introducing this last exchange, the narrator describes a considerably more positive interlocutor. A scribe has heard Jesus' remarks to the other group and approves them (12:28). The mention of hearing (ἀκούσας) with a good response (καλῶς) should encourage the audience to look with favor on this individual as a possible representative of the good earth, even though he is identified with a group (the scribes) who consistently reject Jesus.

He asks Jesus which commandment is first (12:28) and Jesus answers, not with an argument, but with a quotation from Scripture, Deut. 6:4–5: "Hear, O Israel: The Lord our God, the Lord is one; and you shall love the Lord your God with all your heart, and with all your soul, and with all your mind, and with all your strength" (12:29–30). Indeed, Jesus goes on to answer more than is asked, for he continues with the second commandment, "You shall love your neighbor as yourself" (12:31) and concludes that the two together prevail over all other requirements. The scribe judges Jesus' reply to be correct and true, repeating its salient points for emphasis (12:32–33) and for the sake of the audience's memory. Loving God with all one's heart, understanding, and strength is especially important in the Markan worldview, in which hard-heartedness, lack of understanding, and fear always spell failure to bear fruit; so, the stress on these elements is significant. If the dialogue ended at this point, it would appear as if the scribe held the greater authority in matters of belief, since he exercises the power of ratification over Jesus' words. Of course, the dialogue does not end here, and Jesus is given the parting comment. The scribe may have the power to evaluate Jesus' mastery of the law, but Jesus possesses the greater power, the power to determine that the scribe is "not far from the kingdom of God" (12:34). When Jesus speaks with such divine prerogative, it is little wonder that "after that no one dared to ask him any question."

Having successfully contended with the three questions raised by various Jerusalem groups, Jesus now turns to three teachings, the first of which takes the form of an enthymeme, while the last two are examples (12:35–44). Since Jesus has just articulated the two fundamental commandments for the wise scribe, he proceeds to clarify another central Jewish belief, the relation of the messiah to David (12:35–37). Jesus, as we noted earlier, has been called "Son of David" (10:47–48) and welcomed into the Jerusalem temple with rejoicing over the coming kingdom of David (11:10). Yet his authority is far greater than that of a king. To demonstrate that this higher identity is confirmed by Scripture, Jesus interprets an accepted messianic text enthymematically. He begins by stating the view of the scribes, which he intends to refute, "that the Christ is the son of David" (12:35), and then constructs his scriptural enthymeme with a suppressed major premise drawn from customary mores:

> *Suppressed major premise:* Fathers do not address their sons with titles of respect like "sir" or "master."
> *Minor premise:* David declared, "The Lord said to my master, 'Sit at my right hand, till I put your enemies under your feet'" (Mark 12:36).
> *Conclusion:* The one David calls master cannot be his son.

Because fathers do not call their sons masters, David's reference to the Christ as my master (or "my lord") proves that the Christ cannot be David's son in any traditional sense. It is possible to understand Jesus as "Son of David" only if one recognizes that title as describing one aspect of Jesus' broader role as heir of the vineyard. Further, Jesus' enthymeme seems to challenge any literal attempt to trace Davidic lineage as a test of messiahship,[41] for the Christ is not David's traditional son but his master and lord. The Christ is God's heir, not David's.

Jesus completes his teaching in the temple with two examples of religious practice, the first disjunctive, detailing what one should *not* do (12:38–40), and the second conjunctive, showing what one should do (12:41–44). Not surprisingly, given Mark's typical patterns of characterization, the bad example of cultic participation is illustrated by scribes and the good example by a nameless poor widow. In Greco-Roman rhetoric, examples (Gk.: παράδειγμα) were usually drawn from myths, nature, or well-known past history. As George Kennedy points out, "In the New Testament they are most commonly taken from Jewish history or from everyday life and nature."[42] Moreover, rarely are the applications of Jesus' examples, the generalized conclusions they convey, made explicit for the audience;[43] instead, in line with Demetrius's advice,[44] they are left for the audience to work out on their own. In the case of these two examples, the scribes who desire fame, honor, and high repute while at the same time victimizing the weak and the anonymous poor widow who gives her whole living to God so obviously embody the disparate ethical stances of self-aggrandizement versus doing the will of God, which have been repeatedly depicted in the preceding episodes, that the audience should have no difficulty perceiving the intended general lesson.

That the two teachings (12:35–37, 38–40) that immediately follow the episode with the wise scribe (12:28–34) detail the false teachings and hypocritical actions of *scribes* (12:35, 38) is probably designed to reinforce the negative characterization of the group as a whole, while still allowing that one individual may be able to surmount the type. Indeed, the Gospel often seems to describe good actions or good responses as *individual* actions, whereas groups are portrayed neutrally or negatively. Those healed are single individuals emerging from the crowds; the true offering of the *one* poor widow is contrasted to the abundance of the *many* rich people (12:41–42); the one wise scribe stands apart from the typical beliefs and actions of scribes in general; and the opponents of Jesus are mainly collectives like the Pharisees, the Herodians, the Sadducees, the elders, the scribes, the chief priests, and, of course, the disciples. This bias on behalf of individuals over against groups is additionally supported, as we shall see, by the increasing

41. That proving Jesus' Davidic lineage was a problem for the early Christians may be indicated by the two different genealogies that Matthew and Luke evidently thought it necessary to devise (see Matt. 1:1–17 and Luke 3:23–38).

42. *Rhetorical Criticism,* 16.

43. Ibid.

44. *On Style* 222: "Not all possible points should be punctiliously and tediously elaborated, but some should be left to the comprehension and inference of the hearer."

isolation of Jesus as he nears the moment of crucifixion. He must go his way alone, without the sustenance of family or disciples.

Although the two examples of cultic practice that close the tests and teachings inside the temple do not cite Scripture, the theme of Jesus as the heir of the scriptural traditions of Israel extends throughout the recognition sequence. In some cases Jesus indicates that an event is occurring "as it is written," even though no actual scriptural text appears to lie behind the references (e.g., 14:21, 49), while in others he quotes Scripture as the guide to what is happening (e.g., 14:27; 15:34). Moreover, the narrator weaves allusions to Psalms 22 and 69 throughout the crucifixion scene itself (15:21–39). All of these instances are designed to demonstrate that Jesus is the heir of the vineyard not only as the supreme interpreter of Israel's scriptural tradition but also as the one in whom that tradition finds its ultimate fulfillment. However, his embodiment of Scripture is not limited to matters of the law or cultic practice, for he is also portrayed as a prophet of the end time. Both the law and the prophets find their true heir in Jesus.

Mark 13:1–37—The Rejected Stone and the Temple Stones

Although Jesus' major prophetic utterance is the Apocalyptic Discourse in Mark 13:1–37, the fulfillment of which lies outside the Gospel narrative, a number of other illustrations of Jesus' prescient ability find completion in Division Two to establish beyond question his dependability as a prophet. Along with other aspects of the recognition sequence, the first indication of this role occurs in the introduction to the Division, Mark 11:1–11. While Jesus has been portrayed with the power to read the minds and motivations of others earlier in the Gospel (e.g., 2:8; 8:17) and the detail of his triple Passion predictions argued for their reliability, it is not until the entry into Jerusalem that Jesus' capacity to forecast events is given emphatic proof. Jesus instructs two of his disciples in direct discourse to "Go into the village opposite you, and immediately as you enter it you will find a colt tied, on which no one has ever sat; untie it and bring it. If any one says to you, 'Why are you doing this?' say, 'The Lord has need of it and will send it back here immediately'" (11:2–3). The disciples do as Jesus asks and find everything, including the challenge from some bystanders, exactly as Jesus predicted (11:4–6). Indeed, more space in the episode is actually devoted to securing the colt than to entering the city and temple. This conspicuous prediction-fulfillment interlude both validates Jesus' credentials as prophet and signals the increased importance of this role for Division Two as a whole.

A quite similar interlude follows soon after the Apocalyptic Discourse in Mark 13, probably to reiterate the dependability of Jesus' words concerning future events. To prepare for the Passover meal, Jesus instructs two of his disciples to "Go into the city, and a man carrying a jar of water will meet you; follow him, and wherever he enters, say to the householder, 'The Teacher says, Where is my guest room, where I am to eat the passover with my disciples?' And he will show you a large upper room furnished and ready; there prepare for us" (14:13–15). Again, they find everything as he predicted (14:16). The detail of the actions in both interludes, evocative of the remarkable detail of God's proof to Saul that he was to be king of Israel (1 Sam. 10:1–9), stresses dramatically the extent of Jesus' prescience. To historicize the incidents, as some commentators have tried to do, by suggesting that Jesus must have prearranged the events[45] is to miss entirely Mark's point in depicting these foretellings. Both stories show that Jesus is a prophet of amazing capability whose words about the future are to be believed and whose orders are to be obeyed.

Since in both detailed prediction-fulfillment instances, it is two disciples who receive and carry out the instructions and, as we shall see, four disciples who hear the Apocalyptic Discourse, it is all the more striking—though thoroughly characteristic of their typology—that Peter and the disciples refuse to believe Jesus' forewarning concerning their actions in the final prediction-fulfillment sequence of the Gospel. After the Passover dinner Jesus tells the disciples, "You will all fall away; for it is written, 'I will strike the shepherd, and the sheep will be scattered.' But after I am raised up, I will go before you to Galilee" (14:27–28). Peter vehemently objects, drawing upon his head an individual prediction concerning his triple denials of Jesus (14:29–30),[46] but all the disciples join in the rejection of Jesus' forecast (14:31). From the perspective of the audience, such disputing of Jesus' words constitutes only a further display of the disciples' hard-heartedness and not at all a reflection on Jesus' reliability. So, it comes as no surprise to the audience that Jesus' disciples do flee when he is arrested (14:49–52) and Peter does indeed deny Jesus three times before the cock crows twice (14:54, 66–72). Again, the complication of the prediction (*three* denials before the *second* cock crow), like the details of the earlier actions, emphasizes the omniscience of Jesus' prescience.

Underscoring that omniscience is vital to establishing the believability of those predictions whose fulfillments are *not* part of the narrative itself. It could be argued that the three prediction-fulfillment episodes, including the dramatic portrayal of Peter's denials, combined with the triple Passion predictions and their fulfillment in the trial and crucifixion scenes, all serve

45. See, e.g., Taylor, *The Gospel According to St. Mark,* 452, 454, 535–38.
46. See above, pp. 212–13, 217–18.

an ancillary purpose: to verify beyond doubt to the audience the accuracy and thoroughness of Jesus' prophetic announcements, so that those prophecies unfulfilled in the Gospel and thus directed especially toward the audience would win acceptance and belief. Although the unfulfilled prophecies are delivered to the disciples (13:1–5; 14:28), the Jerusalem council (14:62), and the women (16:7), since their subject is the apocalyptic coming of the Son of man and the events that will precede it, their import concerns the audience and not the characters in the story world. Yet, only to the degree that Jesus has been shown as reliable in the story world can the audience grant plausibility to his forecasts beyond that world. Even then, the transfer of belief from story to reality is always chancy and would depend heavily on the agreement between the actual lived experience of the actual audience and the story's formulations about the future.[47] It may be partially for this reason that the bulk of the material in Jesus' discussion of the eschaton describes the tribulations that *precede* the coming of the Son of man (13:5–23) rather than the coming itself (13:24–27) and that the other references to seeing that event (14:62; 16:7) are brief.

Jesus' major prophetic utterance is found in Mark 13 as the final teaching on that long day in and around the temple. He sits on the Mount of Olives opposite the temple and speaks privately to Peter, James, John, and Andrew, a location and companions that tie this scene to Gethsemane and the arrest (14:32–52) where Peter, James, and John so blatantly fail to heed Jesus' warnings to watch and pray, lest one be found asleep when the hour comes (13:35–37//14:34, 37–41). Although these predictions are articulated before the somber evening of supper, Gethsemane, arrest, and trial that leads directly to the crucifixion, by remembering the parable of the Tenants the authorial audience can perceive the proper chain of causality. After the tenants seize the heir, kill him, and throw him out of the vineyard (12:8), Jesus says that the Lord of the vineyard will come, destroy these tenants, and give the vineyard to others. "Have you not read this scripture: 'The very stone (λίθον) which the builders (οἱ οἰκοδομοῦντες) rejected has become the head of the corner'?" (12:9–10). In structuring the opening exchange of the Apocalyptic Discourse with a chiastic repetition of the key words "stones" (λίθοι) and "buildings" (οἰκοδομαί), the implied author signals the authorial audience that the discussion to follow will explain how the rejected stone becomes "the head of the corner":

---

47. Because the persuasiveness of the Gospel's message about the future depends to a large degree on the agreement between the actual audience's experience and these predictions, scholars have generally been correct to recognize the Apocalyptic Discourse in Mark 13 as a primary source for reconstructing the Gospel's audience—or at least its authorial audience; see, e.g., Weeden, *Mark—Traditions in Conflict*, 72–100; and Pesch, *Naherwartungen*, 74–243.

One of his disciples says to him,

Teacher, look! wonderful stones (λίθοι)[a] and wonderful

buildings (οἰκοδομαί)[b]!

Jesus said to him,

See (βλέπεις) these great buildings (οἰκοδομάς)[b']? There will

not be left here a stone (λίθος) upon a stone (λίθον)[a'] that

will not be thrown down. (Mark 13:1–2)

As the parable of the Tenants implies and the opening of the Apocalyptic Discourse confirms, for the rejected stone to become the new centerpiece, the buildings presently standing must first be completely dismantled and the tenants presently in control must first be destroyed; only then can the new edifice rise and the faithful tenants be installed. Until that longed-for time arrives, the evil that dominates temple and vineyard will continue. Hence the crucial question for the faithful, posed in the narrative privately by four of the disciples, the two sets of brothers (1:16, 19), Peter and Andrew, James and John, is *when* all this will take place and what sign will mark the event (13:4). In responding to their question, Jesus delivers the Apocalyptic Discourse,[48] which is divided rhetorically into three sections: (1) the tribulations preceding the coming (13:5–23), which are surrounded by an *inclusio* that is formed by "see" (βλέπετε, vv. 5, 23) and "lead astray" (πλανήσῃ, πλανήσουσιν, vv. 5–6, and ἀποπλανᾶν, v. 22) and that concerns the appearance of false leaders using the name of Christ; (2) the actual coming of the Son of man in the clouds (13:24–27); and (3) the parables of the Fig Tree and the Lord of the House (13:28–37), which admonish watchfulness through the indefinite but limited time still dominated by this generation.

The tribulations, the longest and in many ways most important section of the Discourse, appear to take place in two stages: the period of political and natural disruptions that mark the "beginning of the birth-pangs," in which the faithful must see to themselves (13:7–13), and the period of the great tribulation initiated by the setting up of the "desolating sacrilege" (13:14–20). Common to both periods, as the enclosing *inclusio* indicates, are people coming in the name of Christ (13:6) or false Christs and false

48. Needless to say, Mark 13 has been the subject of numerous studies, most of which have focused primary attention on the possible sources behind the present text; see, e.g., Taylor, *The Gospel According to St. Mark*, 498–500; J. Lambrecht, *Die Redacktion der Markus-Apokalypse* (AB 28; Rome: Pontifical Biblical Institute, 1967); and L. Hartman, *Prophecy Interpreted: The Formation of Some Jewish Apocalyptic Texts and of the Eschatological Discourse Mark 13* (Coniectanea Biblica, NTS 1; Lund: C. W. K. Gleerup, 1966); and Pesch, *Naherwartungen.*

prophets (13:21) trying to lead astray the faithful by claiming identity with Christ or performing "signs and wonders" (13:22). These people evidently pose as leaders of the Christian movement with special authority and powers, but Jesus stresses that they are false leaders and will only lead the faithful astray. This polemic accords well with the whole thrust of the Gospel's typology, which has characterized desires for power, authority, name, and reputation—in everyone from the disciples to the Jerusalem leaders and Herod—as accompaniments of hard-heartedness and rejection of the word. Moreover, employing "signs and wonders" to persuade others to believe is an obvious perversion of Jesus' interactive practice in which faith is the prerequisite of miracles. Jesus shuns performing signs (8:11–12), tries to suppress his spreading fame, and never exercises control over others.[49] The false Christs and false prophets, on the other hand, are predatory leaders whose values, like those of the disciples, stem from self-aggrandizement. Such leaders permeate the entire time prior to the coming of the Son of man, and the faithful must beware of succumbing to their wiles.

The first stage in the movement toward the goal or end ($\tau\grave{o}$ $\tau\acute{\epsilon}\lambda os$, 13:7) of God's coming kingdom, the period of "the beginning of the birth-pangs" (13:8), is delineated by social, political, and natural disasters such as wars, earthquakes, and famines (13:7–8) and requires the faithful to see ($\beta\lambda\acute{\epsilon}\pi\epsilon\tau\epsilon$) to their own actions (13:9), for they will be persecuted and hated "by all"; yet, only those who remain faithful throughout will be saved (13:13). The immediate causes of these sufferings are the governors, kings, and authorities, the present tenants controlling the vineyard, who pit nation against nation and kingdom against kingdom while at the same time harrowing the faithful with beatings, arrests, trials, and death. Although famines may well result from wars, the mention of earthquakes is a subtle reminder that behind this evil generation also stand demonic cosmic powers intent upon destroying God's good earth. The situation depicted in this first stage is not only the ugly condition of the world faced by the later followers of Jesus but is likewise the precise situation now confronting Jesus and his disciples in Jerusalem.

Jesus himself is about to be delivered to councils ($\epsilon\mathring{\iota}s$ $\sigma\upsilon\nu\acute{\epsilon}\delta\rho\iota\alpha$, 13:9 // $\mathring{o}\lambda o\nu$ $\tau\grave{o}$ $\sigma\upsilon\nu\acute{\epsilon}\delta\rho\iota o\nu$, 14:55) for trial, to stand before governors (15:1–5), to be beaten (14:65), and to be hated and mocked by all (14:64–65; 15:11–14, 19–20, 29–32). While those who will bear testimony ($\mathring{\eta}$ $\mu\alpha\rho\tau\upsilon\rho\acute{\iota}\alpha$, 14:59) against him cannot agree, his "testimony before them" ($\epsilon\mathring{\iota}s$ $\mu\alpha\rho\tau\acute{\upsilon}\rho\iota o\nu$ $\alpha\mathring{\upsilon}\tau o\hat{\iota}s$, 13:9), inspired by the Holy Spirit (13:11), is the ringing affirmation of his true identity, "I am," to the high priest's question, "Are you the

---

49. Jesus may command people to do one thing or another, but they are quite obviously free to obey or not. Jesus does not control the actions of those he meets (see, e.g., Mark 1:44–45; 3:4–5; 10:21–22).

Christ, the Son of the Blessed?" (14:61–62). Furthermore, just as later
followers will be delivered up (παραδώσει, 13:12) to death by fathers, children, and brothers, perhaps like the two sets of brothers listening to this
Discourse, just so will Jesus be delivered up (παραδίδοται, 14:41) by Judas,
his disciple and supposed brother in the family of God (see 3:34–35). Thus
the period of "the beginning of the birth-pangs" includes both Jesus' time
and that of his later followers, so that the descriptions of how he "endures
to the end" (13:13) and how the disciples fail to do so can function as
positive and negative examples to all who are willing to take up their crosses
and follow.

Since the author of Mark uses so many of the images and admonitions
from the Apocalyptic Discourse to portray the willing obedience of Jesus
through his arrest, trials, beatings, mockings, and death on the cross as well
as the failure of the disciples at Gethsemane (13:32–37//14:37–41), the
reason for positioning the Discourse immediately before the events of
the Passion is quite obvious. The audience is encouraged to understand the
Passion not only as the death of the heir that will trigger the coming of
the lord of the vineyard but also as an example of how the inevitable
persecutions perpetrated by this evil generation on the followers of Jesus are
to be endured faithfully—or how they may fail to be endured through fear.
Moreover, that Jesus' tomb is found empty and the young man proclaims
that he is risen, "as he told you" (16:7), stands as a final reassurance of
Jesus' promise that one who endures to the end *will be saved* (13:13).

Further, it is from this double perspective on Jesus' death, as both trigger
and example, that his earlier saying, "For the Son of man also came not to
be served but to serve, and to give his life as a ransom for many" (10:45),
should be viewed. For Mark, Jesus' death is *not* the innocent sacrifice
demanded by a righteous and angry God to atone for the sinful state of
humankind;[50] instead, Jesus' suffering and death are the inescapable results
of challenging the authority of the present tenants of the vineyard in order
to sow the good news of the nearness of God's kingdom to the nations.
While it is true that Jesus' crucifixion is the act that will finally prompt the
coming of that kingdom in all its glory and wrath, God did not send Jesus
in order that he might die; rather, the lord of the vineyard sent the final
messenger, the beloved son, in the divinely foolish hope that the tenants
would revere the son (12:6) and experience a change of heart. Jesus' life is
given as a ransom to the murderous authorities of this generation, the price
required to sow the word abroad, to awaken the good earth into abundant

---

50. Here I am in strong agreement with scholars like Howard Clark Kee (*Community of the New Age*, 47–48, 135–36) who deny that Mark contains an atonement
view of Jesus' death drawn from Isaiah 53, though my reasons are somewhat different
from theirs. For the opposite view, based I suspect more on Matthew's revision of
Mark than on Mark, see Williams, *Gospel Against Parable*, 44–50.

fruitfulness. His service in giving his life for the sake of the gospel must be emulated by any who would follow him, for the gospel must be preached to all nations (13:10), and its bearers will surely face the same evil opposition Jesus encounters. Like him, they must endure their persecutions faithfully, relying on the Holy Spirit to supply the words and direction they need. Not only do they have his resurrection as a guarantee that they too will be saved, but they also have the knowledge that his death is the final provocation for the coming of that kingdom; so, their period of suffering is limited, for the end is now in sight.

Unfortunately, however, things will get worse before they get better. Although Jesus' death at the hands of the Jerusalem authorities ultimately seals the fate of those murderous tenants, before the Son of man comes on the clouds one final, horrible tribulation, "as has not been from the beginning of the creation which God created until now, and never will be" (13:19), will break out upon the earth. The tenants will apparently rampage in an orgy of death and destruction over all creation. The sign that will mark the shift to this second stage in the period preceding the coming is when one sees "the desolating sacrilege set up where it ought not to be" (13:14). The reference to "the desolating sacrilege" (τὸ βδέλυγμα τῆς ἐρημώσεως) is drawn from Dan. 12:11 (LXX; cf. Dan. 9:27; 11:31), where it seemingly described the pagan altar constructed in the temple by Antiochus Epiphanes in 168 B.C.E. (see 1 Macc. 1:54) in the veiled language typical of apocalyptic writing. Mark, oddly, modifies the singular neuter noun, τὸ βδέλυγμα, with a masculine participle, ἑστηκότα ("set up"), suggesting perhaps a personal agent rather than an object behind this new "desolating sacrilege."[51]

What the image of "the desolating sacrilege set up where it ought not to be" precisely describes is not revealed in the narrative at all; instead, the strange allusion is followed immediately by the unique—and thus extraordinary—"wink" to the reader by the author: "let the reader understand." In the midst of Jesus' words to other characters in second degree narrative, the implied author/narrator of first degree narrative interrupts to address directly the implied reader/narratee for the only time in the entire Gospel. Whether the reader so addressed is the public lector, reading aloud to the group, or any reader/hearer of the story, the use of such an unusual narrative strategy clearly indicates the special nature of the material in Mark 13:14. The reader or hearer of Mark is supposed to understand something about this reference to "the desolating sacrilege set up where it ought not to be" that the narrative itself does not give. In other words, "the desolating sacrilege" is an esoteric image, the proper interpretation of which depends

51. See the discussion in Taylor, *The Gospel According to St. Mark*, 511–12. Many commentators have noted the similarities in Mark's vision and that found in 2 Thess. 2:3–10, which warns of the antichrist.

on knowledge supplied, not by the story, but by information obtained from some external, initiated group. For modern readers, separated by centuries from that knowledgeable group, entering the ranks of the authorial audience of Mark 13:14 becomes an impossibility. We do not know and probably cannot know for sure what "the desolating sacrilege" was supposed to represent. Nevertheless, the blatant narrative signal provided for this one esoteric element confers an element of reassurance concerning the public nature of the Gospel as a whole. For most of its length, the Gospel of Mark intends to present an exoteric story, available and accessible to a wide audience, and not a veiled writing open only to the initiated few.

Whatever "the desolating sacrilege set up where it ought not to be" refers to, its appearance should generate an immediate flight for safety. People should flee Judea for the mountains without taking time to collect their possessions or even pick up their coats (13:15–16), much as the Maccabees had fled at the beginning of their war against the Syrians (1 Macc. 2:28). And this greatest of tribulations, like all the lesser tribulations of world history, will fall most brutally on mothers and children, the perennial victims of human abuse, rage, and violence (13:17). While Jesus enjoins the faithful to pray "that it may not happen in winter" (13:18), the catastrophic nature of the event could hardly be mitigated by seasonal difference, for it will be the most ruinous oppression the human race has ever released on creation. Indeed, Jesus reveals that all flesh would be destroyed were it not for God's intervention (13:20). For the sake of the faithful, the elect, God will not permit this evil to run its full course unchecked. As an act of grace the Lord will shorten the days, thereby saving those who do not fall away during the tribulation (4:17) but endure to the end (13:13).

The frightful nature of this final assault by the tenants on all existence and the continuous period of persecutions of the faithful leading up to it underscore yet again why for the Gospel of Mark fear is the most persistent obstacle to faith. The world in which Jesus and his followers live is a bleak, ugly, and painful place filled with wars, persecutions, trials, betrayals, death, and a yet to be experienced last bloodbath of cosmic dimensions.[52] A desire for self-preservation, much less self-enhancement, would certainly deem fear an appropriate response in the face of such a scenario; yet, as Jesus earlier warned the disciples, "whoever would save his life will lose it; and whoever loses his life for my sake and the gospel's will save it" (Mark 8:35), for this scenario, as terrible as it most surely is, is but a passing interlude before the coming of the Son of man on the clouds and life eternal for the

52. For an early and insightful discussion of Mark's negative view of world history, see H. Conzelmann, "Geschichte und Eschaton nach MK 13," *ZNW* 50 (1959): 210–21.

faithful. That coming is the good news of the Gospel of Mark, and it is a welcome word for a captive earth groaning under the domination of this evil generation.

Moreover, since that good news must be preached to all the nations (13:10) in order for the elect (13:22, 27), the good earth, to reveal themselves in fruitful production before the Son of man comes to end the present reign of terror, the pressing task for all the followers of Jesus is to sow the word as far and wide as Jesus himself has been doing. Yet, also like Jesus, their sowing of the word will inevitably bring upon them the wrath of the corrupt authorities of this world and thus their preaching too must be a taking up of their crosses (8:34) in faith. What motivates their march into suffering and persecution is their knowledge that God's kingdom has already come in their lives with abundant and powerful fruit and their belief that it will soon come in full glory throughout the cosmos, finally ending the evil control of the present authorities. The sooner the gospel is preached to all nations, the sooner the kingdom will arrive and all suffering will cease. Indeed, as we shall suggest more fully later, the writing of the Gospel of Mark itself might have been an attempt at spreading the word and thus hastening the coming of that deeply desired new age. *That* the Son of man will come is assured by this generation's rejection and murder of the heir; *when* he will come is known only by "the Father" (13:10) but is at least partially dependent on the urgency with which Jesus' followers preach the word to all nations (13:10). Hence, sowing the gospel abroad becomes the one human act that can expedite the demise of this present evil, oppressive, and suffering-filled existence.

Mark 13:24–37

After the great tribulation brought about by the combined depravity of human and cosmic evil, at the hour set by the Father, the Son of man will come to gather and thus protect the elect from destruction. The coming itself (13:24–27) is narrated briefly, using imagery drawn mainly from Isaiah for the heavenly accompaniments (vv. 24–25) of divine intervention (cf. Isa. 13:10; 34:4) and from Dan. 7:13 for the Son of man himself (v. 26). Since the focus of the Gospel is primarily on the present ugly world situation facing Jesus and his followers, presumably including members of the authorial audience as well, that material has been presented at length, while this concluding action need only be sketched quickly. Nevertheless, three points are worth noting about Mark's understanding of the coming of the Son of man in the clouds.

First, quite unlike Matt. 25:31–46, the Gospel of Mark does *not* portray the coming as a judgment on the nations.[53] Rather, the Son of man sends out the angels to bring together the elect "from the ends of the earth to the ends of heaven" (Mark 13:27) in order to save them from the slaughter of the great tribulation (13:20). The coming is one of protection for those who have endured faithfully to the end (13:13). The meting out of divine punishment on the murderous authorities of this generation is unnecessary, for by plunging the world into that ultimate bloodbath of violence they bring down judgment on their own heads, securing their own demise. Rampant evil finally destroys even itself. The coming, then, is a saving, protective, and totally positive event; for Mark, it carries with it no threat of divine anger on the Christian community. What threat exists for Jesus and his would-be followers arises from the fearful persecutions and tribulations of this present age, which they must endure with faith and not flee from in fear, for only such faithful endurance demonstrates their membership in "the elect."

Thus, second, while "the elect" may in some sense be elected by God (13:20), they are most clearly elected by their own behavior. Those who respond to the word with faith and willingly take up the crosses forced upon them by the current world order show themselves to be the elect, the new family of Jesus who do the will of God, the fruitful ground of the kingdom. The language of election, which appears only here in the Apocalyptic Discourse of Mark, does not imply some concept of predestination underlying the Gospel, if interpreted within its narrative context. The elect of Mark 13:20, 22, and 27 are obviously those who endured the persecutions of 13:9–13 faithfully with the help of the Holy Spirit and were not led astray by false prophets and Christ imitators (13:21–22). Their actions declare their election. Concomitantly, the reason why it is necessary for the word to be preached to the nations is so that the elect "from the ends of the earth" (13:27) may reveal themselves by their faithful response to the word before the Son of man comes. The Gospel of Mark never suggests that some special people are predestined by divine will to accept Jesus' word while others are preordained to reject it. Instead, it describes a world in which some do in fact accept and others do reject and attempts to dramatize the human characteristics that foster those responses, so that they can be better understood and thus either emulated or avoided. The whole point of contrasting the positive examples of Jesus, the sower, and the good earth with the negative examples of the various unproductive earths would be lost if individuals possessed no ability whatsoever to choose which way to follow.

---

53. Luke's version of the coming as a protection or redemption (Luke 21:25–28) conveys much the same sense as Mark's, although one might infer some aspect of a judgment from Luke 21:36.

Furthermore, unlike Israel as the chosen people, for Mark the elect of the kingdom are defined solely by doing the will of God and not by national, racial, social, or sexual categories, for responses of faith have come from women (e.g., 5:26–34; 7:25–30), foreigners (e.g., 5:1–20; 7:25–30), and the poor (e.g., 10:46–52) as well as from scribes (e.g., 12:28–34) and synagogue leaders (e.g., 5:21, 35–43). Hence the elect of the new age include Jew and Greek, slave and free, male and female (cf. Gal. 3:28).

Third, the language of seeing the Son of man coming in the clouds with power is repeated later in Jesus' affirmation of his true identity before the chief priests and the Jerusalem council (Mark 14:61–62). Before those opponents, however, the promise of preserving the elect is omitted, for although all will see the glorious coming, only the faithful will be saved from destruction by its advent. While the repetition of the image should remind the audience of the fuller description provided by the Apocalyptic Discourse, the purpose of using it to respond to the chief priest is mainly to assert Jesus' authority and power as God's heir. Whatever the evil present generation may do to him now, their days are numbered because no human authority, neither Jewish, Roman, nor any other, will finally possess the inheritance that rightfully belongs to the son. Of course, as the parable of the Tenants indicated, as soon as the current establishment recognizes the heir for who he is, they decide to kill him, and that action is precisely what Jesus' assertion before the council brings about (14:63–64).

The final segment of the Apocalyptic Discourse, Mark 13:28–37, is composed of two short parables, the Fig Tree (13:28–31) and the Lord of the House (13:32–37), which close the Discourse with both assurance and warning, not only for the listening disciples but for "all" (13:37). The disciples had originally asked Jesus when these things would take place and what sign would indicate the coming (13:3). Only now at the end of the Discourse, after describing at length the sorry state of the world leading up to the advent of the Son of man, does Jesus address their concern about the timing of events, and he does so indirectly by means of the brief example of a fig tree coming into leaf as a sign of approaching summer (13:28). The image of a barren and fruitless fig tree opened this segment of Division Two (11:12–25) as Jesus confronted the corrupt state of the Jerusalem temple and religious hierarchy; however, it is a fig tree about to burst into the full bloom of summer that closes the segment with its promise to the faithful of the gloriously fruitful season just about to arrive. The winter of suffering, persecutions, and terrible tribulations will soon make way for a new summer of eternal life just as surely as nature's ordered cycle predictably causes the sap to rise in the barren fig tree, the branches to grow, and leaves to appear.

When they see the things Jesus has described taking place, Jesus' followers will know that the Son of man is on the threshold (13:29). Since, indeed, the situation of trials, beatings, hatred, betrayal, and death, which Jesus called "the beginning of the birth-pangs" (13:8), will soon engulf Jesus himself, some of the signs of the coming are already occurring in the lifetime of Jesus; so, the culmination of this evil state cannot be far away. Yet, as Jesus also warns, until all these events take place, this murderous, faithless generation will remain in charge of the vineyard (13:30). The term "this generation" (ἡ γενεὰ αὕτη) is used throughout the Gospel of Mark only in a negative sense, always referring to the present authorities and groups opposing Jesus' word and way (8:12, 38; 9:19; 13:30). Thus, when Mark 13:30 is read within the narrative context of the Gospel as a whole, it refers *not* to the disciples or first followers of Jesus, as some commentators suggest,[54] but rather to the present evil tenants who control the vineyard and harrow the faithful. Their perverse authority will not cease until all the terrible events Jesus has foretold happen and the Son of man arrives to rescue the elect. Nevertheless, this warning reminder of the current dominance of evil is linked to an emphatic promise by Jesus: "Heaven and earth will pass away, but my words will not pass away" (13:31). The power of this generation is limited, even if it destroys the earth and shakes the heavens; only Jesus' words are eternal, and on them the elect may depend without reserve or fear.

The Apocalyptic Discourse closes with a final parable exhorting Jesus' followers to watch, stay alert, and look, for "of that day or that hour no one knows, not even the angels in heaven, nor the Son, but only the Father" (13:32). The information the disciples actually sought from Jesus—*when* these things would occur—is the one fact Jesus cannot provide, because even he does not know it.[55] What he does know is the amount of suffering and tribulation his followers must endure before the hour comes, but that information conforms so well to the three earlier predictions of his own passion and his teachings on the necessity for cross-bearing discipleship, which the Twelve have already failed to understand or actually rejected, that their ability to comprehend this forecast and heed his warnings is doubtful. Indeed, the upcoming Gethsemane episode (14:32–42), which closes the account book on the rocky ground type,[56] by repeating the vocabulary

---

54. See, e.g., Taylor, *The Gospel According to St. Mark,* 521.

55. Mark 13:32 supplies one of the clearest indications of Mark's consistent recognition of the distinction between God and Jesus. For the Gospel of Mark, Jesus is God's son and heir, an identity that gives him special status and power, but Jesus is *not* God. The identification of Jesus as one with God found, e.g., in the Gospel of John or of Jesus as "God-with-us" found in the Gospel of Matthew constitute much "higher" Christologies than anything suggested by Mark.

56. See above, pp. 214–18.

("watch," "asleep," "hour," "come")[57] of the parable of the Lord of the House and depicting the disciples as asleep when Jesus' hour comes confirms their inability to endure and thus their exclusion from the elect. By employing the images of the Lord of the House for the Gethsemane passage, the implied author also adds another dimension of meaning to this hour that the faithful must watch for: it represents not only the consummate hour when the Father sends the Son of man with the angels to gather the elect but it also represents that individual hour of suffering, persecution, and tribulation, which will inevitably come to test the faith of each follower, just as it does Jesus and the disciples, and which will best be endured by imitating Jesus' advice and example to watch and pray while avoiding the disciples' tendency to sleep.

At the conclusion of the Apocalyptic Discourse, however, this more personal and individual meaning of the coming hour has yet to be developed,[58] so that the parable of the Lord of the House in the context of Mark 13 functions as a general admonition to all to carry out their duties faithfully, "for you do not know when the time will come" (13:33). The parable itself (13:34–36) is divided into two parts. The first part describes the typical situation of a person placing servants in charge of the house while away on a journey (v. 34), while the second, by switching to the imperative, identifies those hearing the story with the servants (vv. 35–36). Since the servants do not know when the lord of the house will come, they must pursue their tasks conscientiously and faithfully in order to be ready at any moment for the return. For Jesus' disciples and followers the exhortation is to assiduous dedication in preaching the word to all nations and to courageous faith in enduring the persecutions which that proclamation will inevitably provoke. Although this admonition is wasted on the disciples of second degree narrative, for they will soon flee in fear, it is directly addressed as well to the audience listening to the story: "And what I say to you I say to all: Watch" (13:37).

The typical situation the parable narrates, that of a person away from home on a journey, if applied to Jesus' death and later return, raises a debated issue in Markan research: whether the Gospel of Mark understands the risen Jesus to be present or absent from the community of his followers during the time between his resurrection and his coming again as Son of man in the clouds.[59] On the basis of the reference in the parable of the

---

57. The parable's mention of the lord coming "at cockcrow" (13:35) connects it also to Peter's denial, which was to occur before the second cock crow in Mark 14:30, 72.

58. Some suggestion of this individual meaning of the hour may be present at Mark 13:11. See below, pp. 275–77.

59. See, e.g., J. D. Crossan, "Empty Tomb and Absent Lord (Mark 16:1–8)," in

Tenants to the heir being cast out of the vineyard after his death (12:8) and on the basis of the consistency with which the Gospel as a whole supports that reference, we wish to agree with those who view Jesus himself as absent from his followers still struggling in the vineyard until that time when the Father sends the Son of man to gather the elect. The parable of the Tenants reports that the tenants "took him and killed him, and cast him out of the vineyard" (12:8). In the Gospel narrative Jesus ceases to be a speaking character or the subject of active verbs in main clauses when he utters a loud cry and breathes his last on the cross (15:37). From the moment of his death Jesus is absent; others may speak for him (16:6–7) or about him (15:39, 43–45), but his active presence has ended. Unlike the Gospels of Matthew and Luke with their conspicuous resurrection appearance stories, the Jesus of Mark's Gospel leaves this mismanaged and suffering-filled vineyard at his death not to return again until the hour set by the Father. For Mark, of course, that hour is not far off, and in the meantime, his followers have his example, eternal words (13:23, 31), and the guidance of the Holy Spirit (13:11) to assist them. Most of all, both Jesus and his followers have the assurance of a faithful God, who will not forsake them even at death, an issue Jesus' own death will raise explicitly.[60]

The Passion in Mark: Studies on Mark 14—16, ed. W. H. Kelber (Philadelphia: Fortress Press, 1976), 135–52.

60. See below, pp. 282–88.

11

The Death
of the Heir

By the time the authorial audience reaches the last section of the Gospel of Mark, containing the Passion narrative or recognition sequence proper, their understanding of the unfolding events is focused by two interrelated perspectives. First, the plot summary supplied by the parable of the Tenants has informed them that as soon as the tenants recognize the final messenger, the beloved son, as the rightful heir, they will decide to kill him (12:7), and their act of seizing him, killing him, and casting him out of the vineyard (12:8), while not the intention of the owner in sending his son (12:6), will be the act that finally provokes the lord of the vineyard to come and put out this murderous generation (12:9). Thus the death of Jesus is the instigation for the coming end of this age. Second, in the Apocalyptic Discourse Jesus described the kinds of events that his followers must face in sowing the word to the nations (13:9–13: trials before councils, governors, and kings; beaten; delivered to death by brothers, fathers, and children; hated by all) and admonished them to endure these things faithfully and watchfully (13:32–37). By repeating many of those situations in Jesus' own passion, the author provides the audience with a concrete example of how one can endure steadfastly, while by dramatizing the fear and failure of the disciples, how one cannot endure to the point of becoming implicated in the evil designs of the establishment through betrayal and denial. Hence Jesus' way of death also provides the paradigm for doing the will of God to the end.

The Gospel's final section is set off by two episodes of anointing (14:1–9 and 16:1–8), both of which are introduced by definite time references (14:1; 16:1), involve unnamed or named women characters, and are explicitly tied to Jesus' burial (14:8; 16:2–3). The careful time plotting that distinguishes Division Two throughout, as it often does the recognition sequences of the ancient erotic novels, dominates the episodes of this closing section, with the crucifixion itself even being marked off in hours (15:25, 33, 34) and carefully crafted rhetorically. The rhetorical outline of the section as a whole is as follows (for the complete outline of the Gospel, see Appendix A):

III. Division Two—Jesus, the Heir of the Vineyard—Mark 11:1—16:8
    A. Introduction—11:1-11
    B. 11:12—13:37
    C. 14:1—16:8
        1. 14:1-11—time reference; death plot; unnamed woman anoints Jesus for burial
            a. 14:1-2—plot against Jesus
            b. 14:3-9—unnamed woman anoints Jesus for burial
            c. 14:10-11—Judas joins plot
        2. 14:12-26a—the supper
            a. 14:12-16—prediction and preparation
            b. 14:17-21—dialogue with disciples on betrayal
            c. 14:22-26a—monologue of institution: bread, cup, hymn
        3. 14:26b-52—on the Mount of Olives
            a. 14:26b-31—dialogue with disciples on falling away
            b. 14:32-42—monologue in Gethsemane
            c. 14:43-52—betrayal, arrest, and flight
        4. 14:53-72—Jesus affirms identity; Peter denies
            a. 14:53-54—Peter follows Jesus to courtyard
            b. 14:55-65—Jesus before council: affirms identity
            c. 14:66-72—Peter's three denials in courtyard
        5. 15:1-15—Jesus before Pilate
            a. 15:1-5—Pilate questions Jesus
            b. 15:6-15—Pilate's three attempts to release Jesus fail
        6. 15:16-39—the crucifixion
            a. 15:16-20—soldiers mock Jesus
            b. 15:21-22—compel passerby to help to Golgotha
            c. 15:23—offer wine
            d. 15:24a—crucify him
            e. 15:24b—divide his garments
              f. 15:25-27—3d hour—King of Jews
              g. 15:29-32—ironic mocking
              f'. 15:33—6th to 9th hour—darkness
              g'. 15:34—Jesus' cry to God

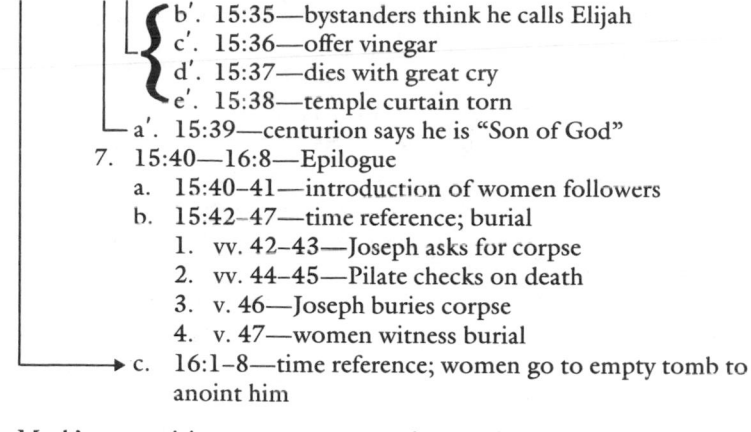

    b'. 15:35—bystanders think he calls Elijah
    c'. 15:36—offer vinegar
    d'. 15:37—dies with great cry
    e'. 15:38—temple curtain torn
   a'. 15:39—centurion says he is "Son of God"
  7. 15:40—16:8—Epilogue
   a. 15:40-41—introduction of women followers
   b. 15:42-47—time reference; burial
    1. vv. 42-43—Joseph asks for corpse
    2. vv. 44-45—Pilate checks on death
    3. v. 46—Joseph buries corpse
    4. v. 47—women witness burial
   c. 16:1-8—time reference; women go to empty tomb to anoint him

Mark's recognition sequence not only reveals publicly the true identity of Jesus as God's heir but also establishes with finality the rocky hardness of the disciples in their betrayal, flight, and denial and the monolithic rejection of the religious hierarchy in their charge of blasphemy and death plot. The types of unproductive ground embodied by each group are fully exposed in these closing scenes. Even the type of the thorny ground reappears in the characterization of Pilate to play its part in the death of the heir. Pilate, like King Herod before him (6:14–29),[1] initially responds positively to the man in his custody. Pilate, indeed, as the narrator informs the audience, recognizes that the accusation against Jesus arises out of the envy of the chief priests (15:10) rather than out of any crime Jesus has committed and seeks to release him (15:9, 12, 14).[2] However, also as with King Herod, Pilate's nobler instincts collapse under the press of expediency: "So Pilate, wishing to satisfy the crowd, released for them Barabbas; and having scourged Jesus, he delivered him to be crucified" (15:15). The "cares of the world . . . enter in and choke the word" (4:19).

The only example of the good earth type to be found amidst the final dark days is the unnamed woman of the opening episode (14:3–9). Her ano-

---

1. See above, pp. 157–58.
2. Pilate's questions and three attempts to release Jesus immediately follow Peter's three denials of Jesus during questioning. Whereas Peter's scene is an antirecognition scene (see above, pp. 75–76, 217–18), Pilate's episode takes the form of a near-recognition scene, for he does acknowledge Jesus as king of the Jews and knows that the charges against him are false. Yet, ultimately *both* Peter and Pilate fail in their opportunities to recognize and acknowledge who Jesus is and who they are in relation to Jesus. The contrasting ways in which they fail, however, relate to the types of ground they embody: Peter's absolute denial of truth demonstrates his rockiness, while Pilate's partial recognition shows the underlying fertility of the thorny ground.

I owe this intriguing comparison of Peter's and Pilate's episodes to Jeffrey T. Tucker, a Ph.D. candidate in Vanderbilt University's Graduate Department of Religion.

nymity and act of love in anointing Jesus' head with costly oil proclaim her affinity with the faithful ones healed in the earlier days of the Galilean ministry.[3] Jesus interprets her act as the anointing of his body beforehand for burial. In that light, her action becomes a faithful response to his words, for he has three times asserted that he will be killed (8:31; 9:31; 10:34) in Jerusalem. She cannot prevent what she believes will happen, but she does what she can (14:8a), and such loving generosity with no prospect of material or even moral return (unlike giving money to the poor, 14:5) prompts Jesus to commend her action to all who hear the gospel preached "in memory of her" (14:9). With perhaps some slight irony but also with utter consistency from the Markan perspective, this memory will not bring name and fame to a special individual but will instead serve to memorialize the anonymity of loving kindness.

The rarity of such faithfulness during the Jerusalem period is emphasized narratively by surrounding the anointing episode with the developing plot against Jesus (14:1–2 and 10–11) and countering the woman's act itself with a controversy over the proper object of generosity (14:4–5). Some who are with Jesus in the house of Simon the leper object that the expensive ointment should have been sold and the money given to the poor rather than simply being wasted on Jesus. Jesus' reply (14:6–9) *neither* divinely ordains the perpetual existence of poverty *nor* denigrates the importance of helping those in need; rather, his reply indicates that social action on behalf of suffering humanity is not a substitute for personal gestures of love to individuals, and vice versa. Both special deeds in response to particular circumstances and general ventures of charity are part of doing the will of God. One should not be reproached for performing one rather than the other, just as performing one does not remove the obligation for the other. But whatever the moral choices involved in using money for various loving ends, giving money to purchase betrayal and accepting money to deliver up your teacher to his enemies is clearly evil. The contrast between the generosity of the anonymous woman and the deal of Judas ("who was one of the twelve") with the chief priests to exchange Jesus for money (14:10–11) dramatizes starkly the different production of good earth and rocky ground. And just as his followers will be later (13:12), Jesus is to be

3. The ointment the woman pours on Jesus is described as consisting of νάρδου πιστικῆς, often translated as "pure nard" (Mark 14:3). The meaning and even the derivation of the adjective πιστικῆς (πιστικός, ή, όν) is extremely uncertain (see, e.g., Taylor, *The Gospel According to St. Mark,* 530–31), and in the New Testament the word appears only here and at John 12:3. Whether it is actually derived from πιστὸς ("faithful, true") or not, the lexical similarity of πιστικός to the family of words describing faith and belief in Mark may have provided the authorial audience with an additional clue to the affiliation of this woman's act with the faithful responses of the good earth type narrated earlier in the Gospel.

delivered up to death by his "brother" in the family of God, one who was appointed "to be with him" (3:14).

Much of the material in these closing episodes has already been discussed at length in detailing the falling away of the rocky ground type, and we need not repeat those conclusions here.[4] Rather, since our focus now is on the death of the heir itself, we must look mostly at the portrayal of Jesus at Gethsemane, the trial, and the crucifixion. Although Jesus has been depicted throughout Mark as the special messenger of God, who is also son and heir, having striking omniscient and prescient abilities, he has at the same time been shown as limited in power (e.g., 6:5–6), influence (e.g., 1:44–45; 10:21–22), and knowledge (e.g., 13:32). Such a mixed portrait reflects theologically Jesus' status as both a human and a divine figure, but perhaps more important for Mark, whose theological or conceptual concerns appear generally to be rather modest, it is the human side of Jesus that permits him to fulfill his narrative function as an example of faithful, watchful endurance through suffering, persecution, and even death. If the image of Jesus on the mount of transfiguration with Elijah and Moses (9:2–8) is the surest vision of Jesus' divinity, then the image of Jesus praying on the Mount of Olives (14:32–42) and on the cross (15:34) is Jesus at his most human. That the humanity of Jesus should be stressed during his passion is especially appropriate for presenting Jesus' way of death as one to be emulated by his followers, who are themselves, after all, only human.

Mark 14:32—15:5

As we indicated earlier,[5] repeating the vocabulary of the parable of the Lord of the House (13:32–37) in the Gethsemane scene and locating Gethsemane on the Mount of Olives (14:26), where Jesus had just delivered the Apocalyptic Discourse (13:3), encourages the audience to contrast Jesus' watchfulness and prayer with the disciples' sleep as examples of good and bad ways to prepare for the coming hour, an hour in this case of personal temptation and trial. Jesus' interior monologue, echoing as it does the heroic tradition in Greek literature,[6] voices his dismay at the future he is facing and requests that God spare him (14:35–36a). Jesus does not desire death, nor should his followers. It is no lack of courage or faith to experience distress at the thought of persecution or to pray that some different means might be substituted for one's own death, for only fools, charlatans,[7]

4. See above, pp. 211–18.
5. See above, pp. 268–69.
6. See above, pp. 76, 214–16.
7. In Lucian's *The Passing of Peregrinus,* one of the proofs that Peregrinus is a false philosopher is his ardent lust for death—and a glorious or spectacular death at that.

or masochists seek out suffering.[8] The heroic ideal, however, and for Mark the Christian ideal as well, is to resolve one's distress by firmly subordinating one's own desires to the overarching requirements of the hour: but not what I want but what you want (14:36b). Jesus' honest acknowledgment of his apprehension and his resolution to act as God wills despite it is the epitome of courage, a courage thoroughly imitable by the elect. Alternatively, the disciples sleep through their three final opportunities to assess their condition and prepare themselves for what is to come. That the hour finds them to be betrayers, fleers, and deniers is, sadly, no surprise at all.

After Jesus is betrayed by one of the Twelve and all the others flee (14:43–52), he is delivered up to the council (συνέδριον) to bear testimony (14:55–64), beaten (14:65), and led before Pilate, the governor[9] (5:1–5). At his crucifixion he is mocked and despised by all, even the two criminals being crucified along with him (15:16–32). All these events dramatize concretely the scenarios Jesus forecast for his followers in the Apocalyptic Discourse: "They will deliver you up to councils; and you will be beaten in synagogues; and you will stand before governors and kings for my sake, to bear testimony before them. . . . And when they bring you to trial and deliver you up, do not be anxious beforehand what you are to say; but say whatever is given you in that hour, for it is not you who speak, but the Holy Spirit. And brother will deliver up brother to death, and the father his child, and children will rise against parents and have them put to death; and you will be hated by all for my name's sake" (13:9, 11–13). They will have nothing to face that Jesus has not himself endured courageously and faithfully. In addition to paralleling the later experiences of the elect, the events of Jesus' passion fulfill his earlier predictions (8:31; 9:31; 10:33–34) and replicate the parabolic type of the son and heir before the tenants (12:6–8). The combination of these previous perspectives molds Jesus' arrest, trial, and death into patterns the authorial audience both expects and can also learn from.

Jesus' trial before the Jerusalem council (14:53, 55–65) fulfills a number of these expectations.[10] He is delivered up to councils, as the elect will be,

---

8. The problem of voluntary martyrdom plagued the Christian movement throughout its early centuries. Although some groups like the Montanists often encouraged believers to provoke their own martyrdoms, the early church generally rejected such actions.

9. Mark never names Pilate's position or office, but both Matthew and Luke refer to him as "governor" (ἡγεμών) in Matt. 27:2 and Luke 3:1.

10. The many scholarly debates over the historicity of the account of the trial (e.g., whether or not the council could meet at night, or meet twice; whether or not proper legal rules for testimony and evidence were followed; etc.) may again miss the point that Mark is making in depicting Jesus' passion as both example and fulfillment of Jesus' own predictions. For a lucid and balanced assessment of all the problems with the trial proceedings (much of the evidence coming from material considerably later

and answers only at the crucial moment to reveal his true identity and assert his authority (14:61–62), just as the elect will be able to rely upon the Holy Spirit to help them do in their hour (13:11). Moreover, that answer, as the parable of the Tenants indicated (12:7), immediately prompts the authorities to condemn him to death (14:63–64), and he is beaten (14:65), not in synagogues (13:9), but in the high priest's house, a fair substitute. The final, and most detailed, of Jesus' three Passion predictions had forecast this program as well: "Behold, we are going up to Jerusalem; and the Son of man will be delivered to the chief priests and the scribes, and they will condemn him to death, and deliver him to the Gentiles; and they will mock him, and spit upon him, and scourge him, and kill him; and after three days he will rise" (10:33–34).

The authorial audience is explicitly reminded of these earlier predictions by the only other direct discourse, besides Jesus' exchange with the chief priest, in the trial scene, the false testimony of the witnesses: "And some stood up and bore false witness against him, saying, 'We heard him say, "I will destroy this temple that is made with hands, and in three days I will build another, not made with hands"'" (14:57–58). The narrator surrounds this statement with reiterations of its untruth (14:56, 59) but leaves it to the audience to recognize what makes it false. The witnesses have pulled out of context words that Jesus did say, scrambled them together, and elaborated the whole. Jesus did say the temple would be destroyed (13:1–2), although he did not say he would do it, and he did speak of something special happening "in three days" (8:31; 9:31; 10:34), though it was not related to the temple. Knowing that the testimony is false, the audience is encouraged to hear the key phrases "destroy this temple" and "in three days" and remember their true contexts, the Apocalyptic Discourse and the Passion predictions. Furthermore, the "in three days" is the first of two overt allusions to Jesus' predicted resurrection in the midst of the death story, the other occurring during the mocking at the cross (15:29). While the events of trial, beatings, delivery to Pilate, mocking, and crucifixion themselves fulfill Jesus' previous prophecies concerning his future, it is important for the audience to recall during these evil experiences the final clause in those prophecies: "after three days he will rise" (10:34; also 8:31 and 9:31).

The trial episode also features prominently a Markan device that has permeated the depiction of the disciples in the Gospel and will now dominate the account of Jesus' death: irony. The mild irony of false witnesses

than the Gospel of Mark), see Juel, *Messiah and Temple,* 1–39; see also Donahue, *Are You the Christ?* 5–30. For a different and intriguing look at the trial narrative, see M. A. Beavis, "The Trial Before the Sanhedrin (Mark 14:53–65): Reader Response and Greco-Roman Readers," *CBQ* 49 (1987): 581–96.

manufacturing false testimony that does not even agree with itself (14:56, 59), which casts Jesus' opponents as a rather inept group, is overshadowed by the heavy irony of their final word to Jesus, "Prophesy" (14:65). The audience knows that the very acts his enemies are committing in trying, condemning, beating, and spitting upon him *are* fulfillments of his prophecies. Hence their mocking call for him to "prophesy" itself demonstrates the efficacy of Jesus as prophet. The effect of irony on an audience, as we have already noted,[11] is to distance the audience from the unwitting victims of the irony, in this case the chief priest, the scribes, the elders, and the whole council, while solidifying their identification with the narrator/ implied author's perspective. Yet irony not only separates insiders from outsiders, it also encourages insiders to appreciate the superiority of their knowledge over that of the ironic victims and to disdain the others' limitations. In the context of the Markan Passion narrative, such a response bonds the audience even more closely with Jesus, who shares the implied author's ideology, and repels the audience away from all of Jesus' opponents, who are depicted as vicious, violent, envious, mean-spirited, hardhearted, and narrow men. Thus, not only the acts of arrest, trial, and condemnation but the rhetorical devices used to portray these acts narratively invite a reaction from the audience of scorn and repugnance toward the Jerusalem Jewish authorities, a reaction the Christian church, to its profound discredit, has occasionally used through the centuries to promote anti-Semitism.

The shout at Jesus to "prophesy" is quite appropriately (and ironically) the point at which the narrator returns to Peter in the courtyard below and relates Peter's three denials before the second cock crow (14:66–72), just as Jesus had predicted them.[12] Jesus' affirmation of his own identity stands in utter contrast to Peter's series of denials, one as an example of faith under trial, the other as an example of fear in retreat. With Jesus' identity as the Christ, the Son of God now publicly announced, he has nothing more to admit to the present tenants of the vineyard. He responds to Pilate's question concerning the charge that he claims to be King of the Jews with the ambiguous, You are saying (15:2), and then silence (15:5). And that silence continues to the grave and beyond with one exception: his cry to God from the cross (15:34). All the direct discourse of others during the crucifixion scene up until that cry either further implicates the Jerusalem council and crowds[13] in bringing about Jesus' death (15:9–14) or increases the ironic

11. See above, pp. 98–99, 103.
12. See above, pp. 217–18, 258.
13. It is probably closer to the conventional expectations of the authorial audience to view the crowds as a narrative chorus whose main function is to reflect whatever action is dominating the story at the moment (much the same role played by the

portrait of Jesus' enemies, be they Roman soldiers (15:18), bystanders (15:29–30), or chief priests and scribes (15:31–32).[14]

Mark 15:16–39

The crucifixion scene itself (15:16–39) is rhetorically shaped by blocks of parallel material arranged in a chiastic pattern with the events of the third to the ninth hour (15:25–34) at the center:

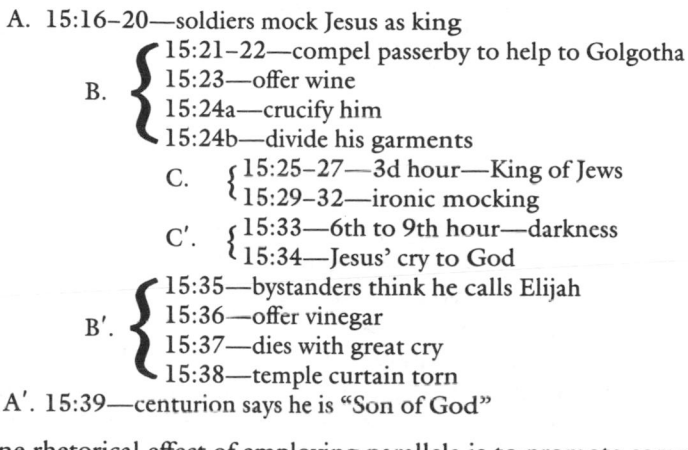

A. 15:16–20—soldiers mock Jesus as king

B. { 15:21–22—compel passerby to help to Golgotha
15:23—offer wine
15:24a—crucify him
15:24b—divide his garments

C. { 15:25–27—3d hour—King of Jews
15:29–32—ironic mocking

C'. { 15:33—6th to 9th hour—darkness
15:34—Jesus' cry to God

B'. { 15:35—bystanders think he calls Elijah
15:36—offer vinegar
15:37—dies with great cry
15:38—temple curtain torn

A'. 15:39—centurion says he is "Son of God"

One rhetorical effect of employing parallels is to promote comparison and contrast, as we saw in the paralleled structures of the Gospel's opening chapters.[15] Here the pervasive contrast is between events understood only in the limited, distorted view of this generation's human world (A, B, C) and events directed toward and informed by the cosmic, divine realm (C', B', A'). Whereas the soldiers dress Jesus in purple robes and a crown of thorns to hail him as a competitor of Caesar's (A—15:16–20), the centurion standing opposite the cross and observing his death recognizes not a human king but a divine son, God's heir (A'—15:39). Whereas the soldiers compel a certain Simon, a passerby, to carry the cross for him to Golgotha (B—15:21–22), after Jesus' cry to God, those standing near hope to see him assisted by Elijah returning from heaven (B'—15:35–36). Whereas when they crucify him the soldiers divide his human garments among themselves by casting lots, a direct reference to Ps. 22:18–19 (B—15:24), when Jesus expels his last breath with a great shout, the curtain of the temple tears in two (B'—15:37–38).

---

chorus in Greek tragedy) than to see them as a character group in Mark who supported Jesus earlier but who now with great fickleness turn against him.

14. For a discussion of the verbal irony of the crucifixion scene, see above, p. 99.

15. See above, pp. 131–42.

That last parallel, the divided garments and the torn temple curtain, requires further explication to suggest how the authorial audience might have construed the comparison. Mark has never before mentioned the curtain (τὸ καταπέτασμα) of the temple, although he has talked of the temple stones being thrown down (13:2), and perhaps the torn curtain is intended to remind the audience of that prophecy, as some commentators have suggested.[16] However, the parallel with Jesus' divided garments offers another possibility for understanding the torn curtain, which, while not contradicting an allusion to destroying the temple, enriches its meaning. Throughout the Gospel, Jesus' garments have functioned symbolically to indicate his power or state of being: touching the hem of his garments was sufficient to heal those with faith (5:27–31; 6:56); his garments became intensely white beyond the power of any human bleach as he was transfigured (9:3); and just prior to dividing his garments, the soldiers had replaced them with purple robes to mock him as king (15:16–20). His garments have been used, then, to symbolize who Jesus is and what state he is in (i.e., powerful healer, transfigured divine son, mocked human king). Moreover, the garments of others throughout the Gospel have also exhibited figurative dimensions: the young man dropped his covering and ran away naked to emphasize his panicked flight (14:51–52); the high priest tore his garments to signify his horror at Jesus' blasphemy (15:63); and the disciples were instructed to go out on their preaching mission without concern for their own welfare or comfort, including not wearing two tunics (6:8–9). Hence clothes in the Gospel of Mark generally bear emblematic connotations.

The dividing up of Jesus' human clothes at his death indicates figuratively his departure from the human world; indeed, the only covering his body will again receive is a linen shroud, the clothes of the grave (15:46). By reporting the distribution of his garments at his crucifixion, the narrator symbolically confirms the parable of the Tenant's assertion that the heir would be killed and cast out of the vineyard (12:8). As a parallel to this figure for Jesus' change of state, the tearing of the temple curtain from top to bottom may also signify his transit from the human world to the heavenly. The curtain that Mark intends is probably the one separating the Holy of Holies from the rest of the temple or Holy Place, for it bore definite symbolic and ritual significance.[17] The Jewish historian Josephus in inter-

16. See, e.g., Juel, *Messiah and Temple*, 127–39; Donahue, *Are You the Christ?* 45, 113–47; and Robinson, *The Problem of History in Mark*, 63–67.

17. This point is much debated (see, e.g., the discussion in Taylor, *The Gospel According to St. Mark*, 596–97). The temple had two major types of curtains: the inner curtain separating the Holy Place from the Holy of Holies, most often called τὸ καταπέτασμα (Heb. 6:19; 9:3; 10:20; Mark 15:38), and the large outer curtain dividing the whole temple from the courtyard, generally called κάλυμμα (Exod. 27:16). The

preting the temple for Greco-Roman readers assimilated its three major divisions to the cosmogony, in which the first two, the court and the Holy Place, represent land and sea, the abode of humanity, while the third, the Holy of Holies, represents heaven, the abode of God.[18] The curtain separating the Holy Place from the Holy of Holies, then, signifies the barrier between the human world and the divine. At Jesus' death that barrier is split apart, opening the way for Jesus' passage and indeed his later return as Son of man with the angels.

Some confirmation of this suggestion may be found in the verb used to describe the tearing of the curtain ($\sigma\chi\ell\zeta\omega$, 15:38). That verb is employed only one other time in all of the Gospel at Mark 1:10 when the heavens split open for the Spirit to descend on Jesus at his baptism.[19] The rending of the heavens and the rending of the temple curtain may describe similar transportations from realm to realm, one literally and the other symbolically. The special value of the symbolic representation is that by indicating the thoroughness of the tear, "in two, from top to bottom" (15:38), it implies a permanent breach in the divide, allowing freer access to the divine world by the elect and portending an earlier return to the human world by the lord of the vineyard. Moreover, the prologue to the Gospel (1:1–13), which contains the account of the heaven's splitting, is itself, like the crucifixion scene, structured rhetorically by a chiastic pattern that generally contrasts the human and cosmic dimensions of Mark's story.[20] In that initial chiasm the cosmic realm surrounded the human (A A' vs. B B'), while at the end of the story the chiasm moves from the human to the divine (A B C vs. C' B' A'), emphasizing through the events of the crucifixion the underlying cosmic import of Jesus' message, life, and death. Even though the present human generation controlling the vineyard has done its worst, the culmination of the story depends on the divine realm.

names, however, were not rigidly applied, so their use cannot be taken as certain evidence for which curtain was meant. The outside curtain had no ritual significance, and the recent suggestion by H. Jackson ("The Death of Jesus in Mark and the Miracle from the Cross," *NTS* 33 [1987]: 16–37) that the outer curtain must have been intended because it was the only one the centurion might actually have been able to see from Golgotha (p. 24) assumes a level of narrative realism more appropriate to twentieth-century writing than first century.

18. Josephus, *Antiquities* 3.6.4 and 3.7.7. Josephus is actually talking about the tabernacle that Moses constructed, but since it had no court or first division, the model he is using must be the Herodian temple in Jerusalem.

On the use of cosmogonic patterns for temple construction, see M. Eliade, *The Sacred and the Profane: The Nature of Religion*, trans. W. Trask (New York: Harcourt, Brace & World, 1959), 58–62.

19. Both Jackson ("The Death of Jesus in Mark and the Miracle from the Cross," 23–24) and S. Motyer ("The Rending of the Veil: A Markan Pentecost," *NTS* 33 [1987]: 155–56) recognize the parallel between Mark 15:38 and 1:10, but they develop it in ways different from the one suggested here.

20. See above, pp. 108–13.

Finally, the Greek word naming the curtain, καταπέτασμα (lit.: something spread out *down*), and the Greek description of the tear, ἀπ᾽ ἄνωθεν ἕως κάτω (from top to *bottom*), in Mark 15:38 form the culmination of a whole series of plays (paronomasia[21]) on words—mainly verbs—compounded with κατα (down) prefixes that runs throughout the central portion of the crucifixion episode to contrast this generation's view of salvation and Jesus' view. In Mark 15:29–30, passers-by ridicule Jesus by insisting that as one who could tear *down* (καταλύων) the temple, he ought to be able to save himself by coming *down* (καταβὰς) from the cross. Similarly, in 15:32 the chief priests and the scribes taunt him to come *down* (καταβάτω) from the cross so they can see and believe. Even later, after Jesus' cry from the cross, bystanders hope to see divine aid in the form of Elijah take Jesus *down* (καθελεῖν) off the cross in 15:36. Alternately, Jesus' own words in 15:34 question in the strongest possible way why God has left him *behind* (ἐγκατέλιπές[22]) in this evil vineyard. In the blind view of Jesus' human opponents, for him to be saved (15:30–31) would require that he come *down* from the cross to rejoin the human world; however, Jesus' cry implies that his heartfelt desire is to rejoin God in the divine realm instead of being left *down* here in the vineyard. Reporting the splitting of the curtain from top to bottom (15:38) immediately after Jesus' death as the conclusion of this series of wordplays connects the tear with Jesus' cry and further supports its symbolic role as an image of transportation from realm to realm.

The mention of Jesus' call from the cross brings us to the center of the crucifixion episode, where the narrative clock slows to an hourly count (C C'—15:25–34). This central unit contains both Jesus' words (C'—15:33–34) and the direct-discourse mocking of the bystanders, scribes, and chief priests (C—15:25–32). The mocking of Jesus on the cross by his opponents is, as we have already explained, a classic example of verbal irony.[23] What these characters call out to Jesus in derision, the audience knows to be true, and thus their mockery falls on their own heads. Jesus' cry to God, his very last words in the Gospel and ones additionally stressed by Mark's presentation of them twice, first in a Hebraized Aramaic transliteration and then in Greek translation, compose a much more complex irony, moving toward paradox. That Jesus should suggest that God has forsaken him on the cross has disturbed many Markan commentators. Since the words Jesus

21. On this type of "loose" punning, see *Rhetorica ad Herennium* 4.22.30.
22. The additional ἐγ prefix on the Greek καταλείπω is an intensification: Jesus is *utterly* forsaken.
On the meaning of the cry, see below, pp. 286–88.
23. See above, p. 99.

uses, "My God, my God, why hast thou forsaken me?" are a close rendition of the opening verse of Psalm 22, which begins in sadness but ends in assurance, some have argued that the whole psalm is being called to mind, and consequently the cry should be interpreted as triumph over desolation. Such a view, however, does little justice to the words as they stand. Had Mark wanted Jesus to express triumph or confidence from the cross, his final words could have been shaped quite differently, as in fact they are in the Gospels of Luke and John. Indeed, quoting the words initially in transliterated Aramaic, "Eloi, Eloi, lama sabachthani," besides providing the link to Elijah in v. 35, would undoubtedly have increased their strangeness or distinctiveness to a Greek-speaking audience, hence decreasing the audience's likelihood of immediately recognizing a scriptural quotation.

Although most of the verbal and situational ironies throughout the Gospel have been employed, often quite blatantly, to distance the audience from negative characters and solidify their identification with the narrator and Jesus, to touch Jesus' last words with irony creates a much more complicated dynamic. The audience has been led by the implied author, narrator, and Jesus to believe that God loves Jesus as a son (1:11; 9:7; 12:6) and is faithful in responding to those who pray in faith (11:22–24). With such prior knowledge it would be extremely hard for the audience to believe that God would forsake Jesus on the cross.[24] Jesus must be wrong. But the narrative has also convinced the audience that Jesus is never wrong—at least not in relation to the cosmic or divine realm. How is this dilemma to be adjudicated? The form of the cry itself may provide the key: Jesus implies that he has been abandoned by God in the form of a prayer/petition *to God*. In other words, Jesus addresses his words to the very One whom he claims has deserted him. Yet, if God is truly absent, why call upon God, for calling upon God indicates that God is not truly absent. Consequently, the form of Jesus' words undercuts their content, and the audience's dilemma is mirrored in the saying itself. The irony created by the conflict of form and content in Jesus' cry to God moves very close to paradox, in which two contradictory positions are both held to be true. Jesus is forsaken by God, and at the same time God is available to be called upon. Why the author should wish to confirm the continued presence of God, implied by the form of the saying, is quite obvious, but why Jesus' experience of abandonment, expressed in the content, should be equally emphasized requires explication. The context for that explication is to be found in the Markan understanding of suffering.

---

24. For a discussion of conflicts of belief or knowledge as the basis for stable irony, see Booth, *A Rhetoric of Irony*, 61–67, 73–76.

Suffering and Alienation

That the Gospel of Mark presents Jesus as a suffering Messiah has earned almost the status of a commonplace in Markan studies. Indeed, evidence for the claim is abundant: John the Baptist, Jesus' predecessor and foil, is arrested and later beheaded after baptizing a repentant Judea and Jerusalem (1:5, 15; 6:17–29); Jesus' opponents begin to plot his death very early in his ministry (3:6), and his betrayal by one of his own chosen twelve is disclosed the moment they are selected (3:19); and Jesus himself predicts his suffering, arrest, trial, and death several times (8:31; 9:31; 10:33–34), with the actual narration of these events coming as an expected confirmation in the final recognition sequence. Moreover, Jesus forecasts a similar way of suffering for all of his followers (13:9–13). The reason or cause of this suffering, which has not always been so clear to those Markan scholars who have read the Gospel of Mark through Matthew's or Luke's eyes or as a piece of modern realistic narrative, is revealed typologically in the parables of the Sower and the Tenants and dramatized by the characterization of the Jewish and Roman authorities: God's realm, the lovingly created vineyard, is under the control of an evil, murderous, and faithless generation who, backed by the forces of Satan, refuse to produce the fruits of the vineyard for its Creator. Anyone who attempts to speak out for the Creator and demand production from the earth can expect only persecution, tribulation, and suffering from the present establishment. Cosmically, the Gospel of Mark concerns the battle for control of creation between God and the forces of Satan, a battle that God will ultimately win, just as Jesus always dominates the evil spirits he encounters. Humanly, the Gospel of Mark depicts the corruption of the current generation with its lust for power, fame, money, and glory and its utter opposition to the good news of God's coming rule, an opposition that, while it lasts, will always ravage God's messengers of the gospel. Suffering, then, is the inevitable consequence of preaching the good news of God's imminent coup d'état in a world now oppressed by power-greedy human tyrants.[25]

Even though the inescapability of suffering for those sowing the gospel on ground, three quarters of which is unfruitful because of hardness, underlying rockiness, or weed growth, may not be difficult to grasp, the full dimensions of that suffering are greater than might first appear. While it surely includes the physical pain inflicted by beatings, torture, and death, for Mark the fullness of suffering goes far beyond physical agony. Indeed, none of the canonical Gospels especially emphasizes Jesus' bodily pain dur-

---

25. For Mark, the lust for power, fame, and prestige even infects the Christian movement itself (see especially Mark 10:42–45), and Jesus must warn his followers to beware of false leaders who will try to lead them astray (Mark 13:6, 21–22).

ing his trial and crucifixion;[26] our modern tendency to concentrate on physical distress as the epitome of suffering is more the result of later Easter sermons, plays, movies, and now television dramas, which linger on the drops of blood from thorns and whips and the sound of hammering at Golgotha for sensational effect, than of anything related by the Gospels. Actually, for the ancient world—and for the modern post-Holocaust world as well—six hours of hanging on a cross, even if it were conceived to be the most brutal form of torture possible (which it was *not*), would hardly qualify as the apex of physical agony. Many people throughout human history have suffered more terrible tortures and abuse for far longer periods than six hours. Nor does the claim that Jesus was innocent or willingly died for others make his pain unique, for the innocent are often the victims of foul acts and many brave people have died willingly to save family, nation, or comrades. The Greco-Roman world was a cruel and harsh place, beset with illness, famine, military conflict, slavery, and torture. Crucifixion, while an onerous way to die, was neither rare nor especially dreaded, although in those cases where it took the crucified person days to die, the cruelty of the method was obvious, but such was not the case with Jesus. Six hours on a cross would certainly not have impressed the authorial audience as an unusual degree of physical suffering.

Yet the Gospel of Mark stresses the theme of suffering for Jesus and his followers. If the portrayal of Jesus' physical agony was not particularly extraordinary for that cultural milieu, what, then, really constitutes this suffering? Mark's crucifixion account itself suggests the answer. The center of the episode contains not only Jesus' cry of abandonment but also the extensive direct-discourse mocking of bystanders, accusers, and even fellow prisoners (cf. 15:25–32). Thus the period preceding his death when Jesus hangs on the cross is filled narratively, not by details of execution or physical pain, but by the taunting of an abusive, disdaining tide of humanity. It is Jesus' isolation and rejection that Mark emphasizes in the crucifixion. Furthermore, this abusive rejection of Jesus stands as the culmination of a whole pattern of rejection, alienation, and progressive isolation that reaches back into the early days of Jesus' Galilean ministry. From his first encounters with the religious leaders of his tradition, they contested his words and actions (e.g., 2:1–12, 16–17, 23–28) and were soon plotting his death (3:1–6). His immediate family misunderstood him (e.g., 3:20–22, 31–32), and his neighbors and kin rejected him outright (6:1–6). Even the Twelve, whom he had appointed to be with him and who had accompanied

26. The Gospel of John mentions the nail holes in Jesus' hands and the spear cut in his side during his resurrection appearances (John 20:25, 27), and a variant reading at Luke 22:44 has Jesus sweat drops of blood, but these details are as graphic as the canonical Gospels ever get concerning Jesus' physical agony.

him through all of his preaching ministry, fled when active persecution arose in Jerusalem. Indeed, although such desertion would have been bad enough, Jesus experienced worse, for one disciple actively participated in his arrest by betraying him and another violently repudiated him in triple denials. Condemned and disdained by his enemies, rejected by his family and neighbors, betrayed, abandoned, and denied by his disciples, Jesus went to the cross utterly alone, cut off and isolated from humanity.

It is this alienation from the entire human community, and especially that segment of the community that normally is expected to provide the support, care, and love each human being desperately needs in times of trouble—family, neighbors, friends, and kin—that reveals the deeper dimensions of the suffering Jesus must endure. And not only Jesus, for all those who follow after him must walk this solitary road as well. In addition to arrests by councils and beatings in synagogues (13:9), Jesus predicted that his followers would be delivered to death by their brothers, or children, or parents (13:12). Traditional relationships, ties of blood and love, will turn into murderous hatred for those who, like Jesus, preach the gospel to the nations. For Mark, the most profound agony of the human spirit is not that engendered by the enmity of one's opponents but rather that caused by the betrayal and hatred of one's intimates. As Jesus declared early in his ministry, those who speak out for God are not despised *except* in their own homeland, among their own kin, and in their own houses (6:4).

Moreover, the suffering brought about by separation, alienation, and isolation from family, homeland, and friends would strike a familiar chord in the Greco-Roman world out of which the Gospel of Mark comes. As we reviewed generally in Part I,[27] the Hellenistic period saw the increasing growth of huge, multinational urban centers like Antioch, Alexandria, Ephesus, and Rome, drawing people away from native lands and established tribal traditions. These cities, the breeding grounds for early Christianity as well as many other Hellenistic cults, offered their inhabitants no sense of community as citizens, which the old Greek polis had provided, and little opportunity to preserve familial or tribal solidarity. Such a situation encouraged a sense of anxiety, insecurity, and alienation, forcing the isolated individual on a solitary quest for security in a radically insecure world. As with Mark's Jesus, past religious traditions, family relationships, native communities, and newfound friends could not be relied upon to render support or help in troubled times. But surely in God, one could find a safe harbor, an escape from the seas of anxiety and alienation, an abiding presence to banish loneliness.

Yet it is not to be so for Jesus. The fullness of suffering for the Gospel of Mark is the experience of being abandoned, left behind not only by all

27. See above, pp. 37–40.

humanity but also by divinity. Although the voice from the clouds had named him beloved Son at the baptism, had confirmed his status to unperceptive disciples at the transfiguration, and had heard his prayer at Gethsemane while the disciples slept, here at the ninth hour, after three hours of taunting and three hours of the darkest evil enveloping all the earth (ἐφ᾽ ὅλην τὴν γῆν, 15:33), Jesus cries out from the cross to ask why *God* has forsaken him. In that moment he expresses the agony of utter isolation in the cosmos, rejected by humanity and deserted by divinity. A state of such consummate loneliness and alienation is nothing short of hell itself, for it probes the most dreadful fear of all, the fear of the absence of God. No follower of Jesus need worry that she or he will be required to suffer more than the Son of man, for no loneliness is more profound than the beloved Son of God abandoned by God. The way of Jesus is not nor can it be an *escape* from suffering, given the present corrupt state of the world. Jesus' own example proves that alienation is inevitable, even from—or perhaps, especially from—the closest circles of the human family, and for Jesus the fullness of such suffering is still greater, as the divine Parent leaves behind the dying Son. Instead of retreating from the torments of this world, the way that Jesus builds for each individual to follow is a faithful march straight into and through them. The content of Jesus' cry from the cross, his expression of abandonment by God, stands as an assurance to his followers that the worst desolation imaginable, cosmic isolation, can be endured faithfully. What is separation from family and betrayal or denial by friends in comparison to that timeless moment of nothingness when God's Son is deserted by God?

Nevertheless, the *form* of Jesus' cry, a prayer *to* God, suggests that the experience of absence may carry within it the possibility of its own resolution, for Jesus himself earlier taught that whatever is requested in faithful prayer will be given (11:22–24). That the great shout (φωνῇ μεγάλῃ, 15:34) which accompanies Jesus' prayer is repeated moments later to describe his sudden death (φωνὴν μεγάλην, 15:37) connects the death to Jesus' request; he is no longer left behind, abandoned by God to this faithless and murderous generation (see 9:19), for the temple curtain is split (15:38), and the barrier between the human world and the divine is symbolically removed.[28] Jesus' prayer is answered. The centurion, standing opposite the cross and observing the sudden death after the loud petition to God, speaks for the authorial audience as well as for the author of Mark when he declares: Truly this man was Son of God (15:39). God's Son is reunited with the divine Parent; God does indeed save those who endure to the end (13:13), regardless of the rejection, betrayal, and failure provided by most of humanity in this corrupt and hard-hearted world.

28. On the symbolism of the temple curtain, see above, pp. 280–82.

Even though Jesus' active role in the narrative ends with the crucifixion and even though the centurion's declaration recognizes conclusively and publicly Jesus' true identity as Son of God, resolving the major issue of the Passion narrative or recognition sequence, Mark does not close the story at this apparently fitting point. Two reasons may be suggested for the addition of the final scenes of burial and empty tomb (15:40—16:8). First, the major emphasis of the crucifixion scene has focused on the rejection, alienation, and suffering of Jesus. While God's positive response to Jesus' prayer in opening the way out of the human world is symbolically represented by the tearing of the temple curtain and rhetorically implied by the wordplays on κατα-compounds,[29] its overt expression in the Passion narrative is minimal. Since Jesus predicted that he would be resurrected in three days (e.g., 8:31; 9:31; 10:34) and the audience was reminded of that prediction several times in the passion sequence itself (14:28, 58; 15:29), narrating the proof that his resurrection did occur confirms absolutely the faithfulness of God in saving those who endure their trials and persecutions. The symbolism of the Passion becomes the documentation of the empty tomb.[30] Second, if the Gospel of Mark is as fully a rhetorical document as we have argued and tried to demonstrate throughout this study, then its purpose must be less the simple communication of information and more the persuasion of its audience to follow the way that Jesus has built. In other words, the experience of hearing the gospel of Jesus Christ (1:1) should lead to action, and it is the desire to provoke this action that crafts the final scenes.

Mark 15:40—16:8—The Ending As Epilogue

One of the more crucial differences between the ancient world and our contemporary one concerns assumptions about the basic nature of language. For the ancients, language was understood "as a force acting on the world,"[31] a source of real power. Because language was power, because it could affect people's beliefs and actions, the value of learning the most persuasive uses of language, that is, of studying rhetoric, was self-evident to Greco-Roman society. Furthermore, since language could actually change life, its morality or ethical import was a matter of urgent appraisal, as Plato

29. See above, p. 282.

30. E. Bickerman argued years ago that empty tomb stories were a conventional device in ancient literature to prove the assumption of the hero into heaven ("Das leere Grab," *ZNW* 23 [1924]: 281–92).

31. J. P. Tompkins, "The Reader in History: The Changing Shape of Literary Response," in Tompkins, ed., *Reader-Response Criticism: From Formalism to Post-Structuralism* (Baltimore: Johns Hopkins University Press, 1980), 203. Much of the following discussion is drawn from pp. 201–6 of this excellent article.

obviously reflects in banishing poets from his ideal state. In contrast, for readers in the twentieth and probably the twenty-first century, language is mostly conceived "as a series of signs to be deciphered."[32] Our contemporary obsession is with the *meaning* of a text, whether we choose to locate that meaning in the text itself or in the reader or somewhere in between. What it *means,* rather than what it *does,* is the concern of modern critics and exegetes, requiring them always to be involved in the task of interpretation. Indeed, although we have consciously attempted to hear the Gospel of Mark in the light of the literary and rhetorical conventions of its own Hellenistic milieu, our very intention of interpreting the text and clarifying its meaning brands this study quite clearly as a modern, twentieth-century exploration of an ancient text and not as an imitation or replication of the reading/hearing experience of any first-century audience. From an ancient perspective,

> The text as an object of study or contemplation has no importance, . . . for literature is thought of as existing primarily in order to produce results and not as an end in itself. A literary work is not so much an object, therefore, as a unit of force whose power is exerted upon the world in a particular direction.[33]

Nowhere is it more vital to recognize the Gospel of Mark as "a unit of force whose power is exerted upon the world in a particular direction" than in evaluating its ending. Although the whole configuration of an ancient plot should be fashioned so as to move its audience, most rhetorical handbooks and studies of rhetoric singled out the epilogue as having, besides its function of recapitulation, a special responsibility to arouse the emotions of the audience, to excite them to action.[34] In addition, the rhetorical handbooks, in concert with Aristotle's analysis of tragedy in the *Poetics,*[35] suggested that one of the best strategies for stimulating this response was the depiction of a reversal in fortune from good to bad.[36] Actually, the handbooks, as they often did, were in this case simply codifying a fairly common observation about human experience: we are more aroused if raised expectations are dashed than if no expectations had been raised in the first place. The disciples as a group in Mark—the rocky ground type—exemplify such a procedure; their final failure is more painful to witness because of their

32. Ibid., 203.
33. Ibid., 204.
34. See, e.g., Aristotle, *Rhetoric* 3.19.1 and 2.8.10–11; *Rhetorica ad Herennium* 2.31.50 and 3.5.9; Cicero, *De inventione* 1.55.106—56.109; and *Rhetorica ad Alexandrum* 1445a.
35. *Poetics* 1453a.
36. See, e.g., *Rhetorica ad Herennium* 2.31.50; Aristotle, *Rhetoric* 3.19.3 and 2.8.10–11; and Cicero, *De partitione oratoria* 17.57.

initial promise than it would have been had they—like the Jerusalem authorities—rejected Jesus from the beginning. If things look well (good fortune) and then collapse (bad fortune), the fall is more affecting than had they never looked well at all. However, by the time of Jesus' crucifixion and unexpectedly sudden death on the cross, all the active character groups from earlier sections of the story—the Jerusalem authorities, Jesus' neighbors and kin, and the Twelve—have supplied graphic evidence of their failure and basic identity with the various kinds of unfruitful grounds. Whatever expectations they may have embodied have now been fully demolished and their eternal bad fortune guaranteed. Consequently, Mark begins the epilogue of the Gospel by introducing a previously unknown group: "women looking on from afar, . . . who, when he was in Galilee, followed him, and ministered to him" (15:40–41). In fact, with the exception of Pilate and the centurion (15:43–45), all the actors in the epilogue are new to the Gospel story, and their newness permits a renewal of hope in human fruition just when it appears that all such hope was lost.

The epilogue is structured by the triple appearance of three (or two) named women at crucial points of witness: at the crucifixion (15:40), at the burial (15:47), and at the empty tomb on the morning of the first day of the week (16:1–2). Moreover, the chronology of events is carefully charted by three explicit time references before the burial and before the trip to the tomb: "when evening had come, since it was the day of Preparation, that is, the day before the sabbath" (15:42);[37] "when the sabbath was past" (16:1); and "very early on the first day of the week . . . when the sun had risen" (16:2).[38] These three references unmistakably demonstrate the passage of three days, the day before the Sabbath, the Sabbath, and the day after the Sabbath, alerting the authorial audience, who had been only recently

37. The Sabbath was celebrated from sundown Friday to sundown Saturday. By indicating that it was evening, Mark suggests the rapid approach of the Sabbath. By having to explain the meaning of "day of Preparation" the author shows again that the authorial audience was not primarily Jewish Christians. Also, the detail of having Joseph purchase a linen cloth (Mark 15:46) for the body, an action that Jewish law prohibited on a festival day, may be more evidence of the author's own unsure grasp of Jewish tradition, law, and custom.

38. Since λίαν πρωΐ ("very early") can refer in Hellenistic Greek to the period before sunrise (around 3 A.M.), commentators often understand it to conflict with "when the sun had risen" (see, e.g., Taylor, *The Gospel According to St. Mark,* 604–5), occasionally to the point of suggesting a confluence of sources in 16:2, which the author was too inept to smooth out. Mark uses the phrase one other time at 1:35: πρωΐ ἔννυχα λίαν (very early at night). If Mark viewed the Greek "very early" to refer to a period before sunrise, this first usage is unnecessarily redundant: very early *at night.* Rather than accusing the author of redundancy on one hand (1:35) and contradiction on the other (16:2), might it not be simpler to suggest that whatever meaning the phrase might have had in other writings, for the author of Mark λίαν πρωΐ indicated only a generally early time in the morning, and whether it was still dark or first light had to be additionally specified?

reminded of Jesus' prediction that something significant would happen "in three days" (15:29), to the importance of the women's visit to the tomb and what they were likely to find—or rather *not* to find—there. The epilogue can be outlined rhetorically as follows:[39]

7. 15:40—16:8—Epilogue
    a. 15:40–41—introduction of women followers
    b. 15:42–47—time reference; burial
        1. vv. 42–43—Joseph asks for corpse
        2. vv. 44–45—Pilate checks on death
        3. v. 46—Joseph buries corpse
        4. v. 47—women witness burial
    c. 16:1–8—time reference; women go to empty tomb to anoint Jesus

Initiating the final tomb visit with the report that "Mary Magdalene, and Mary the mother of James, and Salome, bought spices, so that they might go and anoint him" (16:1) connects the ending with the opening scene of the recognition sequence, in which an unnamed woman poured ointment on Jesus' head, anointing his body beforehand for burying (14:3–9), and also reveals the ambiguity Mark constructs throughout the epilogue: paralleling the action of the named women with that of the unnamed woman so highly praised by Jesus (see 14:8–9) places their quest in a favorable light; yet, if Jesus has already been anointed for burial, is it appropriate for a second anointing to occur? Ambiguity stalks the characterization of these women much as it earlier did the portrait of the Twelve.

In contrast to the rejection and alienation emphasized by the mocking and by Jesus' cry from the cross, the introduction of a faithful group of followers comes like the glow of dawn after a dark night. While the authorial audience may infer that God has responded to Jesus' distress (15:37–38), it would be hopeful to hear that some of Jesus' human associates had fared better than the disastrous twelve, and such seems to be the case when the narrator notes that women who had followed Jesus and ministered to him in Galilee are watching the crucifixion (15:40–41). They have not betrayed, denied, and fled, as did the male disciples, but have remained with Jesus through tribulation and persecution. Although some scholars treat the

---

39. Studies of the ending of Mark are very numerous. Some of the most important current ones include the following: Crossan, "Empty Tomb and Absent Lord (Mark 16:1–8)," in *The Passion in Mark: Studies on Mark 14—16*, ed. Kelber, 135–52; R. H. Fuller, *The Formation of the Resurrection Narratives* (New York: Macmillan Co., 1971; Philadelphia: Fortress Press, 1980); N. Perrin, *The Resurrection According to Matthew, Mark, and Luke* (Philadelphia: Fortress Press, 1977), 14–38; and N. Petersen, "When Is the End Not the End? Literary Reflections on the Ending of Mark's Narrative," *Interpretation* 34 (1980): 151–66.

women basically as surrogates or stand-ins for the disciples[40] and presenting three named women along with a larger group certainly invites such an approach, *when* the women appear, *how* they are described, and their identity *as women* all depict a group similar to but *much better than* the Twelve. They are not surrogates but superiors. The Twelve revealed themselves fully as rocky ground by their responses when active persecution started in Jerusalem; these women, on the other hand, "who came up with him to Jerusalem," follow Jesus to the cross and beyond. Moreover, Jesus himself rebuked James's and John's wish for glory by teaching that even the Son of man came to minister (διακονῆσαι, 10:45), and these women are characterized as ones who ministered (διηκόνουν, 15:41) in Galilee. Further, with the blatant exception of Herodias and her daughter (6:17–25), female characters throughout the Gospel have consistently embodied the good earth type (e.g., 1:30–31; 5:25–34; 7:25–30; 12:41–44; 14:3–9).[41] Thus, as women, as ministers, and as those who have followed Jesus along the way of the cross, these women appear to represent the good earth, that fruitful minority of humanity whose faithfulness demonstrates affinity with the kingdom of God.[42]

Rhetorically, the juxtaposition of a positively depicted group with the human evil and failure which dominates the Passion narrative places these women in striking relief. They appear all the better because they follow the disciples' nadir, enduring where the Twelve have not. According to Aristotle's careful analysis of various scenarios for the reversal of fortune, audiences are most deeply affected by the plight of those who are neither preeminently virtuous nor obviously evil but appear better than the mean and whose shift from good to bad fortune is due to some flaw or sin (ἁμαρτία) in themselves.[43] Mark's portrayal of these women conforms remarkably well to Aristotle's recommendations.[44] Even in their initially positive delineation two small but worrying notes may be heard: they watched the crucifixion from far away (μακρόθεν, 15:40), and they are *named*. Unlike Jesus'

40. See, e.g., Perrin, *The Resurrection*, 28–30.

41. Major women characters in the ancient erotic novels were also consistently portrayed as more moral, faithful, and good than their male counterparts; see above, Part I, p. 73.

42. Several feminist scholars have rightly noted this "better than" characterization of the women followers in Mark; see, e.g., E. Schüssler Fiorenza, *In Memory of Her: A Feminist Theological Reconstruction of Christian Origins* (New York: Crossroad, 1983), 138–39; E. S. Malbon, "Fallible Followers: Women and Men in the Gospel of Mark," 28–48; M. Schierling, "Women as Leaders in the Marcan Communities," *Listening* 15 (1980): 250–56; and W. Munro, "Women Disciples in Mark?" *CBQ* 44 (1982): 225–41.

43. *Poetics* 1453a.

44. This does not necessarily mean that no historical reminiscence lies behind these scenes; it does suggest, however, that whatever historical material may be present has been thoroughly shaped by the rhetorician's or storyteller's art.

opponents who were nearby or passed by or stood opposite the cross, these women, while not totally absent as were the male disciples, were nevertheless keeping well away from the center of the action. Also, naming three of them casts a possible shadow on their natures, for throughout the Gospel naming has often been associated with the human desire for fame, glory, status, and authority, all longings that harden the heart and encourage fear rather than faith. The authorial audience must remember that both the good earth *and* the rocky ground are initially positive; which type these women represent will only be fully recognized in their response to the word.

The burial itself is carried out by another new character, Joseph of Arimathea, whom the narrator describes as "a respected member of the council, who was also himself looking for the kingdom of God" (15:43). Since *all* of the council had earlier condemned Jesus to death (see 14:55, 64), Joseph must be among Jesus' former opponents who rejected his claim to be "the Son of the Blessed" (14:61–62). Yet he, like Jesus, longs for the coming of God's rule and shows compassion for the body or corpse (πτῶμα, 15:45) of his former enemy. That Jesus must be buried not only by a stranger but by an opponent casts additional shame on his absent male disciples—after all, John the Baptist's disciples had at least buried him (see 6:29)—and perhaps even impugns the women followers, who see what happens but again take no active role (15:47). The narrative report of Pilate's summons to the centurion (15:44–45) serves the dual purpose of confirming Jesus' death and reiterating its surprising suddenness, a suddenness resulting from God's response to Jesus' despairing prayer at being left behind.[45] Joseph may wrap the corpse in a shroud, bury it in a rock cave, and roll a stone across the door (15:46),[46] but Jesus' destiny is now under divine control and the human world can hold him back no longer.

The final episode in the Gospel of Mark, 16:1–8,[47] turns the women from

45. This repetition of the theme of the unexpectedly sudden nature of Jesus' death tends to confirm our reading of the reason for the centurion's declaration that Jesus was truly God's Son. What the centurion observed was the impassioned cry followed by the sudden death. God had answered Jesus' prayer.

46. Mark fills this section with vocabulary that evokes the whole Jerusalem tragedy: the rock (πέτρα) of the tomb reminds one of the rocky ground of Peter and the disciples; the linen shroud (σινδών) echoes the linen cloth dropped by the fleeing disciple (Mark 14:51–52); and the stone (λίθον) is reminiscent of the stones of the temple (13:1–12) and the rejected stone that becomes the centerpiece (12:10).

47. That the original version of the Gospel ended at 16:8 is supported by both textual evidence from some of our earliest Greek manuscripts and also from the internal evidence of vocabulary and style. By the end of the second century, additional endings to the Gospel had been added to some manuscripts. The so-called Longer Ending, vv. 9–20, and the Shorter Ending along with the Freer Logion are three of the options provided in later manuscripts. For a discussion of the issue, see Taylor, *The Gospel According to St. Mark*, 610–15. For a sympathetic reassessment of the evidence

observers to actors and reveals the type of ground, productive or unfruitful, they embody. Their very act of buying spices and going to the tomb to anoint Jesus raises troubling questions. If they had followed Jesus in Galilee and heard his predictions, they, like the authorial audience, should expect that he will be raised in three days. Are they going, then, to perform the ritual offices on a dead corpse or to anoint a risen Messiah-King? Mark seems purposely to leave the exact nature of their mission ambiguous so that the audience cannot determine at the outset whether the women are faithful followers going to welcome the risen Messiah or unbelievers intent on decently burying the dead. Interestingly, the Gospels of Matthew and Luke resolve Mark's ambiguity but in opposite directions. By omitting any reference to the purchase of spices, Matthew asserts that the visit of the two Marys was simply "to see" what was happening, implying their belief that something would indeed happen (Matt. 28:1) and rewarding their action by an encounter with the risen Jesus (Matt. 28:9–10). Conversely, Luke twice repeats their preparation of spices and ointments for emphasis (Luke 23:56—24:1), has the two men at the tomb explicitly rebuke the women for seeking "the living among the dead" (Luke 24:5), and belittles their true witness by having the apostles disbelieve it (Luke 24:11). For Mark, the women's denouement must wait until the very last words of the Gospel in order to build up the highest hopes possible in the audience before thoroughly disappointing them. Still, having the only words the women are ever given to speak concern who will roll the stone away from the door for them (Mark 16:3) does appear to hint at a more mundane level of their expectations for the trip.

When they enter the tomb, after finding the worrisome stone—a very large one—rolled back (16:4), they discover "a young man sitting on the right side, dressed in a white robe" (16:5). Since Mark used a white robe to symbolize a divine state in Jesus' transfiguration (9:3) and the position of sitting on the right was conventionally associated with special power (see, e.g., 10:37; 14:62), the young man's description, while appropriately vague, clearly conveys his divine pedigree. The women's amazement, another inkling of their possible typology, permits the young man to proclaim, in a series of asyndeta for rhetorical effect, the resounding affirmation of Mark's good news: "You seek Jesus of Nazareth, who was crucified. He has risen, he is not here; see the place where they laid him" (16:6). God's salvation for those who endure faithfully to the end is definitely established; Jesus has been raised, as he promised he would be, and his followers can be certain of their own ultimate eternal life. However treacherous humanity

for the Longer Ending, which still must conclude that the evidence for inclusion is insufficient, see W. Farmer, *The Last Twelve Verses of Mark* (Cambridge: Cambridge University Press, 1974).

may be, God can be trusted; while the Gospel of Mark may depict a human tragedy, it is also most surely a divine comedy.

The young man then proceeds to give the woman a direct command, which begins with "Go" (ὑπάγετε, 16:7), the order most often addressed to those healed, the good earth (e.g., 1:44; 2:11; 5:19, 34; 7:29; 10:52). He instructs them to "tell his disciples and Peter that he is going before you to Galilee; there you will see him, as he told you" (16:7). Only the Gerasene demoniac has previously been told to go and tell (5:19–20), but his home was foreign ground and Jesus had no need to worry that the demoniac's preaching would shorten his time of sowing. Now, of course, all need for secrecy is past. The tenants have identified the heir, killed him, and he has been removed from the vineyard. The event that will initiate the coming of the lord of the vineyard has occurred, and all that remains to be done before this evil and murderous generation is put out of power is for the good news of God's rule to be spread to all nations (13:10), as the demoniac himself successfully began to do. The narrator then reports the women's response to this auspicious message: "And they went out and fled from the tomb; for trembling and astonishment had come upon them; and they said nothing to any one, for they were afraid" (16:8). The seed has fallen on rocky ground once again, as fear, not faith, motivates their actions. Like the Twelve before them, the women too flee in silence. Earlier, the woman with the flow of blood had also experienced fear and trembling, but she had spoken up despite those problems and been rewarded with healing (5:33–34). The demoniac, when commanded to tell, had preached to the Decapolis, and even those ordered to be silent had spoken out (see 1:44–45; 7:36). Here in the final irony of the Gospel, with all need for secrecy gone, those who are directed to go and tell run away in fear, saying nothing to anyone.

In attempting imaginatively to enter the ranks of Mark's authorial audience, we need to ask, not what this ending *means,* but what it *does.* At a fairly basic level, the story of the named women recapitulates the rocky ground type, the most complex of the hearing-response typologies illustrated by the Gospel and the one embodied also by the disciples, the most important characters in the narrative next to Jesus himself. Such a reiteration of major themes fulfills one of the necessary functions of an epilogue, reminding the audience in brief of the foregoing plot.[48] However, this ending is crafted to do much more than merely recall the disciples' failures. It is intended to

48. Both Chariton's and Xenophon's novels end with the motif of the finally reunited lovers telling each other or their families about their various adventures. This device of briefly retelling the story as a narrative epilogue probably owes its origin to Homer's *Odyssey,* in which Odysseus relates his adventures to his wife and family at the conclusion of his struggles. The device is so conventional by Xenophon's time that he simply reports that Anthia and Habrocomes tell each other what happened without repeating any of it.

move its hearers to respond, to excite their emotions on behalf of Jesus and the gospel message. Jesus' agony in Gethsemane, his courage at the trial, and his despair on the cross create a deep empathy for him in the audience, augmenting the already firm identification with his views established by the implied author's/narrator's reliable commentary throughout the Gospel. Moreover, through irony the author has pilloried both the Twelve and Jesus' opponents, encouraging the audience to look elsewhere for those who will prove faithful to Jesus' heroic example in the face of glaring injustice and evil.

When the women are introduced, they become the focus of these hopes, for one so badly wants someone to do well by Jesus. Although the typology of the parable of the Sower warns that the majority of those who hear will be unproductive and Jesus' own disciples have demonstrated that sad truth, it is almost impossible to believe that these women also fail, both because they have already shown themselves to be more faithful than the male disciples and because the audience's expectation and desire for them to succeed is so strong.[49] Indeed, the whole history of the later interpretation of Mark's Gospel from the early centuries to the present is littered with attempts to make the ending come out right, to make it satisfy the expectations it raises in its audience. The resurrection appearances and concomitant reclamation of the male disciples provided by Matthew and Luke, the additional endings tacked on to some manuscript copies of Mark by later editors or copyists, and even some recent scholarly attempts to remove the negativity of the final verses[50]—all testify to the rhetorical power of the epilogue. Why, then, did the author not resolve the expectations raised by the women's appearance and supply generations of "pleromatists"[51] (fulfillment seekers) with

49. Aristotle argued that the best plot for arousing the emotions of the audience was one that presented an unexpected incident that was at the same time fully in harmony with what has gone before; see *Poetics* 1452a. The women's failure is unexpected and yet at the same time predictable, given the overall Gospel story.

50. From the earlier suggestions that the evangelist might have died or been arrested just as he finished writing 16:8 and before he could properly conclude the Gospel to the more recent suggestions that silence is an appropriately worshipful response to an angelophany (Fuller, *The Formation of the Resurrection Narratives,* 52–53), or that the women did not tell just anyone but only the special people they were instructed to tell (D. Catchpole, "The Fearful Silence of the Women at the Tomb: A Study in Mark Theology," *Journal of Theology for Southern Africa* 18 [1977]: 3–10), or that the plotted narrative may end at 16:8 but the story world resolves the rift between Jesus and Peter in the audience's imagination (Petersen, "When Is the End Not the End?" 151–66)—all of these hypotheses attempt to make the story work out satisfactorily, that is, to make it satisfy the desires of the reader that some group serve Jesus faithfully and truly in the end. Every one of these sometimes clever, sometimes insightful, sometimes silly theories witnesses to the rhetorical power of the Markan epilogue.

51. Kermode's wonderful term for all of us human readers and hearers of stories (*The Genesis of Secrecy,* 64–65).

the gratifying closure they desire? The reason is quite simply but also quite profoundly that the Gospel of Mark intended to be "a unit of force whose power is exerted upon the world in a particular direction"[52] and not a comfortably concluded aesthetic experience.

If the women frustrate the hopes of the authorial audience for individuals to prove faithful to the courageous example of Jesus and follow his way by going out and sowing the word abroad, is there anyone else available to fulfill that task? Is there anyone else who has heard Jesus' teaching in Galilee, seen his miraculous feedings, witnessed his transfiguration, understood his conception of discipleship, listened to his predictions concerning the coming of the Son of man, remained awake at Gethsemane, followed him through the trial by the Jerusalem council and Pilate's interrogation, stood by him on the cross, watched his burial, and received the joyous confirmation of his resurrection? Of course there is: the audience itself. By involving the audience in the narrative time of Jesus' life and death, by aligning their evaluative perspective with that of the narrator and Jesus, by permitting them to share superior knowledge from the beginning of who Jesus was and what he was in the world to do, Mark has created in the role of the authorial audience the perfect disciple. Furthermore, that the audience was allowed to see the fearful responses of the various unfruitful grounds, especially the type that initially appears productive, and, by observing their actions, gain insight into the human traits that lead to hard-hearted failure encourages the reader/hearer of the Gospel to reject such traits and embrace instead the humility, anonymity, unconcern for self-enhancement, freedom from rigid traditionalism, and ministry to others embodied by Jesus and those of the good earth.

The narrator opened the Gospel of Mark by announcing to the hearer/reader the beginning of the good news about Jesus Christ, Son of God (1:1), and shortly after that, the character Jesus opened his ministry by coming into Galilee preaching the good news about God (1:14–15). The parallel established by these references to "the gospel" in first degree narration and then in second degree narration attests corresponding goals. Just as Jesus preached his performative word to the crowds of Galilee, just so does the Gospel of Mark as a whole seek to be a performative word for its audience. And as Jesus' sowing revealed the various types of earth present around him, from the monolithically hard-hearted ground of the path, whose violence and opposition eventually led to his crucifixion, to the abundant fruitfulness of the good earth, whose healings demonstrated the kingdom of God already come in power, in the same manner will Mark's seed fall on a variety of types of earth throughout the nations, disclosing

52. Tompkins, "The Reader in History," 204.

both the elect and those wedded to the values of this present power-greedy generation.

For the elect, the message of the young man at the tomb, to "tell his disciples and Peter that he is going before you to Galilee; there you will see him, as he told you" (16:7), is a clear call to go to Galilee, the location of Jesus' sowing of the word and the start of his preaching ministry. Literal geography is not the point, for Galilee represents the time of sowing,[53] and the message of the empty tomb is that the time of sowing still continues, even perhaps for hard to cultivate types like the rocky Peter, although the failure of the character Peter and the Twelve to produce good fruit under the constant, patient tillage of Jesus himself suggests that for those specific individuals the hour may have passed, but there may be other "Rocks" among the nations who will heed the call to discipleship before time runs out. And time will, indeed, run out, for the heir's death itself is the final provocation bringing the kingdom of God in all its glory to end the dominance of this evil generation and to install new tenants who will provide the fruit of the vineyard for its Creator. At some moment, in the midst of the terrible persecutions and tribulations that spreading the seed will inevitably entail, the faithful followers will "see" ($\check{o}\psi\epsilon\sigma\theta\epsilon$, 16:7) Jesus, as he promised, return on the clouds of heaven with the angels as Son of man to gather his elect from the four winds (13:23, 26–27; 14:62).[54]

The time for sowing the good news of this coming glory may linger yet awhile, but the new age is on the horizon. Each individual who hears the word sown by the Gospel of Mark, the word that human corruption and suffering will now finally be abolished by the glory of God's kingdom, is given the opportunity—as have all the characters in the story—to respond in faith or in fear. The problem posed by the epilogue in strong rhetorical

53. The symbolic nature of this reference has been argued by many scholars; see, e.g., Lightfoot, *Locality and Doctrine;* Perrin, *The Resurrection,* 26–27; and N. Q. Hamilton, *Recovery of the Protestant Adventure* (New York: Seabury Press, 1981), 118–22; others still opt for literal geography, as, e.g., W. Marxsen, *Introduction to the New Testament,* trans. G. Buswell (Philadelphia: Fortress Press, 1968), 141–42; and Kelber, *Mark's Story of Jesus,* 89–95.

54. That seeing Jesus in Mark 16:7 refers to the coming of the Son of man and not to a resurrection appearance (as Matthew makes it) is supported both by the general understanding of resurrection as an abiding aspect of God's action in the past and present that Mark seems to hold (see above, pp. 253–54) and by the word used for "see," $\check{o}\psi\epsilon\sigma\theta\epsilon$. The same verb is used for seeing the coming of the Son of man on the clouds in 13:26 ($\check{o}\psi o\nu\tau\alpha\iota$) and in 14:62 ($\check{o}\psi\epsilon\sigma\theta\epsilon$). The reference in the apocalyptic discourse also includes the notice that Jesus has told them all these things beforehand (13:23).

A number of other scholars also understand the reference in 16:7 to refer to the Parousia; see, e.g., Perrin, *The Resurrection,* 25–27; and Marxsen, *Introduction to the New Testament,* 142; for the view that a resurrection appearance is intended, see, e.g., Taylor, *The Gospel According to St. Mark,* 608–9; and Fuller, *The Formation of the Resurrection Narratives,* 63–64.

terms through the unfulfilled expectations raised by the named women is, If these followers will not go and tell, who will? In the end, Mark's Gospel purposely leaves each reader or hearer with the urgent and disturbing question: What type of earth am *I*? Will *I* go and tell? Indeed, one's response to the seed sown by the Gospel of Mark reveals in each listener's heart, as did Jesus' earlier preaching, the presence of God's ground or Satan's.

Conclusion

The Gospel of Mark comes from an ancient culture whose languages, customs, governments, and people are all now long dead. We may sense some inkling of "the glory that was Greece and the grandeur that was Rome" in the fragments of statues, mosaics, or jewelry housed in today's museums or in the excavated ruins of cities that once dominated the Mediterranean world, but we can bring that time back to life only very partially and only in the imagination. This literary-historical study of the Gospel of Mark has attempted to participate in such an imaginative endeavor. To do so we have had to unearth, sometimes very laboriously, conventions of writing and hearing that would have been a natural part of the common discourse to a Greek- speaking man or woman of the first century C.E. Even with that effort our results can never be other than tentative and hypothetical because so much from that distant age is lost to us. To enter fully the ranks of the authorial audience of the Gospel of Mark is an impossibility. Indeed, just the aim of trying to interpret Mark within its own literary milieu stamps our analysis as a modern reading of the Gospel and not an ancient one. Nevertheless, by drawing on whatever stylistically similar literature we can find, by culling the rhetorical handbooks that shaped (or perhaps reflected) the way Greco-Roman society wrote and spoke, we have been able to read the Gospel of Mark with ears slightly more attuned to its narrative rhythms.

What has emerged from our study is a typological, episodic, rhetorically molded religious tract that intends to sow abroad the good news of God's imminent coup d'état over the murderous authorities of this generation, in order to disclose the good earth of God's kingdom before the coming of the Son of man on the clouds of glory. It is an apocalyptic message in a popular narrative framework, replete with all the "helps for hearers" an ancient audience needed and would have expected: repetitions, amplifications of major themes, plot summaries, foreshadowings, and recapitulations. Its characters embody general types and illustrate the various human traits that accompany success or failure, thus showing the audience what to emulate and what to avoid. Its purpose is not to provide information for reflection or analysis but to persuade its hearers to have faith in the gospel of Jesus Christ, to follow the way he forged into inevitable persecutions, the cross, but also eternal life, and to become themselves sowers of the good news of God's coming kingdom.

We have discovered, in fact, a remarkably coherent worldview inspired by a deeply pessimistic assessment of the present human condition with its love of power, status, fame, and glory and its evil exercise of authority to pervert God's good creation. So thorough is the corruption of this generation that only God can put a stop to it, but Mark's good news arises at precisely this point: God is going to put a stop to it very soon. The killing of Jesus, God's beloved son and last messenger, was the final provocation for God to act. While the exact hour may be unknown, its arrival is inescapable. In the meantime, those who hear the word and believe, even though they be a minority, can experience the abundant power of that kingdom now with the assurance of eternal life in the future. Furthermore, their one task to hasten the glorious day, a task in which the Gospel of Mark itself participates, is to preach the gospel to the nations.

Read within the conventions of its own Greco-Roman milieu, the Gospel is neither esoteric nor muddled but rather accessible, forthright, and even fairly simple. However, the dust of centuries, the demands of Christian dogma, and some of the tendencies of biblical scholarship have made what was clear to ancient ears appear obscure to modern eyes. *We* have often created the muddle by tearing the story into fragments or trying to force it into the quite different perspectives of Matthew and Luke; by placing it solely against a Jewish or Hebrew Bible background and then deciphering it through a network of mostly illusory allusions; or by insisting anachronistically that it conform to current standards of historical accuracy, realism, psychological character development, and narrative subtlety. Such procedures have additionally served our contemporary love for enigma and mystification, but puzzles and games are hardly appropriate media for sowing the word of God's imminent coup, as the author of Mark well understood. Still, some of the issues raised by recent biblical scholarship may be addressed on the basis of this literary-historical interpretation.

Before we close our study of Mark, let us speculate briefly on what this analysis suggests about the historical setting of the Gospel, its *Vorleben,* and its *Nachleben.*

The Historical Setting

Particularly since the rise of redaction criticism in the 1950s and 1960s, one of the major areas of discussion concerning the Gospel of Mark has been the community out of which the Gospel came or to which it was directed.[1] The geographical setting of that community has been debated between northern Palestine and Rome, and even specific conflicts within the community have been postulated as the cause for writing the Gospel. The assumption underlying all of this work—an assumption that has never really received careful scrutiny—is that some identifiable, individualized local group—that is, a *specific* community—and its problems provide the setting for Mark and, for that matter, for all the other canonical Gospels as well.[2] This assumption was initially imported into the arena of Gospel studies from Pauline scholarship,[3] where attempts to understand the problems Paul was trying to address in his letters to different churches had yielded considerable insight into Paul's theology. However, one of the central principles of biblical form criticism ought to have raised questions from the beginning about the appropriateness of applying this Pauline model to the Gospels, for form critics argued that different genres imply different functions and different settings. While a letter may be an effective medium for directly challenging a community's practice or correcting its theological views, a Gospel, a narrative purporting to relate the actions, words, and views of characters from an earlier time, clearly is not.

Theories that connect Mark to the conflicts of one special Christian community have never adequately accounted for the development of the *narrative* format, since stories with their concern for entertainment are not well suited for debating theoretical issues. What narratives do well is enlist the sympathy of an audience on behalf of the hero, portray the universal forces affecting the success or failure of human existence in concrete situations, and create alternative worlds in hopes of altering or maintaining the

---

1. For theories about the community, see, e.g., Marxsen, *Mark the Evangelist,* 106–16; Weeden, *Mark—Traditions in Conflict;* Kelber, *Mark's Story of Jesus,* 92–95; and Kee, *Community of the New Age.*

2. Attempts to specify a community for the Gospel of Luke especially have been notoriously unsuccessful. John has had the most extensive community theories attached to it; see, e.g., R. E. Brown, *The Community of the Beloved Disciple* (New York: Paulist Press, 1979).

3. See, e.g., Weeden's use of theories concerning the Corinthian community in his study of Mark (*Mark—Traditions in Conflict,* 54–69).

status quo. If the author of Mark wished to correct the Christology of his audience, he selected a very poor design for it; if, however, the author wanted to spread the gospel by arousing the emotions of the audience in Jesus' behalf, his choice was excellent. On the basis of our literary-historical interpretation, we suggest that the Gospel of Mark was *not* written in response to the problems of a specific, local community but was instead intended, as were the ancient erotic novels, for a wide readership. It was written to individuals, not to groups, and individuals in primarily two general categories: individual Christians experiencing persecutions because of their faith who were in need of encouragement and individuals interested in Christianity but not yet fully committed who needed to be persuaded. Mark's rhetorical goals are exhortation and proselytizing.[4]

Moreover, Mark's understanding of Christianity supports these goals. To demonstrate one's participation in the elect, one needs only to hear the word of God's coming kingdom and believe. No extensive training is necessary; no special rituals are mandatory, although they are certainly not prohibited unless they work against spreading the word. The good earth of the kingdom may come from any national or racial background, Jew or Greek, either gender, male or female, and any status or station in life. Naturally it would be more difficult for someone with wealth, political power, or high reputation to follow the way of Jesus, but even that scenario was possible provided the heart-hardening desires for power, authority, riches, and fame were rejected. Serving the needs of others, sowing the gospel abroad, and enduring the persecutions of the evil establishment faithfully were the crucial elements of the Christian life in this brief period before the arrival of the Son of man.

Besides persecutions from current religious and political establishments, the only other widespread issues facing Christians that the Gospel appears to reflect by its repetitions of themes are faulty leadership among Christians (through both the specific characterization of the disciples, the dominance of the rocky ground type in general, and the warnings in the Apocalyptic Discourse) and conflicts over eating rituals or regulations (through a number of controversy stories concerning fasting, hand washing, eating consecrated food, etc.). However, since salvation is a matter of individual faith in the Gospel and personal willingness to take up one's cross, the failure of glory-seeking leaders or arguments over ritual meals have no ultimate significance for the humble, anonymous Christian following the way of Jesus. In fact, making those who initially respond favorably to the Gospel but then collapse under pressure be one of the four universal types of response to the word establishes a certain sad inevitability about Christian defections. They

---

4. For a comparable view of the missionary dimension of Mark, see especially D. Senior, "The Struggle to be Universal: Mission as Vantage Point for New Testament Investigation," *CBQ* 46 (1984): 63–81.

must be expected to occur and thus should not cause any crisis in the belief of others; those who betray or deny when threatened were simply rocky ground in the first place.

Proposing that the Gospel was not written to a specific local community does not, of course, mean that it was not written in a certain place. A strong pro-Roman apologetic tone pervades the narrative. It can be seen, for example, in having a centurion make the final public declaration of Jesus' identity, in fashioning the Roman-linked leaders Herod and Pilate into the thorny ground type, which, while still finally failing, possesses some aspect of fertility, and in excusing them from responsibility for the deaths of John the Baptist and Jesus, which they actually controlled, by creating an evil woman trickster,[5] Herodias, and an evil Jewish religious establishment to take the blame. Although this apologetic certainly lends some weight to the ancient tradition of Mark's Roman provenance and although, coupled with the "Latinisms"[6] in vocabulary, the shaky hold on Jewish tradition and Palestinian geography argues against a northern Palestinian setting, in truth on the basis of the story alone almost any city in the Mediterranean area might be its author's home.

Nevertheless, considering Rome or another large city under Roman rule of the late first century as the place of origin may supply a concrete historical context to explain why a religion that relied so heavily on preaching and oral tradition might see the value of a written manuscript. Rome from the time of the Flavians onward discouraged public religious gatherings and periodically persecuted Christian preachers. Such actions caused Christian missionaries to cease preaching and public assemblies to halt.[7] Individual, word-of-mouth contact from one person to another in the marketplace was a very slow method of spreading the word. Having a tract that could be passed from extended household to household might be one way of avoiding the wrath of Roman authorities while at the same time sowing the word more broadly and quickly. The only requirement would be that each household have someone associated with it who had the ability to read, and considering the simplicity of Mark's Greek style, that ability would not need to be particularly sophisticated. If the Gospel were composed for such

5. Herodias, like many female characters, has her access to direct power blocked by a superior male figure. To get her way she must resort to the wily action of a trickster. On women as trickster figures, see all of *Semeia* 42 (1988): "Reasoning with the Foxes—Female Wit in a World of Male Power," ed. J. Cheryl Exum.

6. For a listing and discussion of Mark's "Latin" words, see Taylor, *The Gospel According to St. Mark*, 44–45.

7. Whether it was the threat of persecution or actual persecution that silenced Christian preachers and missionaries, the fact is that "after Saint Paul, the church had no mission, it made no organized or official approach to unbelievers; rather, it left everything to the individual," in R. MacMullen, *Christianizing the Roman Empire (A.D. 100–400)* (New Haven: Yale University Press, 1984), 34. See MacMullen's full discussion in pp. 32–42. See also Nock, *Conversion*, 202–4.

a function, it would also account for its wide dissemination in a relatively brief time. Moreover, if first-century Christians understood Mark as a proselytizing tract for spreading the news of the speedy approach of God's kingdom, rather than a sacred repository of Jesus' words or a careful account of his historical ministry, the freedom with which Matthew, Luke, and perhaps John alter, omit, and add to Mark's story becomes thoroughly credible. Finally, if listening to the Gospel of Mark had comforted a generation of early Christians suffering persecution or brought some of them into the Christian fold in the first place, it makes more sensible their preservation of the Gospel even after its apocalyptic, antiestablishment message was no longer religiously or politically relevant.

The *Vorleben*

Without doubt the author of Mark had some sources, probably mostly oral, available to draw upon in composing the Gospel. However, it is equally clear on the basis of this study that whatever "traditional" material the author used was reworked to fit the overall rhetorical aims and typology of the plot. Along with Werner Kelber,[8] we want to argue in the strongest terms that the Gospel of Mark is the result of a definitive creative enterprise on the part of its author and not the natural end product of a gradually coalescing body of oral tradition. The two long parables, the Sower and the Tenants, which reveal for the audience the allegorical or typological[9] level of the story, are good cases in point. It is possible that these parables or some variation of them existed in Christian oral tradition prior to Mark. Yet they are so crucial to the organization of the Gospel and to the molding of so much other material that it is hard to believe the author did not shape them to fit his requirements. The Interpretation of the parable of the Sower, with its point-by-point expansion and repetition of the parable, is especially likely to have come from the author's own hand.

Whether created by the author or overwritten to fit the demands of the narrative, all the episodes and characters in the Gospel, as we have seen, cohere to the basic plot line. Recognizing this narrative unity has far-reaching effects on attempts to move behind the written Gospel to oral tradition and to trace that oral tradition back, perhaps, to Jesus. Since no

---

8. For Kelber's excellent discussion of this position, see *The Oral and the Written Gospel*, 1–34.

9. Throughout this study, I have generally used the word "typology" instead of "allegory" to refer to the parables. The parables in Mark as stories that present universal types which can be adapted to many different specific situations would be obviously allegorical to an ancient audience. However, modern readers often have such a narrow view of allegory as an artificial form with a rigid one-to-one correspondence and a specific single referent that I have avoided the term in order to try to prevent misunderstanding.

simple division between redaction and tradition is generally possible, *if* an oral tradition prior to Mark is to be discovered—and that may well be an impossibility[10]—much more sophisticated forms of analysis must be developed than are now being employed by many biblical form critics and historians. On the basis of this study and others, the naive view that Mark, or any other New Testament document, reflects what was happening with only minimal ideological, polemical, or rhetorical distortion can no longer be justified.

The *Nachleben*

While the message of the Gospel of Mark would have had obvious appeal to the persecuted members of a small apocalyptic sect urgently hoping for God's protective intervention in the evil exercises of those presently in religious or political authority, as time passed without that intervention occurring and, perhaps even more important, as members of the sect ceased being persecuted and became themselves those in religious and political authority, Mark's message could easily become an embarrassment. Negative criticism of the Gospel is clearly implied in Papias's defensive remarks about Mark writing down all he could remember but not "in order."[11] By the end of the first century Mark's conviction concerning the imminent return of the Son of man on the clouds of heaven would already be seriously questioned, and by the "triumph of Christianity" through Constantine in the fourth century, Mark's absolute insistence on the corruption accompanying fame, power, status, and wealth—even for Christians—was wildly inappropriate. The antiestablishment stance of a marginal religious sect had no place in the worldview of the religion of the empire. That Augustine dismissed Mark as the abbreviator of Matthew made considerably more political than literary sense, and Christianity, the dominant religion of the Western world, manifestly had no inclination to reverse that evaluation over the last fifteen centuries. Actually, the really surprising thing about the Gospel of Mark is that it was preserved at all!

It probably would not have been preserved, so problematic became its message, had it not been effectively neutralized by the writings of Matthew and Luke. Although we may not be able to prove conclusively that both Matthew and Luke—for somewhat different reasons and in different ways—purposely intended to refute and supplant Mark's understanding of

10. Because of the difficulty in the sources, Schweitzer announced the death of the quest for the historical Jesus at the beginning of this century. For the same reason, Bultmann announced it again around the middle of the century. Needless to say, I am not especially sanguine that another announcement now for the same reason will be any more effective.

11. See Eusebius, *Historia ecclesiastica* 3.39.15.

the Christian gospel, we can confidently assert that such a supersedure was the net result of their efforts. By using much or most of what Mark created for quite disparate ends, they overshadowed Mark's earlier and less acceptable version. While it is beyond the scope of this study to analyze the projects of Matthew and Luke in detail, a few general points of disagreement with Mark's views may be tentatively suggested by way of illustration. For Mark, the main focus of concern was Jesus' message about the coming near of God's kingdom; the importance of Jesus himself rested in his role as the final messenger, the beloved Son, whose death at the hands of this faithless generation assured God's intervention, and his function as example to all his followers of faithful endurance to the end. For both Matthew and Luke, the *person* of Jesus himself is much more the focus of concern than the coming of God's kingdom. Through their additions of quite different birth stories, resurrection appearance stories, and extensive teachings, they emphasize Jesus Christ as the savior of the world, the founder of a new religion, with John the Baptist as the apocalyptic messenger. The coming of God's kingdom is still hoped for, but its advent for both Matthew and Luke is much farther off in the future while the primary concern of the present is reconciliation or salvation through Jesus Christ.

If Matthew and Luke agree in shifting the focus from the message to the person, they disagree on other aspects of Mark's position. For Matthew, Mark's negative assessment of the Jews, of those desiring power and status, and of the general state of the world is fairly accurate. Indeed, Matthew often appears to be as suspicious of the unfortunate proclivities of human nature—even the human nature of Christians—as Mark is and more willing to place blame: in Matthew's world the sheep and the goats are sharply divided. However, Mark's idea that a response of faith to hearing the word is sufficient training for the Christian life is totally unacceptable to Matthew. Mark's rocky ground becomes Matthew's learners. The disciples are still depicted as often failing Jesus, but their failures are related to their need to learn how to lead the Christian life. They must be painstakingly taught an authoritative tradition, and then, after the resurrection and their reconciliation with Jesus, they themselves can be commissioned to go out and teach this tradition to others. For Matthew, Christian faith is not the discovery of one's true nature as God's good earth[12] but a process of formation through the learning of a tradition that reaches back to Jesus himself.

---

12. While Mark is not afflicted by the sharp division of the spiritual world from the material that characterized most Gnostic Christianity of the second to the fourth centuries C.E., the Gospel's understanding of salvation as the discovery or disclosure of one's true nature as God's ground bears clear affinities to some later Gnostic positions. For an attempt to relate Mark to Gnostic documents, see J. M. Robinson, "On the *Gattung* of Mark (and John)" and "Gnosticism and the New Testament" in *The Problem of History in Mark and Other Marcan Studies,* 11–39 and 40–53.

For Luke, it is not Mark's lack of concern with the authority of tradition that causes problems but his uncompromisingly malign regard for the present world. Although Luke willingly admits that bad things happen in this life—innocent people are executed, followers lie, deny, or under Satan's influence betray—still history is redeemable. God can work through this present existence for the good of all in God's own way. Luke is much more optimistic about the structures of society and the ultimate success of God's plan despite the weakness, lack of faith, recalcitrance, or misgivings of God's human agents than Mark could ever be. Where Mark portrays an utterly corrupt age that can be changed only by its total annihilation, Luke fashions an imperfect but malleable creation that has strayed from God's intended path as revealed in Scripture but can be led back by following the example of Jesus, the universal savior. Though both Matthew and Luke, the earliest reflections of the *Nachleben* of the Gospel of Mark, may have succeeded in substituting their understandings of Christianity for Mark's, it is important to recognize they are no less the children of Greco-Roman society than Mark is. They too develop typologies, sketch illustrative characters, evolve episodic plots, and write rhetorically powerful stories, even if their final goals, like their portrayals of the Christian story, are somewhat different from Mark's. A literary-historical perspective may be especially critical in interpreting Luke, for of all the New Testament authors, Luke is the most accomplished writer and stylist and the most polished rhetorician.

We have tried to read the Gospel of Mark in the light of its own Hellenistic milieu, to enter imaginatively the ranks of its authorial audience. Yet we are not people of the first century. What, if anything, has Mark to say to the society of the twentieth and twenty-first centuries? To the degree that the Gospel continues as a living document of the Christian religion, it is certainly permissible for modern-day Christians to read it on their own terms, actualizing its potential for today, without special regard for its original setting. Such a reading, though, should be carried out with integrity, by the honest admission from the outset that the contemporary context and not the ancient one will dominate. If, alternatively, one wishes to maintain the historical conditionedness of the text, what wisdom might it confer at this juncture in time? First, the intrinsic nature of typological narrative gives it a certain transferability. To the extent that Mark's four types of responses to the word do describe a kind of universal human pattern, they can be applied to people in the present. The danger of typology, well exemplified by the history of interpretation of all the Gospels, is that ages like our own, unused to illustrative narration, may petrify typology into history. Thus, we begin to think that the hard earth of the path is identified once and for all by the Jerusalem Jewish authorities, and by destroying the Jews we rid ourselves of this negative response. The despicable evil of anti-Semitism is fed by such thinking, and the Christian Gospels have much to answer for in this regard. What a typological narrative ought to do is warn us that the hard-hearted path, the rocky ground, and the thorny earth are always with us, offering constant temptations to failure and fear. The good earth is now and always has been in the minority, but by their fruits we will know them.

Second, in a period beset by Star Wars, nuclear weapons, acid rain, widespread famine, revolution, and war, Mark's unrelentingly negative analysis of the human world seems like clear-eyed realism. By observing institutions from universities and churches to corporations and governments around the globe, we can easily testify that power, wealth, status, fame, and authority still corrupt humanity and harden hearts to the suffering of others. The difficulty Mark furnishes for modern appropriation is not its negative assessment of the human situation but its solution to the problem. Mark argues that only direct divine intervention can preserve the elect from the mess this generation is making of the cosmos. While some even now may wish to continue affirming Mark's view, such acquiescence has unfortunately permitted this generation to keep increasing the mess for almost two thousand years. Mark's analysis should be valued, but Christians today must work, not individually, but in solidarity with others to bring to fruition this abundant and lovingly created vineyard that is God's intended kingdom. Our alternative may well be Mark's other vision of the future: "such tribulation as has not been from the beginning of the creation which God created until now, and never will be" (13:19). We have the power to become responsible tenants or to destroy the vineyard absolutely. Which is it to be?

Appendix A

RHETORICAL STRUCTURE OF MARK

I. Prologue—Mark 1:1–13
   A. 1:1–3
   B. 1:4–8
   B′. 1:9–10
   A′. 1:11–13

II. DIVISION ONE—Jesus, the Sower of the Word—Mark 1:14—10:52
   A. Introduction—1:14–15
   B. 1:16—3:6
      1. 1:16–20—calls disciples
         a. 1:21–28—healing in synagogue
         b. 1:29–34—healing of Simon's mother-in-law and crowds
            [1:35–39—prayer alone]
         c. 1:40–45—healing of leper
         d. 2:1–12—healing of paralytic/controversy with scribes
      2. 2:13–14—calls disciple
         a. 2:15–17—controversy over eating with sinners
         b. 2:18–22—controversy over fasting
         c. 2:23–28—controversy over picking grain on Sabbath
         d. 3:1–6—controversy/healing on Sabbath
   C. 3:7—6:34
      1. 3:7–35
         a. 3:7–12—by sea, crowds from named towns, boat, heal
         b. 3:13–19a—calls and appoints the Twelve
         c. 3:19b–35
            1. 3:19b–30—controversy with "those near him" and Jerusalem scribes
            2. 3:31–35—rejects old family, establishes rule for new
      2. 4:1—5:43
         a. 4:1–34—parables

311

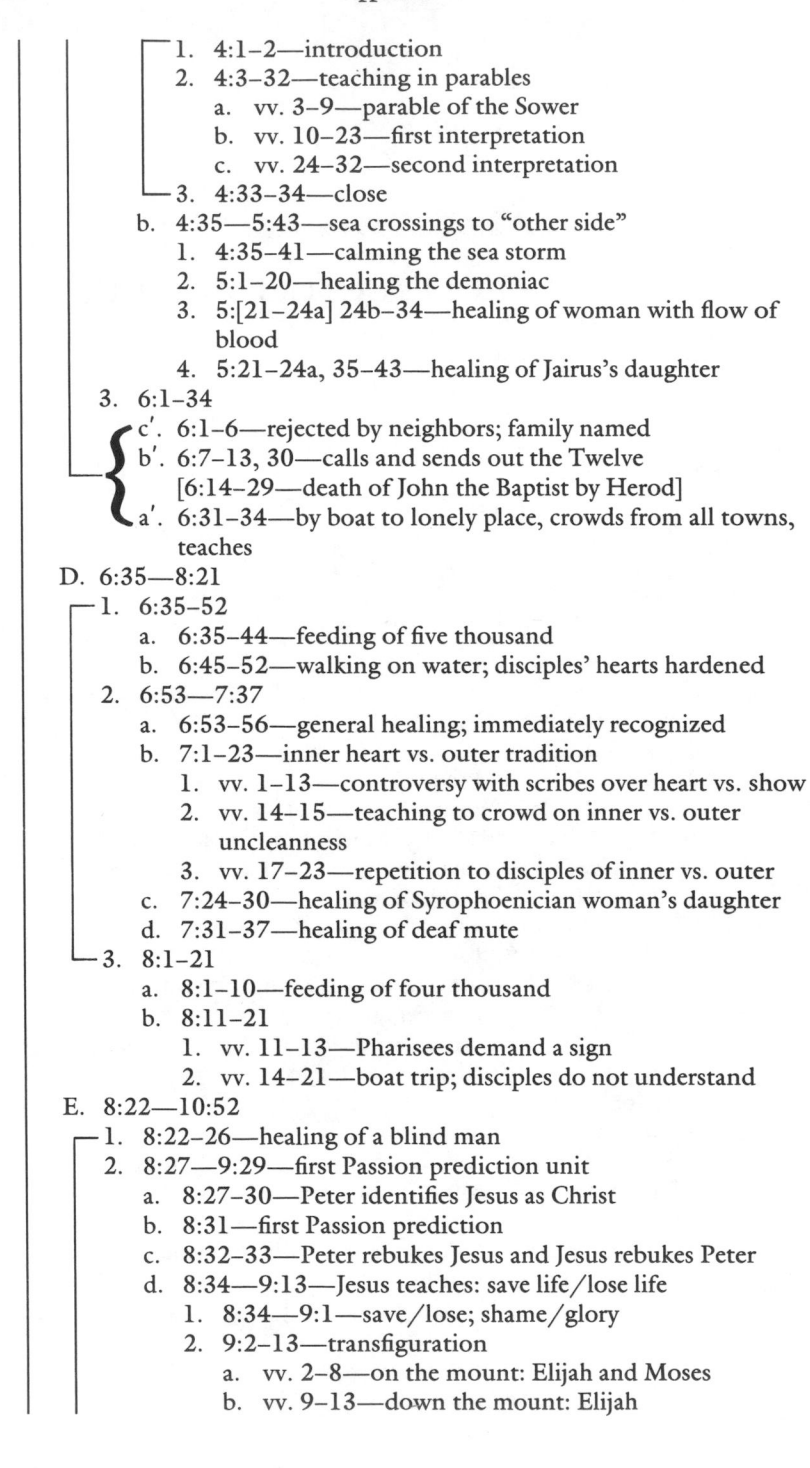

1. 4:1–2—introduction
2. 4:3–32—teaching in parables
   a. vv. 3–9—parable of the Sower
   b. vv. 10–23—first interpretation
   c. vv. 24–32—second interpretation
3. 4:33–34—close
   b. 4:35—5:43—sea crossings to "other side"
   1. 4:35–41—calming the sea storm
   2. 5:1–20—healing the demoniac
   3. 5:[21–24a] 24b–34—healing of woman with flow of blood
   4. 5:21–24a, 35–43—healing of Jairus's daughter
3. 6:1–34
   c′. 6:1–6—rejected by neighbors; family named
   b′. 6:7–13, 30—calls and sends out the Twelve
   [6:14–29—death of John the Baptist by Herod]
   a′. 6:31–34—by boat to lonely place, crowds from all towns, teaches
D. 6:35—8:21
   1. 6:35–52
      a. 6:35–44—feeding of five thousand
      b. 6:45–52—walking on water; disciples' hearts hardened
   2. 6:53—7:37
      a. 6:53–56—general healing; immediately recognized
      b. 7:1–23—inner heart vs. outer tradition
         1. vv. 1–13—controversy with scribes over heart vs. show
         2. vv. 14–15—teaching to crowd on inner vs. outer uncleanness
         3. vv. 17–23—repetition to disciples of inner vs. outer
      c. 7:24–30—healing of Syrophoenician woman's daughter
      d. 7:31–37—healing of deaf mute
   3. 8:1–21
      a. 8:1–10—feeding of four thousand
      b. 8:11–21
         1. vv. 11–13—Pharisees demand a sign
         2. vv. 14–21—boat trip; disciples do not understand
E. 8:22—10:52
   1. 8:22–26—healing of a blind man
   2. 8:27—9:29—first Passion prediction unit
      a. 8:27–30—Peter identifies Jesus as Christ
      b. 8:31—first Passion prediction
      c. 8:32–33—Peter rebukes Jesus and Jesus rebukes Peter
      d. 8:34—9:13—Jesus teaches: save life/lose life
         1. 8:34—9:1—save/lose; shame/glory
         2. 9:2–13—transfiguration
            a. vv. 2–8—on the mount: Elijah and Moses
            b. vv. 9–13—down the mount: Elijah

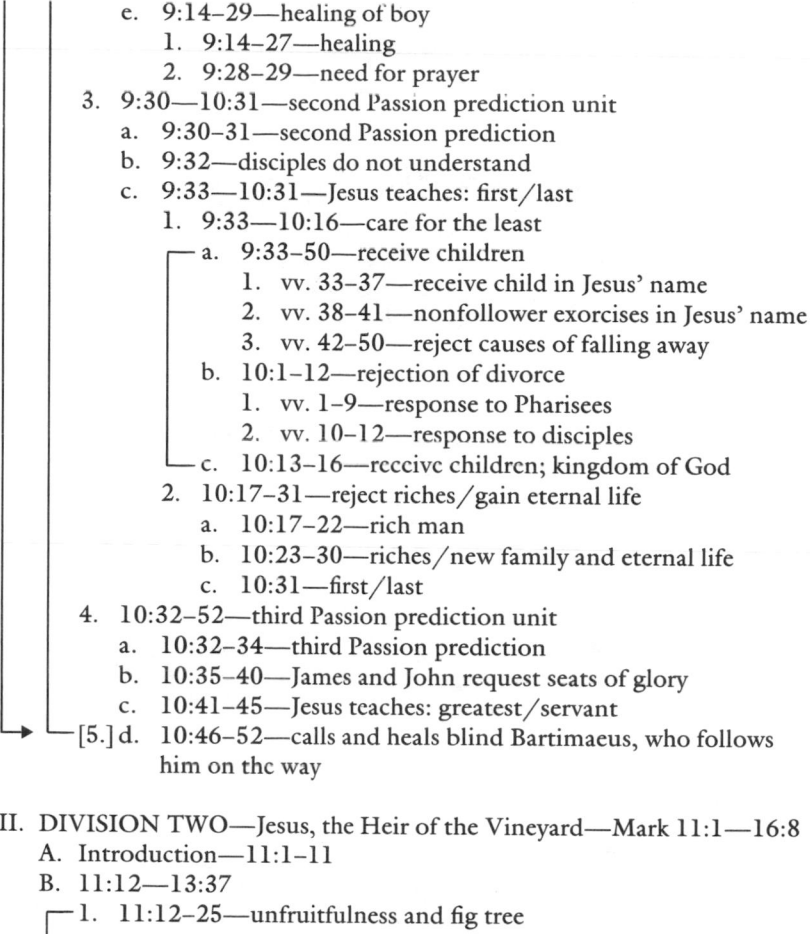

        e. 9:14–29—healing of boy
            1. 9:14–27—healing
            2. 9:28–29—need for prayer
    3. 9:30—10:31—second Passion prediction unit
        a. 9:30–31—second Passion prediction
        b. 9:32—disciples do not understand
        c. 9:33—10:31—Jesus teaches: first/last
            1. 9:33—10:16—care for the least
                a. 9:33–50—receive children
                    1. vv. 33–37—receive child in Jesus' name
                    2. vv. 38–41—nonfollower exorcises in Jesus' name
                    3. vv. 42–50—reject causes of falling away
                b. 10:1–12—rejection of divorce
                    1. vv. 1–9—response to Pharisees
                    2. vv. 10–12—response to disciples
                c. 10:13–16—receive children; kingdom of God
            2. 10:17–31—reject riches/gain eternal life
                a. 10:17–22—rich man
                b. 10:23–30—riches/new family and eternal life
                c. 10:31—first/last
    4. 10:32–52—third Passion prediction unit
        a. 10:32–34—third Passion prediction
        b. 10:35–40—James and John request seats of glory
        c. 10:41–45—Jesus teaches: greatest/servant
[5.] d. 10:46–52—calls and heals blind Bartimaeus, who follows
         him on the way

III. DIVISION TWO—Jesus, the Heir of the Vineyard—Mark 11:1—16:8
    A. Introduction—11:1–11
    B. 11:12—13:37
        1. 11:12–25—unfruitfulness and fig tree
            a. 11:12–14—failure of fig tree
            b. 11:15–19—cleansing of temple
            c. 11:20–25—fig tree and faith
        2. 11:27—12:12—Jesus' and John's authority
            a. 11:27–33—controversy over authority
            b. 12:1–12—parable of the Vineyard and the Tenants
        3. 12:13–44—tests and teachings
            a. 12:13–34—three controversies to test Jesus
                1. 12:13–17—payment of taxes
                2. 12:18–27—resurrection
                3. 12:28–34—Great Commandment
            b. 12:35–44—three teachings by Jesus
                1. 12:35–37—David's Lord
                2. 12:38–40—hypocrisy of scribes
                3. 12:41–44—widow's offering

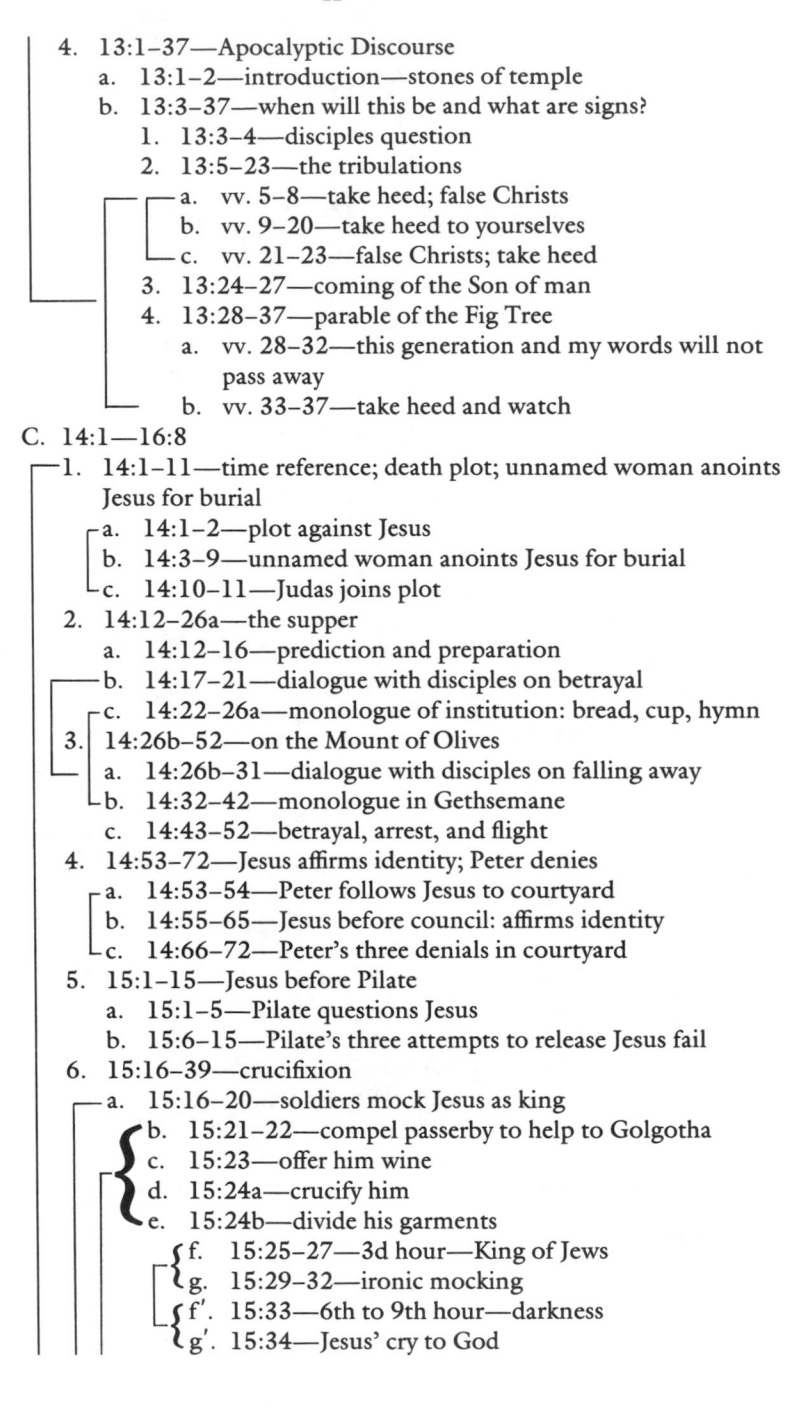

  4. 13:1–37—Apocalyptic Discourse
      a. 13:1–2—introduction—stones of temple
      b. 13:3–37—when will this be and what are signs?
          1. 13:3–4—disciples question
          2. 13:5–23—the tribulations
              a. vv. 5–8—take heed; false Christs
              b. vv. 9–20—take heed to yourselves
              c. vv. 21–23—false Christs; take heed
          3. 13:24–27—coming of the Son of man
          4. 13:28–37—parable of the Fig Tree
              a. vv. 28–32—this generation and my words will not
                  pass away
              b. vv. 33–37—take heed and watch
C. 14:1—16:8
  1. 14:1–11—time reference; death plot; unnamed woman anoints
      Jesus for burial
      a. 14:1–2—plot against Jesus
      b. 14:3–9—unnamed woman anoints Jesus for burial
      c. 14:10–11—Judas joins plot
  2. 14:12–26a—the supper
      a. 14:12–16—prediction and preparation
      b. 14:17–21—dialogue with disciples on betrayal
      c. 14:22–26a—monologue of institution: bread, cup, hymn
  3. 14:26b–52—on the Mount of Olives
      a. 14:26b–31—dialogue with disciples on falling away
      b. 14:32–42—monologue in Gethsemane
      c. 14:43–52—betrayal, arrest, and flight
  4. 14:53–72—Jesus affirms identity; Peter denies
      a. 14:53–54—Peter follows Jesus to courtyard
      b. 14:55–65—Jesus before council: affirms identity
      c. 14:66–72—Peter's three denials in courtyard
  5. 15:1–15—Jesus before Pilate
      a. 15:1–5—Pilate questions Jesus
      b. 15:6–15—Pilate's three attempts to release Jesus fail
  6. 15:16–39—crucifixion
      a. 15:16–20—soldiers mock Jesus as king
      b. 15:21–22—compel passerby to help to Golgotha
      c. 15:23—offer him wine
      d. 15:24a—crucify him
      e. 15:24b—divide his garments
          f. 15:25–27—3d hour—King of Jews
          g. 15:29–32—ironic mocking
          f'. 15:33—6th to 9th hour—darkness
          g'. 15:34—Jesus' cry to God

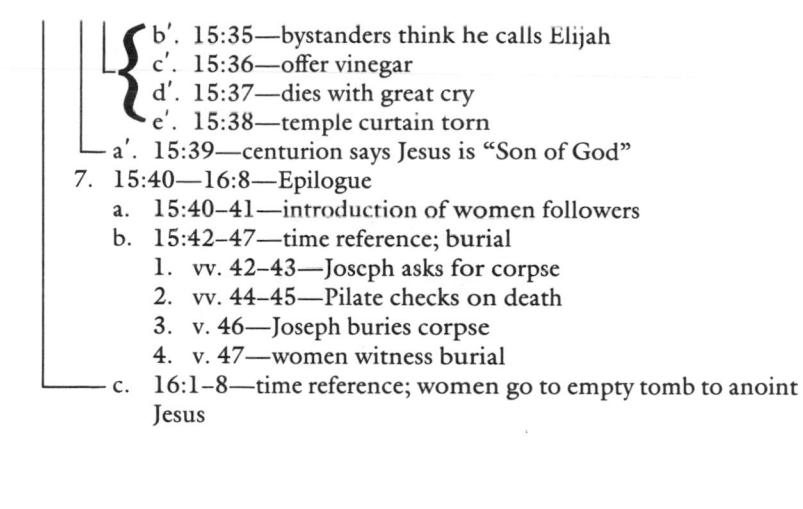

b'. 15:35—bystanders think he calls Elijah
c'. 15:36—offer vinegar
d'. 15:37—dies with great cry
e'. 15:38—temple curtain torn
a'. 15:39—centurion says Jesus is "Son of God"

7. 15:40—16:8—Epilogue
   a. 15:40–41—introduction of women followers
   b. 15:42–47—time reference; burial
      1. vv. 42-43—Joseph asks for corpse
      2. vv. 44-45—Pilate checks on death
      3. v. 46—Joseph buries corpse
      4. v. 47—women witness burial
   c. 16:1–8—time reference; women go to empty tomb to anoint Jesus

Appendix B

THE PROLOGUE: MARK 1:1–13

Greek Structure

A   Ἀρχὴ τοῦ εὐαγγελίου Ἰησοῦ Χριστοῦ υἱοῦ θεοῦ

Καθὼς γέγραπται ἐν τῷ Ἠσαΐᾳ τῷ προφήτῃ,

   Ἰδοὺ ἀποστέλλω τὸν ἄγγελόν μου πρὸ προσώπου σου,

   ὃς κατασκευάσει τὴν ὁδόν σου·

φωνὴ βοῶντος ἐν τῇ ἐρήμῳ,

   Ἑτοιμάσατε τὴν ὁδὸν κυρίου,

   εὐθείας ποιεῖτε τὰς τρίβους αὐτοῦ—

B   ἐγένετο Ἰωάννης βαπτίζων ἐν τῇ ἐρήμῳ καὶ κηρύσσων βάπτισμα μετανοίας εἰς ἄφεσιν ἁμαρτιῶν. καὶ ἐξεπορεύετο πρὸς αὐτὸν πᾶσα ἡ Ἰουδαία χώρα καὶ οἱ Ἱεροσολυμῖται πάντες, καὶ ἐβαπτίζοντο ὑπ᾽ αὐτοῦ ἐν τῷ Ἰορδάνῃ ποταμῷ ἐξομολογούμενοι τὰς ἁμαρτίας αὐτῶν. καὶ ἦν ὁ Ἰωάννης ἐνδεδυμένος τρίχας καμήλου καὶ ζώνην δερματίνην περὶ τὴν ὀσφὺν αὐτοῦ, καὶ ἐσθίων ἀκρίδας καὶ μέλι ἄγριον. καὶ ἐκήρυσσεν λέγων, Ἔρχεται ὁ ἰσχυρότερός μου ὀπίσω μου, οὗ οὐκ εἰμὶ ἱκανὸς κύψας λῦσαι τὸν ἱμάντα τῶν ὑποδημάτων αὐτοῦ· ἐγὼ ἐβάπτισα ὑμᾶς ὕδατι, αὐτὸς δὲ βαπτίσει ὑμᾶς ἐν πνεύματι ἁγίῳ.

B′   Καὶ ἐγένετο ἐν ἐκείναις ταῖς ἡμέραις ἦλθεν Ἰησοῦς ἀπὸ Ναζαρὲτ τῆς
Γαλιλαίας καὶ ἐβαπτίσθη εἰς τὸν Ἰορδάνην ὑπὸ Ἰωάννου. καὶ εὐθὺς
ἀναβαίνων ἐκ τοῦ ὕδατος εἶδεν σχιζομένους τοὺς οὐρανοὺς καὶ τὸ πνεῦμα ὡς
περιστερὰν καταβαῖνον εἰς αὐτόν·

A′   καὶ φωνὴ ἐγένετο ἐκ τῶν οὐρανῶν, Σὺ εἶ ὁ υἱός μου ὁ ἀγαπητός, ἐν σοὶ
εὐδόκησα. Καὶ εὐθὺς τὸ πνεῦμα αὐτὸν ἐκβάλλει εἰς τὴν ἔρημον. καὶ ἦν ἐν τῇ
ἐρήμῳ τεσσαράκοντα ἡμέρας πειραζόμενος ὑπὸ τοῦ Σατανᾶ, καὶ ἦν μετὰ τῶν
θηρίων, καὶ οἱ ἄγγελοι διηκόνουν αὐτῷ.

KEY: Anaphora   ═══════

      Anastrophe   ─────────

      Chiastic parallels   · · · · · · · , ─ ─ ─ ─ ─ ─

Index of Biblical and Ancient Sources

The Gospel of Mark

1:1	2, 28 n.12; 94, *110 n.43*; 116, 200, 227, 248, 288, 297
1:1-3	*239–48*
1:1-13	*108–13*, 234, 281
1:1—16:8	*120*
1:2	*110 n.44*
1:4	116, 197 n.34; 244, 247
1:4-5	224, 236
1:4-8	198
1:4-13	116
1:5	114, 116 n.56; 208, 246, 284
1:6	208
1:7	242, 243
1:7-8	244
1:9	114
1:9-11	244
1:10	281
1:11	51, 94, 201, 239, 248, 283
1:12-13	244
1:13	137 n.20
1:14a	208
1:14	234, 246
1:14-15	108 n.37; *114–18*, 119, 122, 131, 229, 240, 247, 297
1:14—8:26	114 n.52
1:14—10:52	107, 231
1:15	135, 164, 173, 197 n.34; 244, 284
1:16	116, 131, 260
1:16-20	132, 141, 154, 190, 192, *196*
1:16—2:12	131–32
1:16—3:6	*131–48*, 142
1:16—6:34	196
1:16—10:52	108 n.37
1:17	202 n.44
1:18	190
1:19	260
1:20	154 n.43; 190
1:21	132
1:21-28	132, *135–36*, 136–37 n.19; 233
1:21—2:12	*135–39*, 165, 227
1:22	136
1:24	201
1:25	201
1:27	136
1:28	137
1:29-34	132, 141
1:30-31	135, 292

319

Hebrew Bible

New Testament

Ancient Authors and Writings

Index
of Authors

329

Index of
Literary and
Rhetorical Terms

Foreign Policy and the Democratic Dilemmas THIRD EDITION

Foreign Policy and the Democratic Dilemmas THIRD EDITION

John Spanier
University of Florida

Eric M. Uslaner
University of Maryland

Holt, Rinehart and Winston
New York   Chicago   San Francisco   Philadelphia   Montreal
Toronto   London   Sydney   Tokyo   Mexico City   Rio de Janeiro
Madrid

Library of Congress Cataloging in Publication Data

Spanier, John W.
  Foreign policy and the democratic dilemmas.

  Previously published as: How American foreign policy
is made.
  Bibliography: p.
  Includes index.
  1. United States—Foreign relations administration.
I. Uslaner, Eric M.   II.   Title.
JX1706.A4 1982   353.0089'2   81-6683
ISBN 0-03-060141-X   AACR2

CBS COLLEGE PUBLISHING
Holt, Rinehart and Winston
The Dryden Press
Saunders College Publishing

In memory of
William and Liesel Spanier
and
Abe and Irene Uslaner

Preface

This is the third edition of *How American Foreign Policy is Made.* The change in title from the second edition reflects our somewhat greater emphasis in this edition on the dilemmas that the United States faces as a democracy conducting its foreign policy. While this issue was introduced in the first edition, our discussion of it in this edition is more elaborate and analyzed more explicitly.

Our original purpose in writing this book was to explain the ways in which foreign policy (further subdivided into crisis and noncrisis security policies) is made differently than is domestic policy. At that time, most texts on the policy process focused on *domestic* policymaking. *How American Foreign Policy Is Made* was written to fill the need for an introduction to the actors and elements in the foreign policy decision process and to the analytic approaches most useful in understanding and criticizing it. In the last edition, we added intermestic policy as a further category to our two types of foreign policies because of the increasing erosion of the distinction between foreign and domestic policy in this area. This three-fold distinction is maintained in this book and examined in greater detail by additional case studies.

Contemporary conflict over foreign policy demands, too, that we not only deal with the processes of foreign policy-making but also confront the question of whether the outcome of these processes can be both effective and democratic. We felt this issue critical enough that we have explained it at greater length in terms of what we call the "three dilemmas" of democratic policy-making. For this purpose, we examine the variations in the constitutional and political power of the president and Congress in both domestic and foreign policy formation. We also examine the actual access to foreign policy decision roles and various possible participants, the parts that may be played by congressmen, parties, and interest groups, and the impact of the media and expressions of public opinion.

The rational-actor and bureaucratic models of decision-making are suggested as aids to a clearer understanding of the interaction of all these forces. The utility of these models is demonstrated in five case studies: the Cuban missile crisis of 1962, the Iranian hostage crisis of 1979–81, the process of enacting the anti-ballistic missile (ABM) legislation in the Johnson and Nixon administrations (which largely focuses on the bureaucracy), the Strategic Arms Limitation Treaty or the "defeat" of SALT II in the U.S. Senate (which focuses on executive-legislative relations), and the fate of energy legislation in the Congress.

The recent past suggests that presidential dominance has become a "given" in American foreign policy-making, so our concluding chapter returns to the question: Can policy formulation be both effective and democratic? Drawing on American foreign policy experience we ask: How might events have been altered by enlarged Congressional participation? Would the outcomes in fact have conformed to the democratic expectations of today's reformers?

These are complex issues, and we do not claim to have resolved them. Rather, our goal is more modest: to outline for the introductory student of American government or of American foreign policy the foreign policy-making process and to highlight the problems we believe are the most important. In any such endeavor, particularly a joint one, some arguments are bound to remain somewhat incomplete in the eyes of the specialist. Our problem was somewhat compounded by differing views on what would constitute a "good" foreign policy—and, indeed, on how much of a say Congress should have. Such disagreements have led us to produce balanced arguments on different sides of critical issues—and also to examine the feasibility of proposed reforms regardless of our personal biases.

J.S.
E.M.U.

Contents

ix

7 Balancing the Scales? 217

Notes 241

Suggestions for Further Reading 253

Index 256

Foreign Policy in a Democracy

1

The Three Dilemmas of Democratic Foreign Policy

The United States officially has one president, but he occupies two presidencies.[1] One deals with the domestic political system, the other with the international one. Inherent in that division lies one of the three major dilemmas which the United States, as a democracy and as a superpower, faces as she conducts her foreign policy. This fundamental dilemma might be summed up as *governmental checks and balances versus presidential concentration of power*. In domestic matters, it has always been considered vital to limit presidential power to preserve the constitutional design of American democracy. The nation's historical tradition has been one of fear and suspicion of concentrated power, whether it existed in the governmental or economic area. The possession of power has been equated with its potential abuse, and power was therefore domestically distributed vertically between the federal government and the states, and within the federal government it was separated horizontally among the executive, legislative, and judicial branches.

By contrast, the conduct of foreign policy—whose principal aim is safeguarding the nation's security so that its way of life at home may be preserved and enjoyed—requires a concentration of executive power. In

1

the international, or state, system, in which each state is its own protector and must rely primarily upon its own resources and strength, it is the chief executive who is usually considered the defender of the "national interests." This was as true in the days before democracy, under the rule of the Crown, as it is in contemporary democracies, authoritarian, and totalitarian states. Survival in an essentially anarchical international system whose principal rule is self-help requires a single source of authority so that a state can, if necessary, act speedily, secretly, with continuity of purpose or, when demanded, with flexibility. From the beginning of the modern state system it was taken for granted that legislatures, especially as the democratic representatives of the people, were incapable of the serious conduct of foreign affairs; public opinion was felt to be too ignorant, too impassioned, and too unstable. Parliaments as legislative institutions were by their very nature thought to be incapable of rapid decisions; to pass wise legislation, they were expected to debate at some length and reconcile conflicting interests and viewpoints. In short, the primacy of the executive in foreign policy was essentially a response to the nature of the state system.

Because of the domestic system's requirements to restrain executive power and the state system's need for ample executive power, tension between the two U.S. presidencies is inevitable.[2] On the one hand, if the president is limited sufficiently to protect American democracy the danger is that he might also become so enfeebled that he will not be able to effectively defend the nation's interests. On the other hand, if the president accumulates enough power to act with the necessary authority, dispatch, and secrecy to protect the nation he might become so powerful that he will erode the restraints on his power which were intended to preserve the constitutional nature of the American political system. Thus what is a virtue domestically might become a vice internationally, as the nation falls victim to its democratic organization; and what is a virtue externally might become a vice internally, as the nation loses its democratic soul in seeking to protect its democratic order from foreign threats.

Interestingly enough, this fundamental dilemma of how the United States can preserve a democratic order at home while investing the government and especially the presidency with enough authority to effectively guard the nation's security and welfare was first noted by the English political philosopher, John Locke, who is usually regarded as the theorist whose political philosophy underlies the Declaration of Independence and the Constitution. Locke asserted that man possessed certain natural or inalienable rights which in society would be protected by the election of representatives who, through the legislature, would restrain the executive from abusing these rights and undermining the democratic nature of society. Externally, however, nations continued to live in a "state of nature" with one another, and therefore the executive—which in the conduct of foreign affairs, Locke called the federative power—could not be similarly contained.

> These two powers, executive and federative, though they be really distinct in themselves, yet one comprehending the executive of the municipal laws of the society within itself . . . ; the other the management of the security and interests of the public without. . . . And though this federative power in the well or ill management of it be of great moment to the commonwealth, yet it is much less capable to be directed by antecedent, standing, positive laws than the executive; and so must necessarily be left to the prudence and wisdom of those whose hands it is in, to be managed for the public good.[3]

It was Locke, then, who first distinguished between the two presidencies—the executive and the federative—which are both embodied in one man: the president, situated at the crossroads where the domestic and international systems meet and overlap.

The second, and closely related, dilemma might be summed up as *process versus output*. The American government is supposed to represent the "will of the people." This will is expressed in many different ways: a nationwide election every four years for the president, the only nationally elected figure in the United States; biannual elections for one third of the Senate and the entire House; the ability of those who hold grievances they seek to remedy and aspirations they wish to realize, to organize themselves, express their legitimate interests and, as interest groups, work for them by supporting candidates for office during elections and, in between elections, by bringing their influence to bear at the legislative, executive, and judicial levels of government (both state and federal). Clearly, in domestic policy, the emphasis is on widespread participation of the many different groups and interests in society and government and the reconciliation of these diverse and conflicting interests represented in the bureaucracy, Congress, and interest groups. The preferences of the majority emerge through this political process.

In foreign policy, as in domestic policy, the executive and legislative branches share responsibility and power. This does not, however, necessarily produce the "right" policies. The concern for producing the "correct" foreign policies—or at least not the wrong ones—is certainly understandable, especially in this highly combustible era. President Kennedy once said that foreign policy can kill us, while domestic policies can set us back. This description may be overdrawn. Not all foreign policies are likely to result in nuclear war nor are all domestic policies necessarily salvageable and correctible if mistakes are made. But Kennedy did state an elemental truth hanging over foreign and domestic policies; the former, unlike the latter, may be irreversible and result in the destruction of American society—indeed, much of the world. Kennedy's own estimate in the early 1960s was that 100 million Americans, 100 million Europeans, and 100 million Russians would become casualties in the opening hours of an all-out American-Russian nuclear war. More recent figures have placed U.S. casualties at 140 million and Russian at about 110 million. The margin for error has certainly drastically declined since the United States became a world power.

From the beginning of the cold war there was agreement that foreign policy should therefore be decided differently than domestic policies. Indeed, there was some precedence. In wartime, as from 1941–45, the balance between the president and Congress was virtually suspended and the president given emergency powers for the duration of the conflict; then, after hostilities had ceased, the Congress reasserted itself. Not surprisingly, the concentration of power in the presidency was, therefore, considered the most effective way to conduct the cold war. Partisan rivalry and executive-legislative conflict—the norms in domestic policy—would play havoc with foreign policy. Presidential primacy and congressional and bipartisan support would provide a more effective pattern.

Moreover, the cold war, being neither war nor peace (as usually understood), meant that instead of wielding emergency powers temporarily, to be relinquished once the emergency was over, the president had to exercise these emergency powers on a continuing basis. This was a novel situation. The United States had overnight become the leader of the "free world" with extensive and long-term commitments in many areas of the world; many of the situations it confronted, and could expect to confront, needed speedy decision and action for delay could be costly, and the issues which had to be dealt with were varied and complex. American foreign policy required that the president be given the authority he needed. Only he had the capacity to act quickly and, thanks to the large bureaucracy whose responsibility it was to deal with the world beyond America, he also possessed the expertise. He did, however, need legislative support, for the correct policies were not always the popular ones. Conflicts between the president and Congress and between the two political parties, on the other hand, would undermine such support and were, therefore, intolerable. "A nation which excuses its own failures by the sacred untouchableness of its own habits can excuse itself into complete disaster."[4] The domestic ways of making policy were unfit for making foreign policy.

Successive presidents—with the general support of Congress—expanded the powers of the office to avoid such disaster. After the United States became deeply involved in the Vietnam War, however, it was precisely this growth of presidential power which was held to blame for the war. The "imperial presidency" was now said to be responsible for a policy which had overcommitted the United States and led to a policy of "global policemanship" beyond the capacity of America's "limited power." Vietnam was considered the logical conclusion of this policy. In turn, the imperial presidency was said to be the offspring of the disregard for prescribed procedure. Said Senator J. William Fulbright (D., Ark.), the former chairman of the Senate Foreign Relations Committee:

> Out of a well-intended but misconceived notion of what patriotism and responsibility require in a time of world crisis, Congress has permitted the president to take over the two vital foreign policy powers which the Constitution vested in Congress: the power to initiate war and the Senate's power to consent or withhold consent from significant commitments. . . . So completely have these two powers been taken over by the president that it is no exaggeration to say that . . . the United States has . . . become . . . a presidential dictatorship.[5]

Recent presidents, Fulbright said, had claimed the "unlimited right" to use the armed forces as they saw fit under an inflated interpretation of their commander in chief powers and ignored Congress' authority to declare war.[6] Similarly, the Senate's treaty power had been weakened by: contracting obligations with other nations by executive agreements or declarations; the interpretation of existing treaties in "extravagant and unwarranted ways"; and the revision of treaties by executive agreements after Senate approval of the treaties.[7] Fulbright's charges received widespread agreement at the time.

Within a few years, however, as disillusionment with détente grew, the demands for the weakening or removal of at least some of the restraints placed upon presidential power in the wake of Vietnam grew again since these restraints seemed to be obstacles to the conduct of a more vigorous, assertive foreign policy seemingly required by the continued expansion of Soviet influence, the demands of the developing nations for a new international economic order, and the growing importance of the Persian Gulf-Indian Ocean area for American and Western security and economic viability. The fear now was that the imperial presidency had become the "imperilled presidency," and that if the shift of power from the presidency to the Congress that occurred after Vietnam was not partially reversed, the United States' ability to define and defend its vital security and economic interests might be jeopardized. In short, greater congressional participation in foreign policy was compatible with a more limited American role in the world but this larger legislative involvement, or what the critics called congressional "interference" and "restraint," was not compatible with the enlarged global role that seemed to be the lot of the United States in the 1980s.

The third dilemma follows from the other two: *broad democratic participation versus foreign-policy making by a small elite.* The ethos of the American political system points to the widespread involvement of the many actors involved on a particular issue. Certainly domestic policies follow this practice. The emphasis is on representativeness. In foreign policy, it is on expertise. "Too many cooks spoil the broth" seems to be the adage. Most cooks are assumed to be amateurs. Those who are professionally skilled in foreign affairs—the small number of people to whom foreign affairs are not "furrin"—should be in charge and be the president's advisor. By contrast, the foreign policies of a president who feels he must reflect public opinion, as represented by the polls and Congress, will be short-term and erratic, for the public's mood tends to change rapidly. We are then condemned to "diplomacy by dilettantism," as one expert has called it.[8]

The degree of participation is critical in the two principal models of decision making presented in this book (Chapter 5): bureaucratic/ governmental politics and rational. The first part of the former is so named because the most important domestic policies and virtually all foreign policies are initiated in the executive branch; whether the ideas for the policies are the president's own brainchildren or not, it is the bureaucracy that spells out the details of proposed policies (and later administers them). Governmental refers to the wider participation in the policy process of other actors such as Congress, interest groups, and affected segments of public opinion. And the word politics is included because with so many actors with different views and interests at stake, the only way of arriving at a decision is by negotiations and compromise—that is, "politics." If the necessary accommodations are attained, most of the participants will gain something, although most likely not all they wanted. This is, then, considered a satisfactory solution even though the policy output may not be the best one in terms of solving a particular problem. There clearly is no such thing as a correct policy. The issue is how to reconcile conflicting interpretations of what the correct policy ought to be. The result of the compromises made is bound to be a watered down version of what rationally would be the best policy solution.

The rational model refers to precisely that—the best solution to a particular problem. The focus, instead of being on the internal dynamics of the policy process which seeks to give everyone "a piece of the action," is on the specific issue at hand and the most appropriate way of enhancing the value or goal which the policy-makers select. Which way can they attain such a goal, for example, the nation's security or welfare? Of the several possible alternative means usually available, which option is the most likely to achieve this end? The search is for a successful policy, not necessarily a popular one; the emphasis is on the solution to the problem, not the attempt to satisfy the many players involved, which all too often results in a policy no participant fully favors.

In our scheme, the bureaucratic/governmental politics model best explains the domestic policy process while the rational actor model is most useful in explaining foreign policy crisis situations. Our other two policies, noncrisis security policies and intermestic policies, which are a mixture of inter(national) and (do)mestic policies, are also best understood by the bureaucratic/governmental politics model. While rational policy stands largely by itself, the other policies are part of a continuum.

Crisis policy, then, is made by the few deciding rationally; other policies by the many arriving at a decision politically. The more a policy resembles domestic policy, the larger the number of actors and the more intense the bargaining is likely to be. At the cost of some repetition, let us be clear about the distinction. Crisis policy focuses on the external situation confronting the nation and on finding a correct response in the sense that after a full examination of the alternative ways in which the national security or welfare can be protected in the situation at hand, the most effective means which will achieve that goal at the least possible cost is chosen. Noncrisis security and other policies, by contrast, focus on the preferences of the many participating actors in the bureaucracy and legislature, their varying and differing policy preferences and purposes, the negotiations among them, and the policy "outcomes" that occur as a result of the compromises struck. In short, the latter emphasizes the dynamics of the decision-making process and its central feature, the constant bargaining and trade-offs arranged among the players. It ought to be added that crisis policy, decided quickly by a few men at the pinnacle of the executive branch, resembles policies made by authoritarian regimes while noncrisis policy, characterized by the widespread participation of the bureaucracy and Congress over a fairly lengthy time period, tends to be highly democratic.

Our third dilemma for most security policies has been summed up as follows:

> A democratic government must accomplish two tasks: On the one hand, it must pursue policies which maximize the chances for success; on the other hand, it must secure the approval of its people for these foreign policies. . . . The necessity to perform these tasks simultaneously faces a democratic government with a dilemma; for the conditions under which popular support can be obtained for a foreign policy are not necessarily identical with the conditions under which such a policy can be successfully pursued. A popular foreign policy is not necessarily a good one.[9]

TABLE 1-1

Rational Decision-Making	Bureaucratic/Governmental Politics		
Crisis Policies	Noncrisis Security Policies	Intermestic Policies	Domestic Policies

Increasing number of actors and bargaining involved
in the policy-making process

The Growth of Presidential Primacy

In an effort to strike a balance between the demands of the state system—or what Paul Seabury has called the "intrinsic authoritarian necessities of foreign affairs"[10]—and the democratic needs of the internal order, the framers of the U.S. Constitution vested exclusive responsibility for the conduct of foreign policy in the federal government and then divided its authority in this field, as in the domestic, between the president and Congress. The president could receive and send ambassadors—that is, deal with representatives of foreign powers—but the Senate had to give its consent to treaties by a two-thirds vote and confirm top diplomatic, military, and political appointments. The president was appointed commander in chief of the armed forces, but only Congress was empowered to declare war, appropriate funds for the maintenance of military forces, and regulate commerce with other nations. It could also investigate the operations of the various executive departments that participated in the formulation and implementation of the foreign policy of the United States.

Thus, while this sharing of the foreign policy power by separate institutions was to ensure a check on presidential power, the president clearly was constitutionally the nation's chief diplomat and commander in chief. But a number of changes in the social and economic environment increasingly upset the balance between the executive and legislative branches and shifted power toward the president. Most of these new conditions have affected the conduct of both foreign and domestic affairs in all nations, but particularly in those of the West. First, and perhaps most fundamental, is the general growth of Big Government—which has usually meant "executive government." Running a highly urbanized, complex, industrial society has required big government and large bureaucracies to serve its manifold needs. The mass vote and the mobilization of new groups and classes into the political process have multiplied demands upon government for services ranging from unending economic growth, high employment, subsidies of all types, stabilization of the economy, and redistributing power, status, and money to create a more equitable society, protection of the environment, to such specifics as abortion, control of hospital costs, reducing violence in the streets, and elimination of hazardous toys. The list is endless.

Indeed, it was the growth of the role of the government in the domestic economy, as much as any international event, which, in the United States, marked the sharp shift in the balance between the president and the Congress. The Great Depression of the 1930s focused people's attention on Washington. The traditional forces of the marketplace had failed to readjust themselves to an era of great ecomonic crisis and the administration of Franklin D. Roosevelt, which began in 1933, committed the national government to direct intervention in the economy on a massive scale. Even during the earlier pre-World War I administration of Woodrow Wilson, known for his liberal economic policies (which he called the "New Freedom"), total federal expenditures constituted less than 2 percent of the gross national product—or GNP—the value of all goods and services produced in the country. Half of those expenditures went for defense. By the 1930s, the figure for total spending rose to 7.7 percent, most of which (4.9 percent) was domestically oriented. The federal share of the GNP has continued to rise so that it now approaches 25 percent. This great increase in federal spending gave broad new responsibilities to the national government—and to the president who proposes and (at least indirectly) administers the programs. And presidents have not shied away from claiming credit for these programs, thus enhancing their power even further.

Presidents and prime ministers in the relatively open societies of the West, as leaders of political parties from whom the electorate expects the satisfaction of certain demands, have become the central figures; as heads of their party and government, they draw up the social and economic programs, as well as foreign policies, to be submitted to the legislature, and it becomes their responsibility to shepherd bills through Congress or Parliament. Legislatures do not as a matter of fact act on their own. They wait for the executive to submit his program. And it is upon this record of achievement that the parties and their leaders run in the next election and seek to renew their mandate to govern.

Even nations that are neither democratic nor economically developed share this global trend toward executive government. States that, like the Soviet Union, do not possess a constitutional tradition may have a legislature, but such a body has no independent status and power. The executive has complete authority and governs unchallenged. In the new, ex-colonial, economically underdeveloped countries, too, power is centralized in the executive to try and hold the new fragmentary nation together and organize its human and material resources for modernization. One-party governments and military regimes exist throughout the Third World; parliamentary bodies, with few exceptions, are in decay, if they still survive. Executive dominance, whether justified by efficiency, ideology, or impatience, has everywhere emerged as the way to ensure results.

In the case of the United States another obvious fact needs to be noted in this regard. The president is nationally elected, and he, more than any other figure, represents the national mood and is the spokesman for the nation's interests, domestic and foreign. Congress, on the other hand, represents local interests; its representatives in the House and "ambassadors from the states" in the Senate respond mainly to their constituents' interests. By contrast, in Great Britain elections are organized around the parties and their national platforms. One votes for a member of Parliament because he represents one of the parties whose leader, if the party wins, becomes prime minister. But, unlike in Britain, the U.S. chief executive is also chief of state. He is more than a partisan leader and chief of government. In short, when he occupies the office of the presidency, he becomes the symbol of national unity and can thus draw upon most citizens' patriotism and loyalty. In England, the monarch is chief of state and stands above politics and differences over public policy, while the prime minister is chief of government. Therefore a United States citizen may often feel politically schizophrenic, hating and loving the president at one and the same time (as a partisan and American). In England, the citizen can hate the prime minister and still love, respect, and feel patriotic about his king or queen, although a great first minister of the Crown such as Churchill may elicit much the same feelings. Not surprisingly, though, a president combining these two functions is constantly in the limelight and has a large corps of media correspondents assigned to him.

Only the president can instantly communicate with the people. Television, especially, has done much to expand the president's powers, but even in the days before the widespread use of radio, Theodore Roosevelt referred to the White House as a "bully pulpit." This is all the more true today when the people look toward the president for everything from national defense to social justice. Harry Truman once said that the president is the lobbyist for all the people. As chief of state, whether receiving a distinguished foreign dignitary or visiting other nations, he is covered by the press and television cameras—and therefore he can remain first in his nation's eyes, if not always in its heart. All in all, foreign policy, with its wars, crises, and glamor, magnifies the public's awareness of the president's leading role and its need for his leadership.

Since World War II and the advent of the atomic era, the president's foreign policy role has reinforced his central role in government to the point where he is no longer merely the "first among equals"; during the cold war he became, as one writer has said of the English prime minister, the "sun around which planets revolve."[11] The Constitution gave the presidency specific grants of authority with a great potential for expansion. These grants, such as that of commander in chief, were written in such a way that they were open to future interpretations as circumstances changed. In a real sense, what was not said in the Constitution "proved ultimately more important than what was."[12] Often called the Constitution's "great silences," they gave presidents—especially strong presidents such as Lincoln, the two Roosevelts, Truman, Kennedy, Johnson, and Nixon—freedom to do what they thought needed to be done in unprecedented circumstances on behalf of the nation's interests as they defined these, and to test the powers and limits of the office.

There were, to put it simply, "missing powers" in the Constitution. For example, the Constitution did not say where the powers to recognize other states or to proclaim neutrality were located. If the president and

Senate must cooperate in the negotiation and ratification of a treaty, did they both have to agree also when terminating a treaty? If Congress must declare war, does it also make peace? Who proclaims neutrality, the president because he is commander in chief, or Congress because of its authority to declare war and regulate commerce? One frequent manner of determining who exercises these powers has been to assume that the foreign affairs powers explicitly granted imply other powers: The president's power to appoint and receive ambassadors, for example, implies the power to recognize or withhold recognition from other states. The "implied powers" doctrine, however, leaves much room for struggles between the executive and legislative branches for control of the conduct of foreign affairs—as the former enhanced its powers, especially during this century. As Louis Henkin has noted, the powers specifically allocated to the president are so few that "a stranger reading the Constitution would get little inkling of such large presidential authority, for the powers explicitly vested in him are few and seem modest, far fewer and more modest, than those bestowed upon Congress.[13] . . . It seems incredible that these few meager grants support the most powerful office in the world and the multivaried, wide-flung web-work of foreign activity of the most powerful nation in the world."[14] One obvious reason for this is that the Founding Fathers did not foresee the United States soon playing an active and major role in international politics. In his Farewell Address, President Washington counseled his countrymen to take advantage of America's "detached and distant situation" from Europe and stay isolated from the "toils of European ambition, Rivalship, Interest, Humor or Caprice."[15]

Thus we return to our question: Can a democratic American domestic order be reconciled with an executive powerful enough to safeguard the nation's security so that it can continue to enjoy its way of life? Former Senator Fulbright admitted he was a pessimist. "I for one am fairly well convinced that neither constitutional government nor democratic freedoms can survive indefinitely in a country chronically at war [presumably the cold war], as America has been for the last three decades. Sooner or later, war will lead to dictatorship."[16] Has post-World War II American foreign policy—the means to protect the security of American democracy—subverted the very aims it was intended to serve? Let us take a closer look at the basic types of policies and the principal characteristics of each corresponding foreign policy process. It is our contention that there are three different types of foreign policies and that each is made in a different way.

Security, Crisis, and Intermestic Policies

All states need a foreign policy because they all exist in an essentially anarchical world in which each state lives in fear and must seek its own security.[17] There is no world government which protects the individual states. Each must guard itself in a system in which states tend to view each other as potential adversaries rather than friends. As in the proverbial town of the "old West" where there was no "law and order," men lived in fear of one another and wore guns to protect themselves against those who might want to rob them, take away their land, or who were just "plain ornery" and mean. State A might look at its neighbor B and see it is arming itself. Is B strengthening itself to deter a possible attack (a defensive action), or is it preparing to attack (an offensive action)? B might declare that its intentions are peaceful and that it is increasing its military power only to ensure that A or other states will not attack it. But why should A believe that statement? Once B's capabilities have grown, he may attack; the declaration of peaceful intent may have been deceitful. Or, even if B had been sincere about its defensive intentions earlier, he can, after all, change his mind once he realizes his improved power position.

The point of this simple analogy is that, in general, states distrust one another. Even when one state extends the hand of friendship, the other wonders why. Is he trying to deceive him and put him off his guard in order to strike later when he is relaxed? Where their security is concerned, if not their survival, states are very cautious and careful. No one guarantees them either; each is its own guardian. States, therefore, rarely take chances. The stakes are too high. The basic rule is "protect yourself." This is fundamental since security is regarded as the prerequisite for enjoying a nation's way of life. Forgetting this basic rule is to risk endangering one's territorial integrity and political independence.

The principal mechanism to ensure one's safety is in fact the balance of power. If one state matches another state in strength, neither is likely to attack the other; but an imbalance may entice the stronger one to attack. Consequently, in the state system, in which each state sees an increase in power and security for another state as a loss of power and security for itself—a loss which it regards as unacceptable—preserving the balance of power constitutes the heart of its foreign policy. American foreign policy since World War II has been largely concerned with the central balance with its principal adversary, the Soviet Union, and a series of regional balances in Europe, Asia, the Middle East, and, since the 1970s, sub-Sahara Africa. Thus the United States is involved in virtually every area of the world with many different nations as adversaries, allies, and underdeveloped countries. Military power—the threat and the actual use of force—have played a major deterrent and coercive role in this foreign policy, although other instruments such as economic aid to strengthen an ally or friend have also been widely used.

While American foreign policy is thus primarily concerned with assuring the nation's security, we refer to the more specific policies which seek to do this as security policies. This includes (but is not limited to) such policy areas as the defense budget (procurement and deployment of arms and men), arms control, limited war, alliances, arms transfers to allies and other countries, economic and technical aid, and intelligence operations against other states. Most of these policies are continuing ones because they involve long-run interests. The United States, as one of the world's two nuclear superpowers, has an additional interest in not only balancing Soviet military strength, but in seeking to reduce the intensity of the arms competition and stabilize the balance in an environment of rapid technological innovation in weaponry. Foreign aid programs and arms transfers go on from year to year, although the recipients and the amounts they receive may change. Limited wars obviously—and fortunately—are not an everyday concern, but when they have occurred, as in Korea and Vietnam, the fighting has gone on for periods of three to eight years and they have consequently required major commitments of men, arms, and money.

Crisis policies, by contrast, are distinguished by their relative infrequency and their short duration. But they make up for their lack of numbers by the utter seriousness and great danger when they do happen. Frequently characterized by surprise, crisis policies are even more prominently featured by the perceived threat to a nation's vital interests and the lack of time the policy-makers feel they have to deal with it. If they do not act quickly, the crisis situation, which in all probability took them by surprise and is in any case seen by them as endangering the country's fundamental security, will go against them. In these circumstances, the most critical element of a crisis is that the possibility of the threat of force or actual use of violence—which underlies much of traditional international politics—is very high. In short, the likelihood of war erupting suddenly becomes a real danger. Even if in the case of a Soviet-American crisis, which most crises in which the United States has been involved since World War II have been, the initial clash is at the level of threats or low levels of force, the possibility of escalation to a nuclear confrontation is always present. The art of crisis management is, therefore, defending the interests threatened (usually by invoking the threat of force) while simultaneously avoiding nuclear war.[18]

If these two policies comprise what is sometimes today called the "old" international politics, intermestic policies constitute the "new" global politics. The "new" foreign policy revolves around economics, specifically the issue of prosperity. Earlier, we already noted that the major domestic cause for governmental growth, and especially the power of the presidency and executive branch, has been the increasing demand by citizens for more and more services. Governments all over the world, especially in democratic states where the electorate can hold its representatives accountable if they do not respond to its demands, are held responsible for the welfare of their peoples and for satisfying their ever higher expectations. This "welfare state" must, therefore, concern itself with economic growth rates, creation of jobs, higher incomes, and social programs for the disadvantaged. If political leaders do not want to lose office, their concern with social services is at least as great as with the military services. Security issues, except in moments of crisis, rarely touch the mass of the electorate personally, even if they are aware of important foreign policy events from watching the television news or reading the newspaper. But employment, salaries, and prices affect their pocketbooks. Bread-and-butter issues arouse them quickly, certainly in time for the next election.

The problem is that, increasingly, nations do not have the natural resources or industrial/agricultural capacity to ensure their own prosperity. They must import raw materials, manufactured goods, and food items. Nations, and especially their economies, are thus increasingly a part of an interdependent world. Even a government like that of the United States, a country possessing many of the resources it needs, an enormous industry, and productive agriculture, no longer controls its economic destiny. Ever since 1973 and the quadrupling of oil prices from $3 a barrel to $12 a barrel by the Organization of Petroleum Exporting Countries (OPEC), it has become clear that the economic prosperity of the United States depends on decisions made overseas. America's welfare can be undermined if, for example, a less developed country possessing a vital resource such as oil withholds that resource or dramatically raises the price. OPEC's 1973 price increase has lowered America's living standards (as the same amount of money must be stretched for the higher cost of heating, air conditioning, transportation, and oil-based products from clothes to records), increased inflation, precipitated the worst recession since the 1930s, made it more difficult to resume a rapid rate of economic growth, and posed a danger to democracy's social peace and political stability which had always been based largely on a growing economic "pie" and the expectation of all social groups for increased prosperity.

The increasing vulnerability of the United States to disruptions or reductions in oil production and sizable price increases was clearly shown after the Shah's fall in Iran in early 1979. Even though other oil-producing countries made up for the loss of Iranian oil (about half of which was later restored), the continued increase in the world demand for oil meant that production was barely enough to keep up with the demand. Indeed, as some of the Arab sheiks watched what happened to the Shah, they became convinced that he was overthrown because he had too rapidly tried to modernize his society and had thereby created immense social dislocation and instability which even his despotic role could not control. The lesson seemed to be the slower development of their societies; this in turn required less—not more—oil production since they did not need to earn ever higher incomes.

The relationship of supply and demand thus became "tight." Moreover, it proved enormously profitable. The world could not do without oil. Neither coal, nuclear, or solar energy, nor enormous non-OPEC oil supplies, were available to substitute for or supplement OPEC's oil. Countries, especially the Western industrial countries (including Japan), scrambled for the available oil, driving prices ever upward. In just over a year after the Shah's collapse, oil prices doubled from approximately $15 a barrel to over $30. By mid-1980 they stood close to $35 a barrel. The United States by the beginning of the new decade imported 45 percent of its oil. Only twenty years earlier it had been an oil exporter. In 1979 it paid out about $60 billion to pay for oil imports; the 1980 figure was expected to be nearer $90 billion. If the country is not to go bankrupt, it has to earn the money to pay for this oil, an increasingly impossible task reflected by the growing U.S. trade deficits. No wonder that the dollar, the medium for paying the oil-producing states, was flooding the international market, creating a glut of dollars and declining in value.

Domestic affairs thus became deeply involved in foreign affairs. The oil issue erased the distinction between domestic and foreign policies. Caught up in both, it could best be characterized as "intermestic."[19] Above all, it meant that a nation no longer fully controlled its own economic destiny; what Washington decided to do about inflation or recession might be less important than what Saudi Arabia decided. Oil was not the only symptom of this increasingly interdependent world in which economic currents swept across frontiers; there were other scarce raw materials, as well as such issues as population, food, and pollution. In a world of underdeveloped countries with a rapidly growing population whose feeding depends on an oil-based, high technology domestic farming, plus imports from the West in years of shortages, and of repeated large Soviet demands for grain, food has also become intertwined with foreign policy. American food exports now earn much of the money needed to pay for OPEC oil; it can also be used to advance political purposes (for instance, to bolster détente with Russia or provide Egypt with an incentive to orient her foreign policy toward the United States), and, in cases of starvation, for humanitarian aims. As American consumers compete for food with Indians and Russians, United States food prices, already raised by the higher price of oil, rise even further. In the interdependent world of the new international politics, disruptions of supplies, major price changes, and unexpected demands for relatively limited goods can dislocate entire economies, change life-styles, and affect tens of millions of people in their daily lives. Whereas in the old international politics, the emphasis was on the independence of states, their concern with security, and their tendency to view one another as rivals, on these bread-and-butter issues states presumably share a larger degree of common interest. If each is to prosper, they need to cooperate; they either prosper together or are hurt together.

Policies and Stakes

A key element in any situation in which any of these policies may be invoked is how the various actors involved in decision making perceive the consequences of their actions. The differences between foreign and domestic policy-making are due, at least in part, to the different stakes involved and how the actors perceive them. In domestic policy-making, participants can often differentiate between the "winners" and the "losers." In foreign policy-making, on the other hand, the entire nation is usually seen as either "winning" or "losing." Most foreign policy decisions do not result with one group in the population gaining at the expense of others.* In domestic policy, the most clear-cut example of the winners-losers dichotomy may be the antipoverty program. This program is specifically designed to provide aid to an identifiable group in the population (the poor), who are classified as "losers" by such standards as income or housing. The poor are viewed as a "have-not" group, and the debate surrounding the antipoverty program is marked by arguments about what the government should do to aid disadvantaged groups at the expense (in taxes or prerogatives) of the "haves" in society—those people who have more or less "made it" in society. The goal, then, is to turn some of the "losers" into "winners."

On the traditional questions of foreign policy, however, decisions are not generally viewed in terms of "winners" against "losers." Foreign policy decisions are more frequently viewed in terms of the entire country (rather than any particular group in the population) winning or losing. This is most noticeable when a country goes to war or is involved in a crisis. The winners and losers are the nations (or alliances) involved, not specific groups like the oil companies, the farmers, or the poor. Tensions within the country on domestic legislation are put aside as the population "rallies around the flag" in support of the president's actions as commander in chief.[20] Simply stated, the stakes are very different in foreign and domestic politics.

In domestic politics, there are a multitude of interest groups concerned with the decisions of government and attempting to influence them. Each group wants to be a winner rather than a loser or a nonwinner. Even though the president initiates more domestic legislation than does Congress, the chief executive's hands are tied to a much greater extent in domestic politics than in foreign politics. Groups and individuals looking out for their own interests attempt to influence Congress on how money

---

*Not everybody sees foreign policy in this way. Notably, radical critics (on both the left and the right) do see foreign policy decisions as involving domestic winners and losers. Critics on the left, for example, may view foreign-policy decision-making as a conflict between capitalists and the workers (just as they do in domestic politics).

should be spent, which tax loopholes should be closed or left untouched, and how business and labor should be regulated. The process of raising revenue and spending it for domestic programs is marked by a relatively high degree of conflict among the groups contending for special benefits. The mediating actors in domestic politics are Congress and the executive departments that draw up the federal budget. To some extent, the very large scope of the demands made can also serve to moderate these demands made by interest groups. The president simply cannot spend his time listening to all of these demands. He is willing in most cases to give up a large part of his power to Congress.

All of these conflicts and more are found on intermestic issues. In addition to the aforementioned actors on domestic policy, we find the president trying to balance a whole series of conflicting interests: the vitality of the American economy, the coherence of American policy, and the various pressures from multinational companies who often have divided loyalties. The president will have to balance the American demand for oil against the traditional policy of providing strong support for Israel. Oil companies, as well as other businesses operating abroad, find themselves active participants in the intermestic policy process. To meet their goal of making as large a profit as possible, they might pursue policies (such as advocating a tilt in Middle Eastern policy toward the Arabs) which might be at odds with that of official United States policy.

There are, then, so many different actors, foreign and domestic, and the issues involved may be vital to the nation's security and certainly to its economic well-being. International politics and economics, as well as intermestic policies, clearly involve very high stakes. There are "winners," "losers," and sometimes "nonwinners" as well—groups which might not be affected by a particular change in policy through careful strategic planning (someone who has shifted from oil to natural gas for home heating or air conditioning) or simple happenstance. Indeed, we find not only "winners" and "losers" but also many "high rollers"—actors willing to take major risks, such as the oil-producing nations which have steadily raised their prices since 1973 in the belief that their strategic position is superior. What makes intermestic politics so complicated is that it encompasses not only the divisions we find on domestic policies, but also the "we-they" conflicts of foreign policy.

The situation is quite different with crisis and, to a large extent, security policies. Since foreign policy decisions are not perceived either by the public or by the decision-makers as involving methods of "dividing up the spoils," the conflict over decisions made will involve a much smaller circle of actors. Interest groups become mobilized only when they see the potential to "win" something for themselves, but on most foreign policy issues either the entire country wins or the country loses. This is not to deny that some citizens or groups may differ vastly on foreign policy questions from other citizens or groups. But, significantly, each group views its own position as the one which is in the "national" (or even "international") interest.

The basic distinction, then, between conflicts over domestic and over foreign affairs concerns the way participants view the stakes of the policy process. On most domestic policies, including intermestic policies, there are more likely to be winners and nonwinners than winners and losers. These policies, also called "distributive" policies, are "perceived to confer direct benefits upon one or more groups [but are] determined with little or no conflict over the passage of the legislation but only over the size and specific distribution of the shares."[21] On crisis decisions, however, the whole nation either wins or loses, and the nature of the conflict on such policies will be quite different. Conflict on these crisis decisions is most likely to resemble the less frequent but loudly argued cases of domestic policies which propose to redistribute income from the "haves" in society to the "have-nots," where again we see a clash between inevitable winners and losers. Security policies involve many actors who may have diverse goals and different perceptions of the stakes involved. Crisis decisions, on the other hand, involve only a small number of actors, and the stakes involved are generally quite clear. Indeed, the high stakes involved in crisis decisions are a key reason why the president is the dominant actor in this area: The president is the only actor in the American political system capable of the swift and decisive action required in crises.

Characteristics of Foreign-Policy Decision-Making

The principal characteristics of decision making in the foreign policy sphere may be summed up as follows:

1. The actors and processes of foreign-policy decision-making differ for each of the three types of foreign policy decisions: crisis decisions, security decisions, and intermestic policy decisions.

    Crisis decisions, as noted, usually involve an element of surprise. The leaders have not been anticipating a threat from a foreign power; when the threat does occur, they perceive the need for a quick response lest the situation deteriorate to the detriment of the nation's security, and violence might ensue. For this reason, crisis decisions are made by the small number of actors at the very top of the executive "policy-making machine."

    Security decisions, on the other hand, involve long-run policies. Most security policies, although formulated by the president and the various foreign policy bureaucracies, involve money and thus require congressional approval. Because many actors must participate, these policies may require lengthy deliberation. Furthermore, because security policies express continuing goals and commitments, they tend to involve stable sets of actors.

Intermestic decisions may involve both short-term and long-term considerations. Energy, for example, is an issue of enduring importance but it may also be subject to short-run factors such as an oil embargo or temporary loss of supplies. These issues affect both relations among nations and politics within nations. Intermestic issues, therefore, mobilize all the actors that domestic policies usually do: the executive agencies whose jurisdiction is basically domestic, Congress, interest groups, and public opinion. Consequently, the State Department, articulating the "national interest," will hardly be heard above the din of voices of the Departments of Treasury, Agriculture, Labor, and Commerce, their respective congressional committees, and interest groups in each of these and other policy areas. All these actors feel expert in these areas, possess major stakes and can articulate their viewpoints, and usually have a good deal of clout since they represent specific, well-organized and well-financed groups who normally represent millions of voters.

2. The foreign policy elite is a relatively small group located in the executive branch, primarily the political leadership and the professional officers of the principal foreign policy bureaucracies. More specifically, this includes the president (politically elected), special assistants on National Security Affairs, secretaries, under secretaries and assistant secretaries (political appointees), as well as senior professional officers of both the Departments of State and Defense and the Central Intelligence Agency. On a secondary level, there are the upper ranks of the Arms Control and Disarmament Agency, the International Communication Agency, and the Agency for International Development, as well as other departments and agencies that have an intermittent interest in specific foreign policy issues, such as the Department of the Treasury's interest in monetary policy or the Department of Agriculture's desire to export food products.

3. Most noncrisis foreign policy decisions are arrived at through bureaucratic politics. Different bureaucracies have different perspectives and training for their professional staffs, a need to believe in and justify their tasks, and an understandable need to enhance their prestige, budgets, and influence—the more so if they are convinced of the importance of their contribution to the nation's security and well-being. The different departments and agencies, in short, may see the same problem differently, or even focus on different parts of the same problem and, therefore, come up with varying and conflicting policy recommendations. The result, on the one hand, is bureaucratic conflict; on the other hand, the need to make a decision produces a "strain toward agreement or consensus."[22] Policy, therefore, results from a process of bargaining and compromising. This is particularly the case

on intermestic issues, where even more diverse interests are involved than we find for security policy or most domestic issues. This multiplicity of actors, many of them outside of the executive branch, makes bargaining particularly difficult—and there is no guarantee that a satisfactory compromise will be reached. Stalemate remains a strong possibility.

4. The central and key figure in the foreign policy process is the president. Although noncrisis policy is largely the product of bureaucratic conflict, this does not mean—as models of bureaucratic struggle often imply—that the president is merely one player among many, one chief among many departmental chiefs. He is more than merely a first among equals; he is by far the most important player.[23] He, after all, appoints the chiefs; presumably to a large degree they reflect his values and owe him, as well as their departments, a degree of loyalty. They can be fired if they no longer serve the president's purposes. He can also "stack the deck" by assigning a policy to a particular chief and department or set of men. If he selects "hawks" to investigate whether to intervene militarily in Vietnam, as Kennedy did, he is likely to receive a report favoring intervention; had he chosen "doves" he would in all probability have gotten back quite a different answer.

Moreover, many problems require the consideration of so many political, economic, social, and psychological elements that nowhere short of the presidential level can these factors really be balanced off against one another and integrated into an overall policy. But perhaps the most important factor—in an era in which presidents have grown increasingly fond of being their own secretaries of state—is that presidents will seize for themselves specific areas of policy (for instance, arms control) or policies (for instance, negotiating an end to the war in Vietnam). "The ability of bureaucracies to independently establish policies is a function of presidential attention. Presidential attention is a function of presidential values. The chief executive involves himself in those areas which he determines to be important."[24] Bureaucratic power is thus to a large degree a function of presidential—and, even further, congressional and public—inattention. In practice this means bureaucracy plays its largest role in routine day-to-day matters, its smallest during crisis periods.

The comparative presidential ability to gain legislative support for his foreign as distinct from his domestic policy has been summed up by one leading scholar of American politics as follows:

The president's normal problem with domestic policy is to get congressional support for the programs he prefers. In foreign affairs, in contrast, he can almost always get support for policies that he believes will protect the nation—but his problem is to find a viable policy. . . .

In the realm of foreign policy there has not been a single major issue on which presidents, when they were serious and determined, have failed. The list of their victories is impressive: entry into the United Nations, the Marshall Plan, NATO, the Truman Doctrine, the decisions to stay out of Indochina in 1954 and to intervene in Vietnam in the 1960s, aid to Poland and Yugoslavia, the test-ban treaty, and many more. Serious setbacks to the president in controlling foreign policy are extraordinary and unusual.[25]

On intermestic policies, not surprisingly, the president's ability to initiate, lead, and maneuver will, as in domestic policies in general, be more constrained than on security issues. As one writer, referring to the growth of intermestic issues which he calls nondefense issues, has said:

> . . . there is likely to be an increasing emphasis on nondefense foreign policy issues, most of which will have a great impact on domestic politics and great attraction for domestic interest groups. Problems with the monetary system, trade deficits and surpluses, energy policy, and the import or export of things such as inflation, unemployment, technology, and pollution will consume more and more of the foreign policy effort. This will occur . . . because these nondefense issues will have a larger absolute impact on American society. . . . As post-Vietnam foreign policy becomes more oriented to nonsecurity affairs, the president's choices will become more constrained, on the one hand, by independent foreign actors he will not be able to outmaneuver, such as economic institutions and foreign governments' economic policies, and on the other hand, by the fact that his decisions will have real domestic impact. . . . Indeed, the seamlessness of the distinction between foreign economic and domestic economic policy may simply extend the president's weakness in domestic policy to foreign policy as well.[26]

5. The Congress has been traditionally supportive of the president in foreign policy. Congressmen to a large extent felt a lack of familiarity and sense of incompetence on foreign affairs. Viewing them as esoteric matters beyond their personal experience, in contrast to farm or labor problems, confronted with expert civilian and military witnesses at committee hearings, they usually tend to subordinate their own presumed expertise—political judgment of the feasibility and acceptability of administration policies—to that of the president and his phalanx of bureaucratic help.

But since Vietnam, Congress has become more assertive and less willing to accept presidential dominance on foreign policy. There has been a renewed concern for the establishment of a balance of power between the president and Congress in policy-making, although this reassertion of congressional power does not mean that the legislature has become an equal partner with the president. While more members of the Congress are more interested in foreign policy today than at any time in recent history, they are still a substantial minority within the Congress. Most legislators are primarily concerned with domestic policies—and with their own reelection campaigns. Foreign policy questions are not salient to most voters, so members of Congress tend to downplay their importance and devote their time to issues and services which are more rewarding. Thus, only a minority of the legislators are strongly concerned about foreign policy and even they still are supportive of the president in crisis situations. There are more challenges than before on security decisions, but the greatest congressional involvement is found on intermestic policies. These issues (energy, trade) have great impacts on the day-to-day lives of the people in members' districts and the stakes are perceived as very high. Each member sees himself as the only protector of his district's interests and the key intermestic policy battles are fought in the legislature where presidential programs are often held hostage and do not always escape alive. The regional and economic controversies surrounding intermestic politics are clearly reflected in the localism of Congress and its decentralized (many say parochial) system of committees and subcommittees.

6. Interest group representation, articulation, and influence, while pervasive in domestic politics, are not nearly as extensive or intense in the traditional area of foreign policy concerned with security issues. In this area interest groups tend to lack the interest, experience, and, above all, the knowledge they possess on domestic issues. Nonetheless, ethnic groups in a nation of immigrants have in the past often pressed for policies favorable to the former mother country; now that Germany and Italy are allies instead of enemies, however, the principal ethnic group with influence is the Jewish community, which has lobbied very successfully for American diplomatic, economic, and military support for Israel. In contrast, as already suggested, on intermestic issues so many groups have interests in the outcome of policies and see the stakes as so high that these groups may control much of the policy process. Business, agricultural, shipping interests, and labor organizations have a natural interest in trade, foreign investment, and tariff issues. Virtually nobody fails to perceive a critical interest in energy policy (Chapter 6).

7. The public has, like the Congress, largely been supportive of the president's conduct of foreign policy, particularly before Vietnam. One reason is that most Americans simply are poorly informed and uninterested in foreign policy issues. Their knowledge and experience, like that of most senators and representatives, relate to affairs nearer home, such as family and professional life; the political opinions they do hold are more likely to be about national politics. At best, policy-makers may sense a general mood, which may set broad limits on what they regard as feasible and permissible, but they do not receive specific operational cues. In general, it would be more accurate to say that public opinion on foreign policy is a response to the policy-makers' decisions and to public presentation of the issues. On intermestic issues, however, much of the public does not make a clear-cut

distinction between domestic and foreign policy considerations. Thus, these issues can easily become a source of great controversy since citizens may expect that domestic political factors will determine how to resolve questions such as the state of the economy and the need to allocate scarce energy supplies. The public is less supportive of the president during times of domestic hardship, for they expect him to provide immediate relief for these sorts of pocketbook problems and display little patience when he cannot do so.

8. The role of parties in foreign policy has been defined in terms quite different from those applied to domestic policy by politicians themselves, as well as by journalists and scholars. Largely stirred by the memory of the defeat of the Versailles treaty following World War I in the conflict between a Democratic president and a Republican Senate, the post-World War II assumption was partisanship and the usual type of political considerations, it was held, had no place in the conduct of foreign affairs. The national interest was to be placed ahead of party interest. In protecting the nation against external threats the president deserved the support of both parties. "Bipartisanship" became the new slogan and the patriotic thing to do; partisanship was to be confined strictly to domestic affairs. Executive-legislative hostility and party controversy over foreign policy might undermine the stability and continuity of U.S. policy, make it impossible to speak with one national voice in world affairs, and erode the nation's credibility in its dealing with friends and foes.

Support for bipartisanship has not always been forthcoming. In the era since Vietnam, attacks on the idea of bipartisanship itself have been particularly sharp; these challenges were made by party leaders in the Congress and thus represented major breaks with the past. Throughout the era, however, there coexisted deep divisions within the parties on foreign policy. Vietnam, more than any other issue, was responsible for these divisions. The growth of interest group strength has further weakened the American parties. Even as the parties have become more divided over security questions, they can no longer rally large numbers of supporters in the electorate behind their programs. The intermestic issue of trade, which was traditionally a highly partisan issue (with Democrats supporting lower tariffs and Republicans seeking industry protection) and energy have cut across party lines; on these issues, regional and economic interests predominate over parties. But, for all of its weaknesses, the party system is still viewed by many as the most coherent way of sorting out a complex set of issues to present to the electorate in the quest for democratic control of policy making on both the domestic and foreign fronts.

To sum up: All three types of policies revolve around the central question of democratic decision-making on foreign policy: How much participation, and by which actors, do we want or can we tolerate? The larger the number of participants involved in making decisions, the more difficult it will be to reach a consensus on what ought to be done and the longer it will take to reach a decision. In a crisis, such widespread participation may incapacitate an entire government and may also lead (as it almost did in the Cuban missile crisis) to public pressure to adopt policies which might have plunged the world into a nuclear war. In such situations presidents feel that they ought to be free of restraints from the Congress, political parties, interest groups, the press, and even public opinion. Was democracy designed for domestic policies only? Can it serve foreign policy decisions as well—and should foreign policy always follow the most open, participatory model?

Presidential Preeminence in the Making of Foreign Policy

2

Presidential Primacy in Foreign Affairs

The preeminence of presidents in the domain of foreign policy is visible in the names attached to specific policies: Washington's Farewell Address, Jefferson's Embargo, the Monroe Doctrine, Theodore Roosevelt's "Big Stick," Wilson's Fourteen Points, Franklin Roosevelt's Good Neighbor Policy, the Truman Doctrine, the Eisenhower Doctrine, and—inevitably—the Nixon Doctrine. During his years in office, President Nixon issued an annual State of the World message to supplement the yearly State of the Union message. The latter formerly included a president's assessments and general recommendations on foreign and domestic policies; Nixon separated the two. President Carter made "human rights" the dominant theme of his first years; later, in 1980, after the Soviet invasion of Afghanistan, he declared the Carter Doctrine, which committed the U.S. to preserving the independence of the oil producing states bordering the Persian Gulf. President Reagan, as demonstrated in his early days in the White House, emphasized human rights less and the adversary U.S.-Soviet relationship and the balance of power far more.

Indeed, since the end of World War II, most of our presidents have been primarily interested and concerned with foreign policy issues. Truman had little choice; circumstances made it necessary for him to give most of his time to foreign policy and, having chosen excellent advisers, he will be remembered by history primarily as a great or near-great president for his foreign policy. President Eisenhower, the general who had led Allied armies to victory in Europe, was elected during the frustrations of Nationalist China's collapse and the protracted Korean War, which he promised to end. John Kennedy left no doubt that he sought his fame and reputation by his handling of foreign policy; in his inaugural address he confidently asserted that the United States "shall pay any price, bear any burden, meet any hardship, support any friend, oppose any foe to assure the survival and the success of liberty."[1] President Nixon, too, clearly considered foreign policy his particular area of expertise and showed far less interest in domestic affairs. Before his inauguration, he was quoted as saying that the country needed a president for the conduct of foreign policy; the cabinet could take care of domestic policies. His reorientation of American policy toward Communist China and his negotiations with Russia on a broad front from arms control to trade preoccupied the President in his attempt to lay the foundation of a "generation of peace."

By contrast, President Johnson's fate tragically symbolized the plight of a president whose principal experience was domestic and whose fundamental wish was to enact a social reform program to rival that of his mentor, Franklin Roosevelt. Unfortunately the world would not go away. Thus Johnson, upon succeeding President Kennedy after the latter's assassination, pushed more liberal social legislation through Congress than any president in the twentieth century, including Franklin Roosevelt. But foreign policy proved his undoing. Vietnam not only forced him from office in 1968, but has seemingly stained his historical reputation.

Ford, too, had little experience in foreign policy. After long service in the House, he became president only by the rarest of circumstances. First, the Vice-President was forced to resign because of alleged kickbacks he had taken while governor of Maryland and, second, the President left office because he would have been impeached had he not quit. Ford, however, had a very experienced and forceful secretary of state. Carter was the first governor in the post-war period to become president. Even though he had served on the Trilateral Commission, the purpose of which was to bring about closer relations between the United States and her democratic and industrial allies in Western Europe and Japan, he had no foreign policy experience and relied heavily on a number of advisers. The point, however, is clear: Whatever the president's background and however much or little he is interested in foreign policy, he soon becomes immersed in foreign policy issues. One of the ironies of the Carter presidency in this respect, was that the President was widely perceived as having failed as a manager of the economy and that his achievements really were in the foreign policy area: the Panama Canal treaties, Camp David and the Israeli-Egyptian peace treaty, the official recognition of the People's Republic of China, and the SALT II treaty (even though the Senate did not approve it afterward). And President Reagan, another governor, soon after his inauguration, received as many, if not more, headlines for his views of the Soviet leaders and policies "to stop Communism" in El Salvador as for his economic policies and budget-cutting measures.

The Recruitment of Presidential Candidates

The central role for the president in foreign affairs has been reflected during the post-World War II period—from the eruption of the cold war to the end of the war in Vietnam—by the pattern of recruitment of presidential candidates. Until World War II, the governorship had supplied a long list of presidential candidates. Since the end of the Civil War, the list includes Wilson, Harding, Coolidge, and Franklin D. Roosevelt. While the United States was largely an isolationist country, this training ground for presidents was incomparable. It was at the state level that they gained experience in dealing with the problems of pre-Depression domestic America; four of the presidents since 1945 have come from the Senate. At a time when the United States was one of the two leading powers in the world, when nuclear weapons meant the deaths of tens of millions of Americans if war erupted, this is not really surprising. The expertise for dealing with these key issues of war and peace was in Washington, not state capitals. And in Washington, the Senate is the senior legislative body and is more involved in foreign policy-making than the House. Thus the emergence of the Senate as a launching platform for presidential candidates is natural. Truman was a senator, although he was not selected by Roosevelt as vice-president in 1944 because of his knowledge of foreign affairs. But what is very striking about post-Truman presidential and most vice-presidential candidates until 1976—especially the winners of each nomination in both parties—is (1) the predominance of U.S. senators and (2) membership of those senators on either the Foreign Relations Committee or the Armed Services Committee, with a slight edge for the former. The standout exception was Eisenhower, a military officer and public servant with much experience in foreign policy and diplomacy.

Two senators who were unsuccessful in their first tries for a place on their parties' national tickets and were successful the second time had in the interim become members of the key Senate committees. John Kennedy (D., Mass.) in 1956 was a member of the Senate Government Operations

TABLE 2–1. Major Party Presidential and Vice-Presidential Candidates 1952–80

Year	Presidential		Vice-Presidential	
1952 DEM.	Stevenson*		Sparkman	Sen. F.R.
	Kefauver	Sen. A.S.		
	Barkley	Sen. F.R.		
	Russell	Sen. A.S. (Chairman)		
	Harriman	Sec. of Commerce and Committee on Foreign Aid (in executive to evaluate U.S. capability for Marshall Plan aid)		
1952 REP.	Eisenhower		Nixon	House Un-American, Select Committee Foreign Aid, 80th Congress
	Taft			
1956 DEM.	Stevenson		Kefauver	See 1952
	Harriman	See 1952	Kennedy	Sen. Gov't. Operations
	Kefauver		Humphrey	Sen. F.R.
1956 REP.	Eisenhower		Nixon	See 1952
			Stassen	Disarmament adviser
1960 DEM.	Kennedy	Sen. F.R.	Johnson	Sen. A.S.
	Humphrey	Sen. F.R.		
	Johnson	Sen. A.S.		
	Symington	Sen. A.S.		
1960 REP.	Nixon	See 1952	Lodge	Sen. F.R. 80th U.S. Ambassador to U.N.
	Goldwater			
	Rockefeller			
1964 DEM.	Johnson	See 1960	Humphrey	See 1960
1964 REP.	Goldwater	Sen. A.S.	Miller	
	Scranton			
	Rockefeller			
	Romney			
	Lodge	See 1960		
1968 DEM.	Humphrey	See 1960	Muskie	Sen. Gov't. Operations
	McCarthy	Sen. F.R.		
	R. Kennedy			

TABLE 2–1. (Continued)

Year	Presidential		Vice-Presidential	
	McGovern	Director, Food for Peace		
1968 REP.	*Nixon*	See 1952	*Agnew*	
	Romney			
	Rockefeller			
	Reagan			
1972 DEM.	*McGovern*	See 1968	Shriver	Director, Peace Corps
	Muskie	Sen. F.R.	Eagleton	
	Humphrey	See 1960		
	Jackson	Sen. A.S.		
	Wallace			
	Lindsay			
1972 REP.	*Nixon*	See 1952	*Agnew*	
1976 DEM.	*Carter*		*Mondale*	Select Sen. Intelligence
	Brown			
	Church	Sen. F.R. Select Sen. Intelligence, chairman		
	Udall			
	Jackson	See 1972		
	Wallace			
1976 REP.	*Ford*		*Dole*	
	Reagan		Schweiker	Select Sen. Intelligence
1980 DEM.	*Carter*	See 1976	*Mondale*	See 1976
	E. Kennedy	Chairman, Senate Judiciary Committee, Subcommittee on Immigration		
	Brown			
1980	*Reagan*		*Bush*	Director, CIA, U.S. Envoy, China
	Bush	Director, CIA, U.S. Envoy, China		
	Baker	Sen. F.R.		
	Connally	Sec. of Treasury, Sec. of Army		
	Dole			
	Crane			
	Anderson			

*Party nominees in italics; F.R. = Foreign Relations Committee; A.S. = Armed Services Committee.

Committee when he sought the Democratic vice-presidency; four years later, when he became his party's presidential nominee, he was on the Foreign Relations Committee. Barry Goldwater (R., Ariz.), unsuccessful in 1960, was successful in 1964 and had in the meantime become a Senate Armed Services Committee member. Edmund Muskie (D., Me.), the Democratic vice-presidential candidate in 1968, joined Foreign Relations before the next election, when in the early going he was considered the front-runner for the Democratic presidential nomination.

Governors were generally unsuccessful from 1945 to 1976—until after Vietnam and the resulting disillusionment with foreign policy and increasing domestic economic concerns. Two governors were nominated during the cold war: Thomas Dewey (R., N.Y.) in 1948 and Adlai Stevenson (D., Ill.) in 1952 and 1956. The latter had some foreign policy experience. State executives who made presidential bids and failed—Nelson Rockefeller, William Scranton, and W. Averell Harriman—had considerable foreign policy experience. But most governors did not; because their experience was primarily domestic, they were not even nominated. A state's chief executive who demonstrated an interest in foreign policy but also an inability to handle international problems was even worse off than a governor who stressed domestic concerns almost to the exclusion of foreign policy. A case in point is former Michigan Governor George Romney. Romney was considered the front-runner for the Republican nomination in 1968 until he stated that the Johnson administration had succeeded in "brainwashing" him on the proper course of action in Vietnam. The charge backfired on Romney, who appeared to many to be too gullible on any policy. The first governor actually elected on a national ticket in the postwar years was Spiro T. Agnew in 1968 and 1972, who had not aspired to the post and was rather surprised at being selected by candidate Nixon in 1968 to balance the GOP ticket geographically and ideologically. Both Nixon and Agnew, of course, left office involuntarily; Agnew was then replaced by Nelson Rockefeller who, as noted, had considerable foreign policy experience (indeed, he introduced Kissinger to national political life). At the time of his nomination, he was serving as the head of a self-financed research organization analyzing both foreign and domestic policy alternatives.

As surveys indicated a declining trust in the federal government by the citizenry, however, Washington experience became a less critical factor for candidates seeking the presidency. In 1976, former Governor Jimmy Carter of Georgia gained the Democratic nomination for president by running against the "Washington establishment." Four years later, facing Carter the incumbent, former Governor Ronald Reagan of California won the Republican nomination which had so long eluded him in the days when Washington experience was more highly valued. To be sure, each candidate benefited from the extensive use of the media in presidential campaigns and the party reforms of the 1970s which more than doubled the number of presidential primary elections held throughout the nation. The campaign for president now extended over almost an entire term, with formal announcements occurring as early as two years before the election. As wealthy men with no formal commitments, Carter and Reagan were able to pursue the nominations of their parties full-time for two years, while their challengers in both 1976 and 1980, such as Frank Church (D., Idaho), Edward M. Kennedy (D., Mass.), and Howard Baker (R., Tenn.) remained tied to their Senate duties. But the success of outsider candidates goes beyond the long campaign: George Bush, with considerable Washington experience and an extensive foreign policy background (former director of the Central Intelligence Agency and U.S. representative to the People's Republic of China), did not fare well in the campaign against Reagan. Bush throughout the primary campaign had heavily stressed his Washington experience and was perceived, perhaps unfairly, to be out of step ideologically with the Republican party of 1980.

From Truman until Carter, presidents have been so involved with foreign policy problems, including crises when the fear of nuclear war became especially acute, that domestic problems were bound to suffer neglect. The fact that there are only so many hours per day and that the president can pay attention to only some of the many problems that he should deal with, had he unlimited time, means that he has to make a choice, and when the external danger is perceived as high by the president and his advisers, foreign policy will preoccupy them. Since throughout most of the post-1945 period the threat from Russia and China (from 1950–72) was seen as global in scope, it is not surprising that domestic affairs were assigned to a secondary status. One analyst has even asserted that "foreign policy concerns tended to drive out domestic policy."[2] Indeed, in a situation where even potential foreign crises like Vietnam did not receive sufficient attention, and therefore tended to blow up into full-fledged crises, domestic affairs often seemed to gain consideration only when they too became critical. Sometimes, in fact, it appeared as if only domestic violence would attract sufficient attention and bring results, as, for example, when black rioting, burning, and looting dramatically demonstrated the frustration and anger among American blacks at their status and treatment one hundred years after the Emancipation Proclamation.

This subordination of domestic to foreign policy has occurred with increasing frequency during this century, as the world more and more has been unwilling to leave America alone to attend to its domestic needs. Every president who has come into office bent on reform at home has sooner or later found himself confronted by external threats, which came to preoccupy his attention and led to the neglect of domestic problems. Wilson's New Freedom program was overtaken by the German menace and World War I; Franklin Roosevelt, or "Dr. New Deal," as he called himself, became "Dr. Win-the-War" early in his third term, as Hitler, Mussolini, and Tojo made it impossible to complete domestic reforms; after 1945 Truman's Fair Deal quickly became subordinated to containment; Kennedy's New Frontier became a victim of one foreign crisis after another; and Johnson's Great Society was devoured by Vietnam.

This does not mean that, without the appearance and perception of external threats, presidents supported by Congress would have spent the resources used up by recurrent military preparations on domestic problems and reforms of various kinds. Roosevelt's New Deal program was stalled in Congress by 1938. Truman's Fair Deal made modest progress in 1949–50, but was overshadowed by congressional criticism of the Korean War in the last two years of his administration. Eisenhower had no social program to speak of, and Kennedy's New Frontier remained largely rhetoric since Congress wanted no part of it. Johnson's Great Society was the exception, and it was made possible by the exceptional circumstances of his immense persuasive skills, a landslide presidential victory that also elected a sizable number of Democratic congressmen, and the president's concentration on the enactment of his social legislation while trying to conduct the escalating Vietnam War in a "business as usual" atmosphere that demanded no sacrifices from the American people. This strategy worked until the 1966 mid-term election and the recapture by the Republicans of many of their former House seats. Nixon, in his turn, had few domestic interests except to dismantle much of his predecessor's social programs. But the widespread disenchantment with foreign policy and increasing concern with domestic affairs at a time of very high *inflation* and unemployment and a *stagnating* economy—even though this *stagflation* was largely due to a rapidly growing U.S. oil dependence on overseas countries—may mean that senators will no longer have the inside track on being nominated for the presidency. Carter, of course, was renominated; Senator Edward Kennedy challenged the President, but questions about the senator's character drew attention away from his stress on Carter's management of the economy for most primary voters. Reagan in the Republican party had the field virtually to himself; he was an old campaigner, the darling of the conservatives, and had almost taken the nomination away from President Ford in 1976. Ford withdrew from the 1980 field after his defeat that year. After his nomination in 1980, however, presidential candidate Reagan, inexperienced as he was in the area, stressed foreign policy heavily.

Like Carter, it was predictable that Reagan, if elected, would have to pay much of his attention to foreign policy. He would, like his predecessor, have to learn on the job. As already noted, there is an irony to former Governor Carter's record as president—if he had any successes they were in foreign policy, not domestic affairs. He was the father of the Israeli-Egyptian peace, two countries which had fought four wars in twenty-five years; he negotiated a strategic arms limitation treaty with Russia (which then got stalled in the Senate and the President temporarily withdrew the treaty after the Soviet invasion of Afghanistan); he formally recognized the People's Republic of China; he negotiated a new status for the Panama Canal; and he was active in seeking a peaceful solution for

Rhodesia, governed by the small white minority (Britain, whose colony Rhodesia had been, finally negotiated a solution for black majority rule in the renamed state of Zimbabwe). By contrast, the energy problem, unemployment, and inflation remained. Not that Carter did not devise programs to manage these problems; but Congress was not very helpful in cooperating with the President. Yet the fact remains that Carter was widely perceived as an incompetent president and, most ironic of all, it was his handling of the Iranian hostage issue and Afghanistan that rallied the country around him, helped stifle Kennedy's campaign on domestic issues, and raised the President's ratings which helped him through all but the late presidential primaries without emerging from the White House to campaign actively.

Indeed, Reagan's campaign against Carter in 1980 very much resembled Carter's own race against Ford in 1976. Carter, with a limited background in foreign policy, chose a popular figure with a Washington background and foreign policy experience as his running mate and capitalized on Ford's blunder in the foreign policy debate between the two presidential candidates. He also campaigned as an outsider against the "Washington establishment" candidate (Ford). Four years later, he found himself the "insider" candidate against Reagan, who had also chosen a running mate (George Bush) with Washington experience and an extensive foreign policy background. Like Carter in 1976, Reagan attempted to make up for his lack of foreign policy background by surrounding himself with knowledgeable assistants and no shortage of policy statements. The experience itself would be gained on the job. Independent candidate Representative John Anderson (Ill.), who had sought the GOP nomination unsuccessfully, strove to bring his campaign greater credibility and visibility by traveling to the Middle East and Europe and meeting with several heads of state while Reagan was being nominated by the Republicans at their convention. The outsider strategy which has come to be so prominent in the last several years does have disturbing consequences for the conduct of foreign policy, some of which we alluded to above and others which will be discussed later in this chapter. Specifically, we wonder whether this strategy might produce presidential candidates who are far better at running for office than at filling the position—that is, winning elections but not governing.

Presidential Stakes in Foreign Policy

Foreign policy and presidential authority are organically and intimately tied together. While the welfare state is one reason for the enormous growth of presidential power, foreign policy is clearly the primary one. Presidents have clearly benefited from America's global role; during the cold war, they achieved a clear-cut primacy while Congress subordinated itself to a secondary, if not peripheral, role. In the post-Vietnam, Watergate phase, the congressional attempts to restrain the president were linked to attacks on America's cold war role as "global policeman." A more limited presidential role was tied to a policy more consistent with America's "limited power"; so was an institutionally greater congressional role. In short, the executive-legislative conflict revolved around America's world role. A strong presidency had a vested interest in not retreating from its overseas position; a strong Congress—reasserting itself at the cost of the presidency—had a vested interest in precisely such a retreat to what was called a more responsible, discriminating foreign policy.

It may also be true that while Democratic presidents have been in the forefront of expanding executive authority, it has been Republican presidents who, until President Carter, may have had an even greater vested interest in making foreign policy their strong suit. For the Democrats were in power when the United States became involved in World Wars I and II, the Korean War, and the Vietnam War; the Democrats were sometimes accused of being the "war party." Democrats could, however, also run on their domestic record—the New Deal, the Fair Deal, the New Frontier, and the Great Society. By contrast, the Republicans, the party of Herbert Hoover and the Depression, had no domestic record on which to run; they had to run on foreign policy and demonstrate to the nation that they could more effectively manage the country's foreign affairs. Thus Eisenhower was urged to run by the Eastern, moderate, internationalist wing of the Republican party. Senator Taft (R., Ohio), the leader of the dominant conservative, nationalist-isolationist, mid-Western wing of the party, was favored as the party's presidential candidate. Eisenhower, elected after three years of the Korean War, was followed eight years later by Nixon, elected after three years of the Vietnam War. Nixon's only interest was foreign policy. Détente with Russia, with SALT I as its centerpiece, rapprochement with Communist China, a gradual disengagement from Vietnam which left the anti-Communist Thieu regime in power in Saigon, was a record which saw Nixon win every state in 1972 except Massachusetts.

Thus presidential interest in foreign policy is more than a matter of America's stakes in the world and more than a matter of personal interest; it is also a matter of political self-interest. It is their foreign policy record which has allowed them to establish a reputation for leadership and for the effective stewardship of the nation's affairs in this tumultuous world; this also obviously helps their party's reputation and fortunes. In contrast to domestic policy, where in the past the more active congressional and interest group participation limited the possibilities of presidential leadership, and the multitude of "veto points" in the two houses of Congress often paralyzed the decision-making system, making it impossible to respond effectively to the nation's internal problems, foreign policy until Vietnam permitted the president to exercise a degree of initiative and possess a degree of autonomy he simply did not possess in domestic affairs. By and large, the president could count on public support and congressional deference on foreign policy issues. The temptation to be an activist president in foreign policy in thus very great; so is the satisfaction derived from playing this role.

If proof were needed of presidential interest in foreign policy in order to achieve a successful record upon which to run victoriously every four years, one need but look at President Carter. Unable to establish such a record on domestic policy where his years in office witnessed a major increase in both unemployment and inflation; unable to get along with Congress even on such nationally vital legislation as energy, Carter's achievements were largely limited to foreign policy. While these achievements were not beyond criticism, and the Carter foreign policy was hardly one of unbroken successes, it was not a bad record, certainly compared to his domestic achievements. Foreign policy actions tended to revive those flagging public opinion polls presidents begin to receive within a few months of assuming office. For Carter this was particularly true. Iran's seizure of U.S. hostages and Russia's invasion of Afghanistan for a while raised the President's public ratings, although a few months later the polls dropped again (see Chapter 5).

There has long been widespread disagreement as to the precise impact of foreign policy issues on presidential elections in the United States. Many observers contend that the outcome of a presidential race turns primarily on domestic issues—such matters as the price of wheat, the level of unemployment, or the cost of groceries in the supermarket. Others argue for the salience of foreign policy in the race for the White House, and point to the elections of 1952 and 1968, when the Korean and Vietnam wars seemed to exert a major influence upon voting behavior. What seems beyond dispute is the fact that the voters are very much concerned over the relative capacity of rival presidential candidates to deal effectively with foreign policy issues, even though they may have little knowledge of, or concern for, the substance of these issues. Clearly, presidential candidates themselves believe this to be the case. One of the chief ways in which presidential hopefuls demonstrate their qualifications for the high office they seek is by exhibiting knowledge and competence in matters affecting the national security of the United States. When a candidate fails to radiate a reassuring image in foreign affairs, his campaign is gravely damaged.[3]

Presidents and Foreign Policy Advisers

One result of the trend toward concentration on foreign affairs and the stakes a president has in the conduct of foreign policy has been that presidents have increasingly become their own secretaries of state. Wilson set the precedent; he clearly overshadowed William Jennings Bryan, the former Democratic presidential candidate and great orator, as well as Bryan's successor, Robert Lansing. Franklin Roosevelt hardly even paid any attention to his secretary of state, Cordell Hull. During World War II, in his meetings with Prime Minister Churchill and Premier Stalin, he usually left Hull at home and uninformed. Kennedy deliberately selected a relatively weak secretary of state, Dean Rusk, a former assistant secretary of state during the Truman years, and Nixon from 1969 to 1973 chose a friend, William Rogers, precisely because he had no experience in foreign affairs at all. Only Truman and Eisenhower had strong secretaries of state, Acheson and Dulles, respectively. Nixon replaced Rogers with Kissinger, a strong figure, at the beginning of his second administration, and Kissinger served President Ford after Nixon resigned his office.

As presidents have increasingly exercised their authority as the nation's chief diplomat, they have also increasingly relied upon a personal adviser who, starting with Eisenhower, came to be called a special assistant on National Security Affairs. Wilson had his Colonel House, and Franklin Roosevelt his Harry Hopkins. Kennedy appointed McGeorge Bundy from Harvard; because of Bundy's credentials he first attracted attention to the position. Johnson appointed Walt Rostow from MIT after Bundy resigned, and Nixon chose Kissinger, also from Harvard. Under Nixon the position became institutionalized, and a sizable foreign policy staff of about fifty under Kissinger's direction was assembled in the White House (Bundy had twelve). This marks perhaps better than anything else the pre-Reagan shift of the locus of foreign-policy decision-making to the White House. Even when appointed secretary of state, Kissinger kept his White House position until the Congress in 1976 forced the controversial secretary to give up his position as National Security adviser to Nixon's replacement, Ford. Yet, the new security adviser was General Brent Snowcroft, Kissinger's deputy. Carter followed the traditional pattern of employing an academic adviser on foreign policy, Zbigniew Brzezinski of Columbia.

In a real sense, the national security assistant became a second secretary of state. This was not the original intention; the assistant was merely to arrange meetings of the National Security Council (NSC) and manage the paperwork. Created in 1947 to coordinate the political and military strands of foreign policy, the NSC did not initially play a prominent role. Truman and Eisenhower's assistants remain unknown figures; the two presidents relied upon their secretaries of state, Dean Acheson and John Foster Dulles respectively, both very strong personalities who would not have tolerated anyone between themselves and the president. But Kennedy, wishing to play a more direct foreign policy role than his two predecessors, made the assistant's position more prominent by appointing the dean of the Harvard faculty, McGeorge

Bundy. The latter did, however, largely stay out of the limelight. The assistant's job was to ensure that the president would receive all the necessary information and full range of options he needed to make decisions; coordinate the work of all departments involved; and ensure that presidential decisions would be carried out. He was to be a largely anonymous manager. Kissinger (with a staff of over sixty) and Brzezinski (even with a smaller staff of about thirty–thirty-five) have given the position great prominence. Kissinger was in charge of the Vietnamese peace negotiations, SALT, China and, after the 1973 Yom Kippur War, the first Israeli-Egyptian steps toward peace in the Middle East. Brzezinski has not been quite as dominant, although he was active, especially on China policies. A "hard-liner" concerned about Russia's rapidly growing military power and expansion of influence, his advice became more prominent after the Soviet invasion of Afghanistan disillusioned Carter with Russia's behavior and Secretary of State Vance's more accommodating stance.

Thus one of the results of appointing a prominent national security assistant has been friction with the secretary of state, officially the president's chief foreign policy adviser. Conflicting policy statements from the president's assistant and secretary of state also raise questions among friends and foes about what the foreign policy of the United States is and who is in charge. Another result is tension with Congress, which does not confirm the assistant's appointment; as the president's assistant he cannot be called upon to testify before congressional committees, even though he may give television or newspaper interviews. A cabinet officer is confirmed and has to testify (at best, the assistant meets informally with the Senate Foreign Relations Committee, for instance, or individual members of Congress). Perhaps the greatest danger is that the national assistant, if he is a man with strong policy preferences of his own, will not ensure that all points of view on issues reach the president. It has been said that Rostow shielded Johnson from critical views on the Vietnamese war; Rostow was considered a "hawk" on the war. The assistant cannot be both policy advocate and neutral policy manager. Institutionally, it is impossible; it is not primarily a matter of personality.

Not surprisingly, it has been suggested that the national security assistant's position should be either abolished or downgraded to the basically neutral manager and the secretary of state restored to the position as the president's chief adviser on foreign policy. Interestingly enough, after he left office Kissinger himself, came out against a strong national security assistant and recommended a strong secretary of state. An active assistant, he said, is bound to reduce the secretary of state's prestige and influence. If the president does not have confidence in his secretary of state, Kissinger claims, he should replace him. Secretary Vance too, after he resigned from office, urged that there be only two spokesmen for the government on foreign policy issues: the president and the secretary of state. Reagan, who was advised by Kissinger among others and reflected on the frequent Vance (and later Muskie)-Brzezinski tugs of war during his predecessor's tenure, chose General Alexander Haig, Kissinger's former assistant and later NATO's commander in chief, a position in which he had gained diplomatic experience. Haig, a strong personality, would presumably establish himself as Reagan's chief foreign-policy maker, which the President said he wanted, and prevent the rise of a rival like a Kissinger or a Haig in the White House. The appointment of Richard Allen, not previously well known as a foreign policy activist, appeared to ensure this goal. The fact that the national security adviser would no longer report directly to the president as did his predecessors, and that the president's counselor, Edwin Meese, who would serve with cabinet rank and would be in charge of both the national security and domestic policy staffs underlined the determination to avoid having what amounted to two secretaries of state. How this arrangement would work out in practice remains to be seen.

A strong secretary of state may not, however, be able to avoid conflict with the security assistant. First, departments deal with policy only from their own perspective; this is as true for the State Department as of other departments. By contrast, the assistant sitting next to the president at the apex of the governmental structure is in a better position to form a broader perspective, integrating the many strands of foreign policy.

Second, State has a reputataon of being cautious, often timid, unimaginative, and slow. It also lacks the capability for long range planning; its Policy Planning Staff, which is supposed to do this, has neither the power nor prestige to do so and gain the cooperation of other responsible departments. This raises a question about the desirability of State acting as the president's chief adviser on foreign policy; indeed, Presidents Kennedy and Nixon questioned whether State has the ability to act in this capacity. One reason for the growth of the assistant's authority is precisely that presidents have felt they could not depend on State for quick, sound advice. Recent presidents have felt the need for someone besides the secretary of state to ask for his judgements; the "president's intellectual" has been that individual.

Third, even if State could be the primary spokesman, it would not be the only one—nor the most powerful. Defense and—now that economic issues have become as prominent as political-strategic ones—Agriculture, Treasury, Commerce, are all more powerful spokesmen for their viewpoints than is State. These agencies all represent major sectors of the society and economy such as the defense industries, farming, the banking, or business community, all of which have political clout and can mobilize support for their views in Congress and among the public in general. State, even though it represents the "national interest," has no constituency. Its chances of determining policy through coordinating the varying views of the different departments is, therefore, likely to be contested. The Reagan administration's decision to establish three senior interdepartmental groups (SIGs)—one dealing with foreign policy, one with defense policy, and a third with intelligence, each directed respectively by the secretary of state, secretary of defense, and the director of the Central Intelligence Agency—is unlikely to avoid bureaucratic struggle.

Thus the national security assistant is likely to remain in a powerful position, helping the president achieve an overall view and giving the president counsel when he seeks it. It is the president, at whose pleasure the assistant serves, who defines the job and the balance he wants between his assistant and the secretary of state. He may dislike conflict, as Nixon did, and appoint a figurehead to the State Department; or he may, as Carter, welcome diverse advice and conflict, which leaves him greater freedom to choose (Franklin Roosevelt used to encourage conflict among all his advisers, domestic and foreign!); or he may not give him direct access, as Reagan did. But it is unlikely he can do without him. For in the words of the Senate Subcommittee on National Security Organization:

> The President at all times should have the help and protection of a small staff whose members work outside the system, who are sensitive to the President's information needs, and who can assist him in asking relevant questions of his departmental chief, in making suggestions for policy initiatives not emerging from the operating departments and in spotting gaps in policy execution.[4]

These reasons may be reinforced by differences of opinion among the president's cabinet members. In the absence of a consensus, the national security adviser may well be the person asked by the president to present the options and his own preferences. Thus, conflict between the NSC assistant and the secretary of state may not be avoidable, not because of the personalities involved but because of the structure of decision making. Symptomatic perhaps of future problems was the initial clash between the Reagan White House and Secretary of State Haig after the new administration had only been in office for nine weeks.

Haig was supposed to be the administration's number one foreign policy-maker and spokesman. The new President wanted to avoid the Brzezinski-Vance tug of war of his predecessor. Thus, Haig believed that he and State should be in charge not only of daily policy but also of crises when they arose. But the White House asserted that crisis management was, as in the past, within its jurisdiction, and it placed Vice-President Bush in charge (rather than the national security assistant, Richard Allen, as had been done in the past). Still, the Vice-President has virtually no staff and he would thus have to depend upon the NSC staff if a crisis erupted. But what about situations leading to crises? Even the preparation for the Western Economic Summit Conference in the summer of 1981 was handled under Mr. Bush's supervision after Mr. Reagan expressed dissatisfaction with the State Department's preparation for his visit to Canada shortly after his inauguration. Hence, the jurisdictional struggle over directing American foreign policy continues.

Presidential Power and Executive-Legislative Relations

Foreign policy favors the growth of executive power; but this growth has also come about as a result of the difficulties of conducting a responsible, steady, long-range, yet adaptable foreign policy under a separation of powers system. To put it more bluntly: A major cause in the growth of presidential power has been congressional obstructionism. Three phases of U.S. policy in this century need to be mentioned if it is to be understood not only why the presidency has established such preeminence in the conduct of foreign policy, but, equally important, why until Vietnam, this trend received popular approval and academic blessings.

The starting point is the Versailles Treaty which both concluded World War I and established the League of Nations. The intensity of the conflict between President Wilson, a Democrat, and the Senate, controlled by the Republicans and directed by Senator Henry Cabot Lodge (Mass.), resulted in the treaty's defeat. Executive-legislative rivalry, partisan considerations, and personal hatred of the two men towards each other were thus involved in the U.S. withdrawal from an active world role after the war. Since Britain and France had already proven too weak to contain Germany in the war and it had taken U.S. intervention to defeat her finally, the American return to isolationism was felt by many Americans later on to be partly responsible for the outbreak of World War II. The defeat of this treaty thus dramatically raised the question of America's ability, with its institutions, to conduct a foreign policy to protect American interests.

The second period, from the German defeat of France in the spring of 1940 to Pearl Harbor in late 1941, reinforced this concern.[5] This was a period in which the President had to confront the threat of an increasingly powerful Germany while Congress remained in the grip of isolationism. Indeed, during the 1930s the Congress had passed a series of neutrality laws which were supposed to keep the United States out of any future European war. On the eve of that war in 1939, when the administration asked for changes which would allow the government to sell arms to the allies who seemed less well prepared than the Nazis, Senator William Borah (R., Ida.), chairman of the Foreign Relations Committee and himself an ardent isolationist, not only rejected the request, but asserted that *his* sources of information were superior to those of the State Department, and that they had told him there would be no war!

After hostilities erupted despite Borah's prediction, the problem for

President Roosevelt was how to do the "right thing" and be able to do it despite the continued isolationist sentiment in the Congress. For Roosevelt, the "right thing" meant supporting Britain after the fall of France, the low countries (the Netherlands, Belgium, and Luxembourg), and Denmark and Norway. American policy-makers have historically defined the domination of Western Europe by a single power as a potential threat to American security. Even Thomas Jefferson, a Francophile, voiced the possibility of aligning with England as Napoleon proceeded to conquer Europe. In Roosevelt's words, the defense of American democracy would be difficult and would certainly result in the sacrifice of the democratic ingredient if the United States were to become a lone island of peace surrounded by a world of brute force (German, Italian, and Japanese). America would have to turn herself into a garrison state; the Atlantic Ocean was no longer a barrier to attack but a highway to the Western Hemisphere.

The President therefore wanted to help Britain, first of all, to defend herself against a possible German invasion. But despite entreaties by Prime Minister Churchill for some old World War I vintage destroyers to help defend the English Channel and other waters surrounding England, Roosevelt, at a time of great emergency, procrastinated. The Congress, anticipating him, had imposed a legal barrier in his way by decreeing that the President could not transfer the destroyers unless the chief of Naval Operations certified that such ships were not needed for U.S. defense. The distrust of the President was abundantly clear. The President finally outflanked the Congress with an executive agreement, but only after four months of hesitation, after he had received a pledge from the Republican presidential nominee that he would not make the transaction a political issue, after the Committee to Defend America by Aiding the Allies had mobilized domestic support through intensive propaganda, and after Churchill had agreed that in return for the destroyers the United States could lease bases on British islands in the Atlantic and Caribbean. This allowed Roosevelt to present the destroyer deal basically as an American acquisition of bases and thus a means of enhancing American security; the destroyer transfer was hardly mentioned in Roosevelt's speech to the country. What would have happened had the Germans invaded, as expected, during these months?

After his reelection, Roosevelt was successful in obtaining congressional support for the Lend-Lease Act by which Britain, soon unable to pay for American arms and ammunition, could acquire these on a lease basis. The United States was to become "the great arsenal of democracy." The Congress went along with the President because of the view— probably shared by Roosevelt too—that the best chance of staying out of the war was by helping England to strengthen herself and win the war. "Give us the tools and we will finish the job" was Churchill's cry. But the key problem was getting the supplies to Britain. In the Battle of the

Atlantic, the Germans were sinking British and Canadian merchant ships faster than they could be built. But Britain's survival remained the critical issue. Yet, what was the point of giving the arms to the British if they never got to England? Roosevelt felt inhibited, however, from doing anything. He had, in the summer of 1941, sent the marines to Iceland to prevent the Germans from stationing air reconnaissance and submarines there to cut Britain's lifeline to America. But he continued to hesitate in authorizing American warships to take supplies and mail to the marines from convoying allied ships to Iceland, even though that would relieve the already thinly stretched British navy (which would then have to convoy ships only the last half of their journey across the Atlantic). One senator had introduced a resolution specifically forbidding the President from authorizing convoys. Again, not until after several months of hesitation did Roosevelt as commander in chief of the armed forces authorize such protection.

He did so only after a German submarine had attacked the U.S. destroyer *Greer*. In publicly explaining that the navy would from then escort all merchant ships and "shoot-on-sight" at German submarines and raiders, the President was in effect involving the United States in a limited naval war in the western Atlantic. But he did not explain in his "undeclared war" speech that the destroyers had for several hours pursued the German submarine, that in desperation to escape, the submarine had turned on the destroyer and fired its torpedoes, after which the destroyer had dropped depth charges on the submarine. Thus a German act, which could not have been anticipated, finally permitted the United States to do what was needed to ensure that the arms required by England—America's first line of defense—would get there. Had the submarine been able to slip away and had other German submarines not sunk several other American ships, what could the President have done? For congressional sentiment on the eve of World War II was clearly shown in two separate votes—one on extending the Selective Service Act which passed the House by only one vote, and the other, squeezed through in a very narrow House majority of 212–194 and Senate majority of 50–37, on finally repealing the last major neutrality law constraint blocking American ships from carrying supplies directly to British ports. These last two votes came right after a German submarine had torpedoed a U.S. destroyer near Iceland.

Franklin Roosevelt thus set a precedent for his successors. He felt compelled to resort to executive agreements to get around the treaty obstacle and expand the commander in chief powers. His problem, as he saw it, was that if he did not undertake the various measures he did to help Britain, Hitler might win in Europe and then threaten the United States. If he had sought to gain congressional approval for such steps as the Destroyer Deal or convoying of allied merchant ships by U.S. warships as far as Iceland, he might have failed, eroding his own authority and effectiveness as President and encouraging Hitler while sapping the hopes of Churchill and his countrymen in their finest hour. Indeed, had he come out more openly for intervention he might have lost his unprecedented third-term bid for the presidency.

It is interesting that even the critics of the president's war powers do not question Roosevelt's judgment of the peril to national security (probably because they share his liberal values as incorporated in the New Deal and view World War II as a "good war"). But they do question the constitutional propriety of his actions. Thus, quite typically, Merlo Pusey, after admitting that had the President gone to Congress he would have been turned down even though "human freedom was gravely endangered on a global scale," says: "On grounds of expediency and of international power politics, the argument [for the actions Roosevelt took] is very impressive. But where does it leave us in terms of democratic principles and the maintenance of constitutional government?"[6] By the juxtaposition of such loaded terms as "expediency" and "power politics" with "principles" and "democracy," Pusey stacks the odds and avoids the issue of (1) what Roosevelt should have done and (2) how to reconcile American democratic government with the protection of national security. Pusey dismisses this concern as "one of the inescapable risks in democratic government."[7] The worst, he says, that would have happened had Roosevelt gone to Congress for support and been rejected, would have been more aggressive behavior by the Nazis on the assumption that the United States would do nothing to stop them; they might even have struck the first blow, as Japan finally did.

What Pusey, in short, argues is that U.S. institutions could not cope with the critical situation in 1940–41; they could not take the initiative to protect U.S. security, but could only react to the enemy's initiatives. But no matter. America's paralysis would have provoked its enemies so that after they had attacked this country Congress could legally have declared war.[8] The integrity of the Constitution in these circumstances could have been preserved. In other words, American democracy—separation of powers style—unable to act wisely would be saved by its enemies' stupidity.

But this avoids the central issue of the effectiveness of American institutions in meeting critical foreign policy situations and of the ability of the political process to produce the "correct" policy outcome. What would have happened had the Japanese bypassed Hawaii and had Hitler not declared war on America? Could Roosevelt have mobilized sufficient congressional and public support to declare war on the Axis powers? It is doubtful, even though by late 1941 Germany had conquered all of Western Europe except England, stood at the gates of Moscow and Leningrad, had captured much of North Africa, and was soon to move within sight of the Suez Canal, while Japan was poised for the conquest of British, French, and Dutch colonies in the Far East with a possible linkup via India with the Germans in the Middle East. But for German and Japanese mistakes, these two powers might have finished off their opponents and then confronted a psychologically and militarily unprepared America at the peak of their power and self-confidence. The ultimate decision—to make war on the United States—was made by Japan and Germany. The United States did not make this decision for itself despite the fact that the balances of power in Asia and Europe were at stake. As Robert Divine has aptly said:

> ... From the first signs of aggression in the 1930's to the attack on Pearl Harbor, the United States refused to attack until there was no other choice. ... Although it was the single most powerful nation on the globe, the United States abdicated its responsibilities and became a creature of history rather than its molder. By surrendering the initiative to Germany and Japan, the nation imperiled its security and very nearly permitted the Axis powers to win the war. In the last analysis the United States was saved only by the Japanese miscalculation in attacking Pearl Harbor.[9]

Given the experience of 1940–41, it is not surprising that students of American foreign policy have often noted the executive-legislative relationship as a chief obstacle to the formation of a sound American foreign policy in the postwar era.

Presidential Primacy and the Cold War

The triumphant victories over Germany, Italy, and Japan under Franklin Roosevelt's majestic leadership only reinforced the trend toward strong presidential leadership. This strong leadership would allow the United States to act with authority, speed, steadiness, and, when necessary, flexibility. A congressionally active role raised the possibility that U.S. foreign policy would be characterized by divided counsel, frequent policy changes, if not occasional paralysis, slow reactions, and inability to exploit rapidly changing situations—all of which would raise questions as the cold war began about U.S. leadership and reliability. The country under the new circumstances of American-Soviet conflict could not afford constant executive-legislative quarrels; indeed, as noted earlier, it was in recognition that this would be harmful that bipartisanship or "nonpartisanship" was advocated as a solution.

The bipartisan formula which accepted presidential primacy and congressional acquiescence in a subordinate role was probably unavoidable during the cold war, even had the memories of Versailles faded and those of 1940–41 been less vivid. For the cold war was attended by an almost universal American perception that the country's security was under threat. It was not called "cold war" for nothing. The United States was engaged in a war, even if it was not a hot one. But the adversary was as much, if not more, of a threat than Germany had been. Russia was the other "super-power," the only nation in the world which could threaten our security—indeed, our survival. And she was a threat not only because Russia was a great power but because Soviet Russia was also a totalitarian state which represented beliefs and values completely antithetical to those of American and Western democracy. The Soviet challenge, like the German ones which preceded it, thus constituted a menace to America's physical and political survival.

Second, this perception of threat was reinforced by frequent high tensions. Each superpower watched the other carefully lest any shift of power would give his opponent an irreversible superiority. This had to be prevented to preserve the balance. Frequent confrontation and crises were the result: Greece and Turkey 1946—47, Berlin 1948—49, the Korean War 1950—53, Quemoy-Matsu 1954—55, the Suez War and Hungarian uprising 1956, Quemoy-Matsu 1958, Berlin 1958—62, Cuba 1961—62, and the deepening Vietnam involvement after 1961 and finally, war after 1965. Short time and the need to make rapid decisions often meant that presidents spent most of their time consulting with their advisers; they then usually informed Congress of their decisions. When there was more time for consultation between the two branches of government, policy might be modified. Congress frequently put its imprint on the president's policy, but the essence of executive policy remained intact. In any event, the recurrence of crisis brought home the perceived danger to America and reinforced the popular and congressional rallying-around-the-flag phenomenon that external danger always encourages.

Third, Congress recognizes the executive's expertise in foreign policy. The president has at hand a large bureaucracy to help him. Senators and congressmen, therefore, rely upon executive officials for information and interpretation of events. Members of Congress lack the confidence they have on domestic matters. As citizens and representatives, they hold views on many of the problems their constituents experience, be it inflation, unemployment, busing, education, subsidies or health care; whatever their own professions, they presumably have wide acquaintanceship in their constituencies with individuals in other walks of life and their specific problems as doctors, farmers, or workers. Moreover, they can call on a whole range of interest groups for other views of the facts and alternative policy views. But foreign problems—the question of Sino-Soviet relations, Soviet intentions, Third World nationalism, military strategy, force levels, and weapons systems—are for most congressmen just that, "foreign." This is also true for most interest groups; their expertise is essentially domestic. Deference to executive judgments followed logically. Congress tends to be not only supportive, therefore, but permissive in giving the executive a good deal of leeway.

Finally, and very important, congressional subordination was the result of a consensus on foreign policy. For over two decades the president and Congress shared a common set of beliefs about the role and objectives of the United States in the world: The central conflict in international politics was the conflict between the Communist world led by the Soviet Union and the "free world" led by the United States; that any expansion of Communist influence and power was a loss of influence and power for the "free world"; that the fundamental role for American and Western policy, therefore, was to oppose such expansion; that the United States, by far the strongest Western power, had the primary responsibility for containing communism; that military power was a principal tool for preserving the strategic balance between the superpowers and deterring a Soviet first strike against the United States and her European allies, as well as for opposing any limited Communist aggression around the Sino-Soviet periphery; that firmness in negotiations was essential because concessions only whetted the unlimited ambitions of the totalitarian rulers of Russia and China and would not therefore resolve key issues but lead to further demands; that other means for waging the struggle against communism—ranging from economic aid and arms sales to subversion—were legitimate in what was essentially a global competition between two giants whose rivalry would determine which of the two antithetical ways of life would dominate the world—freedom or despotism. Permeating this consensus was the feeling that this conflict between despotism and democracy was a struggle between the forces of good and evil. This set of "shared images" between the two branches of government meant that conflict between them largely revolved around the problem of means. The ends or objectives of American policy were agreed upon; controversy was focused on the implementation.

All of the above reasons favored presidential leadership and Congress' willingness to accept, or at least acquiesce in a secondary—if not at times peripheral—role in foreign policy-making. Ironically, therefore, the problem of executive-legislative relations which many observers in the mid to late 1940s expected would obstruct the formation of a policy responsive to America's international needs was largely—although not completely—avoided.[10] There was only one exception to this largely bipartisan cold war consensus: American policy in Asia. Its occurrence was a constant reminder of what could happen to United States foreign policy in a situation of congressional assertiveness and partisan rivalry. For its effects on policy was twofold: one, to transform United States policy in Asia into a rigid anti-Communist Chinese mold, deepen Sino-American enmity and delay a reconciliation between the two countries which from the early 1960s on shared a common interest in containing Russia until the early 1970s; and two, to help precipitate the tragic American intervention in Vietnam. Whether Vietnam was avoidable is debatable; what is not debatable is that congressional pressures, and the anticipation of such pressures by Presidents Kennedy and Johnson, made Vietnam inevitable.

Domestic Politics and "Toughness" in Foreign Policy: The Example of U.S.-Asian Policy

Since presidents run for office, wish to be reelected, or want successors elected who will keep control of the White House in their party, foreign policy cannot be divorced from domestic politics. This is not to say that foreign policy positions are adopted only, or primarily for, domestic political reasons, but it does say that the latter may, to varying degrees, depending on the president and international and domestic circumstances, influence the conduct of the nation's international behavior.

Nowhere was this clearer than in America's post-World War II Asian policy.[11] After three defeats of Republican presidential nominees in 1940, 1944, and 1948—elections in which the Republicans were led by candidates from the moderate-liberal Eastern wing of their party—Republican conservatives felt that only a presidential candidate from their wing of the party could regain control of the White House. A conservative candidate would give the country "a choice, not an echo." Since the party of Herbert Hoover and the Depression was hardly likely to attract a popular majority on domestic issues, foreign policy became the target. The collapse of Nationalist China presented the opportunity. Until then the Republicans had supported containment in Europe and not been very critical about U.S. policy toward China. But when Nationalist China disintegrated because of its war-weariness, corruption, inefficiency, and brutality it was exploited by the Republican conservatives and led to vicious attacks upon the Democrats. China, it was charged, had been sold out; the administration had "coddled communism" and "appeased" the Kremlin; Communists and "Communist dupes" in the State Department and other high places in government—whether they had infiltrated or been appointed by Roosevelt or Truman—had betrayed an ally and friend, as well as their own country. China, in brief, had not fallen because the Nationalists had been incompetent or because Communist morale, organization, and fighting ability had been superior; it was "lost" because of a deliberate conspiracy within the Democratic administration to lose Nationalist China.

The results of these vicious and continuing attacks had profound consequences for U.S. policy. They particularly affected the Democrats. In order to avoid further charges of betrayal, of selling out allies, they were disposed to preempt such a charge with strong anti-Communist policies, military intervention, and escalation and, at all times, no diplomatic recognition of Communist China. Thus during the Korean War, once the North Koreans had been driven back to the 38th parallel where they had begun their attack upon South Korea, an end to the war based upon the prewar status quo was attacked as appeasement. Undoubtedly, such attacks on a solution short of total victory influenced the Truman administration to advance into North Korea. Its neighbor, Communist China, seeing American armies march toward its frontier, then intervened and enlarged the war. When the Korean War had started, the Republicans had already exacted a price from the Democrats for political support and domestic unity: the protection of the island of Formosa (Taiwan) to which Chiang had fled. Thus the United States, which had finally washed its hands of Chiang and his losing cause in January 1950, had reintervened in that civil war by June. No wonder that the new China, seeing the United States protect the rival claimant to legitimate authority over all of China, and American armies advancing toward its borders, defined the United States as its enemy and intervened to protect itself. But this intervention embittered U.S.-Chinese relations for two decades and played into the hands of those opposing any reconciliation.

One can only speculate whether the Chinese intervention in the Korean War, the escalation of the hostilities, and the subsequent rancorous Sino-American relations could have been avoided had the United States had its own diplomatic representatives in China. Chinese warnings of intervention if the United States advanced toward the Korea-Chinese frontier were dismissed in Washington as a bluff. Would American personnel in China not have told Washington that these warnings had to be taken seriously? If one cannot with certainty argue that two of the costs of American nonrecognition of the People's Republic were the intense fighting in Korea, plus the political alienation of the two countries, there is much less uncertainty that two additional costs were the Vietnam War and the failure to recognize and exploit the Sino-Soviet dispute by the late 1950s. Instead, even as late as the early to middle 1960s, any moves toward the diplomatic recognition of the People's Republic of China were politically dangerous—indeed, for the Democrats, suicidal. Not surprisingly, without personnel in China, the differences between Russia and China were often dismissed as tactical rather than fundamental, and North Vietnam viewed as essentially a tool of an expansionist, oppressive China. Hanoi was not perceived as nationalistic and independent of both Moscow and Peking. Surely, American observers in Peking would have known better and so advised the U.S. government. The Vietnam War may thus have been the ultimate price the United States paid for the congressional hard-line attitude toward recognition of Peking.

The decision to intervene with U.S. military forces was made by President Johnson. He did so because by early 1965 U.S. options had run out. His predecessors had still possessed them and each had, therefore, stalled and done only what each had judged necessary to prevent the loss of South Vietnam. For each postwar president the increasing involvement in Indochina leading to the final military intervention in 1965 was calculated as *less costly domestically* than doing nothing and writing it off as an unwinnable situation in the long-run and, therefore, from a rational cost-and-benefit analysis, a place from which to disengage. In the context of American domestic politics and a government characterized by a separation of powers, the acceptance of defeat was believed to be unacceptable. The costs of nonintervention in terms of the loss of congressional and public support was measured as exceeding the cost of intervention severalfold. The basic rule was "Don't lose Indochina." As Daniel Ellsberg summed up this imperative for each White House incumbent: "This is a bad year for me to lose Vietnam to communism."[12] Thus, each time the possibility of disaster stared an administration in the face, it escalated the involvement and commitment to *not* losing Vietnam.

Note the negative nature of the goal: to prevent a disaster. It was hoped that if they could not win, the North Vietnamese would eventually desist. Even before the French defeat in 1954, the Truman administration, by the time of the Korean War, was sending aid to help the French and prevent a Communist victory. The Eisenhower administration, while not intervening militarily, talked a great deal in public about the strategic importance of Vietnam, raised the U.S. financial contribution to the French conduct of the war, and organized and supported the new anti-Communist Diem government in Saigon politically, economically, and militarily. The Kennedy administration fortified this commitment with U.S. military "advisers" and tacitly consented to the South Vietnam military's overthrow of the increasingly despotic and ineffective Diem regime, thereby tightening the link between the United States and the survival of the U.S.-encouraged military government in Saigon which Washington hoped could conduct the war more effectively than its predecessor. For the Johnson administration, however, time and options—other than the politically difficult withdrawal from South Vietnam—ran out. So Johnson sent in the military to prevent the collapse of South Vietnam. The intervention was the logical culmination of the acts of his predecessors; with the exception of Eisenhower, none of them had to make a decision about the use of force in Vietnam to prevent Communist domination. Johnson did; he could not avoid it. But each of Johnson's predecessors was responsible for an increasing commitment and escalation in Vietnam; but if each one was one of the architects of intervention, each was also a "part, and prisoner of the larger political system that fed on itself, trapping all its participants in a war they could not afford to lose and were unable to win quickly."[13]

Why was it that charges of "appeasement" from the opposition party made it impossible to recognize the People's Republic after its birth, negotiate with it on a continuing basis on outstanding issues, and later exploit China's quarrel with Russia? Why was American diplomacy frozen into a rigid anti-Communist posture that finally led the nation into the quagmire of Vietnam? Because "if nation X collapses," a president lays himself open to political attack by the opposition party. One of the resulting casualties may be his prestige and reputation. For a man who has sought the presidency, worked for it and sacrificed for it and perhaps long dreamed about it, a major failure is a blow to the strong ego that drove him to the top and made him believe that he could be a successful president. Even after they leave office, presidents are not forgotten; they become immortal because their heads appear on postage stamps, and their records go into the history books. So major political criticisms of alleged failure which might endanger their reputations, so to speak, are not desirable. In Johnson's words, he was not going to be the first president in American history to lose a war.

But more than personal prestige is at stake for any president. He has to be concerned with his own reelection or, if he does not run again, his successor's election. In a democracy, the president's focus on his own political fortunes and that of his party cannot be neglected; to suggest that there is something immoral about such considerations is to ignore how U.S. politics works. Moreover, it needs to be stressed that if there had not been an election and the public had not "punished" the president at the polls for the "loss" of country X, this would not have affected the president's calculations about the possible electoral impact during the next presidential election and, it ought to be added, the mid-term election. What is of crucial importance is what presidents believe might happen. Laurence Radway has said that "American incumbents tend to overinsure against even a remote possibility of defeat. They can be sobered to the point of paranoia by the realization that quite a few congressional elections and fully 50 percent of all presidential elections since World War II have been decided by only a handful of votes."[14]

Closely related is another cost: the president's domestic program. The fall of China, followed by the Korean War, killed Truman's Fair Deal and then his reelection chances (he withdrew from renomination), followed by a Democratic defeat in 1952; and Kennedy's record in Laos, Cuba (Bay of Pigs), and Berlin at the time the Wall was built did not help him achieve his New Frontier. Johnson did not want to jeopardize his Great Society program. Consequently, he did not want to be tagged as the president who "lost Indochina" as Truman had "lost China." Conservatives in both parties were opposed to liberal /social programs anyway, but the fact that the President was on the defensive and growing weaker strengthened their ability to block or dilute his proposed legislative proposals.

Obviously the foreign policies of an administration are also fair game for attack. Thus a "loss" of a China or Vietnam or other countries may endanger U.S. policies toward other areas. No wonder, confronted by such electoral pressures and partisan attacks, the president calculates that tough foreign policy postures, including intervention or nonrecognition of an "evil" government, are preferable to more accommodating and noninterventionist postures, and will be *less* costly politically at home. Even before congressional or partisan pressures are exercized, the mere anticipation of such pressures will have a "pre-natal" effect on the president's conduct of foreign policy, leading to irrational policies ranging from the pretense that Nationalist China's government on the island of Taiwan was still the government of all of China to the escalation of the U.S. involvement in South Vietnam. During both of the limited wars the United States has fought in Asia, Korea, and Vietnam, Truman and Johnson felt that they were pressured from the right to escalate even further. It has been said with great perceptiveness that Congress, like the Strategic Air Command, possesses both the power of deterrence to prevent the president from doing what Congress feels he should not do (such as recognizing the new regime in Communist China), and the threat of "massive retaliation" if he does what Congress wants him not to do (such as lose South Vietnam, which Congress in the early-middle 1960s was as much opposed to as the president).*

By contrast, conservative presidents were able to withstand domestic pressures for intervention and escalation (although they might also do so for international reasons) and could meet and negotiate with Communists. Thus Eisenhower could sign a Korean peace treaty on the basis of the *status quo ante bellum*, which Truman had been unable to do. Confronted by the possible collapse of the French position in Indochina in 1954, Eisenhower threatened intervention but then decided against it! And no one accused him of a "sell-out." In 1955 he became the first cold war president to meet the Soviet leaders—without being labeled "procommunist." And Nixon, while escalating the air war in Vietnam, could bring U.S. ground forces out and eventually disengage the United States from that war. Above all, he initiated a détente with Moscow to negotiate seriously over a whole range of issues, including strategic arms limitation and a rapprochement with Peking. The latter particularly would have been impossible for a more liberal president. More conservative presidents, immune to attacks of appeasement and coddling communism, have a far greater flexibility in the conduct of foreign policy.

Not that they are immune to attacks. To protect himself from the right wing of his own party, Eisenhower resorted to tough talk of "liberation" and "unleashing Chiang" and "massive retaliation"; initially

---

*Even in areas other than Asia they were susceptible to doing whatever was necessary to avoid such political attacks. Thus after becoming President, John Kennedy discovered the CIA plans for the Bay of Pigs operation. He felt uneasy about the feasibility of the operation but proceeded anyway lest he subsequently be accused of weakness and cowardice compared to Eisenhower, his predecessor, who had conceived of the operation and presumably would have gone ahead with it and carried it out successfully (or left that to his heir apparent, Richard Nixon). Similarly, when, in 1965, "pro-Castro communists" were allegedly involved with the opposition in an attempted overthrow of the Dominican Republic's right-wing military-supported government, Lyndon Johnson intervened. The Democrats had to avoid the accusation of having "allowed another Cuba."

permitted Senator Joseph McCarthy (R., Wisc.) a virtually free hand in his general witch-hunt for alleged security risks, demoralizing the State Department and the U.S. Information Agency, as well as lowering his own presidential prestige as many wondered who was in charge—Eisenhower or McCarthy; and allowed congressional Republican leaders in the Senate to constrain his foreign policy options. Even in Indochina, while Eisenhower did not intervene in 1954, he did not disengage the United States either. Rather, he substituted an American presence for that of France; American dollars, military equipment, and men to train South Vietnamese forces flowed to the new half-country, and the SEATO alliance was formed to permit a unilateral U.S. intervention if it failed to deter future "communist aggression." Eisenhower, in Gelb and Betts' neat summation, "kept America out of war, and he kept America in Vietnam."[15]

Similarly, when Eisenhower's former vice-president, Nixon, came into office in 1969 at a time of growing disillusionment with anticommunism, he made the initial moves toward opening relations with China secretly and presented his trip as a *fait accompli* so that any opposition would not have time to organize itself. And the final withdrawal from Vietnam and peace negotiations were well covered after Hanoi's 1972 spring offensive by the very heavy bombing of North Vietnam, including a pounding of Hanoi itself by B-52's during the Christmas season. Even Nixon and Kissinger were haunted by the fear of another right-wing, appeasement type of attack at home if they "sold out" in Vietnam.

In short, Congress' cold war record is one of militant anticommunism, of nonnegotiation with or "building of bridges" to the Communists, of emphasizing military power, and frequently embracing right-wing dictatorial regimes. This should give pause to anyone placing his faith in the ability of Congress to restrain a too aggressive president. Even a conservative president like Nixon, with an impeccable anti-Communist record (as defined by the right), moved toward a long overdue recognition of Communist China without consulting Congress or allowing his move to leak out to the press, and "covered" the end of the war in Vietnam with what was a compromise settlement and not a traditional military victory with a massive demonstration of American air power over North Vietnam.

In any event, a consistent pattern emerges: election pressures, party competition, and executive-legislative rivalry have, more frequently than not, led to pressures for "tough" positions, inflexible policies, and militant rhetoric rather than conciliatory policies and an accommodating tone. One need look no farther than the 1980 presidential campaign where, in anticipation of the election, President Carter took on increasingly hard-line positions on Iran and, especially after Afghanistan, toward the Soviet Union, keeping the United States out of the summer Olympic games in Moscow, imposing economic sanctions, and increasing the defense budget. In fact, in the subsequent election campaign in which Reagan accused the President of weakness on foreign policy and neglect of American military strength, Carter charged Reagan with not being tough enough since the Republican nominee had not favored the wheat embargo and draft registration, and had waffled on the Olympic boycott. On the eve of Carter's renomination, it became known that the administration was reconsidering its earlier decision not to build a new bomber to replace the B-52 and, more significantly, had switched its nuclear strategy of deterrence to encompass—reportedly like Soviet military strategy—a war-fighting capacity (also favored by Reagan's advisers); the Democratic platform also endorsed the President's decision to build a new MX missile to implement that strategy and make American missiles less vulnerable to a Soviet first strike.

The Ability to Act: Information as a Political Resource

One of the reasons why the president has possessed an advantage over Congress in foreign policy is the vast amounts of information he has at his fingertips. "Power is knowledge," and the foreign policy bureaucracy possesses such knowledge. The president can call upon the State and Defense Departments, the Central Intelligence Agency, the Arms Control and Disarmament Agency, the U.S. International Communication Agency (propaganda), the Agency for International Development (economic aid), and the foreign staffs in such other departments as Commerce, Treasury, and Agriculture. All these agencies are represented in the embassies abroad and participate in the making of foreign policy in Washington; abroad, they are also amply represented outside the embassies, often by delegations of at least equal size to that of the State Department's foreign service. Indeed, the State Department, of the major agencies, is the smallest one. Note the figures (Table 2–2) just before the outbreak of World War II, at the height of the cold war in 1948, and as the cold war was fading and being replaced by Nixon's détente. In the White House alone the president has the help of special bureaus on a whole range of topics—the National Security Council, Office of Special Representative for Trade Negotiations, Office of Science and Technology, Council of Economic Advisers, and Council on Environmental Quality.

It is not surprising that in these circumstances Congress should be dependent upon the executive for its information. This is particularly true when compared to domestic affairs. Here, as already noted, a representative or senator can call upon the appropriate executive departments dealing with the problem and numerous interest groups, as well as rely upon his own familiarity with the problems being considered by the committee (for instance, congressmen from agricultural areas may serve on the agriculture committee). He has, in brief, means not only to check

TABLE 2–2. Staffing the Department of State

Category	1938	1948	1969
Secretary's Office (including secretariat and under secretaries)	21	186	342
Geographic political offices*	112	318	980
Functional offices Economic, Intelligence, UN, Educational, Scientific, Legal, Protocol, etc.	387	881	1,645
Administrative offices (including consular divisions)	443	2,813	3,307
Miscellaneous (personnel seconded to other agencies, in training, on leave status)	—	—	600
Totals	963	4,198	6,874

*African Affairs, Inter-American Affairs, East Asian and Pacific Affairs, European Affairs, Near Eastern and South Asian Affairs.
SOURCE: Table 2 of *The Foreign Affairs Fudge Factory*, by John Campbell, © 1971 by Basic Books, Inc., Publishers, New York.

out what "the facts" really are, but also experience from which to gain his own sense of perspective on executive policy recommendations. But on foreign policy issues Congress has relied primarily upon information supplied by the president and the foreign policy bureaucracy. And given the facts of life for most congressmen—that they must devote a lot of time to their constituents' affairs—they are members of one or more committees in which most of Congress' work is accomplished; and they themselves feel that they have far less competence and knowledge of external than of internal problems—this reliance is understandable.

This reliance is, in fact, twofold. First, it applies to the "facts" which most congressmen do not even have the time to digest. Thus, when Congress was deciding on the Marshall Plan for the reconstruction of postwar Europe, a highly imaginative policy that signaled a revolutionary shift of American policy from its prewar isolationism to a postwar commitment to Europe—a course Congress had rejected in 1919—this exchange occurred between the Staff Director of the Republican Policy Committee and Republican Senator Homer Ferguson (Mich.):

> MR. SMITH: Now, Senators, for your amusement as well as to bear out my point on the impossible work load put upon members of Congress, I have gathered here a group of the books and reports, limited solely to an official character, which you should be reading now on the Marshall Plan.
> [MR. SMITH here presented a stack of material 18 inches high.]
> You are going to take the momentous step in the history of this

country when you pass upon the Marshall plan. . . . That is what you ought to be studying. It contains the Krug report, the Harriman report, the State Department report, the reports of the Herter committee, the Foreign Relations Committee digest; it includes part of the hearings just completed of the Foreign Relations Committee. It does not include hearings yet to be held by the Appropriations Committees. This is one work load you have now on a single problem out of the many problems you have to decide.

SENATOR FERGUSON: How long would it take in your opinion . . . for a person to read it?

MR. SMITH: Well, Senator, I have been reading for the last 35 years, nearly all my life, in the field of research; and if I could do an intelligent job on that in 2 months of solid reading excluding myself from everything else. . . . I would credit myself with great efficiency.

SENATOR FERGUSON: A normal person would probably take 4 to 5 months.[16]

How in these circumstances can a legislator become familiar with such intricate problems as the strategic arms limitation negotiations, the nature of nationalism in some Third World region, the intentions of Russia toward the major non-Communist states, or the strategic doctrine, force levels, and arms composition of the U.S. military? These and the multiple other issues confronting Congress are issues on which even the experts may not have all the facts and on which, even with sufficient facts, they would disagree as to meaning, consequences, and what ought to be done.

Of course, all of this assumes that Congress gets the information. After it was disclosed in 1973 that the United States had been secretly bombing Cambodia during 1969–70, a number of senators were critical of Secretary of State Rogers for not discussing this issue with them fully at the time. A State Department spokesman said in reply that Rogers had mentioned the raids on two occasions while testifying before the Foreign Relations Committee, although he admitted the secretary had not volunteered information on the magnitude of the raids. He added that if Rogers had been asked for details of the bombing, the secretary would have provided any requested information! But how were senators to ask questions about a military operation of which they were unaware and about which they had learned only a few details from The New York Times? The utter dependence of senators on the executive for information could not be more clearly illustrated than by this admittedly exceptional example. If the executive withholds information, Congress is likely to remain ignorant.

But Congress is dependent upon the executive not only for "the facts" but for their interpretation as well. For example, in 1947 the Truman administration had to reach a decision about intervening in the eastern Mediterranean, where the Russians were putting great pressure on Turkey for control of the Dardanelles and on Greece, where a civil war involving the Greek Communists was raging. There was little precedent for American involvement in that area of the world. While Congress had become increasingly anti-Russian during spats with Moscow in 1946, it was also in a fierce budget-cutting mood and averse to vast, expensive external commitments in January 1947. Thus when in February the British informed the State Department that they could no longer support both endangered countries, the Truman administration decided that American power had to contain what it perceived to be Russian expansion. As the states of Europe collapsed, symbolized by Britain's collapse, the postwar bipolar balance emerged.

On the Eurasian continent, Russia was emerging as the dominant state; only the United States, separated from Eurasia by the Atlantic and Pacific oceans, could supply the countervailing power. President Truman called together a congressional delegation to declare his intentions, but it initially reacted skeptically and interpreted Truman's proposed action as pulling British chestnuts out of the fire. Secretary of State Marshall and Under Secretary Acheson contested this interpretation, and Acheson particularly stressed American security considerations. Convinced, the congressmen insisted Truman explain his dramatic reversal of traditional American policy before Congress and the nation. In an address to a joint session of both houses, Truman informed Congress of the situations in Turkey and Greece and then outlined the basis of the new containment policy. He disguised the basic power realities motivating U.S. actions, however, and justified them on ideological grounds.[17] The Truman Doctrine was, for the United States, the beginning of the cold war.

Another pertinent example is the American involvement in Vietnam which was to end the cold war. Johnson inherited a situation in which only *ad hoc* decisions had been made in response to immediate problems; the Kennedy administration, Arthur Schlesinger, Jr., has suggested, was occupied with other more urgent issues, such as the abortive Cuban invasion, the Berlin Wall, crises in Laos and the Congo, the Alliance for Progress, and the Limited Nuclear Test Ban.[18] Only piecemeal economic and military commitments had been made; each constituted the minimally necessary step to prevent a Communist victory. At no point were the fundamental questions and long-range implications of an increasing Vietnam involvement analyzed: Was South Vietnam vital to American security? Would its fall represent the consolidation of one country under a nationalist leader or constitute a "falling domino" in the Communization of all of Southeast Asia? Did the political situation in South Vietnam warrant or preclude American intervention? Were political conditions both in the United States and in South Vietnam conducive to effective military action? How large a commitment would the United States be required to make, and what costs should be expected? What role should Saigon and its forces play?

If these questions were even asked by President Kennedy and his advisers, the answers did not provide guidelines for the policies that were ultimately followed. The assumption was that South Vietnam was vital, a test of the credibility of America's commitments and power. Policy was built upon that assumption. The approach was incremental and, as the overall situation deteriorated badly, Johnson, like Kennedy, continued to react to the symptoms of the problem and applied short-range solutions: first covert operations, then increasingly frequent "retaliatory" air strikes against North Vietnam, followed by around-the-clock bombing and, finally, the use of U.S. ground forces in South Vietnam as Johnson saw no other options, yet felt committed by his predecessors' actions.

What is noticeable, in retrospect, is not only the administration's lack of questions, but also Congress'. Congressmen may not always know the facts or be sufficiently expert in foreign policy, but their expertise is supposed to be something more fundamental, a political judgment as to the viability of policy, an ability to question the experts' views based upon specialized knowledge. But neither the Senate nor any of its committees, including Foreign Relations and Armed Services, raised any of the fundamental questions that should have been answered before the 1965 intervention. As before, the Senate and House followed the executive's lead; their criticism came after the intervention, and then only after the intervention went sour.

It is unlikely that the information and interpretation "gap" between the executive and legislative branches will disappear. It has, to be sure, been narrowed as congressional committees have obtained larger and better staffs to develop their own sources of information and policy advice, taken more investigative trips abroad, and have been critical in cross-examining administration witnesses. The Vietnam War has led the Congress, particularly the Senate, to concern itself more with the assumptions underlying specific policies and the likely consequences of their adoption. Still, the resources of the executive remain overwhelming by comparison. An administration which insists that its policies are of vital importance to the national interest will probably still prevail.

The Willingness to Act

The Chief Diplomat and the Constitution

Besides the advantage of knowledge, the president possesses the further advantage of being able to act. It is, of course, this capacity to initiate action—especially the commitment of U.S. forces when the president deems it necessary—that has been greatly responsible for the expansion of presidential power in foreign policy since the Nazi and Japanese threats of the late 1930s; and it is this capacity that is at the heart of the contemporary controversy over the extent of presidential powers. Not that this expansion started in the 1930s. For example, the Constitution stated that the president could receive and send ambassadors. President

Washington interpreted this as conferring upon the presidency the power of diplomatic recognition by receiving Citizen Genêt of the French Republic. Congress, of course, has on occasion exerted its influence on this issue, as it did after 1949, when it consistently warned successive presidents not to extend recognition to Communist China. Still, a determined President Nixon, with his surprise 1971 announcement that he would visit Peking, quickly turned the tables on the opponents of recognizing Communist China and showed once again that it is largely the president who determines the question of recognizing foreign governments. By seizing the initiative, he left the congressional opponents no time to organize. The president's subsequent steps—his visits with Mao Tse-tung and Chou En-lai and the 1973 opening of Chinese and American "liaison missions" in Washington and Peking, respectively—established formal diplomatic relations in all but name.

President Carter extended full diplomatic recognition in 1979. The decision did not go unchallenged. Opponents of the recognition of China, which involved withdrawing it from the Nationalists on Taiwan, took the issue to the courts. Senator Goldwater, who brought the lawsuit, argued that since the Senate had given its consent to the 1955 mutual security treaty with Taiwan (the treaty would be null and void one year after the transfer of recognition), the Senate had to consent to ending the treaty and, by implication, the recognition of the People's Republic of China.[19] A federal judge ruled that the Senate had to approve the president's decision by a two-thirds vote or a majority of both houses of Congress, even though the treaty contained the standard clause allowing either party to withdraw from the treaty at any time after proper notification of the other party (a clause approved by the Senate with the rest of the treaty). But on appeal, the judge was overruled and the president's right to recognize a nation by accrediting diplomats was upheld. This is a legal right which a president will exercise when political circumstances are favorable or, at least, not hostile to a recognition.* On China, Congress had for thirty years opposed recognition and made it very clear that the president would recognize Peking as the legal government of China at his risk. The resulting Asian policy bordered on the irrational, reflecting emotions, even hysteria, not hard calculations of what American national interests required. But presidents refused to exercise their power for fear of Congress; only after a costly and divisive war and the election of a conservative president who was beyond the pale of being accused of appeasement could U.S. policy once more be set on a path of rational calculation—and then only stealthily.

Presidents not only exploited the "great silences" of the Constitution

---

*The Supreme Court has never ruled on this question. The judges have always hesitated to interfere in foreign policy and left such issues to be settled politically.

to "make foreign policy" and enhance the powers of their office, but also used their position as the nation's chief diplomat to seize the initiative and strengthen their position against Congress. In this connection, presidents have long resorted to setting policy in declarations or by their behavior. A Monroe announces his famous Doctrine or a Truman declares, as he did in early 1947, that it must be the policy of the United States to support free peoples who are resisting attempted subjugation by armed minorities or outside pressure; and, more recently, the Carter Doctrine committed the U.S. in the Persian Gulf-Indian Ocean area. Or a president may visit West Berlin, as Kennedy did, thus reinforcing in the minds of his NATO allies and Soviet adversary the American commitment to that city and Western Europe; he may visit the capital of a nation not previously recognized, as Nixon did on his trip to Peking, signaling a radical shift of policy; or go to the Middle East, especially Egypt and Syria, to indicate U.S. interest in the area and a more evenhanded policy between Israel and the Arab states. Or he may as Carter did after the Soviet invasion of Afghanistan decide that the U.S. should boycott the 1980 summer Olympic game in Moscow. Or, like Reagan early in his administration, he can make his concern known about Communist arms shipments to El Salvador, a small country torn apart by civil war, in order to send Russia's leaders the message that the U.S. will no longer tolerate such interventions to expand Soviet influence in less developed countries. Similarly, a president can express sentiments of support for a particular state so often, as every American president has in fact done with regard to Israel, so that a virtual commitment of defense seems to exist even though no treaty to this effect has ever been approved by the Senate. Indeed, former Senator Fulbright used to suggest that the United States sign a treaty in order to delimit our unspoken commitment.

The point of these examples is threefold: one, the president, by what he says and does—and, on occasion, by not saying or not doing—sets the direction and tone of U.S. foreign policy; two, by exercising his initiative the president usually leaves Congress with little option but to follow him, unless it wishes publicly to humiliate him and undermine his position as the nation's spokesman in international affairs; and three, the president has an array of tools—informal, such as the ones just discussed, as well as more formal ones—at his disposal, which enable him to use his advantages.

One of the more formal tools the president can use to draw public attention to certain issues and his suggested solutions is the draft treaty. Although the Senate may be consulted during the drafting and negotiating of a treaty and may give its consent when it is submitted, the end of the negotiating process with the other country involved really commits the United States, unless the Senate wants to erode other nations' confidence in the president's ability to represent and articulate American interests internationally. Ever since defeat of the Versailles Treaty concluding World War I, the Senate has been reluctant to deny ratification. For example, when a president is negotiating a limitation of strategic arms, the publicity alone by the time the treaty reaches the Senate floor makes the draft difficult to defeat. Arms control measures are probably particularly so. If an administration has initialed a draft treaty that has the support—or at least the acquiescence—of the various interested executive agencies involved, such as the Joint Chiefs of Staff, it can "sell" such measures to Congress and the public, because arms control often takes on the appearance of a combination of motherhood and salvation and can be easily identified with that most cherished of values, peace. When such a measure is signed in Moscow by the president himself, as Nixon did with the Strategic Arms Limitations Treaty (SALT I) and this is fully covered by television (as were the President's return to the United States and his immediate journey to Capitol Hill to report the success of his negotiations in building a more stable "structure of peace"), who can really do more than raise some objections and then approve such a clearly worthy enterprise when the president has already gone over Congress' head to the country?

SALT II, however, reaped considerable opposition even though the Carter administration consulted Congress, especially the Senate, far more than Nixon or Ford had for the earlier arms control negotiations. Despite that opposition, which ranged from liberals who thought the number of strategic weapons allowed each side were so high that SALT II hardly constituted arms control, to conservatives who felt that it ratified Soviet strategic superiority and endangered U.S. deterrence capability, to moderates who found the treaty acceptable if the administration would simultaneously increase defense spending 5 percent per year (over inflation costs), especially on conventional forces (meaning mainly European defense), Carter was probably short of the magic sixty-seven votes he needed when events overtook him and jeopardized passage of the treaty—his own inept handling of the issue of a Soviet brigade in Cuba, the Shah's collapse in Iran which eliminated a vital intelligence post for observing Soviet missile testing, and especially Moscow's invasion of Afghanistan. Carter used this event to toughen his policy toward the Soviet Union, invoking a number of diplomatic and economic sanctions, and withdrawing SALT II before—in its anti-Soviet mood—the Senate would now certainly defeat it (see Chapter 6).

Although some of the most fundamental U.S. policies since 1945 have been submitted to the Senate in order to let the American people know what commitments their government has undertaken on their behalf and to signal to the adversary the nature of American interests, treaties are few and far between. Presidents often bypass the Senate, with its demand for a two-thirds majority approval of treaties. In a Senate representing 50 states, it takes only 34 votes out of 100 to defeat a treaty. That means a majority of senators may in fact favor a treaty, which was certainly true of SALT II. Indeed, given the fact that a highly urbanized state with a large population has the same representation as a rural state with a smaller population, the 34 senators opposing the treaty may in fact represent less than 5 percent of the population. The two-thirds majority required for treaties in fact places a premium on opposition so that the president, in order to mobilize those 16 votes he needs over a 51 majority, has to literally "buy" these votes by acquiescing or supporting policy decisions such as increasing the defense budget or a pet project in a state which a senator wants for his state. These may add millions, if not billions, to the nation's federal budget.

Given the uncertainty of Senate treaty approval, the length of time it usually takes to strike all the bargains, the cost in the president's time to conduct or supervise all these negotiations (including the neglect of other issues), and the possible economic price for the nation as a whole, it is understandable why presidents prefer to use executive agreements which do not need legislative approval. (Executive agreements may, of course, also be negotiated and signed in pursuance of a particular objective authorized by Congress—for instance, specific tariff agreements with individual countries after Congress has approved a general tariff bill.) Indeed, executive agreements outnumber treaties.

Between January 1, 1946 and December 31, 1976, the United States signed 7201 agreements with the other nations of the world. According to Johnson and McCormick, about 6 percent of these were embodied in treaties; 87 percent were executive agreements to implement congressional legislation or congressional-executive agreements; and only 7 percent were executive agreements based on the executive branch's constitutional authority.[20] Seven percent may be a small number, but these agreements may be the most significant of all the executive agreements, and indeed more important than most of the treaties, for they may commit the United States to the defense of other countries or involve it in situations that may involve the use of force. Thus, for example, a series of executive agreements with Spain for American military bases since 1953 are virtually tantamount to a military commitment to Spain, even though the Senate in 1970 adopted a nonbinding resolution expressing the view that the 1970 executive agreement signed by Spain and the Nixon administration should not be construed as a U.S. commitment to the defense of Spain. In 1976, an agreement for the continued use of American bases in Spain was finally put in treaty form, giving the United States the opportunity to deny the existence of a defense commitment to Spain. (Of course, whether such a commitment does not in fact exist once American forces in Spain are attacked, regardless of a Senate resolution or treaty denying such an obligation, is another question.) The trend toward executive agreements on important issues is demonstrated by two other Nixon agreements: The Paris peace agreement ending the Vietnam War (at least, officially) and the five-year freeze on offensive arms negotiated as part of the SALT I package were both executive agreements (although the ABM limitation was incorporated in a treaty, as is likely to happen with a SALT II offensive weapons agreement, if one is reached).

No executive agreement is ever likely to be more dramatic than the Franklin Roosevelt destroyer deal of 1940 referred to earlier. One more example, perhaps more of presidential ability to commit the United States than of executive agreement, was a letter President Nixon sent President Thieu of South Vietnam to soften his opposition to the Vietnam peace agreement. While such letters do not usually constitute executive agreements, Nixon assured Thieu that if North Vietnam did not abide by the terms of the agreement, he would "take swift and severe retaliatory action."[21] Nixon repeated this assurance at a later date. Confronted by these reassurances and faced with U.S. determination to go ahead and sign the cease-fire agreement on its own and disengage from the war, Thieu signed too. Nixon had just been reelected by a very large majority; he had won all states except Massachusetts. At the zenith of his power, Thieu obviously believed Nixon's premise was credible. Watergate and the War Powers resolution were to undermine that promise.

The Commander in Chief Wields the Sword

But it is the president's authority as commander in chief that has become the greatest source of his expanded power in this century. In 1900 President McKinley sent troops to China to join an international army to crush the Boxer Rebellion, which had besieged foreign embassies in Peking. Theodore Roosevelt, Wilson, and Coolidge used the marines at will throughout the Caribbean. Woodrow Wilson sent troops into Mexico to pursue Pancho Villa and had Vera Cruz bombarded before the outbreak of World War I. In early 1917, when the Germans declared unrestricted submarine warfare on all shipping, belligerent and neutral, to starve Britain into submission, Wilson armed American merchant marines taking supplies to England. Wilson acted after the Senate refused to sanction the President's request for authorizing armaments for the self-defense of the ships. When, during the later Russian Civil War, the Japanese sought to exploit that conflict and establish themselves in Siberia by landing troops, Wilson sent American troops to keep an eye on the Japanese. After the eruption of World War II and the fall of France, President Roosevelt, as we already know, used American warships to escort the English and Canadian merchant ships as far as Iceland, where the British Royal Navy took over, and ordered American ships to "shoot on sight" at German raiders or submarines.

Since World War II, recurrent crises—with the potential of exploding into nuclear war—as well as two limited wars, have built on these precedents and further expanded the president's authority as commander in chief. When the Russians blockaded Berlin in 1948, President Truman responded with an airlift to supply the population of the Western half of the city. When the North Koreans attacked South Korea in 1950, the President ordered first air support for the South Korean Army and then the landing of American ground forces in Korea when the air support seemed unable to stem the invaders. Congressional leaders were informed of these decisions by the President, but he did not ask for their approval. Truman felt that as commander in chief he already possessed the authority to commit U.S. forces when he believed American security was endangered. After Communist China's intervention in Korea, he sent several divisions to Western Europe to enhance Western strength and deter a possible Russian move in Moscow's "front yard" while America was becoming more deeply involved in Asia; again Congress was not asked for approval.

Both Eisenhower and Kennedy, as we know, made commitments to South Vietnam. The former initiated a large-scale program of economic and military assistance to support the non-Communist government there. "The United States had gradually developed a special commitment in South Vietnam. It was certainly not absolutely binding—but the commitment was there."[22] Kennedy would enlarge this into what the Pentagon Papers refer to as a "broad commitment"[23] and would leave his successor feeling that this commitment was virtually binding. Kennedy also launched the Eisenhower-planned invasion of Cuba in 1961 and blockaded the island a year later to compel the Soviets to withdraw their missiles. After his assassination, his successor intervened in the Dominican Republic in 1965 with troops to forestall "another Cuba" (Eisenhower had earlier, in 1954, covertly used the CIA, rather than the marines, to overthrow the government of Guatemala when it was feared to be moving in Moscow's direction).

It was, however, the increasing unpopularity of America's first modern limited war, the Korean War, that led President Eisenhower, after the Democrats had been defeated in 1952, to ask for congressional resolutions granting him legislative support to use the armed forces when he felt this to be necessary in the national interest. The administration's idea was that "the resolution process, by involving Congress in the take-off, would incriminate it in a crash-landing."[24] In other words, a principal purpose was to ward off the type of later congressional criticism and retribution that had hurt the Truman administration. These resolutions did not, however, indicate that Eisenhower, any more than his predecessors or successors, felt that in the absence of congressional support he did not possess the legal authority to use the armed forces as he saw fit—as, for example, in Lebanon or the Formosa Straits. In any event, Congress gave him virtually a blank check; in fact, it was more an expression of approval than a grant of authority.

Johnson, in 1964, received a similar broad grant known as the Tonkin Resolution, after the gulf where North Vietnamese torpedo boats allegedly attacked two American destroyers. This is how in part it was worded:

> [Be it] Resolved by the Senate and House of Representatives of the United States of America in Congress assembled, that the Congress approves and supports the determination of the President, as Commander in Chief, to take all necessary measures to repel any armed attack against the forces of the United States and to prevent further aggression.
>
> The United States regards as vital to its national interest and to world peace the maintenance of international peace and security in Southeast Asia. Consonant with the Constitution and the Charter of the United Nations and in accordance with its obligations under the Southeast Asia Collective Defense Treaty, the United States is, therefore, prepared, as the President determines, to take all necessary steps, including the use of armed force, to assist any member or protocol state of the Southeast Asia Collective Defense Treaty requesting assistance in defense of its freedom.[25]

Johnson, unfortunately for the nation as well as himself, was neither lucky nor shrewd.[26] Both he and Eisenhower requested congressional resolutions for the areas in which action was contemplated when tensions there appeared to be quite high. In each case Congress, once the President had publicly requested its support, could hardly turn him down unless it wished to seem unpatriotic. Eisenhower, however, was either lucky or shrewd. In neither crisis was he required to use force overtly. In the Middle East, troops landed in Lebanon but were not involved in any fighting, and in the Formosa Straits the Seventh Fleet "showed the flag" but did not need to shoot. Johnson, however, followed with 500,000 troops!

Johnson had hoped that the Tonkin Resolution, passed by the Senate with only two dissenting votes and by the House unanimously, would be read by Hanoi as an indication of American determination to prevent a Communist takeover of South Vietnam and that it would therefore desist from attempting to do so. But neither the resolution nor some retaliatory strikes after Tonkin and, later, Pleiku, led Hanoi to "leave its neighbor alone," as Secretary of State Dean Rusk phrased the American objective. More punitive moves, it was felt, were needed to attain this aim. Sustained air attacks that avoided bombing cities were launched in the spring of 1965; when those also did not frighten off Hanoi, presumed to be the organizer and director of the war in the South, Johnson felt he had no choice but to send American troops into South Vietnam as the military situation there deteriorated rapidly and the Vietcong appeared to be within reach of victory. But as the increasingly Americanized war dragged on and victory seemed more and more to be an illusion, congressional and public support for the war declined, as it had earlier for the war in Korea. As the criticism mounted, Johnson was not protected by the Tonkin Resolution. The conclusion would, therefore, seem to be that congressional support in the form of a resolution for presidential use of force is politically largely immaterial. If a president is successful, he will receive little or no criticism—indeed much praise—even without a congressional resolution; if he is unsuccessful, he will reap large amounts of criticism and abuse, even if he possesses hundreds of congressional resolutions.

In any event, once the country is involved in a war, whether it is legally declared by the Congress or not, presidents make the basic political decisions and choose the appropriate military strategy to achieve the chosen political objectives. Thus, Roosevelt during World War II decided that Germany should be defeated before Japan since Germany was the stronger power and the United States, as a belligerent, had allies whose existence was threatened primarily by Germany, not Japan. Later, Roosevelt chose to invade continental Europe through France rather than, as Churchill wanted, to drive into the Balkans from northern Italy and Yugoslavia, thereby trying to limit the Russian army's advance and Soviet influence to Eastern Europe. A cross-channel invasion, which would come to grips with the German army on the plains of Europe where it could be defeated, seemed to Roosevelt a more feasible way to end the war quickly; it undoubtedly was, but it did mean that the Russian army stood in the heart of Europe after Germany's collapse.

During the Korean War, President Truman, who had already made the key decisions to drop two atomic bombs to force Japan's surrender and to intervene in Korea, made two further significant decisions: one, to cross the 38th parallel dividing North and South Korea after the North Korean army had been defeated; and two, not to extend the war even farther by bombing and blockading China after the Chinese had responded to the U.S. invasion of North Korea by intervening, just as the North Korean invasion of the South had precipitated American intervention. This brought Truman into a fierce confrontation with the commanding general, General Douglas MacArthur, a great war hero who was supported by the conservative and dominant wing of the Republican party in Congress. When MacArthur refused to stop publicly criticizing the administration's policy and strategy in Korea with the assertion that there was "no substitute for victory," Truman fired him amid a public furor.[27]

For Johnson, of course, all the decisions in Vietnam proved fateful: the decision in 1965 to escalate the American intervention with air power and troops until U.S. forces in Vietnam stood at over five hundred thousand men; further decisions to escalate in order to appease congressional hawks and de-escalate to satisfy the doves; and the decision to fight a "painless war" until 1967 by deferring students and postponing a war tax to counter the rising inflation, among other measures. But as the intervention turned sour, it stained Johnson's historical reputation, precipitated an executive-legislative struggle, badly divided the nation, compelled Johnson to foreswear renomination as the Democrat's presidential candidate in 1968, deeply divided the Democratic party, and helped the Republicans win the presidency that year.

After President Nixon had come into office, the Senate repealed the

Tonkin Resolution not once but twice! Nixon even supported this move, claiming that he did not need it, and thereby added insult to the injury the Senate already felt at what it claimed was Johnson's deception at the time he requested the Tonkin Resolution. Although it had given him a broad grant of authority, senatorial critics now asserted, it had done so on the assumption that Johnson would use it only for his retaliatory strikes, not to justify the widening of the war with large-scale American intervention.[28] But Nixon, whose policy was to withdraw U.S. ground forces gradually while letting the South Vietnamese army increasingly take over the fighting as its capability to do so was presumably enhanced by better training and more weapons, claimed that as commander in chief he had the authority to use the armed forces in any way he wished to protect the remaining American forces in Vietnam.

As more troops were pulled out and Hanoi's temptation to attack in South Vietnam increased, Nixon undertook a number of actions—vigorously criticized in the Senate—under the commander in chief authority he had claimed. He ordered American forces into Cambodia to search for and destroy North Vietnamese supplies. (Before this action in 1970, as noted earlier, U.S. bombers had long carried on bombing attacks in Cambodia, which were hidden from congressional and public scrutiny.) Nixon also sent American planes from time to time for "protective reaction" raids on the North; authorized the mining of North Vietnamese ports and heavy bombing of Hanoi and Haiphong after Hanoi launched a large conventional attack on South Vietnam; and, when the Paris peace negotiations stalled, launched B-52's during the Christmas season to compel a settlement (in January 1973, a settlement was signed). After the Paris peace agreement, when the understanding that a cease-fire and withdrawal of U.S. forces from South Vietnam would be followed shortly by cease-fires in Laos and Cambodia failed to materialize in Cambodia, B-52's were used to stem the successful Communist forces. Since the President could no longer invoke his need to protect American troops after they had departed, he claimed that the failure of the Communists to abide by the Paris agreement meant that he could wage the war in Cambodia until a cease-fire had been agreed upon. He had possessed the authority to wage the war in Vietnam; this authority continued until the war in Cambodia ended as it had in South Vietnam. The Congress disagreed and cut off funds for further bombing in 1973.

In an attempt to terminate the bombing even before the cut-off date, a suit was brought in federal court on the basis that Congress had not declared a war in Cambodia and that consequently the President's action was unconstitutional. The suit was eventually unsuccessful, but at some point it is likely that the Supreme Court will have to rule on the whole issue of the president's war power. In the past, the Court has generally been reluctant to challenge the president's exercise of his power, even when he has exercised it in unprecedented ways. Whether it can or will continue this general abstention on the crucial, central issue of the force remains to be seen.

The War Powers Resolution

In the wake of the Vietnam War, the Congress took a number of actions to hold the executive more accountable. Collectively, they constituted a congressional assertion to play a larger and more active foreign policy role than before and, simultaneously, to restrain the president from presumably getting the country into another Vietnam. "No more Vietnams" was the slogan and the mood of the country throughout the 1970s. Closer supervision of presidents was viewed as the best means of keeping the country out of new and costly overseas "adventures." America was no longer to be the "world's policeman;" it was to play a more limited role only. To ensure this was Congress' responsibility.

Congress' determination to play a more energetic part in the process was reflected in the following actions:

1. The War Powers resolution which was passed by the Senate and the House over President Nixon's veto in 1973 was to restore Congress' role in decisions involving the use of force.
2. Executive agreements had to be reported to Congress and the Congress has tended to insist that important agreements be submitted as treaties.
3. An increasing number of restrictions have been imposed on security or military assistance, including a congressional veto of specific arms transfers over a few million dollars.
4. Intelligence operations—that is, CIA covert interventions or subversions—must now be reported to a number of Senate and House committees.

We shall focus on the War Powers resolution because it is as commander in chief that presidents have enormously expanded the powers of their office, and it was the Vietnam War which led to the legislative decision to reassert its responsibilities in the use of force. The resolution states that the president shall, in every possible instance, consult with Congress before using U.S. armed forces. The resolution also provides for three emergency situations in which the president can commit American forces without prior congressional declaration of war: to repel or forestall an attack upon the United States; to repel or forestall an attack upon American forces located outside the country; to rescue endangered American citizens in carefully defined circumstances; beyond these emergency categories, the president would need "specific statutory authorization."[29] This requirement aims to replace the blank-check resolution such as the Gulf of Tonkin with precisely worded resolutions, jointly devised by Congress and the president. Even when the president uses his emergency powers, he must immediately make a full report to Congress and obtain congressional authority to continue the action after sixty days, with an extension of thirty additional days if troops are in danger. If he fails to receive legislative concurrence, he must terminate the action at that time. Even before this sixty-day deadline Congress can terminate the action through a concurrent resolution, which would not be subject to a presidential veto. As one of the bill's sponsors said, "The real danger is that presidents can—and do—shoot from the hip. If the collective judgment of the president and Congress is required to go to war, it will call for responsible action by the Congress for which each member must answer individually and for restraint by both the Congress and the presidents."[30] The War Powers resolution, in short, grants the Congress the potential to play a greater role in decisions involving the use of force. Indeed, it not only grants it; the resolution no longer permits Congress to avoid its political responsibility.

In reality, however, has much changed? The act, in a sense, recognized "reality," for it changed the Constitution from reading that war cannot be waged without the consent of Congress to the president can wage war until Congress stops him. When the U.S. merchant ship *Mayaguez* was seized in what the American government claimed to be the high seas by the Cambodians shortly after the final collapse of South Vietnam in 1975, the President used American military forces to recover the ship and its crew on the island where they were and, to prevent any retaliation, ordered some bombing of certain airfields and port targets on the mainland. President Ford did inform the Congress, as the War Powers Resolution required, of what had occurred and what he was going to do about it. But he no more consulted Congress than had his predecessors. The ship and crew were recovered, although at the time the rescue operation began, unknown to the United States, the crew was being released. Despite loss of life and equipment, the action was generally applauded as successful and had saved a tattered American prestige, which had been badly deflated by the demise of South Vietnam and was widely judged as further deflated by Cambodia's action. Therefore, a mini-power such as Cambodia, could not be permitted to seize and hold a U.S. ship with impunity without lowering American self-esteem—and, perhaps, prestige as seen in Moscow and elsewhere. Ford had rescued this prestige and, as a result, his popularity in the country rose to his highest yet. Thus, instead of being criticized by the Congress he had essentially bypassed, he was praised by Republicans and Democrats alike.

The lesson appears clear and is probably no comfort to the proponents of the War Powers Resolution. If a president is unsuccessful when he uses force, he will be damned even if he has legislative support; if successful, he will be acclaimed even if he does not possess congressional support. Perhaps the real test of the War Powers Resolution will come when the president confronts a situation involving a more sustained and far bigger military involvement than the rescue of the *Mayaguez* required, or the later rescue mission of the U.S. hostages in Iran in April 1980. (Chapter 5) An intervention in a larger and longer-lasting war will, of course, require the Congress to stand up and be counted—"Put blood on our hands, too," as Senator Jacob Javits (R., N.Y.) reportedly said—instead of hiding behind the president and letting him take sole responsibility.[31] But, of course, the Congress has always possessed the power to intervene if it had not approved of the president's actions by not appropriating funds for the conduct of hostilities. The real test of the War Powers resolution, as of general executive-legislative relations, is still to come.[32]

What happens if the president and Congress differ in their respective definitions of a "national emergency"—that is, whether a crisis exists? Would the Congress have accepted Roosevelt's definition of the German threat after the fall of France as a menace to U.S. security and supported the transfer of destroyers to England, the convoying of British merchant ships by U.S. warships as far as Iceland, or the "shoot on sight" order against German raiders? The War Powers resolution simply assumed the unassumable, that a crisis is a crisis, clear to any beholder and therefore not needing any definition. This may not always be true.

Even if they agree on what an emergency is, how from a practical point of view can the president be given sufficient authority and flexibility to act without evading congressional involvement and responsibility to participate in key decisions affecting war and peace; or can this be insured only by eliminating presidential discretion and carefully defining the circumstances in which he can act? In short, how can one find the spot halfway between authority which is too broad and that which is too narrow, between giving the president the flexibility he needs to protect American interests and handcuffing him so that he does not involve the country in needless conflict? In the weeks before the spring, 1980, abortive rescue attempt of the American hostages held in Iran, the Senate Foreign Relations Committee chairman and ranking minority members insisted that the Carter administration consult with the committee before using force. Rumors were rife that Iran's ports were about to be mined in an effort to increase economic pressure on Iran. But how can any administration consult the Congress in advance on plans for the use of force without placing the world on notice, giving its adversary time to mobilize international opinion (including American opinion) against such an effort, and placing its military forces on alert to foil the American effort? Is this any way for a great power to conduct its foreign policy and protect its interests?

A third problem remains equally vexing: How can Congress really participate in crisis decision-making? President Ford after the *Mayaguez* said that it could not and cited several reasons, some of which President Kennedy before him and Carter after him also cited.[33]

1. Key legislators were out of town and communicating with them was difficult, slow, and in some instances impossible. (Kennedy had the

Air Force pick up the important congressional figures and return them to Washington during the Cuban missile crisis).

2. Congressmen have a multitude of concerns which prevent them from focusing over a period of time only, or primarily, on one issue.

3. Time is of the essence and this requirement is incompatible with developing a consensus among congressional leaders in case of disagreement, especially if they are not in town.

4. Even if a consensus were reached, many congressmen among today's independent-minded legislators might not accept it.

5. The likelihood of information leaking out from some members of Congress about a forthcoming military operation inhibits any executive consultation with the Congress or with more than just a very few members.

One might add to these reasons cited by President Ford that in the contemporary Congress it is doubtful that many members would consider presidential consultation with key congressional leaders sufficient. The days during which a few men could speak for the president appear to be over. Paradoxically, however, one might question how many congressmen really want to know what the president is planning. It is one thing to blame him for failure afterwards and suggest that had he consulted Congress this failure could have been avoided; it is another matter to also be held accountable for disaster. Perhaps it is for this reason that not too many voices were raised in protest about the lack of consultation after the failure of the mission to rescue the hostages in Iran in the spring of 1980.

The War Powers resolution and the increasing concern of the Congress for limiting presidential discretion on foreign policy call our attention to another critical aspect of the chief executive's position: his personality and ability to work with the Congress on questions of national policy. An activist president may have little interest in the Congress and attempt to govern, particularly on international issues, as if the legislature were not at all powerful. This sort of behavior will lead to a clashing of wills and perhaps, as occurred in the Nixon presidency, very bitter personal clashes between the president and key members of Congress. To what extent does the personality of the chief executive dictate his fitness for office—and can we predict in advance what sort of president an individual might be? We now turn to these questions.

Personality and the Search for a President: Why Not the Best?

Increasing presidential power has spawned a heightened concern for the type of men who have occupied—and will occupy—the highest office in the land and perhaps the world. Most schoolchildren can recite a list of "great" presidents such as Washington, Jefferson, Lincoln, Wilson, and the two Roosevelts, Theodore and Franklin. Discredited chief executives also come to mind quickly: Andrew Johnson, who was impeached and almost convicted (he survived as president by a single vote in the conviction trial in the Senate), and Nixon, who resigned on the verge of impeachment and probable conviction a century later. We hear substantially less about other presidents and virtually nothing at all about vice-presidents. In 1972, the McGovern presidential campaign suffered a major setback when it became known that the vice-presidential nominee, Senator Thomas Eagleton (D., Mo.), had undergone psychiatric treatment earlier in his life. Eagleton was ultimately forced to withdraw from the ticket although he has continued to serve quite effectively in the Senate. There was considerable controversy at the time about Eagleton's capacity to serve as vice-president (and possibly some day as president). In an era of the strong presidency, the demands placed upon nominees' personal traits are being critically scrutinized by the press, the public, and scholars. There is little evidence that the public would stand for a presidential candidate who would give the country a "government as good as its people," in the words of one Jimmy Carter.

The tensions of Vietnam and Watergate have made Americans somewhat fearful of presidential power. In turn, these events have called attention to the problem of determining in advance who might be an exceptional president, or at least a very good one, in contrast to the failed Johnson and Nixon administrations. To be sure, there were many observers who quite accurately observed that a country boy like Lyndon Johnson would not adapt well to international politics. Johnson found himself uncomfortable with most of the advisers from the academy that he inherited from Kennedy, many of whom were more at home in Paris than on the bank of the Pedernales and Johnson City, Texas. On the other hand, Nixon was a master of international politics, a match for any Soviet or Chinese leader (or even Charles de Gaulle of France), but again there were many who remembered his dirty political campaigns of the 1940s and 1950s, when he falsely accused his opponents of being soft on communism—in his 1946 race for the Senate in California he called Democratic Representative Helen Gahagan Douglas the "pink lady"—and many refused to believe in 1968 that there was a "new Nixon." Before his second term had passed its midpoint, it was clear that this emperor did not have any new clothes. But is a close scrutiny of the personal attributes of the candidates enough? It would hardly seem so since many of those who most strongly supported Nixon in 1968 argued that he would restore the confidence in government that was lost in the Vietnam quagmire of Johnson.

The joint occurrence of Vietnam, the Eagleton affair, and Watergate within less than a decade highlighted the nation's concern for ensuring that the highest office would be filled with someone who was capable of handling the job. Could there be a prescreening, a sort of Presidential Leadership Test, which might not guarantee us great leaders, but perhaps save us from our previous errors? At least one school of thought leads to a positive answer to this question. Called "psychohistory" or "psychobiography," this approach to studying leadership is based upon the development of personality in potential leaders and the use of psychoanalytic methods of investigation to determine what led some leaders to success and others to failure. The 1970s did not mark the beginning of psychohistory, but rather a renewed and enlarged concern for the capacity of academic research to guide us in screening out potentially bad presidents.

Psychobiography has been applied to such diverse figures as Luther and Woodrow Wilson. But in 1972, James David Barber's book, *The Presidential Character*, the first psychohistory of American presidents, was published.[34] Barber's analysis: (1) dealt with presidents comparatively; (2) presented a framework for classifying presidents; (3) claimed to have predictive utility; and (4) specifically and rather strikingly predicted the failure of the Nixon presidency. Barber's argument is itself complex, so we shall necessarily oversimplify it here.

Barber clearly maintains that the early development of a president's personality is the key to understanding how he will perform in office.[35] In examining this personality through the tools of psychoanalysis, we must be careful to avoid accounts which are too popular (press reports or biographies which may be overly critical or flattering) and obtain detailed information on the future leader's early development. What is one to look for in examining whether someone will be a successful leader? *Style* involves the way the president balances rhetoric, personal relationships, and detailed "homework"—ranging from the very intense patterns of Nixon, Johnson, and Wilson to the more relaxed style of Eisenhower and particularly Coolidge, who would not miss his daily nap. *World view* consists of the president's perception of what the great issues of the time are and what forces shape them, including both Franklin Roosevelt's dictum that "We have nothing to fear but fear itself" to Nixon's (and Johnson's) identification of such struggles as involving good and evil, white and black, the forces of incumbency versus the challenge from without and sometimes even within, from what Dan Rather has called "the palace guard."[36] Finally, there is the element of *character*, the president's outlook on life and his role in the world "not for the moment, but enduringly."[37] From these considerations Barber outlines two basic dimensions of the presidential character: activity-passivity and positive-negative affect toward one's activity. On the question of activity, style is stressed. Affect toward activity reflects world view and character; more specifically, affect poses the question: Does the (potential) president enjoy the job and have a positive outlook toward his capacity to handling the problems he confronts?

Putting these two dimensions together, Barber constructs four types of presidential character. The active-positive chief executive puts much effort into the job and enjoys doing it. He values productivity and sees himself as developing over time to meet new challenges within well-defined personal goals. There is an emphasis on rationality; such a president sees events in terms of diverse factors and the political battles that must be won, within the contexts of rational action, to achieve productivity.[38] Among the active-positive presidents have been Franklin Roosevelt, Harry Truman, John Kennedy, Gerald Ford, and Jimmy Carter. In contrast, the active-negatives have a conflict between a very strong effort to succeed and low emotional reward for that attempt. Activity is compulsive, the president himself ambitious and aggressive. Unlike the active-positive, who relates well to others who may oppose his policies, the active-negative retreats from opposition, often into a lonely inner struggle which produces confrontation and despair for the leader and isolates him from the nation.[39] Such presidents include Wilson, Johnson, Herbert Hoover, and Nixon. All had unhappy childhoods, including poor relationships with their parents, and a pressing need to succeed against what seemed to be a highly imperfect and often hostile world.

The passive-positive president is simultaneously optimistic and agreeable, friendly and compliant. Such a leader has a positive outlook on the job of being president but does not believe that much is demanded of him personally in terms of commitment to new programs or national leadership. The emphasis is on personality, as Barber argues regarding the ever-smiling William Howard Taft and Warren Harding during the "return to normalcy" after World War I, a period of relative calm in the country. A passive-positive is popular because of what he does not do and because of what he is—either a hero to the nation or a likable sort of person (Harding). A passive-negative, in contrast, would rather be almost anything but president. He is in politics because he believes he ought to be. The job is unrewarding and this type of leader has little patience for it. The classic case is Coolidge, who slept through more than half of his administration; another, less clear-cut example, is Dwight Eisenhower.[40] Neither sought the position. Coolidge simply walked away from renomination when he said, "I do not choose to run." Eisenhower, with not much of a world view (he was not registered in either political party for most of his adult life), turned down the Democratic nomination in 1948, while the battle on his behalf for the Republican nomination was largely waged without his efforts.

In the era of strong presidents, however, passive chief executives are increasingly unlikely to be selected. Rather, Barber sees the major struggle in American politics as one between active-positives and active-negatives. The former are, of course, almost ideal types. The great presidents were all active-positives and others who fit into this category are viewed at least as reasonably successful. All were well adjusted and did not allow the office of the presidency to insulate them from the nation, whatever their other failings may have been. Active-negatives, on the other hand, are self-destructive and thus potentially fatal to the nation. Their world vision is limited by their concern for their respective places in history and their insistence that each of them has the answers to the nation's problems. Opponents are simply wrong. Barber predicted in 1972 that Nixon's presidency would come to an unhappy end, and the utility of his framework was established for many.[41] In 1980, he predicted that if elected, Reagan would be a "jelly bean"—a softie—rather than the Darth Vader that President Carter was trying to portray him as. Reagan, according to Barber, would be a nine-to-five president. His passivity has been shown by his lifetime practice of taking it easy; his positive side is evident in his generally cheerful, optimistic attitude. Reagan hates to fight and seeks to please and may cave in to pressure; the greatest danger will be that as his passive-positive predecessors, the president may be done in by his friends. Who his presidential friends will be is thus critical and a considerably more important issue to consider than it would be for a president possessing a different character.

The strengths of the approach of psychohistory are its comparative evaluation of presidents and its recognition of the role of childhood development on a leader's personality. The active-passives are well adjusted and the active-negatives poorly adjusted. But historical records, even psychoanalytic ones, are subject to multiple interpretations. The same evidence can be used to adduce either a positive or a negative evaluation of even childhood experiences.[42] Often value judgments are a function of hindsight. Truman seems to be a much better president now than he did when he was in office; then, he was too common; today he is viewed as a man of the people. Revisionist psychohistory in progress may leapfrog Eisenhower from a borderline passive-negative to a passive-positive.[43] Reagan's high profile and very effective bargaining style during his first several months in office seemed to dispute the widespread predictions of his passivity. Psychohistory is certainly a useful way of generalizing about leadership which has previously been beyond the political scientists' scope. But what happens when not just the journalists but the specialists, the psychohistorians, disagree on what the evidence means? Furthermore, Barber's linkage of the presidential character to early childhood experiences and teenage development seems to belie the traditional notion of a president "growing into the job." How much more likely is someone with earlier emotional problems to develop into an active-negative president? Has the country actually been better served by ensuring that Eagleton will never be elected to either the presidency or the vice-presidency? How do we determine the most appropriate methods of evaluating the evidence? Psychoanalysis is hardly an exact science.[44]

What kind of a foreign policy president will a particular personality type make? It is in this area that there is the greatest potential for further development, because handling foreign affairs from the White House necessarily involves on-the-job training. Two classic active-negatives, Wilson and Johnson, failed on key foreign policy issues important to them. Wilson lost a pitched battle with the Senate over American entry into the League of Nations while Johnson was overcome by events in Vietnam. Both presidents had been primarily interested in domestic politics—and, despite Barber's analysis, Wilson is often listed in both public and academic surveys as one of the nation's great presidents.[45] The disparity lies in Wilson's remarkable achievements in social welfare legislation, his New Freedom, mostly accomplished during his first administration (1913—17). Johnson was also a leader in domestic politics, where he sought "to heal and to build" and was a compassionate champion of civil rights and war against poverty, not people. Probably more social legislation was passed during 1965—66 than in the rest of this century (including the New Freedom and Franklin Roosevelt's New Deal). Could Johnson have been an active-positive president on domestic policy but not on foreign policy? On the other hand, Nixon's foreign policy accomplishments kept his personal popularity at levels which let him retain the presidency for at least several months longer than would otherwise be the case. (Chapter 4) As much as Wilson and Johnson disliked the conduct of foreign policy and sought refuge in social welfare legislation, Nixon believed that his world centered around international events.

These questions are not meant to disparage the contributions of psychohistory, but only to recognize the limitations of any approach which seeks to determine who might be a great president or even an acceptable one. A good president on foreign policy is not necessarily the same as a strong leader on domestic policy. Perhaps the personality types involved in each are sufficiently different so that we expect the impossible. Traditional foreign policy leadership requires a command style, the establishment of a hierarchy so that there is a single leader for the nation. Domestic policy success, on the other hand, requires strong bargaining skills, an ability to deal with legislators on their own terms, and, most critically, an understanding of the complex political relationships among members of Congress and the president. One style emphasizes almost complete control over a situation; the other tremendous flexibility. It is a rare president, particularly in these days of an increasingly interdependent world, who possesses both traits. Perhaps only Franklin Roosevelt achieved such success.

Another problem that psychohistorical approaches have not stressed is the increasing divergence between the traits necessary to get elected and those useful in governing. In the 1970s, politicians have run for national office—both the presidency and Congress—by running against Washington.[46] The theme was sounded clearly by Carter in 1976 and then turned against him by Reagan in 1980! The lack of enthusiasm for both major party nominees in 1980—and 1976, to be sure—has been traced directly to our system of nominating the president. This reformed system is marked by widespread public participation in the selection process, so that the number of primaries in each party has more than doubled from the prereform year of 1968 to 1980. David S. Broder has commented:[47]

> The selection system . . . largely determines the kind of candidates you get. Carters and Reagans—men who are capable free-lance campaigners of somewhat idiosyncratic background and views, self-proclaimed outsiders, most remarkable for their dogged ambition and relentless energy, prepared to spend years of their lives seeking the presidential prize, but not viewed by their political peers—or by much of the public—as unusually gifted in governmental leadership.

Both Carter and Reagan spent several years not holding any public office in search of their parties' nominations, as did George Bush in 1980. In contrast, Republican Howard Baker and Democrats Walter Mondale and Edward M. Kennedy, each of whom would in all likelihood have been much more acceptable in 1980 to their legislative parties, had to spend so much time as incumbents (Senators or the vice-president) that they had little time to roam the country seeking political support over a four-year period.

Parliamentary systems, such as those of Great Britain or Germany, select their chief executives from the legislative parties. One can argue that the people selected by the major parties in such systems would probably not have emerged from a system of primaries such as we have in the United States. Parliamentary parties select as leaders people with widespread support within the party machinery and with demonstrated ability to lead in the legislature. It is virtually inconceivable for such a system to pick a Reagan or a Carter as chief executive. Meg Greenfield was even less sanguine than Broder: "We have developed something new in our politics: the professional amateur. . . .You succeed in this line of activity by declaring your aversion to and unfitness for it. That will bring you the cheers of the multitude. It will also bring in time . . . the kind of troubles the Carter presidency has sustained and seemed, almost perversely, to compound."[48]

To be more specific: The nomination process favors temperaments and methods that do not equip the candidate for political life in Washington. As presidential candidates increasingly appeal to the party faithful in primaries, their world view or ideology may not only differ from the congressional party but it further weakens the political ties between the president and his party. Michael Krasner has aptly noted that "The resources essential to capturing the nomination—a strong personal organization, an effective television image, and an appealing campaign theme—are not central to the conflict and bargaining that permeate national policy-making."[49] Once in power, why should the president change the habits which have brought him the highest secular political reward: "to go it alone, to keep his own counsel, to rely on his personal staff, to set himself apart from other politicians, to rely on persuasion and media appeals, to treat issues as separate problems"[50] without much sense of priorities? But these qualities are likely to make a president a poor political leader—to get things done, especially in mobilizing congressional support for his legislative proposals—because he has not learned to bargain and negotiate. He will come up with specific proposals on issues and he will expect these proposals to be accepted on the basis of their merit. Having not come up through the party, owing party leaders little, his views may not only differ significantly from the party mainstream, thus intensifying executive-legislative conflict, but his campaigning may not have prepared him for the need to mend fences, deal with others in terms of their interests, build support where he can, and compromise where he must and to do so on a continuing basis.

How new is this phenomenon? The tension between seeking elective office and governing effectively predates the dominance of the executive branch over the legislative branch in American politics. In the days of the weak president, Woodrow Wilson lamented: ". . . administration is regarded as something which an old soldier, an ex-diplomatist (sic), or a popular politician may be trusted to take by instinct. No man of tolerable talents need despair of having been born a Presidential candidate."[51] Three decades later, in 1915, the English observer Lord Bryce titled a chapter in his famous *The American Commonwealth* "Why Great Men Are Not Chosen Presidents," and warned that "the merits of a President are one thing and those of a candidate another thing."[52] Somewhat presciently, he argued against psychohistorical predictions "because the previous career of the possible candidates has generally made it easier to say who will succeed as a candidate than who will succeed as a President."[53]

But these words were written before the era of the strong president; among the traits that Bryce believed were not necessary for a good president to possess were brilliance and eloquence. What was required included honesty, firmness, and common sense—the same traits that a man would need to run a moderate-sized company.[54] The demands of a world view, an activist style, and a firm character arose with the strong chief executive. But what has not changed fundamentally is the nature of political man. If anything, the greater demands on a president's talents brought on by a more complex world less dominated by a few powers and the new technology of media politics have made the gap between the talents needed for election and effective governing even wider. The issue we confront is the classic one of democratic political systems: How can we reconcile a process which is fundamentally based upon popular consent and control with the demands of running a nation efficiently and with some vision of an ideal policy? The demagogue who makes the trains run on time may ultimately destroy the democratic regime he purports to serve, but the quiet legislative leader studying strategies and policy alternatives may, when he enters the forum of national political competition, be left waiting at the station.

Congress: How Silent a Partner?

3

The First Branch of Government

The president is the major actor not only in foreign policy, but in domestic policy as well. But the intentions of the Founders of the American republic had not envisaged this. The legislative branch is the first one discussed in the Constitution and this was not accidental.[1] The type of government envisaged by the Founders was one of legislative dominance. The Constitution gives the Congress a large number of specifically enumerated powers and a wide-ranging grant of "implied powers." In contrast, as noted earlier, the president has constitutionally been given only three specific powers: (1) his position as commander in chief of the armed forces and as the principal officer in each of the executive departments; (2) his power to negotiate treaties and to appoint ambassadors, in each case with the "advice and consent" of the Senate; and (3) the power to make executive appointments during periods when the Senate is in recess.

Two of the three powers specifically granted to the president deal with questions of foreign policy, but this hardly is evidence that the Founders expected the executive branch to dominate policy making in this arena. George Washington's "Farewell Address" to the nation warned against the country becoming involved in "entangling alliances" and the Founders generally expected the president to execute the laws of the country as passed by the Congress in domestic policy. The scope of foreign policy-making was viewed as quite limited—and not terribly important to a new nation thousands of miles away from the European powers. Foreign policy was simply too inconsequential to take up much of the time of the Congress, the first branch of government. In the unlikely event of armed conflict, however, the legislature retained the sole power to declare war on foreign countries.

Two centuries later, however, presidential preeminence on foreign policy was unquestioned at least in fact. The impetus of decision making had shifted dramatically and many members of the Congress after Vietnam sought to reclaim their historical role as at least a coequal policy-maker on foreign policy. The arguments raised in this debate over which branch should be most powerful have been reminiscent of those which marked the original debate over the Constitution. The Founders selected a president rather than a king because they did not want one individual to accumulate so much power as to be unchecked. The powerful president, so highly regarded when people liked the men occupying the office, became in the 1960s and 1970s the "imperial Presidency,"[2] an American king. Congress, in contrast, was the "voice of the people," the men and women directly elected by the mass public. As such, a representative government should place great emphasis on reflecting public opinion in policy making.[3]

A president, sitting in Washington, might become too isolated from public opinion and carry out policies which do not have widespread support. The Congress, on the other hand, might prove to be too parochial: members of the House of Representatives are elected from legislative districts and thus have little incentive to consider the great issues of international politics. There are two senators representing each state and, initially, senators were chosen by state legislatures rather than by popular vote. The Senate possesses more formal foreign policy powers than the House because the Founders feared what a political body so closely linked to mass opinions might do. The House, with its smaller districts and biannual elections, would tailor its policies to the popular sentiment of the moment. The Senate, chosen for six-year terms and supposedly the more elite body, would be more concerned with the long-term consequences of its decisions. For it is, or at least calls itself, the "world's greatest deliberative body."

How, then, should policy be made? Should it follow the will of the public or are the masses too uninformed and unconcerned to be trusted? What differences are there between foreign and domestic policy formation? These are the large issues which concern us in this and succeeding chapters. Furthermore, since the Congress has taken many steps to reassert its power in foreign policy, what is the actual balance between legislative and executive initiatives on foreign policy? Can a bicameral legislature with 535 members formulate any sort of policy? If not, what is the most appropriate role for the legislature to play?

The constitutional theories of legislative supremacy, or at least equal sharing of decision making by the two branches, are discussed more these days in the literature on Congress than on foreign-policy making. Indeed, the dominant model of foreign-policy decision-making is that of the concentric circles.[4] In these circles (see Figure 3−1), the central decision-making locus on foreign policy is the president and his key advisers. In the second circle are the bureaucracies in the major foreign policy agencies and the armed services, the second-rank and less influential foreign policy departments, presidential advisers, and cabinet members whose primary responsibility is in the domestic sphere but who may be consulted on foreign policy questions, and scientists. The innermost circle is composed of a select few members of the administration; the outer circles have successively more members and, correspondingly, less impact on foreign policy decisions. Traditionally we have placed Congress in the third circle, together with political parties and interest groups; the fourth, outer circle comprises public opinion and the media.

Foreign-policy decision-making has been viewed, as represented in the concentric circles, as basically hierarchical. There is one president and then there is everyone else. Occasionally, as the situation warrants, an

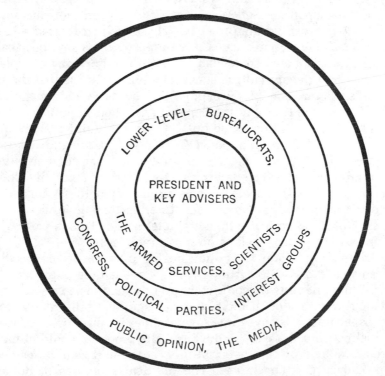

FIGURE 3−1 The Concentric Circles of Power in Foreign-Policy Decision-Making.

adviser might move into the first circle from the second. But the norm is that the president, as the only nationally elected politician, chooses whomever he wishes, to occupy the innermost circle with him. The outer circles are expected to be at the beck and call of those in the inner circle, thus establishing the hierarchy. The difference is highlighted by a story involving Johnson and Senator Frank Church, not yet chairman of the Senate Foreign Relations Committee, at a White House reception. Johnson queried the senator, an early opponent of the Vietnam War, as to where he was getting his information on the war effort. Church replied that his information came from the columns of the noted journalist Walter Lippman (now deceased). The President reportedly replied, "Well, the next time you want a dam in Idaho, ask Walter Lippman for it."

The concentric circles analogy stands in sharp contrast to the decision-making process in domestic policies. Here lines of authority cut across the national, state, and local levels and across the executive, legislative, and judicial branches as well. The stakes are generally perceived as less critical and policies are, at least in principle, more easily reversible. The actions taken are viewed as the results of bargaining and coalition building by actors who are intensely interested in their own priorities and often could not care less about other issues. Thus a legislator from the Midwest will fight long and hard for agriculture subsidies to wheat farmers and work with representatives of farmers' groups and the Department of Agriculture (the relevant bureaucracy) to ensure that their programs are protected. These well-structured relationships among legislators, bureaucrats, and interest groups have been called "policy subsystems"[5] and, somewhat less admiringly, "cozy triangles."[6] The dilemma that the agriculture subsystem has to face is that the farm bloc in the legislature is not large enough to provide a voting majority on the floor of either the House or the Senate to get their programs enacted. Thus, they are forced into seeking out votes from "uninterested" members[7]—such as legislators from New York City or Cleveland, who may want public housing projects or government-backed loans to their cities to prevent imminent bankruptcy. Intermestic policies are much like domestic policies, at least with respect to decision-making patterns. Indeed, the number of actors may be greater on some intermestic policies because the decisions involved affect more than a single nation. This is particularly true on energy politics, as well as on most trade issues.

Legislators thus trade votes and, ideally, interests are not in direct conflict so that most major groups can get what they want from the Congress. When interests do conflict, a group which feels very intensely about its position can often block the passage of a bill adverse to its position, as the railroads have done several times in the effort to construct a coal pipeline from the West to the East. The pipeline would eliminate the railroad's monopoly of transportation of coal, but it would lower costs to the producers and consumers. The political processes of domestic politics hardly guarantee good policies. Instead, they are designed to insure that each important group gets heard before a decision is reached.[8] The power of an interest lies in how often it can get its way and how strong its ties are to legislators and bureaucrats who formulate and administer the policies which affect the routines of the interest. Bargaining takes place among equals, although as George Orwell has reminded us, some are more equal than others. But every legislator, no matter how much power or seniority he or she might have, still has to face the electorate every two (six) years. Once elected, or reelected, each has the same mandate as every other.

The concentric circles, then, indicate the amount of centralization or hierarchy in decision making on foreign policy. Restriction of foreign policy initiatives to the innermost circle, the president and his closest advisers, fits the hierarchical model nicely and best describes crisis decision-making. (Chapter 5) On the other hand, congressional action on foreign policy necessarily includes more actors and since the legislature is itself not hierarchically structured, the potential for widespread participation by legislators and their supporting and opposing constituents (interest groups, political parties, public opinion, and the media) is enhanced. But what does this do to the quality of decisions made on foreign policy?

We note that in contrast to the executive branch, congressional decision-making is parochial rather than national or global in focus, with members rarely putting their districts' concerns out of mind; indeed, because members rely so heavily upon constituency contacts rather than strong national parties for reelection, this local focus may be inevitable in the Congress. Second, the executive branch can respond quickly to changing events; the legislature is a "deliberative" body (or, as critics might have it, an obstructionist one which succeeds by employing delaying tactics). Third, the Congress is not particularly interested in foreign policy, does not have the staff expertise on international questions that the administration does, has had weak foreign policy committees in the House of Representatives, and has not developed the resource base in terms of information that the executive branch has on foreign policy issues. We shall now examine each of these issues. But we first turn to a discussion of perhaps the most important occurrence of recent years: the increased activism of Congress on international issues.

Congress and Foreign Policy: Revival Fires

The Congress has become more involved in foreign policy in recent years. The most celebrated action it has taken, as noted earlier, is the War Powers Resolution. Other actions have also been largely directed toward amending, or restraining, executive initiatives. Congress has not taken upon itself the problem of formulating alternative policies. That is, as we shall see shortly, simply impractical. But the legislature can be an effective check on the executive branch: In 1974, for example, it passed what has been called the Hughes-Ryan amendment, after former Senator Harold Hughes (D., Ia.) and the late Representative Leo Ryan (D., Cal.), which significantly restrained the president's leeway to use the Central Intelligence Agency as he wished.[9] The bill forbade the CIA to use public funds for foreign operations, excluding the gathering of intelligence, unless the president decides that the activity is important to the national security. Even in that event, the chief executive was required to report such actions to committees in the House and the Senate, totaling as many as eight (the foreign policy committees, Armed Services, the military subcommittees of Appropriations, and the intelligence committees) at one point before it was finally limited to two (House and Senate Intelligence) in 1980. Furthermore, the Case-Zablocki Act of 1972, named after Senator Clifford Case (R., N.J.) and Rep. Clement Zablocki (D., Wis.), established new requirements for the reporting of executive agreements to the Congress. An amendment sponsored by Senator Gaylord Nelson (D., Wis.) and Rep. Jonathan Bingham (D., N.Y.) established procedures for reporting arms sales to the Congress and provided for a legislative veto over some sales. Although this 1974 legislation had a rather large loophole (only sales of over $5,000 had to be reported, so that multiple sales of $4,999.99 could go undetected) and there were relatively few instances of administration proposals actually being defeated, the impact of the amendment should not be underestimated. Despite an unsuccessful effort to prevent the sale of jet fighters in 1978 to Egypt and Saudi Arabia by leading Jewish groups and many members of Congress, arms sales to Turkey, Chile, Argentina, Libya, Iraq, and other nations were either defeated or stalled in committee so that the administration did not press further for them. In some cases, such as Libya and Iraq, the issue was not strictly over military sales but about the purchase of aircraft which had potential military applications. In several cases, including Turkish aid, the increased congressional role threatened to disrupt the NATO alliance while in others, such as the cutback of aid to Nicaragua in 1980 following the revolution in that country, the legislative actions ran directly contrary to the Carter administration's announced foreign policy toward developing nations.

Other legislative initiatives include an amendment, sponsored by Rep. Thomas Harkin (D., Ia.) in 1975, which established criteria for determining aid eligibility on the basis of a nation's human rights record. Except in a few cases (mostly in Latin America), the Congress did not exercise the veto power it granted itself over executive decisions that could waive this provision. In 1973, Senator Henry Jackson (D., Wash.) and Rep. Charles Vanik (D., Ohio) shepherded through the Congress an amendment which linked favorable trade relations with the Soviet Union to more liberal emigration procedures by that country, particularly for religious (notably Jewish) dissidents. Many of these actions occurred during the Nixon administration and constituted a congressional assault on the President's refusal to be forthcoming with the Democrats who controlled the Congress on both foreign and domestic questions. Nixon strongly believed in the command style of decision making and was also much more interested in foreign policy than domestic issues. The foreign policy clashes thus were part of a pattern of poor legislative-executive relations that marked his administration. But the roots of the congressional resurgence and assertiveness go deeper—to Vietnam and a reluctance to have the United States too widely committed throughout the world and especially to become involved in wars that might not be winnable (Angola in 1976) or in countries where the leadership may have been only marginally more popular than that in Vietnam. The cry was "No more Vietnams."

While the examples point to attempts by Congress to regain control over foreign policy and indicate that the president may well face strong constraints (as demonstrated especially the two very close Senate votes on the Panama Canal treaty in April 1978), the greatest challenge to presidential preeminence on foreign policy occurred in 1979 on the second Strategic Arms Limitation Treaty or SALT II (see Chapter 6 for a detailed analysis). The second SALT treaty was favorably viewed by the Senate Foreign Relations Committee, but faced considerable opposition from that body's Armed Services Committee, a much more hawkish group of legislators. Jackson, a senior member of Armed Services who had been offered the position of secretary of defense in the Nixon administration, joined several conservative senators from both parties in opposing the treaty. Some moderate Republicans, including ranking minority member of Foreign Relations, Jacob Javits, supported the treaty, and press reports variously indicated that the treaty would either pass with several votes to spare, or be roundly defeated. The administration's political problems were compounded by the decision of Minority Leader Howard Baker to oppose SALT II. Baker had been a key, if not decisive, backer of the Panama Canal treaties, maintaining the tradition of bipartisanship in foreign policy that dated back to at least the administration of Franklin D. Roosevelt. But in 1979 Baker specifically argued that it was time to reassess the wisdom of restraining partisan criticism of presidential foreign policy decisions. After Baker announced his position, press estimates of vote counts in the Senate tilted heavily toward defeat of SALT II. The minority leader may not have made his decision based upon the desirability of bipartisanship in foreign policy; Baker was on the verge of announcing his own bid for the Republican nomination for president and had been roundly criticized by GOP conservatives for supporting the

Panama Canal treaties. Following the Soviet Union's invasion of Afghanistan in December 1979, Carter asked the Senate to defer further consideration of SALT II. While it was a presidential initiative which took the treaty off the Senate calendar there was little doubt that Carter's action was taken as much to prevent his own political embarrassment as punish the Russians.

The bipartisan consensus on foreign policy which had crumbled during the Johnson administration as political conflict over Vietnam crossed party lines, and deeply divided the Democrats, has not been restored. When Nixon had assumed office in 1969, the Asian war had become a "Republican war," which was widely criticized by Democrats of various political persuasions. These challenges not only reflect a willingness of Congress to assert itself more vigorously on foreign policy (during the entire eight years of the Nixon and Ford presidencies the Congress was controlled by Democrats), but also indicate that some of the traditional differences in terms of congressional determination to participate in policy making between domestic and foreign policy are weakening. Domestic policy has traditionally involved multiple groups and interests. All of these forces are represented in the Congress, where their spokesmen argue forcefully for their positions. There is no presumption of greater administration experience and expertise on domestic policy as on foreign policy. A member of the House Education and Labor Committee, interviewed by Richard F. Fenno, Jr. in the 1960s, made the point dramatically—and it is certainly still valid today.[10]

> Hell, everyone thinks he's an expert on the questions before our Committee. On education, the problem is everyone went to school. They all think that makes them experts on that. And labor matters are so polarized that everyone is committed. You take sides first and then you acquire expertise. So no one accepts anyone as impartial.

In contrast, there is still the "we-they" attitude on foreign policy issues, with the United States pitted against other nations. A president's popularity increases whenever he is involved in a major foreign policy achievement or a crisis. There were virtually no critics of Carter following the Camp David accord between Israel and Egypt and a confrontation with the President over the handling of the Iranian hostage issue was viewed as unpatriotic. Indeed, Mondale charged Kennedy with a lack of sufficient patriotism when the Massachusetts senator told a San Francisco television station that the President should not have let the Shah back into the United States for cancer treatment when there were indications that such a decision might lead to problems at the American embassy in Teheran. As the Congress moves toward greater activism in foreign policy, we must consider the institutional capacity of Congress to take concerted action in this arena.

The Reelection Imperative: "Afghanistan's Not in My District"

As foreign policy-making moves beyond the innermost circle to include participation by the Congress, more actors and perspectives become involved in making decisions. While Congress has become more active on foreign policy to check a potential "imperial President," greater participation has its costs as well. In particular, members of the House and Senate tend to see policy alternatives in terms of the districts and states they represent. In the words of House Speaker Thomas P. (Tip) O'Neill, Jr. (D., Mass.): "All politics is local."[11] Representatives and senators see the stakes in terms of the people they represent and the views of a Midwest farmer are not necessarily similar to those of a New Yorker or a Floridian.

Unlike most parliamentary systems, the American Congress is elected by congressional district (states in the Senate). Representatives face constant reelection battles, while senators are more insulated from the mass public. House members always face the electorate at the same time as the president, but they also must run in even-numbered years when the president is not on the ballot. Only one third of the Senate is elected at the same time as the president. This type of electoral system puts even stronger pressures on legislators to pay more attention to local issues than to national concerns. Furthermore, the United States does not have strong political parties. (Chapter 4) There is no country in the world where individual legislators are as free of pressures from national political parties and where the ties to local constituencies are as strong as the United States. The electoral system and weak parties reinforce localism in American politics. And it is difficult, if not impossible, to conduct a coherent national foreign policy if decision-makers do not see the stakes in the same way.

In international crises, support for the president by the public and the Congress is generally strong and lasts for a considerable amount of time. On more routine foreign policy issues, legislators from different regions with different types of constituencies will, as on domestic policy questions, see questions in terms of alternative stakes. Consumers want lower prices at the grocery stores, farmers protection from meat and vegetables which sell at lower prices in other nations. Steel and automobile workers also fear foreign competition and clamor for protection against cheaper imported materials and products from Europe and Japan, in the latter instance as demonstrated by the "voluntary" reduction in imports from Japan negotiated by President Reagan in May 1981, while automobile manufacturers—who might favor higher tariffs on foreign cars—might fight any move to restrict imports of less expensive steel. Legislators from the steel-mining area of Pittsburgh and the automotive center of Detroit, although representing the same political party and both espousing the "national interest," will see the stakes in foreign-policy decision-making quite differently. It is unlikely that they will perceive the issues as involving primarily foreign policy issues, since the economic well-being of their constituents is at stake. Indeed, Rep. Jerome Ambro (D., N.Y.) has gone so far as to admit that his primary legislative concern on any issue is: What's in it for Long Island?[12] This localism kept him in office representing a traditionally Republican district from 1975 to 1981, but ultimately did not shield him from the Republican tide of 1980.

The electoral cycle and the weak party system explain much of the parochialism of members of the Congress, but so do the attitudes of members toward their jobs and their constituencies. Former Representative Frank Smith (D., Miss.) stated: "All members have a primary interest in being reelected. Some members have no other interest."[13] For representatives, the reelection drive begins the day after the previous contest ends. The overwhelming majority of members of Congress, and particularly the House, not only seek reelection but attain it. In 1978, over three quarters of the House incumbents seeking another term were reelected with 60 percent or more of the vote in their districts.

How do members get reelected? In the past, congressional elections were referenda on the standings of the political parties. Within Congress, the parties and their leaders dominated the Congress in the late nineteenth and early twentieth centuries. In the House, the Speaker appointed members of all standing committees and controlled the flow of legislation; members voted the party line in the vast majority of instances.[14] But in 1910–11, a revolt against the strong Speakership by the Progressive wing of the Republican majority and the minority Democrats stripped the leader of the House of much of his power and transferred it to committees. Since then, committee and party leaders have struggled for dominance in the Congress, with the former being victorious much of the time. The growth of subcommittee government has further weakened the congressional parties, as members are free to pursue their own policy interests without much concern for formal positions of power. When a member cannot obtain some jurisdiction over a bill in subcommittee, he or she is likely to propose an amendment to it on the House or Senate floor. This is a role which was proscribed for junior members in the past. But today independence is valued more highly than party or committee discipline. As the congressional parties have weakened, so have the parties in the mass electorate. There is more ticket-splitting and fewer strong attachments among voters to political parties today than at any time in our recent history and to many, political parties are anachronisms.[15]

Taking the place of parties have been single-interest groups, such as pro and anti abortion forces, antigun control activists, environmentalists, opponents of the Panama Canal treaties, and so forth. While it is unclear what impact such forces have on actual election returns, the proliferation of these "political action committees" has changed the political landscape. Candidates for office no longer can depend upon strong party organizations to turn out loyal supporters, but many do not lament the passing of the parties. The increased incumbency advantage for members seeking reelection can be traced to some of the perquisites of office that members have provided for themselves: in 1954, the Congress had a staff of about 5000 people; by 1978, the figure had risen to over 17,000. Thirty years ago, House members were limited to five members on their personal staffs and senators six. These figures are very generous by comparison with virtually any other legislative body in the world. In Britain, for example, all but the most senior members of the majority party have their correspondence handled by a typing pool. The contemporary House, however, allows members to hire up to twenty-two personal staff members at a cost to the public of about $300,000 for each representative. Senators' staffs are based upon the population of the states the members represent but allocations today range from a low of $500,000 to a high of over $1 million. In addition to personal staffs, members of both chambers who chair committees or subcommittees have access to several more staff assistants through their committee positions. Senator Edward Kennedy had over one hundred people working for his various offices (personal staff, the Judiciary Committee he previously chaired, and subcommittee aides) prior to 1981 and still has over fifty staffers.

These staff assistants do work on legislation, to be sure, but many concentrate on "casework," providing services to constituents such as finding lost Social Security checks, writing letters of congratulations or condolence, or sending out copies of government publications. Many staffers do little more than answer mail from constituents—on two consecutive days in July 1979, the Senate alone received 500,000 pieces of mail and every letter writer expects an answer. The flow of mail back to constituents has risen from about 40 million letters and parcels in 1954 to over 250 million a year today. And this massive postal bill is not paid for by the members themselves. Correspondence dealing with the "official business" of the Congress can be mailed without postage under the member's signature (called the "frank"); other mail, much of it oriented toward reelection, does require stamps, but the members have very generous postage allowances.[16]

In the quest for reelection, there is no place like home. Members of the House are authorized twenty-six trips back to their districts at government expense every year, but most members go back every weekend or at least three out of four a month. Senators, who go home less frequently, are authorized forty trips home each year. Many senators believe that they do not have to pay such close attention to their constituents because they face the electorate only once every six years compared to their House colleagues; furthermore, most senators would clearly prefer to be interviewed on "Face the Nation" or "Meet the Press" than discuss some constituent's personal problem at a garden club meeting back home. Yet, senators who neglect this advice are becoming increasingly vulnerable to challengers who promise better constituency service.[17] Not only is it important for legislators to make frequent trips home, but members also find it more advantageous to keep larger portions of their staff in the district or state. In 1960, only 14 percent of representatives' staffs were located in home district offices; by 1974, the figure had jumped to 34 percent. Not only has the percentage of staff assigned to the district increased, but so has the total number of staff members. This at least doubles the impact of the increase.

Such close attention to the constituency no doubt helps the members gain reelection, but it also reinforces parochialism in congressional decision-making. To members of the Senate and particularly the House, the national interest is usually defined in terms of local priorities. The reelection imperative as well as the success that members have in exploiting these advantages work against the development of a national or international perspective. In a rare burst of introspection, a survey of representatives conducted by the House in 1977 found that 57 percent of the legislators believed that constituent demands interfere with other aspects of the job, especially the legislative role.[18] By contrast, the president is the only nationally elected political leader and thus has greater leeway to balance competing interests in both domestic and foreign policy. The chief executive can thus take a more detached view of policy alternatives and can, indeed must, consider the reactions of our allies and enemies to foreign policy decisions as well as the long-term consequences of decisions.[19] The vast foreign policy bureaucracy serves the president and his secretary of state—who, in turn, can be dismissed at any time the president chooses.

Reelection is not the only goal of members of Congress, however. Fenno examined three other major goals which characterized legislators to varying degrees: (1) seeking influence within the House or Senate; (2) making good public policy; and (3) a career in politics beyond the House or Senate.[20] (For House members, this career generally means the Senate or a governorship, for senators the goal is the White House.) Indeed, some members, a minority to be sure, try to strive for the making of sound national and international policy without excessive concern for the parochial interests of their own districts or even the political consequences of their decisions. A somewhat jaundiced member of the House commented to Fenno:[21]

> All some House members are interested in is "the folks." They think "the folks" are the second coming. They would no longer do anything to displease "the folks" than they would fly. They spend all their time trying to find out what "the folks" want. I imagine if they get five letters on one side and five letters on the other side, they die.

The goal of making good public policy is held in varying degrees by all members. But what is good policy? For many, it is meeting the needs of the district. It is hardly surprising to find that a member from the Midwest or South would be primarily concerned with agriculture policy or that a black representative from New York or Chicago would be most interested in civil rights and labor policy. For most members, what is good for his district is good for the country—and, to a certain extent, each is correct. The country cannot have a healthy economy without a productive agricultural (mining, and so forth) sector. But the balance between district demands and the nation's priorities is difficult to determine. The policy-oriented member must not neglect his or her district, but he or she is also compelled to consider the claims of other members. Domestic policy-making is generally not discussed in these terms. Legislators, who must face constituencies back home as well as among their fellow members, prefer policies which produce only "winners" and "nonwinners," the politics of the pork barrel and the agriculture and housing subsidies. Probably only a small minority of elected officials are concerned with resolving the issues involving "winners" and "losers," the sorts of questions that arose when over one hundred thousand Cuban refugees entered the United States during the 1980 recession. When unemployment is rising, how do you distribute jobs to the new Americans? An even smaller number direct their attention to foreign affairs. Those who do, often have studied international relations in college and traveled extensively.[22] In the House, they tend to come from urban areas and have relatively safe seats, and they are also more likely to be members of ethnic groups particularly concerned with foreign policy (Jews regarding Israel and blacks on Africa). In addition, as noted earlier (Chapter 2), many members of the foreign policy committees have ambitions beyond the Congress.

These diverse member goals may often come into conflict. Particularly on questions of foreign policy, legislators recognize that concern for foreign policy is often not appreciated back home. A Democratic member of the House Foreign Affairs Committee in the 1950s and 1960s told Fenno:[23]

The first few weeks I was here I would go home on the weekend to see constituents. One night, there must have been 45 people waiting to see me, this big ward leader came in, big fat guy, a head taller than me. He said, "What's the big idea keeping me waiting?" I tried to explain to him that, gee whiz, we had a committee meeting. Berlin was falling apart, the Secretary of State was briefing the Committee on Berlin, and I didn't feel that I, as a new member, should be rude to him by walking out. I said, "John Foster Dulles appeared before the committee, the meeting went a little overtime, and I missed the plane." He said, "John Foster Dulles. Hell, he wasn't even with us last time out!" There's no relation between your committee work and back home.

A Senate member of Foreign Relations commented similarly:[24]

> It's a political liability. . . . You have no constituency. In my reelection campaign last fall, the main thing they used against me was that because of my interest in foreign relations, I was more interested in what happened to the people of Abyssinia and Afghanistan than in what happened to the good people of my state.

Do the generalizations of the 1960s apply to the 1980s?

The answer is a most emphatic "yes." If anything, politics is more locally oriented than before. Senators who concentrate on foreign affairs or who cast controversial roll calls against vocal groups in their constituencies may suffer electorally for their decisions. On the two Panama Canal treaties, Senator Thomas McIntyre, a liberal Democrat from New Hampshire, received threats from conservative groups in his state that a vote in favor would provoke severe political consequences. McIntyre, who had survived such challenges before, went to the Senate floor to denounce the right wing and proclaimed himself a profile in courage who would vote his conscience. He was also comfortably ahead in the polls at the time against a virtually unknown challenger. Senator Jennings Randolph, a moderate Democrat from West Virginia, waited until a sufficient number of "yea" votes had been cast for each treaty before voting "nay" on each. At the time, he was either slightly behind, or at best even in his reelection contest against a very popular former governor. McIntyre lost and Randolph won in the 1978 general elections. In the next Congress, McIntyre's Democratic colleague from New Hampshire, John Durkin, followed a much more conservative, noninternationalist position on many foreign policy votes but was still defeated in 1980.

In 1978, Senator Dick Clark (D., Ia.) concentrated on African politics as chairman of the African Affairs subcommittee of Foreign Relations. Like McIntyre, he made relatively few trips home, while Randolph was among the most diligent senators in keeping up contacts with his constituents.[25] Clark also lost and his chairmanship devolved to George McGovern who, himself, faced a difficult reelection fight in 1980. His opponents charged him with being more concerned with international issues—which had led the senator to seek the presidency in 1972—than with issues of concern to South Dakota. McGovern, like Clark, did not hesitate to speak out on foreign policy questions, but did not pay disproportionate attention to Africa; when he was back home, he stressed his position on the Senate Agriculture Committee more than his foreign policy credentials. In this regard, he followed the political strategy of one of the most powerful Senate Foreign Relations Committee chairmen, J. William Fulbright, whose porkbarreling instincts saved him in several elections from an electorate which had little concern or sympathy for his internationalist (and anti-Vietnam war) policy positions in the 1960s. Another erstwhile presidential candidate, Frank Church, assumed the chairmanship of the Senate committee in 1979, a year before his most difficult political campaign. During 1979, he served as the administration's major Senate advocate of SALT II; once that treaty was doomed, he concentrated on sugar policy and land conservation, of greater interest to his Idaho constituents.

The difficulties of serving on a foreign policy committee were very evident in the 1980 Senate elections. Four of the five members of the Foreign Relations Committee who were seeking reelection were defeated—including chairman Church and ranking minority member Javits as well as McGovern and freshman Richard Stone (D., Fla.). The Panama Canal issue was prominently raised in the campaigns against Church, McGovern, and Stone—and was particularly important in the latter race since Panama's government is friendly with Cuba and there is no place in the country with as much concern (and fear) about Fidel Castro's motivations as in Florida. The concern for foreign policy was particularly damaging to McGovern, who had earlier sold his house in South Dakota (much as McIntyre had done two years earlier in New Hampshire) and was increasingly associated with international rather than state or local problems. The only Foreign Relations member to survive the Republican sweep in the Senate in 1980 was John Glenn (D., Ohio), whose previous career as an astronaut made him an international celebrity as well as a spokesman on foreign policy. The personal appeal of the former astronaut played a key role in his overwhelming victory in 1980, but the senator received diffused criticism from the right for his opposition to SALT II on the grounds that it was unverifiable. Even the new chairman of Foreign Relations, Charles R. Percy (R., Ill.), long identified with the moderate-liberal wing of his party, has taken a more hawkish stand since his own brush with electoral defeat in 1978.

By contrast, the House Foreign Affairs Committee remains classified as a "minor" committee by the party organizations which assign members to committee positions. A member on a minor committee can also serve on another committee. The additional committee assignment of most House Foreign Affairs members is more politically beneficial to them; unlike senators, therefore, they do not become too infamous for their foreign policy concerns. Furthermore, the lower profile of the House on foreign policy also helps to protect members in this regard, as does the greater attention House members give to their constituents compared to senators.[26]

For senators, then, the goal of making good public policy generally conflicts with that for reelection, at least in the area of foreign policy. This is not quite the case in the House, but probably because those members attracted to the House Foreign Affairs Committee are among the most electorally secure members. The Senate Foreign Relations Committee is a high-profile committee; Foreign Affairs is almost invisible. It seems to have an identity crisis within the House. Indeed, in an attempt to call greater attention to its role, the committee changed its name in 1971 to International Relations. A senior committee member commented: "We were sick of that old [former senator and vice-president] Alben Barkley joke, the House committee only had affairs, not relations. Basically, we were considered a throwaway committee—our only bill was foreign aid. So we changed our name to change our image."[27] But, despite the increasing activism of the body, the House did not stand up and take notice, so the name was changed back to Foreign Affairs in 1979 because members found the new title confusing and "difficult to remember."

Perhaps because so many senators seek (or wish to seek) the presidency, the Senate Foreign Relations Committee has served to help members attain institutional power. The House Foreign Affairs Committee is not the road to power in the House although there is at least some limited evidence that members of Foreign Affairs are motivated to seek higher office: Five of the thirty-eight members serving during 1970 ran for the Senate, three of them successfully, during the 1970s. Most House members on the committee who run for the Senate are relatively junior; those who pass up the opportunity generally do not opt for more "desirable" committees but stay on Foreign Affairs, which has among the highest level of continuous service of all House committees.[28] But this longevity may be both a blessing and a curse for coherent foreign policy formation. Members who have served many years are less likely to provoke a confrontation with the executive branch; they recognize that foreign policy must be conducted with considerable continuity and at best only a modicum of partisanship.

The low rate of turnover, except for the politically ambitious junior members, also means that the Foreign Affairs committee will be more reluctant to challenge the president when the chief executive (including Nixon) may overextend his power—or simply make bad decisions. Foreign policy initiatives in the House are limited by the nature of the major committee on foreign policy, as we shall now discuss in greater detail, and by the lack of incentives for members to adopt international perspectives when their votes are cast in constituencies of about five hundred thousand voters.

The Senate, long the bastion of both reasoned and unprincipled opposition—and support—for administration foreign policy, is now becoming more and more like the House. Senators are finding foreign policy concerns to be politically costly. The goals of members of Congress may often be conflicting and in cases such as McIntyre, legislators may be called upon to decide whether to cast a vote in favor of a controversial foreign policy issue supported by the president (as the Panama Canal treaties) or to ensure their reelection or quest for higher office. In a parliamentary system, Howard Baker, now the Senate Majority Leader, would have been the odds-on choice to gain the Republican nomination for president (or party leader) in 1980. Instead, an outsider to the legislative party, Ronald Reagan, captured his party's nomination with ease and Baker took considerable criticism within his own party for supporting the Canal treaties—a move that might in itself have cost him the vice-presidential nomination that year.

The ideological attacks by conservative groups on senators who supported the foreign policy of the recent Democratic *and* Republican administrations have increased Senate parochialism on foreign policy. Foreign policy is less important in House contests because representatives have paid more attention to their constituents than have senators and because House members have not expressed a very strong concern for foreign policy issues. The prevailing attitude has been: Let sleeping dogs lie. When the House has taken initiatives on foreign policy, it has generally done so in response to some sort of constituency pressure—from the demands of ethnic lobbies to economic interests in the district. One of the ultimate ironies of recent Congresses has been the tremendous increase in size of House and Senate staffs, but the lack of new efforts to challenge the executive branch in terms of staff expertise on foreign policy. Congressional staffs concentrate on public relations activities designed to aid reelection efforts but, when they are concerned with policy, it is domestic issues. The reason is straightforward: most members of Congress do not have a primary or even a strong interest in foreign policy. The issues raised stand in the way of reelection and often institutional power. Since each member can allocate his staff resources and his own time and interests as he wishes, the Congress is capable of producing 535 separate foreign policies, each based upon a different conception of national and local interests with no strong organizing force such as political parties to produce more coherent choices.

The Congress, then, represents primarily domestic interest groups and its members have a responsibility to protect the economic well-being of their constituents. A president can afford to ignore the views of many citizens. For expeditious decision-making, this may be a virtue. But such a president cannot claim to represent "all of the people" any more than can a collection of representatives and senators. The president, to be sure, is in a better strategic position to take into account the global interests of the country. But someone must look after the constituencies in a democracy. Thus the president, but particularly the Congress, face the dilemma posed at the beginning of the *Talmud*, the book of Jewish interpretations of the first five books of the Old Testament: "If I am not for myself, who will be for me? If I am for myself alone, what am I?"

Committees: Centers of Congressional Power

A camel, it is said, is a horse designed by a committee. Congressional government is committee government—and, in recent years, government by subcommittees, the littlest legislatures of them all. The camel analogy is quite appropriate since committee government does not move much faster than that desert animal. Whereas foreign policy, or at least crisis decision-making, is marked by the need for action which is both *unified* and *quick*, responsiveness to public opinion and allowances for maximum feasible participation in decision making are characterized by a slow process of bargaining, negotiations, and compromises. Senators particularly like to call this process "deliberation." Others might see it as an attempt to stalemate the opposition by responding so slowly that the opponent in the policy-making process may simply give way to what he perceives as a variant on Chinese water torture.

Congressional government by committees is also parochial government. In the Congress, committees are organized largely on the basis of constituency interests: Education and Labor, Agriculture, Interior, Public Works and Transportation, Energy and Commerce, Judiciary, and Small Business are typical House committees. Public Works is a much sought-after body, especially for junior members who want to engage in porkbarrel politics for their districts; it is the committee which constructs dams and produces hydroelectric energy. Judiciary, of course, handles civil rights legislation, but also the more politically salient questions of resolving claims against the government and expediting immigration and naturalization procedures. Interior is the guardian of the national parks, as well as the protector of the environment. Energy and Commerce handles not only much, although not all, energy legislation, but also virtually everything that can be sold, bartered, or regulated—from the nation's airwaves to health care to railroads. These committees attract members from districts most directly affected by their principal subjects. While jurisdictions are not always clearly defined, membership on a committee which seems most relevant to one's district concerns can be of great benefit in reelection drives. Precisely because jurisdictions are not always clear-cut, the potential for slowing the progress of a major bill—or even stopping it completely—is very real in the Congress. A bill selected at random from all of those introduced in any given Congress (almost twenty thousand now in the House alone) may not have as good a chance of passage as a camel trying to find an oasis in the desert. The long and tortuous path that a bill must take, involving at least one committee and one subcommittee in both the House and the Senate, makes enactment of a bill into a public law a major event, complete with an elaborate White House ceremony to mark the occasion if the bill—or its sponsor—is deemed sufficiently important.

The "big three" committees in the House are Appropriations, Ways and Means, and Rules. Members assigned to any of these committees are generally not given any additional committee assignments. They are considered "power committees," bodies where members who want to gather institutional power jockey for positions. These committees are important because they handle the key aspects of legislative decision-making: money and procedure. All bills which provide for the direct spending of money must go to the House and Senate Appropriations committees. The money, in turn, must come from somewhere: taxes, which are handled by Ways and Means in the House and Finance in the Senate. In the House, but not the Senate, most important bills *must* be sent to the Rules Committee which determines which amendments (if any) can be offered on the floor and what the ground rules (including time limitations) for debate will be. The Rules Committee also serves as the arbiter when there are conflicting claims among committees over alternative bills—or simply which body ought to have jurisdiction over a specific piece of legislation. Some bills are "privileged" in that they can go directly to the House floor without getting a rule; these include appropriations bills, but the power of the Rules Committee to restrict the amendments which might be offered provides strong incentives for virtually all committees to seek rules for debate for their bills. The situation is different in the Senate. Time limits can only be established by unanimous consent (the norm) or by a motion of cloture to break a filibuster, a prolonged period of "debate" designed to kill a bill. During a filibuster, members may argue the merits of a piece of legislation for days, weeks, or even months; in earlier days, the quality of Senate debates during filibusters varied widely as some members cited the arguments on their side of the bill and others read from telephone books merely to consume time. Senate procedures restricting amendments are so weak that a powerful committee such as the House Rules Committee could never develop. There is a Rules Committee in the Senate, but it deals with internal housekeeping (like the House Administration Committee), not the resolution of critical procedural issues.

The slow pace of congressional decision-making is perhaps best illustrated by a change in House procedures in 1974 to permit greater participation in its decision making by junior members. In previous years, committees had been dominated by strong chairmen such as Wilbur Mills of Ways and Means and Howard "Judge" Smith of Rules. Mills had long served as the major expert in Congress on taxation and developed a reputation for being a hard worker and an extremely fair chairman.[29] He finally lost power in 1975 following a sex scandal. Smith, who chaired Rules during the 1940s through the 1960s before he lost his party's primary in 1966 in his own district, held on to his position because of continuous service on the committee—the seniority principle—and was viewed by many as ruthless and not willing to work with his party's leadership. His major preoccupation was the blocking of civil rights legislation in the House and he would use such tactics as refusing to call committee meetings (even absenting himself from Washington when necessary) to ensure that such bills would not receive rules. The seniority system—and indeed the entire committee system—was systematically weakened through a series of reforms (which we shall discuss below). But the change in referral procedures in the House in 1974 to make this chamber's procedures similar to those in the Senate dramatically demonstrates how the drive for power by a large number of actors can lead to a legislative stalemate. The situation is made even more cumbersome by the constituency politics that marks the fight over which committees and subcommittees get control over a piece of legislation.

The change in referral procedure permitted more actors to get involved in the processing of each bill. Previously, a bill was filed by a member and then the clerk of the House, acting through the Speaker, would assign it to a committee. In several key instances, this referral procedure permitted the leadership to avoid recalcitrant chairmen. The Civil Rights Act of 1964, for example, faced an uncertain future in the Senate because the chairman of the Judiciary Committee, James Eastland (D., Miss.), was unalterably opposed to the bill. Since the legislation dealt with discrimination which might arise in businesses engaged in interstate commerce, the Senate bill was referred to the Commerce Committee rather than Judiciary and was ultimately enacted into law. But the reform of 1974 in the House, following similar action in the Senate, now permitted several different types of bill referral, including joint, sequential, and split referrals. The first permitted several committees to consider a bill simultaneously; the second allowed several committees to handle a bill in sequence; while the latter let the Speaker break a bill into several components and assign them to different committees.

While the rationale behind this proposal was to increase participation by all House members on legislation in which they were particularly interested, the reform had one major drawback: politically, the Speaker could hardly reject the demand of any committee (or of a subcommittee through the full committee) as long as jurisdiction, determined by House rules, gave the committee a legitimate claim to the subject matter of the bill. The new participatory environment gave virtually every member the opportunity to have some say on a policy decision of concern to him or her. What ensued over the next several years was a series of jurisdictional conflicts that Rep. Toby Moffett (D., Conn.) called "jungle warfare."[30] Thus virtually every committee could claim jurisdiction over energy policy. (Chapter 6) The situation is even worse on health policy where national health insurance is the concern of the Health subcommittee of Energy and Commerce and a similar subcommittee on Ways and Means (which has primary jurisdiction over Medicare, a Social Security program financed through taxes); in addition every special interest committee (Veterans' Affairs, Small Business, Merchant Marine and Fisheries, Education and Labor, Interior, and so forth) controls decision making on health care within its general jurisdictions. The situation is no better on foreign policy where questions of restrictions on foreign trade were matters of concern to Ways and Means (primary jurisdiction over trade policy), Foreign Affairs, Government Operations (oversight of both commerce and national security), Agriculture (food exports), Small Business, and Energy and Commerce—at a minimum. Should any of these committees, or the relevant subcommittees, refuse to report the bill to the Rules Committee, the legislation would die unless extraordinary measures were taken to rescue it.

The increasing use of multiple referral procedures in both the House and the Senate and the greater emphasis on the reelection goal have both served to weaken congressional initiatives in policy making. According to data compiled by the Congressional Research Service of the Library of Congress for the Select Committee on Committees, a reform effort which failed in 1979, 1885 measures were multiply referred in the House in the Ninety-fifth Congress (1977–78) for a total of 4184 referrals considered by more than one committee. Thus, about 20 percent of all committee business in that House were bills multiply referred. Such legislation was half as likely to be reported from committee compared to bills singly referred and less than a third as likely to be passed by the full House. Bills so handled also took up more time than singly referred bills (21.8 hours in hearings on an average, compared to five hours) and were four times as likely to be amended on the House floor.[31]

The Foreign Affairs Committee ranks considerably above the mean for all committees in the number of bills multiply referred; it shares the Food for Peace program with Agriculture, foreign intelligence activities with Armed Services and the Select Committee on Intelligence, international banking with Banking, Finance, and Urban Affairs, the ACTION program (including the Peace Corps) and other education programs as well as the United Nation's International Labor Organization with Education and Labor, immigration, claims, and passports with Judiciary, international fishing rights and environmental legislation and the Panama Canal with Merchant Marine and Fisheries, and trade with Ways and Means. The referral system clearly adds many delays to the Congressional process and may be particularly problematic in foreign policy, where quick responses to changes in the international system may often be required. The more actors who become involved in foreign policy, the less expeditiously the nation can act.

Congressional decision-making is also slowed down by the lack of any committee similar to the House Rules Committee in the Senate, where debate may continue at great length on virtually any subject. The lack of a strong procedure limiting amendments in the Senate means that a foreign policy question can be attached as a "rider" (an amendment not directly connected to the bill under consideration) to any other piece of legislation. There are rules in both houses prohibiting new legislation in an appropriations bill, so that it should not be possible to constrain, say, foreign trade on a foreign aid appropriation. However, virtually every subject imaginable involves the expenditure of money; all programs require someone to manage them at the least, and these managers must be paid salaries. So the jurisdictional lines become even more blurred and the process can be delayed at virtually any time for almost any reason.

Multiple referral of bills not only complicates the policy process; so does a 1971 reform which greatly eased the requirements for roll call votes. Prior to that action, there were approximately 150 to 200 recorded votes a year; now there are about 800 such votes. Each vote takes between fifteen minutes and half an hour (often longer in Senate, where computerized voting has been resisted), adding yet further delays to the slow process. It is small wonder, then, that members often do not know the details of the bills on which they are voting; much of the time, they do not even know what the basic substance of the bill is and rush to the floor from their offices or committee meetings, ask a trusted colleague who has followed the proceedings what the bill is and how he or she is voting, and vote accordingly.[32]

The concern for maximum possible participation, then, clearly slows down the legislative process and gives many more outside interests, as well as members themselves, the opportunity to block legislation before it can be adopted. But the commitment to a greater role for individual members, which led to the change in House referral procedures, is a hallmark of the open politics of the Congress of the 1970s and most likely the 1980s. Until 1980 the president, as cited earlier, had to report covert CIA activities to eight committees of the Congress, four each in the House and the Senate. No member trusted the others in making policy decisions for the country. Speed and coherence became clearly secondary goals to those of openness and participation. Critics charged that such a philosophy of policy making might prevent an "imperial Presidency," but would also militate against a chief executive who could command enough authority and respect within his administration, as well as his own congressional party, to demand the attention and loyalty of our allies in international politics. The bill referral reform is but one of the factors which makes legislative decision-making on foreign policy so less expeditious than executive policy formation. The congressional reforms of the 1970s led to an increased policy activism in both the House and the Senate. We shall discuss these reforms shortly. But here we stress that this very activism and the longer deliberations that precede any final action on behalf of the nation have led foreign leaders, both in friendly and adversary countries, to wonder who exactly is in charge of our foreign policy—if anyone. A former British foreign minister reportedly once suggested, and not completely in jest, that foreign embassies ought to be built across from the Congress. For example, was Senator Dennis DeConcini (D., Ariz.) or Carter principally responsible for the final agreements on the Panama Canal treaty? Or does the government in Nicaragua negotiate for foreign aid with the president and secretary of state, the chairmen of the Foreign Affairs/Foreign Relations committees, or the heads of the Foreign Operations subcommittees of Appropriations in each House? In 1980, Rep. Clarence Long (D., Md.), who chairs the House Appropriations subcommittee, led the fight against increased aid to Nicaragua and largely succeeded in getting his way despite bitter opposition from the Carter administration and other congressional leaders.

In 1979, both the House and the Senate voted to restore diplomatic relations with Taiwan after the administration broke such relations to recognize the People's Republic of China; the fight over congressional prerogatives in this area was finally settled in the administration's favor but not until the Supreme Court refused to overturn a decision by the U.S. Court of Appeals that while initial recognition of Taiwan was accomplished by legislative action, the president could reverse that decision without congressional assent. Had the Court ruled otherwise, the newly established relations with China might well have been broken; they surely would have been very strained. During 1978 and 1979, the Congress wrestled with an amendment proposed by Senator Jesse Helms (R., N.C.) which would have repealed American participation in the United Nations trade embargo on the white minority government of Rhodesia, a policy endorsed by every other nation except South Africa. Rhodesia, now a black majority-controlled nation called Zimbabwe, had been involved in a bloody civil war for over a decade since the tiny white minority had unilaterally declared independence from Britain. The Carter administration, working with the British government under a United Nations mandate, was attempting to resolve the impasse in that African nation. Repeal of the embargo would certainly have set back such efforts, but in the eyes of the Senate supporters it would also have freed the United States from virtually complete dependence upon the Soviet Union for chrome imports. The Helms amendment cleared the Senate by a wide margin, but administration and party leadership pressure finally prevailed as the House refused to go along with the upper chamber.

The Panama Canal, Nicaraguan aid, Chinese relations, and Rhodesian embargo issues all took many months of congressional time. The legislative process is designed to be deliberative rather than expeditious. There is a far greater premium placed upon hearing diverse points of view and reflecting constituency opinion than upon quick, coordinated action. The refusal of House Democrats to permit the Democratic caucus to take binding policy stands in 1975 is perhaps the most dramatic example of this concern. The Senate, to be sure, is even slower than the House. The upper chamber has 18 committees and, like the House, about 140 subcommittees. But there are only 100 senators compared to 435 members of the House. Thus while most House members serve on one or two committees, senators generally have three to five committee assignments and eight to ten subcommittee positions are not unusual. A senator running from one committee meeting to another, having to ask what the subject matter of today's hearing is, is commonplace.

While both representatives and senators have large staffs and the Congress has provided itself with three research organizations, the General Accounting Office, the Office of Technology Assessment, and the Congressional Research Service of the Library of Congress (as well as the Congressional Budget Office), even these facilities are dwarfed by the administrative bureaucracies of the Executive Office of the President, the

Office of Management and Budget, and the State Department. Also, each congressional research unit serves all 535 members of the House and Senate and examines not only foreign policy questions, but domestic ones as well. Furthermore, the congressional Research Service does many studies of internal congressional organization and fulfills specific research requests from members' offices which may have been forwarded from constituents needing information.

Could the Congress establish a research and investigative arm for foreign (and domestic) policy that would rival that of the executive branch? Probably not, given the vast resources of the entire federal bureaucracy available to the White House. Even with its recent increases of staff and strengthening of its research organizations, jurisdictional conflicts have arisen to weaken the potential for real coordination. So does the subcommittee system, a set of governments numbering over three hundred in the House and Senate, which has replaced committees as the center of congressional power. The growth of subcommittee autonomy, together with other reforms of the 1970s, have meant that policy specialists are now not only competing with the executive branch but also with each other. We turn now to an examination of these reforms and their impact.

The New Congress: The Impact of Reforms

In the 1970s, committee government gave way to subcommittee domination. A series of reforms in the 1971−75 period radically changed the way in which the House of Representatives conducted its business. Committee chairmen were no longer automatically selected by the seniority principle, the length of continuous service on a committee. Democratic party members were no longer to be assigned to positions by the Ways and Means Committee; instead, a party organization, the Steering and Policy Committee, a third of whose members are appointed by the Speaker, controlled appointments to committees and the naming of chairmen. The Democratic caucus, composed of all party members in the House, then voted upon the recommendations of Steering and Policy, and agreement was not automatic. Furthermore, in an attempt to control the agenda, the Rules Committee was brought under party control. The Speaker was given the authority to appoint all Democratic members of Rules directly. In 1974, Appropriations also fell prey to the party leadership when its subcommittee chairmen were to be appointed by Steering and Policy, subject to caucus approval.

Other reforms of even greater import include the "subcommittee bill of rights" and the creation, in both the House and the Senate, of Budget committees which were designed to rationalize the relationship between spending and revenue raising. The first has had the greatest impact and is the most widely discussed.[33] In 1971, the Democratic caucus began the process which liberated junior members from the tyrannical chairman formerly typified by "Judge" Smith. The initial reforms restricted Democratic members from chairing more than one legislative subcommittee (although a member could retain a second chair of an investigative body which did not report original legislation) and guaranteed subcommittees the power to hire their own professional staff members. The biggest block of reforms occurred two years later when the selection of subcommittee members was made the responsibility of the full committee caucus and could not be dominated by the committee chairmen; subcommittees were also guaranteed fixed jurisdictions, so that full committee chairmen could not create new subcommittees at will to reward friends and punish enemies; committee members were guaranteed their choice, based upon seniority, of subcommittee assignments; and subcommittees were forced to have ratios of party members which reflected the full committee party balances, so that conservative chairmen could not stack certain subcommittees, for instance, with Republicans and overbalance other, less powerful ones with liberal Democrats.

In December 1974, in addition to the change in Appropriations subcommittee chairmanship appointments, the caucus mandated the following reforms: committees with more than twenty members (Ways and Means) but with no subcommittees would have to establish at least four such bodies; numbered subcommittees, such as those on Armed Services, were abolished so that the conservative chairman could no longer prevent some of the new liberal members of the committee from serving on subcommittees that were examining racial and sexual discrimination in the armed forces by assigning bills to subcommittees without specific subject jurisdictions; committees were required to establish an oversight subcommittee; and members would be restricted to membership on two subcommittees in each full committee on which they serve (four years later, they would be restricted to five subcommittees in total—at least in principle).

These reforms encompassing the "subcommittee bill of rights" were not intended to "punish" all chairmen of full committees because many were very highly regarded by the other members. The major objective of this reform, which was enormously successful, was to disperse power within the House. The focal point of activity shifted from the 22 standing committees to the approximately 140 subcommittees. The prestige of the title "Mr. (or Madame) Chairman" was somewhat reduced since almost two thirds of the Democrats in the House now hold it. The days of the strong chairmen were over. The younger members who had been entering the House since the late 1960s found their cause bolstered by the Democratic landslide of 1974, which brought into the Congress a large bloc of post-Vietnam politicians distrustful of highly-structured decision-making.

The demise of the strong committees opened up two possibilities for future congressional decision-making: an increased role for the two parties or an extreme decentralization so that each member would, in essence, become a sovereign. In the mid-1970s a resurgence of party government seemed possible. The Democratic caucus had gone on record three times (1971, 1973, and 1975) calling for a withdrawal of American troops from Vietnam and many in the party saw the prospect of using the caucus as a forum for coordinating policy making in Congress. But the old-line conservatives, including many chairmen of full committees who had seen their power eroded, feared that the caucus would impose a liberal orthodoxy on the congressional party. The newer, more progressive members, on the other hand, were distrustful of any hierarchical decision-making structure, and they, too, opposed an increased role for the caucus. Thus, in early 1975, the caucus forbade itself from binding members to specific voting stands on the House floor and then, it voted additionally to open future meetings to the public in order to stem any possibility that party leaders might try to resurrect the caucus as an internal forum for policy decisions.

One measure designed to centralize decision making in the Congress was the Budget and Impoundment Control Act of 1974 which created Budget committees in the House and the Senate and also a Congressional Budget Office to formulate an alternative budget to that of the president and to coordinate spending and revenue raising in the Congress. The idea of a legislative budget was initiated as one of the anti-Nixon reforms of the Democratic Congress, but it drew support from liberals and conservatives alike. Each saw the potential for the Congress to put its budgetary process in some sort of order, for the new law required the Budget committees to propose and enact a legislative budget. The limits established for expenditures in the final act passed each year could not be exceeded by the Appropriations committee of either House for any of the approximately twenty categories of federal spending.

The existing expenditure process was a classic example of group politics designed to produce many "winners" and few real "losers." Before any money could be expended, it must first be *authorized*, that is, made legal. Authorizations are determined by the substantive policy committees of the House and the Senate, so that Armed Services in each chamber would determine a maximum (and also possibly a minimum) amount to be spent on the military, while Education and Labor (House) and Labor and Human Resources (Senate) would set spending limits for federal aid to education, and so forth. Should the two houses disagree, as they usually do, a *conference committee* would be appointed by the Speaker of the House and the Senate party leadership (generally the majority and minority leaders working together) to work out a compromise within the limits of the original House and Senate bills. The conferees are, virtually without exception, members of the (sub-) committee(s) that handled the original legislation. House and Senate conferees each had to vote as a bloc and no bill would be enacted unless both groups reached agreement. Once agreement was reached, the House and Senate could only vote to accept or reject the conference report; no amendments are allowed. Failure to pass the report by either House would require the convening of another conference.

Even assuming that the conference report is accepted by the two houses, the spending process is far from over. Authorizations do not provide for the expenditure of any money; all that they do is to make it legal for the Appropriations committees in the House and Senate to propose actual expenditures, as restricted by the authorizations bills' maximum (or minimum) amounts. But at this point tension arises: The Appropriations committees are faced with authorizations that, when added up, would break any conceivable budget. Thus they work to cut back the authorized amounts from the special interest committees to produce a more coherent relationship between taxing and spending. The House Appropriations Committee, therefore, has historically served as the budget-cutter in the expenditure process, with the Senate body as a "court of last resort" for the authorizing committees and their supporting constituency groups.[34] The Armed Services committees have been notably active in pursuing their claims for more money and, an extremely unusual move in 1980, Carter's chairman of the Joint Chiefs of Staff of the armed services, David Jones, opposed his own President's budget recommendations and supported the authorizing committees' recommendations for further increases in military spending. While the Appropriations committees did, then, serve to restrain spending somewhat, the entire budget was never discussed in terms of overall priorities. The new Budget committees were designed to remedy this flaw in fiscal planning. To date, however, the success of these committees has been greatly limited. Budget resolutions often did not pass the Congress and the norm became a system in which spending limits on particular programs were simply waived by legislative acts. The early resolutions of the budget resolutions supported by President Reagan in 1981 suggest that the process can indeed work when disciplined majorities exist in the House and Senate. But it was the very lack of such discipline that led to the formation of the budget committees in 1974.

While the reforms of the 1970s could have produced either a more centralized or a more decentralized Congress, the weakness of the party system and the reluctance of the members to subordinate their newly liberated subcommittees to party leadership tilted the balance strongly in favor of fractionalized allegiances. Individual members, motivated by power, sought the overthrow of the committee barons who replaced the strong Speaker of the late nineteenth and early twentieth centuries. The upshot of this move toward greater participation in decision making within the Congress has led to a situation in which the only real power is the ability to block consideration of proposed legislation. If domestic authorizations and appropriations are not passed, highly salient political programs (such as agriculture, housing, and transportation subsidies) will come to a sudden halt and federal paychecks will bounce. In contrast, failure to act on key foreign policy issues will leave the executive unchecked; diplomacy will not cease. Enormous costs may, therefore, result from congressional failure to act, but these will not be directly borne by angry constituents in most instances. Foreign policy has a much smaller and less organized constituency than do most domestic programs. However, when Congress does not act on foreign policy, the president might gain so much leverage that the policy does not reflect popular opinion. What Congress does best is to represent the views of organized groups within the electorate. We can debate the wisdom of making policy, either domestic or foreign, through such group demands, but the American system has been based upon this concept of politics.[35] We shall turn to an examination of how well Congress might perform this representation function after discussing the structure of foreign-policy decision-making in Congress.

The Foreign Policy Committees

Table 3–1 presents the full range of dispersion of foreign-policy decision-making in the Congress. Jurisdictional lines are often not as clear-cut as the table indicates, but the very large number of bodies with significant foreign policy authority is staggering. It is small wonder that Congress rarely takes the lead in initiating foreign policy. The key foreign policy committees are Foreign Relations (Senate), Foreign Affairs (House), Armed Services and Appropriations in each chamber, Governmental Affairs (Senate), and Government Operations (House). In addition to these standing committees, there are *select* Intelligence committees in both the House and the Senate. Select committees usually are established within each House for a specified time period and are restricted to either general oversight of the administration or the reporting of very few pieces of legislation. The Intelligence committees, however, have been established (as of 1977 for both houses) as permanent select committees and in 1979–80 considered a proposal to establish a charter for the Central Intelligence Agency.

The key committees are Foreign Relations and Foreign Affairs and an examination of each highlights the different ways in which senators and representatives perceive foreign policy. Foreign Relations is a highly desired committee slot; members often wait years to obtain a seat on it and there are many disputes among members as to who is entitled to serve on that prestigious body. Some analysts rank Foreign Relations as the most prestigious committee in the Senate. The body has attracted the "best and the brightest" of the Senate and both chairmen and ranking minority members have achieved great stature in the Senate, including Arthur Vandenburg (R., Mich.)—principal spokesman for the post-World War II bipartisan foreign policy under the Truman administration, J. William Fulbright, Frank Church, and Jacob Javits. Following Fulbright's primary election defeat in 1974 and before Church's elevation to the chairmanship five years later, John Sparkman (D., Ala.) chaired the committee. Unlike his predecessor or his successor, Sparkman was not an activist chairman. He believed that his principal duty was to work with the president to conduct a bipartisan foreign policy. But he was a leader well respected in the Senate. Originally a moderate from the South, he was close enough to the mainstream of the party to be selected as Adlai Stevenson's running mate in the 1952 presidential election. Sparkman had become more conservative over the next two decades but, when he finally achieved the leadership position on Foreign Relations, he did not attempt to impose his own views on the full committee. As a respected member of the Senate, he let individual members have a great deal of leeway, thereby strengthening subcommittee autonomy by the time Church assumed power. The de facto leader of the committee during Sparkman's era, to the extent that there was one, was Javits, a moderate-liberal Republican often more in step with Democrats than his own party. Overall, the Senate Foreign Relations Committee has developed a reputation for foreign policy activism, tilted toward the left of center in both parties, and strong and influential leadership. Under Percy, the committee will still be marked by leadership which is in the tradition of bipartisan internationalism, but the overall balance of power has shifted sharply to the right with the new Republican majority. Percy, wary of his own minority position in the party, is at best a moderating force between his own party's positions and those of President Reagan. Indeed, he even voted in committee against the nomination of Ernest Lefever as assistant secretary of state for human rights and humanitarian affairs in June 1981. Percy was joined by a majority of committee Republicans in the 13–4 vote, leading to Lefever's withdrawal. The Democratic ranking minority member, Claiborne Pell (D., R.I.), is a thoughtful and widely respected member who is both electorally safe and committed to the continuation of a strong human rights policy. But, despite his reputation within the Congress, Pell is not as widely known throughout the country as either Church or Javits were and he will find it difficult to replace them.

In contrast, the leadership of the House committee reflects the lower prestige of that body within the chamber. The more senior members generally opt for chairmanships of subcommittees on their second committees rather than on Foreign Affairs. The committee has a reputation for concentrating on only one piece of legislation a year, foreign aid, and there are few less salient or popular issues among the mass public. The

TABLE 3–1 Committees of Congress Dealing With Foreign Policy Issues

Committee	Subjects
Foreign Relations (Senate)	General conduct of foreign policy; declarations of war; executive agreements; treaties
Foreign Affairs (House)	Same as Senate Foreign Relations except for treaties
Armed Services (Senate and House)	Military affairs; defense budget; national security; arms exports
Energy and Commerce (House)	Energy; international economic policy; telecommunications; transportation; shipping
Commerce, Science, and Transportation (Senate)	International economic policy; telecommunications; transportation; shipping; ocean and fishing rights; nonmilitary space programs; merchant marine
Merchant Marine and Fisheries (House)	Merchant marine; ocean and fishing rights; offshore oil; law of the sea; Panama Canal
Appropriations (Senate and House)	All programs requiring funding; defense budget; budget for running bureaucracies
Budget (Senate and House)	Overall spending levels and spending within specific categories
Banking, Housing, and Urban Affairs (Senate) /Banking, Finance, and Urban Affairs (House)	International monetary policy; international commerce; authorizations for Export-Import Bank, and World Bank

Committee	Jurisdiction
Intelligence (Senate and House)	Oversight of intelligence agencies (select committees)
Science and Technology (House)	Space program; energy research and development
Energy and Natural Resources (Senate)	Energy policy; energy research and development
Environment and Public Works (Senate)	Environmental policy; water resources; nuclear energy regulation
Interior and Insular Affairs (House)	Environmental policy; nuclear energy regulation; coal mining
Public Works and Transportation (House)	Aviation; water resources; hydroelectric energy; transportation
Finance (Senate)/Ways and Means (House)	Reciprocal trade agreements; tariffs; import quotas; customs
Agriculture, Nutrition, and Forestry (Senate)/Agriculture (House)	Price supports; international food policy; food exports; Food for Peace
Governmental Affairs (Senate)	General oversight; nuclear energy and export; executive branch organization
Government Operations (House)	General oversight; energy policy; trade oversight (including embargos)
Rules (House)	Setting of legislative agenda for House bills
Education and Labor (House)/Labor and Human Resources (Senate)	ACTION (including Peace Corps); International Labor Organization; migration and immigration
Judiciary (Senate and House)	Immigration policy
Joint Economic Committee (Senate and House)	International economic policy (no legislative authority; research function only)

committee has eight subcommittees, four dealing with general issue areas and four arranged on geographic locales. For many years the dominant premise was to resist conflict with the administration, even to the point of inaction. One member told Fenno in the 1960s:[36]

> I've been on the Europe subcommittee for five months and I haven't even heard NATO mentioned, haven't even heard the word. I read my hometown newspaper to find out what's happening to NATO. . . . The subcommittees have displayed absolute irrelevancy in foreign affairs, amazing irrelevancy.

The chairman from 1958 to 1977 was Thomas "Doc" Morgan (D., Pa.), who was succeeded by Clement Zablocki. Morgan believed that the proper role of the committee was to pass the president's foreign aid request and little more.[37] He rarely interfered with subcommittee chairmen and gave them considerable leeway in the 1970s when several members, including Zablocki, became more activist. Zablocki cosponsored (with Senator Clifford Case) a successful move to require prompt reporting to the Congress of executive agreements. But the greatest degree of activism came from other members, mostly representatives from relatively safe seats: Benjamin Rosenthal, Jonathan Bingham, Stephen J. Solarz, and Lester Wolff (all D., N.Y.); John Brademas (D., Ind.), Paul Sarbanes (D., Md.), Lee Hamilton (D., Ind.), Donald Fraser (D., Minn.), and Pierre DuPont (R., Del.). All were ambitious: Rosenthal unsuccessfully challenged Zablocki for the chairmanship in the 1977 Democratic caucus; Sarbanes and Fraser ran for the Senate; DuPont was elected governor; and Brademas was selected House Democratic Whip in 1977.

Despite Zablocki's own action in 1972, the Wisconsin Democrat did not move to change the basic decision-making strategy of the committee. Like Morgan, he is not a mover and a shaker nor is he nearly as liberal as most of his party colleagues on the committee. One account of his career maintains: "He owes this position mainly to seniority; there is little likelihood that he would have been elected to it de novo."[38] Serving beside him and Morgan as ranking minority member is William S. Broomfield (R., Mich.), first elected to the House in 1956 and a rather quiet member who generally follows his party's line in both domestic and foreign policy. Neither Zablocki nor Broomfield have taken an active role in encouraging or discouraging subcommittee members from initiating foreign policy. One liberal activist, who will likely be chairman in this decade, is Dante Fascell (D., Fla.). Under Fascell, the approach of the entire committee may change.

The challenges to the war in Vietnam, as well as the War Powers Act, originated in the Senate committee. During the late 1960s and throughout the first half-decade of the 1970s, several attempts were made by Foreign Relations members to cut off funds for fighting the war in Vietnam, notably by Senators Church, McGovern, Case, and John Sherman Cooper (R., Ky.). This bipartisan effort, in various forms, passed the Senate many times, but always failed in the House where members were reluctant to challenge presidential authority. Whereas Foreign Relations chairman Fulbright was a leading spokesman on behalf of these efforts, Morgan quietly led the opposition in the House. An amendment to forbid funding for military operations in Cambodia did pass both houses in 1975, but by that time the troops were already out. The only real success of a congressional amendment to terminate the American involvement in Vietnam occurred *after* the Paris peace agreement, when all U.S. forces had been withdrawn from Vietnam and all prisoners of war returned to America. Only then did *both* houses cut off funds for the administration's continued bombing in Cambodia, where no cease-fire had yet occurred. Yet, the legislative success was qualified, because Nixon vetoed the appropriations bill to which the cut-off on funds was attached. The President's need for funds for several executive agencies led to a compromise delaying the end of the bombing for several weeks. This gave Washington and Hanoi another chance to negotiate a Cambodian cease-fire and await the onset of the monsoon season, which would make further fighting very difficult.

The Senate, through the Foreign Relations Committee, consistently took the lead in the efforts to restrain the executive in Vietnam (as well as in Angola) in the 1960s and 1970s. The most prominent House committee initiative on foreign policy occurred on an issue which in many ways resembles the classic constituency politics of domestic policy more than the global issues of foreign policy—aid to Turkey. In July 1975, Turkey intervened militarily in Cyprus, a Mediterranean island populated by people of Turkish and Greek descent, after the Greek military government had attempted to unite Greece and Cyprus. The two countries were historical rivals, but both were NATO members. The situation was further complicated by the fact that Turkish troops used American-supplied arms in their attack. The dilemma posed to American interests was readily resolved when two factors were taken into account: (1) Turkey had not been cooperative with the United States in restricting the growth of poppy seeds, the source of heroin, despite repeated American overtures and assistance on this issue; and (2) there are many more Greek-Americans than Turkish-Americans and these Greek-Americans tend to live in the larger cities and vote Democratic. Just as American Jewish groups have pressed for congressional and administration support for aid to Israel through the American-Israel Public Affairs Committee (AIPAC), Greek-Americans established the American Hellenic Educational Progressive Association (AHEPA) and the American Hellenic Institute Public Affairs Committee (AHIPAC) to lobby for a pro-Greek foreign policy.

Americans of Jewish and Greek background had traditionally gotten along quite well together, so Jewish members of Congress readily lent their support to the AHEPA-AHIPAC move to cut off military aid to Turkey.[39] The key House backers of the move were Rosenthal (Jewish) and

DuPont in the foreground, and Brademas and Sarbanes, both of Greek descent, in the background. The initial move on the boycott came in the Senate but the Appropriations Committee of that body weakened the language introduced in the House to permit the President to restore aid when Turkey showed good faith in attempting to reach an agreement with Greece. The House clearly took the lead in responding to this foreign policy initiative with strong constituency politics elements. From a position of strength, the House insisted upon its position and won in the conference with the Senate although it agreed to delay the embargo until February 1976—when arms shipments were finally cut off.

The success of the House in foreign policy-making was, however, short-lived. By the fall of 1976, the good faith effort language of the Senate was adopted by both houses. The ban was finally lifted in 1978, when Carter was basking in the glory of the Camp David accord between Israel and Egypt. Earlier, AIPAC had suffered a stinging defeat when the Congress refused to block the sale of jet fighters to Egypt and Saudi Arabia. Several key Jewish members of the House and the Senate, convinced that the sale would aid the Camp David agreements because it would attract Saudi support for the peace process, bolted AIPAC. The ethnic lobbies also lost on the arms embargo issue when global political considerations, including rampant unemployment and violence in Turkey and a series of unstable governments in that country, led a traditional leader in the Greek-Jewish alliance, Solarz, to manage the administration's embargo repeal effort in the House. Senate agreement followed quickly.

Thus, the House Foreign Affairs Committee is no match for either the president or the Senate Foreign Relations body. There is increasing activism and occasionally strong challenges to the administration, including votes in both committees—even the Republican-dominated Senate one—in April and May of 1981 to try to limit military aid by the Reagan administration to El Salvador, but the committee still seems to be without an established direction. The Senate Foreign Relations Committee has been more powerful in the past fifteen years than its House counterpart, but this committee has traditionally been quite powerful. In the past, it served as the bulwark of the bipartisan foreign policy. As it has come to challenge the president more often in recent years, its power base has been more widely noticed. Under Carter, however, Foreign Relations was quite cooperative on most issues. It is likely that the President felt constrained in several key policy areas, including aid to Pakistan and the level of support given to Israel, by the Senate committee and chose to work with the members rather than confront them with a battle he was not sure he could win.

In contrast, the Armed Services committees have pushed the president to the right rather than the left in recent years. The Senate body was chaired until 1981 by John Stennis (D., Miss.), one of the strongest defenders of the military in the Congress. Right behind him in seniority was Jackson, sometimes called the "Senator from Boeing" because of his support for high levels of military spending which would benefit that company and Lockheed, both of which have large numbers of employees in the Seattle area. The new chairman is conservative Republican John Tower (Tex.), who differs little from his Democratic colleagues on key defense issues. All three are formidable forces in Senate politics. The House committee is chaired by a moderate Democrat, Melvin Price (Ill.)—a marked departure from previous leaders Mendel Rivers (D., S.C.) and F. Edward Hébert (D., La.).

With only a few exceptions, the Democratic and Republican members of the committee are all strong backers of the military and work diligently in the pursuit of two goals: (1) increasing the defense budget; and (2) ensuring that their districts are granted at least their fair share of defense contracts and subcontracts. The same description applies to members of the Defense subcommittees of House and Senate Appropriations. On House Armed Services, three prominent liberals first elected in 1974 have taken policy initiatives: Bob Carr (D., Mich.), a former pilot himself, was, until his surprise defeat in 1980, a consistent critic of defense spending and led the fight in 1975, as a freshman, to cut off funds for Cambodia; Patricia Schroeder (D., Colo.), one of the less predictable members of Congress on most issues but a leading advocate of increased opportunities for women in the armed forces and perhaps the most vociferous opponent of reinstating the draft in the lower house; and Ronald Dellums (D., Cal.), a critic of defense spending and a vociferous spokesman for racial equality in the services (as elsewhere). But these members, together with a few other liberals and moderates appointed in later congresses, form a distinct minority in the committee. They have learned, as the first and most persistent critic of defense spending on the committee, Les Aspin (D., Wisc.), that their major impact is through the publicity that their disclosures of waste and improper practices uncover rather than in committee decision-making.

The Senate body is clearly more powerful than its House counterpart. It often stands in opposition to presidential policies, as was the case with the B−1 bomber (which it failed to get enacted) and SALT II (where opposition within the committee may have weakened the already precarious position of the treaty in the Senate). Senator Sam Nunn (D., Ga.), one of the most diligent and respected supporters of the military in Congress, is a leading spokesman for increased defense spending, and his influence among colleagues is so strong that many believe that he can bargain successfully for higher expenditures in return for support on other key foreign policy questions, such as the Panama Canal treaties. While Carter faced a more compliant Foreign Relations Committee than did his three predecessors, the pressure of Armed Services was just as disturbing to executive dominance over foreign policy-making. The executive may be better off fighting this body than Foreign Relations, however, since the latter committee is more directly involved in decisions affecting foreign commitments. But a challenge from Armed Services cannot be easily dismissed since it is a double-barreled threat: The president cannot use a "divide and conquer" strategy among Senate committees. Prior to 1981 Stennis chaired both Armed Services and the Defense subcommittee of Appropriations. This could not happen in the House since Appropriations is an exclusive committee and, under normal circumstances, a member would not serve on any other committee; even if this rule should be breached, a chairman of one committee could not chair another legislative subcommittee. The new chairman of Armed Services, Tower, does not serve on Appropriations. But the chairman of the Defense subcommittee on Appropriations is now the Majority Whip in the Senate, Ted Stevens of Alaska—long considered a moderate in his party despite a conservative voting record but nevertheless one of the earlier supporters of Reagan's bid for the presidency in 1980. The smaller number of members of the Senate thus serves to concentrate power to a greater extent than we find in the House.

The remaining major foreign policy committees have substantially less clout than do Foreign Relations/Foreign Affairs, Armed Services, and the Senate Defense subcommittee of Appropriations. While each might exercise considerable power on specific issues from time to time, none has either an institutional structure or a powerful leadership to propel it into the mainstream of decision making on foreign and defense policy. The Intelligence committees have largely faded from public view and failed badly in their 1979–80 attempt to write a charter for the CIA; the bodies did, however, prevent outright repeal of many of the Hughes-Ryan provisions, as urged by members who thought that the restrictions might have contributed to the failure of the government to respond to the revolutions in Iran and Nicaragua. The Carter administration supported the charter, but there is little evidence that the select committees have had significant impacts on the activities of the intelligence agencies.

The many different committees which have jurisdiction over aspects of foreign policy weaken the ability of Congress as an institution to propose and carry out an alternative foreign policy. But they also provide opportunities for the administration to seek support from different constituencies within the Congress for its foreign policy as well as pitfalls for the implementation of some policies. In many instances, the administration only needs to block a restive committee effort to undermine the president's program and, as stressed before, it is much easier to defeat something in Congress than to pass a bill. But when congressional support is required, the battle may become more difficult to win, as the examples of SALT II, the Panama Canal treaties, and even the Turkish arms embargo indicate. Trade-offs on other questions of foreign policy or on domestic issues may have to be employed and in this sense foreign policy formation by—or with—Congress comes to resemble the constituency politics of domestic policy.

Can Congress Make an Effective Foreign Policy?

For all of the increased activism of Congress in recent years, it would be a mistake to conclude that the legislative branch has assumed a role in foreign policy similar to its concern for domestic policy. The stakes are too different for that to happen and the data would not support such a conclusion. We present in Table 3−2 a comparison of the number of treaties and executive agreements over the past four decades. While the number of treaties has not increased dramatically, executive agreements have become much more frequent.[40] A study of executive agreements formulated between 1946 and 1972 found that the overwhelming majority of them (87 percent) had been authorized by congressional statute.[41] But this analysis indicates only a greater procedural role for Congress in enacting legislation which permits the agreements to be signed. An agreement signed in 1980 may have been authorized by statute twenty years earlier. Furthermore, the study produced no evidence—and, indeed considerable skepticism—that such statutory grants were based upon a knowledge of what types of agreements were to follow. Indeed, Carter threatened to implement the Panama Canal legislation as an executive agreement had the Senate defeated the treaties. This suggestion led to heavy criticism of the President and was promptly withdrawn—although Carter's threat may have alleviated some momentum building at the time among treaty opponents. In any event, the idea was unrealistic since the treaties required implementing legislation which appropriated funds to pay Panama for the operation of the canal in the years before the land

TABLE 3−2

Year	Treaties	Executive Agreements	Year	Treaties	Executive Agreements
1930	25	11	1970	20	183
1935	25	10	1971	17	214
1940	12	20	1972	20	287
1944	1	74	1973	17	241
1945	6	54	1974	13	229
1946	19	139	1975	13	264
1950	11	157	1976	13	402
1955	7	297	1977	17	424
1960	5	266	1978	15	417
1965	14	204	1979	30	360

reverts to Panamanian sovereignty. The critical House roll call on this funding in 1979 passed by only a single vote. The administration had assumed that the battle had been won after the Senate consented to the treaties. It could not have been more mistaken. The assertiveness of the Congress on foreign policy questions may not occur often, but at least often enough *on important issues* that the legislative branch can no longer be consigned to a third circle of decision making.

Can Congress make foreign policy? Not by itself, to be sure. Should Congress make foreign policy? The members themselves have answered that question in the affirmative. The president is still the leading spokesman on foreign policy questions, but there is little doubt that his power will not be unchecked in the future. Indeed, the increasing popularity of the "legislative veto," through which either House (or both) can reverse an administrative action by simple roll call votes, may be extended even further to foreign policy issues. It is presently used for military sales and the Congress has imposed a two-house veto on the controversial domestic agency, the Federal Trade Commission. Should the use of this procedure spread, a much greater role will follow for Congress in foreign policy in the future. How desirable is such a trend? Crisis decision-making is unlikely to be affected, since the Congress, as well as the mass public, tends to rally around the president during such moments. However, for noncrisis decision-making, the question comes down to a very difficult choice which lies at the heart of the problem of foreign-policy decision-making in a democracy: How can we reconcile the need for swift and united national action and the demand for a set of policy goals which is responsive to public opinion and also meets the requirements of constitutional government? There are inherent tensions here and every increase in speed and flexibility leads to a decrease in public participation. On the other hand, the greater the degree of public and legislative initiatives in foreign policy, the more difficult it might be for the administration to negotiate (particularly when secret talks are required) with foreign governments and conduct its foreign policy.

The issue of expeditious action versus reflecting public preferences is, however, more complex. The Congress certainly does reflect what its members believe to be public opinion in their districts (or states for senators). Some legislators go so far as to make such opinions the deciding factor in their policy decisions, as Senator Edward Zorinsky (D., Neb.) did on the Panama Canal treaties in 1978. Zorinsky pledged that he would be bound by poll results he obtained and even went so far in support of the treaties as to convince Carter to invite 250 Nebraska residents to the White House to increase support among influential citizens in the state.[42] The polls consistently showed a majority against the treaties and Zorinsky reluctantly followed public sentiment. This localism in congressional foreign policy-making is clearly aided by the large staffs and tremendous expenditures for offices, supplies, and trips back home in the congressional politics in the era of strong incumbents. The resources available to members have changed dramatically. Contrast this with the concern of Robert A. Dahl over thirty years ago over how to make foreign policy-making in Congress in greater accord with public opinion:[43]

> Representative Jacob Javits employed the Roper agency to poll opinion in the Twenty-first Congressional district of New York prior to the 1948 elections. But this is not a readily available technique; the expense rules it out as more than a rare device. One polling agency estimates that it would cost $2,000 to $2,500 to poll a "typical" Congressional district—pretty clearly an expense not many Congressmen or local party organizations can often afford.

In contemporary politics, virtually every candidate for Congress conducts polls which are a regular part of the campaign. Even at inflated prices, polls are now regarded as necessities and well within campaign budgets, which are well over $100,000 for most challengers in the House (and even greater for incumbents) and about $1 million in the Senate.[44] This increased use of polling certainly induces more localism into decision making, including that on foreign policy.

However, it would be all too facile to assume that presidents are immune from public pressure in the conduct of foreign policy. Indeed, in his first major speech after resigning in protest as secretary of state in the Carter administration, Cyrus Vance charged in June 1980 that the administration's policies regarding SALT II, Afghanistan, the Middle East, and human rights were based more upon election year political considerations—public opinion—than on global political considerations.[45] Carter spent the better part of his early campaign in the White House during the 1980 Democratic party primaries, in which Kennedy challenged him, stressing his role as President. To be sure, the President argued that he was preoccupied with the crisis in Iran, but when he felt that political pressures forced him to resume active campaigning, the hostages were still not free.

In 1972, Nixon made his historic trip to China and traveled to Moscow to sign SALT I before the Republican convention—and the ensuing general election campaign. Presidents, no less than members of Congress, are political animals and have a keen sense of how to use the advantage of incumbency to increase their standing in public opinion polls. Foreign policy initiatives—or even crises—are particularly useful in this regard since they focus directly upon the president in a "we-they" perspective. The chief executive is seen dealing with other heads of state, thus avoiding a direct confrontation with political rivals. To a certain extent, a president serving his second term is shielded from such political pressures, but we should not overestimate the impact of the two-term limitation mandated by the Twenty-second Amendment to the Constitution. For no president wants to leave office unpopular—and perhaps charged with electing a successor of the opposite party because his policies were out of step with public opinion.

The question, in the final analysis, is which institution better represents public opinion? In turn, we must ask: Is there a single national opinion to be represented, as defenders of the strong presidency maintain, or is the nation composed largely of groups of citizens with different interests? The answer we give largely determines which institution should dominate foreign-policy decision-making, assuming that one wants to argue that foreign policy, like domestic policy, should be subject to such public concern and influences. Perhaps the major questions each of us must ask ourselves are whether the two types of policy making require basically similar or different approaches and whether the benefits of participation by the legislative branch in foreign policy-making, thus checking a potential "imperial president," are greater, equal to, or less than, the costs imposed by the concern of Congress with issues of interest to the constituencies and by the delays (deliberations) involved in participatory decision-making.

The Decision-Making Arena: The Cast of Characters

The Circles of Power: A Recapitulation

Because the stakes in foreign-policy decision-making are generally seen as quite different from those in domestic policies, it is not surprising to find that some of the major actors on domestic policy such as political parties, interest groups, and public opinion play a lesser role in foreign-policy decision-making. It is the presidency which is well suited as an office for handling questions that have high stakes and may require quick and decisive action. But the Congress has taken an increasingly active role in foreign policy in the past decade.

In the previous chapter, we presented a model of foreign-policy decision-making based upon a set of concentric circles.[1] We indicated that the role of Congress has changed, but otherwise the hierarchical model still fits most activity in this arena. The smallest, inner circle (see Figure 3–1) contains the actors who actually make the decisions on most foreign-policy questions. Here we find the president and his closest advisers. The Congress traditionally was placed in one of the outer circles, but the more aggressive legislature of the 1980s now must be considered to be part of the innermost circle in many critical instances. The delineation of power between the legislative and executive branches is

119

not as clear-cut as it was a decade ago. The more a foreign policy decision affects domestic interests as, for example, in limited war,[2] the greater is the role that Congress will play on that policy—and the more the legislature will belong in the innermost circle.

On other issues, primarily those involving crises or security questions, the Congress, while more assertive, has tended, with some notable exceptions, to provide more support for the president's policies or engage in some degree of oversight. Examples include the 1975 interim accord in the Sinai between Egypt and Israel to monitor the possibility that either country might launch a surprise attack against the other, which resulted in a rather detailed grilling of Kissinger by the Senate Foreign Relations Committee, followed by overwhelming legislative approval of the plan, and the oversight of intelligence operations abroad, including the *Mayaguez* incident in 1975 and the attempt to rescue the American hostages in Iran in 1980, when the President (as required by the Hughes-Ryan amendment) consulted with key congressional leaders but did not directly involve them in decision making. Here Congress is found in the second circle, where there are also the bureaucracies in the major foreign policy agencies and the armed services, the second-rank and less influential foreign policy departments, presidential advisers and cabinet members whose primary responsibility is in the domestic sphere but who may be consulted on foreign policy questions, and scientists. In the third circle, we find political parties and interest groups; and in the fourth, outer circle are public opinion and the media.

The Inner Circle: Presidential Dominance

At the center of the inner circle, of course, stands the president. In addition, this circle includes the vice-president and the secretaries of defense and state, the director of the Central Intelligence Agency and the chairman of the Joint Chiefs of Staff. Others often attending are the president's national security adviser, the director of the Office of Management and Budget, secretary of the Treasury, chairman of the Council of Economic Advisers, and such other advisers as the president might choose such as the directors of the International Communication Agency and the Arms Control and Disarmament Agency. The rationale behind the establishment of the National Security Council (NSC), which was founded in 1947 by the same act that established an independent Air Force, the Defense Department, and the Central Intelligence Agency, was to centralize decision making on national security issues, to ensure that the political and military strands of foreign policy issues would be more related to one another than formerly, and to make certain that the major foreign policy advisers would be included in the decision-making process. Under Franklin D. Roosevelt, the decision on which high officials or agencies to include and not include in a specific decision was entirely in the president's hands. As a result, political and strategic issues had often not been coordinated. The NSC was supposed to be a check against such presidential discretion and lack of coordination.

Most recent presidents have circumvented the NSC as the formal or actual locus of foreign-policy decision-making. Instead, they have formed their own informal circle of advisers whose membership may be somewhat broader than the statutory membership of the NSC. This is not to say that the *actors* who comprise the NSC are not in the president's own special circle; on the contrary, most of them usually are. Rather, membership on the NSC does not guarantee an actor a place in the informal circle; in addition, actors not on the NSC but whom the president is close to, may be included. The chief executive has a great deal of leeway in deciding whom to include. Kennedy included his brother, Attorney General Robert Kennedy, as well as staff aides Theodore C. Sorensen and Arthur M. Schlesinger, Jr. Lyndon Johnson retained many of Kennedy's advisers and also consulted a group of "wise men," people with extensive backgrounds in foreign relations who held no formal positions in the government. Perhaps the most prominent was former Secretary of State Dean Acheson. Nixon, on the other hand, kept his inner circle more restricted. Henry Kissinger, national security adviser from 1969 to 1973 and thereafter secretary of state, dominated virtually everybody else. Gerald R. Ford also relied almost exclusively on Kissinger.

Carter's closest advisers were his wife Rosalyn, Vice-President Mondale, Secretary of State Cyrus Vance, National Security Adviser Zbigniew Brzezinski (recruited from the academic community like McGeorge Bundy, W. W. Rostow, and Kissinger), United Nations Ambassador Andrew Young, Chief of Staff Hamilton Jordan (who masterminded the Iranian hostage issue from its beginning), and Robert Strauss—who held a variety of positions from chairman of the Democratic National Committee to Special Representative for World Trade negotiations, to Special Middle East envoy, to campaign chairman of the reelection effort. Unlike Ford or Nixon, Carter had a large inner circle and expanded it to include different people on different issues, such as Ellsworth Bunker on the Panama Canal negotiations, Elliot Richardson on the Law of the Sea Conference, Gerard Smith on SALT II, and so forth.

However, the fiercest conflict among this large group of advisers occurred among Vance, Brzezinski, and Young. Young, a former civil rights activist and the first black representative from the South elected since Reconstruction, was unable to refrain from speaking his mind when he disagreed with the administration and was ultimately dismissed for his impolitic remarks. Vance resigned following the Iranian hostage rescue mission, which he alone among Carter's top advisers had opposed. He had been feuding with Brzezinski almost from the beginning of their service with Carter's administration and had begun to lose influence by late 1979.

Vance was replaced by Senator Edmund Muskie, a very popular figure both in the Congress and among the public. Jordan was also to take a leave of absence from the administration to run the day-to-day operations of the reelection effort, although he continued to speak on behalf of the President on domestic and foreign policy questions from that post.

Why have not most recent presidents made greater use of the NSC? The answer is relatively simple. The act that created the NSC attempted to *impose* an inner circle on the president by granting various actors *ex officio* entry. Nevertheless, most presidents simply did not accept the idea that they *had* to consult certain actors and *only* those actors on foreign policy questions. They wanted to include in the inner circle close personal advisers and others whose opinions they respected. Furthermore, no president has been equally close to all members of the NSC. Indeed, few have been close to their vice-presidents at all. The vice-presidential candidate is usually chosen more for his vote-getting ability than for his ability to succeed the president. Vice-presidents have not played a major role in foreign policy. The inner circle thus provides the president with a less formal means of accomplishing the same basic goal as the NSC—formulation of major foreign policy decisions. Thus high-level officials have not been systematically excluded from the decision-making process since the Roosevelt administration

The informal circle is especially prominent in crisis decision-making. This is where the alternatives are discussed and either accepted or rejected. The tendency of certain officeholders to remain in the inner circle from administration to administration (the secretaries of defense and state, the director of the CIA, the national security adviser, and the chairman of the Joint Chiefs of Staff) derives from their functions. They are the men charged with carrying out presidential decisions and thus can hardly be excluded from participating in the formulation of the decisions. However, being a member of this circle does not automatically imply that all advisers are equally influential. Truman and Eisenhower relied far more heavily on their secretaries of state—Acheson and John Foster Dulles, respectively—than on their secretaries of defense. Nixon and, to a lesser extent, Kennedy played down the role of the secretary of state. Nixon relied primarily on Kissinger, while Kennedy depended upon his secretary of defense. Indeed, Robert S. McNamara, who was secretary of defense under both Kennedy and Johnson, was among the closest and most persuasive advisers to each president until his opposition to the conduct of the Vietnam War alienated him from Johnson. Even then, Johnson did not entirely stop listening to McNamara.

By contrast, the Iranian crisis led to a break between Carter and Vance, with the secretary of state resigning in protest over the abortive rescue effort. As is typical in crisis decision-making, Carter relied most heavily upon his most trusted aides and friends—including Jordan, Brzezinski, Jack Watson (later to become White House Chief of Staff), and his wife Rosalyn. At the beginning of the crisis, Carter called together a secret group of top foreign policy advisers in previous administrations in a move to create a national consensus: Among those who later spoke out and revealed at least their own identities were Rusk and Kissinger. There was little evidence that these leaders had any lasting impact, as Johnson's "wise men" did. Indeed, Kissinger later became a vocal critic of the President for not doing enough to save the pro-American regime of the Shah in Iran.

High-ranking officials in the inner circle often find themselves in dual roles when advising the president. On the one hand, they were selected by the president to advise him. On the other hand, as representatives of their agencies or departments they come into meetings of the inner circle with a point of view at least partially shaped by their daily experiences, views and interests of their departments. The secretary of state is faced with problems of diplomacy, while the secretary of defense is more concerned in his daily routine with questions of military policy. Each may be faced with a dilemma of either expressing his own advice to the president or representing his department. Often there is no conflict between the two roles.[3] However, the institutional environments of the various agencies can easily compel such a choice. Kennedy chose McNamara as secretary of defense because of his success in applying modern management techniques at the Ford Motor Company. He expected the secretary to apply the same techniques of measuring cost-effectiveness to the Pentagon. The new secretary immediately ran into problems with the heads of the various services, who resented the attempt by a civilian—and an outsider to the Pentagon at that—to tell the military what its organization and strategy should be. He battled with the services throughout his tenure as he took on more the role of presidential adviser than representative of his agency. John Foster Dulles, similarly, never bothered to penetrate into the daily workings of the State Department, choosing instead to represent his own views before Eisenhower. Nixon, by contrast, viewed the position of secretary of defense as less an advisory than a managerial post. In 1973, he selected Elliot Richardson, secretary of health, education, and welfare, to run the Pentagon. Richardson was soon shifted to the Justice Department. He was, quite simply, a superb administrator who could cut through organizational red tape and assert his command position. When a department needed reorganizing, he was Nixon's choice to head it. He later served as secretary of commerce under Ford and accepted a diplomatic position offered by Carter in early 1977.

Despite the fact the presidential styles are the basic determinant of how the inner circle will be composed, some continuities can be found throughout the post-World War II presidencies. As we have noted, no president before Carter has relied heavily on his vice-president. Each president will include in his innermost circle, although not in the NSC, several key members of Congress, notably those on the Armed Services and Foreign Relations committees. Truman relied heavily upon Republican Senator Arthur Vandenberg (Mich.) for support for his bipartisan foreign policy. Eisenhower, faced with a Democratic congressional majority during six of his eight years in office and a hostile Republican majority during the other two, paid great heed to the advice of Democratic floor leader Lyndon Johnson (Tex.). Kennedy was close to Fulbright, but had an unbreakable commitment to House Armed Services Chairman Carl Vinson (D., Ga.). Vinson had almost forced himself into the President's innermost circle. A strong domestic conservative during his many years in Congress, he shifted ground under Kennedy and supported the President's domestic program in return for increased influence on military policy, particularly the defense budget. Johnson relied heavily upon the advice of two members of the Senate Armed Services Committee, with whom he had served while in that chamber: Chairman Richard Russell (D., Ga.) and the second-ranking Democrat, John Stennis. Nixon, facing a Democratic Congress throughout his administration, relied upon Stennis (then chairman of the committee) and Jackson (D., Wash.).

Carter, in contrast, rapidly acquired a reputation for not consulting key congressional leaders. He did not display the contempt for the Congress that Nixon had, but simply did not establish close liaisons with important legislators. Instead, he dealt with members of Congress on specific foreign policy matters—and this sometimes put him at a strategic disadvantage, as was the case on the Panama Canal with Senator DeConcini and on SALT II with Minority Leader Howard Baker, Jackson, and even Majority Leader Robert Byrd (D., W.Va.) (who wanted to work to save the treaty but was not always informed by the White House on the current legislative strategy). Carter did gain much support from Byrd and Foreign Relations Chairman Church anyway but, unlike previous presidents, could not dominate the Congress even on foreign policy questions.

Since Kennedy raided the Harvard faculty in 1961, there has also been a steady stream of academics into the president's inner circle. Some, like Kissinger under Eisenhower, Kennedy, Johnson, and Nixon, have been informal advisers and also held official governmental positions dealing with foreign policy. Others have occupied other executive positions, such as Schlesinger under Kennedy and John Roche under Johnson, in which their functions were not limited to foreign policy. Despite Kennedy's widespread use of nationally recognized academics such as Schlesinger, McGeorge Bundy, John Kenneth Galbraith, and Roger Hilsman, and the continuation of this policy by Johnson, no academic appears to have made the mark upon policy formation and public opinion that Kissinger has under Nixon and Ford.

Brzezinski's influence increased after Afghanistan, which seemed to confirm his more "hawkish" view of Russia, but, like the advisers gathered by Ronald Reagan in his 1980 election campaign (notably Fred Iklé as well as professors from generally conservative institutions such as

Georgetown University and United Nations ambassador Jeanne Kirkpatrick), their public visibility was no match for that of Kissinger—even after the latter was out of office. The rationale for bringing academics into the policy-making process was highlighted in the Kennedy administration: the academic community consists of specialists in information and policy analysis, and also draws conclusions from the past, commodities that are essential for informed decision-making. Furthermore, academics are not tied to institutional loyalties in the same way that bureaucrats (including secretaries and department heads) are. They can therefore bring an independent perspective to the policy-making process.[4] While many academicians have filled positions in the bureaucracy or have been consulted by it, the tendency has been to appoint such men as special appoint such men as special advisers to the president.

When an administration changes, a change in the top-level foreign policy positions generally occurs. This does not mean, however, that the inner circle changes dramatically from one administration to another. Rather, members of the inner circle tend to be "in-and-outers," to hold one position in one administration and a different one in another.[5] Perhaps the best example is W. Averell Harriman, who served every Democratic president since Roosevelt. During the eight years of the Eisenhower administration, he was not in the inner circle. The most common type of "in-and-outer" is the man who has served only when his party held the White House. When a change of party occurs, he will return to private life, most likely as either a businessman or an academic. Many academics do not go back to universities but take positions with "think tanks," such as the Brookings Institution, the Center for the Study of Democratic Institutions, the Rand Corporation, and the Hudson Institute. Indeed, Brookings is often considered a kind of "government in exile" for Democrats when their party is out of power, while its Washington neighbor, the American Enterprise Institute (AEI), performs a similar function for the Republicans. To be sure, this portrait is somewhat exaggerated as Brookings and AEI have both moved somewhat closer to the center in recent years and have even sponsored joint conferences. But despite this cross-fertilization, the general stereotypes of these organizations have not vanished and were even reinforced in 1981 as half a dozen AEI scholars obtained positions in the Reagan administration and several key Carter aides joined Brookings, at least temporarily.

The "in-and-outers" help bring continuity to foreign-policy decision-making, so that the policy will not change radically from one administration to another. Johnson relied very heavily on a council of "wise men" with whom he regularly discussed major foreign policy questions. Included in this group were Acheson, Harriman, Cyrus Vance (formerly deputy secretary of defense), General Maxwell Taylor (Chairman of the Joint Chiefs of Staff under Kennedy and ambassador to Vietnam for Johnson), and United Nations ambassador Arthur Goldberg.

Not every "in-and-outer," however, has served only one party; several, including Kissinger, Henry Stimson, John McCloy, and Allen Dulles have served presidents of both parties. This is another factor in the continuity of foreign policy decisions from one administration to the next: the lack of partisanship on foreign policy.

Perhaps no president has relied as heavily on advisers who served previous administrations as Carter. In 1976, he ran as a candidate opposed to the "Washington establishment"; in 1977, however, the new President appointed foreign policy advisers who were prominent members of that establishment! Vance and Brzezinski were the most prominent former members of the Kennedy and Johnson administrations. Secretary of Defense Harold Brown, Treasury Secretary Michael Blumenthal, Charles Schultze of the Council of Economic Advisers, and arms control head Paul Warnke also had been part of what the press called the "junior varsity" of the earlier Democratic administrations. Schultze returned to the government from Brookings, as did many lesser officials. Harriman and Clark Clifford, who succeeded McNamara as secretary of defense under Johnson, served as presidential advisers. Carter also sought the counsel of men who had served Republican administrations, including Richardson and Ellsworth Bunker. The "new faces" promised by Carter during the 1976 presidential campaign were domestic policy advisers. In the "intermestic" area of energy policy, however, Carter's chief adviser was James Schlesinger, former defense secretary under Ford.

Whatever changes in the decision-making process do occur with changes in administrations are due more to each president's style than to the changes he makes in personnel. Kennedy, for example, did not have a single inner circle for all issues. Rather, he selected different advisers for different problem areas. Nixon, on the other hand, just about reduced the circle to himself and Kissinger. Nixon had the distinction of selecting his secretary of state precisely because of his lack of knowledge of foreign policy. The mechanism of the NSC ensures that the circle will always be relatively permeable by at least those charged with the formal tasks of foreign policy formation. How successful each member is, depends ultimately upon his relationship with his superior, the president.

Reagan appeared to believe that he would succeed where his predecessors had failed. Nixon and Carter too had emphasized that they would rely on "cabinet government." But, as might have been expected, the secretaries soon found themselves as spokesmen for their departments and different priorities—and therefore in conflict. More and more, the White House staffs achieved prominence, if not preeminence, as the president's early belief that his cabinet colleagues would rise above partisan departmental views foundered rather predictably as an illusion. During the Carter years, the frequency of cabinet meetings dropped strikingly. In 1977 they were held weekly; in 1978, biweekly, and during 1979–80, they were held on the average of once every six weeks.

Precedent, at least, would suggest that Reagan's closest personal advisers will gain the most influence, not the cabinet. Indeed, the attempted assassination of the President less than two months after his inauguration led to an open rift between Secretary of State Alexander Haig and Defense Secretary Caspar Weinberger over the chain of command—a dispute in which both men lost stature to White House advisers Edwin Meese and Lyn Nofziger as well as to Vice-President George Bush. Meese, counselor to the President, Chief of Staff James A. Baker, and his deputy Michael Deaver formed a triumvirate of Reagan's closest advisers on both foreign and domestic policy early in the new administration. Nofziger appeared to have an independent but very powerful base of influence, as did the deputy secretary of state, William Clark, a long-time Reagan associate. Bush was also prominent in foreign policy and traveled throughout the world, thereby exacerbating rumors of rifts between Haig and the White House.

The Second Circle: Bureaucrats and Advisers

We discussed the role of the Congress in the previous chapter and noted that often the legislative branch is part of the innermost circle on foreign policy decisions. Here we concentrate on another aspect of foreign-policy decision-making: handling of the day-to-day functions of the process which actually constitute most of the decision making which takes place.

While the secretaries of state and defense—and often their under secretaries and assistant secretaries—and the director of the CIA are attending meetings of the president's inner circle, one may wonder, "Who's minding the store?" Each department has a set of lower-level leaders—deputy assistant secretaries and other officials. There are also the ambassadors under the wing of the State Department (including the ambassador to the United Nations) and the military and civilian officials in the army, navy, and air force in the Pentagon. In addition, there are secondary foreign policy agencies which cannot match the political influence of State, Defense, or the CIA. These less powerful foreign policy bureaucracies include the Arms Control and Disarmament Agency (ACDA), the United States International Communication Agency (USICA), the Agency for International Development (AID), the military services, and the scientific and academic advisers to the president and the major foreign policy bureaucracies. Among these advisers, for example, are the Rand Corporation, a "think tank" for scientists in California; the Harvard Center for International Affairs; and similar academic centers at other major universities.

Another set of actors in this second circle are cabinet members who are only partially concerned with foreign policy issues. The Department of Commerce plays a major role in all aspects of international trade as well as in matters of immigration. The Department of the Treasury is a key actor in such decisions as the devaluation of the dollar in the international money market and, of course, has an abiding interest in the cost of U.S. foreign policy. The Agriculture Department is consulted on such issues as wheat sales to the Soviet Union and China and the use of surplus commodities in the foreign aid program. The Energy Department is also a major actor on foreign policy issues. The first secretary of energy, James Schlesinger, had served as secretary of defense under Carter's predecessor; when Schlesinger himself became too controversial for Carter to maintain on the job, the President selected Charles Duncan, another man with Pentagon experience.

Compared to the inner circle, there is greater continuity among the lower-level officials. A new administration does not mean massive changes in the executive departments. In particular, the military service personnel are quite durable. The country desks at State, the scientists at the Pentagon, the small staff at ACDA, and many career diplomats who have obtained their posts by rising through the Foreign Service remain in place as the men at the top change. The second circle thus provides a continuing organizational basis for foreign-policy decision-making at lower levels. However, the bureaucrats at the various country desks (for instance, the African desk, the Western Europe desk, and so forth) at State and in the three services at Defense also develop vested interests to protect. They served in their departments before their respective secretaries, under secretaries, and assistant secretaries were appointed and have established their own "standard operating procedures."

A change in the men at the top may mean at least a minor shake-up of bureaucratic procedures. The lower-level officials may attempt to resist such changes, as the services did under McNamara. If a member of the inner circle also is occupied with settling problems and conflicts in his own department, he faces the problem of presenting a unified departmental position to the White House. The problem is particularly acute for secretaries of state. The various desks not only have their own operating procedures, but also their own policy positions and these often conflict with the views of the secretaries. The Middle East desk, for instance, has long been charged with displaying a pro-Arab and anti-Israel bias, while most secretaries of state have been disposed the other way. Furthermore, there was much criticism of that desk, as well as of the intelligence community, especially the CIA, for developing such close ties with the Shah that the staff could not objectively foresee the rising anger of the Iranian population which led to the revolution of 1978–79.

The function of the second circle is to provide ideas, information on policy alternatives, and to make policy recommendations that the members of the inner circle can discuss among themselves. The second circle also carries out the day-to-day operations of the nation's foreign and military policies. It does not play a direct role in crisis decision-making or even in most foreign policy decisions, but it serves the members of the inner circle by providing background information and analyses to decision-makers. In 1962, during the debate on sending American troops into Laos, the State Department's Bureau of Intelligence and Research, the Policy Planning staff of the CIA, and logistics experts connected with Defense all prepared studies for their respective department heads.[6]

How well the members of this second circle perform their information functions may affect how influential their spokesmen in the inner circle are. The president wants accurate information and sound analysis from his principal advisers—who in turn must rely upon their departments. The State Department has fared less well than Defense in the role of providing key information to its top-level bureaucrats. The large bureaucracy at State, with vested interests in the country desks, leads activist presidents to circumvent the department in making foreign policy innovations. Because the department is compartmentalized into sections dealing with specific geographical areas and functional areas, there is the virtually insurmountable problem of coming up with a unified position on foreign policy. As is the case with Congress—or with the Agriculture Department, which is segmented by crop—there are simply too many vested interests in the department to achieve a consensus on what ought to be done and to arrive at one set of recommendations on how to do it. The policy statements that the secretary of state receives from his subordinates therefore often take a long time in writing and tend to be ambiguous and lacking in references to short-run consequences. On the other hand, the policy recommendations of Defense tend to be produced relatively quickly and are quite specific, taking into account the short-run and long-range consequences of the alternatives.

The Pentagon is not without its own vested interests: there are strong inter-service rivalries and, indeed, even vigorous intra-service rivalries (such as that between the Strategic and Tactical Air Commands in the Air Force). But the Defense Department's policy recommendations to the president are more specific than those of State because much of the rivalry among the services is found on the more basic questions of which weapons to build rather than how to use the weapons at the nation's disposal if necessary. Because the study of which weapons system to deploy is a "harder" science than the study of the behavior of actors in the international system, Defense can make more precise statements than State. For the same reason, the views espoused by the Defense Department are more likely to be seen by the president as reliable because they appear more "scientific." Furthermore, if one of the services sharply disagrees with the recommendations of the secretary of defense, its Chief of Staff can state his objections directly to the president, for the Joint Chiefs of Staff are almost always in the inner circle. In contrast, the secretary of state *may* be the only representative of that department in the inner circle. Even if the under secretary and assistant secretaries are on occasion in the inner circle, they do not ordinarily have the same influence as the Joint Chiefs.

Interestingly enough, Defense is not necessarily influential when it comes to the use of force. The military advisers were usually divided, as were their civilian counterparts. ". . . military leaders were less anxious than the majority of involved civilians to initiate United States commitments about as often as they were aggressive. Joint Chiefs of Staff (JCS) members' views were virtually the same as the dominant civilian attitude more than half the time. . . . In no case did a fully united set of military advisers oppose united civilians." The real difference was that once a commitment was made the military wanted to employ force massively and quickly in order to win. Ironically, the "only cases in which military recommendations on use of force were considered irresistible were the instances in which they opposed intervention."[7]

The difficulties State has in developing clear-cut policy proposals further weaken the stature of the department in the inner circle by leading activist presidents who assume the political functions of the department. After all, diplomacy is something presidents think they know something about. Bargaining and accommodation between conflicting interests is the essence of the political process—whose summit they reached in the White House. This "pre-emption" further lowers departmental morale. As Henry T. Nash has stated: "To the extent that crises in Asia and the Middle East have been 'managed' by the president's White House staff, the skills of state have eroded through disuse."[8] As Kissinger himself argued before taking on his duties with the Nixon administration:

> Because management of the bureaucracy takes so much energy and precisely because changing course is so difficult, many of the most important decisions are taken by extra-bureaucratic means. Some of the most important decisions are kept to a very small circle while the bureaucracy happily continues working away in ignorance of the fact that decisions are being made, or the fact that a decision is being made in a particular area. One reason for keeping the decisions to small groups is that when bureaucracies are so unwieldy and when their internal morale becomes a serious problem, an unpopular decision may be fought by brutal means, such as leaks to the press or to congressional committees.[9]

We thus have a kind of "vicious circle" in which the ambiguous policy recommendations of State are rejected and in which this rejection leads to a further weakening of the power of State in the inner circle. The public image of State is a function of the department's performance, of what people believe it stands for, and of how the department is viewed in comparison with Defense. The public, including Congress, sees State as representing foreign interests rather than American labor or business or agriculture. State brings a troubled world to the door of American citizens. Instead of facing a complex world, it is easier to make State a scapegoat. The department is frequently called "Foggy Bottom." Originally this term referred to the haze surrounding the department's building in a valley in the District of Columbia; in recent years, the term has been used to characterize the type of thinking in the department. The public's view of State is not one of admiration. Frances E. Rourke has noted that:

> . . . the nonmilitary sector of the foreign affairs bureaucracy has been on the defensive before the bar of public opinion, confronted with a deficit of public support rather than the surplus which the military ordinarily enjoys. Over virtually the entire period of the cold war the State Department had been in a precarious position with respect to its public image.[10]

On the other hand, "the military role exerts a symbolic appeal that is as rare among bureaucratic organizations in the United States as it is in other societies. The identification of the military with national pride and achievement—in a word, with patriotism—is a quite extraordinary bureaucratic resource—setting the Defense Department apart from all other executive agencies in the country."[11]

While State is less powerful in the inner circle because of its weakness when compared to Defense, there are even weaker agencies in the second circle. The functions of ACDA overlap with those of State, which is concerned with overall political position of the United States, and Defense, which is charged with devising military strategy and evaluating the level and kind of armaments needed to defend the country. Therefore, ACDA, small by comparison with State and a midget compared to the giant-sized Defense Department, must walk a very thin line between these agencies and at the same time serve the president. ACDA's fortunes have gone up and down. In the 1960s, as arms control became a prominent issue, its influence rose; in the SALT I negotiations, its influence reached its highest levels (although much of the negotiating on key issues was done not by ACDA's director but by Kissinger negotiating in the "back-channels" with the Soviet ambassador in Washington). But after SALT I, its influence declined as Kissinger completely took over the arms control negotiations. Later, under Carter, ACDA's director again conducted most of the negotiations. But with the growing disillusionment with détente, the renewed emphasis by the President and Congress on building up military strength, and the apparent end of SALT II and other arms control negotiations, the stature of ACDA went down sharply. The question was even raised on whether it was needed at all; the agency could be integrated into the State Department or abolished altogether. Influence varies, among other things, with time and circumstances.

The second circle thus provides decision-makers with information on policy questions. It also runs the bureaucracies which—in turn—gather the information for the mid-level officials. This circle has its own sphere of decision making as well, but its decisions concern more routine types of foreign policy questions, which the president and his inner circle have neither the time nor the inclination to answer. Will the administration agree to a particular request for foreign aid? Will it send a trade mission to a newly emerging country? These are the questions usually reserved for the bureaucracies.

The distinction between the actors in the first and second circles is not clear-cut over all decisions on foreign policy questions. Because the lines between the inner and second circles are porous, a sudden crisis in a remote area in the world can elevate a bureaucrat—for example, a Soviet specialist—to the inner circle. Or, if one president pays more attention to the recommendations of his secretary of state and another to his secretary of defense, different policy areas or issues may find the same actors in different circles.

In this connection, it is worth emphasizing a function of the NSC which is normally overlooked. A lower level official may write a policy paper on either an issue that he foresees occurring or on current policy. As it slowly makes its way up the vertical channels to the top of his department or across the horizontal channels between departments sharing responsibilities for a problem, it is likely to be increasingly watered down or, at some point, be buried. It is NSC staff members, dealing with specific areas, who usually know other members throughout the executive branch also working in these areas. They can cut across bureaucratic lines (in our concentric circles), establish informal links with those they believe able (given these links, the latter will also take the initiative and send their papers or talk to the NSC staff), thereby enlisting the "best and brightest" in the process of policy formation. Brzezinski reportedly encouraged this process.

The Third Circle: Political Parties and Interest Groups

The third circle is comprised of the political parties and pressure groups. It is somewhat farther removed from the policy-making process than the second. In crisis situations, the third circle plays a minor role at best in the policy-making process. Partisan cleavages are relatively rare and interest groups have less at stake in most foreign policy decisions than they do in domestic politics. Yet, when certain foreign policy decisions have an impact upon domestic policies, the actors in this third circle play a more important role in the policy-making process. Furthermore the increased role of Congress in foreign-policy decision-making has led to more group activity in this arena. We shall examine parties and interest groups in turn.

Political Parties

In contrast to many parliamentary systems, the political party system in the United States has not been marked by either ideologically distinct or internally cohesive legislative parties. Most roll call votes in the House of Commons in Great Britain are along strictly party lines. Indeed, a member who deviates from the party position can be thrown out of the party, although this rarely happens in practice. In the United States, however, the only votes that can be safely predicted to come out along strictly partisan lines are those that choose the leaders of each House of Congress.

Nevertheless, on domestic policies that are primarily distributive—general appropriations measures, agriculture price supports, public works bills, legislation relating to the size of the bureaucracy and the overall level of government spending, and (until recently) military appropriations measures—party unity has been relatively strong. These issue areas involve the spending of money by the government and find the Democrats as the "big spenders" and the Republicans as the "guardians of the nation's purse." The differences between the parties on distributive issues are quite real. Throughout the 1950s and 1960s, issues involving government management of the economy and agriculture were consistently very partisan compared to voting on social welfare, civil liberties, and particularly international relations.[12] However, as the North-South split within the Democratic party dissipated in the 1970s, issues concerning social welfare and civil liberties also became very partisan, while differences between the congressional parties on economics and farm issues continued to exist.[13] Nevertheless, more recently, the ideological distance between the parties on domestic policy may be declining.[14]

On foreign policy, there has been a search for consensus across the parties because political parties have traditionally been much weaker organizations and because the sharing of powers among the executive, legislative, and judicial branches makes coherent policy making more difficult. First, the legislative and executive branches may be controlled by different political parties. Second, the lack of strong national political parties provides a weak basis for overcoming regional and ideological disagreements of key members of the same party.

The aim of a bipartisan foreign policy, is, in the words of Assistant Secretary of State for Congressional Relations Ernest A. Gross in 1949, "to make it virtually impossible for 'momentous divisions' to occur in our foreign affairs" and to provide a "continuity and consistency"[15] in decision making from one administration to another. Franklin D. Roosevelt had moved toward a bipartisan foreign policy as early as 1940 by naming Republicans Henry Stimson and Frank Knox as secretaries of war and of the navy, respectively. By appointing members of the opposition party to high-level government positions, Roosevelt sought to dramatize the idea that the stakes in foreign-policy decision-making involved the welfare of the entire nation and transcended any partisan lines. Truman continued the bipartisan foreign policy after World War II. James Forrestal and Robert A. Lovett, both Republicans, served as secretary of defense under Truman, and Lovett also served as under secretary of state. Kennedy appointed McNamara as secretary of defense, William C.

Foster as head of ACDA, John A. McCone as head of the CIA, and Henry Cabot Lodge as ambassador to Saigon—among others. Democrats have followed this pattern of bipartisanship more than the Republicans have, probably because Democratic presidents have been more concerned with warding off charges of being too "soft" toward Communist regimes than have Republicans (the charges, after all, have come mainly from Republicans). A Democratic administration with Republicans playing a major role in the formation of foreign policy, Democrats believed, would be less susceptible to such attacks. Indeed, Dulles negotiated the World War II peace treaty with Japan, while Vandenberg, chairman of the Senate Foreign Relations Committee, participated in American delegations to the United Nations, negotiating teams for the peace treaties with the Eastern European countries after World War II, and the establishment of the North Atlantic Treaty Organization.

The appointment of opposition party members was just one method presidents used to gain bipartisan support for their foreign policy. Truman worked rather closely with Vandenberg, particularly during 1947–48, when the Republicans controlled Congress. The White House openly brought Congress into the decision-making process on foreign policy. The Marshall Plan and the establishment of NATO probably marked the high points of congressional involvement in foreign policy-making. Truman pursued a bipartisan foreign policy not only because he believed that the international stakes were extremely high and that they transcended partisan grounds, but also because his party simply did not have the strength in Congress to adopt his proposals. In 1947–48 particularly, cooperation with the Republicans was a necessity.

In this respect, Republican chief executives did resemble their Democratic counterparts. Eisenhower had to deal with a Democratic Congress during six of his eight years in the White House, and he found Senate Majority Leader Lyndon B. Johnson's support of his foreign policy more dependable than that of his own party leaders. Democrats have generally been more cohesive on foreign policy votes in Congress than have Republicans. Furthermore, Eisenhower's dealings with his own party majority in 1953–54 were rather strained. Senator Robert Taft (R., Ohio) was Eisenhower's first majority leader; Taft had been Eisenhower's main competitor for the 1952 Republican nomination, and the two men sharply disagreed on foreign policy questions. Following Taft's death, the President received only slightly more support from Majority Leader William Knowland (R., Cal.), who had presidential ambitions of his own. In 1953, the bipartisan foreign policy of more than a decade was almost upset by the efforts of Republican Senator John W. Bricker (Ohio) to limit severely the president's authority to conduct foreign policy by amending the Constitution to prohibit the executive from entering into any agreement that committed American troops to any foreign conflict without express congressional approval. Knowland, in a rare spirit of cooperation with Eisenhower, agreed to be the floor leader for an administration-sponsored substitute to the Bricker amendment. Until recent years, bipartisan foreign policy was accentuated when control of the White House and Congress was split between the two parties.

Indeed, it appeared that there would have to be a bipartisan foreign policy if the nation were to have any type of coherent foreign policy in a situation of divided control. When one party controls both the executive and legislative branches, as occurred in 1949–55, 1961–69, and 1977–81, criticism of foreign policy may increase because bipartisan support is no longer strictly necessary; conversely, when the opposition controls Congress, it may well be reluctant to oppose the president outright, for he can then accuse it of subordinating the nation's interests to partisan politics and advantage. Yet a president cannot be sure in advance from which direction criticism will come. Eisenhower received the bulk of his criticism from fellow Republicans, Johnson from other Democrats. Kennedy and Truman, on the other hand, found their own parties more united in their support and the opposition split.

By contrast, the 1950s and 1960s showed remarkably little party voting in Congress on questions of foreign policy, where domestic "winners" and "losers" are more difficult to identify than on domestic policies. There was a slight increase in party voting in Congress on foreign policy during the Nixon administration, as Democrats tried to blame the Republican President for the Vietnam War, but this soon dissipated and the majority party became even more factionalized than in earlier years, when a president could call upon legislators not only to support the foreign policy of the nation but also of the party.[16] The Vietnam War appears to have shattered the traditional two-party support for presidential foreign policy, but not by pitting one party against each other. What has happened is that conflict over foreign policy has become more intense within both parties, as more Democrats have become willing (since Vietnam) to advocate international positions of restraint, while an increasing bloc of conservative Republicans in the House and particularly in the Senate, has charged that the nation has for too long refrained from a more activist role in maintaining world order. What we now see is a set of deep cleavages on foreign policy within each party so that neither Majority Leader Byrd nor Minority Leader Baker could deliver large blocs of senators in favor of such a critical issue as the Panama Canal Treaty. On SALT II, there was substantial opposition to the treaty within the Democratic party and Baker, jockeying for position in the presidential primaries, was of no help to Carter. In fact, he went so far as to argue that the country might be better off if there were more clear-cut differences between the foreign policy platforms of the parties. The era of Vandenberg, he argued, had ended.

Partisanship has been the most intense on foreign policies which more closely resemble domestic issues. The parties have been traditionally divided over the size of the defense budget, with the Democrats supporting increases in military spending and the Republicans calling for cutbacks. This is not to suggest that the Democrats have been traditionally more "hawkish" than the Republicans. Rather, the Democrats have generally been more willing to support higher levels of expenditures *across the board* than have Republicans. Recent years have witnessed a reversal of this pattern of behavior. The defense budget is no longer viewed as just another part of the budget, but rather as a major element of the nation's foreign policy, as well as a key issue of foreign/domestic priorities. Another area of foreign policy that has often (though not always) divided the congressional parties is reciprocal trade legislation.[17] The Democrats have generally also supported lower tariff barriers, with the Republicans taking the opposite position. However, recent years again indicate somewhat of a shift in this polarization. American companies have been hurt by many imported goods that are sold at prices below their own. Strong pressure from both labor and management has created a great deal of bipartisan support for more restrictive tariffs on many items. This support is not yet a dominant protectionist coalition, but it does indicate that the old partisan coalitions are breaking down.

During the recession of 1980, demands for protection for such depressed industries as steel and automobiles were made not only by industries but also by the unions, composed of voters who normally cast Democratic ballots. Union members were being laid off as the companies which employed them found themselves unable to compete effectively with foreign producers, particularly those in Japan and West Germany. Foreign policy considerations prevailed and increased tariffs were avoided, but there were continuing pressures for such action. Automotive workers had successfully pressed for federal aid to the financially strapped Chrysler Corporation much as Lockheed workers had pressed the fight for federal loan guarantees in 1971. The Chrysler and Lockheed loans had succeeded, while demands for protection failed because the former involved only domestic considerations while increased tariffs would have led to complications in an already difficult era with two of America's strongest allies. Yet by 1981 the reverberations throughout the economy of the auto industry's depression led a "free trade" president to persuade Japan to restrict imports voluntarily.

On some other intermestic policies, notably energy (Chapter 6), regional considerations predominate over party—making coherent policy formation close to impossible. The American political parties are not as homogeneous as those of most parliamentary systems. Indeed, the Democrats have been the dominant party for most of the past half-century because they have appeared to be "all things to all people." When a bipartisan consensus on critical foreign policy problems could be achieved, this relieved the majority party from having to accept complete responsibility for its actions. On the one hand, the divisions on intermestic policies which have produced partisan splits have not generally hurt the Democrats electorally. The extent of the battle on energy, on the other hand, does provide the potential for prolonged conflict within the society. Thus, the issue would clearly benefit from a clarification of the alternatives—but politicans who do not want to alienate some bloc of voters are reluctant to do just that. Given the weakness of the American party system, one should not expect that a breakdown in bipartisanship would lead to clearly defined positions for each of the major parties. Instead, many different coalitions within each party are likely to develop, making debate on foreign policy more intense and more difficult to manage.

Interest Groups

In domestic politics, weak political parties generally indicate the presence of strong interest groups.[18] Particularly when the stakes involve "winners" and "nonwinners" rather than "winners" and "lowers," interest groups are key actors. Thus, farmers' lobbies have an important say on agriculture bills; veterans' organizations are forceful proponents of their demands for more government services; and business lobbies are rather successful in maintaining tax loopholes in the Internal Revenue Service code. In foreign policy, however, interest groups are less numerous and less powerful.

One critical reason why interest groups are weaker on foreign policy questions than on domestic policy is that lobbyists specialize in the provision of information to members of Congress and the bureaucracy. Spokesmen for organized interests, Lester W. Milbrath has noted, "communicate to government what is happening or what is likely to happen to their clients. They advocate policies and points of view before both Congress and the executive agencies. They stimulate others to communicate with government."[19] If information is the lobbyist's basic resource, it is not difficult to see why interest groups are relatively powerless in foreign policy. As Milbrath states:

> Domestic policies often have direct economic consequences for citizens; these consequences are fairly easily demonstrable in a message. Foreign issues, on the other hand, usually have more indirect consequences . . . and it is difficult to demonstrate in a message how a group might be hurt.[20]

Indeed, the stakes in foreign policy appear once again to be quite different from those in domestic policy. But so is the problem of the interest group. On matters of domestic policy, the lobbyist may well have information that the bureaucrat or member of Congress does not have. The interest groups can generate their own sources of information on questions such as the effect of an increased minimum wage or of a restriction of agriculture price supports to $20,000 per farmer. On foreign policy questions, interest groups seem no better off than Congress in terms of the amount of information each has and in a considerably weaker position than either the State or the Defense Department.

The weakness of most pressure groups in foreign policy questions can be demonstrated by the example of reciprocal trade legislation—a foreign policy issue with strong domestic policy implications. Since a less restrictive tariff will lower the prices of many American products, and also because tariff legislation is one area of foreign-policy decision-making in which affected groups might be expected to have a great deal of information to peddle to members of Congress and the executive branch, it might also be thought that interest group activity would be very strong on this type of legislation. Indeed, the larger corporations do make attempts to contact members of Congress on trade legislation; and the larger the business, the more likely it is that the company will have made some contact on Capitol Hill.[21]

However, they have tended to concentrate their efforts on members of Congress, who agreed with their own stands. Free-trade supporters made contact with members of Congress with similar views; protectionist corporations spoke to protectionist members. Furthermore, the many corporations were just as likely to be opposed to one another as to present a unified front. Lower import duties on crude oil might have the support of the major oil firms but would be opposed by producers of alternative sources of energy, such as natural gas. On trade legislation, Raymond Bauer (et al.) have commented:

> The stereotype notion of omnipotent pressure groups becomes completely untenable once there are groups aligned on both sides. The result of opposing omnipotent forces is stalemate. But, even taken by themselves, the groups did not appear to have the raw material of great power. We noted shortages of money, men, information, and time.[22]

Indeed, many large companies acknowledged that a liberalized trade bill would help part of their business and harm part of it.

Another area of foreign-policy decision-making in which the role of interest groups might be presumed to be relatively strong is the defense budget. With an annual defense budget approaching $200 billion, it is not unreasonable to assume that military contractors would attempt to play a major role in the defense budgetary process. And it is indeed the case that military contractors have supported specific services in their competition for funds and weapons. However, the military services are not themselves united over which weapons should be built: the navy wants more ships, the army more tanks, the air force more jets. Not all can be purchased and rivalries among the services are fierce. Members of Congress do fight for military projects for their districts, but even in this realm there is no strong evidence to support a linkage between serving on the Armed Services committees and getting more than a "fair share" of military expenditures in one's district or state.[23] Legislators do a better job of protecting military installations already in their districts than in obtaining new bases. Cost-effectiveness is one criterion: as military expenses increase, so does inflation and most of the military budget now is spent on personnel. So there is simply less flexibility in locating installations for political purposes. Furthermore, there are some other restrictions that we tend to gloss over: you cannot locate a naval base in Kansas.

The "intermestic" policies of food and energy also involve group conflict, just as trade and the defense budget do. However, the policy-making process on these issues is considerably more complex. In addition to the range of domestic interest groups involved, there are foreign actors who can restrict the range of alternative policies from which a decision can be made. There are also multinational corporations, such as the oil companies or telecommunications giants such as AT&T, ITT, or IBM, which operate both in the consuming nations (particularly the United States) and the producing nations (such as the OPEC countries). These corporations are, of course, among the domestic interests involved in the policy-making process—thus having a greater impact than might occur on most domestic policies. But multinational corporations are not easily controlled by the American government. They can act in concert with the producing nations (as the oil companies cooperate with the OPEC nations) and are not subject to United States regulations outside the American borders. Pharmaceutical firms can market products abroad which have not been approved by American authorities. The leverage that the United States has over such companies is limited, since the multinationals can threaten to move their bases of operation abroad. The policy-making process on these issues becomes much more complex—and often the result is no coordinated policy at all.

As energy prices soar and inflationary pressures grip most of the developing nations of the Third World, these countries become increasingly dependent upon outside financial support. But support for foreign aid has plummeted among the American public—and thus in the Congress—and direct grants are more difficult to obtain, more widely dispersed among nations, and more urgently needed by the developing nations. Filling the role formerly occupied by governments are the banks, many themselves multinational corporations. Traveling abroad, it is virtually no longer a shock to see offices of Citibank, the Bank of America, or the First National Bank of Chicago, among others. These financial institutions have become the principal financiers of development and, in turn, have large numbers of "petrodollars" on deposit from oil-producing nations. Many of these loans have been made to developing nations strongly allied with the United States, such as Zaire and Turkey, which are in very precarious financial situations themselves. Other loans have been made to the Communist nations of Eastern Europe—and the Soviet Union itself. By making these loans, the banks not only make calculated business decisions but foreign policy as well.

Privately made loans often serve the same functions that government loans or direct aid would, were Congress more generous in providing foreign assistance. Just as critically, many of these loans are made to facilitate purchases of American goods by foreign nations. The banks, then, control the flow of international commerce and international banking regulations are few in number and difficult to enforce. When Carter froze Iranian assets in American banks (including overseas branches) following the seizure of hostages, observers in the financial community wondered whether the banks would go along and many doubted that foreign branches could comply. The banks did not challenge the President, however, and the allies were quite supportive in permitting American branches in their nations to follow presidential orders. An international, financial, and political crisis might have developed otherwise. The issue was resolved without substantial difficulty because most banks involved also were holding unpaid notes from the Shah's government and it was far from clear that the new Islamic government would honor past debts. The possibility that the government might have to bail out some banks which lost large amounts of money through loans to American allies was fortunately avoided in the Iranian case, but it is a question that worries both policy-makers and bankers. It is far from clear what the government would do should a major nation default or refuse to pay its debts—nor is it immediately evident whether the government of the United States or the banks, which control much of the domestic money supply, would ultimately emerge from such a struggle as the dominant actor.[24] The government won the first round of what promised to be a protracted legal battle when the Supreme Court ruled unanimously in July 1981 that President Carter had authority under the Constitution to conclude the agreement which finally won the hostages' release (see Chapter 5).

Ideological interest groups, such as the Committee of One Million and the Women's Strike for Peace, played a major role in the foreign policy of the 1950s and 1960s. The former group consistently battled to prevent the recognition of the Peking government of China, whereas the latter organization pressed for nuclear disarmament. Neither of these groups was successful in its goal, and both have largely disappeared from public view. Some ethnic lobbies have also been weakened. The typical "ethnic lobby" of the 1950s and 1960s was the Eastern European immigrant organization (the Ukrainians, Latvians, Lithuanians, and Estonians) seeking demonstrations of congressional support for freedom for their fellow countrymen who reside in formerly independent states that are now part of the Soviet Union. These groups still exist, but they no longer occupy the privileged position on Capitol Hill that they did during the cold war days.

Other ethnic lobbies are even stronger than they were in the 1950s and 1960s. The more prominent ethnic lobbies, as already discussed, are the Jewish organizations, particularly the American Israel Public Affairs

Committee, and the Greek lobbyists, the American Hellenic Institute Public Affairs Committee and the American Hellenic Educational Progressive Association. These groups are generally regarded as the most effective and well organized in Washington, particularly AIPAC. The Jewish organizations (AIPAC, the American Jewish Committee, and the B'nai Brith Anti-Defamation League) are concerned almost exclusively with American policy toward Israel, although emigration of Soviet Jews has also been a major focus of their efforts. While these organizations have been unusually successful, they are not always victorious. The failure to block the jet sales to Egypt and Saudi Arabia in 1978 is one such example, but the House in 1980 did vote to cut off all aid to Syria, an Arab nation which has bitterly denounced the Camp David accords. The Jewish lobbies have succeeded in most of their efforts, sometimes without solid Jewish support in the Congress—as occurred on the Syrian vote, when several Jewish members voted to permit the President to determine whether such aid might induce the Syrians to moderate their opposition to Egyptian-Israeli negotiations. The power of these groups has been bitterly denounced by some senators, including Mike Gravel (D., Ala.) and Adlai Stevenson III (D., Ill.). Gravel admitted that he might be giving up financial support from Jewish groups in the 1980 elections,[25] but there are very few Jewish people in Alaska. This potential ethnic bloc is much more powerful in Illinois, however, but Stevenson had already announced his intention not to run for another term.

The strength of Jewish and Greek groups is not a new phenomenon in American politics. Ethnic groups have played a major role in foreign policy debates throughout the twentieth century. Irish groups, which disliked Britain intensely, argued against American participation in World War I and later opposed U.S. entry into the League of Nations. Italian and German groups were active opponents of American entry into both world wars. Indeed, Germanic groups were extremely powerful in the Midwest throughout the century, electing several senators and members of the House. While often quite liberal on domestic policies, the midwestern members of Congress elected from districts with heavy concentrations of Germans were decidedly isolationist in their foreign policy. Their rationale for not fighting a war against Germany was that the United States should not attempt to resolve what essentially were conflicts between other nations. Isolationist strength reached its peak between the two wars, when Robert LaFollette, Sr., ran for president on a third-party label in 1924. Although LaFollette carried only his home state of Wisconsin, he ran a close second in several midwestern states and compiled what was then the second largest number of votes a third-party candidate had ever received for president. The strength of the LaFollette movement raised serious questions about American entry into World War II before Pearl Harbor. The Irish, Italian, and German groups failed because they each opposed the government's established policies, whereas the Jewish groups have been more successful because of the government's official position of support toward Israel. On those issues where AIPAC has been least successful, it faced strong opposition from the administration.

In addition to Jewish and Greek groups, ethnic lobbies of blacks (Transafrica) and Arab-Americans have become increasingly vocal on behalf of African and Arab nations respectively. Blacks have played a major role in the establishment of stronger American ties with such key African nations as Tanzania and in the drive for a peaceful settlement in Zimbabwe. They have also urged the United States to impose a trade embargo on the white minority government in South Africa. Blacks, like Jews and Greeks, have achieved a large measure of success because: (1) they constitute a large bloc of voters whose support has been consistent and important to the maintenance of the Democratic electoral coalition and were wooed, with more than usual success, by Reagan in 1980; and (2) at least under the Carter administration, the policies advocated by black groups were also supported by the President.

In contrast, the Association of Arab-Americans, although quite vociferous, has met only with very modest success. American policy has not tilted toward the Arab position on Middle Eastern issues, at least not to the point of disrupting relations with Israel. It is not surprising that this organization has not been successful, given the much greater resources of the American Petroleum Institute (API), which represents 350 corporations, and which has been lobbying for a shift in American Middle Eastern policy for about a decade.[26] The API is primarily concerned with oil politics, of course, but it has acted in the not unreasonable belief that American relations with the oil-producing nations are related to the willingness of the country to consider alternative political solutions in the Middle East. The oil companies have not been able to dictate foreign policy to the president or the Congress. Indeed, this poor record of influencing policies suggests that any view of foreign policy based upon economic determinism is a vast oversimplification. Economic interest groups have been active on foreign policy issues, but Bernard Cohen found that they obtain what they want if these demands *do not conflict with preestablished policies of the government.*[27] An economic interest group may benefit from a foreign policy decision, but this does not imply anything about the role that the group actually played in the formulation of the decision. A good example of this is the economic boom that some farmers and grain speculators reaped from the decision of the United States to make major wheat sales to the Soviet Union in 1973, without having initiated or lobbied for the deal.

However, a threat to the traditional American support for Israel arose in 1979 when several major black civil rights leaders, including the Reverend Jesse Jackson and nonvoting House Delegate Walter Fauntroy (Washington, D.C.), made visits to the Middle East and made statements in support of the Palestine Liberation Organization (PLO). The civil rights leaders were upset when United Nations Ambassador Andrew Young, the first black to hold a major foreign policy position in the American government, was forced to resign following an unauthorized meeting with a PLO representative at the United Nations. Jackson, Fauntroy, and others visited the Middle East and met with key Arab leaders, including Yasser Arafat of the PLO, but did not meet with Israeli Prime Minister Menachem Begin. The black leaders did not indicate much of a desire to meet with Begin, but the Israeli Prime Minister was even less forthcoming toward the Americans who had just met—and hugged—Arafat. Upon returning home, the black leaders made strong statements in support of Palestinian rights and on the need for a cease-fire in the areas under military threat. Black-Jewish tensions were exacerbated by some poll data showing a weakening in the traditional black support for Israel and by revelations that Arab groups had made donations to black civil rights organizations. The traditional black-Jewish alliance was in danger and there were serious questions of what the impact upon foreign policy in both the Middle East and Africa might be. Other black leaders reasserted traditional support for Israel and rejected the argument that blacks must be concerned with Palestinian rights because in any conflict involving American armed intervention in the Middle East, an interruption of oil supplies would most adversely affect the most disadvantaged economic groups, notably blacks.

Several factors worked to defuse the conflict, at least temporarily. One was the strong defense of Israel and the need for a continuation of the black-Jewish alliance made by Urban League President Vernon Jordan, a widely respected figure in the black community. A second was the revelation of financial inducements made by Arab groups and allegedly demanded by some black leaders in return for political support. Finally, the takeover of the American embassy in Iran by Islamic militants united black and white Americans in support of the President's policies. It is thus far from clear that these issues between blacks and Jews have been resolved. A major conflict between these two important constituent groups, both strongly associated with the Democratic party, might affect policy through the ballot box: Should the party lose the support of either group, it could not hope to gain a majority in presidential elections for years to come. The loss of both groups would virtually guarantee it perpetual minority status. But neither group is likely to defect permanently to the Republicans, so an element of instability in elections could lead to a foreign policy which fluctuates from election to election.

An ethnic group which has been receiving considerable attention in recent years is the Hispanics. People of Mexican, Puerto Rican, and Cuban backgrounds have all been active in pressing for policy shifts for these areas. However, a united Hispanic coalition seems unlikely because of differences among them. Most Mexicans and Puerto Ricans in the United States have come from lower-class backgrounds and have been advocating that the government take positions on foreign policy issues which favor a redistribution of wealth and power. On the other hand, the Cuban immigrants have tended to be somewhat more affluent and educated. Unlike other Hispanics, they vote Republican most of the time and also hope to return to their homeland eventually.

The potential power of economic and ethnic interests which press for policies that will further their interests and perhaps especially single-issue organizations such as those which opposed the Panama Canal treaties and SALT II (Chapter 6) raise important issues related to the democratic dilemma on foreign-policy decision-making. Specifically, the question becomes: What price might our foreign policy pay for its openness? Does the opportunity for groups to participate mean that they might come to dominate the policy-making process and seek ends which only they find desirable (or profitable)? While most economic interests cannot dominate foreign policy-making, some can. An argument for the thesis that economics may on occasion determine policy choices can be made by examples.[28] The attempt by the International Telephone and Telegraph Company to rig the 1970 election for president of Chile against the Socialist Salvadore Allende to protect its financial interests there is a case in point. While Nixon and Kissinger specifically rejected a plan that would have entailed the cooperation of the White House in what proved to be an unsuccessful attempt to prevent Allende from becoming president, in 1973 the CIA "destabilized" the Allende government. While there is no direct evidence that multinational corporations were also involved in the 1973 incident, Nixon did know about the CIA involvement. Thus, even if there was no firm conspiracy between business and the government, in this instance, at least, American foreign and economic policies certainly coincided. In this instance, however, we do not know whether ITT was aiding the government or if the government abetted ITT. Fortunately, such instances seem relatively unusual. But we must always be concerned about the potential for a private interest to determine public policy. On the other hand, grass-roots organizations such as the Emergency Coalition to Save the Panama Canal do attempt to mobilize support in the Congress to persuade members to espouse certain policy positions on the basis of public opinion. In such efforts, as in the ethnic lobbies, foreign policy-making resembles domestic policy formation.

The actors in the third circle of decision making are strongest on foreign policy when they respond to the same pressures as found in domestic and even intermestic policies. However, a bipartisan foreign policy aids the executive branch in its battle with the Congress since the president can build a new coalition of his own on each foreign policy roll call. Furthermore, the leaders of both parties can generally be counted upon to seek out support for the president's positions. As the traditional bipartisanship is threatened, so is the president's strategic advantage. Particularly when such consensus may be replaced by conflicts among traditional allies—the members of the Democratic coalition—and when American foreign policy might become more dependent upon international economic conditions (as have the policies of Western Europe and Japan on Middle Eastern issues), the executive branch faces severe challenges ahead. The Congress is not in a position to fill any such leadership vacuum because it has not resolved, and hardly seems willing to try to resolve, the difficult question of which interests are ultimately to be represented.

The Outermost Circle: Public Opinion and the Media

Public opinion and the media stand at the periphery of the foreign-policy decision-making process. Public opinion tends to be permissive and supportive of presidential decisions in foreign policy. Indeed, the level of public support for the president, as measured by polls, increases dramatically in a foreign policy crisis—whether the resolution of the crisis is favorable to the American position or not![29] Furthermore, public opinion is not always marked by consistency: Polls may indicate that a large percentage of the American people consider a specific policy decision to be a mistake but nevertheless will support a presidential decision with which it disagrees. Critics of the policy can cite the first set of poll results, the administration the second. Each is partially correct, but the net result of the confusion is that the president can cite public support for his actions and use the power of his office to continue pursuing his chosen policies. Our discussion of public opinion will begin with a consideration of the broad limiting role of public viewpoints—of when public opinion is weak, when it becomes stronger, and the forces pushing it in various directions. We shall then consider the role of public opinion in a somewhat different context—the ways in which public opinion might be translated into policy decisions.

Support of and Opposition to the President and His Policies

The role of public opinion in foreign policy is, as we have noted, permissive and supportive of presidential discretion. The principal reason is that the vast majority of Americans are poorly informed about and uninterested in foreign policy. Most foreign policy issues are simply too far removed from their everyday frames of reference. A voter, who may be a worker, a farmer, a businessman, or a professor, will have (or will believe that he has) a certain degree of knowledge and familiarity in dealing with issues related to his sphere of livelihood (for instance, unemployment and job security or farm price subsidies), and he is also likely to hold views on various topics that relate to him as a citizen, parent, and so forth (open housing, equal job opportunity, police protection, drugs, the quality and cost of medical care and education). On domestic policies he will therefore be more likely to hold his own views, even if they should differ from those of the president. On foreign policy issues, however, most voters do not have the knowledge, frame of reference, or sense of personal competence they do with affairs that are less remote.[30] This lack of factual content and intellectual structure of public opinion means that the mass public reacts to foreign policy issues in terms of moods and seeks guidance from the president.

> The general public looks for *cues* and *responses* in public discussions of foreign policy. It does not listen to the content of discussion but to its tone. A presidential statement that a crisis exists will ordinarily be registered in the form of apprehension. A reassuring statement will be received with complacency reactions. In both cases, the reaction has no depth and no structure.[31]

Two things should be clear. First, it is the president to whom the public looks for information and interpretation of the outside world and how it affects American security interests. This means that he has considerable freedom to set his direction and mold public opinion. Second, public opinion does not usually guide the president; it is more frequently formed as a response to presidential action, not only because of public ignorance but because in foreign policy presidents frequently have to act *before* any firm public opinion has been formed. Perhaps the best way of summing up the role of public opinion in foreign policy is to emphasize its followership.

Since the Truman Doctrine in 1947, public opinion has been responsive to presidential leadership and, therefore, has been as rigid or flexible as presidential policy. It has supported hardline anti-Soviet and anti-Chinese policies when they were official policy (as they were from Truman's day right through to Johnson), and it has supported moves toward a relaxation of tensions and negotiating conflicts of interests (as during the Nixon era). Both kinds of moves received widespread popular acclaim. The public looked to the president for its cues. In a crisis this phenomenon is particularly noticeable; the public rallies around the president even if the crisis was bungled by the president, as Kennedy with the ill-fated refugee invasion of Cuba in 1961. During the opening periods of the two limited wars in which the United States has become engaged since World War II, the initial commitments received very high levels of public and congressional support, and they stayed high despite great costs, including high casualty rates, during the opening phase of the war. The fact that presidential action is a prerequisite to the formation of public opinion on foreign policy issues was especially clear during the Vietnam War. There was little in the way of any opinion—either for or against—during the Kennedy administration's incremental commitment of advisers, or even after the Gulf of Tonkin. Extensive public awareness of Vietnam came only with the sudden, visible commitment of more than

500,000 men. But perhaps a more astounding example of public opinion's followership role and inconsistency occurred with President Nixon's decision to send American troops into Cambodia. Just prior to the decision, only 7 percent of the respondents favored such a move; after the move 50 percent approved! Ford's approval rating jumped 11 percent immediately after the *Mayaguez* incident. Indeed, the public is so predisposed to view the foreign policy postures of chief executives positively that a July 1974 Gallup poll found 54 percent of the respondents approving of how Nixon handled foreign policy. The President, who was to resign within a month in the midst of the Watergate scandal, had an overall approval rating of only 26 percent of favorable responses.

Yet, while permissive and supportive, public support is not unlimited.[32] If a president's policies are not successful, if they fail to achieve their objectives in a reasonable amount of time and at a tolerable cost, the public reserves the right to punish the president and his party at election time. Military interventions provide a dramatic example. When the president first announces an intervention the public—and Congress—will support him. Indeed, this recurrent phenomenon has led John Mueller to suggest that as long as presidents can commit troops, proposals that wars can be avoided if Congress were required to vote its approval are unlikely to work, for once the commitment has been made the tendency will be to "rally around the flag."[33] An intervention such as the Dominican conflict in 1965 may be widely criticized by foreign policy experts in and out of government, congressmen, and journalists, but if it is brought to a successful conclusion, or at least what appears to be a successful conclusion, relatively quickly, the president will suffer no electoral reprisals. On the other hand, popular support for a Korean or Vietnamese war will decline over time if the price appears to be disproportionate to the objectives sought.

Public and congressional support for the conduct of the war does not decrease significantly, despite high casualties and/or taxes, while the general belief in a reasonably short war and success on the battlefield remains prevalent. Conversely, this support erodes as hostilities drag on and the continued high costs of the conflict appear increasingly pointless as the expectation of victory disappears. In Korea, Chinese entry into the war led to a major drop of support for Truman five months after the American intervention; in Vietnam, the drop took longer, starting in the spring of 1965 and reaching a low point in late 1967, which, after a brief upsurge, was reconfirmed by the Communist Tet offensive in early 1968.[34] Even President Johnson, a skillful manipulator, could not hold off the cost of the war forever; he had postponed this cost by not drafting most American middle- and upper-class males, mainly students; not calling up the reserves; and postponing a war surcharge tax. But the support eroded, and Tet was the final proof that victory was no nearer than before and that the high costs of the war were fruitless.

Thus, in limited wars, public opinion does become relevant. Support for the wars in Vietnam and Korea declined as the costs, especially the casualty rates, increased over time. The impact of the casualty rate on the level of opposition to the war was considerably stronger for the Vietnam War than for Korea.[35] That may be an indication that the nightly exposure of Vietnam casualties by the television networks had a considerable effect on the increase in opposition to the war.

The Iranian crisis produced a similar pattern of public support to that of Korea and Vietnam although, with the exception of the few who died in the abortive rescue mission, no Americans died. The situation began like that of the Cuban missile crisis, an act of aggression by a former ally against the United States. The crisis occurred at the nadir of Carter's popularity as President and at the low point of his perceived ability to handle foreign policy well. The latter figure had dropped to below 30 percent, compared to the high of almost 55 percent after the Camp David accords had been signed in 1978. Few observers at the time gave him much chance of defeating Kennedy for the Democratic nomination for president, which would have made him the first president in over a century elected in his own right to be denied renomination by his party. Following the seizure of the hostages, the President's approval rating jumped from about 30 percent to over 60 percent, while satisfaction with his handling of foreign policy increased to almost 50 percent.

Approval of the President's handling of the Iranian crisis stood at almost 80 percent in December 1979. But as the hostage situation wore on without resolution, public confidence in the President declined. By April 1980, support for the way Carter was handling the crisis had dropped to 39 percent, overall job performance to 40 percent, and foreign policy performance to just over 30 percent.[36] The President had picked up enough political momentum in the meantime virtually to ensure himself the Democratic nomination for president for a second time, but his overall political base had been greatly weakened. The initial charges that critics might not be as patriotic as they thought gave way to attacks from both the right and the left as a regular part of the political process. The Iranian crisis had almost become "Vietnamized" politically, as Kennedy and John Anderson, a Republican soon to turn Independent candidate for president, attacked the President's militarism and the various Republican candidates, especially nominee Ronald Reagan, charged that the President was not responding strongly enough in the crisis.

The Iranian situation, then, initially resembled a crisis such as the Cuban missile crisis where public opinion was strongly united around the president. What was somewhat unusual about this crisis is that public support for the President remained very strong for several months following the seizure of the hostages and then began a precipitous decline, much more pronounced and rapid than occurred in the Korean and Vietnam wars. However, like Vietnam, the constant media exposure of the Iranian situation served to highlight the President's inability to resolve the issue. To be sure, Carter focused attention on himself by holding many press conferences, insisting that he could not leave the White House to campaign or even to meet with other public officials outside Washington. But the media also paid a great deal of attention to Iran, with ABC television news scheduling a nightly program on the events (or nonevents) of the day. Americans became very familiar with the militants holding the hostages at the embassy and their spokeswoman, called Mary, generally had higher late-night television ratings on ABC than Johnny Carson did on NBC. The Iranian situation and the response of the mass public ultimately resembled Vietnam and Korea more than Cuba. As in Korea and Vietnam, the evaporation of presidential support permitted other sources of information to gain a public following.

The two principal alternative sources are congressional hearings and the media. Lacking the power to change the president's Vietnam policies, Senator Fulbright used the mechanism of his Foreign Relations Committee hearings to dramatize opposition to the war. At times, the major television networks would carry live coverage of these hearings. At a minimum, the hearings would be covered on the evening network news programs and in the major newspapers across the country. The influence of such hearings—which are often long and tedious and may not bring out any new information—may be slight, but it is often almost all that opponents of a policy have in their attempt to affect public opinion. With the growth of the medium of television, the roles of the congressional committee hearings and the media have become ever more closely intertwined. Television gives opponents of a policy a more direct line to the public than did newspapers or radio—it provides for visual contact as well as the reporting of events. However, the gains that opponents of a policy have made through this newest medium have also accrued to the president. Indeed, the chief executive can always obtain free network time for an address to the nation, and he can use such speeches to rally public opinion behind his policies. On balance, the advent of television probably has meant more to opponents of a president's policy than to the chief executive himself. Since public opinion is generally permissive and supportive of presidential initiatives, any gain in exposure of the opposition's point of view may well enhance the opponents' strength. A president simply needs less exposure to rally support for his position than does the opposition.

The media are more than just devices for presenting alternative views of public officials to the mass public or, in turn, representing the mass public to the foreign policy establishment. The media also have their own impact on public opinion. Although most voters are not terribly concerned with foreign policy issues, the nightly television coverage of events in Vietnam brought an overseas war into millions of American homes each night as did the reports on Iran a half decade after American involvement in Vietnam ended. Furthermore, the media have not always presented presidential decisions in a favorable light. Virtually every president of the United States in recent years has believed that the press was hostile to him, "out to get him." Indeed, the Nixon administration brought its hostilities toward the media—the television networks and national news magazines as well as the newspapers—out into the open. Johnson was less hostile to the press but did criticize several reporters and nationally syndicated columnists for their opposition to his Vietnam policies.

Presidents respond in different ways to criticism by the press. At one extreme, Nixon was so angered by the *Washington Post's* coverage of the Watergate crisis, which ultimately brought his administration down, that he threatened to have the Federal Communications Commission deny the applications for license renewals of two television stations the *Post* owned in Florida. At the other extreme was the reaction of Kennedy, who cancelled his subscription to the *New York Herald Tribune* following a series of uncomplimentary articles the paper ran about him. The subscription was quietly renewed when the incident embarrassed the President, a former reporter himself. Carter, withdrawing from criticism of his handling of foreign and domestic policy before the hostage crisis, refused to hold press conferences in Washington for several months, traveling to distant locales where the local press might be somewhat more sympathetic to his situation. After the hostages were seized, however, Carter actively sought out the press, even as his popularity was declining. Reagan, a former actor with superb communication skills, has frequently used the press conference to build support for his programs and to disarm the opposition with his quick wit.

Yet, even when public opinion has been mobilized—by the media, the congressional critics, or just by sheer uneasiness over the course of a foreign policy—its role still remains rather limited. The problem is that the public does not always speak with one voice. Sixty-four percent of a November 1965 sample of Americans did *not* think that American involvement in Vietnam was a mistake, as compared to 21 percent who believed that it was. By October 1967, the balance had shifted to the position that the war was a mistake (44 percent in favor, 46 percent opposed to the initial involvement). By the summer of 1968, a sizable majority took the position that the war was a mistake.[37] Yet the pattern of support for proposals to end the war—including both a stepped-up military posture and total withdrawal—had not changed accordingly from 1965 to 1968. Mueller has thus argued that, at any given time, "support should be considered a chord rather than a note."[38] This was no less true of the Iranian situation, where voters critical of the President did not present a clear-cut mandate as to what an alternative policy should be,[39] as in Vietnam. The president can use this pattern of inconsistency among the voters to indicate that there is not enough support for any other alternative policy to warrant a shift in his position. If the lack of consistency in public opinion polls does not provide the president with a distinct message on how to choose foreign policy alternatives, might not the electoral arena? It is to this facet of public opinion's impact on foreign policy—and to the linkage between public opinion and congressional opinion—that we now turn.

Popular Control of Foreign Policy

Public opinion, according to many theorists of democratic government, does not serve as a guide to policy-makers who must choose among alternative courses of action every day. Rather, at election time the citizenry is called upon to choose its leaders and then to let those leaders determine policy choices until the next election. The electoral mechanism thus gives the voter what has been called "popular control of government." The voter, according to this thesis, does not instruct the men and women he chooses at the ballot box on what policies to adopt. Rather, he selects a candidate who represents policy positions closest to his own. This is the electoral function of public opinion.[40] An even stronger demand upon public opinion is made by other democratic theorists: that public opinion should be "converted" into public policy by the representative system of government. These theorists expect a member of Congress to represent—or, "re-present"—the views of his constituency in his voting behavior in Congress. How well the public's viewpoints are translated into policy decisions of their representatives gives us an idea of how well the democratic political system is working. This "conversion" function of public opinion demands more than the electoral function. The latter merely assumes that the voter can replace an officeholder whose views he does not like at the next election. The conversion function assumes that it is the task of the officeholder to represent faithfully the majority position in his constituency between elections as well.[41] In this section, we shall examine both views of the function of public opinion.

The concept of the electoral system as a choice between two competing sets of policy choices does indeed seem to hold true for the 1952 election. The evidence is rather straightforward that Truman's decline in popularity and the subsequent Republican victory in 1952 can be attributed to the public's adverse reaction to the Korean War.[42] In general, however, there appears to be no great amount of policy voting on either domestic or foreign policy issues. On the one hand, the two parties have not usually offered the voter a clear-cut choice on policy alternatives. On the other hand, there is even less evidence that voters are aware of whatever differences there may be between two candidates for an office.

Since voters tend to be less interested in questions of foreign policy than in domestic policies, it is not surprising to find that policy voting on foreign affairs questions is rather rare. A study of voters in the 1956 and 1960 presidential elections led Warren E. Miller to conclude that, at an absolute maximum, the net contribution of the parties' foreign policy stands toward changes in voting behavior from one election to the next was one-half of 1 percent.[43] In an election as close as the 1960 contest, this margin may be substantial. When looked at by itself, however, the effect of policy stands on voting is negligible. A Roper poll reported that in the 1976 elections, voters saw domestic issues as more important in their voting decisions than foreign policy issues by a margin of more than 12−1. The results for foreign policy of more recent studies are no more heartening for the advocate of a political system that converts public opinion on foreign policy into public policy through elections. A study by Gerald M. Pomper found that, from 1956 to 1972, voter attitudes and partisan affiliation became more strongly associated in five areas of domestic policy but did not change for the one foreign policy measure (foreign aid) he examined.[44] There remained in 1972, as there had been in 1956, 1960, 1964, and 1968, virtually no relationship between public opinion and party identification on this foreign policy measure.

In presidential elections, voters seem to be looking for some indication that the candidate they prefer: (1) is capable of handling foreign policy; and (2) will not adopt some extreme policies which might provoke a world war or other major international confrontation. Negative perceptions on both questions clearly hurt McGovern in 1972,[45] while positive responses helped John F. Kennedy in 1960 and Carter in 1976. The latter candidates, despite their lack of foreign policy experience, gained the upper hand on this issue by scoring very well in televised debates with their "more experienced" opponents. Despite the increased salience of foreign policy among members of Congress, there is no indication that foreign policy plays any role in congressional elections. In 1978, less than 1 percent of all voters cited foreign policy issues as the most important questions facing the nation, while none cited foreign policy as the most important campaign issues.[46] To the extent that foreign policy plays any role in races for the Congress, it is through paying too much attention to international affairs and not enough to those which are important in one's district or state. Occasionally, an issue such as the Panama Canal treaties may be raised in a Senate race, but there is no hard evidence that a particular vote could by itself affect the outcome of a Senate race. Those senators who lost in 1978 not only paid a lot of attention to foreign policy, but also did not pay enough attention to their own constituents.[47]

Studies of how members of the House of Representatives voted on foreign policy from surveys conducted in the 1950s did not indicate that legislators followed their constituents' preferences on foreign policy. No similar studies have been conducted on this direct linkage since then, but the evidence we have suggests that the impact of foreign policy on congressional elections has not increased—and may actually have declined—in the last few decades. The small number of voters who express a strong concern for foreign policy, particularly in congressional elections, makes the linkage between masses and legislators difficult to establish. If voters are not interested in these issues, the chances are quite high that they will not make up their minds in the voting booth on the basis of those policies. Furthermore (as we argued in Chapter 3), legislators themselves are mostly not terribly interested in foreign affairs because they do not see much of an electoral payoff in tackling these questions. Foreign policy issues are peripheral to the general problem of representation because neither the representatives nor the represented give it a high priority.

Measures designed to strengthen the role of Congress in the foreign policy process will not, therefore, necessarily bring foreign policy more in line with public opinion. If anything, public opinion seems to follow presidential opinion more than it does congressional opinion. Even when guided by opinion leaders in opposition to the president, the public tends to be more responsive to the chief executive. Yet, when opinions do become divided on a policy area, such as the war in Vietnam, the failure of the party system to play the role of opinion leader serves as a strong check on the conversion of public preferences into public policy in the foreign policy arena.

Still, a president cannot forget public opinion before he makes decisions; he is indeed very conscious of it, as it affects his desire to be reelected or for his party's candidate to win, and he is therefore quite aware of what might happen if the citizen-consumer does not like his policy-products. (Carl Friedrich has called this "the law of anticipated reaction.") Before World War II, the isolationist consensus set the constraints within which foreign policy decisions had to be made. Even joining the International Court of Justice became impossible; Roosevelt's call in 1937 for the democracies to "quarantine" the aggressors met with a public furor. After World War II, Truman did not oppose the rapid demobilization of the armed forces despite increasing tensions with the Soviet Union. The public wanted to relax, to bring boys back home, to concentrate once more on domestic and private affairs. Not until eighteen months after the war against Japan had ended, after the perception of repeated demonstrations of Soviet hostility and numerous vetoes in the United Nations, did the Soviet threat appear sufficiently clear that Truman felt he could go before Congress and the public and ask them to support the policy of containment. The reaction to Vietnam and America's frequently criticized role as world policeman led presidents to assume a "lower profile" in order to retain public—and congressional—support.

For most of the cold war period, however, presidential candidates have felt that the public wanted the United States not to withdraw from the world or play a lesser role in it, but employ a tougher posture. Even the post-Vietnam mood of disillusionment with extensive international involvement has partially receded. Soviet behavior which appeared to contrast starkly with how most Americans understood détente and the enormous Soviet military buildup were two factors; but it was the seizure by the Iranians of the U.S. diplomatic hostages, followed shortly thereafter by the Russian army's invasion of Afghanistan, which did most to arouse once more a generally strong nationalist mood. Carter, reflecting this change in mood, adopted a harder line toward Russia, imposing economic sanctions and pulling the United States out of the Moscow Olympic games in the summer of 1980. He was also anticipating a strong Reagan accusation of his foreign policy as being one of weakness and too much accommodation—ironically, these were not only the Reagan charges against Ford in the Republican party contest in 1976, but also Carter's own accusations against Ford in the presidential election campaign that year. Thus public opinion is generally supportive and does look to the president for its cues on foreign policy.

This does not, however, mean that presidents manipulate public opinion or that the relationship between the president and foreign policy is a one-way relationship. The "anticipated reaction" or "pre-natal" effects of public opinion—the presidential perception of possible reward or punishment by the public in the election booths for his actions—make it very much a two-way or reciprocal relationship. As Larry Radway has noted: "Even if voters do not exercise to the full their right to constrain politicians by retaliating at the polls, it is enough that candidates believe they may, or that some of them may, and 'some' need not be 'many,' since American incumbents tend to overinsure against the possibility of (electoral) defeat."[48]

What Kind of Foreign Policy Does the Public Want?

We have concentrated on describing the various actors in the foreign policy-making process and their relative strengths in this and other policy arenas. The picture we have drawn is one of an imbalance of power between the president and Congress, with other actors (the bureaucracy, political parties, public opinion, interest groups, and the media) having even less influence. Furthermore, to the extent that other actors do have influence, they exert their strength on behalf of particular interests. The problem of popular control of foreign policy is a particularly difficult one, since these issues more than any other encourage many different perspectives on what views ought to prevail—from those of our allies and adversaries in the international arena to localistic concerns in the constituencies of members of Congress. But is popular control really so difficult and elusive? What sort of balance among the actors does the public want and what types of policies might emerge if a greater role for public opinion on foreign-policy decision-making existed?

We answer these questions by comparing the results of two surveys conducted in late 1978-to-early 1979 by the Gallup poll organization under contract to the prestigious Chicago Council on Foreign Relations, a nonpartisan research and educational organization (with membership open to the general public). The first poll surveyed over 1500 American citizens aged 18 and over throughout the nation; the second poll asked the same questions as the first, but the respondents were members of a "foreign policy elite": 366 individuals believed to represent Americans who are knowledgeable and influential in foreign policy, including senators and representatives, officials of the State Department and other high-level bureaucracies dealing with international problems, business leaders, as well as representatives of the media, educational institutions, labor unions, and ethnic and religious groups. The elite sample thus consists of the major actors (outside of the White House) whom we have discussed in this and the preceding chapter. We have argued that legislators often act parochially on foreign policy issues because such issues are not salient to the constituents and interest groups back home. Thus, we would expect that the elite sample would be more supportive of presidential leadership on foreign policy and more "internationalist" in its positions on questions of foreign policy than would the mass public sample. Of course, since the elite sample consists partially of business and labor leaders, as well as those representing ethnic groups, we would not expect either sample to be unconcerned with self-interest. But, even in such groups as business, labor, and ethnic groups, leaders have traditionally been more trusting of presidential initiatives while followers have been more enthusiastic in their demands for higher tariffs and decreased executive leverage in dealing with foreign countries associated with ethnic lobbies; Jewish leaders, for example, have often been more tolerant toward presidential initiatives toward the Arab nations than rank-and-file Jewish voters since these leaders, many of whom frequently interact with high-ranking policy makers, understand more clearly the complexities of international negotiations.

We examine first the responses of each group to a set of questions asking whether various actors are perceived as either "very important" or "important" in foreign policy-making and whether each actor *should be* this important. The results are presented in Table 4−1.* It is hardly surprising that the president is seen by both samples as the most important actor, although three quarters of the general public has this perception compared to almost the entire elite sample. Almost equally

*The data from the Chicago Council on Foreign Relations surveys are reported in Robert W. Oldenick and Barbara A. Bardes, "A Cross-Time Comparison of Mass and Elite Foreign Policy Attitudes," paper prepared for delivery at the 1980 Annual Meeting of the American Political Science Association, Washington, D.C., August 1980. We are grateful to Professor Bardes for her permission to use some of her computations here.

TABLE 4-1 The Importance of Various Actors in Foreign Policy Making: The Chicago Council on Foreign Relations Mass and Elite Surveys, 1978-79

Actor	Actor Perceived as Important*		Actor Should Be Important	
	Mass	Elite	Mass	Elite
President	74.1	93.7	45.5	20.5
Secretary of State	65.9	63.4	36.8	28.6
State Department	49.8	34.0	38.9	31.7
Congress	47.9	45.1	45.0	31.6
Military	43.6	29.6	30.9	10.6
Public Opinion	28.0	20.3	66.9	44.3
United Nations	34.4	2.7	42.7	35.3
American Business	45.5	22.2	29.5	21.7
Labor Unions	28.7	6.6	18.9	13.0
Private Organizations	18.2	6.2	15.5	25.9
Central Intelligence Agency	36.3	18.0	21.5	14.1

*In percentages.

powerful from the public's perspective—and still a strong second in the eyes of the elite—is the secretary of state. Slightly less than half of each sample sees an important role for Congress—this represents a considerable shift from a similar survey taken in late 1974 when less than 20 percent of the elites and about 40 percent of the public perceived Congress as playing an important role on foreign policy. What is striking from this table is that most of the actors, ranging from the bureaucrats at State to the United Nations to labor and business as well as the military and the CIA, are perceived as less important by the elites than they are by the mass public. The elites thus tend to view the foreign-policy making-process in terms of dominance by the president and the secretary of state, with some power for Congress and more limited influence by the bureaucrats, the military, public opinion, and the military. On the other hand, the public acknowledges executive dominance on foreign policy but also sees a substantial role for most other actors. But, most of the public does not perceive public opinion to be as powerful in foreign policy as Congress, the military, the State Department, or business.

While the public does not see its own opinions as very powerful, it does believe (by a margin of two-thirds) that it should be the most important determinant of foreign policy-making. The president and Congress are virtually tied for a distant second in the ranking of which actors should be important, followed (somewhat surprisingly) by the United Nations. The public is more willing to entrust policy making to business than to labor or other private organizations, but it already sees each of these actors as having more power than desirable. In contrast, the elites prefer an even more widespread dispersion of power than the public, although neither favors strongly centralized decision-making. The elites acknowledge that the president is dominant, followed by the secretary of state, but do not approve of such concentrated power. There is also slightly less support for strong roles for the United Nations, the State Department, and Congress among the elites than among the mass public. Since many members of the former sample come from the Congress, it may be surprising to note the greater support for Congress among the mass public. But legislators may not only want to limit executive power, but also understand very well the problems of investing the Congress with too much authority to initiate foreign policy.

Both the public and the elites, however, place public opinion at the top of the list of actors which should be important. What sorts of changes from a policy currently made by elites would there be, if any? We recognize that the direction of foreign policy is set in the White House and that these leaders are not included in the elite survey of the Chicago Council on Foreign Relations, but nevertheless it seems reasonable to assume that the values of executive leaders are closer to those of other elites than they are to the views of the mass public. Our comparison of policy positions espoused by the mass and elite samples is presented in Table 4−2. There we find that the elites are much more supportive of an active role on world affairs and of our economic and military commitments to developing nations and our allies than is the mass public. On the other hand, the elites are less committed to the idea that we should stop the spread of communism whenever it appears. They are more willing than the mass public to support some human rights activities (such as opposing apartheid in South Africa) through moral persuasion but are more reticent to send in the military to protect American businesses abroad or to erect tariff barriers to protect American workers' jobs in the face of increased competition from abroad. Furthermore, the elites are more likely than the mass public to agree with the position generally associated with the president and State Department that the treatment of Soviet Jewry is not the business of the United States.

A greater role for public opinion on foreign policy would thus, at least given the data we present above, suggest a more nationalistic policy for the United States overall: an increased concern for the spread of communism (and perhaps a stronger reaction to Soviet activities in Africa and Afghanistan), greater protection (both economic and military) for American businesses both abroad and at home, and more emphasis on human rights issues in nations which do not ally themselves with us and less emphasis on such issues in countries which do identify with the United States. Many of these positions directly confront the bipartisan positions of foreign policy of past decades, but they also reflect at least one wing of the "dissensus" of the 1980s—as reflected in the Democratic and Republican party platforms in 1980. The positions of the public reflect more closely those of Republican Ronald Reagan—and it is

TABLE 4-2 Foreign Policy Orientations of the Mass Public and Elites: Chicago Council on Foreign Relations Surveys, 1978-79

Policy Position	Mass Response*	Elite Response
United States should take an active role in world affairs	59.2	97.0
United States should provide economic aid to needy countries**	37.8	64.8
Containing communism is a critical goal for U.S.	63.7	45.2
Defending allies is a critical goal for U.S.	54.0	78.0
United States should protect American business abroad	47.6	26.7
United States should protect jobs of American workers (by using tariffs)	81.0	35.1
United should be more active in opposing apartheid in South Africa	47.5	69.3
Treatment of Soviet Jews is not the business of the United States	54.0	68.8

*Entries are percentages agreeing with each statement.
**Question taken from 1974 surveys; not asked in 1978-79.

somewhat ironic that much of the 1980 campaign revolved around whether these policies might get the United States into trouble in the world, if not into a war.

More ironic is the fact that the elite generally supports the policies of the presidents of the 1960s and 1970s, but believes that there should be a shift away from executive dominance of the foreign policy process and an increase in the importance of public opinion. Were this to happen, it would be likely that the policies espoused by the elite sample—in many cases quite strongly—would be reversed. It is one thing to argue that public opinion ought to be followed in theory, but quite another to call for a foreign policy based upon the specific policies favored by the mass public. It is far from clear that the elites would be quite so willing to entrust more power in the masses if they knew what the policy consequences might be. As Jimmy Carter found out, promising voters a "government as good as its people" (which sounds good initially) is quite different from expecting the voters to approve of a performance which is far closer to "average" than it is to "outstanding." We do not have an answer to this dilemma, but the data from these two samples once again point to the difficulty in resolving the issues of process versus "correct" decision making and of how much control the public should have over the policy-making process.

To sum up: The four circles of power we have proposed do seem to indicate the relative impact of each set of actors on the foreign policy process. The president, because he can listen to whom he wishes, and because he can generally command the support of the public (and Congress as well), stands at the center of the decision-making process. Surrounding him are key personal advisers and the leaders of the major foreign policy agencies in the government. These leaders in turn depend upon the actors immediately below them in their respective departments for detailed advice and recommendations, which they carry into the innermost circle.

Standing at somewhat greater distance from the center of power are the political parties and interest groups. While each may attempt to perform some role in decision making, their successes are far outnumbered by those of the president. Congress has asserted itself on foreign policy questions, but it has yet to find the mechanism to obtain more power. Congress and the media may try to lead the voters, but the voters do not seem to follow. Constituents' positions are often poorly articulated, and even when they become clearer on occasion there is no guarantee that anyone in a position of authority will be there to listen. The dilemma the average voter faces also affects Congress in its role as an opinion leader: It is well expressed by John Dewey in a 1926 statement that "the Public seems to be lost; it is certainly bewildered."[49]

The Rational Actor Model and Crisis Decisions

Two Models of Policy Making

How do the various actors who participate in foreign policy-making interact? To examine this question, we will analyze two models of the policy-making process. The first model we shall examine is the *rational actor* approach; the second is that of *bureaucratic* politics. These models are devices by which we, as outside observers and analysts, organize our perceptions about how decisions are made. We do not assume that the various actors necessarily "choose" one model or the other and then make their decisions on the basis of that model. Rather, we describe possible methods of decision making when we posit the models. We will then examine several specific foreign policy decisions in light of these models.

The rational actor model is based upon the assumption of rational decision-making and assumes that there is some agreed-upon goal to be attained; the problem, then, is to find the most effective way to reach that goal. This is most useful in studying crisis decision-making as we shall indicate below. In contrast, the bureaucratic politics model assumes that there are a multiplicity of actors, each with different goals who see the stakes involved in a situation in different terms. The outcome reached will be one which is most politically feasible, the result of a bargaining

161

agreement among the parties involved. This model best fits noncrisis decisions involving security policies and particularly those policies which are intermestic—partly international, partly domestic. The characteristics of the policy-making process on each of these types of policies are detailed in Table 5-1.

Crisis decision-making involves a response to a perceived threat, a rational calculation of what to do given the actions of an opponent. Such situations involve relatively few actors, with the president preeminent, and require the capacity for both swift and careful planning. To paraphrase the Cuban revolutionary Ché Guevara, crisis decision-making is not a dinner party. A great degree of cooperation within the national government is required; there is little room for dissent or prolonged discussion within the legislature or among the mass public about what the appropriate response to a crisis should be. All actors perceive—or at least are expected to perceive—a common stake in responding to another nation or alliance and they are also expected to present a united front. Furthermore, there is a great deal of emphasis on arriving at the most effective solution to the question of how to respond. Otherwise, many lives might be lost and the international system might be disrupted even further. The rational actor approach and crisis decision-making thus stress a strong executive, the ability to act swiftly and to arrive at the appropriate decision, and the need to present a united front. Clearly, then, the rational actor model emphasizes one set of values embodied in our democratic dilemma.

The bureaucratic politics model, on the other hand, emphasizes the other values: checks and balances, fair opportunities for bargaining among diverse actors, and the need for widespread participation by as many interested parties as possible. The emphasis here is on the representation of diverse interests, each of whom may see the stakes involved in a decision-making situation differently. There is no unique "best" outcome. The decision is evaluated on the basis of the opportunities that various actors have to influence the bargaining that produces some outcome—which may very well be no change in the *status quo* because each of the various participants may check and balance each other too effectively for any to emerge as dominant. This model applies to noncrisis policies—security issues such as arms race politics within the United States—and even better, to intermestic policies (for instance, energy) since the origin of this model lies in the domestic policy process.

To return to the rational actor model: The term *rational* has a very specific meaning. It refers to a decision-making process and involves four steps: (1) select the objectives and values that a given policy is supposed to achieve and maximize; (2) consider the various alternative means to achieve these purposes; (3) calculate the likely consequences of each alternative course; and (4) choose the course that is most likely to attain the objectives originally selected. Furthermore, the government is usually

TABLE 5–1 Policy Characteristics

Type of Policy	Chief Characteristics	Primary Actors	Principal Decision-maker	Role of Congress	Role of Interest Groups	Role of Public Opinion	Relationship among Actors
Crisis	Short run; bureaucracy and Congress short-circuited. Common stake: all win or lose together	President, responsible officials, and ad hoc individuals from in and out of government	Executive (presidential preeminence)	Postcrisis legitimization	None	Supportive; legitimization	Cooperation
Noncrisis (security)	Long run; bureaucratic-legislative participation; winners and losers	President; executive agencies; Congress; interest groups; public opinion	Executive bureaucracy	Congressional participation	Low to moderate	Low to moderate	Competition and bargaining
Intermestic (welfare)	Long run; bureaucratic-legislative participation; winners, non-winners, and losers	President; executive agencies; Congress; interest groups; public opinion	Executive-congressional sharing	High	High	High	Competition and bargaining

This table is modeled on one in Randall B. Ripley and Grace A. Franklin, *Congress, the Bureaucracy, and Public Policy* (Homewood, Ill.: Dorsey, 1976), p. 17.

viewed as a unitary actor when the rational actor model is used. This is implicit in the phrases we use or read: "The United States has decided . . . ," "It is believed that Moscow seeks . . . ," and "China has announced. . . ."

Decision-makers have goals and attempt to maximize them in the policy-making arena. Deterrence of nuclear war, for example, assumes that a potential aggressor will not attack if the price of destroying his adversary is far higher than any conceivable gains he might make.[1] Nuclear devastation is clearly a price totally disproportionate to any possible profit. Deterrence thus rests upon the assumption that the party to be deterred is rational and that he will reject alternative courses of action—that is, he will not attack and commit suicide or choose a third course such as refusing to defend his own interests and withdrawing into isolationism. Or, consider the rationale for limited war. In 1957, Henry A. Kissinger published a book, *Nuclear Weapons and Foreign Policy*, in which he argued that since the United States' strategy of massive retaliation gave the president only two options—deterrence or, if challenged, fighting a total war—America's adversary (then still perceived as a united Sino-Soviet bloc) would be able to confront him with limited challenges in areas of vital interest to the United States.[2] This would then put Washington up against a dilemma: either respond completely and risk nuclear immolation, or don't respond and appease or yield. The rational alternative in these circumstances was to have a limited war capability to respond to such less than total challenges.

The rational actor model has been dominant in explaining international politics—to a far greater degree than in domestic politics.[3] Because most decisions studied in international politics have involved relations among nations, students of international politics have tended to view nations as unitary actors. It is our view that for crisis decision-making, this assumption is a reasonable one. In a crisis, the scope of the decision-making arena is rather small. The inner circle makes the decisions and is almost invariably supported by Congress, the bureaucracies, and public opinion. This is less true for noncrisis security decisions, and we shall see in the next chapter that these present a different model for explaining and understanding the decision-making process in more normal or everyday type of security policies.

In contrast to the "rational actor" model, the "bureaucratic" politics model does not assume that the government is a unitary actor.[4] It does not use phrases such as "the U.S.," or "the Soviet Union"; or refer to Paris or London as shorthand terms for their governments. Government is the sum of many parts. The executive branch of the U.S. government consists of more than the office of the presidency—it is also, as we know, composed of the senior foreign policy departments such as State, Defense, and the CIA; junior foreign policy departments, such as the International Communication Agency, Arms Control and Disarmament Agency; and such essentially domestic departments as Commerce, Labor, Agriculture, and Treasury, all of whom have some interest in foreign policy because they wish to enhance exports, protect U.S. labor, or seek a favorable balance of trade. Similarly, as we saw also earlier, the Congress is composed of two houses, each of which is further decentralized into committees which, in turn, fragment into a multitude of subcommittees. And in this context, a whole host of interest groups representing every conceivable group from business and labor to environmentalist and other self-styled public interest groups are additional actors.

Second, each of these actors—the presidency, executive departments, committees, subcommittees, and interest groups—approaches a problem or issue somewhat differently. This should not be surprising. They have different responsibilities; often they have received training to fulfill these responsibilities; they view the world from different perspectives and their stakes are different as well. It is surely understandable that each "actor" should believe that what he is doing is important—otherwise, why bother?—and that he should actively seek to gain the adoption of his solution for the problem being confronted. There is a phrase for this: Where you stand depends upon where you sit. A State Department Foreign Service officer not unnaturally believes that given patience, and the kinds of skills he possesses, almost any problem can be resolved by diplomacy. By contrast, a military officer is more prone to dismiss the possibilities of a compromise settlement and feel that the use of force or threat of force is more likely to yield fruitful results. Similarly, a congressional committee concerned with foreign affairs may well see a specific issue quite differently than one concerned with military affairs.

Actually, government can be broken down even further. Thus the State Department, as noted earlier, is hardly a single actor, even if the secretary of state officially presents his viewpoint. For State in turn is composed of desks representing each major area of the world. Thus, as often happened in the past, the European desk and the African would be at odds. If a colony were seeking its independence, as often happened after World War II, the African desk would urge U.S. support of the independence movement, even if it annoyed one of our European allies, while the European desk would recommend caution; preserving the cohesiveness of NATO against Russia was from its point of view more critical. Similarly, the Defense Department is composed of the air force, army, and navy, each of which quite naturally feels that its contribution to the defense and security of the United States is the most important and, therefore, seeks the larger share of the budget in order to best equip itself for any tasks it might be called upon to do. Therefore, not only are the three services rivals, but each is subject to further conflict, for example, between the Strategic Air Command, Tactical Air Command, and Military Air Transport (air force); armor, artillery, and infantry (army); and aircraft carriers, regular surface navy, and nuclear submarines (navy). The United

States thus has three navies! The aircraft carrier navy, which has been dominant since World War II, believes that should war occur with Russia it can best project U.S. naval power; and in limited war and crisis situations it can bring U.S. air power to bear even if land bases are absent. The surface navy is preoccupied with control of the sea lanes in case of war so that American troops and munitions can be shipped to Western Europe, and that American industry continues to have access to the raw materials it needs from all regions of the world. The nuclear submarine navy, of course, feels it is the most important of these three navies since its task is the deterrence of war and, should that fail, to retaliate and destroy Russia for striking the United States. To repeat: Where you stand depends upon where you sit.

Third, the inevitable result of so many executive and legislative actors, each with a different stake in an issue and therefore viewing it differently, is conflict. Making a decision is thus not a matter of selecting a particular value or goal, calculating the various means by which it can be attained, and then selecting the one means which will most fully realize it at the least possible cost. Rather than reflecting a calm, considered, dignified, and reasoned process, decision making resembles a brawl, usually an unseemly one at that. For the issue is not whose policy position and recommendation is correct. There is no single correct policy which, but for every actor's narrow and self-interested perspective, would clearly emerge. Let us be clear about this: There is no objective "national interest" which would be clearly visible to all policy-makers if they would but give priority to a broader, unselfish, patriotic view and subordinate their own parochial and selfish perception of a problem and do "what's right for the country." The issue is not who is right but how to reconcile—if that is even possible—many conflicting interpretations of what the correct policy should be.

The reason the term "bureaucratic politics" is used more frequently than "governmental politics" should be obvious from our earlier analysis: The executive branch has the primary responsibility in the formulation and implementation of foreign policy. Thus the focus of the policy struggle is among the many executive actors; the conflict is between the various bureaucracies. But, as is also clear from our earlier discussion, the Congress can never be neglected in noncrisis decisions; since Vietnam, indeed, interested legislative actors have participated more consistently and assertively than before. Hence, our emphasis on governmental politics, encompassing all the decision-making circles. In nondemocratic societies like Russia, of course, one could focus only on the executive.

Fourth, as noted, this pluralism of actors, interests, and views means that the policy process is one of attempting to reconcile these conflicting perspectives and building a consensus or majority coalition so that a decision can be made. This is not done by considering only whose policy recommendation has the most merit; it is also a question of which actor is the more powerful. Indeed, the degree of an actor's influence, skill in negotiating, ability to attract some actors and accommodate others, are probably more important than the wisdom of his position. Indeed, the reason for the use of the word "politics" in the terms "governmental politics" or "bureaucratic politics" reflects the fact that a policy emerges from a process of simultaneous conflict and accommodation among a multitude of actors with competing viewpoints and possessing different amounts of "power." Policy making means bargaining; negotiations are required and compromises must be struck. Those for a policy and those opposing the policy negotiate with other actors, seeking to organize a coalition of a majority of the actors to advance their collective policy interests or oppose a change of policy. Negotiations thus occur throughout the executive branch as officials, bureaus, and agencies in one department seek support in another; attracting the president and/or some of his advisors is especially important and is, therefore, a cause of fierce struggle. Policy making is thus a matter of widening the base of support within the executive while also seeking allies within Congress, through the constant modification of the proposed policy as concessions are made to potential allies in order to satisfy their needs and overcome their objections in the hope of building a majority coalition. Coalition building, in short, crosses institutional lines.

Fifth, the characteristics of the conflict and the coalition-building process affect the policy output. One of the most important results of this continuous bargaining within the "policy machine" is that policy moves forward one step at a time and tends to focus on momentary concerns and short-range aims. This is usually called incrementalism. Another word is "satisficing." This word suggests that policy-makers do not, each time they have to make a decision, sit down and go through the rational procedure of decision making. Policy-makers have neither the time nor the resources to go through this process. Instead, they pick the policy that is likely to be the most satisfactory; and they judge this by whether a policy has been successful in the past. If a policy has been satisfactory up to that point, why not take another step forward on the same path? The presumption is that what worked in the past will work now, as well as in the future. In addition, once a majority coalition has been forged after hard struggle, a "winning" coalition will normally prefer modification of existing policy to another major fight. The assumption is, of course, that there will be policy decisions. This is not necessarily true. The negotiating process among different groups with conflicting perspectives and vested interests can produce a stalemate and paralysis of policy—that is, no policy at all.

Sixth, a further characteristic of the policy process, and implicit in our analysis so far, is its time-consuming nature. Incrementalism suggests a policy machine in low gear, moving along a well-defined road rather slowly in response to specific short-run stimuli. A proposed policy is normally discussed first within the executive. It then passes through official channels, where it receives "clearances" and modifications as it gathers a broader base of support on its way "up" the executive hierarchy to the president. The constant conferences and negotiations among departments clearly slow the pace. The process takes even longer when a policy needs congressional and public approval. Potential opponents can occupy many "veto points" to block legislation within Congress; such veto points are in the House Rules Committee, the House and Senate committees and a multitude of subcommittees, and on the floor during debates and votes in both chambers. The advantage normally lies with those who oppose a specific policy, because it is difficult to jump all the hurdles along its route of legislative enactment. An additional result, given this slow-negotiating policy process, the formidable obstacles and great effort needed to pass major policy, is that old policies and the old assumptions upon which they are based, tend to survive longer than the conditions which produced these policies initially.

Seventh, one further characteristic of American foreign-policy decision-making is that it is usually public in nature. In a democracy, this is inevitable. While policy may be made primarily by the executive, the confines of this policy are established by public opinion. No American government before the fall of France could have intervened in Europe to preserve the balance of power. During World War II and most of the cold war, however, Congress and public opinion tended to be permissive and supportive as far as the presidential conduct of foreign policy was concerned. Aware of their lack of knowledge, information, and competence in an area remote from their everyday involvement—in the more familiar area of domestic policies, public opinion is much more structured and knowledgeable—the legislature and public looked to the president for leadership. Only when setbacks arose or painful experiences that pinched the voters' toes occurred would Congress and public opinion react, broadly clarify the limits of its tolerance, and perhaps punish the party in power. But even if most of the time public opinion did not act as a restraining factor, policy-makers were always aware of its existence. Because mass opinion does not tend to take shape until *after* some foreign event has occurred, it can hardly act as a guide for those who must make the policy; nonetheless, the latter will take into account what they think "the traffic will bear," because they know that if a decision is significant enough, there is likely to be some crystallization of opinion and, possibly, retribution at the polls. Since Vietnam, this has changed considerably. There is more widespread skepticism of presidential wisdom, greater congressional capability, more extensive public concern about dangerous involvements; and the emergence of intermestic policies with their pocketbook effects on voters arouses their congressmen and interest groups. Congress and public opinion tend to be both less permissive and supportive of presidents now; presidential capacity for leadership has become more constrained.

We shall examine the "bureaucratic" politics model as it relates to the anti-ballistic missile system (ABM), strategic arms limitation talks, and energy politics in the next chapter. But we shall first focus on the rational actor model and its application to crisis decision-making on Cuba and Iran in this chapter.

The Cuban Missile and Iranian Hostage Crises

Crises, as we have seen, are characterized by a number of features: a perceived threat to vital interests, usually surprise, and a sense of urgency to make decisions.[5] But the principal characteristic of crises in which one of the superpowers demands a change in the *status quo* and the other resists, is the threat of violence—possibly nuclear war—is very much present. This possibility of military action is also likely when the United States is involved with secondary states, whether they are Communists (for instance, the unexpected North Koreans' attack on South Korea in 1950) or non-Communists (for instance, the Iranian seizure of the U.S. Embassy in Teheran in 1979). Time may not be quite as critical a factor (Iran dragged on for 444 days) but the importance of the issues at stake for both sides virtually guarantees the use of the threat, if not the actual employment, of force.

It is these characteristics of a crisis which influence the decision-making process. The suddenness of being confronted by a critical situation, the vital interests perceived to be involved, and the very great danger present as a result of the consequences of using force which are never completely predictable, guarantees that the key decisions will be made at the very top level of government by the president and his closest advisers. Some will be his statutory advisers, such as the secretaries of his chief foreign policy agencies, others men both in and out of government whose judgment the president particularly trusts. Thus, during the potentially very explosive Cuban missile crisis of 1962,[6] which occurred after the Russians had sent approximately seventy intermediate and medium-range missiles to the island, the Executive Committee, which managed the crisis, listed as its members the President and Vice-President, the secretaries of state and defense; their seconds in command; the director of the CIA; the Chairman of the Joint Chiefs of Staff; the President's special assistant for National Security Affairs; the secretary of the treasury; the Attorney General (the President's brother); his special counsel (perhaps the President's closest friend among his advisers); an ambassador just returned from Moscow; and President Truman's former secretary of state. And after the so-called militant Islamic students had taken over the American Embassy and its personnel in late 1979, President Carter was advised chiefly by his national security assistant, and the secretaries of state and defense; he appears also to have sought or received advice from Hamilton Jordan, White House Chief of Staff, and Jody Powell, the White

House press secretary, two men close to him who were also actively directing his campaign for renomination and reelection.

Note a difference between Presidents Kennedy and Carter. Kennedy, who demanded that Russia dismantle the missiles which would, within a very short time, become operational, assembled a special group of advisers to help him manage this particular crisis; this *ad hoc* group's function would end with the resolution of the crisis. But for the duration of the crisis, it was a full-time group. Members who were high officials of various departments were relieved of their regular responsibilities. Business unrelated to the crisis was left to lower-level officials or remained undecided. The point was that confronting a situation of war or peace, Kennedy wanted a small group of able and trusted men to give him their best advice about what to do. To do this they were to concentrate totally on the crisis at hand; they were to check their regular departmental business at the door to the White House. Had these men been asked to assist the President in the crisis as well as carry out their normal duties, they could have given the Cuban situation only superficial attention—quite frankly, the kind of attention most high level officials are able to devote to problems due to their frequent occurrence.

The Iranian crisis, which erupted in November 1979, and ended on inauguration day, January 1981, was quite different. One reason was that the use of force did not hang over this situation in the same way. The Embassy was in downtown Teheran. An Entebbe-type rescue mission (in which the Israelis rescued their citizens captured when their French plane was hijacked by the PLO and flown to Uganda's Entebbe Airport) could thus not be carried out. It was one thing for the Israelis to send troops to an airport located many miles from a city; with enough soldiers and an element of surprise, they could overwhelm the hostages' guards, liberate the hostages, and fly them out before reinforcements could be brought in. The West Germans could do the same thing in Somalia. But not only was the U.S. Embassy located in the heart of Iran's capital city, but armed student guards were swarming over the Embassy grounds, and tens of thousands—sometimes hundreds of thousands—paraded around the Embassy grounds screaming anti-American slogans and praising the Ayatollah Khomeini, the religious leader of the Islamic revolution, who had a few months before overthrown the pro-American Shah and bestowed his blessings on the students who had invaded American territory. (An embassy is considered the territory of the country occupying it, and its seizure can, therefore, be considered an act of war, one reason why it is rarely done.) A rescue mission in these circumstances was initially rejected; many of the hostages might be killed and the troops would suffer heavy casualties, if they could get into the Embassy—and out as well. In one sense, this crisis does not fit our definition in a key respect, but given the intense concern in the United States about the safety of the sixty-three hostages and the public outrage which their seizure stirred, President Carter and his principal foreign policy advisers had to give it immediate and full attention. Even as it became apparent that the hostages would not be released soon, this crisis maintained its sense of the urgency because of frequent threats of trials and constant concern about their lives, and top-level officials continued to give the situation in Teheran priority. Thus, despite the critical difference from a U.S.-Soviet crisis in which the survival of the entire society is at stake, this "lower-level" type of crisis management may become more frequent in an increasingly unstable and multipolar world.

This also applied to some of the President's domestic policy advisers. For Carter's public opinion ratings stood at an all-time low; while widely perceived as an honest and decent man, the President was also believed to be generally incompetent, not capable of handling the demanding job he had so eagerly sought. Most members of his party in Congress were hoping Senator Kennedy would run for the nomination and become the Democrats' standard-bearer; the Kennedy magic would hopefully help them get elected at a time when the economy was in terrible straits, suffering simultaneously from high inflation and a recession. With Carter as its nominee, the fear was that the Democrats would lose both the presidency and many congressional seats against an attractive Republican candidate who was an effective campaigner. The Iranians' seizure of U.S. hostages could not have been better timed for Carter. In such moments the country tends to unite and the president is the beneficiary of this rallying-around-the-flag phenomenon. A crisis focuses virtually everyone's attention on the president and thus Carter's handling of the hostage issue gave him an unexpected opportunity to erase his image as a bumbler and substitute for it the image of a leader who deserved to be reelected. Together with the Soviet invasion of Afghanistan a few weeks later at Christmastime, 1979, Carter's handling of foreign policy now seemed to be his path for secular electoral salvation.

President Kennedy in 1962, of course, was not running for reelection. Yet he did confront the midterm congressional election. Cuba had been a hot issue since Castro came to power. It became an issue in one of the Nixon-Kennedy TV debates; Kennedy's position was militantly anti-Castro. The failure of the subsequent Bay of Pigs operation, planned by the Eisenhower administration and reluctantly carried out by a Kennedy dubious about the feasibility of this covert CIA operation, hurt him as well as the nation's prestige. If nothing succeeds like success, nothing fails like failure. Kennedy was also under attack on the Cuba issue by Republican senators who declared that rumors from Cuba were saying that the Russians were installing missiles. Since there were no hard intelligence data supporting this contention, the President denied it and issued a statement that the United States would not tolerate missiles in Cuba. When the rumors turned out to be fact, inaction would undoubtedly have hurt Kennedy's reputation in the nation, Congress, and within the executive branch. Thus a tough reaction was politically required by U.S. politics.[7]

In a democratic system, awareness of the possible electoral consequences can hardly be avoided. This is especially true in a system like that of the United States where some sort of election is always occurring or about to occur. How much awareness of domestic politics is allowed to intrude into foreign policy considerations and decisions, however, depends on the president. For if the first characteristic of crises is that decision making flows upward to the top, while at the same time being narrowed to relatively few participants, the second characteristic is the central role of the president; it is he who, more than anyone else, interprets events and evaluates the stakes in the crisis. Kennedy's and Nixon's "readings" of the nature of the situations they confronted, the consequences these situations might have upon U.S. security, and their own political futures and ability to lead the nation, were responsible for their actions. (The latter two considerations can hardly be separated, for the external challenges, as presidents see them, do not really leave them with a choice of accepting a personal loss of prestige without accepting as well a loss of national prestige. For a president of the United States, personal and national cost calculations tend to become identical.) Kennedy saw the installation of Soviet missiles in Cuba as a personal challenge with damaging national effects. Since, in response to earlier congressional and public clamor about possible offensive missiles in Cuba, Kennedy had publicly declared that the United States would not tolerate offensive missiles on the island ninety miles off the Florida coast, he had to act. Kennedy's statement had clearly been understood in Moscow which had responded that it had no intention of placing missiles in Cuba; Russia had more than enough missiles at home. Thus the President, having initially deemphasized the possibility that the Russians would install such weapons in Cuba, and Moscow having then signaled that it understood Kennedy's declaration, Kennedy was publicly pledged to act if the Russians lied—as it turned out they had—unless he wished to be publicly humiliated. If he did not act in these circumstances, the Soviet leader, Nikita Khrushchev, would not believe other pledges and commitments the President had made or was obligated to fulfill by virtue of their existence when he had acceded to the presidency. At least, this is how the President perceived the situation.

The consequences were judged as very dangerous by Kennedy, who already feared that Khrushchev interpreted previous acts by Kennedy not as acts of restraint but as signs of a lack of will, an absence of sufficient resolution and determination on the part of the United States to defend its vital interests. During the abortive CIA-supported refugee invasion of Cuba in 1961, Kennedy had refused to commit U.S. forces once the invasion appeared doomed, although Washington had wanted to eliminate Castro. During the building of the Berlin Wall the same year,

American forces had stood by as the wall went up. Khrushchev began to talk openly of America's failure of nerve. The United States apparently talked loudly but carried a small stick. Thus failure to act in the Caribbean, which has traditionally been an area within America's sphere of influence (as Eastern Europe was Russia's and so in East Germany in 1953 and Hungary in 1956—as in Czechoslovakia in 1968—the United States kept its hands off during Russia's times of trouble), would have immense and damaging consequences. It was not so much the effect of the Soviet missiles upon the military equation between the two powers, although that was important; it was the political consequences of the *appearance* of a change in the balance of power that were deemed critical by Kennedy. The Soviet Union was supposed to be on the short end of the missile gap. But American inaction would, Kennedy feared, be widely recognized as a persuasive answer to the U.S. claims of missile superiority, would lead allied governments to fear that in the new situation, with America highly vulnerable to nuclear devastation, they could no longer count on the United States to defend them. In these circumstances the Soviets would be tempted to exploit the situation and seek to disintegrate America's alliances—especially NATO since Khrushchev had already restated his determination to eject the Western allies from West Berlin. Thus, while the risks of action in Cuba were obviously great, the risks of escalation as a result of inaction were also perceived as great. If Khrushchev got away with Cuba, why should he take seriously Kennedy's pledge to defend West Berlin? And if he did not, would not Soviet and American troops soon be clashing in an area where they would be hard to separate?

The real irony of the Cuban missile crisis is that Kennedy was also determined that during his years in office he would try to seek a more stable and restrained basis of coexistence with the Soviet Union. This long-range goal, which hardly had the massive support it has today, could not be realized if Khrushchev would not take Kennedy seriously or felt he could push Kennedy around; then serious negotiations, recognizing each other's legitimate interests, would be impossible. Thus a major change in the cold war atmosphere was at stake, in addition to America's reputation for power and willingness to keep commitments. If Khrushchev viewed him as a weakling, he would continue to pressure and push; such a lack of respect for the United States could only be dangerous, for if he raised the pressure too much and pushed too far on the assumption that the President was too fearful of risking a confrontation, a Soviet miscalculation could well spark a military conflict. Aware of the fact that his prestige was identical with the prestige of the United States, that he, Kennedy— chief of party and government—was also the symbol of the United States whose Chief of State he was, the President's prime considerations were clearly concerned with the foreign policy effects of his inaction. He would, in short, have reacted to the Soviet missiles even if domestic politics had not pointed in the same direction. His blockade of Cuba was basically a rational response to the demands of the external situation as he perceived and defined that situation.

Having made the key decision that the stakes were high and required the Soviet Union to dismantle its missiles and take them out of Cuba, the President also made the critical decisions on how to gain Soviet compliance. The U.S. alternatives ranged from diplomatic pressure, a secret approach to Castro, a surgical air strike on the missiles, invasion, and blockade. However, feeling strongly that he had to act in order to impress Khrushchev, Kennedy chose the blockade as the option most likely to attain the removal of the Soviet missiles. While the blockade could not by itself achieve this objective, it (1) was a sign of American determination; (2) permitted the United States the option of increasing the pressure on Moscow later if Moscow would not remove its missiles; (3) provided a relatively safe middle course between inaction and invasion or an air strike, which might provoke the Russians; and (4) placed on Khrushchev the responsibility of deciding whether to escalate or de-escalate. It is significant to note that, thanks to a U-2 "spy plane," the administration had an entire week in which to debate the meaning and significance of the Russian move, what its military and political effects were likely to be on U.S. security interests, what the different courses of actions open to the United States were, and which was most likely to achieve the removal of the Soviet missiles without precipitating nuclear war. Many crises simply do not allow such time for preparation and the careful consideration of the many alternative actions that can be undertaken. Even during the missile crisis, the initial reaction of most of the President's advisers was to bomb the missile sites. Slowing down the momentum of events becomes crucial if impulsive actions are to be avoided.

If Kennedy, like Carter in the Iranian crisis, did not deliberately define the Soviet missiles in Cuba as a crisis for domestic reasons, Carter, unlike Kennedy, confronted a much longer-term situation. The missile crisis was over in slightly less than a week after the President delivered his speech revealing the presence of the Soviet missiles in Cuba. Carter was not so lucky. The longer the hostages remained in Iranian hands, the more impotent and helpless the country appeared to many Americans and the greater the public impatience became; the President's standing in the polls dropped as well. Initially, however, Carter's handling of the crisis gained great domestic approval. Before the hostages' seizure, as noted earlier, the President's popularity had stood at an all-time low approval rating of only 30 percent. Senator Kennedy had led Carter by 54 to 20 percent among Democrats nationally. After the seizure, Carter's rating shot upward. By February 1980, 48 percent of the public approved of his conduct of foreign policy in general and 53 percent approved of his handling of the presidency.[8] By then, Carter had abandoned his active campaign for the Democratic renomination. The suspicion remains that he did so only partly for the reason he stated—to focus his full attention on the hostage situation and not appear to be "playing politics" while American citizens were being held hostages and their lives endangered. The real reason appears to have been that by staying in the White House and "being presidential," Carter felt he could best resurrect his fallen image. This "Rose Garden" strategy would also avoid the embarrassment of refusing to debate Senator Kennedy or being beaten on television by the senator, who in his campaign was heavily emphasizing the President's dismal economic record. The best politics for Carter, in short, was to pretend that he was not playing politics but being a statesman tending the nation's business at a critical moment.

There really was not much Carter could do to get the hostages freed. Since force seemed to the President to be the most likely way to get them killed, the President's objective in this crisis dictated a policy of restraint and gradually applying sanctions to make it more costly for Iran to hold the hostages. This policy of "tightening the screws" bit by bit was widely hailed in the United States, as well as among our allies, as a responsible policy. What were the objectives this policy of patience and incremental pressure was supposed to achieve? One was simply to impress upon the Iranians that the United States would not pay the price they set for ending the crisis. The Ayatollah and the student militants demanded the return of the Shah to stand trial for his "crimes against the Iranian people." He had been allowed into this country for the treatment of cancer. Indeed, the Shah was hustled out of this country to Panama as soon as he had recuperated from his operation. This was supposed to impress upon the Iranians that a deal would no longer be possible, but it failed to do so. The demands for his return and, after his death from cancer, for the billions of dollars he was supposed to have taken with him or sent over here in earlier years continued until nearly the end.

A second goal was the freeing of the hostages. Their lives were the key objective. A third objective was to protect the West's political friends and economic interests in the area. The conservative sheiks in Saudi Arabia and other oil kingdoms on the Arabian peninsula were badly shaken by the downfall of the Shah. Most of these states, including Saudi Arabia, were also politically vulnerable to internal disturbances, coups d'états, or revolutions. The likelihood of such occurrences gave nightmares to the United States, Western Europe, and Japan, all of whom depended upon the area's oil to maintain their economies. A U.S. attack on Iran might set off a strong wave of anti-Americanism which might endanger these pro-Western but shaky regimes. The Ayatollah repeatedly condemned the United States as a "satanic power" and Western influence as corrupt and destructive of traditional Moslem values and religion; although he was a Shiite Moslem and this sect was only a minority in the Moslem world, he was appealing to the Moslem (mainly Sunni) masses to overthrow American political and cultural influence. Thus recourse to force was even less likely; even if Carter had been willing to risk sacrificing the lives of the hostages, and even had U.S. forces been capable of an immediate large-scale military operation against Iran, the possible danger to the conservative Islamic governments friendly to the United States, and the protection of their oil—upon which America's allies were far more dependent than the U.S.—counseled against using large-scale violence if it were at all avoidable.

But Carter's various maneuvers were all to fail over the next six months. He tried one thing after another: He cut off Iranian oil imports (a symbolic gesture since we did not import as much as the Europeans, and we could buy that amount elsewhere now while "our" oil would be sold to someone else). He froze all Iranian funds in United States banks at home and abroad (several billion dollars) and sought and gained a UN Security Council resolution (supported by Russia as well as several Islamic nations) calling on Iran to release the hostages; enlisted both the International Court of Justice and the Pope for the same purpose; and agreed to an Iranian demand for a commission of inquiry to investigate the Shah's rule and American support for him. (In fact, the Iranians did not want *any* report but clearly one that condemned both.) These and other efforts all came to naught. As economic sanctions were now organized and the United States pressured its industrial allies to cooperate, mostly without success; and, as the first reports of mining Iran's harbor became public, the administration attempted a rescue mission which failed due to poor organization of the rescue force, several malfunctioning helicopters, and poor weather conditions.

The President had been patient but in vain; the polls showed a declining confidence in his handling of the Iranian situation. Indeed, the first time the polls had started to go down, Carter was rescued by Afghanistan; his tough measures against the Soviet Union after its invasion of that country raised his standing again. But the public's sense of helplessness and humiliation and patience ran out. Senator Kennedy was still contesting the President's renomination; in the eastern industrial states his emphasis on inflation and unemployment was being heard even though Kennedy won few primaries. And the chaos in Iran appeared to be spreading as various nationalities sought greater autonomy, Iran and Iraq clashed, left-wing students fought with Khomeini's "revolutionary guards" on the streets of Teheran, and the Revolutionary Council which governed Iran remained divided. Clearly, the hostages were being used by the various factions competing for power in Iran and they would, therefore, not be released soon. Under these circumstances, a rescue mission appealed to the President. Success would make him an instant hero, restore the nation's dignity and pride, and relieve our allies of cooperating with sanctions they only most reluctantly and slowly accepted. While most Americans agreed with the President's decision to attempt the rescue mission, the failure seemed to symbolize the widespread perception of the administration's ineptness. The polls plummeted again (see Chapter 4 for details). The one thing the abortive rescue mission did accomplish was bringing the President out of the White House and onto the campaign trail again, although he had earlier said that he would not do so until the hostages' release. Carter clearly was seeking to maximize his delegate strength in the primaries as much as possible to ward off embarrassing and divisive challenges from Kennedy at the convention; the senator's delegate strength had to be kept down.

Carter won the nomination but the hostage issue came back to haunt him in the closing days of the presidential campaign. As the Iranians announced their terms for the hostages' release and hopes for their quick release rose again—only to be quickly dimmed—the nation was vividly reminded of the President's failure to secure their release. Whether fair or not, the post-election *New York Times*/CBS News Poll showed a last minute change of mind on whom to vote for or whether or not to vote at all; three-fifths of these voters decided to vote against Carter. Twenty-three percent of these switchers cited Iran.[9]

A third characteristic of crises and the accompanying sense of urgency to make a decision, as well as the perception by the policy-makers that the nation's security is at stake and the possibility of war looms so threateningly, is the subordination of bureaucratic interests to the need to make a decision to safeguard the "national interest." Crisis decision-making takes place at the top level of the government, and the men in these positions, while reflecting their departmental viewpoints, do not necessarily feel themselves limited to representing these perspectives. Organizational affiliation is not per se a good predictor of their stands.[10] McNamara did not reflect the Joint Chiefs' impulse to bomb and invade during the missile crisis (as later in Vietnam, he was increasingly to disagree with their views and recommendations); he became the leading advocate of the blockade.

Bureaucracy becomes important mainly in the implementation of decisions. Standard operating procedures and departmental interests tend to rise to the fore. Potentially this may be dangerous. A bureaucracy reflects a division of labor; it possesses an expertise in a certain area. Within this area, it manages problems according to standard ways that over time have been found to be successful in resolving such problems. A bureaucracy cannot handle each problem as if it were a new one; it assigns each problem, therefore, to a certain category of problems which it handles and resolves regularly. These are called standard operating procedures (SOP). But in a crisis such SOP designed for the management of daily routines may cause trouble, even spark a conflagration. Thus the U.S. Navy wanted to place the blockade 800 miles away from Cuba, outside of the range of Cuban jet fighters. But Kennedy, while concerned about the safety of the U.S. ships, was even more concerned that the Soviet leaders should be given as much time as possible to consider their options and actions; too short a time might lead them to hasty and ill-considered action. He therefore insisted that the Navy pull its blockade back to 500 miles to give the Kremlin extra hours in the hope it would realize the gravity and danger of the situation and do nothing rash.

Similarly, Kennedy would not stop the first two ships that would approach the blockade line. One was a Soviet ship and the other an East German one; neither carried missiles. Neither did the third ship but the President did stop it—a U.S.-built World War II Liberty ship, Panamanian owned and registered in Lebanon under charter to the Soviet Union. Stopping that ship as the first one would be less provocative to the Soviets. Kennedy did the same thing to the Air Force. Asked by the President if it could carry out a "surgical strike" against the missiles, the Air Force dusted off an old plan, part of an invasion plan, requiring several hundred sorties and widespread bombing. Clearly, such an operation might have killed hundreds of the thousands of Russians in Cuba. Would this not cause Khrushchev to react militarily? Could he really tolerate such loss of life and do nothing?

In short, Kennedy not only made the key decision about the U.S. objectives, but supervised the implementation of the plans to achieve them in detail. He did not hesitate to interfere in the military chain of command. While this made some military officers unhappy with such "political interference," especially the Chief of Naval Operations, the President knew that if he were not aware of all the plans and did not ask all the right questions, he could not be assured that his objectives could be achieved—the withdrawal of the Soviet missiles *and* the avoidance of a nuclear war. Since the military was in charge of operations, he wanted to be certain he knew as much as possible about what they were going to do so as to ensure that these actions were consistent with his aims.

President Carter, by contrast, appears not to have similarly closely supervised the preparations for the Iranian rescue mission. Given the stakes a president has in a successful outcome of a crisis, he cannot avoid becoming familiar with each facet of the operation—except at his peril. He cannot entirely rely on either the experts or trusted advisers. Few details about the rescue mission are admittedly known besides the fact that three of the eight helicopters broke down (the minimum required number was six); that the helicopters needed refueling on the ground and landed at a desert strip to do so (so close to a road that a busload of Iranians had to be detained to keep the mission secret!); and that during this refueling stop one helicopter's propeller blades struck a C–130 transport plane filled with fuel, causing both to burst into flames. Other details seem to be:[11] that the President may have cut the operation back from a 400-man force and 35 helicopters because he was unwilling to risk a major military confrontation; that the Navy maintenance for the eight helicopters may have been carried out in a rather routine fashion; and that despite the fact that helicopters are rather delicate, an insufficient number of helicopters were provided, and questions about the age and experience of the Navy's helicopter crews, especially in regard to night flying, remain unanswered.

One major possible cause for failure may have been intraservice rivalry and fragmented command. Instead of sending a special commando unit carefully trained in antiterrorist activities and unified under a single command, like those in Israel and West Germany, the rescue force was an *ad hoc* group composed of the three military branches which had been trained for only a few months; the force did not even have a full dress rehearsal so that at the refueling stop the men did not know who the commanding officer was, and some, therefore, refused to obey orders. The overall impression remains of poor coordination among the services and unclear lines of authority during the operation. (The speculation is that another reason why the President reduced the size of the mission was that he could call it off if, for some reason, he changed his mind; indeed, there have been suggestions that he lost his nerve and latched onto the helicopter failures as an excuse to call the mission off.)

Finally, despite the War Powers Resolution, crisis decision-making is characterized by minimal, if any, congressional involvement. Before Vietnam, congressional leaders were usually called in and informed of the president's decision just before he announced it publicly. This was done as a matter of courtesy. But their advice was not requested. Presidents considered themselves more representative than any senator or House member and as representative as Congress as a whole. Moreover, as the term "crisis" suggests, such occurrences were—and continue to be—perceived by one side as affecting vital interests and frequently happen suddenly and unexpectedly, leaving decision-makers with a sharp sense that they have to make rapid decisions lest the situation deteriorate further. A lack of decision time tends to mean that Congress is bound to be bypassed, except for briefings *after* decisions have been made by the executive. The president has a full-time job—indeed, burns the midnight oil—at such times just consulting his staff and cabinet officers to obtain all possible information on what is happening and interpretations as to the adversary's motives, to canvass the alternative courses of action among which he must choose, and to explore which of these is most likely to achieve his aims without triggering a nuclear exchange. The War Powers Resolution has not yet changed this pattern (see Chapter 2).

Congress may be bypassed for yet another reason. During confrontations of the superpowers, they begin by testing each other's will and determination by some "low-level" action. Thus in Cuba, Kennedy decided on the blockade as an initial move even though it could only prevent the further shipment of missiles to the island, not eliminate the ones already there. But the hope was that Moscow would perceive the blockade as a demonstration of American determination to achieve that objective; if convinced by the blockade, the Soviet Union would withdraw its missiles before Kennedy had to escalate the crisis. He could, for example, have ordered an air strike upon the missiles or an invasion, and these options remained available to him; Moscow knew that and was unwilling to risk such an escalation. In short, crises, precipitated by the attempt of one side to change the *status quo* and the other's equal resolution not to permit such a change, become elaborate maneuvers in which each side seeks to achieve its aim but simultaneously avoid a nuclear exchange. Thus it becomes vital first to start on one of the lower rungs of the "escalation ladder," and second to give the opponent at each higher rung sufficient time to consider risks, costs, and payoffs of either desisting, escalating, or settling the issue at stake through negotiations. These steps must be carefully timed, coordinated, and calculated, for the risks of miscalculation are ever present. It is interesting to note that the first counsel of Kennedy's advisers was to bomb the Soviet missile sites. Only after a week of deliberation did Kennedy and his advisers decide on the blockade; and normally presidents do not have a week's grace to prepare their moves but must decide virtually overnight what to do when unexpectedly they confront a major challenge.

Significantly, however, when a delegation of congressmen was called in to be told of the Russian missiles and what the United States intended to do about them, the delegation's initial reaction was skepticism as to the blockade's ability to compel the withdrawal of the missiles, and it urged an air strike (Fulbright was one of these advocates). Presumably, had Congress been consulted, given the intensely hostile mood of Congress against Castro and Cuba at that time, it would have pressed the administration to bomb or possibly invade the island, thus starting the confrontation near the top of the escalation ladder, attacking Russian installations, killing Russian personnel, and perhaps—if an invasion had occurred—overthrowing a friend and ally of Russia which Moscow had pledged to defend. The risks of these courses, in contrast to the blockade, would have been enormous. Consulting Congress, asking for a supportive resolution, would also have robbed the administration of the advantage of surprise and allowed the USSR to take preemptive steps that might have made it difficult or impossible for Kennedy to act at all. In any event, it is clear that the president has much more room to maneuver if he is not subject to congressional pressures. Congress, on the whole, has not been a force for restraint—except in the later Vietnam years, when Congress climbed off the presidential bandwagon it had occupied earlier.

Carter, too, did not consult Congress about the rescue mission. The fear was of a leak. Ironically, just before the mission the chairman of the Senate Foreign Relations Committee and the ranking minority member, worried by the stories that the President was considering military moves against Iran, sent a letter to the secretary of state insisting on consultation under the War Powers resolution before any force was used. The purpose of invoking this resolution—the first time Congress had done so—was clearly to discourage the administration from mining Iran's harbors or similar moves. If such consultation occurred, it would obviously alarm much of the world by making it appear that action was imminent and, worse from the point of view of operational success, place on alert those against whom the mission was intended. Administration officials did say that military moves were months off since economic and diplomatic sanctions had just been agreed to by America's allies. Nothing was said about the forthcoming rescue effort which the President later called a "humanitarian mission."

Congressional opinion after the mission was divided over the issue of consultation but most, including the senate majority leader, were willing to give the President the benefit of the doubt. President Carter defined the mission as a "humanitarian" one, not a military one, since it involved the rescue of U.S. citizens and only a small force was involved, whose purpose was not to punish Iran by causing great damage. As the acting secretary of state had explained (after Secretary Vance resigned in protest over this rescue mission which he had opposed): the "extraordinary circumstances" surrounding this operation forbade consultation with Congress before its start; if any details of the plan had been revealed, the operation might have been compromised. But had the first stage gone well, "the President had planned to advise appropriate congressional leaders before the next stage." Furthermore, "I want to emphasize," continued the acting secretary, "the administration does not regard the extraordinary circumstances of this case as a precedent for avoiding consultations with the Congress."[12]

Crisis decision-making is thus predominantly characterized by rationality. The fact that vital interests are considered to be at stake, that the decision-makers are usually surprised by the occurrence of the event which gives rise to the crisis, and feel under great pressure to make quick decisions in a situation in which the probability of war erupting is high, ensures that crisis decisions will not be handled as routine. Decision making rises to the top and is narrowed to a few participants who may be organized for the duration of the crisis as a special task force. The president plays the key role; he has a greater opportunity in these circumstances to determine policy than he does in more normal security policies, let alone intermestic policies. He and his specially selected advisers are not hampered by an aroused Congress, irate interest groups, or an inquisitive public. The crisis itself tends to unite everyone; people rally-around-the-flag. There is not enough time to stimulate sufficient opposition. The cabinet officers participating in the decision-making process are usually not fundamentally motivated by the organizational and bureaucratic interests of their departments, as in "normal" policy. Given the threat and urgency of the crisis, they depend on their subordinates to run their departments. In any case, there is normally little time for bargaining among actors with different perspectives. As Lowi said many years ago, "only command positions were involved; the public and its institutions were far removed. . . . In sum, there was hardly any politics at all." The men in these "command positions" are "institutional leaders . . . *without their institutions.*"[13] Thus the U.S. political system ironically may work best when it acts in an authoritarian manner, when the normal democratic participation of the bureaucracy, Congress, interest groups, and public opinion is at a minimum. Some refer to this presidential dominance and freedom from political constraint as "democratic Caesarism."

One final point needs to be discussed briefly: the possibility that when decision making is limited to a few individuals, they will not make rational decisions but will fall victim to "groupthink."[14] This refers to the tendency of a small group of decision-makers to become a cohesive group and the possibility that individual members may silence their doubts and qualifications about the policy views the majority holds; those who disagree tend to be rejected. Thus the consensus reached may be superficial because it does not reflect the sound judgment of the group reached after critical examination; without the give-and-take of debate in which all options are carefully analyzed, this consensus may represent a collective misjudgment—or just plain bad judgments. Groupthink, claims Irving Janis, is a deterioration of the mental efficiency, reality testing, and moral judgment that is the product of group pressure to conform.[15]

In the Cuban missile crisis, the President avoided becoming a victim. First, he absented himself from the executive committee's discussions so that its members would be free to say what they wanted to; had he been present and expressed his views, the tendency would have been for the committee members to take their cue from him. Who, after all, dares to challenge the president's views? Second, the committee was divided into smaller groups who debated and cross-examined one another. In this way, all members became thoroughly familiar with the pros and cons of the arguments for specific options. Robert Kennedy, the attorney-general who was his brother's confidante, often played devil's advocate, probing and asking, what some felt were rude questions that demanded a justification of their position.

If the Cuban missile crisis was handled so well that it has become a classic case study of "crisis management," that is because the administration learned from the disaster of the Bay of Pigs operation a year earlier, when the CIA had sponsored a small army of Cuban refugees to invade Cuba and overthrow Castro. This operation too has become a classic of sorts—of a "perfect failure."[16] The operation was launched upon a series of assumptions, all of which proved wrong. Among these were: No one would discover that the United States was responsible for this invasion; the Cuban Air Force could be knocked out before the invasion started; Castro's army was weak; and that the invasion would touch off uprisings which would probably lead to Castro's overthrow. How could such flimsy assumptions go unchallenged by a group of men who were considered "the best and the brightest"? A number of reasons have been cited, including the fact that the CIA's own intelligence experts and State Department's Cuban desk people who could have predicted the failure of sending 1400 men to Cuba to topple the regime were excluded, and the illusion of these able people that they were invincible and that they were unanimous in their support of the CIA plan. Doubts were not loudly voiced, silence was taken for consent, and any disagreements that surfaced were suppressed by a "mindguard" who guarded the consensus from intellectual assault as a bodyguard would protect an individual from physical injury. Robert Kennedy was one such mindguard.

Was Carter's Iranian rescue mission his "Bay of Pigs"? Were the plans for the mission extensively debated and subjected to rigorous scrutiny? Kennedy not only encouraged vigorous and frank debate in the executive committee but called in some of the "grand old men" who had been active in the early days of containment (Acheson and Lovett, for example). Did Carter ever ask for the opinions of such stalwarts of the previous Democratic administrations as Averell Harriman, Ball, and McNamara? Was the CIA ever consulted or was it only the Joint Chiefs of Staff and the Defense Intelligence Agency (which has a reputation for uncritical judgments since professional officers are generally reluctant to tell their superiors, who will judge their merit and consider their possible promotion, that they do not know what they are talking about)? How feasible really was this operation, however noteworthy and noble its intention? Could the operation have been carried out successfully had the helicopters not broken down, or was the mission itself conceptually faulty? Was its failure due to technical failures—what might perhaps be called "bad luck"—or was the plan itself a "victim of groupthink"?

The Bureaucratic Politics Model and Noncrisis Decisions

6

The bureaucratic/governmental politics model described in Chapter 5 stands in sharp contrast to the rational actor model. Different participants see the stakes in different ways and there is no objective solution to be sought. The outcome is the result of intense bargaining and conflict occurs both within and across the branches of government. Congress, the bureaucracies, interest groups, and public opinion all play key roles—as does, of course, the president—and there is no single actor who is determinative in most cases. In this chapter, we shall outline how decisions are made according to this model. We first discuss Johnson's decision to deploy an antiballistic missile (ABM) system—and contrast that briefly with Nixon's later decision to go forward, on the basis of rational actor logic, with an expanded ABM and the ultimate governmental decision to dismantle the entire system. The emphasis in the ABM case is on the bureaucracy. Then we turn to the politics of arms control in which the stress is on executive-legislative relations. The Strategic Arms Limitation Treaty (SALT II), which had taken the Carter administration over two years to negotiate, was one of the most important treaties the United States had negotiated with the Soviet Union in the postwar period. It needed Senate approval; specifically, as a treaty it needed two-thirds approval, which it failed to obtain. Different opponents saw alternative stakes and found many conflicting reasons for their stands; some thought that the treaty was too strong, others too weak, and many senators tried to barter their support for it in return for favors on pet constituency projects. Even its supporters varied in the intensity of their support.

Finally we consider the Byzantine politics of energy policy internationally and nationally—a classic example of intermestic policy where the stakes are perceived as very high by all actors and there is widespread participation in decision making but virtually no coordination. This lack of coordination fails to produce no international or national energy policy for the developed nations of the world, especially the United States. Energy politics typifies some of the more extreme aspects of the bureaucratic model particularly because participation is so widespread, very few actors have common interests, and the capacity for not reaching a decision is so very great. Indeed, energy policy remains more of a domestic issue because the leading industrial nations—either collectively or individually—have not been able to come to grips with the international politics of oil and other energy supplies. We turn now to each case study.

Johnson, Nixon, and the ABM

In contrast to crisis decision-making, more traditional security decisions such as the military budget and the development of new weapons systems typically involve a multiplicity of actors, different perceptions among the actors as to what is at stake, and a much longer time span in the decision-making process. There is a multiplicity of actors by the very nature of program policies. Such policies are initially developed in the bureaucracies, are sometimes of concern to interest groups (which might be helped or hurt economically by the decision made), and are finally resolved by Congress through an appropriations bill. In the first of the specific program decisions we are considering—Johnson's decision in 1967 to proceed with the procurement of some long-term lead items on an antiballistic missile system—the actors involved included not only the President, his advisers, and other members of the inner circle such as the secretaries of defense and state and the Chairman of the Join Chiefs of Staff, but also lower-level offices in Defense, members of Congress, and (albeit, indirectly) public opinion.[1]

Each actor saw the stakes differently. Indeed, Johnson was more of a neutral actor leaning against deployment. The strongest opposition to an ABM came from Secretary of Defense McNamara. Along with Secretary of State Rusk and the ACDA, he felt that an American decision to deploy an ABM would mean a spiraling and costly arms race that would also destroy all chances for stabilization of the American-Soviet deterrent balance. McNamara contended that an American decision to deploy the ABM would virtually preclude any possibility of initiating arms limitations talks with the Soviets. While Johnson did not agree with McNamara on the likely effects of deployment,[2] he was willing to postpone a final decision on the ABM until he had received word from the Soviets on the possibility of such talks.

McNamara was also skeptical of the feasibility of the proposed ABM. Early versions of the ABM, the Nike-Zeus system was rejected because of its inadequate radar facilities, and the Nike-X had been challenged on similar grounds (among others). The defense secretary, however, was in a minority position within his own department on the question of feasibility. The Pentagon's Offices of Defense Research and Engineering and Systems Analysis both supported deployment. Within Defense, only the Office of International Security Affairs joined McNamara in opposition to the ABM.

The principal supporters of the ABM were the services and key members of the Senate Armed Services Committee. In contrast to most defense budget situations, the ABM debate found the three services united in their support for a weapons system.[3] While the Army, Navy, and Air Force each "saw a different face of ABM and reached different conclusions,"[4] the very fact of this interservice agreement is worth noting. In the past, McNamara had used divisions among the services to prevail on issues of defense spending. However, the united front forced the secretary to appeal above the services directly to the President. General Earle Wheeler, Chairman of the Joint Chiefs of Staff, made no attempt to hide his support for the ABM. Even when the President was on record as opposed to the system, Wheeler made public statements supporting it and criticizing the administration.

Supporting the services were several senior members of the Senate Armed Services Committee, including the chairman, Richard B. Russell, and such other influential members as John Stennis and Henry Jackson. These senators were supporters of Johnson's Vietnam policy and had been friends of the President when he was Democratic leader in the Senate during the Eisenhower administration. Indeed, Johnson had served with them on Armed Services and trusted their judgment. He was particularly close to Russell.

In arguing their case, proponents and adversaries often stressed different factors. Supporters stressed the fact that the Soviets had already developed such a system, that it threatened America's deterrent capacity, and that the ABM would save American lives. The issue of arms limitation talks was not paramount to them. To the extent that they even considered this issue, they argued that an ABM would provide the Americans with an extra bargaining chip in any negotiations on mutual defensive weapons limitations. Opponents, on the other hand, were less concerned about the possibility of Soviet possession of ABMs than they were about the potential for a new arms race. Another factor that concerned the opponents more than the supporters was the price tag. Estimates of the cost of an ABM system ranged from $30 billion to $40 billion. By 1966, even with an unusually large congressional majority, Johnson was experiencing difficulties mobilizing Congress to approve funding for many of the social welfare programs of his Great Society package. With a sharply reduced majority in Congress in 1967, even greater difficulties were anticipated. Many opponents of the ABM—and, indeed, even Johnson—realized that any increase in the military budget could come only at the expense of decreased spending for social welfare programs. Since most of the supporters of the ABM were opposed to Johnson's Great Society package, this aspect of the problem did not trouble them.

Johnson was thus torn between the arguments made by his friends in the Senate that the ABM was needed for the national security and those of McNamara and Rusk that the system was likely to initiate a new arms race. Therefore, he was willing to postpone a decision. Two factors seem to have been particularly important in this respect. The first was that Johnson believed that an arms limitation agreement with the Soviets could change the opinion of the public—and of historians at a later date—on the foreign policy of his administration. Johnson's years in office had been dominated by a seemingly endless war in Vietnam, and the President was hoping for a major breakthrough in some area of international reconciliation. Second, the President wanted to avoid, if at all possible, a direct break with McNamara. The two men were already at odds over Vietnam, but the President still valued his secretary of defense too highly to reject his advice out of hand. Since McNamara viewed the ABM choice as a direct confrontation between himself and the Joint Chiefs of Staff, a decision to deploy the system would be taken as a direct rebuff to the secretary. On the other hand, a negative decision on the ABM would alienate key senators who might proceed to wreak havoc with Johnson's domestic program. While these senators probably opposed much of the Great Society legislation anyway, a negative decision on the ABM might serve to antagonize them still further and thus provoke a sustained effort to cut back domestic programs. Not surprisingly, then, Johnson's instincts "led him to search for a compromise which would minimize the damage to his relations with his advisers."[5]

Ideally, the President would have preferred to let the supporters and opponents reach some kind of compromise among themselves. This was very much the Johnson style—that of the ultimate bargainer—which had been responsible for his tremendous popularity as Senate Democratic leader. It was also the style of Johnson's political mentor, Franklin D. Roosevelt. This course was simply not possible. As Hilsman has argued, a major consequence of "the multiplicity of constituencies involved in [foreign and defense] policy making is that more and more problems are thrown into the White House. It is only the presidency . . . that can consider the whole broad range of interconnections between conflicting interests and demands."[6] The President's only recourse was to make a "minimal decision," one that would not identify either side as a "winner" or a "loser" but would represent some compromise among the competing positions.[7]

The critical question thus became: What would be the nature of this compromise? At least a part of the answer became clear in a meeting Johnson and McNamara had with Soviet Premier Kosygin at Glassboro, New Jersey, in June 1967. Johnson pressed the Soviets for a date for the opening of arms limitation talks but did not receive an answer. Kosygin, in a meeting with both Johnson and McNamara, described the Soviet ABM as a defensive weapon and therefore unobjectionable, hence not a proper subject for arms limitation talks. McNamara's principal objection to the ABM had now been refuted by the Soviets. Consequently, Johnson no longer saw the American ABM as a possible stumbling block to beginning arms limitation talks.[8]

The President was also worried about the possible electoral consequences of a negative decision on the ABM. In late 1966, Michigan Governor George Romney—then believed to be the front-runner for the Republican presidential nomination in 1968—discussed the ABM gap with the Soviet Union on national television. He also indicated that it would be a major issue in the 1968 campaign. Other Republicans made similar charges in Congress. Johnson wanted to quell these complaints. As the vice-presidential candidate on the 1960 ticket that had charged the Eisenhower administration with neglecting the problem of an offensive missile gap, he knew that the issue could be powerful. And it could lead to his own defeat.

Even though the pressure for an ABM from the military and Congress far outweighed the countervailing pressure from McNamara and Rusk, the President was still committed to seeking a compromise. Although the secretary of defense understood the pressures for a decision to deploy the ABM, he remained steadfastly opposed to an anti-Soviet system, which he believed might affect the possibility of an arms control agreement. On September 18, 1967, McNamara announced the administration's opposition to any major ABM deployment:

> The [Soviet ABM] system does not impose any threat to our ability to penetrate and inflict massive and unacceptable damage on the Soviet Union. In other words, it does not presently affect in any significant manner our assured destruction ability. . . . While we have substantially improved our technology in the field, it is important to understand that none of the systems at the present or foreseeable state-of-the-art would provide an impenetrable shield over the United States . . . the $40 billion is not the issue. The money in itself is not the problem. . . . The point for us to keep in mind is that should the [arms limitations] talks fail—and the Soviets decide to expand their present modest ABM deployment into a massive one—our

response must be realistic . . . if the Soviets elect to deploy a heavy ABM system, we must further expand our sophisticated offensive forces.[9]

In brief, not only could an ABM not protect the public, but it could be overcome by saturating the defensive missiles' capability with a large number of ICBMs. If the United States could overcome a Soviet ABM system in this way, presumably the Russians could do the same should the United States deploy a "thick" shield. On other hand, McNamara came out for an anti-Chinese ABM—in case the Chinese, who were at the time perceived as militantly ideological and revolutionary, might be just irrational enough to attempt a nuclear attack upon the United States or its allies in Asia. The new system, called the Sentinel, would have as its major function the defense of American cities.

McNamara's speech clearly indicated that any American reaction to an increased Soviet buildup of the ABM system would be countered by an American increase in offensive missiles. This was a major victory for the secretary against the Joint Chiefs of Staff and ABM supporters in Congress, who favored the more extensive (and more expensive) ABM. The projected cost of the Sentinel was approximately $5 billion. The very fact that McNamara made the speech announcing the administration's support for the ABM indicated that he had by no means suffered a major defeat on this issue. He could view the President's decision as leaving open the possibility that the system would never be deployed at all if the Russians would agree to a mutual defense weapons limitation. The administration had *not* come out in support of deployment, but only for increased funding for the procurement of certain ABM parts, which would require a long lead time. On the other hand, the very fact that the administration had publicly changed its position represented a victory for ABM supporters in Congress and the Joint Chiefs. Proponents of a more extensive "thick" system viewed the administration's change in position as a hopeful sign and expected that they could accomplish their goal later.

Johnson had indeed made another minimal decision, a decision which, on the one hand, postponed the real decision, and, on the other hand, left each side feeling it had won a partial victory. This is evident from McNamara's arguments on behalf of the Sentinel. The interjection of the Chinese threat into the argument seemed to belie the administration's real reasons for supporting the ABM. The Chinese nuclear threat was hardly overwhelming in the fall of 1967: The first atomic bomb was detonated by China in 1964, the next one a year later. In 1965, the Chinese were reported to have detonated two hydrogen bombs, and a third in the spring of 1967. For someone as committed to programs with demonstrated cost-effectiveness, it certainly appeared strange to find McNamara proposing a multi-billion dollar system to oppose what was essentially a minor threat. Clearly, the real purpose of stressing the anti-Chinese nature of the American ABM was to restrict the overall scope of any possible future deployment and especially to prevent the creation of a "thick," anti-Soviet shield. McNamara was particularly anxious to impress the distinction between an anti-Soviet and an anti-Chinese system on American public opinion and mobilize support for the "thin" system. He was also very concerned to communicate this difference to the Kremlin, lest it continue to oppose strategic arms limitation talks and initiate a new offensive arms spiral. Another argument in McNamara's speech is worth noting: the secretary's statement that "the $40 billion is not the issue." Why was it not the issue? Not because Johnson would have been willing to spend that much for an ABM if necessary, but rather because the Sentinel decision no longer required massive outlays of funds. The new program did not dramatically increase the level of defense spending; the estimated cost of $5 billion would not become a major issue until a decision to deploy the Sentinel was made.

The critical point is that McNamara's speech did not address the main arguments of either proponents or opponents of the ABM: The threat of the Soviet ABMs was simply denied in two sentences; the impact of the new system on the potential for arms limitation talks was not even mentioned; the question of national priorities was barely alluded to (by the reference to the $40-billion cost of Nike-X), and the feasibility of the Sentinel system was totally ignored. Under a rational actor model, we would have expected these questions to form the basis for a speech either accepting or rejecting the ABM. They did not. Instead, a side issue—the Chinese "threat"—was made the central concern. Neither the proponents nor the opponents had used this argument in earlier debates over the ABM. The introduction of this argument for the Sentinel clearly represented an attempt to find an *ex post facto* rationale to fit a decision that had been arrived at on the basis of domestic political considerations rather than strategic ones. The Chinese nuclear threat was clearly a "minimal" problem which could be solved by a "minimal" decision. The compromise Johnson was able to reach was hardly satisfactory to any side—but compromises never are. By letting participants outside the executive branch play a major role in determining defense policy, the President had skillfully maneuvered a compromise that neither the supporters nor the opponents of the ABM could reject without risking further losses.

The ABM decision under Johnson thus is a good example of the bureaucratic model. There was, indeed, a multiplicity of actors in the decision-making arena. In contrast to crisis decision-making, not only did Congress play a role on the ABM, but the legislative branch was able to reverse the position the President himself had held. Second, the program decision took a considerable amount of time to be reached. An ABM system had first been proposed in the mid-1950s; Johnson did not act until 1967. Many program policies are resolved in shorter periods: Since the defense budget is annual, at least some programs are reevaluated in a relatively short time span. On the other hand, domestic programs may take even longer: Comprehensive federal aid to education and a system of government-subsidized health care for the aged had each been under consideration in Congress for more than fifty years before Johnson maneuvered them through the Eighty-Ninth Congress in 1965. And finally, the various actors may view the stakes in different ways, a situation which makes compromises possible and minimal decisions likely. The 1967 decision by Johnson let McNamara still believe that the arms race could be limited and let the Joint Chiefs still hope for an expanded ABM. As in all bargaining situations that are successfully terminated, neither side saw itself as a clear loser. In the process of reaching a compromise, however, the value-maximizing approach of the rational actor model was left behind. The 1967 decision did not appear to maximize any of the original values posed by either supporters or opponents of the ABM. Indeed, factors that have no place in a strategic decision made on the basis of rational calculations—such as domestic political considerations—appear to have been dominant in the bureaucratic politics of the Johnson decision.

Perhaps somewhat ironically, Nixon used the Johnson decision to proceed with an ABM to press for a larger system, designed to protect American missiles, two years later. Less than two months after he took office, Nixon proposed the expanded Safeguard system and provoked a sharp confrontation with the Democratic Congress. The President presented the issue as one involving key stakes in our confrontation with the Soviet Union (not China) and refused to bargain at all with the Congress. The decision was presented as the conclusion of a rational calculus and thus the debate in the Congress followed the lines of the rational actor model much more than the bureaucratic politics model.[10] Senator Edward M. Kennedy led the opposition and both sides gathered testimony (and had books published) on why the ABM should (not) be constructed. The debate grew acrimonious and a close vote, at least in the Senate, was expected. So much media attention was given to the debate that Gallup polls taken on April 6 and July 27, 1969 indicated that 69 percent of the respondents had either heard about or read about the ABM—a rather high figure. The surveys also showed, however, that many people were confused about the issue: Only 40 percent of each sample had formed an opinion on the Safeguard system.

Nixon thus employed the decision that Johnson thought he avoided, at least temporarily—building an ABM system. Despite the heated arguments from the Kennedy camp, Nixon easily prevailed in the House (223–141) and narrowly won with a two-vote margin in the Senate on August 6, 1969. The overall coalitions had not changed markedly from the indications of support and opposition in 1967. But the ABM saga was not over.

The strategic arms limitation talks with the Soviets were on the agenda. The United States had no major offensive weapons system for a trade-off at a time when the Russians were leading in the arms race in the number of missiles they were producing. ICBMs with multiple warheads, known as MIRVs, specifically rejected for bargaining purposes because it was seen as the major way of keeping up with Russia's growing number of missiles. (In fact, Moscow in SALT I rejected a trade-off between a reduction of a U.S. *defensive* weapon for a Soviet reduction of *offensive* ICBMs.) Furthermore, U.S. deterrence depended upon the "assured destruction" of Soviet society—its cities, industries, and population. It would have been suicide if they launched an attack on the United States. They, however, had already installed ABMs around Moscow. It was not known whether Moscow was working on a more effective second-generation ABM and might in the future extend it to protect Russia's other major urban areas. But the United States could not presume that this might not occur, for obviously, if they could protect the majority of their population, the American threat to retaliate and destroy Russia as a viable society would lose its credibility. Thus an ABM trade-off was a more likely possibility. SALT I in 1972 did exactly that, limiting each side to two ABM sites for a total of 200 ABMs; in 1974, this figure was cut in half and, for all practical purposes, this indicated the end of ABM defenses and presumably the continuing ability of each superpower to destroy the other's population centers.

In 1975, however, the Democratic leadership in the Congress charged President Ford with spending too much on defense and not enough on social programs and voted accordingly to scrap the one remaining site. Thus, domestic political considerations led to a governmental decision to undo the entire system. Of those voting in 1969, only eight members of the Senate had changed their position from the ballot on the Nixon proposal—five became pro-ABM and all but one were Western Democrats, whose states benefited from contracts and subcontracts for the system. Consider the different perspective (predictable from the bureaucratic politics model) of Senator Quentin Burdick (D., N.D.), a 1969 opponent of the ABM. Dismantling the lone system, however, would mean that Langdon's population would drop from its boom level of 4800 to 2800; it was 2300 before ABM installation began. While North Dakota's other senator, Milton Young, was a strong supporter of the ABM from the beginning, Burdick's position changed to protect the interests of his constituents. By 1975, most of the original opponents of the ABM were more convinced than ever that the program was nothing but a large pork-barrel program for the military. Supporters maintained that the military value of the system was still critical. What accounted for the change in the outcome of the Senate vote? The answer is straightforward: Democrats had picked up several new seats since the 1969 vote and what turnover there was went overwhelmingly against the ABM. The ABM had served the purpose intended for it by Johnson and could be scrapped. A major irony is that the Democrats who provided the margin to dismantle the system had run for office opposing the policies in international politics that Johnson had espoused.

Thus, a defense system which initially (according to the Nixon plan) would have defended many sites was reduced to a bargaining chip in arms limitation talks with the Soviets and then ultimately dismantled in a political battle between the President (and some Democratic senators whose states benefitted from the program) and a Congress controlled by the opposition party. The ultimate fate of the Nixon ABM program was determined not by strategic considerations, but by political ones not fundamentally different from those which led Johnson to his "minimal decision" to deploy a smaller force. There remains, interestingly, talk of a new ABM system which is more reliable than the old one; as the arms race with the Soviets builds up once more and Soviet missiles increasingly threaten the survival potential of American missiles, the ABM is being revived as a possible way of protecting these missiles from a potential Soviet first strike.[11]

Carter and SALT II

The Carter administration, when it came to power in 1977, was committed to the continuation of SALT negotiations.[12] It confronted three problems inherited from its predecessor. One was that SALT I had not been able to provide an agreement on a limitation on offensive weapons. The two powers had simply agreed to "freeze" the numbers of ICBMs each side had in early 1972. The Soviets by then had several hundred more ICBMs than did the United States. The United States, however, had already begun MIRVing or multiplying the number of warheads on many of its ICBMs; and since in addition intercontinental bombers, in which the United States had a considerable quantitative lead, were excluded from SALT I, a rough equality or parity existed. This agreement was to be an interim one, to be replaced after five years by a long-term agreement. The Senate, prodded by Senator Henry Jackson, had gone on record demanding that in SALT II, the United States should not accept force levels lower than those of the Soviet Union.

Second, the strategic balance had changed. Soviet technology, which in the past had not been as sophisticated as that of the United States, had relied on very large missiles. Their size compensated for their inaccuracy. Their warheads were sufficiently big so that when detonated they could destroy their targets even though they might hit a mile or more away from target. The United States concentrated on smaller, more sophisticated and more accurate missiles. However, once the Soviets had overtaken the United States in the number of missiles, the fact that they could carry more "throw-weight" turned out to be very advantageous.

Specifically, as the Soviets began to MIRV their new generation of missiles after SALT I, they could potentially place more and far bigger warheads on them than the United States could on its ICBMs; the Soviets also caught up with the United States in the accuracy of its missile terminal guidance systems. These much larger warheads, plus this enhanced accuracy, meant that Soviet ICBMs could strike at America's land-based missiles. Thus while a U.S. *Minuteman* missile carried three 180,000-ton warheads (later doubled in yield), the USSR's SS−18 carried eight separate megaton (million-ton) range warheads, and the SS−19 six separate 360,000-ton warheads. The SS−18, indeed, had the potential to carry 34 to 40 smaller warheads! There was, therefore, great concern in Washington that the Soviets might be seeking a first-strike counterforce capability rather than a second-strike or retaliatory capability against cities. The experts agreed that the U.S. deterrent would become very vulnerable in the 1980s; theoretically, 95 percent of the land-based *Minutemen* could be destroyed in a first strike.

Third, President Ford had laid the basis for SALT II with the Vladivostok agreement which set an upper ceiling of 2400 launchers (including bombers, land-based ICMBs, and sea-launched ballistic missiles or SLBMs), of which 1320 could be MIRVs. While high, the 2400 ceiling was lower than the total number of Soviet ICBMs and SLBMs, although higher than the U.S. force levels. But SALT II evaded Ford, although he was on the verge of an agreement. The major reason was that in seeking nomination for the presidency in 1976 he had inherited, after Nixon had withdrawn in disgrace after Watergate, his principal challenger—Ronald Reagan—came from the party's right wing. Reagan attacked détente vigorously and Ford, who barely scraped by to beat Reagan for the Republican nomination, dropped the word détente entirely from his political vocabulary, replacing it with the phrase "peace through strength," and hid Kissinger for a while; in the process, Ford did not dare sign SALT II. (In fairness, it ought to be added that Democratic candidate Carter too talked of détente as if it were a giveaway and that the United States had not been tough enough and received better agreements.)

Once in office Carter, who was personally committed to SALT, had to decide whether to sign a SALT II agreement on the basis of the Vladivostok guidelines. Indeed, he had sent word to Moscow before his election that if he became president, he would quickly sign SALT II on the basis of Vladivostok. Once in power, however, Carter and his national security assistant, Zbigniew Brzezinski, decided to go for deeper cuts. This was to be the first of many changes of mind by Carter which over the years were to irritate the Soviets, as well as allies, and give the President a reputation abroad for unreliability. A principal reason for the reversal in this instance was that the two men wished to separate themselves from Kissinger, whose personality and achievements loomed over his successors. Should they now sign an agreement whose outlines had already been negotiated by him? They appeared to want to show they could do better than Kissinger—and, by implication, their Republican predecessors. The latter had accepted ceilings that were at or about U.S. force levels. Instead of these high ceilings, they would make "real cuts." Such personal and partisan considerations were reinforced by the new secretary of defense and others concerned with the Soviets' growing first-strike capability and achievement of nuclear superiority. Deep cuts in Soviet ICBMs, allowing them only as many MIRVs as we had (550 Minutemen were MIRVed), and cutting their huge SS−18s down from the 300 allowed under SALT I to 150, would presumably decrease the Soviet threat to America's 1000 ICBMs (90 percent of which might be destroyed by a Soviet first strike). The new secretary of state, Cyrus Vance, thought that the Soviets would not go for such a proposal. They had agreed to the Vladivostok ceilings and their entire thinking and negotiating posture was tied to Vladivostok. The Soviet bureaucracy would reject the sudden change of terms that had already been agreed upon. The new chief of ACDA and chief SALT II negotiator, Paul Warnke, added that if the Soviets rejected the new Carter deep cuts, and the United States then fell back to the Vladivostok position, the administration would be criticized for retreating.

The Soviets, angered by Carter's early and frequent human rights pronouncements which they saw as largely aimed at them, quickly rejected the deep cuts as a "cheap and shoddy" maneuver to seek a unilateral U.S. advantage. The administration, first defiantly declaring that it would "hang tough," finally changed its mind again and retreated. The final agreement, initialed by Brezhnev and Carter in the spring of 1979, twenty-nine months after Carter had come into office, was based on Vladivostok. It was an agreement that the President could presumably have had earlier which, in turn, would then have allowed him to negotiate major reductions in SALT III. In any event, under the six year agreement signed two and one-half years after Carter had taken office, each side would have 2400 launchers, to be cut down to 2250 by December 31, 1981 (Kissinger had already gained this Soviet concession too). All sorts of subceilings were agreed to: 1320 MIRVs, of which 1200 were to MIRVed ICBMs and SLBMs (which meant that the United States gained an advantage: 120 of its B−52 bombers could each be armed with 20 long-range air-launched cruise missiles, which the Soviets did not yet possess; each B−52 so armed would count as one MIRV); 820 MIRVed ICBMs, of which 308 could be the SS−18 (this 820 subceiling was an effort to limit any attempt by the Soviets, who had most of their throw-weight on their ICBMs, to place even more of their warheads on their big land-based missiles). But the details of the entire SALT II treaty and its pros and cons need concern us less than what happened to the treaty once it was submitted to the Senate for its "advise and consent." Before

President Carter could sign the treaty and ratify it, he needed the Senate's two-thirds approval. Whether he would receive that consent was in doubt from the beginning.

The first hurdle was the treaty procedure, rightfully called by two critics the "treaty trap." An earlier secretary of state, John Hay, had once likened the fate of an administration seeking Senate approval of a treaty to a bull going into an arena: "no one can say just how or when the blow will fall, but one thing is certain—it will never leave the arena alive."[13] It is not that the Senate has defeated most treaties; indeed, only eleven treaties have failed to gain the Senate's consent since 1789. It has, however, defeated a few important ones, the most famous of which was undoubtedly the Versailles Treaty ending World War I and the establishment of the League of Nations. Worse, the possible defeat of a treaty hangs over any administration, making this a very arduous and risky process.

The treaty process was written into the Constitution at a time when the Founding Fathers conceived of the Senate as a wise, deliberate, appointed, and presumably conservative body, not a popularly elected House reflecting the ups and downs of popular passion. In a democracy which does almost everything else by a majority vote—including the declaration of war and the appropriation of billions for defense—the two-thirds provision stands out. It could even be said to be undemocratic in two senses. One, the Senate is composed of two senators from each state regardless of population. This means that the one-third plus one vote could come largely from rural America, representing a minority of the nation's population. Two, the extraordinary size of the Senate majority allows a minority of senators to block a treaty favored by a majority of their colleagues. Not surprisingly, the treaty trap has tempted presidents to either bypass the Senate with executive agreements or simply to do nothing. This latter phenomenon has been referred to as the "pre-natal effect" or "anticipatory reaction"; fearful of what might happen to a treaty, they kill it off before it is born. In the post-Vietnam era, while the Congress has been reasserting itself, executive agreements to bypass the legislature were not in favor. Indeed, when President Carter once floated the idea that he would sign SALT II as an executive agreement and then seek majority approval in both houses by means of a joint resolution, he was quickly rebuffed.

The problem is clearly that in a Senate of 100, it takes only 34 votes to defeat a treaty. On any important treaty, there is likely to be some opposition. It does not take many additional votes to add up to 34. Indeed, the treaty provision places a premium on opposition. The incentive to come out against the treaty is strong because if the administration desperately wants Senate approval, it will have to "buy" those votes by satisfying senators' pet projects (a dam, nuclear power plant, a new weapons system, or some other appropriation). The extra votes—those needed in excess of a simple majority—may be sought not only among senators from one's own party but also among the opposition. Given the lack of party cohesion in the United States, mobilizing support from the opposition party is hardly novel; but a treaty may need more than the usual amount of support from the out-party. This presents an obvious problem for an opposition which hopes to become the in-party by criticism of an administration's record. It may be patriotic to support a treaty but will it not also be politically suicidal for the opposition party? It is the in-party which will claim and gain most of the popular approval for a treaty perceived to be beneficial to the nation.

The international repercussions of the treaty process are even worse. The fact that a president who has negotiated a treaty on behalf of the United States may be repudiated by the Senate, undermines the president's prestige and authority to speak for the United States to the world, weakens America's leadership ability in the world, and raises serious questions among both friends and foes about both the desirability of negotiating with the United States and the reliability of this country. Having arrived at a mutually satisfactory agreement, the United States is presumably thereafter bound to live up to the provisions of that agreement. In which other country can the nation's chief of government be repudiated by another part of the same government? SALT II had been negotiated by three U.S. presidents—Nixon, Ford, and Carter—suggesting both the seriousness and continuity of U.S. purposes. How assured can other nations, especially those with whom the United States has negotiated a treaty, feel that once agreement has been attained, it will be final and receive Senate consent—rather than being renegotiated if the Senate attaches amendments to the treaty? One has only to wonder how Americans would view a treaty with the Soviets which, once negotiated and signed, Moscow would then either want to change or repudiate. Said a Soviet observer:

> . . . With whom in America can we have dealings? If the President needs to coordinate his actions and stand with the Congress, why isn't this done before any international agreement is concluded? Is it really so . . . that for more than six years of talks the U.S. authorities have been unable to decide among themselves what in SALT II they can agree to and what they cannot?. . . Opinions in our government on this or that question may differ, too. But when our representative at negotiations agrees to something, he does so on behalf of the country. . . . In the case of the United States, however, it appears that agreement with the Administration even having a majority in the Congress often counts for little. It comes out that having reached agreement with the Administration, one ought then to enter into separate external relations with the American Congress, and renegotiate, as it were, the agreement reached.[14]

Whether SALT II would finally have received Senate approval or not, had the Soviets not invaded Afghanistan in late December 1979, will never be known. But most observers felt that the reason President Carter "temporarily" withdrew the treaty from Senate consideration at that time was not to punish Moscow for its aggression but to save himself from probable defeat and a stunning political setback in the Senate. From the time the treaty was submitted to the Senate, if not before, the administration appeared on the defensive. The heart of the opposition came from the Armed Services Committee. Although the treaty did not fall within its main jurisdiction, ten of its members issued a report very critical of SALT II over the opposition of its venerable chairman, something which could never have happened a decade earlier. Jackson, one of the committee's members, was one of the Senate's most respected members and known as its leading expert on strategic affairs. Indeed, Jackson had been a strong advocate of deep cuts for SALT II and, asked by Carter, had submitted his guidelines for the SALT negotiations to the President. Carter was aware that he needed Jackson's support. If he decided to adopt parts of the senator's proposal, Jackson would bring with him hard-line senators and the JCS. When Carter had to retreat to the Vladivostok ceilings, Jackson accused the President of retreating, as Paul Warnke had predicted. Indeed, Warnke's appointment as director of ACDA and, in that capacity, chief SALT negotiator, had been an early bitter battle in the Senate, forecasting trouble for the administration on SALT II. Forty senators—six more than needed to defeat a treaty—had voted against Warnke because he was felt to be too soft on arms control; that is, he would not bargain hard enough (58 senators voted for his appointment). The signal sent to the White House was clear: Take a firm stance during the negotiations to get a fair and equitable agreement. The Warnke vote "was a statement of the Senate's determination to exercise independent judgment in assessing the SALT II accords."[15]

As the treaty was being concluded and about to reach the Senate for its consent, the senators could be divided into three main groupings. About 20 senators were completely opposed to any treaty with the Soviet Union; 15 additional senators could be classified as arms control skeptics. Approximately 45 senators could be classified as arms controllers because of their support of the SALT negotiations and belief that an agreement constraining the arms race was preferable to an unrestrained one.[16] A third category of around twenty senators were the swing votes who would be wooed intensely by the administration to make up the needed 67 votes, and by the opposition to stop the vote short of the magic number.

Those opposed to, or skeptical about, SALT II were so because of their anxiety about the mixture of expansionist Soviet-Cuban behavior in Africa and the growing Soviet military arsenal. The Soviets had since SALT I replaced their old missiles with an entire new generation of missiles. Although the SS−19 was considered by the Defense Department as the more dangerous missile because of its greater accuracy, the critics focused on the huge SS−18 and the administration's failure to get Moscow to accept far fewer than just over 300 heavy missiles. By contrast,

Carter had cancelled the B−1 bomber intended as a replacement for the aging B−52, slowed down the development of the new Trident submarines and the Trident I and II SLBMs, remained undecided about the development of a new, larger, mobile MX (X stood for experimental) land-based missile to replace the increasingly vulnerable Minuteman, and had also cancelled—after seeming for a while to be unable to decide—the neutron bomb for NATO forces. SALT II, according to its critics, did not reverse what they saw as a strategic balance shifting in favor of the Soviet Union. The latter had the momentum while the American President cancelled and slowed down necessary replacements or improvements in U.S. weapons. This suggested that the President was unreliable on defense issues.

The great fear for the critics was that the Soviets might be tempted to attack U.S. ICBMs with only a fraction of their force once it was fully MIRVed and equipped with a more accurate terminal guidance system. Knowing that, Soviet policy-makers might try to exert pressure upon the United States, and an administration, knowing the U.S. deterrent's growing vulnerability, might feel compelled to comply with Soviet demands. Distrust of the Soviets was clearly the basic attitude of the critics. It was reflected on other issues as well: the verification of SALT, and the Soviet Backfire bomber (which the critics claimed was an intercontinental bomber, although Moscow denied this).

The treaty was to be managed on the Senate floor by the chairman of the Foreign Relations Committee, Senator Church; but its most effective proponent was the majority whip, Senator Alan Cranston (D., Cal.), who had earlier organized an informal study group of approximately twenty senators, mainly Democrats and arms control supporters, although not all were enthusiastically pro-SALT II. This group received briefings from the President's national security assistant, secretaries of state and defense, director of the CIA and others, and most of them took a major role in replying to the critics' views and presenting the administration's case for SALT II. Fundamentally, the argument was that SALT would advance U.S. security. There was little attempt to oversell the treaty. There were no claims, as with SALT I and Vladivostok, that it would "cap the arms race" or advance détente. The central question was whether the United States would be better or worse off if the treaty were rejected. The critics might wish to reject the treaty because it did not halve the number of SS−18s or include Backfire within the launcher ceiling of 2400; but would rejection enhance U.S. security or reduce it because without a treaty the Soviets could produce more SS−18s, as well as other ICBMs, place more warheads on these missiles, and build more bombers? The critics might also wish to link the treaty to Soviet behavior in various parts of the world, but would we not be hurting ourselves by such a linkage? Were we doing the Soviets a favor with SALT II, or were we signing the treaty because it strengthened our security, regardless of Soviet actions in Africa?

More positively, the SALT supporters could point to the fact that the Soviets would have to scrap several hundred older missiles to reach the 2250 ceiling; limit themselves to one new ICBM (the Soviets have tended to introduce several missiles of a new generation at a time); promise not to produce and deploy the SS–16 ICBM; and limit the number of warheads on ICBMs to ten and SLBMs to 14. In addition, they would not prevent the eventual deployment of the U.S. mobile MX missile (the limit on the number of warheads on Soviet missiles and the proposed deployment of 200 large U.S. MX missiles—to which Carter had finally agreed—would greatly reduce the vulnerability of the missile deterrent); would drop their insistence on a range limitation on the air-launched cruise missile; and would accept the exclusion from SALT II of American forward based systems, such as those in Europe and on aircraft carriers in the Mediterranean, North Sea, and Atlantic, from which aircraft with nuclear bombs could reach Russia. In short, SALT II would be an improvement over no SALT at all. "Passing the SALT" would avoid a new era of uncertainty, accelerated arms competition, and greater defense spending.

Not all senators were either for or against SALT II. There were some liberal senators strongly for arms control who felt that the high ceilings merely legitimated the arms race; SALT neither stopped nor reversed that race. Indeed, it speeded it up. To win sufficient support, as just noted, President Carter had committed himself to the MX at an estimated cost of $40 billion (some estimates were considerable higher). This group even threatened to vote against SALT. There were other senators, many of them members of the swing vote, who generally favored arms control as well, but shared the concern of many critics about the momentum of the arms race in which the Russians were doing the racing and the United States the ambling. The Carter budgets had not increased defense spending as rapidly as domestic expenditures, leading critics to charge that the U.S. strategic posture was vulnerable. Led by Senator Sam Nunn from Georgia, the same state which had produced the President, they wanted a commitment from the administration for a 5 percent real increase (over inflation) in the defense budget over the next five years. Nunn in his few years in the Senate had established a leading reputation in the military area, especially in conventional armaments. He was greatly concerned with NATO's conventional ability to defend itself now that the Soviets had neutralized America's strategic power. Such increases for "guns" rather than "butter," only further annoyed the liberals, intensifying their threat to defect.

The alignments were even more complicated by the 1980 presidential elections. Clearly, a SALT treaty would be a major achievement for the President; such a treaty could be equated with ensuring U.S. security and peace. But the year before a presidential election is not exactly ideal for important but controversial foreign policy moves if the aim is not to lose votes. The Republicans were annoyed with Carter's foreign policy. By and large, they considered it a failure. On the Warnke appointment, 28 of the

Senate's 38 Republicans had voted negatively. This early attack was significant, reflecting both partisanship and genuine concern about the trend of Carter's policies.[17] Simultaneously, they felt that Carter had acted as a strong partisan from the beginning, not only with the deep cuts proposal, but also since he did not give the Republicans the credit they felt they deserved for saving Carter from defeat several times—most importantly on the Panama Canal treaties. Bipartisanship thus was nearing its end; responsible partisanship, as Fred Iklé, former ACDA director under Ford and undersecretary of defense for policy under Reagan, argued in a new Republican journal called *Commonsense*, might well be "the best medicine with which to cure an ailing foreign policy."[18]

Minority Leader Howard Baker, whose support for the Panama Canal treaties had been critical to their successful passage, and upon whose support Carter had again counted for SALT II, had a special problem: He wanted to be president. His vote for Panama had angered many Republicans; if he wanted to be the party's nominee, he had to oppose SALT II. His rivals were all in favor of a treaty but with major changes. Baker thus found SALT II "seriously flawed" and expected to lead his party in the Senate into battle. Especially if the hearings could be televised, Baker would gain a great deal of publicity. The treaty was, therefore, bound to become a key political issue between the parties; and the debate would raise the issue of the broader U.S.-Soviet political context within which SALT II was occurring.

A simple rejection was one way of defeating the treaty. The Senate could also achieve this in another way; by amending the terms of the treaty. This would require renegotiation. The Soviets had already said they would not renegotiate. On the other hand, "understandings" or "interpretations" could be attached without killing the treaty. They clarified to the other contracting party the terms on which the treaty was being signed; they were unilateral declarations not requiring renegotiating. A "reservation," which may limit rather than clarify the consequences of a treaty is also possible; they may, of course, lead the other state to make their own reservations.

What was striking during the Senate debate, and even before, was the activity of pressure groups. The advocate of SALT II was a group called Americans for SALT composed of many distinguished former government officials; the group kept in close touch with the White House and was, in a sense, its unofficial arm. The principal spokesmen and lobbyists for the administration, of course, were the President, Brzezinski, and the secretaries of state and defense; Hamilton Jordan headed the overall public relations effort from the White House, assigning responsibilities to those who were to be in charge of congressional liaison, the general public, and the media. Even though they had no spokesman to match the prestige of the President, the anti-SALT groups, which organized earlier, were the most vocal and gained much of the publicity.

Unlike the administration, which waited until the agreement had been completed to start rallying support, the emerging treaty had already been heavily criticized by the anti-SALT forces. The American Conservative Union, the American Security Council, the Coalition for Peace Through Strength, and perhaps most prominently, the Committee on the Present Danger, whose members included many former high officials who had influence with conservative and moderate members of Congress, all possessed money. Mostly raised by conservative organizations and large corporate contributions, the amount could buy newspaper advertisements and time on television. The Coalition for Peace Through Strength reportedly estimated that it might spend $10 million to defeat SALT, and the American Conservative Union had already raised $400,000 by attacking the treaty over 350 television stations before the superpowers had even announced agreement on SALT II![19] Influential individuals, like President Ford and Henry Kissinger, initially kept quiet but later were critical of the agreement and/or what they perceived to be the Carter administration's weak resistance to the Soviet Union's expansionist policies.

The administration, then, was on the defensive from the very beginning. Even as the treaty came to the Senate floor, it did so only after coming out of the pro-SALT Foreign Relations Committee by a bare 9−6 vote. The President's prestige had sunk to a low point in 1979. As the economy grew worse in a year when oil prices rose 100 percent, the public perception of President Carter's competence declined sharply. This perception had preceded OPEC's frequent price rises and was independent of these increases, although not his management of the economy as inflation rose into the double-digit column—soaring up to 20 percent. The sense that the President held a job beyond his capabilities was not limited to domestic affairs; while the Camp David agreement preceding the Egyptian-Israeli peace treaty brought the President great acclaim, this foreign policy achievement was the exception. The normalization of relations with China, the Panama Canal treaties, and SALT II gained Carter few points in the public opinion polls. By the time of SALT II, it was clear that the President was going to be challenged for the renomination by a member of his own party, Senator Kennedy, who characterized the administration foreign policy as one of "lurching from crisis to crisis." The Kennedy name had long possessed a magic and wide appeal. Reportedly, many senators and congressmen appealed to Kennedy to run; they felt that running with Carter they might go down to defeat. Carter, by the time he was halfway through his first term, stood at a lower popular rating than had Richard Nixon at a comparable point. Kennedy leading the Democratic ticket would be more likely to aid their reelection.

Carter lost further ground when intelligence reports sighted a Soviet combat brigade in Cuba. He had been cruising down the Mississippi River, relaxing as well as campaigning, followed by a vacation at his home in Plains, Georgia. Instead of releasing the information and leading the discussion of its meaning and what it would do about it, the administration informed the Chairman of the Senate Foreign Relations Committee, Senator Church, normally a dove, who was running for reelection in Idaho. So Church took the initiative with a hawkish stance, denouncing the Soviet move and demanding that the Senate put off negotiations on Salt II until Moscow had removed the brigade. He was soon followed by Senator Richard Stone (D., Fla.), also preparing to run for reelection in a state very conscious of Cuba's presence because of its proximity. Carter was caught by surprise and followed suit, calling the Cuban situation "unacceptable." Since he did not want another missile crisis type of confrontation, which was hardly warranted by the brigade anyway (compared to the missiles), he had to retreat from his publicly taken stance and accept Soviet reassurance that the brigade was a training brigade taking its regular field exercises.

The episode seemed to be another example of a President not in charge, and his reputation went down a few more notches. Thus, an issue that did not affect the strategic balance almost torpedoed an issue of far greater priority because of the administration's ineptness, and the President, still short of the needed votes, probably lost one or two more. Above all, the administration lost time—about a month—while SALT II was caught up in the larger issue of Soviet policy, a linkage Carter had resisted from the beginning of his administration; Afghanistan came shortly thereafter. By raising the issue of the Soviet brigade, two senators, who went down to defeat in 1980, cost Carter four weeks and may have destroyed the President's final chance for gaining Senate approval. For the Soviet invasion of Afghanistan was too blatant an act. SALT II, a complex treaty negotiated over a two-year period, finely tuned to both United States and Soviet interests, thus went down to defeat. An election year was hardly a year for its revival unless Moscow pulled its troops out of Afghanistan—which it did not do.

The surprising thing is that despite all this the Carter administration almost gained Senate approval by commitments to: (1) a 5 percent real increase in defense spending for several years; (2) the $40 billion MX; and (3) a major reduction of strategic arsenals in SALT III (while in the meantime both sides would presumably improve their arms in an arms race which had already become qualitative rather than quantitative). President Carter had, to be sure, made more than his share of mistakes, including the initial decision to go for deep cuts rather than sign SALT on the basis of Vladivostok, and later the timing of the U.S. recognition of Communist China; each of these moves at the time annoyed Moscow and stalled negotiations. Carter could have had SALT II early on in his administration while his popularity and prestige were still high; the March proposals thwarted the effort and compelled him to retreat to the Vladivostok guidelines. In the final analysis, however, despite the President's errors, the fact remains that three administrations had negotiated with the Russians on SALT II and shaped the agreement, a reflection that they believed such a treaty was in the national interest. A majority existed in the Senate for the treaty, at least until Afghanistan, and public opinion polls consistently showed a sizable majority of the American people favored SALT II.

Yet the two-thirds Senate majority proved too high an obstacle to overcome. Admittedly, Carter's ways with the Congress, as on other issues, left something to be desired. The President's aides had no experience in Washington and, therefore, no experience in how to deal with the Congress. "They didn't know anything about the Congress, and they don't like the Congress. The price for their amateurism and hostility has been too high. They are learning, but maybe not soon enough," said a sympathetic Democrat who had served in the Congress for many years.[20] Some less sympathetic probably felt Carter never learned. "Carter does good things badly," admitted a member of the administration.[21] In addition, the President was consistently inconsistent, one day aligning himself with his secretary of state who believed that nothing must stand in the way of a SALT agreement and the next day sounding like his national security assistant who, concerned by Soviet behavior, was seeking to link SALT to Soviet foreign policy moves. On the one hand, SALT was important enough to stand by itself and, on the other, SALT was to be viewed as an integral part of the broader pattern of U.S.-Soviet relations.

Still, President Carter did a number of things that should have won him the necessary votes. First, as already noted, was soliciting Jackson's proposals for SALT II. Second, he appointed Lt. Gen. Edward Rowny as representative of the Joint Chiefs of Staff to the SALT delegation. This appointment was striking because Rowny was the first military man to be part of the SALT team and because the general was close to Senator Jackson. In short, Carter was trying to reassure the hard-liners that the Joint Chiefs of Staff would be fully represented. Well intended, this move backfired when Rowney resigned and became an articulate critic of Salt II during the Senate hearings (and was later appointed by Reagan as chief arms control negotiator for the U.S.). Third, Vice-President Mondale, more knowledgeable of the ways of Congress, appointed a group of 14 representatives and 25 senators to serve as advisers to the SALT delegation. Over a third of this group were to spend time with the U.S. delegation at the negotiations in Geneva, Switzerland, and participate in both formal and informal discussion with the Soviet delegation. Clearly, the administration was seeking to involve the Congress and strengthen some senators' vested interests in SALT II in hopes they would become its defendants and proponents in the upper chamber. Indeed, for the Senate as a whole, according to Steve Flanagan, senior Carter officials addressed SALT issues at almost fifty hearings from February 1977 to the 1979

Carter-Brezhnev Vienna summit where the SALT II treaty was signed. A variety of officials briefed senators on 140 occasions and Senate staffers about 100 times. Together, with informed contacts, administration officials kept the Senate fully informed of the state of negotiations.[22] And fourth, in early 1979, in an attempt to defuse conservative critics, Carter replaced Warnke with retired Lt. Gen. George Seignious. A member of a lobby opposed to SALT II, he became an articulate spokesman for the treaty and, unlike his more combative predecessor, got along well with both liberals and conservatives.[23]

The Soviets, of course, share the blame for the demise of SALT II and perhaps the continuing SALT negotiations. In 1972, SALT I had been acclaimed as symbolic of—and an essential ingredient in—détente. But as American-Soviet relations declined over the following years and SALT II dragged on, disillusionment with détente and arms control set in. Soviet actions, often with Cuban military help, in Angola, Ethiopia, South Yemen, and Afghanistan (where there was a Soviet-supported coup in 1978 before the later invasion by the Russian army) all appeared to American perceptions as attempts to exploit détente in Russia's favor; the rapid, enormous, and continuing growth of Soviet strategic as well as conventional power raised widespread concern over Soviet intentions and growing fears of what the Soviets might do with all this new military hardware. Thus by the time SALT II had been agreed upon, there had been a large-scale erosion of confidence in détente and expectations about its benefits. Still, despite all this, SALT II could have received Senate approval. The President, to be sure, was error-prone and proved to be a major obstacle to achieving his desire for SALT II by repeatedly annoying the Russians or the Senate with his decisions. In the final analysis, however, responsibility for the failure of SALT lies clearly with the Senate and the treaty process. A treaty which, from the time the negotiations had begun during the Nixon administration, had taken a total of 50 months to conclude (29 under Carter) and had been judged to be in the national interest of the United States by three presidents, a majority in the Senate, and public opinion, fell victim to the institutional conflict between executive and legislative branches of the federal government and the American political process.

Note also the impact of democratic elections. Confronting competition within the Republican party from Governor Reagan and the right, President Ford dropped détente and SALT II as a hot potato during his campaign for the renomination of his party; then, accused by Carter in the subsequent presidential contest of not having been tough enough with the Russians, he never picked up SALT II again, although Kissinger was close to a final agreement. In short, the year of a presidential election campaign tends to be a year in which controversial foreign policy issues are placed in limbo.

Then the "new team" takes over if the "outs" are elected. Another year may be wasted as the members of this team get to know one another, each other's strengths and weaknesses, how to get along with the bureaucracy and to what extent to trust and follow its experts' advice. The first year of a new administration then tends to be like a shakedown cruise for a new ship, to see how shipshape it is and to work out the bugs and make it a more efficient vessel. Almost invariably, this is the year of the mistakes, for instance, Kennedy's sanctioning of the Bay of Pigs operations and Carter's March SALT II proposals and simultaneous human rights attacks on the Soviet Union.

Only in the second and third years can a new administration expect to get much done. By year four, it is back to the presidential primaries and election. SALT II's demise, while obviously heavily influenced by the increasing disillusionment in the country with Soviet behavior as a result of Soviet-Cuban moves in Africa, Soviet-Vietnamese moves in Cambodia, and Soviet moves in Afghanistan, was also the result of U.S. domestic politics and the four-year presidential cycle. Carter's early moves lost critical time at a moment when a SALT II based on the Vladivostok guidelines could have been concluded and accepted by the Senate. By the time the treaty reached that body, election politics was already beginning and, given that only thirty-four votes were needed to defeat the treaty, the President's task became formidable although not impossible. The Soviet invasion of Afghanistan saved the President from a possible defeat in the Senate and ended hopes for SALT II. Ronald Reagan's election buried the treaty. Concerned with the Soviet influence during the 1970s and perceiving a shift in the strategic balance, the new administration was in no hurry to revive the SALT process. It did not wish to convey an eagerness to negotiate, which might raise the Russian price for a new treaty; instead, it preferred a new arms build-up as a prerequisite for resuming arms control negotiations. Condemning what it saw as its predecessor's use of arms control as a substitute for preserving American military strength, it insisted that any genuinely equitable and fair SALT treaty required greater American strategic capability.

Energy Policy: An Intermestic Issue

In examining energy policy at the international and national levels, we see the democratic dilemma in very straightforward terms. This intermestic policy clearly demonstrates bureaucratic/governmental politics to the ultimate degree, because virtually no participants see the stakes in the way others do and each is in some position to check the actions of most others. What we are studying, then, is nonpolicy making. There are no energy policies, but also there are too many such policies. We find ourselves in the situation of Buridan's ass, which found two bales of hay each so attractive that it starved to death trying to decide which one to devour. On energy policy, however, there are more actors and few mind starving others if that means more of a scarce commodity for themselves. Alas, it does not, however, and what we see is a classic lack of coordination across and within the developed nations—and particularly the United States. When so many actors become so intensively involved in an issue, conflict resolution becomes virtually impossible. When we have both national and international stakes involved, hopeless may be the only way to describe the situation which begs for international coordination.

In any event, in an increasingly interdependent world, the traditional distinctions between foreign and domestic policy-making break down. For many years, policy making on such areas as energy and food was viewed as domestic in scope. To be sure, there were some international implications of these policies—such as the Food for Peace program, trade quotas on specific food commodities particularly when American markets were weak, and the problem of taxing multinational oil companies. But most of the supplies of both energy and food were both produced and consumed in the United States. The energy imported from abroad was extremely cheap—oil was less than a dollar a barrel ten years ago—and plentiful. Thus, there was little concern with the foreign policy implications of resource policy.

The price explosion for oil which followed the outbreak of the Yom Kippur War in the Middle East in 1973, when the member nations of the Organization of Petroleum Exporting Countries (OPEC) imposed an embargo upon nations supporting the political position of Israel, set the stage for international concern for energy prices and availability. Furthermore, the effectiveness of the OPEC embargo brought to the fore the debate over what has been called the New International Economic Order, a demand that the wealthier nations of the West and the East redistribute their wealth and resources to the developing nations of the South (that is, south of the major industrialized nations of North America and Europe). These southern nations, often referred to as the Third World, maintained that the resources of the world rightfully belong to all of its citizens and not just to those who through luck of birthright lived longer and more fulfilling years in the prosperous nations. The ideas underlying the New International Economic Order have gained great currency in organizations such as the United Nations because there are far more poor nations than rich ones. Not surprisingly, the Western and Soviet-led worlds have been somewhat slower to embrace this concept. At least as reluctant have been the nations of OPEC—which includes such diverse states as Saudi Arabia, Kuwait, the United Arab Emirates, Libya, Iraq, Iran, Indonesia, Algeria, Venezuela, and Nigeria (among others) but not exporters such as Mexico, the Soviet Union, or Norway. Most of these countries were either quite poor by world standards or no better than "middle class" when the price explosion started and many still are in the early stages of industrialization and economic development. They had little incentive to redistribute their wealth to the poorest nations, although they have used some of their additional new revenue to provide foreign aid to needy and friendly countries, much as the United States, the Soviet Union, and China have done for many years. But the claims of the poorest nations for a share of oil revenues have generally fallen on deaf ears. This is no less true of OPEC countries than of the West and East, which have been reluctant to redistribute their advantages in agriculture and technology.

Cheap and plentiful energy prior to 1973 had the effect of making energy largely a domestic political issue and not a very salient one at that. The realization in that year that supplies of oil could be shut off *and* that once supplies were resumed the cost would more than quadruple, transformed energy politics into an international issue. There is some question as to whether the embargo of 1973 was intended more as a political or an economic weapon against the West.[24] In any event, it has had mixed results, with Japan and most of Western Europe tilting their foreign policies toward the Arab position in the Middle East and away from that of Israel. These nations are almost entirely dependent upon imported energy supplies and feel themselves particularly vulnerable to future cutoffs; they suffered, to the extent that any country did, more than the United States from the drastic cutback in production and exports from Iran after the revolution which overthrew the Shah. However, the United States, as well as some European nations (Norway and Denmark), refused to change their foreign policy stances in the Middle East and preferred to maintain cordial relations with many OPEC nations on the basis of shared economic development and strategic security issues. But oil politics is complicated indeed, and the United States, which now imports about half of its oil needs, is heavily dependent upon supplies from such radical Arab regimes as Algeria, Iraq, and Libya. Diplomatic relations with the former are at best restrained and the latter two nations do not even have full relations with the United States.

The United States, then, remains very vulnerable to a further embargo of imported oil and seems to be able to do little to prevent whatever price rises the OPEC nations, either individually or collectively, impose upon the consuming nations. The exporting countries have small incentives to maintain prices at existing levels since there is general agreement that oil is rapidly running out and most OPEC nations have economies largely based upon petroleum. Without oil exports, there would be little to distinguish OPEC nations from others in the Third World. As long as demand for oil remains high, prices will continue to rise. Perversely, as demand drops, prices still increase because the OPEC nations have a virtual monopoly on supplies for export. Some price "moderates" such as Saudi Arabia have worked to moderate the level of increases by mantaining high levels of production at *relatively* low costs for substantial periods of time, but even they seem unable or unwilling to stop the upward spiral of prices. The OPEC nations are all striving to industralize before supplies are exhausted.

It is almost beyond question that oil resources will be exhausted long before anyone had previously forecasted, despite huge new discoveries in Mexico and rumors of other sources elsewhere. The major industrial nations which are also oil producers are, with a few exceptions, experiencing substantial drops in domestic production. The Soviet Union, which has been an exporter (to its satellite nations, mostly in Eastern Europe), is expected to become a major importer before the end of the century. Production in the United States has been dropping steadily over the past decade. Unlike food, oil is not a renewable resource—there is not a "new crop" every year. Furthermore, while new areas of arable land can be created by irrigation or other technological breakthroughs, one cannot so easily will another oil field. Energy resources are clearly now an issue of international as well as domestic politics, what have been called "intermestic" policies.[25]

Several problems arise immediately for energy policy. First, there is no coordinated response among the importing nations to the development of OPEC as an international political-economic force. There is an association, the International Energy Agency, which has been established among Western nations to establish a joint strategy for reducing energy consumption and sharing burdens in the event of future shortages. However, domestic political considerations within each of the member nations have precluded effective action. No government can risk facing an electorate after it has agreed to give up some of its scarce energy resources to another and thereby inconvenienced its own citizens—who may have to wait in long gasoline lines (the United States) or, worse, be prohibited from driving at all on certain days (Holland). Many of the strains in establishing a coordinated energy strategy reflect weaknesses in Western alliance. Others, however, stem from economic realities: There are relatively few effective strategies for consuming nations to use against a cartel of producing countries. For economic considerations have tended to overcome political disputes within OPEC. For years Iran and Nigeria, friends of the United States, led the movement for sharp price increases. During the 1973 embargo and the 1979 energy shortage, oil continued to flow from the producing countries to other nations and individual suppliers on what has been called the "spot market," where prices are solely a function of what buyers are willing to pay. It is somewhat ironic that the "spot market" operates out of the Dutch port of Rotterdam, so that a nation which has been most diligent in curbing energy use to reduce consumption finds itself in the situation of being unable to control effectively the price of oil exported from its own ports.

Another problem in the world oil market is the inability of Western nations to agree upon a strategy for conservation. Every nation expects the others to make the major concessions; each has unique problems so that it is conserving as much as can be expected. Furthermore, there is little agreement either among or within nations as to which alternative technologies offer the most promise as an alternative to oil. The issue of nuclear energy has been a more hotly debated political question throughout Europe than in the United States and in most countries pronuclear pluralities or majorities have generally emerged. In several countries, notably Sweden and West Germany, there are powerful antinuclear political parties which threaten to hold the balance of power in the legislatures, thereby making energy choices even more difficult. The attractiveness of nuclear fission varies directly with the lack of other choices available to the country: Nuclear energy is less popular in Germany, where there are ample coal reserves, than in France or Israel, where there are not.

The nuclear issue not only involves questions of threats to health and even life, as the Three Mile Island accident in Pennsylvania demonstrated in 1979, but also with problems of international security: Nuclear energy means not only sources of electricity but also the potential for atomic or hydrogen bombs, as the West discovered in 1974 when India exploded an "atomic device" using materials supplied by Canada and the United States (under the Atoms for Peace program, which quickly died). The potential for controlling nuclear waste for commercial energy remains in doubt, but the problem of proliferation is very real. No one knows how many nations either have nuclear weapons now or will have this potential in the next decade, but the number could be as large as two dozen. Because of its great promise to produce much energy at costs no less staggering than present oil prices, nuclear power is likely to become even more popular in the future especially in countries more concerned with economic development than environmental protection. Somewhat ironically, the countries with the greatest deposits of coal, a major alternative fuel, are also the ones where there are strong concerns about the environmental consequences of increased use of this resource and the health hazards that go hand in hand with mining (the United States and Germany). Complicating the entire situation is the lack of any objective standards for determining which energy strategy is in any scientific or economic sense the optimal one to pursue. Given alternative sets of goals, one can always develop mathematical and statistical models which support one's thesis and, hence, give it scientific standing.[26]

But the most disturbing element in facing an uncertain energy future is the set of political problems in domestic politics which dwarfs the problems in reaching agreement in international politics. One cannot expect an international energy program to be developed in the absence of agreement on a national energy strategy. But, within the United States, the political problems in confronting this issue are overwhelming. The problem is largely one of stakes. The stakes are large indeed, because energy effects everything we do—from driving to school or work to producing the energy itself and the food that sustains us all—as well as shipping that food to where we live. The amount of gasoline wasted when Americans throughout the country waited in gasoline lines in 1973–74 and 1979 is staggering itself! There also are virtually no "winners" in energy shortages—only different levels of losing. To be sure, the oil companies may be profiting immensely as might some other speculators or inventors. But there are few who benefit from shortages; even the oil companies might prefer greater supplies and somewhat lower prices, if for no other reason than to improve their public image, thus preventing their dissolution. Some observers in Washington commented in 1980 that the major oil companies did not press as hard as they might have against Carter's proposal for a tax on the windfall profits they would make as prices became free of government regulation, because they feared that such a show of force might lead to a move to nationalize the companies. Even the capitalist nations of Europe, Canada, and Mexico have either nationalized oil companies or established government-controlled corporations to oversee imports because they have viewed the issue of energy shortages as concerns of overwhelming importance.

But such coordination has eluded the Americans. There have been no major movements to nationalize the oil companies, but Presidents Nixon, Ford, and Carter each proposed at least one comprehensive national energy policy. None met with much success in the Congress. The reason for this lack of action is straightforward: If all politics are local, as Speaker Thomas P. O'Neill of the House has maintained, then energy politics are the most local of them all. The producing areas of the South, especially Texas and Louisiana, have little in common with the consumers of the North and the West. In the former states, temperatures are mild and oil consumption is not nearly so great in the winter as it is in New England. One can drive on the wide Texas freeways and see many cars with bumperstickers reading: "Drive faster, freeze a Yankee!" In Wyoming, where driving at high speeds is seen as a constitutional right, a move was made in 1979 by the state legislature to exempt the state from the national 55-mph speed limit. The governor, Ed Herschler, vetoed the bill, arguing that the state would lose all credits from the national Highway Trust Fund so that no funds would be available to repave periodically the interstate highway system that ran through the state. Other funds might also be withheld by the federal government. But in 1981, Nevada established a miniscule fine of only $5.00 for driving between 55 and 70 mph. The whole issue amused *The New York Times,* located in a city where most residents use public transportation (the subways or buses), which seemed to argue in an editorial that too much exposure to wide open spaces lessens one's concern for fellow citizens.

Not surprisingly, the Congress has reflected these local concerns. Furthermore, the jurisdictional battles in the Congress make a coordinated attack on energy virtually impossible. Congressional committees are based upon jurisdictions which affect major interests in the country: Agriculture, Armed Services, Education and Labor, Banking, Veterans' Affairs, and so forth. These interests are largely, but not exclusively, unaffected directly by each other. Few farming lobbies are concerned with the fate of a housing project for New York or Cleveland. But energy is different. As stated above, it affects everyone. A gallon of gas allocated to New Hampshire means a longer wait on a line in California—unlike the effects of most other policies. So almost every committee in the Congress has some jurisdiction over energy policy: In the Ninety-Fifth Congress (1977–78), eighty-three committees and subcommittees actually held hearings on some aspect of energy policy in the House of Representatives, encompassing every member of the House who serves on a committee.[27] Five committees share jurisdiction over the Department of Energy authorization—Energy and Commerce, Science and Technology, Interior and Insular Affairs, Public Works and Transportation, and Foreign Affairs. The latter body has not exercised its jurisdiction, but still executive spokesmen have to repeat the same testimony to four different authorizing committees in the House—and then appear before Appropriations and Budget in that chamber and Appropriations, Budget, and Energy and the Environment in the Senate.

An attempt to restructure and rationalize energy jurisdictions in the House failed in 1980 because key legislators did not want to yield their power over various aspects of energy legislation and convinced others that power, that goal of all politicians, was not something they should be forced to yield. Perhaps the critical actor was Morris K. Udall, chairman of the House Interior Committee who feared that a new Energy Committee would not exercise sufficient restraint in the regulation of nuclear power plants.[28] Conversely, many House Republicans were concerned that the proposed committee would consist of young, progressive Democrats who would seek to nationalize the oil companies or at least reimpose strict price controls over energy costs. Few people saw the stakes in the same way and the defeat of the proposal was virtually ensured for that very reason: Everyone could find some reason to oppose a new committee. Even the liberal members of the House Education and Labor Committee would lose some jurisdiction: In the previous Congress, the committee held hearings on a synthetic fuels bill because that legislation would have created jobs for the hard-core unemployed under a program authorized by the committee. The jurisdictional lines were somewhat more clearly drawn in the Senate as a result of a 1977 reform which was enacted establishing the Energy and National Resources Committee. However, the committee was so evenly balanced between "liberals" and "conservatives" that most issues were resolved on the Senate floor, where extended debates and the greater ease of offering amendments made the committee system somewhat less important.

Also, much of the important energy legislation involved raising revenue to finance the development of alternative resources and thus was also referred to the Senate's tax committee, Finance, chaired by the powerful Russell Long, from the producing state of Louisiana. Long not only could set much of the agenda from his position on Finance, but also found it somewhat easier to gain a forum for the producers' position in the Senate because of the way the two chambers were apportioned. The House better represented the more populous consuming states of the North and West, whereas the producing states, often smaller, were entitled to the same two senators as New York and California. The Senate Finance Committee remained one of the more conservative bodies in either chamber and Long was one of the most influential members of the Congress. Any legislation opposed by the producers could be either stopped or at least greatly modified in the Senate regardless of what the House did.

This is exactly what happened in 1977–78, when Carter, newly inaugurated, sent to Capitol Hill the most ambitious energy program ever proposed. The new President recognized that he faced severe political problems. When he proposed the program in a televised address to the nation in April 1977, he warned: "I am sure each of you will find something you don't like about the specifics of our proposal. . . . We can be sure that all the special interest groups in the country will attack the part of the plan that affects them directly."[29] He was correct. Business leaders and conservatives generally opposed the program's emphasis on conservation rather than on production. Environmentalists found the level of support for solar energy pitifully low and objected to plans for the development of nuclear technology. Labor thought the program would cut back the number of jobs in energy-related fields and feared that the proposed gasoline tax of fifty cents a gallon would affect only the middle and lower classes; it also argued that further taxation of gas-guzzling cars would take jobs away from the automobile industry—not yet fully recovered from the recession following the oil embargo and certainly not yet anticipating the even worse slump of 1980. Rural members thought the taxes would discriminate against their constituents, while urban legislators believed that the administration's plan to rebate some of the proposed energy taxes signaled an abandonment of the President's commitment to mass transit. The oil companies viewed the program as a consumer plot to keep petroleum prices regulated, but consumer groups felt that the modest energy savings that would be accomplished at great costs to everyone but industry constituted a giant rip-off by the oil companies and OPEC.

Through a complicated and ingenious use of the House rules, Speaker O'Neill bypassed the existing committee system and obtained passage of Carter's energy program virtually intact. The Senate then stalled on the program for almost a year, with much of the time spent in a dispute as to who would replace the swing vote on the Energy and Natural

Resources Committee on the issue of natural gas price decontrol. When the Senate finally resolved this issue, Long and his producer-state allies proceeded to reformulate the entire program and reported a package quite unacceptable to the House. A bitter conference ensued and a "compromise" very similar to the Senate bill finally emerged in 1978, which Carter ultimately agreed to sign because there was no evidence that a veto would produce a better bill.

Little changed in the next couple of years. Many pressures on Carter and the Congress to produce some national energy program continued, but no one could produce a program which was acceptable to 435 members of the House and 100 senators. Senate Majority Leader Robert Byrd (D., W. Va.) summed up the dilemma: "Energy is so divisive, because here all of the parochial—all of the parochial and regional interests surface."[30] Following the long summer of 1979 when residents of California and major cities throughout the country spent thankless hours on gasoline lines, the President proposed a *standby* gasoline rationing plan which could be implemented in the event of a national emergency—not a plan to implement rationing itself, which he opposed (and Kennedy espoused in his bid to deny Carter renomination the following year)—but again parochial, local interests prevailed on the first Carter proposal despite a most unusual plea by the Speaker to members to put aside parochial interests and vote for the plan. In contrast, Rep. Tom Hagedorn (R., Minn.) stated:

> I care less about supplies in the Washington area and more about the citizens of the Second District of Minnesota who would be forced to wait for their ration checks in the mail. . . . I care about the citizens of the Second District who would be forced to pay the white market value for extra coupons that could be sold in downtown Manhattan and brought out to the Midwest and sold for 3 to 4 times as much.[31]

Even more dramatic were the remarks of Rep. Edward Beard (D., R.I.):

> This is not in the interest of my people of the State of Rhode Island. I do not represent California, nor do I represent New York or any other State but Rhode Island, and so for that reason and for the fact that it is very unfair to my State I will vote against this particular bill.[32]

These sorts of comments provided the basis for the only partially tongue-in-cheek line that circulated around Capitol Hill to the effect that the only politically acceptable rationing plan was one that would guarantee *all* of the nation's gasoline to *each* of the 435 congressional districts. A dramatic illustration of this type of constituency-based politics is the Congressional Tourism Caucus, one of the multitude of single-interest/regional interest groups which have formed within the House and Senate in the past several years. Other such groups range from the well-known Black Caucus to Members of Congress for Peace Through Law (founded during the 1960s by anti-Vietnam War members) to the parochial Ball

Bearing Caucus. What distinguishes the Tourism Caucus from the others is the fact that, despite having 231 members (more than either the Sunbelt Caucus or its rival, the Northeast-Midwest Caucus), its staff is paid for largely by the tourism industry. The group is pledged to ensure that energy supplies will remain available for vacation travel by Americans in the event of another gasoline crisis in the United States. All of these caucuses hinder effective policy formation by party leaders and even committees, but the Tourism Caucus seems to be the one most captive of outside organized interests.

The crux of the domestic problem lies in the constituency politics of energy policy and in the supporting base for this type of politics in the Congress. Thus, to a very large extent, international energy politics is a captive of the localism of energy policies in the nation and states. The United States is the world's largest importer of oil and the biggest exporter of food. We could perhaps reach agreement on some national energy policy if: (1) There was any evidence that we could use the food weapon as OPEC has employed the oil weapon, but this is highly questionable because such a small portion of our food exports go to OPEC nations; (2) If such a strategy existed, we could find some way of reaching agreement on a national policy to determine how to allocate the new gains from our agricultural surplus; and (3) We could reconcile such a strategy with the international political environment, since we export so much of our food to our allies and to Third and Fourth World nations, which would then face very high prices for both fuel and food. Could such a strategy bankrupt the international economy on which all nations, but particularly the dominant economic powers such as the United States, Europe, and Saudi Arabia, depend for their prosperity or simple survival? The international energy problem is not likely to be resolved in the immediate future despite the compelling need to do so. But the interconnections between domestic and international considerations makes the political problem seem even less tractable than the technological one.

Balancing the Scales?

7

Where Does the Balance Lie?

The Great Depression, followed by the New Deal and the Nazi threat, followed after Germany's defeat by the cold war, all contributed to the steady growth of presidential power. But for the Vietnam War, this unchallenged growth might have continued. This trend toward increasing presidential power had gone unchallenged because crisis after crisis, domestic and foreign, required strong action and often speedy reaction. The need for a powerful presidency seemed obvious. More than that, the growth of presidential power was identified with the use of this power domestically for progressive social legislation (New Deal, Fair Deal, New Frontier, and Great Society programs) and externally for the defense of what used to be called the Free World, although it included nondemocratic societies. The confrontation of Stalin's Russia—which, not surprisingly so soon after World War II, looked a lot like Hitler's Germany to Western eyes—with the United States, Britain, and France, made the cold war appear to be fundamentally a continuing struggle of totalitarianism against democracy. Thus the expansion of presidential power was identified with liberal causes, with domestic changes to help the underprivileged and to correct social injustices, and a foreign policy to protect liberal values that had first been assaulted by Hitler and then by Stalin. In fact, it had simply come to be assumed that the president is a liberal and that, therefore, he can, like the kings of old, "do no wrong."

During those days it was conservatives who opposed the trend toward increasing presidential power; as exponents of little government and congressional supremacy, they opposed New Deal and other domestic reforms, as well as the conduct of a vigorous foreign policy, all of which required Big Government, especially Big Executive Government. Liberals championed the latter. But Vietnam reversed the liberal attitudes toward presidential power. Liberals, who had always expected "their" presidents to back good causes whether eliminating poverty, doing away with racial injustice, or stopping totalitarian aggression, became schizophrenic as the war escalated. Johnson's domestic record surpassed that of John F. Kennedy, whose style and charm attracted liberals but who by the time of his death had not managed to get Congress to pass even one piece of major social legislation; Johnson got it passed and then began passing his own set of reforms. But Vietnam disillusioned many liberals. A war in defense of an undemocratic government, often fought by methods that repelled men of humane sentiments, springing from commitments made by Presidents Eisenhower and Kennedy and transformed into major war by Johnson, not only seemed incompatible with the very values America proclaimed to the world but was carried on in a way that seemed unconstitutional.

The Gulf of Tonkin Resolution, the blank check Congress gave Johnson but did not expect him to use to initiate a large land war in Asia, only made the war an even more bitter experience. Vietnam, a "presidential war," was perceived to be the culmination of the trend toward increasingly powerful presidents who were not subject to the legislative restraint envisaged by the Founding Fathers; had they not with good reason, in the Constitution, specifically provided against the danger of locating absolute power in the hands of one man by assigning to Congress the authority to "declare war" and the president the authority to "make war"? In the future, asked New York Times journalist Tom Wicker, a critic, "could a president, for example, bomb Lima in order to forestall or retaliate for some act of expropriation by Peru? If Fidel Castro refuses to help put an end to airline hijackings to Cuba, can Mr. Nixon constitutionally bomb Havana to make him negotiate seriously?"[1] Does not the present Constitution, amended by years of presidential practice and congressional acquiescence, read in effect: "The president may conduct a war unless Congress halts him"? Hence, to redress the balance between the executive and legislative, to prevent another Vietnam and avoid a second costly disaster and strain of the American social fabric, a flood of proposals has been put forward, almost all of which aim at a greater role in the making of foreign policy, and especially the use of force, for Congress—and, through it, presumably "the people."

The belief that the presidency—when occupied by bellicose presidents—needs to be restrained by a pacific Congress, acting as the representative of the people, assumes that Congress, especially the Senate, would demonstrate wisdom, moderation, and virtue, qualities that have frequently been lacking in the postwar period.

> This spring the land is filled. . . . with a resounding chorus demanding that the United States Senate reassert its "right" over foreign policy. . . .
>
> But hold on a moment. Which Senate are we speaking of? Are we talking of the Senate which has over and over again balked at constructive foreign initiative, crippled foreign efforts, ignored foreign opportunities? Are we talking of the Senate which blocked American entry into the League of Nations, held back full support for the World Court, is presently cutting back further and further on foreign aid, which has no hesitation over passing resolutions mixing in the affairs of other countries for political rather than diplomatic reasons?
>
> Of course, this is not the Senate which today's "strengthen-the-Senate" advocates have in mind. They visualize an upper chamber full of wisdom and goodwill, a bulwark of reason and foresight in a reckless world. In short, they dream of a Senate which will hew to their own concept of where foreign policy should go and how it should be conducted.[2]

However, these expectations are of a Congress whose foreign policy stance for most of the postwar period has been intensely anti-Communist and nationalistic. Presidents have therefore moved with great caution, if and when they have moved at all, in their relations with Communist countries lest they be tainted as "soft on communism." Even in the 1976 presidential campaign, for example, President Ford dropped the word "détente" as the key phrase describing Soviet-American relations. In the election campaign, Ford and Carter both took a tough line on the issue of the Panama Canal, maintaining that the United States must have complete control over the Canal Zone. Carter changed his policy after his inauguration and Ford joined in the campaign for the ratification of the treaties. Critics worried that Panama would follow the lead of other Latin American countries and take a sharp turn to the left, thereby eliminating American control of the waterway. Similarly, fears that the Sandinista government in Nicaragua would become a Cuban satellite produced a heated debate over foreign aid to that nation in 1980; a restricted version of the aid bill passed by the narrowest of margins in the House, despite considerably easier sailing in the Senate. The critical difference was the support of a moderate Democrat, Edward Zorinsky, in the upper chamber, who believed that the United States had more to lose by alienating Nicaragua than by taking a risk that the new government would be friendly, or at least not hostile, to the United States.

But the fall of pro-American governments in Nicaragua and Iran, as well as the weakness of other friends and allies such as Guatemala, El Salvador, Zaire, Turkey, and Morocco, led to increased demands that the country take a more activist role in international politics. Many of these arguments were heard most loudly in the Congress. The nomination of Ronald Reagan by the Republicans intensified the political debate on foreign policy, especially the growing concern with defense policy. The congressional activism, in contrast to that of the late 1960s and early 1970s, was now once more directed toward an interventionist foreign policy which conflicted with the policies of the President. The Congress of the 1970s was concerned with too much presidential power and prowess, while that of the 1980s, especially the Republican controlled Senate, seems determined to reassert American power. Few members of the Congress during the Vietnam War period could have imagined that a president would not win universal acclaim for pronouncing that no American soldiers had died in overseas combat during his term of office, as Carter often reminded the country.

There is an irony to the post-Vietnam appointment of Congress as the watchdog of presidential temptations to go to war. For it overlooks the fact that Congress approved U.S. participation in both limited wars. Had President Truman requested a declaration of war after North Korea's invasion of South Korea, he would have received it; support for Truman's decision to intervene militarily with U.S. forces received virtually unanimous congressional and popular support. Only after the war became domestically unpopular did a few conservative senators raise the question of its constitutionality. Similarly, President Johnson had the support of large majorities in Congress and the country not only at the time of the Gulf of Tonkin incident during the summer of 1964, but also when the sustained bombing of North Vietnam began in the spring of 1965. If a War Powers Act had existed at the time, it would not have prevented either of the two limited wars in which the United States has become engaged since 1945. Nor would the rule that, sixty days after intervening, the president must desist if he does not receive legislative support after explaining his reason for intervening have changed these outcomes. For this would have been too short a period for any congressional investigation to turn up facts beyond those—as in the North Korean invasion—already evident or explained by the president; Congress' Tonkin Gulf investigation did turn up additional information—three years after the events.

If there is one rule that has become clear in the post-World War II period, it is that during real or alleged crises, Congress and the public turn to the president for information and interpretation. For example, it was Kennedy's interpretation of the impact of Russian missiles in Cuba that precipitated the Cuban missile crisis. Put in different words, the president has a superior ability to manipulate the picture of reality in the short run; this advantageous presidential position is reinforced by an emotional fact of life—namely, that if the president sends troops into action, be it in the name of freedom or security or both, the patriotic feelings that are aroused will make it extremely difficult to oppose him and refuse him the troops and money he requests. In fact, it will take a great deal more willingness on the part of Congress to accept responsibility for its decisions in case history should turn out to vindicate the president.

What Kind of Congress?

What is the proper role for Congress in foreign policy? First we shall consider the possibility of a stronger role for Congress in seizing foreign policy initiatives. Granted that most members of Congress are not strongly interested in doing so, there are nevertheless three major arguments that can be advanced on behalf of this role: (1) The extent of congressional initiatives on foreign policy issues has greatly expanded in the past decade, so that even if most members of Congress are not primarily interested in such issues, a sufficient number are, so that a more important role might be warranted; (2) Congress is, after all, a representative institution and its many actors and different perspectives reflect the sentiments of large numbers of Americans—and they ought to be taken into account in the policy-making process on foreign as well as domestic issues; and (3) There is no guarantee that presidential initiatives on foreign policy will always be wise and in the nation's best interests, so a stronger role for Congress might provide a forum for determining what the country really ought to do while also minimizing the risk of an "imperial Presidency."

Second, the notion of popular control stresses the accountability of decision-makers to the public. Elections, on this view, serve as referenda, not on every detail of foreign (or domestic) policy-making, but on the general thrust of the policies and of the ability of the administration to carry them out. Automatic support for foreign policy is seen as harmful on this view, because it might create the potential for an "imperial Presidency"—or even an "imperial Congress." The critical aspects of popular control are: (1) the voters must be offered some choice between alternative views of what constitutes a good foreign policy; and (2) the administration which they select to implement those policies must actually do so—and thus hold itself accountable to the voters at the next election. One of the most frequently cited violations of the popular control model was the 1964 election, in which Johnson promised not to escalate the war in Vietnam, charged his challenger Goldwater with intending to do so, and then proceeded to follow a Southeast Asian policy which was closer to that of Goldwater's campaign than his own. Similarly, Nixon was a staunch anti-Communist throughout his political career, yet he made the first American breakthrough to China in 1971–72. While such policies may demonstrate the ability to adapt to changing circumstances, they also indicate that there is little control of foreign policy by the public;

furthermore, there is no united voice within each of the congressional parties supporting the nominee for president along with his policies.

Finally, the suggestion that Congress should play primarily an oversight role for executive decisions is a compromise between a stronger Congress and one which is more passive. There is some room for increased participation, but here the Congress is seen as largely reacting to presidential initiatives rather than initiating foreign policy decisions. However, this role for the Congress also recognizes that there may not be a single outcome which is always preferable to others—and permits some participation in the decision-making process by the Congress and other actors. We do not propose a solution to the democratic dilemma here, but shall indicate arguments in favor and against each of the proposals outlined above.

Congress, the Voters, and Foreign Policy

For the first alternative of a stronger role for the Congress in foreign-policy decision-making, one finds support among the members themselves *and* among the general public. A December 1974 Harris poll found that only 39 percent of the respondents believed that Congress had a "very important role" in the implementation of foreign policy, behind that of Secretary of State Kissinger (73 percent), the President (43 percent), and business (42 percent). After attributing a fundamental role for public opinion (58 percent), the respondents believed that Congress (49 percent), more than any other individual or institution, should have a stronger role in foreign-policy decision-making. A survey of members of the House and the Senate by the General Accounting Office, conducted for the subcommittee on International Political and Military Affairs of the House International Relations Committee, found general dissatisfaction with the quantity, quality, and timeliness of executive-branch supplied information.[3] The lone exception occurred in the case of the *Mayaguez*. Yet, what constitutes a stronger role for Congress in the formulation of foreign policy? Recent events indicate that Congress has been most assertive in *reacting* to administration decisions or proposals, but not nearly as successful in initiating foreign policy alternatives. The Congress did block further aid to the regime in South Vietnam as it became evident that the long war was finally coming to an end. It barred funds for military assistance in Angola and cut off aid for several months to Turkey. Some conservative members attempted to repeal a trade embargo against the white-minority government in Rhodesia, while diverse forces were more successful in cutting off military assistance to Turkey and tying a trade agreement with the Soviet Union to increased Jewish immigration from that nation. These are examples of congressional initiatives, but they are atypical of the congressional role in foreign policy in one critical respect: They indicate action initiated by the legislative branch in an attempt to make an independent foreign policy. But even these instances of policy initiation do not necessarily differ from the more typical role of Congress on foreign policy: Reaction to administration requests, such as aid for Nicaragua and passage of the SALT II treaty, is often negative. To be sure, most congressional decisions on foreign policy remain supportive of presidential policies, but the increased role of Congress has included both initiatives which begin within Congress and more frequent negative responses to administration proposals. The Carter administration, for example, met with early defeat in Congress when it was forced to withdraw the nomination of Theodore Sorensen to head the CIA following intense criticism by the Senate Intelligence Committee. Congress was acting negatively rather than initiating any policy; furthermore, most observers did not attribute the negative reaction of the Senate to the new president, but rather to the nominee himself. In contrast, Ernest Lefever's withdrawal of his nomination in 1981 as the human rights official in the Reagan administration reflected not only a negative reaction to the nominee as a person (including the opposition of all four of his brothers) but also a rejection of the Reagan administration's first formulation of its human rights policy. It remains a matter of controversy whether such legislative actions produce better or worse policy outcomes than executive dominance does. What is clear, however, is that the Congress has, to date, been less successful in foreign policy innovations than in restraining what it considers to be executive excess. Instead of participating in innovative foreign policy making, Congress more often simply reacts to administration actions (or anticipated decisions)—for example, the breakthrough to the People's Republic of China (which many members bitterly contested) or the Camp David accords in the Middle East (which virtually all praised profusely). Consequently, we hesitate to judge whether the Congress would do better or worse. Yet, one cannot help but wonder whether the absence of such innovations may be caused by the difficulty of initiating policies with 535 principal decision-makers.

Among the reform proposals favored in the General Accounting Office survey were a system in which information concerning a crisis would automatically flow to the Congress and a requirement that a senior executive official observe executive deliberations during crises and keep the Congress fully informed on the international situation. Two proposals were supported by a narrow margin: (1) granting a small number of members of Congress observer status on the National Security Council or other crisis management groups; and (2) establishing direct participation of members in such crisis decision-making organizations. Yet, there was substantial opposition to the establishment of a special congressional committee to serve as a focal point for information during international crises.[4] Thus, even among the representatives and senators themselves, there is not strong support for giving the legislature an important role in actually making the critical decisions on foreign policy. The members want to be informed, but not the immediate responsibility for making the decisions. There are also institutional difficulties which must be realized by those who would increase the role of Congress in foreign policy initiation: New ventures in foreign policy are difficult for large bodies such as the House or the Senate, or even their committees. These legislative bodies, like their counterparts throughout the world, are primarily concerned with domestic policy-making. Unlike the executive branch, they rarely speak with one voice. And, as we have stressed, they often respond slowly to any policy questions, be they domestic or foreign.

If Congress remains the weak link in the federal government, then it does not make much sense to expect representatives and senators to attempt to "convert" the opinions of their constituents into policy positions. The opinion conversion notion of democratic government makes two critical assumptions: (1) representatives reflect the majority sentiment within their constituencies; and (2) a majority of the representatives can act to formulate public policy. But can a majority act? Sometimes it can, but the bulk of the work in Congress is done in committees and subcommittees. These bodies are not directly accountable to the full House or Senate. While some of the reforms adopted in the early and mid 1970s have strengthened party leadership, the more important ones have spread power so diffusely throughout the Congress that coordinated policy-making is extremely difficult. As a result of the reform of the seniority system, three aging, Southern chairmen of House committees, F. Edward Hébert (D., La.) of Armed Services, W. R. Poage (D., Tex.) of Agriculture, and Wright Patman (D., Tex.) of Banking, were deposed in 1975. Each had reputations for domineering their committees. But the removal of these three leaders neither produced other major upsets in succeeding years—or in the Senate—or a general strengthening of congressional party leadership. The power lost by these chairmen was not centralized by the political parties, but even further diffused among subcommittee leaders. With the growth of subcommittee government and the weakening of the party leadership, the capacity of Congress to mount a unified challenge to the executive branch has actually decreased despite the greater role on foreign policy that the two houses have taken.

If we deny the validity of the second assumption, then it does not seem to matter much whether the first assumption is acceptable. A representative or senator who speaks for his constituency, but is powerless to do anything for them, is not much of an improvement over a legislator who does not even attempt to determine what the will of his constituency is.

Popular Control and Foreign Policy: Bipartisanship Reconsidered

Is there anywhere for a supporter of a stronger congressional role in foreign policy-making to turn? The answer is a tentative "yes." According to another view of democracy, which earlier we called the idea of "popular control of government," the voters select the candidates and parties whose views on the issues are closest to their own. They do not demand that their representative reflect the positions of a majority of his constituents on every issue, but elections are viewed as a check on the positions an administration will adopt. The concept of popular control of government assumes that the positions of the administration can be associated with a particular set of officeholders, particularly the members of Congress of the same party as the president. The opposition party, on the other hand, is associated with a different set of policies. Thus, the voters are offered a choice between competing programs on election day. The voter need not be an "expert" on foreign policy questions. All he would have to know is how he generally reacts to foreign policy issues and which stands each party has taken.

Yet the evidence for popular control of government seems no more substantial than did the claims for the opinion conversion notion of representative government. Issues have not played much of a role in elections, and foreign policy issues are even less important than domestic ones. Defenders of the idea of popular control of government maintain that the voters should not be blamed for not expressing themselves on the issues. The parties, after all, do not offer the voters much of a choice on the issues, particularly on those dealing with foreign policy.

Indeed, issue voting is further frustrated by the post-World War II emphasis on the need for a bipartisan foreign policy. If foreign policy issues transcend party lines, then how can a voter express his dissatisfaction with the policies of a given administration? Until recently, foreign policy votes in Congress have been almost devoid of partisan conflict. The justification for a bipartisan foreign policy has been that partisan conflicts would lead to dramatic shifts in America's relations with the other nations when one party replaced the other in power. Yet it is not only the strong points of a nation's foreign policy—its ability to react quickly to crisis and to pursue consistent policies while maintaining enough flexibility to change policies when the opportunity and need arise—that continue from one administration to the next because of a bipartisan foreign policy. The mistakes of the previous administrations also follow into succeeding ones. Furthermore, the nation's policies often become contradictory, as when the United States tried both to bomb more and to negotiate with the North Vietnamese, because of the compulsion to seek out a moderate course which would command bipartisan support. As James MacGregor Burns has argued:

> The immoderate moderation of American policy, the rigid adherence to a middle-of-the-road course that is often the most dangerous way to travel, stems from a common-sense devotion to consensus. And trying once again to follow a middle course between falsely conceived extremes proved our undoing.[5]

Critics of bipartisanship in foreign-policy decision-making argue that the nation would not be paralyzed in crisis situations even if partisan debate did occur on international issues. During a crisis, public opinion and congressional opinion would undoubtedly rally behind the president as it currently does. The major difference that a more partisan foreign policy would produce is that the administration in power would have to demonstrate to the public that (1) the international event that provoked a presidential response was indeed a crisis; and (2) the administration took the appropriate steps in handling the situation. These appear to be the very concerns that supporters of an increased congressional role have in mind. As Cecil V. Crabb, Jr., has argued, "under bipartisan foreign policy, decisions take on an aura of untouchability." Crabb adds:

> Arguments advanced in behalf of bipartisan foreign policy usually presuppose that by some kind of unexplained process, the government will automatically follow the course best calculated to serve the public interest, if only partisanship can be avoided. . . . Most infrequently is there recognition among supporters of the bipartisan principle that parties, with all their faults, and democratic government are inextricably connected, and that occasional excesses by political parties are part of the price a democracy must pay for the freedom it prizes so highly.

He also maintains that "parties are the most effective mechanism for translating the popular will into governmental policy."[6]

But, if congressional coalitions on foreign policy have been changing in recent years and opposing partisan blocs are becoming prominent in the House of Representatives, it does not seem unreasonable to look at the role of parties in the foreign-policy decision-making process. The first question we must pose is, "What would a stronger party system look like?" Then we shall examine the question of how parties might become more effective participants in foreign-policy decision-making.

Party Responsibility and Foreign Policy

In 1950, a special Committee on Political Parties of the American Political Science Association issued a report sharply critical of the American party system. The committee held:

When there are two parties identifiable by the kinds of action they propose, the voters have an actual choice. On the other hand, the sort of opposition presented by a coalition that cuts across party lines, as a regular thing, tends to deprive the public of a meaningful alternative. When such coalitions are formed after the elections are over, the public usually finds it difficult to understand the new situation and to reconcile it to the purpose of the ballot. Moreover, on that basis it is next to impossible to hold either party responsible for its political record.[7]

The committee's report contained a clear stand in favor of what is called the "doctrine of responsible party government." To enable the voter to hold a party responsible for the actions of the government, each party should present the electorate with clear-cut programs for executive and legislative action. This is the *programmatic* aspect of party responsibility. Secondly, each party should be ideologically distinct from all other parties in the political system, so that the voters have some basis for making a choice on election day. Finally, each party in the legislature should speak with one voice. If the parties are not internally cohesive in the legislature, the voters have a difficult time deciding exactly whom to hold responsible for the decisions of the government. Instead of conflict between the president and the members of his party in Congress, policy decisions should be reached by the legislative and executive wings of the party jointly. The party out of power, as the "loyal opposition," should not only criticize the victors but also offer alternative programs for legislative action. The arguments advanced in favor of party responsibility thus focus on the basic theme that the party system is the *only* mechanism with the potential to serve as a means of translating the public's will into policy decisions.

The emphasis of the responsible party model is, therefore, not upon "balancing the scales" between the president on the one hand and Congress on the other hand. Indeed, party responsibility requires a solid front on the part of a president and his congressional party. Advocates of party responsibility, however, see as the critical question in foreign policy formation "Do the voters have a set of competing policy alternatives from which to choose?" rather than "Are there competing centers of power within the federal government?" For example, if we consider congressional controversy over the Vietnam War, it is obvious that neither party put forward a specific set of proposals for voter approval or disapproval. Indeed, as Republicans and Democrats in the House of Representatives were becoming more ideologically distinct and more internally cohesive in their positions on the war, in the Senate a bipartisan coalition opposing the war was developing. Indeed the Vietnam experience furnishes perhaps the most dramatic example of the lack of party responsibility in contemporary American political history in the election of 1964. Republican presidential candidate Goldwater openly disagreed with Johnson on the proper course of action the United States should pursue in Vietnam. Goldwater favored an increased American role in the war, while Johnson emphatically stated that he would not send American troops into combat in Vietnam. The positions of the two candidates were clearly delineated and each attempted to lead public opinion—as the doctrine of responsible party government prescribes. The Johnson example, while extreme, is not atypical. In 1968, Nixon ran as an ardent anti-Communist; in 1972, his reelection campaign rarely failed to note that he was the first president to establish ties with the People's Republic of China. During the 1976 race, Carter repeatedly charged Ford with conducting foreign policy without consulting the American public and pledged to have an "open" administration. Shortly after taking office in 1977, it was Carter who complained that too many people (including members of Congress) had access to sensitive materials on the conduct of foreign policy—including the names of foreign chiefs of state who had received money from the CIA.

Indeed, the Carter administration vacillated between the more traditional "closed" foreign-policy decision-making and the openness the new chief executive had promised during the campaign. Both Carter and former United Nations ambassador Andrew Young showed a propensity to reveal their thoughts on key international questions to the American public before they so informed foreign leaders. The Soviets, among others, became angered at Carter's public revelation of the terms of a SALT II treaty before the secretary of state had arrived in Moscow to begin negotiations. There were grumblings about openness even from our strongest allies in Western Europe, while both Israelis and Arabs found cause for alarm in the President's public statements on what an acceptable Middle East peace settlement should be. To rectify—or "clarify"—the intent of these public utterances, Carter sought to reassure other nations that policy pronouncements he made were not necessarily binding. But these reassurances took place in closed meetings, usually in private discussions with foreign leaders by Secretary of State Cyrus Vance or his successor Edmund Muskie. Indeed, Vice-President Mondale use to joke that the United States seemed to have a different foreign policy on different days. Carter himself admitted that he talked too much in public (often with inaccurate information) about foreign policy negotiations. Reagan has encountered some similar problems. During the 1980 campaign he promised to restore full diplomatic relations with Taiwan but was forced to retreat from this position after his inauguration. Openness in foreign policy certainly has its limitations, no matter how great the commitment of an administration to it.

The entire question of responsible party government remains an open one as the nation prepares to enter the 1980s. Even if the parties do become more ideologically distinct and programmatic on domestic policy questions, will they do so on foreign policy issues? Robert Dahl has suggested that such a change will depend on the politician's "view of reality." And, in calling for more partisanship on foreign policy issues in particular, he argued:

> It seems entirely doubtful that it is any longer of much profit to a party to avoid taking clear-cut responsibility. Political issues are too important to too many voters for ambiguity and evasiveness to pay large dividends today. The parties themselves may find it increasingly in their own interest to appear before the electorate with a rather well-defined program which, upon election, they will carry through without vast concessions to every minor pressure group. Party responsibility seems likely to prove profitable to the parties themselves.[8]

In the absence of strong partisan cleavages among the electorate on foreign policy issues, however, it does not seem any more likely that electoral factors will induce parties to take more divergent stands on international issues in the 1980s than they did in the 1950s. There are indeed factors, which we shall now consider, that might induce the parties to refrain from being more programmatic on foreign policy issues than on domestic policies. These obstacles are probably not great enough to forestall an increase in party responsibility on foreign policy issues if a similar increase occurs on domestic policies. Yet the electoral arena is but one stumbling block in the way of a more responsible party system. We turn now to a consideration of the various obstacles a party reformer must face.

The Dilemma of the Party System

Even if a more responsible party system were viewed as desirable by party leaders throughout the country, it would be a most difficult task to establish such a party system in the United States. The single greatest obstacle is the fear of the unknown. When a party has nominated a strong ideologue for president—such as Goldwater in 1964 for the GOP and McGovern in 1972 for the Democrats—the result has been disastrous. Even more critical than the fear of the unknown in the electoral arena is the fear of the unknown in policy formation. In a system of responsible party government, a change in party control of the government might mean drastic policy shifts. If the electorate is fickle, however, and turns incumbents out of office with great regularity, then policy formation would be almost schizophrenic. A law passed by the Democrats might be repealed by the Republicans, only to be reinstated when the Democrats came back to power. The consequences of such a situation would be dramatic for domestic policies; they might be cataclysmic for foreign policies. A presidential candidate who opposed the new relationship with mainland China could disrupt American-Chinese relations for decades. Even if such a president were succeeded by an advocate of better relations between the two countries, the damage done by his predecessor may effectively block any initiatives by a new administration. In contrast, a bipartisan foreign policy ensures continued support for the successful policies of the previous administrations (as well as for the failures). The General Accounting Office survey of congressional attitudes on legislative-executive relations on foreign policy confirms the fears of critics of an increased role for political parties. The study, which focuses on the *Mayaguez* incident, shows substantial differences between Democratic and Republican members of Congress: Democrats generally believed that Congress had not been adequately consulted while Republicans were far more satisfied with the performance of a president of their party.[9]

But, even if party leaders were no longer to pay lip service to the old shibboleth that a responsible party is doomed to act "irresponsibly" on foreign policy questions, they still must face several critical stumbling blocks in any attempt to make the American parties more programmatic, ideologically distinct, and internally cohesive. Constitutionally, control over party organizations in the United States rests with the individual states, so a recalcitrant member of a congressional party cannot be denied renomination by the national party, as he can in Britain. This electoral base independent of the national party means that there is little a party can do to ensure itself a high level of cohesion in the national legislative branch. Not even a strong and immensely popular president can effectively intervene in the relationship between a member of Congress and his constituents. Franklin D. Roosevelt attempted to translate his 1936 landslide victory into a mandate for his role as party leader in the 1938 congressional elections by asking voters to "purge" disloyal Democratic representatives and senators. The results may have been the biggest political setback Roosevelt ever suffered. The congressional parties are not without any power over recalcitrant members: The party caucuses can strip mavericks of their seniority rights.* Although this method of punishment has been used infrequently, more responsible parties might find it an effective tactic.

An even more difficult constitutional barrier to surmount in the American political system is the relationship between the president and the legislative branch. In a system of responsible party government, legislative-executive relations are marked by cooperation rather than conflict. The chief executive is the leader of his party, and his party

---

*Democrats stripped of seniority for supporting Goldwater in 1964 were Reps. John Bell Williams (Miss.) and Albert Watson (S.C.). Watson immediately resigned his House seat and won reelection as a Republican. In 1969, House Democrats stripped Rep. John Rarick (La.) of his seniority rights for supporting American Independent candidate George C. Wallace in the 1968 presidential contest.

controls the government. The government stands or falls on the basis of the public's view of the parties. In the United States, however, the legislative and executive branches are separate and supposedly equal according to the Constitution. Because the president is elected every four years, the members of the House every two years, and senators every six years, it is not unusual for one party to win the presidency but not majorities in each house of Congress. From 1947 to 1982, one or the other party controlled both the legislative and executive branches for only 18 years—just half of the time.* When control of the two major branches of the government is divided, domestic policy-making must either involve major concessions by both parties (as occurred under Eisenhower) or virtually grind to a halt (as happened under Truman and Nixon). In neither case is there any room for party responsibility. Indeed, in the area of foreign policy, divided control of the government creates a power vacuum that enhances presidential dominance in the policy-making role.

The separation of powers in the American political system may thus function as the strongest barrier to a more responsible party system in the United States. In contrast, a parliamentary system, such as is found in England and many West European nations, makes responsible parties more feasible. The prime minister is not elected by the people at large but is chosen by the party (or a coalition of parties) that wins the most seats in the legislature. Divided control of the legislative and executive branches of government is therefore impossible. Furthermore, the prime minister, unlike the president, must tailor his policies to the wishes of his parliamentary party. If he refuses to do so, he can conceivably be removed from office by the Parliament—or pressured into resigning. A major failure on a policy decision can result in the formation of a new government. Anthony Eden was replaced as prime minister of Britain in 1956 by Harold Macmillan after a major foreign policy blunder in the Middle East. Eden had committed British troops during the Egyptian-Israeli war to a joint effort with the French to recapture control of the Suez Canal from the Egyptians, who had seized control of the waterway. The British-French attempt failed and Eden resigned. In the United States, on the other hand, Woodrow Wilson argued that

... our system is essentially astronomical. A president's usefulness is measured, not by efficiency, but by calendar months. It is reckoned that if he

*The American voters have been remarkably consistent in returning majorities to the House and the Senate of the same party. Voters returned bare majorities of Republicans (by two in the House, one in the Senate) to Congress in the election of 1930; by the time Congress had actually convened, several Republican deaths allowed the Democrats to organize the House. Not since the adoption of direct election of senators did voters actually split control of the two houses of Congress between the two parties until 1980 when the Republicans won the Senate and the Democrats kept control of the House.

be good at all, he will be good for four years. A prime minister must keep himself in favor with the majority; a president need only keep alive.[10]

American presidents can afford to take actions that risk failure early in their administrations. Because they have as long as three and a half years to recover from their "mistakes," they are virtually unchecked. Even the 1973 vote against Nixon's policies in Cambodia could hardly be taken as a guarantee that the administration's basic foreign policy objectives in Southeast Asia would be altered significantly. A prime minister may find that his very tenure in office is dependent upon the foreign policy risks he chooses to take. Unless he is quite certain the Parliament will support his actions, a prime minister is unlikely to engage in foreign policy adventures that do not directly involve the defense of his own nation.

Responsible party government has been advocated by many academics for more than a century.[11] Indeed, from the 1890s through the second decade of the twentieth century, there was party government in the Congresses. The party leaders appointed all of the members of committees until 1910 and the party caucus still bound members to floor votes for another decade after that. The growth of the committee system weakened the parties in succeeding years and subcommittee government has since further reduced the power of party leaders as well as that of committee heads. But another, more fundamental factor served to weaken the congressional parties: the erosion of the party in the electorate. Voters no longer have strong identifications with political parties compared to just two decades ago. Furthermore, these loose party ties have induced a large amount of ticket-splitting among voters, selecting a candidate of one party for, say, the presidency and of another for the House or Senate.[12] Together with the use of the perquisites of office to maintain the seats of the new members of Congress, this factor means that a House district whose voters identify themselves as Republicans may nevertheless elect Democrats to national office and keep them there for many years. Such a Democrat, elected without any help from the national party, would feel no special obligation to a Democratic president—as Carter found out when he assumed office. This makes coordinated party policy-making terribly difficult and makes us less sanguine about the prospects for achieving party government.

Yet, the idea continues to be popular. A leading liberal economist, Lester W. Thurow, has suggested that a responsible party system might be required to pose the hard choices ahead in setting a new economic course for a nation which seems beset by either high unemployment, inflation, or both.[13] The ultimate paradox may be that as the political system becomes more decentralized and less manageable, the desirability of support for the idea of party government increases, but the prospect for obtaining it is at a minimum. The more people who have power under a decentralized system, the more difficult it will be to get most of them to give up what leverage they have. There is a history of cycles of strong and weak parties, and strong and weak congressional leadership.[14] The pendulum will swing away at some point from extreme decentralization, but two questions remain: (1) How long will this process take? and (2) In which direction will the pendulum swing? It is hardly guaranteed that strong parties will return to American politics, at least any time in the foreseeable future.

The President Proposes, the Congress Reacts?

Perhaps there is a lesser, if not minor, role that Congress can still play in foreign-policy decision-making even if it does not involve anything like equality with the president. Such a role would stress the "oversight" function of Congress, in which the legislative branch investigates the procedures and policies of the executive, makes recommendations for future policy, and even sets guidelines which must be followed. Samuel P. Huntington has argued that Congress is incapable of formulating policy (domestic or foreign) and recommends that it devote most of its resources to oversight.[15] Indeed, the Legislative Reorganization Act of 1970, one of the recent congressional reforms, mandated increased oversight for all committees in the Congress. What are the prospects for oversight and how well can such a function satisfy the critics who insist upon a stronger role on foreign policy for the legislature?

The prospects for oversight can perhaps best be summed up by the traditional refrain. The word oversight has two meanings: critical evaluation of executive performance and a passing thought. In the Congress, where many committee hearings are pretty routine and not very investigative, there has been an overemphasis on the meaning *not* intended by those who want more of a balance of power in the national government. The difficulty is that in too many cases, the regulators (congressional investigators) become the accomplices of the groups or organizations they are supposed to investigate and control.[16] Furthermore, as Morris Ogul argues, the oversight function is not terribly salient to most members of Congress.[17] Even when members do become concerned with their oversight duties, the close working relationships that develop among the legislators, bureaucrats, and interest groups ("those cozy triangles"[18]) are not conducive to critical examinations of the behavior of each other. A staff member of the House Armed Services Committee stated the case simply: "Our committee is a real estate committee."[19]

Yet, there has been an increase in critical oversight in recent years. In particular, both the House and the Senate established oversight committees to investigate the abuses of power of the Central Intelligence Agency and the Federal Bureau of Investigation in the ninety-fourth Congress (1975–76). Yet, the very fact that such committees were

established points to one of the weaknesses in the congressional oversight procedure. Institutional loyalties prevailed, so that no thought was
given to a joint committee—which would have saved duplication of
effort. In each House, a select committee (as opposed to one of the more
traditional standing committees) was formed for the investigations. Yet,
there existed committees on foreign relations, armed services, government operations, and judiciary (in the case of the FBI) in each House
which could just as effectively have conducted the oversight. Why were
select committees employed, then? Again, the question of institutional
loyalties arose within congressional committees, and there was also a
problem of where the ultimate jurisdiction was to be placed.

Once established, the Intelligence committees did not function
smoothly. In the Senate, many critics claimed that Chairman Frank
Church was headline hunting and was trying to conclude the hearings as
quickly as possible to allow him to enter the Democratic presidential
primaries. The committee in the House, known as the Pike committee,
drew better "press notices," but the lower house produced a spectacle of
its own. The original House Intelligence Committee was chaired by Rep.
Lucien Nedzi (D., Mich.). A conflict within the committee developed
when maverick Rep. Michael Harrington (D., Mass.) "leaked" to the press
classified material on the CIA's role in "destabilizing" the Allende
government in Chile in 1973. Nedzi demanded that Harrington be
removed from the committee, and there was a movement within the
House to censure Harrington. The Harrington case was overshadowed by
further leaks to the press and the entire matter was finally closed on a
rather obscure technicality that saved Harrington from possible action by
his fellow House members. Speaker Carl Albert finally resolved the
dispute between supporters of Nedzi and those of Harrington by recon-
stituting the committee without either member. Like its Senate counterpart, the House Intelligence Committee was established as a permanent
committee in 1977.

What did the Intelligence committees accomplish? They did bring to
public attention a large number of abuses of power by the FBI and
particularly by the CIA. Yet, much of this publicity arose through leaks
and much of what we learned about the intelligence agencies came from
newspapers and magazine follow-up stories, rather than from congressional testimony. Indeed, Pike and Ford were at loggerheads on what the
committee could or could not release. The full House ultimately sided
with the President against a moderate Democrat. Much of the impetus for
reform was slowed when Richard Welch, a CIA operative in Greece, was
assassinated. Many people thought that the congressional hearings were
divulging too much information about the agency, thereby making the
intelligence operations of the United States vulnerable throughout the
world. Ultimately, the Congress did take some action: It forbade the CIA
from engaging in domestic intelligence operations and it also passed a

law which made the assassination of foreign leaders illegal—an action that would make few foreign chiefs of state sleep more soundly at night. Attempts to make the CIA budget available to at least the relevant congressional personnel failed. No wide-ranging reorientation of foreign intelligence was mandated by the Congress. The decision in 1977 to place all intelligence operations dealing with foreign policy under a single agency, headed by CIA Director Turner, was made in the White House, not on Capitol Hill.

In 1980 the Congress voted to restrict the number of committees to which the president must report any covert action to two, the Intelligence chambers in the House and the Senate. A congressional move, backed by the Carter administration, to formulate a charter for the CIA failed to win approval, but so did a conservative bid in the Congress to repeal the provisions of the Hughes-Ryan amendment to "unleash" the intelligence community. The actions in 1980 were taken by many as a sign that the CIA and other agencies had learned to live with the new requirements, indeed that the reporting procedures were not particularly onerous. There had been considerable concern that if the president reported to eight committees, leaks of national security information from the Congress would occur, which was the case with the single committee in the House in 1973. So, the administration had simply not informed all relevant committees and subcommittees of foreign intelligence operations.

There were few congressional complaints until the attempt to rescue the hostages from Iran in May 1980 failed and some members of Congress claimed that they had not been given advance notice. But this did not prevent them from restricting the Hughes-Ryan amendment shortly thereafter. Oversight of the CIA, particularly in a period of international tensions when the American will was being severely tried, was not a politically beneficial issue in 1980, and so few members pressed for it. Oversight on foreign policy has thus tended to become regularized since the early 1970s and is not nearly as rewarding as many members thought it might be. Thus, it has taken a lesser role in congressional politics than domestic policy or even other foreign policy issues; and the permanent select committees have not been made standing committees, a move that would indicate greater importance for these bodies within the Congress.

Congressional oversight on foreign policy has not been totally ineffective. Congress did interrogate Kissinger to a greater extent than during any other recent period on the details of the 1975 Sinai accord. As discussed above, Congress has passed, over Nixon's veto, a War Powers Act; and, against the wishes of the Nixon administration, the legislature required the secretary of state to submit the final text of any executive agreement on foreign policy to Congress within sixty days. Yet, oversight does not seem to have strengthened the role of Congress in terms of implementing policy. Oversight has all of the advantages of hindsight, but requires considerably more effort. Those who want to strengthen the role of Congress in determining what the foreign policy of the United States *will be*, as opposed to what it should have been, will demand a more important function for the legislature. But, that brings us full circle to a reconsideration of how powerful the legislative and executive branches of government should be.

The Democratic Dilemma Reconsidered

We have seen that one way of resolving the problem of how much power each branch of the government should have on foreign policy is by strengthening the power of Congress, which can at least in part be accomplished by "reforms" such as the War Powers Act or increased oversight. But, this will not necessarily lead to further congressional *control* over foreign policy decisions. On the other hand, a change that would give Congress more power on foreign policy, strengthening political parties to the point of sharing responsibility with the executive, might not be possible to initiate.

Is there an answer to the problem of foreign-policy decision-making in a democracy? Probably not, if one insists upon a panacea for the failures in foreign policy and a guarantee that successful policies will continue to be chosen. The decision-making process on foreign policy questions appears to work best in crisis situations, when immediate and decisive action is required. Perhaps leaders function best in crises—or perhaps the "followers" are simply more likely to support the leaders. On security and intermestic policies, the system appears to work less well. These issue areas may have high stakes, but they are not perceived in terms of external threats. Furthermore, there is not always agreement about what the stakes are for all actors or what the most desirable outcome is. A democratic political system appears to handle foreign policy decisions best when the fewest actors—the inner circle—are involved in the process of decision making. As more and more actors in all four circles become involved, the conflict between presidential formation of foreign policy and the desires of other actors to have a say in foreign policy becomes intense. In crisis decision-making, the administration chooses a course of action designed to maximize a given goal. The decision that is reached is directly related to that goal. Students of the foreign policy-making process have praised the decisions made in crises and concluded that democratic governments can indeed rival monolithic dictatorships in response to external threats, citing the pattern of rational decision-making in such situations as the reason why the American political system has fared so well in crises. Lowi has stated that

> . . . crisis decisions in foreign policy are made by an elite of formal, official office-holders. Rarely is there time to go further . . . the people who make decisions in times of crisis are largely those who were elected and appointed

to make such decisions. That is to say, *in foreign affairs crises our government has operated pretty much as it was supposed to operate.* There is a normative corollary as well: Since our record of response to crisis is good, then the men in official positions have been acting and are able to act rationally. . . . Indeed, a fundamental feature of crisis decisions is that they involve institution leaders (holders of the top posts) *without their institutions.* Only when time allows does the entire apparatus of the foreign policy establishment come in play.[20]

On security and intermestic policies, however, the decisions reached through bureaucratic/governmental politics are often "minimal" ones; they do not resolve issues one way or the other and often cannot be justified on the basis that they maximize any particular foreign policy goal. Indeed, it is possible that, as in energy policy, bureaucratic/governmental politics may lead to no decisions at all—if the contending forces are each strong enough and obstinate enough to prevent a compromise acceptable to all (or even most) parties.

In addition, in security policies—including limited wars—the objectives of the policy as well as the proposed ways of handling them often lack the clarity of crisis decision-making.* In Vietnam, for example, the objectives of American policy were never clearly delineated. On the one hand, a policy of total war was never seriously considered by the Johnson or Nixon administration. However, neither was the policy of withdrawal of all American troops. Both administrations flatly rejected what might appear to have been a "rational" compromise first suggested by other nations and then advocated by North Vietnam: a coalition government in South Vietnam. The result was a set of minimal decisions: to increase American troop strength during the Johnson administration, but to continue to press for a negotiated settlement to the conflict. By contrast, Nixon reduced American troop strength but increased the bombing of North Vietnam, again continuing to search for a negotiated settlement. Yet the strategies of both administrations involved contradictory policies, producing what Burns has called an "immoderate moderation." The United States finally extricated itself from the war without ever having resolved the question of what goals were accomplished by the many years of costly fighting.

If it is then concluded that decision making works best—produces the "best" results or garners the most public support—in crisis situations, we must, in conclusion, address ourselves again to the democratic dilemma posed at the beginning of the study. To ensure its security in the

---

*Limited wars are much like program policies in that both types of foreign policy decisions (1) involve multiple actors; (2) take a considerable amount of time to reach a conclusion; (3) involve conflicting goals on what a policy is supposed to accomplish; (4) involve bargaining -generally among the combatants rather than domestically—and are ultimately resolved by a negotiated settlement; and (5) are often marked by minimal decisions.

essentially anarchical international system, a state must have a concentration of executive authority so that it can respond quickly and with unity of purpose to events in the international political system. A democratic state, on the other hand, requires a restraint on executive power to preserve the constitutional system. This tension between the needs of international and domestic systems spills over into the distinction between crisis decision-making on the one hand and security and intermestic policies on the other. Decision making in crisis situations very much resembles authoritarian decision-making: Policies are determined by a relatively small number of actors who must act with dispatch and unity. Democratic politics, on the other hand, is often marked by the necessity to compromise, to consider issues at great length in the attempt to reconcile conflicting interests, and to highlight the different goals of the actors involved rather than to assume that the decision-makers all agree upon the goals to be maximized.

The three aspects of the democratic dilemma pervade all aspects of policy making, but are particularly difficult to resolve on foreign policy issues where the stakes are so high and the actors do not all share at least one common goal, the survival and defense of the nation. The need to act quickly on foreign policy issues means that the president, as chief diplomat and commander in chief of the armed forces, must be able to respond to events in the international environment. But presidents may claim many things in the name of national security (Nixon went as far as to include conversations with his aides on the Watergate scandal) and the question remains as to how democratic the nation will be so that the president must protect these claims. What should the proper role of Congress be in foreign-policy decision-making—particularly when the Founding Fathers expected the legislature to dominate domestic politics and domestic policies to dominate the nation's agenda? If the Congress should have some role in foreign policy-making: (1) How great should that role be? (2) Should other actors, such as interest groups, public opinion, and the media, also have their interests represented—as is the case with domestic policy? and (3) Does the Congress, with its more limited resources compared to the vast foreign policy bureaucracy of the executive branch, have the capacity to reach the "correct" foreign policy? In this same regard, how do we determine what the "correct" decision is—and how might we reconcile what we believe to be the proper course of action on an international issue with what popular sentiment might be? When the public is supportive of administration policies, this issue does not arise. But the public and the administration may both be right or may both be wrong. Hindsight is a great teacher, but it gives us little guidance as to how widespread the scope of participation should be for present decisions.

The irony of foreign-policy decision-making is thus that the American political system appears to function best when decisions are made in the very way authoritarian states formulate policies.[21] When foreign policy decisions become more "democratic" by encompassing more actors, the policies selected may not have as clear a relationship to the strategic problem at hand. The democratic dilemma does not admit of a ready answer. The framers of the Constitution did indeed produce a document with "missing powers," allowing for the growth of presidential power to meet changing needs. And by consciously creating a form of government that was inimical to responsible party government,[22] the framers of the Constitution ensured that the legislative branch could not take the foreign policy initiative away from the executive—an initiative they had given him. Believing that the nation would engage in no "entangling alliances," against which George Washington was to admonish the country in his Farewell Address, the Founding Fathers expected the war-making powers given to Congress in the Constitution would provide an adequate check on presidential dominance of the foreign policy process.

The president will, however, remain the dominant actor in foreign-policy decision-making. The conduct of an activist foreign policy—as distinct from a neo-isolationist one—will continue to require a strong foreign policy president. Thus, the basic dilemma remains: What is a virtue internationally may be a vice domestically, and what is a virtue domestically—a restraint on executive power—may become a vice internationally. The basic question is whether the United States can grant its government sufficient authority to safeguard the nation while yet preserving its democratic system. The purpose of America's foreign policy, in the final analysis, is to protect its democratic way of life. Yet, will the policy subvert the very purposes it was intended to serve?

The profound effects that the war in Vietnam had on the relationship between the president and Congress and, indeed, even on the party system will probably serve to restrain future chief executives in foreign policy somewhat. Whether Johnson's personal popularity declined because of the Vietnam situation or because of domestic unrest, it is certain that his place in history will be marred by Vietnam; presumably no future president will wish to repeat this experience. Nor is it probable that presidents will be quite so willing to seek direct confrontations with Congress after Nixon's surprising defeat on the Cambodian and war powers issues in 1973 and the refusal of Congress to authorize funds for Ford's requests on Vietnam and Angola. These acts do not, however, mean that Congress will continue to assert itself on foreign policy. The Democratic party in the House of Representatives, through its caucus, had gone on record as opposing further aid to Vietnam in 1971, 1973, and 1975. The caucus action, however, did not result in legislative action until 1975, by which time the Vietnamese government in the South had almost fallen and public support for continued American aid had virtually evaporated. For Congress, and particularly the congressional parties, to take a stronger role in policy formation, the members would have to translate their policy pronouncements in committees, caucuses, and particularly subcommittees into legislative action which is supported in both the House and the Senate. This is no small task indeed.

The country will continue to rally around the president in crisis situations, although he will probably be less prone to treat some foreign policy decisions as critical international events. On other policies, the roles of the presidency and Congress will depend on at least three circumstances. One is the future course of relations with the Soviet Union. The increasing disillusionment in the United States with what is seen as the Soviet Union's expansionist behavior as exemplified by Ethiopia, South Yemen, Afghanistan, and the Soviet support of Vietnam's invasion of Cambodia, has weakened support for détente in this country. The recent American anxiety about the continuing rapid growth of Soviet military strength, and the increases in American military spending for new weapons systems, are but two symptoms of a renewed concern with checking Soviet influence and matching Soviet power. Second, events in the underdeveloped world may also have an enormous impact. Events in the Persian Gulf-Indian Ocean area—the fall of the Shah in Iran and the subsequent Islamic revolution, the signs of potential internal instability in Saudi Arabia and other oil sheikdoms, and the apparent Soviet encircle-ment of Saudi Arabia—have led an energy-dependent United States to commit itself to the protection of the oil kingdoms. This is one of several signs that instead of withdrawing from many of its commitments, which it is unable to do, the United States has discovered that it has become more involved than during the pre-Vietnam era (with China in Asia, Zimbabwe in southern Africa, as well as the Arab members of the Organization of Petroleum Exporting Countries). Third, because of the Vietnamese war and the subsequent cries of "No More Vietnams," the question is how long the mood of the country, as expressed in this slogan, will constrain a foreign policy which is becoming activist once more and might again include the possibility of military action.

World War I was the "war to end all wars." World War II started only twenty-one years after that earlier conflict had ended. The United States was propelled into this war against Germany and Japan despite congres-sional attempts to constrain presidential freedom of action in order to maintain America's isolationist stance. (Chapter 2) It was not to be the last time that despite a preference for peace the country found itself at war. This long war ended with the detonation of two atomic weapons over Japan and was supposed to underline the dangers of any future interna-tional conflict. A few years later, General Douglas MacArthur, comment-ing on the Korean War, stated that it was sheer folly for the United States to fight a land war in Asia; but that did not prevent Vietnam. As George Santayana noted, any nation that doesn't learn from history is doomed to repeat it. The question is: Which lesson should it learn—the lesson of 1940−41 or that of Vietnam?

Notes

CHAPTER 1

1. Aaron Wildavsky, "The Two Presidencies," *Trans-Action* (December 1966), p. 7.
2. Paul Seabury, in *Power, Freedom and Diplomacy* (New York: Vintage Books, 1967), p. 189, elaborates on this tension.
3. John Locke, *Two Treatises of Government* (Cambridge: Cambridge University Press, 1960), pp. 383–84 (italics and capitalization of nouns omitted).
4. George F. Kennan, *American Diplomacy 1900–1950* (Chicago: University of Chicago Press, 1951), p. 73.
5. J. William Fulbright, *The Crippled Giant* (New York: Vintage Books, 1972), p. 193.
6. *Ibid.*, p. 198.
7. *Ibid.*, p. 218.
8. Kennan, *op. cit.*, pp. 93–94.
9. Hans J. Morgenthau, *A New Foreign Policy for the United States* (New York: Praeger Publishers, 1969), pp. 150–51.
10. Seabury, *op. cit.*, p. 196.
11. Ivor W. Jennings, *Cabinet Government* (Cambridge: Cambridge University Press, 1951), p. 183.
12. Seabury, *Power, Freedom and Diplomacy*, p. 196.
13. Louis Henkin, *Foreign Affairs and the Constitution* (Mineola, N.Y.: The Foundation Press), p. 37.

241

14. *Ibid.*, p. 41.
15. Felix Gilbert, *To the Farewell Address* (Princeton, N.J.: Princeton University Press, 1961), p. 145.
16. Fulbright, *op. cit.*, p. 241.
17. John Spanier, *Games Nations Play*, 4th ed. (New York: Holt, Rinehart and Winston, 1981), Chaps. 2 and especially 5.
18. *Ibid.*, Chap. 9.
19. Bayless Manning, "The Congress, the Executive and Intermestic Affairs: Three Proposals," *Foreign Affairs* (January 1977), pp. 306–24.
20. See Kenneth N. Waltz, *Foreign Policy and Democratic Politics* (Boston: Little, Brown, 1967), pp. 274–75, and John E. Mueller, *War, Presidents, and Public Opinion* (New York: John Wiley, 1973), p. 211.
21. Robert H. Salisbury, "The Analysis of Public Policy: A Search for Theories and Roles," in Austin Ranney, ed., *Political Science and Public Policy* (Chicago: Markham, 1968), p. 158. See also Salisbury and John Heinz, "A Theory of Policy Analysis and Some Preliminary Applications," in Ira Sharkansky, ed., *Policy Analysis and Political Science* (Chicago: Markham, 1970), pp. 39–60.

   On the original distinction between distributive and redistributive policies in the literature of political science, see the pioneering article by Theodore J. Lowi, "American Business, Public Policy, Case Studies, and Political Theory," *World Politics* (July 1964), pp. 677–715. On the applicability of distributive and redistributive policies to the study of foreign policy, see James N. Rosenau, "Foreign Policy as an Issue Area," in Rosenau, ed., *Domestic Sources of Foreign Policy* (New York: The Free Press, 1967), pp. 11–50; and Lowi, "Making Democracy Safe for the World: National Politics and Foreign Policy," in *ibid.*, pp. 295–331.
22. Roger Hilsman, *To Move a Nation* (New York: Doubleday, 1967), p. 541.
23. See Stephen D. Krasner, "Are Bureaucracies Important?" *Foreign Policy* (Summer 1972), pp. 159–79, for an incisive critique of the bureaucratic model.
24. *Ibid.*, p. 168.
25. Wildavsky, "Two Presidencies," pp. 7–8.
26. Donald A. Peppers, " 'The Two Presidencies': Eight Years Later," in Aaron Wildavsky, ed., *Perspectives on the Presidency* (Boston: Little, Brown, 1975), pp. 463–64, 469.

CHAPTER 2

1. *New York Times*, January 21, 1961.
2. Wildavsky, "Two Presidencies," p. 3.
3. Francis E. Rourke, et al. "The Domestic Scene: The President Ascendent," in *Retreat From Empire?* (Baltimore: The Johns Hopkins University Press, 1973), p. 106. Also Leslie H. Gelb and Richard K. Betts, *The Irony of Vietnam* (Washington, D.C.: The Brookings Institution, 1979), pp. 223–24.
4. Quoted in *New York Times*, May 21, 1980. Also see I. M. Destler, "A Job That Doesn't Work." *Foreign Policy*. Spring 1980, pp. 80–88; and Flora Lewis, "The Parts and the Whole." *New York Times*, September 30, 1980.
5. Robert A. Divine, *The Reluctants Belligerent* (New York: John Wiley, 1965); and *idem, Roosevelt and World War II* (Baltimore: Penguin Books, 1969).

6. Merlo J. Pusey, *The Way We Go to War* (Boston: Houghton Mifflin, 1971), p. 74.
7. *Ibid.*, p. 75.
8. *Ibid.*
9. Robert A. Divine, *The Illusion of Neutrality* (Chicago: University of Chicago Press, 1962), pp. 280—81.
10. For example, Daniel S. Cheever and Field H. Haviland, Jr., *American Foreign Policy and the Separation of Powers* (Cambridge, Mass.: Harvard University Press, 1952); and James M. Burns, *Congress on Trial* (New York: Harper & Row, 1949).
11. See Foster Rhea Dulles, *American Foreign Policy Toward Communist China* (New York: Thomas Y. Crowell, 1972); John W. Spanier, *The Truman-MacArthur Controversy and the Korean War*, rev. ed. (New York: W. W. Norton, 1967); and Gelb and Betts, *op. cit.*
12. Daniel Ellsberg, *Papers on the War* (New York: Simon and Schuster, 1972), pp. 101—02.
13. Gelb and Betts, *op. cit.*, p. 25.
14. Laurence I. Radway, "Electoral Pressures on American Foreign Policy," prepared for delivery to the International Studies Association convention, Los Angeles, March 21, 1980, p. 6.
15. Gelb and Betts, *op. cit.*, p. 68.
16. Quoted by Robert A. Dahl, *Congress and Foreign Policy* (New York: Harcourt Brace Jovanovich, 1950), pp. 129—30.
17. Joseph Jones, *The Fifteen Weeks* (New York: Viking Press, 1955), pp. 138—41.
18. Arthur M. Schlesinger, Jr., *The Bitter Heritage* (Greenwich, Conn.: A Fawcett Crest Book, 1967), p. 47.
19. *New York Times*, October 18, 1979.
20. Loch Johnson and James M. McCormick, "Foreign Policy by Executive Fiat," *Foreign Policy*, (Fall 1977), pp. 117—18.
21. Guenter Lewy, *America in Vietnam* (New York: Oxford University Press, 1978), pp. 202—05.
22. Fulbright, *Crippled Giant* (no. 10, Chap. 1), pp. 218—20; and *The Pentagon Papers* (New York: Bantam Books, 1971), p. 25.
23. *Pentagon Papers*, p. 79.
24. Arthur M. Schlesinger, Jr., "Congress and the Making of American Foreign Policy," *Foreign Affairs* (October 1972), p. 98.
25. Quoted by Joseph C. Goulden, *Truth Is the First Casualty* (Chicago: Rand McNally, 1969), pp. 50—55. See also Eugene G. Windchy, *Tonkin Gulf* (New York: Doubleday, 1971).
26. See, for example, David Halberstam, *The Best and the Brightest* (New York: Random House, 1972).
27. Spanier, *The Truman-MacArthur Controversy and the Korean War*.
28. Fulbright, *Crippled Giant*, pp. 188—91.
29. Thomas F. Eagleton, "Whose Power is War Power?" *Foreign Policy* (Fall 1972), pp. 29—31.
30. Jacob Javits in the *New York Times*, February 14, 1972. See also Javits, *Who Makes War* (New York: William Morrow, 1973).
31. Pat M. Holt, *The War Powers Resolution* (Washington, D.C.: American Enterprise Institute, 1978).

32. Cited by Richard G. Head, Frisco W. Short, and Robert C. McFarlane, *Crisis Resolution* (Boulder, Colo.: Westview Press, 1978), p. 254.

33. James David Barber, *The Presidential Character* (Englewood Cliffs, N.J.: Prentice-Hall, 1972). Further citations are to the second edition (1977).

34. Ibid., Chaps. 1 and 10.

35. Dan Rather, and Gary Paul Gates, *The Palace Guard* (New York: Harper & Row, 1974).

36. Barber, *The Presidential Character*, p. 8.

37. *Ibid.*, p. 12.

38. *Ibid.*, Chaps. 2−3.

39. *Ibid.*, Chap. 5.

40. See Alexander George, "Assessing Presidential Character," *World Politics*, vol. 26 (January 1974), pp. 234−82; and James H. Qualls, "Barber's Typological Analysis of Political Leaders," *American Political Science Review*, vol. 71 (March 1977), pp. 182−211.

41. See Robert C. Tucker, "The Georges' Wilson Reexamined," *American Political Science Review*, vol. 71 (June 1977), pp. 606−18.

42. Research on Eisenhower is being conducted by Fred I. Greenstein of Princeton University.

43. Robert E. DiClerico, *The American President* (Englewood Cliffs, N.J.: Prentice-Hall, 1979), p. 305.

44. *Ibid.*, Chap. 9, esp. p. 332.

45. Richard F. Fenno, Jr., "If, as Ralph Nader Says, 'Congress Is the Broken Branch Why Do We Love Our Congressmen So Much?'" in Norman Ornstein, ed., *Congress in Change* (New York: Praeger, 1975), pp. 277−87.

46. David S. Broder, "Would You Prefer a Mondale-Baker Race?" *Washington Post* (June 4, 1980), p. A19.

47. Meg Greenfield, "The Cult of the Amateur," *Washington Post* (June 11, 1980), p. A1.

48. Michael Krasner, "Why Great Presidents Will Become Rare." *Presidential Studies, Quarterly*, Fall 1979, p. 367.

49. *Ibid.*, p. 373.

50. Woodrow Wilson, *Congressional Government* (Cleveland: Meridian Books, 1967), p. 171. Originally published in 1885.

51. James Bryce, *The American Commonwealth*, rev. ed. (New York: Macmillan, 1915), vol. 1, p. 79.

52. *Ibid.*, pp. 79−80.

53. *Ibid.*, p. 80.

CHAPTER 3

1. See Alfred deGrazia, ed., *Congress: The First Branch of Government* (Washington: American Enterprise Institute, 1966).

2. Arthur M. Schlesinger, Jr., *The Imperial Presidency* (Boston: Houghton Mifflin, 1973).

3. Hanna Fenichel Pitkin, *The Concept of Representation* (Berkeley: University of California Press, 1967), Chap. 4.

4. Roger Hilsman, *The Politics of Policy-Making in Defense and Foreign Affairs* (New York: Harper & Row, 1971), pp. 118−20.

5. J. Leiper Freeman, *The Political Process*, rev. ed. (New York: Random House, 1965).

6. Roger H. Davidson, "Breaking Up Those 'Cozy Triangles': An Impossible Dream?" in S. Welch and J. G. Peters, eds., *Legislative Reform and Public Policy* (New York: Praeger, 1977), pp. 30–53.

7. David R. Mayhew, *Party Loyalty Among Congressmen* (Cambridge: Harvard University Press, 1966).

8. Robert A. Dahl, *Polyarchy* (New Haven: Yale University Press, 1971), esp. p. 120.

9. Thomas M. Franck and Edward Weisband, *Foreign Policy By Congress* (New York: Oxford University Press, 1979), pp. 283–84.

10. Richard F. Fenno, Jr., *Congressmen in Committees* (Boston: Little, Brown, 1973), p. 103.

11. "Thomas P. O'Neill, Jr., The Man From Barry's Corner," *Yankee Magazine* (July 1978), p. 99.

12. T. R. Reid, "Ambro's Independence," *Washington Post* (July 5, 1977), p. A7.

13. Frank Smith, *Congressman from Mississippi* (New York: Pantheon, 1964), p. 127. Cf. Mayhew, *Congress: The Electoral Connection* (New Haven: Yale University Press, 1974), esp. Chap. 1.

14. David W. Brady, *Congressional Voting in a Partisan Era* (Lawrence, Kansas: University Press of Kansas, 1973).

15. Walter Dean Burnham, *Critical Elections and the Mainsprings of American Politics* (New York: W. W. Norton, 1970).

16. These data are drawn from Morris P. Fiorina, *Congress: Keystone of the Washington Establishment* (New Haven: Yale University Press, 1977), Chap. 3, and Irwin B. Arieff, "Growing Staff System on Hill Forcing Changes in Congress," *Congressional Quarterly Weekly Report*, vol. 37 (November 24, 1979), pp. 2631–46.

17. Eric M. Uslaner, "The Case of the Vanishing Liberal Senators," *British Journal of Political Science*, vol. 11 (January 1981), pp. 105–113.

18. Data from the House Commission on Administrative Review, 1977, survey of members of the House of Representatives.

19. Samuel P. Huntington, "Congressional Responses to the Twentieth Century," in D. B. Truman, ed., *The Congress and America's Future*, 2d. ed. (Englewood Cliffs, N.J.: Prentice-Hall, 1973), pp. 6–38.

20. Fenno, *Congressmen in Committees*, Chap. 1.

21. Fenno, *Home Style* (Boston: Little, Brown, 1978), p. 160.

22. Fenno, *Congressmen in Committees*, p. 110.

23. *Ibid.*, p. 12.

24. *Ibid.*, p. 141.

25. Uslaner, "The Case of the Vanishing Liberal Senators."

26. *Ibid.*

27. Quoted in Norman J. Ornstein and David W. Rohde, "Shifting Forces, Changing Rules and Political Outcomes," in Robert L. Peabody and Nelson W. Polsby, *New Perspectives on the House of Representatives*, 3d ed. (Chicago: Rand McNally, 1977), p. 222.

28. See the remarks of the Honorable Bob Carr (D., Mich.), *Congressional Record*, Daily Edition, Ninety-sixth Congress, First Session (March 5, 1978), p. E838.

29. On Mills, see John Manley, *The Politics of Finance* (Boston: Little, Brown, 1970).

30. Testimony before the United States House of Representatives Select Committee on Committees, November 14, 1979; quoted in Uslaner, "The Congressional War on Energy," paper prepared for the Conference on Understanding Congressional Leadership sponsored by the Everett McKinley Dirksen Congressional Leadership Research Center, Washington, D.C., June 10–11, 1980, p. 2.
31. Data obtained from the U.S. House Select Committee on Committees; cited in Uslaner, "The Congressional War on Energy," p. 13.
32. See Donald R. Matthews and James A. Stimson, *Yeas and Nays* (New York: John Wiley, 1975).
33. For a general discussion of these reforms, see Leroy N. Rieselbach, *Congressional Reform in the Seventies* (New York: General Learning Press, 1977).
34. Fenno, *The Power of the Purse* (Boston: Little, Brown, 1966), esp. Chap. 11.
35. See Dahl, *Polyarchy*; and Theodore J. Lowi, *The End of Liberalism*, 2d. ed. (New York: W. W. Norton, 1979).
36. Fenno, *Congressmen in Committees*, p. 108.
37. *Ibid.*, pp. 71–72 and 134; cf. Ornstein and Rohde, "Shifting Forces," p. 223.
38. Michael Barone, Grant Ujifusa, and Douglas Matthews, *The Almanac of American Politics, 1940* (New York: E. P. Dutton, 1979), p. 948.
39. Franck and Weisband, *Foreign Policy By Congress*, p. 193.
40. This table is taken from Majorie Ann Browne, "Executive Agreements and the Congress: Issue Brief Number IB75035" (Washington: Congressional Research Service, Library of Congress, 1980), p. 2.
41. Loch Johnson and James M. McCormick, "The Making of International Agreements: A Reappraisal of Congressional Involvement," *Journal of Politics*, vol. 40 (May 1978), pp. 468–78.
42. Franck and Weisband, *Foreign Policy By Congress*, p. 277.
43. Dahl, *Congress and Foreign Policy* (New York: W. W. Norton, 1950), p. 37.
44. These figures computed from the 1978 National Election Study of the Center for Political Studies, University of Michigan, Ann Arbor, Michigan.
45. *New York Times.* (June 6, 1980), p. A12.

CHAPTER 4

1. Roger Hilsman, *The Politics of Policy-Making in Defense and Foreign Affairs* (New York: Harper & Row, 1971), pp. 118–20.
2. Mueller, *War, Presidents, and Public Opinion*, p. 169.
3. Morton H. Halperin and Arnold Kanter call these roles "players" and "organizational participants" in "The Bureaucratic Perspective: A Preliminary Framework," in Halperin and Kanter, eds., *Readings in American Foreign Policy* (Boston: Little, Brown, 1973), pp. 9–10.
4. Yet, as Halberstam noted in *Best and Brightest* (no. 12, Chap. 2), academics like McGeorge Bundy and Rostow quickly became "operators" and lost their independent perspective.
5. Hilsman, *To Move a Nation* pp. 571–72.
6. Hilsman, *Politics of Policy-Making*, pp. 119–20.
7. Richard K. Betts, *Soldiers, Statesmen, and Cold War Crises* (Cambridge, Mass.: Harvard University Press, 1977), pp. 4, 6.
8. Henry T. Nash, *American Foreign Policy: Response to a Sense of Threat* (Homewood, Ill.: Dorsey, 1973), p. 95.

9. Henry A. Kissinger, "Bureaucracy and Policy-Making: The Effects of Insiders and Outsiders on the Policy Process," in Halperin and Kanter, eds., *Readings in American Foreign Policy*, p. 89.

10. Francis E. Rourke, *Bureaucracy and Foreign Policy* (Baltimore: Johns Hopkins University Press, 1973), p. 32.

12. Aage R. Clausen, *How Congressmen Decide* (New York: St. Martin's Press, 1973).

13. Barbara Sinclair, "House Voting Alignments in the 1970s" (Paper delivered at the Annual Meeting of the Midwest Political Science Association, Chicago, Ill., April 1980.)

14. *Ibid.*

15. Ernest A. Gross, "What is a Bipartisan Foreign Policy?" *Department of State Bulletin* (October 3, 1949), pp. 504–5.

16. On parties, see Walter Dean Burnham, *Critical Elections and the Mainsprings of American Politics* (New York: W. W. Norton, 1970). On the changing role of bipartisanship on foreign policy, cf. Richard F. Fenno, *Congressmen in Committees* (Boston: Little, Brown, 1973), with Glenn R. Parker and Suzanne L. Parker, "Factions in Committees," *American Political Science Review*, vol. 73 (March 1979), pp. 85–102.

17. For data on the 1940s and 1950s, see Leroy N. Rieselbach, *The Roots of Isolationism* (Indianapolis: Bobbs-Merrill, 1966).

18. Cf. E. E. Schattschneider, *The Semisovereign People* (New York: Holt, Rinehart and Winston, 1960), esp. Chap. 2.

19. Samuel P. Huntington, *The Common Defense* (New York: Columbia University Press, 1961), pp. 130–31.

20. In the House, there are 45 members of the Appropriations committee, 44 members of Armed Services, and 30 members of the Budget committee. For these 119 positions, there are 104 members (two members of Budget also serve on Armed Services and three on Appropriations). In the Senate, Appropriations has 29 members, Armed Services has 17, and Budget has 22. These 61 positions are filled by 68 individuals (more than half of the entire Senate!), with three members on both Appropriations and Armed Services (including Chairman Tower), on Budget, and one, ranking minority member Stennis, on Appropriations and Armed Services.

21. See Roger H. Davidson and Walter Oleszek, *Congress Against Itself* (Bloomington: Indiana University Press, 1977). On reforms that were adopted, see Leroy N. Rieselbach, *Congressional Reform in the Seventies* (Morristown, N.J.: General Learning Press, 1977).

22. Arnold Kanter, "Congress and the Defense Budget: 1960–1970," *American Political Science Review* (March 1972), p. 132.

23. Bruce Ray, "Congressional Losers in the U.S. Federal Spending Process," *Legislative Studies Quarterly*, vol. 5 (August 1980), pp. 359–72.

24. Jack Zwick and Richard K. Goeltz, "U.S. Banks Are Making Foreign Policy," *New York Times* (March 18, 1979), p. F14.

25. Franck and Weisband, *Foreign Policy By Congress*, p. 190.

26. *Ibid.*, pp. 195–96.

27. Bernard C. Cohen, *The Public's Impact on Foreign Policy* (Boston: Little, Brown, 1973), pp. 98–104.

28. Detailed analysis of American imperialism may be found in, among other books, Carl Oglesby and Richard Shaull, *Containment and Change* (New

York: Macmillan, 1967), and in any of the several volumes by Gabriel Kolko on U.S. foreign policy during World War II and since; a briefer statement of Kolko's view is presented in *The Roots of American Foreign Policy* (Boston: Beacon Press, 1969).

29. See Waltz, *Foreign Policy and Democratic Politics*, pp. 274–75; and Mueller, *War, Presidents, and Public Opinion*, p. 211 (both no. 15, Chap. 1).
30. Rosenau, "Foreign Policy as an Issue Area," pp. 24–36.
31. Gabriel Almond, *The American People and Foreign Policy* (New York: Praeger, 1960), p. 232.
32. Francis E. Rourke, "The Domestic Scene," in Robert E. Osgood, ed., *America and the World* (Baltimore: Johns Hopkins Press; 1970), pp. 149–62. See also "The Domestic Scene: The President's Ascendent," pp. 82–88, and Robert E. Tucker, "The American Outlook: Change and Continuity," pp. 33–38, in Osgood, ed., *Retreat from Empire?* (Baltimore: Johns Hopkins Press, 1973).
33. Mueller, *War, Presidents, and Public Opinion*, p. 53.
34. *Ibid.*; for a more detailed analysis, somewhat at odds with Mueller's reasoning for this loss of presidential (especially Johnson's) support, see Lawrence Elowitz, "The American Political System and Limited War" (unpublished Ph.D. dissertation, University of Florida, 1972).
35. This conclusion is drawn from Table 3.4 of Mueller, *War, Presidents, and Public Opinion*, p. 61. Mueller does not draw his inference himself, but the regression coefficients in the table for opposition to the war do support the claim.
36. Adam Clymer, "Poll Finds Reagan-Carter Choice Unsatisfactory to Half of Public," *New York Times* (April 18, 1980), pp. A1, B5.
37. Mueller, *War, Presidents, and Public Opinion*, pp. 54–55.
38. *Ibid.*, p. 50.
39. Louis Harris, "Carter Rated as 'Failure' In Handling Hostage Crisis," *Washington Post* (March 17, 1980), p. A18.
40. A good statement of this position is found in Austin Ranney and Willmoore Kendall, *Democracy and the American Party System* (New York: Harcourt Brace Jovanovich, 1956), Chap. 4.
41. See Hanna Fenichel Pitkin, *The Concept of Representation* (Berkeley: University of California Press, 1967), Chap. 4.
42. Warren E. Miller, "Voting and Foreign Policy," in Rosenau, *Domestic Sources*, pp. 215–26; and Mueller, *War, Presidents, and Public Opinion*, p. 227.
43. Miller, "Voting and Foreign Policy," p. 229.
44. The five domestic issue areas studies were federal aid to education, medical care, federal job guarantee, fair employment legislation, and school integration. See Gerald M. Pomper, "From Confusion to Clarity: Issues and American Voters, 1956–1968," *American Political Science Review* (June 1972), pp. 415–29.
45. Arthur H. Miller et al., "A Majority Party in Disarray," *American Political Science Review*, vol. 70 (September 1976), pp. 753–78.
46. Computed from the 1978 National Election Study of the Center for Political Studies, University of Michigan, Ann Arbor, Michigan.
47. Uslaner, "The Case of the Vanishing Liberal Senators."
48. Radway, "Electoral Pressures on American Foreign Policy, 1961–80," p. 6.
49. John Dewey, *The Public and its Problems* (Denver: Swallow Press, n.d.), p. 116.

CHAPTER 5

1. Thomas C. Schelling, *Arms and Influence* (New Haven: Yale University Press, 1966).
2. Henry A. Kissinger, *Nuclear Weapons and Foreign Policy* (New York: Harper & Row, 1957).
3. Most prominently, see Hans J. Morgenthau, *Politics Among Nations*, 4th ed. (New York: Alfred A. Knopf, 1967), esp. pp. 5–8.
4. The bureaucratic/government politics model is based on Graham T. Allison, *Essence of Decision* (Boston: Little, Brown, 1971); I. M. Destler, *Presidents, Bureaucrats and Foreign Policy* (Princeton, N.J.: Princeton University Press, 1972); Morton Halperin, *Bureaucratic Politics and Foreign Policy* (Washington, D.C.: Brookings Institution, 1974); and Hilsman, *To Move A Nation*, pp. 3–13, 541–76.
5. Oran R. Young, *The Politics of Force* (Princeton, N.J.: Princeton University Press, 1968), pp. 6–15; Charles F. Hermann, ed., *International Crises* (New York: Free Press, 1972); and Phil Williams, *Crisis Management* (New York: John Wiley, 1976), pp. 59–93.
6. For the Cuban missile crisis, see Elie Abel, *The Missile Crisis* (New York: Bantam Books, 1966); Alexander L. George *et al.*, eds., *The Limits of Coercive Diplomacy* (Boston: Little, Brown, 1971), pp. 86–143; and Robert F. Kennedy, *Thirteen Days* (New York: W. W. Norton, 1971).
7. J. A. Nathan, "The Missile Crisis: His Finest Hour Now," *World Politics*, (January 1975), pp. 262–64.
8. *New York Times,* June 25, 1980.
9. *Ibid.*, November 16, 1980.
10. Morton H. Halperin and Arnold Kanter, eds., *Readings in American Foreign Policy* (Boston: Little, Brown, 1973), pp. 9–10.
11. Richard Burt, "Many Questions, Few Answers on Iran Mission," *New York Times*, May 11, 1980; and William Safire, "Rescue Mission Questions," *Ibid.*, June 5, 1980 after a leak from the Senate Armed Services Committee staff which had made some preliminary inquiries prior to a committee hearing. See also *New York Times Magazine*, May 17, 1981, in which the entire issue is devoted to the Iranian hostage crisis.
12. *New York Times*, May 9, 1980.
13. Theodore Lowi, "Making Democracy Safe for the World," in James Rosenau, ed., *Domestic Sources of Foreign Policy* (New York: Free Press, 1967), p. 301 (italics in original).
14. Irving L. Janis, *Victims of Groupthink* (Boston: Houghton Mifflin, 1972).
15. *Ibid.*, p. 9.
16. *Ibid.*, pp. 14–49; and Theodore C. Sorenson, *Kennedy* (New York: Bantam Books, 1966), pp. 326–46.

CHAPTER 6

1. Morton H. Halperin, "The Decision to Deploy the ABM: Bureaucratic and Domestic Politics in the Johnson Administration," *World Politics* (October 1972), p. 83. On decision making on the ABM, also see Halperin, *Bureaucratic Politics and Foreign Policy* (Washington,: Brookings Institution, 1974); and

Alton Frye, *A Responsible Congress: The Politics of National Security* (New York: McGraw-Hill, 1975), esp. Chap. 2.

2. *Ibid.,* p. 74.
3. *Ibid.,* pp. 67–69.
4. *Ibid.,* p. 69.
5. *Ibid.,* p. 76.
6. Hilsman, *To Move a Nation,* p. 546.
7. Warner R. Schilling, "The H-Bomb Decision: How to Decide without Actually Choosing," in Halperin and Kanter, eds., *Readings in American Foreign Policy* (no. 3, Chap. 3), p. 255.
8. Halperin, "Decision to Deploy," p. 87.
9. Robert S. McNamara, "The Dynamics of Nuclear Strategy," *Department of State Bulletin* (October 9, 1967), pp. 443–51.
10. Abram Chayes and Jerome B. Wiesner, eds., *ABM: An Evaluation of the Decision to Deploy an Antiballistic Missile System* (New York: Harper & Row, 1969), pp. 259–64. Nixon's speech is reproduced on pp. 254–59.
11. Carnes Lord, "The ABM," *Commentary* (May 1980), pp. 31–38 and *New York Times,* August 14, 1980; *U.S. Arms Control Objectives and the Implications for Ballistic Missile Defense* (Center for Science and International Affairs, Harvard University, 1980); Jan M. Lodal, "Deterrence and Nuclear Strategy, *Daedalus,* Fall 1980, pp. 155–76; and William Schneider, Jr., Donald G. Brennan et al., *U.S. Strategic-Nuclear Policy and Ballistic Missile Defense: The 1980s and Beyond* (Cambridge, Mass.: Institute for Foreign Policy Analysis, 1980).
12. This analysis of SALT II is based on Strobe Talbott, *Endgame: The Inside Story of SALT II* (New York: Harper & Row, 1979); Thomas W. Wolfe, *The SALT Experience* (Cambridge, Mass.: Ballinger Publishing Co., 1979); Stephen J. Flanagan, "Congress, the White House and SALT," *The Bulletin of the Atomic Scientists* (November 1978), pp. 34–40, and "Stalemate: The Domestic Politics of SALT II," in John Spanier and Joseph Nogee, eds., *Congress, the Presidency and Foreign Policy* (New York: Pergamon Press, 1981); and Report of the Committee on Foreign Relations, United States Senate. *The SALT II Treaty* (Washington, D.C.: Government Printing Office, 1979).
13. Quoted by Thomas A. Bailey, *A Diplomatic History of the American People,* 7th ed. (New York: Appleton-Century-Croft, 1964), pp. 487–88.
14. Genrik Trofimenko, "Too Many Negotiators," *New York Times,* July 17, 1979.
15. Flanagan, "Congress, The White House and SALT," p. 36.
16. *Ibid.,* pp. 34–5.
17. Quoted by Alton Frye and William D. Rogers, "Linkage Begins at Home," *Foreign Policy* (Summer 1979), pp. 50–1.
18. *Ibid.,* p. 52.
19. *New York Times,* April 13, 1979.
20. Frye and Rogers, *op cit.,* p. 55.
21. *Ibid.*
22. Flanagan, "The Domestic Politics of SALT II."
23. *New York Times,* July 6, 1979.
24. For an argument that American policy in the Middle East played and continues to play a dominant role in OPEC oil strategies, see William B.

Quandt, "The Middle East," in Joseph A. Pechman, ed., *Setting National Priorities: Agenda for the 1980s* (Washington: Brookings Institution, 1980), pp. 317–46. For a contrary position based upon economic arguments, see Charles F. Doran, *Myth, Oil, and Politics* (New York: Free Press, 1977), Chap. 2.

25. Manning, "The Congress, The Executive, and Intermestic Affairs."
26. See Michael J. Malbin, *Unelected Representatives* (New York: Basic Books, 1980), Chap. 9.
27. Data compiled for the United States House of Representatives, Select Committee on Committees, 1979–80. Cited in Uslaner, "The Congressional War on Energy." Much of what follows is based on that work.
28. See Uslaner, "The Congressional War on Energy."
29. Quoted in *Congressional Quarterly Almanac 1977* (Washington, D.C.: Congressional Quarterly, 1977), p. 710.
30. Remarks made on the National Broadcasting Company's *Meet the Press*, February 10, 1980 (Washington: Kelly Press, 1980), p. 8.
31. *Congressional Record, Daily Edition*, Ninety-sixth Congress, First Session, May 10, 1979, p. H2997.
32. *Ibid.*, p. H2992.

CHAPTER 7

1. *New York Times*, January 14, 1973.
2. "Will the Real Senate Stand Up?" *Christian Science Monitor*, May 29–June 1, 1970.
3. Report of the Comptroller General of the United States, *Executive-Legislative Communications and the Role of the Congress During International Crises* (Washington: General Accounting Office, 1976).
4. *Ibid.*, pp. iii–iv.
5. James MacGregor Burns, *Uncommon Sense* (New York: Harper & Row, 1972), p. 53.
6. Cecil V. Crabb, Jr., *Bipartisan Foreign Policy: Myth or Reality?* (White Plains, N.Y.: Row, Peterson, 1957), pp. 241 and 245–46.
7. American Political Science Association, Committee on Political Parties, *Toward a More Responsible Two-Party System, American Political Science Review*, Supplement (1950), vol. 44. p. 19.
8. Robert A. Dahl, *Congress and Foreign Policy* (no. 5. Chap. 2), p. 198.
9. *Executive-Legislative Communications*, Chap. 5.
10. Wilson, *Congressional Government* (Cleveland: Meridian Books, 1967), pp. 167–68. Originally published in 1885.
11. See especially *ibid., passim.*
12. See Norman H. Nie, Sidney Verba, and John R. Petrocik, *The Changing American Voter*, enlarged ed. (Cambridge: Harvard University Press, 1979) and Walter DeVries and V. Lance Tarrance, *The Ticket-Splitter* (Grand Rapids, Mich.: W. B. Eerdman's, 1972).
13. Lester W. Thurow, *The Zero-Sum Society* (New York: Basic Books, 1979), Chap. 8.
14. Lawrence C. Dodd, "Congress, the President, and the Cycles of Power," in Vincent Davis, ed., *The Post-Imperial Presidency* (New Brunswick, N.J.: Transaction Books, 1980).

15. Samuel B. Huntington, "Congressional Responses to the Twentieth Century," in David B. Truman, ed., *The Congress and America's Future*, 2nd ed. (Englewood Cliffs, N.J.: Prentice-Hall, 1973), pp. 6–38.
16. See Seymour Scher, "Conditions for Legislative Control," *Journal of Politics*, vol. 25 (August 1963), pp. 526–51.
17. Morris S. Ogul, *Congress Oversees the Bureaucracy* (Pittsburgh: University of Pittsburgh Press, 1976), esp. Chaps. 1, 6, and 7.
18. See Note 6, Chapter 3.
19. Lewis Anthony Dexter, "Congressmen and the Making of Military Policy," in Robert Peabody and Nelson W. Polsby, eds., *New Perspectives on the House of Representatives*, 2nd ed. (Chicago: Rand McNally, 1969), p. 181.
20. Lowi, "Making Democracy Safe for the World," *Domestic Sources*, p. 301. Emphasis in original. See also Schattschneider, *Party Government*, p. 8.
21. Contrast this argument to the one made by Waltz that democratic institutions in the United States *do not* hinder foreign-policy decision-making; see Waltz, *Foreign Policy and Democratic Politics*, esp. Chap. 11.
22. See Richard Hofstadter, *The Idea of a Party System* (Berkeley: University of California Press, 1970), p. 68.

Suggestions for Further Reading

CHAPTER 1

Henkin, Louis. *Foreign Affairs and the Constitution*. Mineola, N.Y.: Foundation Press, 1973.

Lowi, Theodore, J. "American Business, Public Policy, Case Studies, and Political Theory." *World Politics*, July 1964.

Manning, Bayless. "The Congress, the Executive and Intermestic Affairs: Three Proposals." *Foreign Affairs*, January 1977.

Peppers, Donald A. " 'The Two Presidencies': Eight Years Later," in Wildavsky, Aaron, ed., *Perspectives on the Presidency*. Boston: Little, Brown, 1975.

Wildavsky, Aaron. "The Two Presidencies." *Trans-Action*. December 1966.

CHAPTER 2

Campbell, John F. *The Foreign Affairs Fudge Factory*. New York: Basic Books, 1971.

Fulbright, J. W. *The Crippled Giant*. New York: Random House, 1972.

Halperin, Morton et al. *The Lawless State*. Baltimore, Md.: Penguin Books, 1977.

Spanier, John. *American Foreign Policy Since World War II*, 8th ed. New York: Holt, Rinehart and Winston, 1980.

CHAPTER 3

Fenno, Richard F., Jr. *Home Style: U.S. House Members in Their Districts*. Boston: Little, Brown, 1978.
————. *Congressmen in Committees*. Boston: Little, Brown, 1973.
Fiorina, Morris P. *Congress: Keystone of the Washington Establishment*. New Haven: Yale University Press, 1977.
Franck, Thomas M. and Edward Weisband. *Foreign Policy By Congress*. New York: Oxford University Press, 1979.
Johnson, Loch and James M. McCormick, "The Making of International Agreements: A Reappraisal of Congressional Involvement." *Journal of Politics*, v. 40 (May 1978), pp. 468–478.
Mayhew, David R. *Congress: The Electoral Connection*. New Haven: Yale University Press, 1974.
Spanier, John and Joseph Nogee, eds. *Congress, the Presidency and Foreign Policy*. New York: Pergamon Press, 1981.
Uslaner, Eric M. "The Case of the Vanishing Liberal Senators: The House Did It." *British Journal of Political Science*, v. 11 (January 1981), pp. 105–113.
Wilcox, Francis O. *Congress, the Executive, and Foreign Policy*. New York: Harper & Row, 1971.

CHAPTER 4

Bauer, Raymond A. *et al. American Business and Public Policy*, 2 ed. Chicago: Aldine-Atherton, 1972.
Berkowitz, Morton, P. G. Bock, and Vincent J. Fuccillo, *The Politics of American Foreign Policy*. Englewood Cliffs, N.J.: Prentice-Hall, 1977.
Halperin, Morton H., and Arnold Kanter, eds. *Readings in American Foreign Policy: A Bureaucratic Perspective*. Boston: Little, Brown, 1973.
Huntington, Samuel P. *The Common Defense*. New York: Columbia University Press, 1961.
Mueller, John E. *War, Presidents and Public Opinion*. New York: John Wiley, 1972.
Robinson, James A. *Congress and Foreign Policy*, rev. ed. Homewood, Ill.: Dorsey Press, 1967.
Rosenau, James A., ed. *Domestic Sources of Foreign Policy*. New York: Free Press, 1967.

CHAPTER 5

Allison, Graham. *Essence of Decision*. Boston: Little, Brown, 1971.
Destler, I. M. *Presidents, Bureaucrats, and Foreign Policy*. Princeton, N.J.: Princeton University Press, 1972.
Galucci, Robert L. *Neither Peace Nor Honor*. Baltimore, Md.: The Johns Hopkins University Press, 1975.
Hilsman, Roger. *To Move a Nation*. New York: Doubleday & Co., 1967.
Williams, Phil. *Crisis Management*. New York: John Wiley, 1976.

CHAPTER 6

Congressional Quarterly. Energy Policy. Washington: Congressional Quarterly, 2 ed., 1981.

Davis, David. *Energy Politics,* 2 ed. New York: St. Martin's, 1978.

Doran, Charles F. *Myth, Oil, and Politics.* New York: Free Press, 1977.

Flanagan, Stephen J. "Congress, the White House and SALT." *The Bulletin of Atomic Scientists,* November 1978, pp. 34–40; and "The Domestic Politics of SALT II: Implications for the Foreign Policy Process," in Spanier and Nogee, *op. cit.,* pp. 44–76.

Halperin, Morton. "The Decision to Deploy the ABM: Bureaucratic and Domestic Politics in the Johnson Administration." *World Politics,* October 1972.

————. *Bureaucratic Politics and Foreign Policy.* Washington, D.C.: The Brookings Institution, 1974.

Jones, Charles O. "Congress and the Making of Energy Policy," pp. 161–178 in Robert Lawrence, ed., *New Dimensions to Energy Policy.* Lexington, Mass.: Lexington Books, 1979.

Landsberg, Hans H. "Energy," chap. 4 in Joseph A. Pechman, ed., *Setting National Priorities: Agenda for the 1980s.* Washington: Brookings Institution, 1980.

Schurr, Sam *et al. Energy in America's Future: The Choices Before Us.* Baltimore: Johns Hopkins University Press for Resources for the Future, 1979.

Talbott, Strobe. *Endgame.* New York: Harper & Row, 1979.

Wolfe, Thomas. *The SALT Experience.* Cambridge, Mass.: Ballinger Publishing Co., 1979.

CHAPTER 7

Burns, James MacGregor. *Uncommon Sense.* New York: Harper & Row, 1972.

Crabb, Cecil V., Jr. *Bipartisan Foreign Policy: Myth or Reality?* White Plains, N.Y.: Row, Peterson, & Co., 1957.

Index